Culture and Progress

CULTURE AND PROGRESS

by

WILSON D. WALLIS

PROFESSOR OF ANTHROPOLOGY AND SOCIOLOGY
UNIVERSITY OF MINNESOTA

WHITTLESEY HOUSE
McGRAW-HILL BOOK COMPANY, INC.
NEW YORK · 1930

Published by

WHITTLESEY HOUSE

Trade Division of the
McGraw-Hill Book Company, Inc.
370 Seventh Avenue, New York

Printed in the United States of America by
The Maple Press Company, York, Pa.

To

EDGAR A. SINGER

"The measure of man's coöperation with man . . .
measures progress."

"Of all vulgar modes of escaping from the consideration of the effect of social and moral influences on the human mind, the most vulgar is that of attributing the diversities of conduct and character to inherent natural differences."—John Stuart Mill, *Principles of Political Economy*, I, 390.

"Within the flickering inconsequential acts of our separate selves dwells a sense of the whole which claims and dignifies them. In its presence we put off mortality and live in the universal. The life of the community in which we live and have our being is the fit symbol of this relationship."—John Dewey, *Human Nature and Conduct*, 331–332.

"Man is a tame or civilized animal; nevertheless, he requires proper instruction and a fortunate nature, and then of all animals he becomes the most divine and most civilized; but if he be insufficiently or ill educated he is the most savage of earthly creatures."—Plato, *Laws*, Bk. VI, 766.

"But I think men can help themselves. And I hate men who let things drift, and then, when trouble comes, say that the gods have forsaken them."—Elmer Davis, *Giant-Killer*, 106.

"*Nous devons contempler le passé pour nous en nourrir, le présent pour y vivre et le transformer, l'avenir pour y marcher sans nous y précipiter.*"—Pierre Leroux.

"Ten thousand changes go on, and no one knows where they will end or when they have begun."—Chuan-tze (Chinese philosopher, born 330 B. C.).

Preface

WESTERN civilization is a phase of human culture and can be understood only when viewed in historical and cultural perspective.

The present study deals with human culture, and confines itself neither to contemporary life nor to Western European civilization, although other civilizations and times are utilized mainly as a means of reflecting light upon our own time and civilization. One's own culture, however, must be analyzed as objectively as are other cultures. In interpreting the methods of those who have attempted theoretical reconstructions of culture I have endeavored to be fair and frank. There has been a tendency in this country to compromise with those who are of one's own "school," and there has been singularly little incisive criticism of the methods of fellow-workers. This may show generosity, but certainly, in the end, it benumbs the critical faculty. Vested interests warp the judgment in science as in other fields, and here, too, tradition is stultifying. It seems incredible that no one has challenged the verbal pretensions of those who call themselves adherents of the "historical school" and base their claim on the fact that they proceed without history—if history be taken to mean either chronologically recorded data or a knowledge of the order in which things actually happened. They wish to set themselves apart from, perhaps above, the "evolution school"; hence the verbal tag. But the evolution school was depicting presumed history, and the historical school is depicting presumed evolution. The two schools have the same ambition, namely, an account of the order in which changes actually took place; and they differ little in fundamental procedure. Each uses principles of interpretation which have not been empirically justified, which are useful only if they are true, and which have not been shown to be true. In the main, therefore, their interpretations are but exercises in logic. Some of their alleged principles may be true, but as yet it has not been shown that they are even probably true, and they remain assumptions. If the present work demonstrates the inadequacy of the methods which have been used in interpreting culture and progress, and the necessity of reëxamining most of the problems involved, it will, we believe, be justified. Social science may be on the threshold of important findings in these fields, but at the present time the task has been only begun.

For reading earlier drafts of some of the chapters and for constructive criticisms I am indebted to Professor Edwin R. Guthrie, of the University of Washington, Professor A. L. Kroeber, of the University of California, and Professors Harold D. Lasswell, William F. Ogburn, and Edward Sapir, of the University of Chicago. Dr. Alexander A. Goldenweiser, formerly of the Staff of the "Encyclopaedia of the Social Sciences," has read the manuscript and has given helpful suggestions. For a similar service, and for the drawing, I am indebted to Grace Allen Wallis. For permission to utilize here material which has been published in articles in the *American Anthropologist, Sociology and Social Research*, and the *Scientific Monthly*, I am indebted to the editors of the above named journals.

W. D. W.

MINNEAPOLIS,
September, 1930.

Contents

PART I

Culture and Culture Change

ix

PART II

Theories of Progress

PART III

The Criteria of Progress

PART I
CULTURE AND CULTURE CHANGE

CULTURE AND PROGRESS

INTRODUCTION

The problem of social progress has engaged the attention of many thoughtful men. Some have given interpretations based on conceptions of the development which can be traced or inferred from the past, and have assumed that the future is merely the amplified present. Others, believing culture development definitely limited in possibilities, have assumed that what has been shall be again, for "there is no new thing under the sun." Still others, such as the idealistic Plato and his disciples, have drawn plans for the future, in the assurance that if man discovers the path of progress and is willing to follow it, he can achieve a culture better than any he has known. Some have despaired of progress, some have accounted it actual and even inevitable. Few have assessed its potentiality, and fewer still have defined the criteria for identifying it. There are culture changes and these are sometimes cumulative; and the laws of change, development, and evolution are pertinent to an inquiry into progress; for if culture changes are inevitable or even likely, a theory of progress must take cognizance of them. Culture changes, however, and especially cumulative changes or developments, are not self-revealed, and the identification of them necessitates an interpretation of data. The methods used in reading the past, or in inferring it from present tendencies, likewise merit examination, for faith in results implies confidence in methods. The character of social change depends upon the culture. The possibilities and the limitations inherent in the social life of the ancient Greeks, for example, are to some extent peculiar to them and are nowhere duplicated; for even though the course of Greek culture might have been different, there are limitations in the extent to which, once under way, it could have been different. The potentialities and limitations inherent in culture are, therefore, part of the story of development and progress, and an account of the latter is not complete if it omits the former. There are numerous social developments, but each is specific, unique, and peculiar to the respective culture. An understanding of the development of recent means of transportation, for example, involves an understanding of Western culture before and after the Industrial Revolution. It cannot be understood by

3

studying merely the changes in machinery and in technology. Science, economic organization, and many other phases of the culture are involved. A similar observation applies to political structure, social ideals, institutions, and international relations. Even an understanding of contemporary interpretations involves acquaintance with those of other centuries and cultures. Hindu and Greek, Roman and Egyptian, have interpreted progress, and though their views have much in common, each is to some extent an original interpretation as well as, no doubt, in part a borrowing. Since the Renaissance there have been many interpretations of progress, and acquaintance with them constitutes a proper background for a survey of recent speculation. It is necessary also to examine the presuppositions underlying the concepts of progress, and it is imperative to seek a criterion of it; to inquire to what extent historical developments and recent changes imply progress; and to ascertain to what extent social changes secure and insure values. A survey of the development of cultures contributes to an understanding of these problems. Men will not solve them, but as long as they struggle with obstacles, they will have occasion to ponder them; and a problem understood is already half solved.

Sound procedure involves adherence to the realities; and in social relations these are not reducible to mere individuals. A reality of a unique order exists when men live together in group life and share a common heritage of thought, language, institutions, and technology. Participation in a common heritage is an essential attribute of culture; and an analysis of culture is a prerequisite to an understanding of its heritage. "We seek reality; but what is reality? The physiologists tell us that organisms are formed of cells; the chemists add that cells themselves are formed from atoms. Does this mean that these atoms or these cells constitute reality, or rather the sole reality?" The arrangement of cells which constitutes the unity of the individual is also a reality. "Should a naturalist who had never studied the elephant except by means of the microscope think himself sufficiently acquainted with the animal?"[1] As well hope to understand the elephant by piecing together the information obtained from sections under the microscope as to attempt to understand culture by piecing together information about isolated individuals.

As the complexion of the culture changes, the problems of the individual are remade. Often his world is awry because its parts have not developed harmoniously. The size of the social unit may increase, trade and industry may ramify, the culture may be augmented without an

---

[1] POINCARÉ, HENRI, "The Foundations of Science," p. 217, New York, 1913.

increase in the native ability of the individual and without a comparable increase in the capacity to direct social affairs so as to insure a good life. For culture, like nature, knows nothing of good intentions, and rewards or punishes not motives but actions. The inventor of a new device, such as the telephone or the automobile, may introduce it merely for profit to himself, but the culture may be transformed by it. Since, then,

things are what they are, describe them as we may, and their consequences will be what they will, prophesy of them as we choose; it behooves us to approach the consideration of impending social questions in the spirit of scientific inquiry, and to be impartial investigators of social facts before we become zealous reformers of social wrongs.[1]

Let us first consider the character of culture.

Man alone responds in any considerable degree to the stimulus of human culture; the domesticated animals respond to some of its elements, but the response signifies an adaptation to certain phases of the culture rather than its complete adoption. Thus, language, for example, is a distinctively human attribute, for no other creature responds to the stimulus of speech by attaching conventional meanings to conventional sounds, save within a very limited range, such as the response of the dog, cat, horse, cow, and some other animals, to calls or scoldings. The human infant, however, responds to more varied speech stimuli and to an exceedingly large variety of phonetic elements, combinations, and nuances. But this tendency to respond to phonetic stimuli, and to the situations or meanings which they denote, does not explain the differences between English, Hottentot, German, French, Chinese, and the various languages of mankind. There appears to be no causal relation between the morphology of an Englishman and English, between that of a Hottentot and his language, or between that of a Chinaman and Chinese. No known elements in the physiology or anatomy of the individuals who comprise these respective culture groups are causally related to the respective phonetics, linguistic morphology, or concepts. The morphology of an Englishman appears to be as well adapted to the linguistic form of Chinese or of Hottentot as to that of English, and a like statement holds of all types of mankind with respect to any trait of culture. The explanation of any particular language, then, must be sought in culture terms, i.e., in the social environment, the culture contacts, and the historical background. Physiology and anatomy cannot explain why a specific culture group has its peculiar type of language.

---

[1] BALFOUR, ARTHUR J., "Essays and Addresses," pp. 239–240, 3d ed., Edinburgh, 1905.

The explanation of the individual's language must be sought in his linguistic environment. To explain this environment one must know the culture in which it has developed, the cultures with which it has had direct or indirect contacts, and its historical phases. The study of the individual and of his orientation in his culture may give an insight into individual linguistic accomplishments which are peculiar to him as an English-speaking person, for example, but it cannot explain why the stimuli are English rather than Chinese, Hottentot, or Eskimo. Indeed, for this purpose, psychology is as futile and superfluous as physiology. As Goethe says: "Do not, I beg you, look for anything behind phenomena. *They are themselves their own lesson.*" To search in the laboratories of biology or psychology for the basic factors of social life Wissler significantly compares with "groping behind the scenes and digging under the stage, disregarding the comedies, tragedies, and dramas in plain sight . . . We must deal directly with life itself . . . the realities of social science are what people do."[1] In short, the only avenue to an understanding of the behavior of men in group life is the study of men in group life; and the only avenue to an understanding of culture is the study of culture in its historical and contemporary manifestations. The essence of the matter was well expressed by Ferguson nearly two centuries ago:

If the question be put, "What the mind of man could perform when left to itself, and without the aid of any foreign direction," we are to look for our answer in the history of mankind. Particular experiments which have been found so useful in establishing the principles of other sciences could probably, on this subject, teach us nothing important or new: we are to take the history of every active being from his conduct in the situation to which he is formed, not from his appearance in any forced or uncommon condition; a wild man, therefore, caught in the woods, where he had always lived apart from his species, is a singular instance, not a specimen of any general character. As the anatomy of an eye which had never received the impressions of light, or that of an ear which had never felt the impulse of sounds, would probably exhibit defects in the very structure of the organs themselves, arising from their not being applied to their proper functions, so any particular case of this sort would only show in what degree the powers of apprehension and sentiment could exist where they had not been employed, and what would be the defects and imbecilities of a heart in which the emotions that pertain to society had never been felt . . . We can learn nothing of man's nature from the analogy of other animals. If we would know him, we must attend to himself, to the course of his life, and the tenor of his conduct. With him the society appears to be as old as the individual, and the use of the tongue as universal as that

---

[1] WISSLER, CLARK, "Foreword," in LYND, ROBERT S. and HELEN M., "Middletown: A Study of Contemporary American Culture," New York, 1929.

of the hand or the foot. If there was a time in which he had his acquaintance with his own species to make, and his faculties to acquire, it is a time of which we have no record, and in relation to which our opinions can serve no purpose, and are supported by no evidence . . . Where shall we find the talents which are fit to act with men in a collective body, if we break that body into parts, and confine the observation of each to a separate track?[1]

Again, in his famous discussion of "Nurture and Nature," Galton says:

Man is so educable an animal that it is difficult to distinguish between that part of his character which has been acquired through education and circumstance, and that which was in the original grain of his constitution. His character is exceedingly complex, even in members of the simplest and purest savage race; much more is it so in civilized races, who have long since been exempted from the full rigor of natural selection, and have become more mongrel in their breed than any other animal on the face of the earth. Different aspects of the multifarious character of man respond to different calls from without, so that the same individual and much more the same race may behave very differently at different epochs. There may have been no fundamental change of character, but a different phase or mood of it may have been evoked by special circumstances, or those persons in whom that mood is naturally dominant may through some accident have the opportunity of acting for the time as representatives of the race. The same nation may be seized by a military fervor at one period, and by a commercial one at another; they may be humbly submissive to a monarch, or become outrageous republicans. The love of art, gaiety, adventure, science, religion may be severally paramount at different times. One of the most notable changes that can come over a nation is from a state corresponding to that of our past dark ages into one like that of the Renaissance. In the first case the minds of men are wholly taken up with routine work, and in copying what their predecessors have done they degrade into servile imitators and submissive slaves to the past. In the second case, some circumstance or idea has finally discredited the authorities that impeded intellectual growth, and has unexpectedly revealed new possibilities. Then the mind of the nation is set free, a direction of research is given to it, and all the exploratory and hunting instincts are awakened. These sudden eras of great intellectual progress cannot be due to any alteration in the natural faculties of the race, because there has not been time for that, but to their being directed in productive channels.[2]

A contemporary writer declares "genetic variation . . . a prerequisite for social progress."[3] Not a shred of evidence is adduced or

---

[1] FERGUSON, ADAM, "An Essay on the History of Civil Society," pp. 5, 8–9, 43, Edinburgh, 1767.

[2] GALTON, SIR FRANCIS, "Inquiries into the Human Faculty and Its Development," pp. 128–129, "Everyman's Library," London, n.d.

[3] EAST, EDWARD M., "Heredity and Human Affairs," p. 160, New York, 1927.

can be adduced in support of this statement. No one has discovered a single instance in history in which genetic variation has been a precursor of social progress; and the character of the presumed genetic variation which is capable of bringing social progress has not been even suggested.

In the first half of the nineteenth century the evolution hypothesis was becoming a source of trouble to scientists, historians, and theologians. Since the life of man was found to be diverse, ranging through the whole gamut of misery and happiness, of virtue and sin, speculation regarding the cause and meaning of these divergences was inevitable. Either man has descended from a common parent, the Adam of the Garden of Eden, and has developed into the various creature he now is, or there has been a multiple origin of mankind and some men are not descended from the Adam of biblical tradition. The discovery of human remains of geological age reinforced the theory that man had been upon the earth much longer than commonly had been supposed, and suggested that he was, indeed, antediluvial. This growing conviction paved the way for the assumption that man had gone through a long period of social development. Lord Avebury and Sir Edward B. Taylor showed that man had passed from a lower to a higher culture status. For evidence of this progress they drew largely from the life of contemporary savages, and from the historical civilizations. Almost immediately, however, divergences of view arose, and there were rival schools. All agreed that there had been cultural evolution, but there was diversity of opinion as to the course it had taken. Herbert Spencer suggested that evolution had been from simple to complex, from a simple incoherent undifferentiated homogeneity to a complex differentiated heterogeneity. But Spencer's formula of the course of social evolution is not universally applicable. In language, for example, the course of development frequently, perhaps generally, has been the reverse of that suggested by him. Language "grows" by simplification, by shedding many morphological distinctions and complexities. A similar statement applies to many phases of culture, and this precludes the acceptance of Spencer's theory unless, in the case of the phenomena in question, it can be shown on independent grounds that the course of development has been from simple to complex rather than the reverse.[1] Even when the drift is from simple to complex there are many possible forms of complexity and some insist that the historical method is the only way out of the quandary, and that a knowledge of the course of culture development implies an understanding of the actual historical stages.

---

[1] See further, chap. X.

CHAPTER I

CULTURE AREAS AND CULTURE TRAITS

1. THE NATURE OF CULTURE

It has been said,

A nation's culture, includes the points of view every one has about individual conduct and social relations; his attitude toward government and toward other peoples; his habit of mind about the family, the duty of parents to children and children to parents; his standards of taste and of morals, his store of accepted wisdom which he expresses in proverbs and aphorisms; his venerations and loyalties, his prejudices and biases, his canons of conventionality; the whole group of ideas held in common by most of the people. This body of culture comes to every individual mainly through well-recognized channels, through parents and elders who hand it down by oral tradition, through religion, through schools, and through reading, both of books and of newspapers and periodicals.[1]

This description refers to non-material culture; culture, however, includes material as well as non-material things, and may be defined as the artificial objects, institutions, and modes of life or of thought which are not peculiarly individual but which characterize a group; it is "that complex whole which includes knowledge, belief, art, morals, law, custom, and any other capabilities and habits acquired by man as a member of society."[2] Culture, therefore, is supra-individual. The indi-

---

[1] SULLIVAN, MARK, "Our Times. The United States 1900–1925," vol. II, "America Finding Herself," p. 1, New York, 1927.

[2] TYLOR, EDWARD B., "Primitive Culture," vol. I, p. 1. Professor Odum has proposed the following distinction between the terms *culture* and *civilization:* Culture shall mean "the aggregate or sum total of the products and processes of control. Of course, civilization and culture are always synonomous in parts, but does primitive culture include so markedly the element of conscious direction, telic social organization, or civic drive, or is *culture* a definitive term while *civilization* is descriptive?" *Social Forces,* 6: 40, 1927. O'Leary says: "Culture must be taken in the widest sense to include political, social, and legal intellectual life which show their presence in literature, philosophy, and otherwise, all more or less connected, and all having the common characteristic that they cannot be passed on by physical descent but must be learned in after life. But race, culture, and language resemble one another insofar as it is true that all are multiplex and perpetually interwoven, so that in each the lines of transmission seem rather like a tangled skein than an ordered pattern; results proceed from a conflicting group of causes amongst which it is often difficult to apportion the relative influences." O'LEARY, DE LACY, "Arabic Thought and Its Place in History," p. v., London, 1922.

9

vidual is a carrier and transmitter of it and may modify it, but no individual creates a major portion of the culture in which he participates. A tribe, usually the smallest unit investigated by the ethnographer, is a culture unit, but it has not created all of its culture. Its traits resemble those of neighbors, or of some neighbors, in so many respects that the resemblances cannot be attributed to independent origins, but imply a common source. A culture area, therefore, may include several tribes. Thus the culture traits of the Plains Indians have such marked similarities that the tribes collectively constitute a culture area. The culture of the Eskimo extends over a long narrow strip of the arctic New World and a small portion of the Old World, including many localities which have no direct contacts with one another. Indeed, practically the whole of the known aboriginal New World can be divided into culture areas. An attempt has been made to describe the culture areas of Negro Africa, though not with the same success as in the case of North America, owing, partly perhaps, to the more rapid diffusion of culture traits through much of the African continent, and partly to the nature of the ethnographical data, which are not as adequate for Africa as for North America. There are distinct culture areas in Oceania, notably Polynesia, Melanesia, and Micronesia, and certain culture areas in the Philippines have been identified. Although much of the aboriginal world can be divided into culture areas, there is little information with regard to some large ethnographical areas. Enough is known about aboriginal cultures, however, to justify the following conclusions:

1. A culture is unique. This is true not merely of the larger culture area which includes tribes, but also of each component tribal culture. The culture of the Plains area, for example, is nowhere duplicated. Moreover, no two tribes within the Plains area have identical cultures. Many culture traits of the Omaha are shared by neighbors, but there is no exact counterpart to Omaha culture. The Osage resemble the Ponca and the Kansa in many traits, but each tribal culture has individuality and uniqueness. Throughout the known ethnographical world the respective cultures are unique.

2. A culture does not travel in toto into other culture areas, though the peoples who carry it may extend their territory and so enlarge the geographical boundaries of their culture. Moreover, when people travel to new territory, usually their culture is modified; it does not remain identical with its old self, though of course it may preserve many old traits. Thus the culture of the Old World was not transplanted entire to the New; but only certain traits crossed the Atlantic. No culture area of the New World, therefore, is an exact duplicate of one in the Old World.

3. Despite the uniqueness of tribal culture, no tribe is culturally a self-complete unit. Each is a borrower from others, *i.e.*, the culture is affected by adjacent cultures. The Dakota, for example, were influenced by the art, mythology, and ceremonial organizations of neighbors, and by the latter's use of the horse. Invariably a culture is influenced by the cultures with which it comes into contact. So considerable is this influence that from a knowledge of contiguous cultures one can usually, but not always, correctly predict the general characteristics of a given culture.

4. Though a culture does not travel as a unit, *i.e.*, intact, many culture traits travel. So strong is the tendency for a culture trait to travel beyond the boundaries of the group in which it originated that it is difficult to find examples of culture traits which do not show this disposition. Thus ceramics, art designs, ceremonial organizations, methods of disposing of the dead, birth-rites, naming-customs, styles of dress and of personal adornment, initiation ceremonies, stories and plots, proverbs, omens, portents, animistic interpretations, and a thousand other traits spread from tribe to tribe, and sometimes permeate large culture areas. As a rule, therefore, a culture does not supplant another, but various traits seep into neighboring soil where they take root and sometimes flourish more luxuriantly than in the place of origin—as happened when the messianic religion was introduced from the Paiute into the Plains area, when Christianity was introduced from the Near East into Western Europe, and when maize was introduced into the Plains area by the whites.

5. A culture is a functioning dynamic unit and the various traits which compose it are interdependent. A culture trait does not function in isolation nor independently of other traits of the culture, but each is influenced by a change in any phase of the culture. Thus the Manitoba Dakota recount the order in which the animals and the "elements"— soil, stone, water—were created and this order reflects the hierarchy of the supernatural power of these animals and substances. The folklore and mythology fit into this framework of cosmogony and theology. Fighting, hunting, magic, religion, and ceremonialism are interrelated activities which interdigitate with the Dakota theory of evolution and the philosophy of *wakan*.[1] A similar statement holds for every culture. When, for example, Margaret Mead studied Samoan individuals she found that "a knowledge of the entire culture was essential for the accurate evaluation of any particular individual's behavior."[2] Similarly,

---

[1] See, for example, the writer's "Beliefs and Tales of the Canadian Dakota," *Jour. Amer. Folk-Lore*, **36**; 36–101, 1923.

[2] MEAD, MARGARET, "The Coming of Age in Samoa," New York, 1928.

Malinowski says of the matrilineal system among the Trobriand Islanders: "the whole system is based on mythology, on the native theory of procreation, on certain of their magico-religious beliefs and it pervades all the institutions and customs of the tribe."[1] There are conflicts and maladjustments,[2] but even these imply interdependences and at least a partial unification of tribal life. "A native tribe bound by a code of disconnected inorganic customs would fall to pieces under our very eyes,"[3] as would any culture group.

6. Since the traits which comprise a culture are interrelated, an innovation affects the entire culture. The ethnologist is familiar with many instances in which this has been disastrous. The introduction of the horse doubtless modified many phases of Plains area culture. Later the extinction of the buffalo and the confinement of the Indians to reservations destroyed tribal morale and shattered the culture. When the white man's stove became a part of the culture equipment of the Chilkat of Alaska, the voices of ancestors who had spoken through the crackling of the wood in the open fire no longer came to cheer or to warn descendants, and an important influence in the morale of the tribe disappeared. Degeneration in ethical standards followed and the culture deteriorated. Normally, however, when culture changes are gradual rather than abrupt, there is continuous accommodation to the new trait.

7. Individuals do not participate in the culture to the same degree or in the same way. One individual may be more efficient in art, another in industrial technique, another may be more deeply steeped in tribal lore. Perhaps, "savages are more like one another than are civilized men,"[4] for, as compared with civilized men, the individuals in a primitive group conform more closely to a pattern. If, however, allowance is made for the more limited range of tribal culture, the individualities of men in primitive life are perhaps as marked as those of civilized men.[5]

2. CONTEMPORARY SOCIETY AS A CULTURE PHENOMENON

There are many approaches to the study of social life and each has peculiar advantages. One can approach the study of social phenomena

---

[1] MALINOWSKI, BRONISLAW, "Crime and Custom in Savage Society," p. 75, New York, 1926.

[2] See, for example, ibid., 101ff.

[3] MALINOWSKI, BRONISLAW, "Crime and Custom in Savage Society," pp. 125–126, New York, 1926.

[4] BURNS, C. DELISLE, "Political Ideas, Their Nature and Development," p. 181, Oxford, 1915.

[5] See, for illustrations, RADIN, PAUL, "Crashing Thunder. The Autobiography of an American Indian," New York, 1926; and BARTLETT, FREDERICK C., " Pyschology and Primitive Culture," Cambridge, 1923.

from the psychological angle, ascertain their psychological meanings, and describe them in psychological terminology. Every situation is a stimulus, every appreciation of it is a reaction to it, every mental accretion is a psychological integration, and every mental modification is a psychological reintegration. Thus one can describe any phase of social life in psychological terms, for every social situation is also a psychological situation. One who is predisposed to see things from the historical angle describes social phenomena from that point of view, for every social phenomenon has a historical background, and time will soon make any social phenomenon a matter of history. The social phenomena of today can be described in the history of tomorrow. One may be geographically minded and disposed to describe phenomena in their space distribution, for every social phenomenon happens not merely somewhen but also somewhere, and it has not only a history but also a geography. Geographical configurations include everything which happens, has happened, or will happen. Social life can be delineated on a map in which different tints represent various phases of social life; and it is possible in a series of maps to portray the changes in space distribution during preceding decades, centuries, and millennia. Sometime, no doubt, such a series of maps will be accessible, and they will facilitate a comprehension of the geography of culture phenomena.

Culture is the life of a people as typified in contacts, institutions, and equipment. It includes characteristic concepts and behavior, customs and traditions. No laws of psychology would lead one to expect that the forms of culture would differ much from one group of men to another, or indeed from one century to another; yet so much do they differ that in every politically independent group they are to some extent unique, and as between many culture groups there is in the details of the culture no identity whatever. Western civilization, for example, is a unique phenomenon. A culture has not been previously precisely what it now is, it never has been and presumably it never will be completely duplicated in any other area, and the conclusion is irresistible that it will not remain as it now is. Thus any culture, considered in its totality, is a unique phenomenon, and there is reason to believe that no culture is static, but each changes continually. Certainly this statement holds of contemporary society. The culture approach possesses an especial advantage in the study of social phenomena because in it the relevant phenomena of sociology can be oriented, and their significance can be shown. To one who regards contemporary society as a culture, the play and interplay of traits give ample scope for plot, and the story depicts the life of the group. The culture approach discloses the significance of the respective phases of social life, which as bare entities have little meaning. Thus, for example, a description of the family which omits its orientation in the culture conveys little appreciation of life as it is actually lived by members of the family, for the concrete realities of family life can be ascertained only through knowledge of the culture. The term "contemporary society" is itself a culture concept, for it is used by common consent in our culture to refer to our social life, although this is certainly no more contemporary than thousands of cultures and millions of human beings not included in this term. Contemporary society—we shall give it the usual culture reference—has geographical boundaries. These change and sometimes it is difficult to know precisely where they run. They usually fade away gradually at their margins, and they are not clear-cut like political boundaries.

If one crosses the Canadian boundary west of the Great Lakes one enters, for the most part, no essentially different culture area; but the differences are greater if one crosses the Rio Grande. Mexican culture is of European origin but it differs more from American culture than does that of Western Canada. Indeed one enters another sphere of culture influence before one arrives at the Rio Grande. That fact is indicated by Spanish place names, Spanish dress, the occasional use of the Spanish language, Spanish dishes, Spanish architecture, both of the mud-hut type and of the grandee type, and by many other phases of Spanish-Mexican culture which have percolated into the Southwest and the Pacific West of the United States.

Problems of social reconstruction are largely problems of culture, and they can be dealt with intelligently only by taking due account of culture traits. To attempt to solve, or even to understand, the problems of the family without considering them in their culture setting is only a little more hopeful than attempting to ascertain their real nature by isolating the family group and observing it in a social vacuum.Whatever else it may be, the problem of the family is one of adjustment within the entire culture. Thus the concept of culture brings the phenomena of social life into one frame of reference, and a unifying scheme is devoutly to be desired; it provides an orientation of significant social data and a possibility of bringing order out of chaos. The culture reality must be appreciated in order to understand the significance of social phenomena, for the specific character of an institution can be ascertained only through a knowledge of the culture in which it functions. As the meaning of a word is always to some extent determined by its context, so the meaning of a social situation is always to some extent influenced by the complexion of the social milieu. However much two social phenomena, considered as isolated phenomena, may resemble one another, their setting in the culture may give them specific significance. Thus in one area cannibalism may be supported by economic motives, in another by sentimental attachment to one's kin from whom one is loth to part, in another area it may be based on the concept that thus one acquires the virtues of the deceased. Some of these motives radiate through a goodly portion of the respective cultures, with supporting ethics, mythology, folklore, and perhaps tribal customs. In Western civilization the attitudes toward eating horse flesh, mussels, clams, frog legs, tripe, snails, beans, snakes, sharks, shrimp are largerly matters of culture. Culture traits provide solid ground for investigation, and it may be surmised that the mere placement in culture of some apparently trivial things, such as preference for mussels and rejection of clams in the Old World, and preference for clams and rejection of mussels in the New World, traits which have been characteristic of these respective areas from prehistoric times to the present, will facilitate an appreciation of the basis of social evaluations. Such things as preference for parliamentary and responsible party government or for unresponsible elected representatives, for port or for prohibition, for this or for that religion, party, or principle, are largely matters of culture placement. And if that is the case, then for an understanding of their existence one must go to the culture in which, for which, and because of which they exist. For a hundred thousand years culture has been the foundation on which men have builded. Culture mutations are merely divergences from ancestral type, for culture continuity holds throughout, and it is impossible to believe that it will be otherwise in ages to come. Social life must be builded in and of a culture. And what can it profit men if they gain the whole world of social utopia but lose culture? A social life which is not molded within a culture is as futile as freedom in empty space, as a grammar without a language, and as a language in which no things or concepts correspond with the words. The culture reference gives the fullest meaning to social phenomena.

3. Western Civilization as a Culture and a Composite of Cultures

Western civilization is both a culture and a composite of cultures. The component culture traits include industries, economic activities and organizations, political life, education, literature, science, art, law, ethics, and idealism. The use of the radio, the drinking of tea, the smoking of tobacco, utopian idealism, and the democratic urge are examples of culture traits. Western civilization developed out of Germanic kinship groups and forged ahead only after contact with Græco-Roman culture, and Græco-Roman influence is but a name for the resurrection and diffusion of culture traits. Science, literature, architecture, law, medicine, and education were diffused from Mediterranean civilization to north and west. Germanic peoples were Hellenized or Latinized to the extent that they adopted or revived the culture traits of Greek or Roman civilization. Western civilization is now far-flung and has many specialized forms, some of which extend over large geographical areas. Between these various portions of the culture there are contacts, and culture traits spread from one subsidiary culture area to another. There is an English, a French, a German culture, though each has borrowed traits from all the others. Thus there are culture areas within Western culture. Provinces of American culture, such as portions of the mountain regions of Kentucky and Tennessee, differ in content and in emphasis from other component culture areas, such as portions of New England; and the Pennsylvania Germans, for example, constitute a culture group.

The mechanism by which culture traits spread in civilization has not been investigated, though probably no single problem of culture would yield richer returns. Certain conditions facilitate the adoption of a trait, and an examination of these might disclose some of the main factors responsible for culture change. Some things spread because of their obvious utility—such as matches, firearms, and various military devices; others spread because of their esthetic appeal, such as art in its various forms. Others, again, spread because of an appeal to a sense of the dramatic, or because they contain elements of the comic, as is evidenced in the ubiquity and eternal life of jokes—"What the world needs is a new joke." Intellectual or religious appeal may facilitate the spread of traits, but much depends upon the nature of the soil and the culture potentiality of the trait.

Culture analysis is a profitable approach to the study of contemporary civilization. In the United States there are many culture groups about which little is known. Of their traditions, customs, ideas, ideals, superstitions, intellectual activities, hopes and ambitions, there is little or no information. There is no adequate account of them, and certain phases of the cultures suggest the need of fuller knowledge of the various traits of the cultures in their functioning interdependence. Perhaps the greater portion of the South, the "Bible belt," as Mencken calls it, is a culture area; at any rate, in many portions of the South, such as parts of Texas and of Louisiana, there are fairly distinct culture areas. A series of culture maps of the United States would show the geographical distribution of the respective traits of material culture, of mechanization in its various forms, of travel and transportation and the facilities for them. They would show also the distribution of types of buildings and dwellings, materials used in construction, furnishings, and equipment.

Foods and industrial activities constitute other important culture phases. Foods differ locally, as notably between the southeast and the southwest sections of the country. The Christmas dinner is an illustration of the extent to which food is a matter of culture. The dishes especially appropriate at Christmas differ much from one country to another, though practically every country has a specific Christmas menu. In France it includes chicken and liver pudding, and in Paris, the flesh of goat and donkey. The Spanish serve sweet almonds and cream, then a course of fish which has been broiled in front of the open fire and has been basted with lemon, garlic, and oil. The Germans serve smoked or roast goose stuffed with chestnuts, or apples, pork boiled with sauerkraut, beef with sour sauce, black pudding, and baked apples. This is also the menu in Alsace. Goose is the principal item on the Swiss table, and is supplemented with confectionery, cake, fruit, nut puddings, fritters, fruit-paste, spices, marmalade, eggs, and *kirsch* (cherry brandy). The Russian eats a soup consisting of beef bouillon, boiled cabbage, sour cream, the fermented juice of beetroots, and pork. At the dinner of the Italian, which is eaten in the evening, between eight o'clock and midnight, eels constitute the principal dish, each guest receiving one rolled in a laurel leaf. Serbians, Cubans, and Portuguese serve young pig. The turkey and cranberry sauce of American tables are the result of the transfer of a Thanksgiving dish to the Christmas holiday. In England and in Australia roast beef is served. The distribution of industrial activities, including local variations, is important. Music, art, architecture, landscaping, gardens, parks, and intellectual activities and accomplishments are important culture elements. Libraries, educational and research institutions, museums, and other intellectual stimuli are phases of the culture.

Important, too, is the culture horizon, the extent to which a group participates in a larger culture world. What elements of Eastern and of Western civilization permeate a locality, how much of Egypt, Greece, or Rome can be seen in museum, in architecture, in public or in private libraries? What portion of the larger culture world penetrates through the channels of the press, journals, and travelers who journey to or from the community? To what extent are the traits of the local culture those which are practically world-wide—such as matches, tinned goods, automobiles,—to what extent are they nation-wide, to what extent are they limited to the locality? What are the esthetic, intellectual, economic, and political horizons of the culture, and what are the horizons of its material equipment? The problems of culture must be more adequately and appropriately formulated as one proceeds with the task. They differ from those which confront the ethnographer. He deals with a small and relatively homogeneous group in which contacts with the outside world are narrowly limited, whereas Western civilization is widespread, diverse, and has contacts with almost all other cultures. Compared with the aboriginal civilizations of this continent the present-day civilization of English-speaking North America is uniform throughout—the same newspaper, automobile, soaps, drugs, foods, and so forth. Even so, sectional differences persist, though roads, automobiles, press, telephone, and radio are rapidly making all localities superficially similar throughout the land.

Participants seldom understand their culture, for only an analysis of it reveals the subtle forces of social life to those who live among them. A Bryce gives the best interpretation of American life, an Ostrogorski discloses more about our political parties than we had known, a Lowell explains to Englishmen their own forms of institutions. It is difficult for a people to understand their culture, for it is the medium through which they view the world, and from it they take their standards. Yet culture influences are the most important forces in the world. "Race" prejudice is at basis merely cultural, and nothing does so much to mitigate it as an understanding of one's own culture and that of other peoples. The roots of culture are in the past, though the past is dead, except that part which the present keeps alive. But if the past is dependent upon the present, the present is not less dependent upon the past. To it we go for advice, warning, encouragement, or to confirm our pessimism. The things we do because they were done by our predecessors are more numerous than those we do rationally. Many traits of our culture have been borrowed. Our duodecimal system comes from Babylonia; our calendar, from Egypt; our philosophy, from Greece; our law, from Rome; our religion, from Palestine; Christmas, from Persia, Greece, Rome, and pagan Europe; corn from the Indians; tea and paper from China; kimonos from Japan. If the Mediterranean area were being studied for the first time and the task fell to the lot of the anthropologist, he would describe it, as he describes the aboriginal Caribbean and Central American areas, in terms of culture areas. Egypt with its priesthood, cult of the dead, ethics, and government, is a distinctive culture nowhere duplicated; Babylonian art, science, government, ethics, and religious concepts are peculiar to Mesopotamia and to that period of history; and a similar observation applies to Persia, Greece, and Rome. None of these, however, even in prehistoric times, were isolated cultures, but the early Mediterranean area was a region of fructifying culture contacts. Culture traits spread between Crete and the Greek peninsula, Crete and Asia Minor (Troy), Crete and Egypt, Egypt and Babylonia, and the Hebrews received traits from Egypt, Babylonia, Phœnicia, Greece, and Persia. Since Roman days there have been culture contacts and the diffusion of culture traits between the Mediterranean area and China. Dice, used in ancient Egypt, passed from Rome to China, and silks and porcelains came from China to Rome. Backgammon and chess, probably originating in India, traveled to China, and at about the same time polo spread from Persia to India and to China.

During the long period from Roman times down through the Middle Ages there was a steady give and take. The peach and the apricot, silk and tea, porcelain and paper, playing cards, and probably gunpowder and the compass, were among China's gifts to the West. The grape and alfalfa, the carrot, glass manufacture, Nestorian Christianity and Mohammedanism, the alphabet, and some impulses of Greek art were a few of the things that the countries of the Far East received in return.[1]

Laufer has identified 24 agricultural products, the knowledge of which traveled from China to Persia or beyond during the rule of the Mongols, and a knowledge of 68 were carried in the opposite direction.[2]

Historically, Western European culture is Germanic, but though the background is Germanic there are many culture strata, and upon this Germanic culture traits have been superimposed at different levels. In medieval Europe the principal culture levels were those of the peasantry, the gentry, and the clergy, respectively, the latter two having more in common that the first had with either of the others. The peasantry constituted a culture stratum different from that of the other two classes, and many of its superstitions and customs survive. The gentry developed another culture pattern, though much of the crude superstition of the peasantry flourished there also. Their culture pattern, however, contained more of the intellectual element, and especially more of the formal and conventional. The clergy developed a different pattern, though being recruited mainly from the gentry, it partook largely of the sympathies and outlook of the latter. Nevertheless, in ceremonialism, theology, and the respect, if often superficial and hypocritical, for things religious, its culture pattern was different from that of the gentry, and the legal, social, and ecclesiastical privileges of the clergy emphasized this difference.

In short, the most fruitful conception of Western civilization views it as a culture. An adequate understanding of it involves a knowledge of its historical background, material equipment, and social, political, and economic institutions. The totality of interdependent traits constitutes the culture. Since the various phases of the culture are interdependent one cannot understand political structure or function if one

---

[1] CARTER, THOMAS F., "The Invention of Printing in China and Its Spread Westward," p. 89, New York, 1925.

[2] LAUFER, BERTHOLD, "Sino-Iranica," Chicago, 1919.

knows only political institutions; one cannot understand history, if one is ignorant of other fields of knowledge; one cannot understand man the individual unless one understands men as carriers of culture. As Charles and Mary Beard have said regarding the development of American culture:

> Trained historians have brought under observation single segments of colonial life—economic, political, social, intellectual, artistic—and have written for specialists huge tomes that never find their way into the main stream of American thought. By none of these methods apparently can the intimate essence of American culture be grasped. In reality the heritage, economics, politics, culture, and international affiliations of any civilization are so closely woven by fate into one fabric that no human eye can discern the beginnings of its warp and woof. Any economic interpretation, any political theory, any literary criticism, any esthetic appreciation, which ignores this perplexing fact, is of necessity superficial. That a few students recognize the nature of the problem and are beginning the search for a synthesis is a striking sign of the new epoch in American intellectual development.[1]

Every political event is also a social, economic, psychological, and industrial situation, and the outcome of historical conditions. Every phase of our material, industrial, intellectual, and ethical life is involved in the election of a President of the United States, as is also our history, both as fact and as interpretation. It is influenced by the press, the weather, the radio, story, myth, tradition, the credit system, international relations, religion, education, brass bands, buttons, and by everything bequeathed by the industrial and political revolutions. To interpret intelligently contemporary civilization or any of its phases one must use, in fact if not in name, the concept of culture.

Culture falls into certain patterns in which there is comparative permanence of a few things, which therefore may be called fundamental, and a shifting in details, which may be called ephemeral. Credit, for example, appears fundamental to our present economic organization, although the instruments of credit may change ceaselessly. One cannot predict with much confidence their form a few decades hence; yet it is scarcely possible, while our culture remains essentially what it now is, that it will dispense with a credit system. Education, of some sort, appears to have come to stay, and it is so thoroughly interwoven with the entire culture that no important change in it is possible without readjustments in all phases of the culture. Transportation may become much modified, but one cannot conceive its disappearance. These phases

---

[1] BEARD, CHARLES A. and MARY R., "The Rise of American Civilization," vol. I, p. 124, New York, 1927.

of our civilization illustrate some of the fundamental elements in the pattern of Western culture.

4. THE INTERDEPENDENCE OF CULTURE TRAITS

A cluster of traits which function as a unit is called a complex. The Christmas celebration, in which the tree, the hanging of stockings, the giving of presents, the use of sweets, the attention paid to children, the singing of carols, the use of candles, and other traits, tend to cohere, constitutes the Christmas complex. Similarly with many other celebrations, such as Easter, Hallowe'en, Thanksgiving, Armistice day. The automobile and the traits which cluster about it, such as oil stations and garages, constitute a culture complex, and so, perhaps, does the factory system. The family, the church, the university constitute other culture complexes. A cluster of traits, or a trait complex, illustrates the fact that certain traits are vitally interdependent. As a matter of fact, any trait is dependent upon certain others, and usually a trait is dependent upon a great many, perhaps ultimately upon all, the traits of the culture. Indeed, although a culture can be analyzed into the traits of which it is composed, it cannot be described by merely enumerating the component traits. The traits function, else they become defunct, as of course some traits do. If, therefore, a trait is dropped from the culture the remaining traits are modified. If automobiles, for example, were disbarred from use, many other traits of the culture would be influenced. Remove churches, saloons, educational institutions, newspapers, printing presses, street cars, radios, telephones, private ownership, the wage system, the franchise, the factory system, or any other dominant trait, and the entire culture will be affected.

Similarly, when a new trait is added the entire culture is modified, although some portions of it, *i.e.*, some traits, are influenced more than are others. The automobile, for example, has affected every agency of transportation—railroad, street car, horse-drawn vehicle, and pleasure walking; the telephone has affected a thousand phases of our culture, the radio has affected many phases and promises to affect more. The Industrial Revolution was in essence merely the utilization and improvement of machinery, but every trait in Western culture has been affected by it. A doctrine of equal rights spreads from the original realm of male suffrage based on property, and influences the status of children, the poor, the mentally deficient, and peoples of the cruder cultures. It has influenced educational systems and curricula, and all phases of literature. Slavery eventually influenced every phase of the culture. Thanks to it there are a thousand problems which would not exist, at least not in their present form, had slave labor not been introduced. Social life is a phase of culture and it cannot be divorced, except in thought, from other phases. One can describe contemporary family life without confusing it with the automobile, the radio, or the postal system, but it is impossible to describe the functioning of contemporary family life without reckoning with the automobile, the radio, the postal system, and every other important trait of the culture, for they each and all affect family life. The extension of the suffrage, compulsory education, new legislation with regard to wages and hours of work, the new status of women, playgrounds, the youth movement, these and many other things affect the status of the family and its members. Every hypothesis or conclusion in psychology, ethics, or politics has reverberations in the family circle. Similar observations apply to every aspect of contemporary society: witness the extent to which the churches have been influenced as a result of the introduction of new traits into the culture, whether these were material objects, concepts, theories, or ideals.

In the higher cultures as in the simpler, culture traits are interdependent. They do not function as isolated or independent traits, but each is functionally related to all the others. A complete description of a culture, therefore, includes the interrelations of the component traits. Science affects religion, and religion science. There are interrelations between the press and industrial organizations, political life, educational policies, community spirit, and other phases of the culture. Since each trait influences the others each should be considered in its relation to other traits. The automobile has made many important changes in addition to facilitating traffic, and the telephone does much besides enabling one to speak at a distance. A doctrine of equal rights for all ultimately affects economic classes, the relations between the sexes, and the status of children. A doctrine of evolution in the organic world is applied to mind, morals, religion, and, indeed, to all phases of thought and life.

The interdependence of traits is a universal characteristic of culture. For example, a phase of Western culture consists of technological equipment, which in large part is the product of the Industrial Revolution. Automobiles, railroads, ten-cent stores, screening, warehouses, penny postage, cheap newspapers, airplanes, steambosts, furnaces, cheap pins and nails, are products of the factory system. But industrial development was dependent upon other phases of the culture. All of Western culture helped to make the Industrial Revolution, and the latter in turn influenced all phases of the culture. It was contingent upon developments in science which were under way in the last half of the eighteenth and were increasing apace during the nineteenth century. Machinery presupposed the tempering of iron and the hardening of steel. But until men can utilize coal and make charcoal and coke the smelting processes are handicapped; for iron and steel presuppose the generation and the utilization of intense heat. Development in science must precede any considerable development in manufacturing, and the development of the sciences is in turn contingent upon the maintenance of highly skilled techniques of manufacture. The mounted telescope, the accurate chronometer, the delicate instruments of engineer, oculist, surgeon, and anatomist, are dependent upon the maintenance of highly developed techniques. The Industrial Revolution, moreover, paved the way to universal education, universal suffrage, trade, travel, and credit. Every change in industry influences the culture, and, through social and political controls, the culture affects the trend of industrial changes. By increasing the productiveness of human labor, industrialism increases potential leisure, and when the laboring class becomes also the leisure class there are new culture potentialities. The by-products of industrialism—steel armor, steel cannon, steel shells—place armed rivalry on a new plane, and survival of the fittest becomes translatable into survival of the best manufacturers. The situation, to be sure, is not so simple as this, for it ramifies in all directions: the arms which manipulate the armor may become fatally weaker. In the full picture it would be evident that among interacting traits every action involves a reaction, for the trait which influences is also influenced. The x-ray, for example, was at first an achievement in pure physics, but its applications in surgery and in medicine made it indispensable to every efficiently equipped hospital and clinic. It was utilized in industry to determine the composition of steel and other metals, and now experimental biology employs it.

By treating flies with x-rays, the genes, or hypothetical hereditary particles, are affected, so that mutations can be produced artificially and at will in plants and animals, and the work of the animal and plant breeder will be greatly accelerated. We shall no longer need an empirical genius, such as Burbank, but shall obtain our results by quantitative laboratory methods.

By the use of the x-ray new varieties of tobacco plants have been produced which have a stronger growth and bear more flowers than their cousins descended from parents which have not been thus treated, and it is probable that corn, barley, and other plants respond similarly. The ultraviolet radiation which has been used with much success in the treatment of rickets, as a substitute for the sunlight cut off by modern methods of living, promotes plant growth and increases the production of valuable plant ingredients. Cod liver oil treated with ultraviolet rays is said to invest it with the same value that exposure to the sun possesses for the patient, and thus the beneficial effects of sunlight can be absorbed through the digestive system.[1]

"What would physics and astronomy be like, what our notions of the cosmos and our atmosphere, where would be our telescopes, electrical telegraphs, electric illumination, what would have been the course of navigation and surveying, without the constant and intelligent aid of practical mechanics?"[2] As Dove said

. . . without mathematics we have no astronomy, no geography, no measurement of time, and no systematic navigation, worthy of that name. That is, we have in those departments ignorance or superstition, instead of knowledge . . . The mathematical sciences are absolutely essential to the evolution of mechanics, and mechanical knowledge is absolutely necessary to enable man to turn the earth to the best account.[3]

The concepts of time and the techniques of measuring it are further illustrations of the interplay and interdependence of culture traits. Without a considerable development in mechanics no great accuracy in keeping time is possible. The water vessel would serve well enough if there were accurate methods of measurement; so would the sun-dial; but not until accuracy in measurement is attained can the smaller divisions of the day be precisely determined. A pendulum is accurate, but the utilization of it implies a knowledge of the laws of the pendulum, and also an accuracy in measurement which is not attained in the early civilizations. Later the principle of the wheel is applied, but this presupposes the development of the wheel and the discovery of the power inherent in the flow of water (the water clock). Only the principle of the coiled spring and of cogs with cogs makes possible the small accurate timepiece which can be carried in the pocket. Without accurate methods of keeping time, calendrical, diurnal, and in fractions of seconds, much of the present-day scientific investigation would be impossible. It enables men to predict eclipses, comets, sun-spots, and the weather. It enables them to conduct experiments to test the drag of the ether upon light, and to determine the gravitational influence of the sun upon light-rays. Many experiments in biology, medicine, or physics are impossible without accuracy in measuring time, and some phases of manufacturing are directly dependent upon such accuracy. Contemporary industrial and social life is, indeed, dependent upon the accurate measurement of

[1] Adapted, in part, from "Advances in Biophysics," *Sci. Monthly,* **26**: 189–190, 1928.

[2] HELMHOLTZ, quoted by LOWIE, R. H., "Are We Civilized?" p. 269, New York, 1929.

[3] DOVE, PATRICK E., "The Theory of Human Progression," p. 99, New York, 1910.

time. To banker, shipper, shop-keeper, telegrapher it is indispensable, for we move in orbits of minutes, and a wrong measure may have far-reaching consequences. Indeed, even a new concept of time has far-reaching results. "A new epoch in mathematics began" in 1905, when Albert Einstein published a short paper containing this sentence in the introductory paragraph: "In order that mathematical descriptions may have any physical meaning, it is necessary to have a clear idea of that which one calls Time."[1] Einstein's theory of relativity, originally a purely mathematical conception, has influenced the natural sciences, is now influencing the social sciences, and will influence all studies of social phenomena. Thus, a new concept, like a new trait, may affect the entire culture. Copernicus offers a new interpretation of the relations of the world to the sun and to the planetary and stellar bodies, and certain phases of the culture are greatly influenced. Theology and organized religion react violently, and social and intellectual values are affected. Similarly, when Darwin reinterprets the phenomena of organic life all of the culture is affected. Religion as well as theology opposes, but finally accepts, a Darwinian interpretation of its own field and justifies its persecutions in Darwinian terms. Political science adopts it, and interprets war as a struggle for existence with survival of the best military nations. Ethics becomes concerned with the evolution of conduct and with the survival value of social attitudes. Sociology become Darwinized, uses the biological concepts of selection, counter-selection, struggle, elimination, survival, and adopts a terminology familiar to the Darwinian.

The power of steam saves human energy and steam is used instead of the human arm to turn machines. But the introduction of steam makes changes in home production, the growth of cities, changes in the position of women, new causes for war. It has its effect upon the birth rate, the functions of the church, and the nature of education. If, for illustration, there had not been discovered these sources of power for turning wheels, i.e., if we were still producing by the energy or power of human beings and domesticated animals only, cities would have been few, concentration of production would be largely on the farms and in the home, the position of women would have been much as of old. Some changes would have occurred in education, in religion, and in morals. But there seems to be no doubt that the influences on non-material culture flowing from the use of steam have been profound.[2]

---

[1] Quoted in CURZON, H. E. J., "The History of Mathematics," in CARTER, E. H. (editor), "The New Past and Other Essays on the Development of Civilization," p. 159, Oxford, 1925.

[2] OGBURN, WILLIAM F., "Social Change," pp. 270–271, New York, 1922.

Machinery has influenced transportation, trade, finance, and every phase of our economic and industrial organization. It has influenced also our art, literature, drama, music, and architecture. The monotony and tyranny of the machine have set the style for much of the prevalent realism, and the rhythms, clangs, and whirrings of machinery have prepared the way for the syncopations and weird medleys of modern jazz. Even the stage has felt its influence, and actors impersonate machines; it was, indeed, a playwright, not an inventor, who coined the word *robot* and first gave a description of this automaton. The automobile affects community and economic life in similar ways in Maine, Kansas, or Arizona, because in these areas it makes liaisons with similar culture traits. And what phases of our culture has it not affected? It stimulates road-building; it enlarges the geographical horizon within which the common man moves; it abolishes the industries of the smith and the horse-trader, and stimulates those of the garage and the oil station; it foments new international interests and rivalries—in oil fields and rubber plantations which, after all, are not solely matters of naval convenience; it plays havoc with the bicycle and the horse-drawn vehicle, and helps to create and maintain the golf links; and it introduces new problems into the lives of the young, who suddenly are enabled to escape local surveillance. It creates new forms of social rivalry, new ideals of comfort, brings a new list of casualties and crimes, and a new orientation of finance, especially within the family; and it is the source of a new stimulus to the chamber of commerce. The automobile invades the classroom, the lecture platform, the pulpit, the laboratory, the editorial room, the factory, the palace, and the hovel. Everywhere it is a factor to be reckoned with, and it will leave nothing undisturbed; already it embarrasses preachers as well as horse-traders. The airplane will no doubt have as great transforming influence; and he is bold who ventures to predict that it will leave any phase of culture unchanged. It has influenced international relations; and the end is not yet, in peace or in war. As Madame de Staël pointed out at the close of the eighteenth century, aeronautics may influence every phase of social and economic life: warfare, trade, travel, and international relations.[1]

The diffusion of culture traits and changes in culture proceed without demanding the attention of any one individual or group of individuals. This, perhaps, is accountable for the fact that few are conscious of culture changes, and consequently no one has studied the phenomena as a process which affects culture in its entirety.

---

[1] See below, p. 308.

The minutemen at Concord and Lexington, in 1775, did not realize that they were pointing their guns at the monarchical idea. As little did the Third Estate of France, when it entered the Convention in 1789, realize that its road lay over the ruins of the throne. As little did the pioneers of English freedom, when they began to resist the will of Charles I, foresee that they would be compelled, before they got through, to take his head. In none of these instances, however, has posterity considered that the limited foresight of the pioneers as to the full consequences of their action lessened the world's debt to the crude initiative, without which the fuller triumph would never have come. The logic of the strike meant the overthrow of the irresponsible conduct of industry, whether the strikers knew it or not.[1]

Men do not foresee that the introduction of slavery into new territory may involve civil war later; that a new doctrine of natural rights, or an old one, revived, may involve revolution, democracy, the status of women and children, and family life; or that the radio, because it provides new means of disseminating information and entertainment, may affect every phase of social life. Yet the radio may affect the family as much as the economic independence of women has affected it, for entertainment which previously had to be sought without the home can now be had at home. It suggests new experiments in democracy, since, thanks to the radio, all can hear the discussions of political issues, and eventually the entire electorate may function as a legislature, at least with regard to certain measures. In short, in the course of its adjustment within the culture, and of the adjustment of the culture to it, the radio may influence every phase of culture.

In relation to communication of ideas by radio, the most remote countries are only about one-tenth of a second apart. We all live on a tenth-of-a-second radio world. It does not seem likely that such a world can indefinitely support more than one system of weights and measures. It must only be a question of time, on a tenth-second world, when only one system will supervene.[2]

That these almost instantaneous contacts with all parts of the world will have far-reaching influences is, indeed, a certainty.

Athens was a miniature stage of political developments and transitions. There were changes from monarchy to aristocracy, tyranny, democracy, and empire. Changes in a State are induced by conditions within the State or by external influences; at one time they may be caused by internal conditions, at another, by external factors; and some changes are attributable to an individual. It is, however, difficult to assign any direct or single cause for the changes in form of government

---

[1] BELLAMY, EDWARD, "Equality," p. 208, New York, 1923.

[2] KENNELLY, A. E., "The Metric System of Weights and Measures," *Sci. Monthly*, **26**: 149, 1928.

in Greece. The fact that each city was an independent state responsible for its political affairs made constitutional changes easy and frequent. Plato states that, "infinite time is the maker of cities," and hence of forms of government.

One authority states that the change from monarchy to tyranny was caused by the coinage of native money. Radet believes the new wealthy class was influential in the government, and this wealthy class was made possible by coinage. The first tyrant was the first wealthy citizen or merchant. Similarly the Italian Medici family of the fourteenth and fifteenth centuries were merchants, and in Italy during these centuries "in most cases great wealth was the original source of despotic government."[1] Hence coinage may be a contributory cause of change in form of government. A statement of Solon reflects an opinion of the times:

> But of themselves in their folly the men of the city are willing
> Our great city to wreck, being won by wealth.
> False are the hearts of the people's leaders.

The new rulers who came into power as the result of their wealth were not trained in governmental affairs as were the older aristocracy. This new commercial class established a financial aristocracy which supplanted the old hereditary estates. Theognis states: "The tradesmen reign supreme: the bad lord is over their betters"; "Many a bad man is rich and many a good man poor"; "Most men reckon the only virtue the making of money"; "Everyone honors those who are rich, and despises the needy."[2] Aristotle implies that the early tyrants were successful business men. In Sparta there was no tyrant; the Spartans had no other currency than iron, and Sparta remained rural. Athens mined silver, made coins, and developed large commercial enterprises; and almost immediately there were changes in the form of government. After the Persian wars Athens became the head of the Delian League. Her leadership was made possible by the failure of Sparta and by the personal leadership of Athenians. "Governmental changes and developments must be traced to the movements social and economic, military and religious, which mark the progress or decline of a nation." With the shift in wealth from a landed aristocracy to a commercial or a banking class the social structure changes. The men who are wealthy in money become a new force in the State and demand certain changes. They see in the Government an agency to aid them in making further financial gains. Coinage

---

[1] SYMONDS, J. A., "Age of Despots," p. 103.
[2] See also below, p. 234.

. . . hastened the passing of the collective economic system of the Greek tribal society and the political downfall of the tribal aristocracies whose wealth was based on land-holding. In combination with colonization coinage tended to release latent individual energies and to transmute these into productive effort . . . With the increasing wealth of individuals, household slavery progressed likewise; but this situation was prevalent only in the industrialized cities.[1]

Aristotle states that a change in military power brings a change in the form of government: Oligarchy is allied with cavalry, and light-armed men or infantry with democracy. Religion, too, was an important factor in stimulating changes. While the nobles were able to mediate with the gods in behalf of the people, their power was unbroken, but when the people rejected the gods the mediation of the nobles was no longer needed or effective. The early religion of the Athenians was intimately bound up with tribal life. With the rise of cities tribal bonds were weakened and the earlier religious affiliations were modified. Urbanization effected a change in religious beliefs when the people were no longer attached to the soil but had become the hoi poloi, the populace, of the cities. War may effect coalitions in the Government that are unknown in times of peace. When the State is in extreme danger the entrenched groups are supplanted by the ablest men available. The change from confederacy to empire was effected by a combination of factors which grew out of the Persian wars and the effective leadership of successful Athenians. A change in form of government may be effected by lawgivers, such as Solon, Lycurgus, Draco, Cleisthenes, and others, though men cannot effect these changes unless circumstances are favorable. Although concepts of government which came from across the seas influenced the theories of the Greeks, some writers attribute all changes in the form of government in Greece to the two factors of arms and men. In Athens the form of government went through a series of changes, whereas in Sparta it did not. Sparta was an agricultural State, Athens a commercial urban State. Athens housed merchants from the five seas; Sparta saw none. Athens had abundant contacts with East and West, while Sparta had few, if any. Sparta was the introvert, Athens the extrovert, for Sparta was immune from culture contacts, whereas Athens was an open city. Practically all forms of thought and ideas were current in the schools of Attica, whereas very few took root in Sparta. In identifying the causes responsible for change one must consider the peculiar composition of a nation. Sparta was a closed State, while Athens maintained an open-door policy at all times except during war. No outside contact, no change;

---

[1] "Greek Culture and Thought," in "Encyclopedia of the Social Sciences," vol. I, p. 13, 1930.

many contacts, perhaps much change. Thus, so far as the Greek city-states are concerned, changes in population, coinage, classes, and urbanization have been, severally and conjointly, at least partly responsible for the changes in form of government.[1]

In view, then, of the interdependence of culture traits, of their resilience and reactions to impacts, a social science which acknowledges the dual task of describing the function and the significance of its data cannot proceed fruitfully unless it reckons with the implications of culture. Family organization, as has been said, has little meaning apart from the culture in which it is incorporated. Its significance could not be the same in China, Greece, Rome, and Western civilization, even if the family bonds were identical in these respective areas. In other cultures as in Western civilization, the complexion of family organization changes when other aspects of the culture—social, political, or economic—change. Conversely, the culture gives the emphasis to every phase of life and determines the significance of attitudes. The belligerency of the Dakota and Cree is not that of Germans and Frenchmen. In the one case belligerency means a few scalps taken, a few horses stolen, a few dances and narratives. In the other it means a new agitation of the economic and political order, a new tone in press, pulpit, history, literature, art, music, and international affairs. The belligerency in the respective areas differs in almost every detail. To grasp its significance one must know the culture and follow the reverberations of belligerency within it; for culture has unity and wholeness, and a culture trait in action involves the reaction of the entire culture.

The culture pattern therefore determines the relation between component traits. "All men are born equal" does not mean in French culture what it meant in colonial America. It did not mean in colonial culture what it means in twentieth-century America, nor in Bourbon days what it means in present-day France. And though at any period it may mean various things, the culture orientation is important. When traits function differently the culture pattern changes. The changes which the radio, for example, will bring will depend upon the utilization of the trait. According to the interests and purposes of the respective communities it will make men more musical, more jazzy, more learned in science, in baseball, in weather lore, or in jokes. A radio as a sheer

---

[1] See, for example, GREENRIDGE, A. H. J., "Handbook of Greek Constitutional History," chaps. 1–5; URE, P. N., "The Origin of Tyranny," chaps. 1, 2, 9, 11; WHIBLEY, L., "Greek Oligarchies, Their Character and Organization," chaps. 2–5; FERGUSON, W. S., "Greek Imperialism," chaps. 2, 4.

For the above account of the changes in the form of Greek governments I am indebted to W. A. Lunden, of the University of Minnesota.

device has little significance. But a radio in a culture complex, linked with other traits, and utilized to realize certain ends, becomes part of a culture medium in which it creates new culture patterns and is itself made into a new culture trait. Every new device calls for a psychological adjustment, which of course is a phase of adjustment within the culture.

Every new thing seems strange and rather terrible until it has become part of the human scene, until it has gathered its cluster of association, comic, pathetic, and so forth. Thus our attitude towards automobiles is very different from what it was twenty years ago, when they were still comparatively unfamiliar. Then they were little more than strange disconcerting pieces of mechanism, but now they are almost living creatures. We know that there is drollery, snobbery, pathos, even poetry in our relations with our automobiles. They have become humanized, just as wireless is now rapidly becoming humanized.[1]

A news item of Nov. 29, 1929, states that "radio operators at Glasgow, Scotland, are complaining that their reception is being interfered with by a high-pitched whistle, due to the heterodyne produced by the station at San Sebastian, Spain." And this is not the only type of international problem which the radio creates.

In spite of the diversity in culture there is unity. Of culture traits, too, it may be said that together they stand, divided they fall; for their strength is a function of the extent to which they supplement one another. That is why few things in themselves have much culture significance. What they contribute depends upon how they are utilized and also upon what and how much they utilize; for "he who calls the tune, pays the piper." For any culture,

. . . the danger of electicism lies in the fact that the borrower does not always know what destruction may lurk in the new object he has incorporated into his own culture. So the Plains Indians adopted the horse and completely reorganized their life and many of their cultural values in terms of it. Little did they realize that this strange animal was but the precursor of annihilation.[2]

It may be said, too, that we little knew what we were doing when we adopted the automobile. No one foresaw that, for one thing, we were

---

[1] PRIESTLEY, J. B., "A Mistake about the Future," *Harper's Monthly Mag.*, **115**: 116, 1927.

[2] RADIN, PAUL, "The Story of the American Indian," pp. 316–317, New York, 1927.

perfecting an instrument of destruction more deadly to ourselves than cannon.[1]

5. SUMMARY

Individuals do not live in isolation; everywhere they are members of a social group, such as a family, a town, city, state, or nation. In any group there is a certain amount of likemindedness among the members, otherwise they could not live together. Often there are similarities between individuals who are of different social or political groups, such as the citizens of two adjoining states, or even those of two adjoining nations. They may speak the same language, wear the same kind of clothes, live in the same kind of house, read the same kind of books, newspapers or magazines, and in most respects be essentially similar. When people behave similarly under similar circumstances, have the same tools and material equipment, the same institutions and concepts, they have the same culture. Culture, then, means all those things, institutions, material objects, typical reactions to situations, which characterize a people and distinguish them from other peoples. It is nearly equivalent to civilization, if under that term one includes such types of culture as are found among savages as well as among the civilized, and in early times as well as at the present day. The differences between peoples are essentially differences in culture. It is because the Plains Indians had buffalo hunting, tipis, raw-hide containers, dog transportation, war parties, and the other traits which characterize them, that they differed from Europeans and from all other peoples outside of the Plains area. It is, indeed, because of the language, political institutions, educational system, customs and conventions, that the Englishman is different from the German, the Frenchman, the Italian. It is because we have different ideas, institutions, and material objects, such as automobiles, railroad trains, paved roads, and thousands of other things, that our culture of the present day is different from that of the colonies. Types of culture have specific geographical distributions, though the lines which mark them off are not always identical with the

---

[1] In 1926 automobiles killed 23,264 persons in this country, and in 1927 they were responsible for the death of 24,775. In addition, they injured about 1,200,000 persons during these two years. In 1928 the deaths rose to about 27,500 and this number increased by about 5 per cent in 1929. These figures may be compared with the following: 50,000 American soldiers were killed or died of wounds during the World War and in addition 182,000 were wounded. This record almost justifies the witticism that "if money spent for war could be spent to make people prosperous and happy, there would be cars enough to eliminate the surplus population." Regarding the influence of the automobile see LYND, ROBERT S. and HELEN M., "Middletown: A Study of Contemporary American Culture," chap. XVIII, New York, 1929.

political boundaries. Thus the line between North Dakota and South Dakota is political and not cultural, and the same is true, to a less extent, of the line between North Dakota and Manitoba, but the line between Mexico and the United States is cultural as well as political. One who crosses that boundary passes into a region with different language, customs, conventions, houses, religious organization, and these constitute a different culture. Even so, the contrast is not so great as if one went from the United States to the Eskimo or to a tribal region of Eastern Siberia, for Spanish civilization, which is the basis of Mexican culture, is derived from the same culture background as the civilization which flourishes in the United States. Both have derived their cultures from European civilization, and this common background is responsible for many of the traits which they share in common. There is a historical phase to culture, for culture, like everything else, changes. Our culture is different from that of the last century, which in turn differs from that of colonial days, and a similar statement applies to every culture. In some places, such as China, culture changes slowly, compared with Europe or English-speaking North America, but in China and in every other land the culture changes. Both geographical distribution and historical changes are affected by culture influences from other regions. Since the discovery of the New World, European civilization has spread into almost all parts of the globe, and in some areas, such as most of North America, Australia, New Zealand, much of South Africa, it has largely displaced the earlier cultures of those respective regions. A culture area, like a political area, may increase or may decrease. Of necessity, the spread of one culture means the disappearance, or the submergence, of other cultures. Contact with other areas influences the historical development of a culture. Contacts with Greek and Roman civilization brought a higher culture to the peoples of Northern and Western Europe a thousand years ago, and contacts with the New World gave European culture new products, among them tobacco, the potato, cocoa, while from China it acquired rice, silk, movable type, and the compass. These traits, and many others which came from distant lands, influenced considerably the development of European civilization. For a culture is more than the sum of the things which compose it. Each trait is intimately related to certain other traits, and a change in one influences the others. Indeed, most traits are interdependent, and no one of them can be abolished, or even considerably modified, without the others being affected. The improvement of the stationary engine made possible the locomotive and the steamship, and these in turn affected transportation, commercial routes, trade centers, political issues, international affairs, in short, practically every phase of the culture. At the present time almost every phase of our culture is in some way related to the locomotive and the steamship, and to that other notable application of the engine, the automobile. A change in ideas may have as important results. Thus the doctrine of natural rights which became prevalent in France and in the colonies in the eighteenth century helped to bring a revolution in North America and in France, a Civil War in the United States, and important changes in English social and political life. It affected religion, education, and the family. Social life, therefore, can be understood only by viewing it as a phase of culture and as related to the entire culture; for its character is determined by the culture of which it is a part, and any important change in the culture affects social relations. The improvement of transportation and of communication, for example, has made previously isolated sections of the New World intimate parts of European civilization; and at the present time any important change in culture in any part of the world may affect North America. An assassination in the Balkan peninsula may have as important consequences across the seas as in the obscure province in which it occurs; the identification of the tubercle bacillus by a country physician in Germany proved to be more important for our culture than any law passed by Congress or Parliament.

Chapter II

METHODS OF INFERRING CULTURE DEVELOPMENT

1. The Statistical Approach

There appears to have been some appreciation of the theory of chance in the latter part of the fifteenth century, for Sir John More, father of the author of "Utopia," Sir Thomas More, is said to have declared that "marriage was like dipping one's hand into a bag in which there were twenty snakes and one eel, for it was twenty to one that you caught not the eel." A more explicit application of the probability theory to events is contained in the writings of Mandeville, in the early eighteenth century. In a discussion of chance, Mandeville uses the illustration of the rebound of a tennis ball and also the throw of dice. He says:

To a Man, who knows nothing of the Tennis-Court, the Skips and Rebounds of the Ball seem to be all fortuitous; as he is not able to guess at the several different Directions it will receive, before it comes to the Ground; so, as soon as it has hit the Place, to which it was plainly directed at first, it is Chance to him where it will fall: whereas the experienced Player, knowing perfectly well the Journey the Ball will make, goes directly to the Place, if he is not there already, where it will certainly come within his Reach. Nothing seems to be more the Effect of Chance than a Cast of the Dice: yet they obey the Laws of Gravity and Motion in general, as much as any thing else; and from the Impressions that are given them, it is impossible they should fall otherwise than they do: but the various Directions which they shall receive in the whole Course of the Throw being entirely unknown, and the Rapidity with which they change their Situation being such, that our slow Apprehension cannot trace them, what the Cast will be is a Mystery to human Understanding, at fair Play. But if the same variety of Directions was given to two Cubes of ten Feet each, which a Pair of Dice receive as well from one another as the Box, the Caster's Fingers that cover it, and the Table they are flung upon, from the time they are taken up 'till they lye still, the same Effect would follow; and if the Quantity of Motion, the Force that is imparted to the Box and Dice was exactly known, and the Motion itself was so much retarded in the Performance, that what is done in three or four seconds, should take up an Hour's time, it would be easy to find out the Reason of every Throw, and Men might learn with Certainty to foretell which Side of the Cube would be uppermost. It is evidence then, that the Words *fortuitous* and *casual*, have no other meaning, than what depends upon our want of Knowledge, Foresight and Penetration; the Reflection on which will shew us, by what an Infinity of Degrees all human Capacity falls short of that universal *intuitus*, with which the supreme Being beholds at once every thing without Exception, whether to us it be visible or invisible, past, present, or to come.[1]

The first writer to apply the law of probability to culture phenomena was David Hume. He opens his essay on "The Rise and the Progress of the Arts and Sciences" with the observation: "Nothing requires greater nicety, in our inquiries concerning human affairs, than to distinguish exactly what is owing to *chance*, and what proceeds from causes; nor is there any subject, in which an author is more liable to deceive himself by false subtleties and refinements . . . To say that any event is derived from chance, cuts short all further inquiry concerning it, and leaves the writer in the same state of ignorance with the rest of mankind . . . The distinguishing between chance and causes," he continues, "must depend upon every particular man's sagacity, in considering every particular incident," but nevertheless the principle holds.

If you suppose a die to have any bias, however small, to a particular side, this bias, though, perhaps, it may not appear in a few throws, will certainly prevail in a great number, and will cast the balance entirely to that side. In like manner, when any *causes* beget a particular inclination or passion, at a certain time, and among a certain people; though many individuals may escape the contagion, and be ruled by passions peculiar to themselves; yet the multitude will certainly be seized by the common affection, and be governed by it in all their actions.

That is to say, when a type of event occurs with greater frequency than chance would account for, a persistent cause must be inferred as the explanation. The significance of Hume's observation seems to have escaped subsequent students of culture until the time of Sir Edward B. Tylor. Tylor makes no reference to Hume but he was familiar with the history of social and anthropological theory; that he had read Hume's essay is almost certain; and that he had observed the distinction made by Hume between chance and cause is likewise almost certain. However that may be, Hume's concept is a fitting text for Tylor's statistical method of inferring the course of culture development. Yet if Tylor was familiar with Hume's essay it is surprising that he failed to consider the importance of diffusion, for Hume points out that diffusion may transplant a trait from one culture to another, and in the new culture setting it may flourish contemporaneously with traits which are chronologically as well as logically its antecendents.

---

[1] MANDEVILLE, BERNARD, "Fable of the Bees," vol. II, pp. 262–263, Oxford, 1924.

Imitation also is apt to transport these coarser and more useful arts from one climate to another, and make them precede the refined arts in their progress; though, perhaps, they sprang after them in their first rise and propagation.[1]

There is reason to suppose, said Tylor, that trait A, for example, preceded trait B and that B was followed by trait C. Logical and psychological considerations imply this order, although, by hypothesis, there is no historical evidence that A preceded B nor that B preceded C. In this event one appeals to statistics. If, in a large number of cases, B but not C is associated with A, it appears that A may sometimes give rise to B but not to C, at least not directly. If, further, in many instances C is associated with B, B may be transitional between A and C. The assumption that B is transitional is strengthened if the B cases associated with A are incipient rather than fully developed, and the C cases associated with B are incipient rather than full-fledged. If, in the association of A with B, A is weak when B is more highly developed, and if, in the association of B with C, B is weak when C is vigorous, it becomes more probable that the development was from A to B and from B to C. The tendency for two social features or traits to occur in association Tylor calls "adhesion." Adhesions, then, suggest the course of development, for they imply cause and effect. But in what direction does the cause operate? A may have given rise to B and B to C, or the cause may have operated in the opposite direction and C may have given rise to B and B to A. Unless there is historical and inferential evidence the demonstration of the association of traits does not indicate the order in which they developed, for mere association does not indicate the direction of development. Tylor's data and his problem, therefore, illustrate the difficulty of inferring from concomitant phenomena the direction of culture change. He tabulates the data bearing on the development of exogamy, descent, change of residence, and related traits, particularly the customs of the husband residing in the group of the wife, of the wife residing in the group of the husband, and of both residing in another locality. With change of residence may be causally associated the practice of avoidance, i.e., of the husband not speaking to the wife's relations, or of the wife not speaking to husband's relations. Tylor's data include 350 tribes representing various stages of culture.[2] As regards

[1] HUME, DAVID, "The Rise and the Progress of the Arts and Sciences," In "Essays, Literary, Moral, and Political," p. 72, London, 1870.

[2] TYLOR, EDWARD B., "On a Method of Investigating the Development of Social Institutions," JAI, 18: 245–269, 1889. Reprinted in KROEBER, ALFRED L., and WATERMAN, THOMAS T., "Source Book in Anthropology," pp. 321–342, Berkeley, 1920.

change of residence and the custom of avoidance his analysis yields the
following:

AVOIDANCE

Between H. and W.'s relations,	Mutual,	Between W. and H.'s relations,
45	8	13

TRANSFER OF RESIDENCE

Husband to wife,	Removal to another locality,	Wife to husband,
65	76	141

The husband was an outsider, was regarded as an intruder, and was
treated as a stranger, *i.e.*, he was not "recognized." Since it is more
common for the wife to reside in the husband's group than for him to
reside in hers, if Tylor's supposition that the two practices are causally
related is correct, the custom of avoidance between the husband and
the wife's relations would occur with greater frequency than the custom
of avoidance between the wife and the husband's people. And such is
the case. The data, however, are more significant. "If the customs of
residence and the customs of avoidance were independent, or nearly so,
we should expect to find their coincidence following the ordinary laws of
chance distribution."[1] But the frequency with which the association
occurs is greater than the law of chance would predict. In the 65 tribes
in which the husband resides permanently with the wife's family there
are 14 cases of avoidance between him and her relations, whereas the
expectation based on chance would be 8 cases. In 141 tribes the wife
goes to live in the home of the husband. The law of probability would
assign to these tribes 18 cases of avoidance between husband and wife's
relations, whereas, in fact, there are only 9 such cases. If the 13 cases
of avoidance between wife and husband's relations were distributed
without regard to change of residence, by the law of probability there
would be only 6 cases in which the wife lives in the family of the husband,
whereas, in fact, there are 8 such cases. "Thus there is a well-marked
preponderance, indicating that ceremonial avoidance by the husband
of the wife's family is in some way connected with his living with them;
and *vice versa* as to the wife and husband's family."[1] The following table
compares the correspondences in fact with those predictable by the law of
chance:

---

[1] *Ibid.*

CORRESPONDENCES IN FACT COMPARED WITH CORRESPONDENCES PREDICTABLE BY
THE LAW OF CHANCE

Change of residence	Avoidance	In fact	Predictable by law of chance
H. to W.	H. avoids W.'s relations	14	9
W. to H.	H. avoids W.'s relations	9	18
W. to H.	W. avoids H.'s relations	8	5 to 6
H. to W.	W. avoids H.'s relations	0	2 to 3

Thus the data are consonant with Tylor's theory. Transfer of residence by the husband to the home or group of the wife is associated with
avoidance of her relations in nearly twice the number of cases to be
expected by chance. Also, avoidance by the husband of the wife's people
when she goes to live in his group is found with only half the frequency
which the law of chance would predict. In keeping with these results is
the positive correlation between the wife's avoidance of the husband's
relations and the transfer of residence to his group.[1] Tylor is aware of
limitations in the statistical method. He says:

We pass on to less solid ground in assigning for this connection a reason
which may be only analogous to the real reason, or only indirectly corresponding with it, or only partly expressing it, as its correlation with other connec-
tions may eventually show.[2]

Since conduct is amenable to statistical treatment, explanation should
be "guided in its course and strictly limited in its range by well-marked
lines of fact to which it must conform."[2] It seems clear, however, that
interpretative insight suggested the correlations, for Tylor's statistics
are the outcome of his speculations rather than *vice versa*. After inferring
the course of development and inquiring into the reasons for it he ascer-
tains to what extent correspondences in fact support his inferences.
But the significance of correspondences must be determined. There are
casual as well as causal associations, and the more complex the phenomena the greater the probability that some of it will yield meaningless
correlations. For example, a positive correlation between belief in the
flatness of the earth and in multiplicity of souls does not imply that the
one belief causes the other. The respective beliefs may be due to different
series of causes, and possibly neither phenomenon is responsible for the
genesis or persistence of the other. Statistics, therefore, do not answer the

---

[1] We are here concerned with Tylor's method and not with the statistical value
of the respective numbers of cases, the variability of the data, or the probable error.
[2] *Ibid.*

question of their own value, and to insist that there is a logical, psychological, or historical relation is to rely on something besides sheer statistics. Yet statistics may strengthen the logic of deductions, or may show that they are erroneous. Statistics, therefore, may bring conviction, and conviction may guide statistics; moreover, by demonstrating the character of correlations statistics may indicate causes previously unsuspected. Nevertheless, the fact that two series of events are highly correlated does not imply that the one is the cause of the other, although this knowledge may give an insight into causes. Thus, the April temperatures of previous years may be a good guide to the April temperatures of the coming year but they are not the cause of the latter.

Hobhouse, Wheeler, and Ginsberg[1] point out that diffusion of culture sometimes interferes with normal development, and adds units to the statistical aggregate which, strictly speaking, do not belong there.

A borrowed art is not of the same value as evidence of the mentality of a people as the same art if known to have originated at home, but if we are to pursue this argument too far, in how many cases shall we really be able to say that an art is ultimately of domestic origin? Culture contact, direct or indirect, is in fact the normal not the exceptional process throughout human history. And, on the other hand, how long does it remain true that the importance of a new art is without effect upon the social customs of a people? . . . Upon the whole, therefore, we must take people as we find them, whatever the causes may be which have brought them to their present level.[2]

In their statistical study, then, each tribe which has the designated trait counts as one, whether the trait seems to have arisen independently or appears to have been borrowed. Since, however, the distribution of a given trait throughout contiguous tribes leaves no doubt that diffusion rather than independent origins is responsible for its presence in most of the tribes, the respective tribes should not be counted as units and given equal weight with tribes in regions from which the trait is otherwise absent; for, presumably, in the case of each of the last mentioned tribes the trait has originated independently, while in most of the former tribes its presence is due to diffusion. The data, in short, should be weighted as well as counted. It is possible to weight the evidence by treating as a unit the contiguous tribes in which a given trait appears, rather than count each tribe as one. As a check upon the first method, counting contiguous tribes as a unit, the authors make use of the second method also, and suggest that the results yielded by these two methods

---

[1] "The Social Institutions and Material Culture of the Simpler Peoples," University of London, 1915.
[2] *Ibid.*

are the more convincing if they harmonize. The statistical value of the degree of correspondence will depend upon the number of independent culture areas rather than upon the number of tribes which share the trait in the respective areas. The basis of their correlation, the constant variable, is the method of obtaining food, which distinguishes savagery from civilization as definitively as does any other criterion. The stages recognized are Lower Hunters (*LH*), Higher Hunters (*HH*), Agricultural peoples, and Pastoral peoples; the agricultural stage is subdivided into three types, based on the extent to which agriculture is developed, and the pastoral is divided into two types. This classification does not imply the chronological order in which these economic stages have developed, but is based merely upon the degree of control over the food supply. An analysis of 403 tribes shows a correlation of organized government with economic advance.

Seventeen of the 61 tribes in which there is no government or but little government are among the Lower Hunters, and constitute 47 per cent. of the tribes in that status, while 19 are among the Higher Hunters and constitute 25 per cent. of that group. In 12, or 10 per cent. of the total of Agriculture 2, there is no government, although in Agriculture 3, government is a characteristic of all tribes in a total of 96, and in Pastoral 2, in all tribes in a total of 16. The frequency with which government appears as a trait of tribal culture increases from lower to higher economic stages. Thus, with advance in economic organization there is a tendency toward the consolidation of government and the extension of the area of organized society. In nearly half of the tribes in the lowest economic stages government does not include more than the "primary" group (clan, band, or small local group). "In the highest pastoral and agricultural societies there is organized government in all cases, and in three out of four the organized government includes more than one 'primary' group, and extends to a large village, a tribe, or perhaps a 'nation.' "[1] The administration of justice likewise is positively correlated with economic advance. Self-redress, *i.e.*, absence of law, is found with diminishing frequency from lower to higher stages, while, conversely, public and prescribed punishment for offenses occurs with increasing frequency from lower to higher. In brief:

The sphere of the collective maintenance of justice, viewed as a whole, marks a steady advance from the primary group outwards. Within the primary group, public justice advances upon the whole though less regularly with the advance in material culture. We therefore seem justified in regarding pure

---

[1] *Ibid.*

self-redress as the initial stage of development, and public control as super-imposed by successive stages upon that method of maintaining order.[1]

In 552 tribes the methods of determining guilt indicate a trend toward the adoption of supernatural tests rather than toward rational procedure:

METHODS OF DETERMINING GUILT AT DIFFERENT ECONOMIC STAGES

Economic stage	Trial	Ordeal	Oath
Lower Hunters	5	0[1]	0
Higher Hunters	2	1	0
Dependent Hunters	0	1	0
Agriculture 1	2	3	0
Agriculture 2	7	26	7
Agriculture 3	20	35	8
Pastoral 1	1	1	1
Pastoral 2	6	4	3

[1] Australian spear-throwing ceremonies are omitted.

Thus, taken in their entirety, the data presented by the authors show a correlation of social development with economic development.[2] The lowest societies are small and within the smallest groups there is often no provision for insuring justice. With advance beyond the Lower Hunters there are larger societies, and within these larger social units there is better provision for the maintenance of justice. In a large proportion of tribes in the higher economic stages public justice extends over the whole of a large group. "This brings us to the threshold of civilized order just as economically we have come to the point at which civilization is usually held to begin."[3]

The statistical interpretation of culture is considered also by Mayo-Smith,[4] who calls attention to the complexity of culture phenomena and to the consequent difficulty of selecting factors which are causally related. Since many influences are contemporaneous with a given phenomenon, selection is apt to yield a meaningless association. Quantitative distinctions may reveal laws which apply to masses, though it does not follow that they apply to the individual who is a member of the mass; for "it is not averages that exist, but individuals."[5] When the social environment is complex it is difficult to reduce all phenomena to regularity, for then there is more room for the play of caprice. In civilized

[1] *Ibid.*

[2] We are describing the methods of the authors and are not concerned here with the statistical significance of the data.

[3] *Ibid.*

[4] "Statistics and Sociology," New York, 1895.

[5] WELLS, HERBERT G., "A Modern Utopia," p. 332, New York, n. d.

life the individual is a creative force, and data which apply to the mass
are less likely to apply to component individuals. Though environment
modifies society, with advance in civilization society acquires more
efficient control over physical factors. Statistics can determine the
direction of changes but not the cause or the meaning of them, and it is
incumbent upon the sociologist to discover the social purposes. Statistics,
Mayo-Smith concludes, cannot explain social forces, although it may
reveal their existence by disclosing the regularities of social phenomena.
"Nothing," says Professor Cooley, "is more illuminating or more falla-
cious than statistics. If the underlying material is trustworthy they may
reveal its meaning; but numerical exactitude is often the only thing
scientific about them."[1] And, so, forsooth, "he who sets out in the right
direction with only the stars to guide will reach his goal sooner than one
who goes off in the opposite direction equipped with the most perfect
compass, sextant, and chronometer."[2] Turgot says,

. . . In mathematics, the mind works out a chain of propositions, the one
deduced from the others, the truth of which is demonstrated by their mutual
dependence. It is different with the other sciences, in which it is not through
comparison of ideas between themselves that the truth of knowledge is reached,
but through their conformity with a sequence of real facts. In order to discover truth and to establish it, the point in question is no longer the mere
laying down of a small number of simple principles from which the mind has
only to let itself be carried along the line of consequences; it is necessary to
start from Nature, just as she is, and from that infinite diversity of effects
towards which have occurred so many causes counterbalanced one by another.[3]

Moreover, in investigating social phenomena, however much one may
employ numerical symbols to indicate results, every investigation has
a subjective tinge of meanings and presuppositions. Otherwise the
investigation would not be made, or if made, it would be merely a mathematical procedure with no necessary relation to the facts.[4]

Some professional mathematicians and scientists of a mediocre sort tend
to believe that mathematics is perfect—the "queen" of the sciences, etc.,—and

[1] COOLEY, CHARLES H., "Life and the Student: Roadside Notes on Human
Nature, Society, and Letters," p. 156, New York, 1927.

[2] HOCART, A. M., "Kingship," p. v, Oxford, 1927.

[3] TURGOT, "Discourse at the Sorbonne, Dec. 11, 1750, on the Successive Advances
of the Human Mind." Translated in STEPHENS, W. WALKER, "The Life and Writings
of Turgot," p. 163, London, 1895.

[4] See KASTEN, A. "Gesundheitsstatistik und Soziologie," Jahrb. f. Nationalökonomie und Statistik, 126: 417ff., 1927; THURNWALD, RICHARD, "Die Probleme einer
empirischen Soziologie," Zeitschr. f. Völkerpsychol. und Soziol., 3: 270, 1927; WALLIS,
W. D., "The Problems of an Empirical Sociology," Social Forces, 7: 46–49, 1928.

that if anything is expressed mathematically we must in submissive awe "believe" it, or at least pretend to understand it . . . Orthodox mathematics is no more certain to produce an intelligent result than is orthodox language. That "queen" stuff is obvious nonsense—the protective cloak of the egotistical dogmatist.[1]

The above criticisms, of course, are not directed at the statistical method but only at misapplications of it. The statistical method when it is applicable is probably the most useful device which has been introduced into the social sciences, and to berate it as a method would be sheer obscuranticism. Properly used, *i.e.*, when the data are susceptible of statistical treatment, it provides an objective description of quantitative data which can be achieved by no other means. It is most useful when the problem is understood, and its implications are realized and are brought into the open. The qualitative analysis of the problem is not a function of statistics as such, although statistics frequently reveal or suggest otherwise unsuspected relations; and the demonstration of quantitative relations is possible only through statistical treatment. At the present time, perhaps the larger need in the study of culture phenomena is a more careful and accurate analysis of the data, though each problem has specific demands which, perhaps, cannot be stated under any useful generalization. Certainly "anthropology, social anthropology at least, has a long way to go yet before it can apply mathematical principles as physics does."[2]

2. ETHNOLOGICAL RECONSTRUCTIONS OF CULTURE DEVELOPMENT

In the present century the most notable contributions to method in culture reconstruction have come from four sources: the biological sociologists, the anthropologists and ethnologists, the social psychologists, and the "pure" sociologists. The biological sociologists attempt to reconstruct the course of social development by applying to social life the principles of biological evolution. The categories under which they subsume their data are those of the biologist—struggle for existence, adaptation, selection, counter-selection, and survival of the fittest. But they place too much faith in analogy, assuming rather than demonstrating that the laws which apply to biological phenomena are applicable to social life; for it is a fact that "knowledge of the natural history of the oyster is useless in predicting the behavior and social organization of ants; the natural history of neither enables us to predict man's

---

[1] KLYCE, SCUDDER, "Universe," p. 34, Winchester, Mass., 1921.

[2] ROSE, HERBERT J., "Primitive Culture in Italy," pp. 131–132, New York, 1927. Further reference to the statistical method is made below, pp. 57–58.

behavior."[1] The fields of biology and sociology are on different planes. Principles which hold for the one do not always hold, or hold only with qualification, for the other; there is no thorough-going correspondence between them. As well base biology on sociology as *vice versa*. Biology cannot explain the specific manifestations of culture. G. Elliot Smith says,

It would ill become me as a biologist, to attempt to minimize the vast rôle of heredity in determining the physical structure and the mental and moral aptitudes of every individual, and the variations in the average levels of attainment to which these hereditary qualities are subject in different races. But it is necessary to emphasize the fact that, so far as innate mental and moral characteristics are concerned, it is merely a vaguely defined and more or less generalized aptitude that is inherited, and not any special kind of ability or congenital propensity towards good or evil behavior. The musical genius, however great his aptitude may be to appreciate the subtle symbolism of sound and to acquire the mechanical skill for giving appropriate expression to his knowledge and feelings, could not become a musician unless he is provided with the opportunities for learning the arbitrary conventions of music that obtain in the community where he happens to live.[2]

Aware of the pitfalls of speculation in a science which should be inductive, and of the diversity in savagery, a name which covers a wide range of character and achievement, contemporary ethnologists and anthropologists demand detailed and accurate accounts of culture phenomena. They emphasize the fact that similar conditions may be variously inspired, similar practices arise from different motives, similar customs have varying utility which can be understood only through familiarity with the respective cultures. They depart from the biological and the "pure" sociologists and insist on knowing the facts of social life as they appear to those who approach them without prejudice and without theory to prove or disprove—though, alas! there are no such people. As Czekanowski has said, in ethnological investigations the raw material of observation depends upon the existing state of knowledge and beliefs; and the observations are determined primarily by contemporary interests and evaluations.[3] "Investigators are too apt to forget that the logics of science,—that unattainable ideal of the discovery of pure relations of cause and effect, uncontaminated by any kind of

[1] DORSEY, GEORGE A., "Race and Civilization," in BEARD, CHARLES A. (editor), "Whither Mankind," p. 242, New York, 1928.

[2] SMITH, GRAFTON ELLIOT, "The Evolution of Man," pp. 104–105, London, 1927.

[3] CZEKANOWSKI, JAN, "Objective Kriterien in der Ethnologie," *Korrespondenz-Blatt der Deutschen Gesellschaft für Anthropologie, Ethnologie und Urgeschichte*, **42**: 77, 1911.

emotional bias as well as of unproved opinion,—are not the logics of life."[1] Without the contributions of the ethnographers there can be little advance in an understanding of primitive culture, for without facts one cannot proceed. Mere facts, however, do not solve problems, and at best the accumulation of them merely provides the data for an insight into culture development. The cautious student of primitive culture does not claim that they do more than this. If, however, the search for facts is not guided by fruitful points of view and by significant problems there can be little surety that efforts will prove profitable, for facts are understood only through theory. If theory which takes no account of facts is only idly blowing bubbles, collecting facts without theoretical guidance is only gathering potsherds—though the potsherds may serve a purpose in other hands. Unfortunately, however, little historical material can be gleaned from tribal culture and the anthropologist must proceed non-historically, or must reconstruct history by inference. With few exceptions only the static and not the dynamic life of savages is known, whereas to understand development trend rather than status is essential. And even if the course of development in certain tribes were known, it would be illogical to infer similar developments for other areas—it is not so easy "from one to learn all." The ethnographer, therefore, can supply but scant, though indispensable, assistance to the student to culture development. He can furnish the setting of the problems but, as sheer ethnographer, he has few clues to the solutions of them.

3. SAPIR'S "TIME PERSPECTIVE"

Anthropologists, however, have not given up attempts to define a method for inferring the course of culture developments. Edward Sapir[2] suggests that as we read space perspective into the flat surface of a photograph, so it is possible to read time perspective into the flat surface of American culture, or (by implication) of any culture. A culture, therefore, may be compared to a long-exposure star chart, in which the degree and direction of movement of the nearer bodies are betrayed by short lines. In constructing this time perspective Sapir adduces several principles of interpretation, of which the following will serve as illustrations: The value of native testimony is strengthened by the fact that sometimes things have occurred as alleged, and therefore even native legend may,

---

[1] BOAS, FRANZ, "Primitive Art," p. 2, Oslo, 1927.

[2] SAPIR, EDWARD, "Time Perspective in Aboriginal American Culture, A Study in Method," Ottawa, 1916. This study is the first thorough and critical statement of the problem of time perspective, and certainly is the ablest of them. If any treatment of the problem deserves the name of classic it is, beyond doubt, this brilliant essay.

with caution, be accepted as correct history.[1] There is a principle of logical development, or of "necessary presupposition," by virtue of which the older contemporary traits of culture can sometimes be identified. Thus the throwing-stick of the Southwest is older than the woven rabbit-skin blanket, the former being a simple instrument and characteristic of the culture. The Eskimo make with the drill a circle-and-dot design; hence, the instrument must be older than the design. The more completely and tenaciously a trait adheres to a culture, the older the trait may be assumed to be. "The firmer the association, the older the culture element." By allowing those features of the culture to fall away which of their own accord (!) most easily do so, the oldest is revealed. In this manner the pages of history can be turned.

That, *e.g.* the Beaver-bundle ritual of the Blackfoot, at least in its present form, is of later origin than the sun dance is suggested by its loose superimposition upon the sun dance complex itself. An instructive example is afforded by the comparison of the relative importance or constancy of different dances in the elaborate complex of dances constituting part of the Nootka Wolf ritual. The great majority of these have properly nothing to do with the essential nucleus of the whole ceremony.[2]

Conversely, if a trait is associated with few features of the culture its recent introduction is implied. Adjustment to environment constitutes another criterion. Probably the clumsy elm-bark canoe of the Iroquois is more recent than the finely shaped canoes of the Eastern Woodland Algonkin, because the canoes of the latter are better adapted to the environment. Therefore, one may

risk the guess that the Iroquois bark canoe is an imperfect copy in elm-bark, a characteristically Iroquois material, of the superior Algonkian types, and connect this further with the general culture consideration that the Iroquois were rather more inclined to be cross-country walkers than the neighboring Algonkian tribes, who were more adept river and sea folk.[3]

The prominence of the thunderbird *motif* in the Plains area is in keeping with the prevailing terrific thunderstorms; on the Northwest Coast the thunderbird *motif* is prominent, although environmental conditions would not suggest its presence, since thunder is seldom heard and is distant and mild. One infers, therefore, that the thunderbird

---

[1] Compare Radin: "Legend thus shall lead us by the hand to corroborate what archæology and ethnology have taught and to give us at times glimpses of cultural movements about which archæology and ethnology are unfortunately silent." RADIN, PAUL, "The Story of The American Indian," p. 180, New York, 1927.

[2] SAPIR, *op. cit.*

[3] *Ibid.*

motif of the Northwest Coast came from the Plains area, and persists in an environment to which it is little adapted. A phase of culture which is elaborately developed probably is of relatively great age, but this criterion must be used with caution, since the entire complex to which the trait belongs may have been borrowed. When an element stands out in isolation from the remainder of the culture, as though out of context, apparently having lost its full content of "intelligible relation to the rest of the culture," it may be considered a survival. Survivals, as a rule, pertain to phases of social life which are accepted without questioning their rationality, and are most abundant in ceremonialism.

Survivals, if we can only be sure we really have them, are of great historical interest, as they undoubtedly reach back far into the past; though great caution is needed in the utilization of them. An element of culture may be merely borrowed from another tribe in which its setting is perfectly plain; becoming detached from this setting, it may appear as an isolated survival-like element in the borrowing culture and deceptively suggest great age. Or the element may appear as a survival merely because all the descriptive data required for its elucidation have not been recorded.[1]

The relative age of traits which have been diffused can sometimes be inferred, for, in general, the older the trait, the wider its distribution. Also, relative age can be inferred indirectly from the degree of smoothness of the mechanism of diffusion, from

the relative ease or readiness with which a culture trait is communicated by the borrowing tribe, and the external conditions which favor or militate against the adoption of the trait. Where all three groups of factors are favorable towards the spread of the culture element, the rate of such spread is naturally at a maximum.[1]

Some traits travel faster than others: a humorous story travels faster than a religious ceremony, a simple mechanical device more rapidly than an abstruse concept, a new dance faster than a new method of inheriting property. When age is inferred from relative distribution the probable rate of diffusion must be considered. "It is not difficult to understand why myth plots, spectacular dances, games, and certain decorative designs spread with tremendous rapidity and may, in many cases, cover larger areas of distribution than culture elements of greater age."[1] Hence, "the apparently hoary antiquity of at least some such features, when closely scrutinized, may resolve itself into a relatively recent spread of fashion."[1] The possibility of independent origins must, however, be considered before the criterion of relative age can be applied to widely distributed traits.

---

[1] *Ibid.*

Clark Wissler interprets culture development by criteria similar to those used by Sapir. The area of intensive development is assumed to be the area of origin. If agriculture is most highly developed in Central America, or in Mexico, this region is assumed to be older agriculturally than areas in which agriculture is indifferently practised, and a similar criterion is applied to other culture traits. The degrees of elaboration of a trait indicate the path of diffusion. Uniqueness in the traits and in the patterns of New World cultures implies their origin in the New World rather than diffusion from the Old World.[1]

4. CRITIQUE OF THE "TIME PERSPECTIVE" ARGUMENT

Many of the interpretations suggested by Sapir are susceptible of other reading. The fact, for example, that the statements of natives are sometimes consistent with observed or with implied facts, does not establish the value of inferential native history, since too often it is obviously wrong. As Malinowski says, the savage's "sense of historical accuracy and his interest in reconstructing the past is on the whole extraordinarily weak, as witness the almost complete absence of historical accounts from the immediate past, and the entire unreliability of such tales as can be checked from European chronicles."[2] In the main the channels along which their explanations move, so far as one can check them historically or inferentially, are not trustworthy. Perhaps, as Sapir suggests, the Tewa pueblo of Hano, situated in the Hopi country of Tusayan, correctly traces the origin of its culture to the Rio Grande Valley; but it does not follow that this "should, among other facts of like nature, make us more receptive to the truth of similar movements in native legend."[3] One of the leading-strings of myth-making is the plausible, and one cannot consider a story true merely because it is plausible. The first histories, Turgot observes, are fables invented to supplant ignorance of the origin of empires, arts, and customs; it is easy to recognize their falsity. All such inventions, however, have a certain verisimilitude, for they are in accordance with the presuppositions of the time; and after the account has been given out as the truth, it is not proper to contradict it on the basis of subsequent observations. These fabricators of history crave amusement and glory rather than desire to exaggerate. Even in the time of Herodotus the historian is still a poet. Only later do historians recognize an obligation to adhere

---

[1] A further account of Wissler's method is given below, pp. 70–76.
[2] MALINOWSKI, B., *Sat. Rev. Liter.*, **4**: 738, 1928.
[3] SAPIR, *op. cit.*

to truth.[1] "It is," says Thucydides, "the custom of mankind, nay even where their own country is concerned, to acquiesce with ready credulity in the traditions of former ages, without subjecting them to the test of sedate examination," and he gives some illustrations of the custom.[2] Stefánsson says regarding the Eskimo,

Young men commonly pay very little attention to the stories told by their elders unless they be stories of a religious or miraculous nature . . . The fact that all but one man among the Rae River Eskimo declared stoutly to me that no white man had ever come to Rae River, shows that no great dependence can be placed on negative testimony. Some of these men who denied knowledge of white visitors on Rae River were the sons of the old man Ekallukpik, who himself as a boy of six or eight had seen Richardson when he was followed across the Rae River by the Eskimos in 1848. When later I asked Ekallukpik's sons how it happened that they were ignorant of such an important event that had happened before the eyes of their father, they replied that they no doubt had heard the story often, but had never paid any attention to it "for," they said, "old men tell so many tales."[3]

Mr. Herbert J. Rose examined the Roman myths regarding the kingship with a view to assessing their value as historical records and came to the conclusion that for this purpose they were practically, if not entirely, valueless. After specifying several legends which attribute a divine character to some early or mythical king, he says:

we cannot safely build any theory of the nature of Italian kingship on these stories, for they crumble when we analyze them. The historian can often make a good deal out of tales patently incredible, if he has reason to think them sagas, that is to say, accounts, embroidered by the popular imagination, of real and remembered events. It is long since anyone believed that Minos, King of Crete, was the child of the sky-god, or that his wife gave birth to a monster, half-bull, half-man; but under these curious legends lurk the facts, established by modern archeology, that there were very mighty kings in prehellenic Crete, that bulls played a large part in certain ceremonies, and even that monsters like the fabled Minotaur were often represented in their works of art, and most likely had a religious significance. But these are stories genuinely Greek, the descendents of the more or less true accounts of the Cretan empire which the

---

[1] TURGOT, "Discours sur l'histoire universelle," in DAIRE, EUGÈNE, "Œuvres de Turgot," Tome II, pp. 648–649, Paris, 1844. See the present writer's "History and Psychology," in OGBURN, WILLIAM F., and GOLDENWEISER, ALEXANDER (editors), "The Social Sciences and Their Interrelations," chap. XVIII, New York, 1927.

[2] THUCYDIDES, "The History of the Peloponnesian War," bk. I, transl. by William Smith, vol. I, p. 16, London, 1812.

[3] Vilhjálmur Stefánsson, "The Stefánsson-Anderson Arctic Expedition of the American Museum: Preliminary Ethnological Report," APAMNH, **14**: 35, 1914.

earliest Greek invaders handed down to their posterity. The Italian legends have the great demerit of not being Italian at all.[1]

A similar caution regarding the use of native history was urged by Ferguson:

If conjectures and opinions formed at a distance have not sufficient authority in the history of mankind, the domestic antiquities of every nation must, for this very reason, be received with caution. They are, for most part, the mere conjectures or the fictions of subsequent ages; and even where at first they contained some resemblance of truth, they still vary with the imagination of those by whom they are transmitted, and in every generation receive a different form. They are made to bear the stamp of the times through which they have passed in the form of tradition, not of the ages to which their pretended descriptions relate. The information they bring is not like the light reflected from a mirror, which delineates the object from which it originally came; but, like rays that come broken and dispersed from an opaque or unpolished surface, only give colours and features of the body from which they were last reflected.[2]

Professor Boas has arrived at practically an identical conclusion,[3] and Lowie has dealt with the problem conclusively:

There are few events that can be regarded as equalling in importance the introduction of the horse into America; moreover, this took place within so recent a period, that trustworthy accounts of what happened might reasonably be expected.   Nevertheless we find that the Nez Percé give a perfectly matter-of-fact but wholly erroneous account of the case while the Assiniboine connect the creation of the horse with a cosmogonic hero-myth.[4] If we turn from the origin of the horse to the correlated phenomenon of the first appearance of the whites, corresponding facts stare us in the face. An Assiniboine gives a tale not in the least improbable of the first meeting with whites; only the leader of the Indians at the time is said to be the culture-hero. Among the Lemhi Shoshone I failed to find any recollection of Lewis and Clark's visit, but secured a purely mythical story about a contest between Wolf (or Coyote) as the father of the Indians, and Iron-man, the father of the Whites. Do we fare any better when we turn from these representatives of a cruder culture to peoples who have

---

[1] ROSE, HERBERT J., "Primitive Culture in Italy," pp. 121–122, New York, 1927.

[2] FERGUSON, ADAM, "An Essay on the History of Civil Society," pp. 115–116, Edinburgh, 1767.

[3] BOAS, FRANZ, "Primitive Art," Oslo, 1927.

[4] In the seventies of the last century Smohalla, a chief of the Wanapum tribe, in Washington, declared, "We had ponies long before we ever saw white people. The Great Spirit gave them to us. Our horses were swifter and more enduring, too, in those days, before they were mixed with the white man's horses."—MOONEY, JAMES, "The Ghost Dance Religion," 14th Annual Report of the Bureau of Ethnology, pt. II, p. 724, Washington, 1896.   (Note by W. D. W.)

attained the highest status north of Mexico? Zuñi oral tradition has it that the village at which Niza's negro guide Estevan lost his life, and which Niza himself observed from a distance, was Kiakima. In a masterly paper F. W. Hodge has torn into shreds the arguments advanced on behalf of the aboriginal view. He establishes the fact that the village in question was Hawikuh, and that "Zuñi traditional accounts of events which occurred over three centuries ago are not worthy of consideration as historical or scientific evidence."

The general conclusion is obvious: Indian tradition is historically worthless, because the occurrences, possibly real, which it retains, are of no historical significance; and because it fails to record, or to record accurately, the most momentous happenings. This conclusion is, I am perfectly well aware, an as yet imperfect induction. To examine its ultimate validity, a special inquiry is necessary, for which I should like to outline the guiding principles. The historical sense of primitive peoples can be tested only by a scrutiny of unselected samples of their historical lore. It will not do, as some of our colleagues are wont, to reject manifestly absurd tales and to retain those which do not contravene our notions of physical possibility; for by this process we get, in the first place, a selected series of cases, and, secondly, already prejudge the whole matter by assuming that what is not ridiculously false is historically true. We must rather embrace in our survey every single statement which, whether miraculous or not from our point of view, is to the native psychology a matter of history. To this mass of material we must then apply our canons of trustworthiness; and from a comparison of the cases in which objective evidence supports the native statements with those in which such evidence is contradictory we may arrive at a statistically tenable attitude as to the general probability of their accuracy. Had such a test been made on unselected material, one of my critics would not have dared assert a probability of nine-tenths for the correctness of native statements as to the direction from which a tribe came. In such a test as I propose, aboriginal statements that a certain tribe originated in the very spot in which it now lives must be considered exactly on the same plane as any other tradition.[1]

We cannot accept Sapir's statement that a thinly settled region implies recent occupancy. Much depends on circumstances. It is unjustifiable to assume, on this principle, that Labrador was occupied subsequently to the Maritime Provinces of Canada, or the Plains area after the settlement of Yucatan—now a thinly settled region—and the valley of Mexico. Obviously the principle does not apply to the historical civilizations.

The principle of necessary connection, or of "necessary presupposition," as Sapir calls it, is, as actually applied, a principle of unnecessary presupposition, as, for example, the inference that the dressing of skins

---

[1] LOWIE, ROBERT H., *Jour. Amer. Folk-Lore*, **30**: 164–166, 1917.

is an older technique than tipi covering by buffalo skins, inasmuch as the skins must be dressed before they can be used. The use of skins as tipi covers may have led to the dressing of them. It is, indeed, more probable that the use of skins led to the dressing of them, than that the native first dressed them and then found a use for them. Grinnell says, "The complete and comfortable lodges of modern times were the ultimate development from the windbreaks of undressed hides set up over a frame-work of poles."[1]

We are not convinced by Sapir's assurance that because the Eskimo dot-and-circle design is made by the drill, therefore the Eskimo had the drill before they made the design. The design may have led to the invention of the drill, rather than *vice versa*, or the two may have originated independently and the circle-and-dot design may owe its early development to some instrument other than the drill. In our own culture, for example, in many instances the instrument which makes a design is more recent than the design; as Wissler says, "the mere idea of cutting a spiral does not necessarily involve the mechanical concept of a screw."[2]

Firmness of association is not a good guide to the age of traits, for here, too, much depends upon circumstances. Loosely adhering traits, mere hangers-on, are sometimes of great age—as is true of some survivals. Culture achievement is so essential to adaptation to environment that length of residence cannot be inferred from the degree of adaptation. A people may carry with them, in their culture, the power to adapt themselves to new conditions, or they may not develop the power, however long they live in a locality. Indeed, perhaps the failure to use birch-bark for their canoes implies that the Iroquois did not copy from the Algonkin.

---

[1] GRINNELL, GEORGE B., "The Cheyenne Indians," vol. I, pp. 50, 52, New Haven, 1923. However, the dressing of buffalo hides the Cheyenne are said to have learned from other Plains Indians. Compare Weule: "The skin of the animal which man had slain through cunning or force and which was of no interest, even to his healthy primeval teeth, must soon have appeared well suited to him for covering his own body against cold and rain, as a protection against the dampness of the soil and as a screen against the cutting winds. Unfortunately it became hard and inflexible, and consequently useless long before a new one fell into his hands. Quite instinctively (!) he would then have rubbed and wrung it, perhaps also beaten and tread on it— and behold, the stiff material gradually became as pliable as before. The universal technique of treating skins was indeed invented in this most primitive procedure." WEULE, KARL, "Cultural Element in Mankind: Commencements and Primitive Forms of Material Culture," p. 26, London, 1926. Of course, diffusion must have played a large part in the extension of the technique of dressing hides; and insofar as one must allow for diffusion, Sapir's inference is baseless, because it assumes that both tipi-covering and the dressing of skins developed in the Plains area.

[2] WISSLER, CLARK, "Harpoons and Darts in the Stefánsson Collection," APAMNH, 14: 442, 1916.

There is reason to suppose that the Iroquois used canoes before coming into the area of the birch tree. The more probable inference, therefore, is that elm-bark represents the persistence of a material used in an earlier environment. Dixon, however, follows Sapir in supposing the Iroquois elm-bark canoe the result of diffusion from the eastern Algonkins:

The use of the birch-bark canoe, so characteristic of many of the eastern Algonkian tribes, undoubtedly diffused from them to the Iroquois of New York, in whose territory the birch became gradually less abundant as one went south and west. The Iroquois were therefore forced to replace birch-bark by that of the spruce or elm, which was heavier and less well adapted to the purpose, but this modification of the trait was relatively easily brought about by the gradualness of the change.[1]

Arthur C. Parker, however, does not believe that the Iroquois elm-bark canoe is copied from the birch-bark canoe. He writes:

There are certain things about the structure and sewing which would be considered foreign to the birch-bark canoe. So far as I have been able to determine from archeological excavations and studies among the surviving Iroquois in New York evidence seems to point to a south or southeast origin of the stock. Canoes are mentioned in many of their early myths and traditions and frequently the term "elm-bark canoe" is used. It would seem that this type of canoe was brought with them on their migrations from the lower reaches of the Ohio. In this conclusion I concur with the implied statement which you make.[2]

This is likewise the conclusion of C. M. Barbeau. Mr. Barbeau writes,

I do not believe that the elm-bark canoes were copied from the birch-bark canoes used by the adjacent Algonkins. The technique, for one thing, is entirely different, and seems to have been traditional among them. The Iroquois used two types of canoes, i.e., the dug-out and the elm-bark. They used, besides, the coracle, as most of the interior Indians to the southwest of their habitat.[3]

Nor can one accept the thesis that survivals are of great age. Often the teleological phases of social life, such as family organization, are the oldest. Survivals are created continually; some are recent, some, ancient. The extent of the distribution of a culture trait is not an index to its age. The thousand years required for the spread of bronze through Europe was abbreviated by centuries in the case of iron; aluminum was distributed in a few decades, and the diffusion of radium was a matter of a few years. During these periods probably nothing else spread with the

---

[1] Dixon, Roland B., "The Building of Cultures," pp. 109–110, New York, 1928.

[2] Quoted, by permission, from a letter to the author, dated June 14, 1928. To Sapir, presumably, the references in the myths would have some historical importance.

[3] Quoted, by permission, from a letter to the author, dated June 20, 1928.

rapidity of these respective culture traits. As Sapir himself points out, comparable variations in rate of diffusion are found in savagery. He is aware of the uncertainties which lurk in his criteria. "Everything depends upon the specific conditions of a given problem."[1] One criterion should not be used to the exclusion of another, but all should be utilized. Culture elements must not be abstracted from their psychological and geographical setting; to do so is to lose insight into their probable age. They must be "weighted" before their implications can be understood. But he does not indicate the weight attaching to the respective criteria when they tell different stories; and their testimonies are not always supplementary, but, on the contrary, often are contradictory.

5. The So-called "Historical" Methods of Ethnologists

The conception of culture development which Sapir represents as history is actually theory. Theory makes his history rather than history his theory. Possibly it could not be otherwise; but to the extent that this is the case it contravenes his statement that, "cultural anthropology is more and more rapidly getting to realize itself as a strictly historical science. Its data cannot be understood, either in themselves, or in their relation to one another, except as the end-points of specific sequences of events reaching back into the remote past."[2] But it would be as true to say that they can be understood only as the effort of the Western mind to understand other cultures; for their character—so far as we can know it—depends upon our interpretation.

A similar observation applies to Wissler's and Kroeber's[3] attempts to make history out of theory, to reconstruct the past in accordance with alleged principles of culture development. Like Sapir, they endeavor to arrange traits of primitive culture in a time perspective. If such a perspective represents historical facts theories must be modeled upon it; but until the proper theories are established, it is impossible to reconstruct preliterate history. Even a strictly historical method presupposes criteria of interpretation; but interpretations of culture phenomena

---

[1] Sapir, *op. cit.*

[2] Sapir, *op. cit.* Quite the reverse, says Radin, in effect. "No progress will ever be achieved . . . until scholars rid themselves, once and for all, of the curious notion that everything possesses an evolutionary history; until they realize that certain ideas and certain concepts are as ultimate for man as a social being as specific and physiological reactions are for him as a biological entity. Both doubtless have a history; but in the one case its roots lie in pre-social man and in the other in the lower organisms." Radin, Paul, "Monotheism among Primitive Peoples," pp. 66–67, London, 1924.

[3] Kroeber, Alfred L., "Anthropology," New York, 1923.

emanate from mental patterns which predetermine the nature of the inferred historical background.[1] Perhaps as Dewey says, "we are not likely to get anywhere until events are viewed in relation to their background and social setting";[2] but also we cannot view them without lending to events a tinge of our own philosophy.

When a culture trait is distributed over a contiguous territory and is shared by peoples of different culture levels, is it possible to ascertain without specific history and its implications what people have originated and what people have borrowed the trait? Kroeber answers the question in the affirmative. He says,

The almost unanimous verdict of both history and ethnology is that when a certain art is shared by a number of peoples, and evidence as to its origin is obtainable, it almost always becomes clear that this origin occurred among the more advanced rather than the less advanced peoples of the group; or where both are not equally advanced in general civilization, then among that nation whose civilization is the oldest. On the basis of this well-established principle, it becomes practically certain that the Igorot or Ifugao was not the inventor of the system of irrigation.[3]

Kroeber subsequently reaffirms this "principle": "Normally it is the more advanced culture that affects the other [culture] most."[4] That the method of terracing for irrigation was introduced and is not native to the Philippines may be inferred on other grounds, but not from an alleged "almost unanimous verdict of both history and ethnology" to the effect that a widely spread trait found among both primitive and advanced people has originated among the latter. Since there are more traits to spread from a complex culture a count might show more traits of higher culture among primitive folk than traits of primitive folk among the more complex cultures; but that this would be the result is doubtful, and the exceptions are so numerous, if indeed they are exceptions and not the rule, that the place of origin of a trait cannot be inferred from such a supposititious principle. If there were no history to aid us we should, by Kroeber's principle, infer that the Indians of the Southwest had learned agriculture and irrigation from the whites, that maize came to Indians from whites, that the cultivation and utilization of tobacco, potatoes, coca, cacao, squash, and beans were acquired by the Indians

---

[1] See, for example, the present writer's "Psychology and History," in OGBURN, WILLIAM F., and GOLDENWEISER, ALEXANDER (editors), "The Social Sciences and Their Interrelations," chap. XVIII, New York, 1927.

[2] DEWEY, JOHN, New Republic, **58**: 231, 1929.

[3] KROEBER, ALFRED L., "Peoples of the Philippines," pp. 84–85, American Museum of Natural History, Handbook Series, New York, 1919.

[4] KROEBER, ALFRED L., "Native Culture of the Southwest," UC, **23**: 393, 1928.

from the whites. The Indians have acquired from the whites no traits which are as widespread as numerous traits which the whites have taken from the Indians. The Roosevelt Dam did not inspire the Pueblo Indians to practice irrigation, and the Mexicans and Peruvians did not learn their engineering from the white man. The "principle" which Kroeber announces has not been established, and probably it contradicts the facts.

Christopher Dawson, however, is in general agreement with Kroeber:

> Peoples of primitive culture seldom originate new ideas; they are far more likely to borrow them from the more advanced peoples. On the other hand, the religious beliefs and practices of the higher cultures spread almost automatically among their more primitive neighbors, as we have seen in the case of the religion of the Mother Goddess in Western Asia, and the peasant neolithic cultures of Eastern Europe. Moreover, the distribution of the Megalithic culture differs in a remarkable way from that of any primitive culture that we know. It suggests . . . a movement of maritime colonization like that of the ancient Phœnicians or the modern Portuguese.[1]

Another method of inferring relative age is to posit the priority within a large culture area of those subsidiary culture areas which have relatively few of the widely distributed traits.[2] Thus, if two of six subsidiary culture areas which, in their entirety, comprise one large culture area, have relatively few of the traits which characterize the other four, then these two represent an older culture substratum. Although the units are not of the same geographical magnitude, nevertheless, generally such a rule, it is said, would result in a negative correlation of age with distribution. This is the antithesis of the interpretations of Wissler and Kroeber, and it is scarcely possible that both procedures are correct. In arriving at this conclusion the study referred to assumes that similarities in the details of a trait found in all areas is a better indication of culture contact than is sheer presence of a trait which is of limited distribution in the area. Like the preceding studies, it assumes its principles and then concludes that they are true because the data can be marshaled in accordance with the presuppositions. But, like them also, it does not attempt to establish the truth of the presuppositions. The acceptance of similarities as evidence of historical relationship implies that the similarities have

---

[1] DAWSON, CHRISTOPHER, "The Age of the Gods: A Study in the Origins of Culture in Prehistoric Europe and the Ancient East," p. 200, Boston, 1928.

[2] See CLEMENTS, FOREST E., SCHENCK, SARA M., and BROWN, T. K., "A New Objective Method for Showing Special Relationships," AA, **28**: 585–604, 1926. For a criticism of the same see the present writer's article on "Probability and the Diffusion of Culture Traits," *Ibid.*, **30**: 94–106, 1928, and for a reply, CLEMENTS, FOREST E., "Quantitative Method in Ethnography," *Ibid.*, **30**: 295–310, 1928.

not developed independently—*i.e.*, it takes for granted the truth of the principle which it assumes to demonstrate; and it assumes that traits are weighted by counting as units the elements of which they are composed. But such a method of weighting is not justifiable. A match, for example, which would be counted as one, may be better evidence of culture contacts than is a ceremonial house which is analyzed into twenty (or two hundred) component parts and counted as twenty in weighting the respective evidence of culture contacts. Boas, accordingly, sums up the attempts to solve such ethnographical problems by statistical methods as of "more than doubtful success," because "the fundamental difficulty of this method is our lack of knowledge of historical connection. In order to make a statistical method a success it is essential that the phenomena counted must be independent of one another. If a number of them go back to the same historical sources they cannot be considered as separate units."[1] If they do not go back to the same historical sources, then the similarities which they show do not indicate historical relationship, whereas the study above referred to assumes that the similarities indicate historical relationship, and that all types of similarity should be weighted alike, it being assumed that the trait complex is automatically weighted by breaking it up into its component parts. There is, however, no attempt to show that this principle is true; and its truth must be established before one can accept it as a guide in making historical reconstructions.

Paul Radin[2] infers by a different method the relative age of the respective cultures in aboriginal America. He takes as his starting point the larger culture areas—the Eskimo, the Plains Indians, the Mound Builders, the peoples of the Southwest, the Aztecs, the Mayas, and others. Historical records are supplemented by archeology, which in many cases points to the area of origin of certain culture traits and may be taken as the culture weather-vane which indicates the direction of the winds of influence. Thus he infers that the cultures of the Southwest and those of the Lower Mississippi, including the Mound Builders, received influences from the Maya. Archeology takes the searcher for origins to the southeast of Mexico, where the civilization arose which later found its way to the region near the present Mexico City. Southeastern Mexican civilization had, in turn, been inspired by the Maya civilization of Yucatan, which is therefore the original stimulus of much of the culture which spread far into North America. The Maya developed the cultivation of maize, and without maize there could be no settled abode, no

---

[1] BOAS, FRANZ, "Anthropology and Statistics," in OGBURN and GOLDENWEISER, *op. cit.*, p. 120.

[2] RADIN, PAUL, "Story of the American Indian," New York, 1927.

large villages or cities, nor much development of political or social life. With these traits are associated priesthood and elaborate ceremonialism, which likewise are indirectly dependent upon the cultivation of maize. Thus, in inferring the age of culture traits, Radin does not, like Wissler, Sapir, and Kroeber, isolate the traits, but treats culture areas as units. He does not imply, however, that a culture moves as a unit, nor that a trait may not detach itself from the culture and travel alone into other culture areas.

Laufer adduces domestication as an example of culture traits which can be reconstructed from the past by a study of contemporary cultures, and attempts "to demonstrate by a few practical examples . . . that it is possible to reconstruct by means of purely ethnological data and methods mental processes and culture phases of the past which cannot be reached by historical and archeological methods."[1] In Eastern Asia, for example, there is no dairy economy, although milk-producing animals—cows, sheep, goats, buffaloes, mares, donkeys, camels—are kept, whereas in Tibet, India, Western Asia, and throughout Europe dairy economy is important. Its absence from Eastern Asia is a positive trait, for these peoples know that others utilize the milk of animals, but to them the idea is repellent. He accounts for the facts as follows: In the earlier period of domestication the use of milk was unknown. Subsequently Western Asia developed a dairy economy.

This new development remained confined to the West, but it did not affect Eastern Asia, and must therefore have taken place at a time when the East was definitely settled in its culture pattern and was no longer ready to absorb extraneous ideas. It bespeaks a lengthy prehistoric cultural development in the East independently of the West . . . I . . . cite this case as an illustration of how ethnological methods may carry us into the remotest past and help us to discover and unravel ideas of which no record has been preserved.[2]

They "carry us into the past," to be sure, but how they "help us to discover and unravel ideas of which no record has been preserved," depends, of necessity, upon our criteria for inferring the past. Since the trait of domestication is more elaborately developed in Western Asia and in Europe than in Eastern Asia, the Western area is, by Wissler's criterion, the area of origin, and the Eastern area, in which the trait is less intensively developed, is peripheral. Archeologically the earliest evidence of domestication is in Europe, though this fact, of course, may be

---

[1] LAUFER, BERTHOLD, "Methods in the Study of Domestication," *Sci. Monthly,* **25**: 251–255, 1927.

[2] *Ibid.*

due to the paucity of archeological evidence from Asia. Yet if Western Asia developed a dairy economy before the spread of domestication eastward, supposing that domestication originated in Europe, why did the Eastern peoples subsequently accept domestication but reject the dairy economy? Laufer emphasizes the fact that for millennia the latter have refused to adopt a dairy economy; may they not have refused with equal persistence at an earlier day?

Laufer, significantly, does not mention the historical or the primitive cattle-using cultures of India. In India as in Egypt the use of milk is old, and it is utilized by one of the primitive cultures in the Nilghiri hills, the Toda. Many African tribes adopted dairy economy without adopting the utilization of cattle, or buffalo, as means of transportation or as beasts of burden, and without utilizing their flesh as food. May not the peoples of Eastern Asia have adopted from western neighbors a part of the domestication complex without taking all of it? Laufer does not answer these questions. His inference is but one plausible interpretation. We are, however, not concerned with plausible interpretations, but with the problem of whether the evidence justifies inference of the specific historical development, and, if so, whether we should follow Laufer or Wissler; for their respective methods lead, at least in this instance, to diametrically opposite conclusions; and, as Laufer himself has said, "possibilities are not historical facts."[1] The problem raised by Laufer was considered many years ago by Eduard Hahn, who concluded that China had acquired the trait of domestication from the Western world. The failure to use cattle for food or for transportation, or to utilize their milk or that of other animals, indicates, for him, an early borrowing of the trait of domestication before the animals were utilized in this fashion in the Western world. The culture trait became fixed in the form in which they had acquired it, hence their failure to adopt the later pattern of the trait when it subsequently came to them from Western culture.[2]

The first to point out the totally non-historical character of the "historical" reconstructions of Boas and others were, so far as we are aware, Kroeber and Radin. Radin says: "the so-called historical method of Professor Boas is really a purely logical one and is naïvely unhistorical."[3] And Kroeber observes: "History is what Dr. Boas, in this ["Pri-

[1] LAUFER, BERTHOLD, "The Eskimo Screw as a Cultural-Historical Problem," AA, 17: 398, 1915.

[2] See HAHN, EDUARD, "Die Haustiere und ihre Beziehungen zur Wirtschaft des Menschen," pp. 492–493, Leipzig, 1896. For a similar interpretation see LOWIE, ROBERT H., "Are We Civilized?" p. 62, New York, 1929.

[3] RADIN, PAUL, "History of Ethnological Theories," AA, 31: 16, 1929.

mitive Art"] as in all his work, with one or two brief and hesitant exceptions, has avoided doing, and apparently sheers off from distrustfully."[1] Kroeber, however, defends what he calls "the historical conclusions of Wissler, Spinden, and Kroeber, which after all are inductively founded in generalizations drawn from data in their natural space-time relations."[2] But Kroeber's assurance is not convincing. In these reconstructions, at least in those of Wissler and Kroeber, there is nothing that savors of induction, unless fitting data into a gratuitously preconceived generalization is induction. They have not treated data in their space-time relations but have ascertained their space relations and have inferred the time relations by using a generalization which, so far as we are aware, they have not even attempted to establish empirically or inductively, but have merely assumed, and have then fitted the data into the *a priori* scheme. Fitting the data into exactly the contrary generalization would be equally inductive. The theory would work equally well in the opposite direction, for they have adduced no historical evidence to support their conclusion, which in reality is a premise, not a conclusion. They merely assume that the premise is correct; and if one admits the premise, the conclusion follows. But for any pretence of induction this puts the theologian to shame! "Not all his gains will compensate for the guilt of his sin"; for there are no gains unless the "principles" are at least probably true.

We agree with Radcliffe-Brown that

it is impossible to reach a complete understanding of any element of culture—language, art, religion, social organization,—without a profound and extensive study of history. But it must be real history, not conjectural history. We must know in detail how languages, etc., actually have changed. We cannot be helped, I believe, but rather we shall be hindered, at any rate at the present stage of anthropological studies, by conjectures as to how they may have changed. Hypothetical reconstructions of an unknown past do not and cannot add anything at all to our understanding of the nature of culture and the laws of its growth and change, but, on the contrary, must necessarily be based on assumptions as to that nature and those laws.[3]

The thesis of the ethnologists whom Radcliffe-Brown criticizes, contains an implicit assumption of a fundamental sameness in human nature, or at least in culture, so far as response to similar conditions is concerned. This assumption cannot be proved or disproved, for the means of demonstration are lacking and presumably always will be.

---

[1] KROEBER, ALFRED L., "Review of Franz Boas' 'Primitive Art,'" AA, **31**: 140, 1929.

[2] *Ibid.*

[3] RADCLIFFE-BROWN, A. R., "Bilateral Descent," *Man*, **29**: 200, 1929.

Thus these writers construct an ethnological Garden of Eden to illustrate what they assume happened in the days when there was no recorder but when prehistoric human nature was nevertheless contemporaneously human. If the past will not reveal its secrets they can be imagined and dramatized, and the fiction can be given the name of history, for it seems consonant with the facts and it may be true. Meanwhile the attitude of Robert Recorde has grown antiquated—"though I might of my scholar some credence require, yet except I show reason I do not desire it."

MAGNITUDE OF DISTRIBUTION, CENTRIFUGAL SPREAD, AND CENTRIPEDAL ELABORATION OF CULTURE TRAITS

1. MAGNITUDE OF DISTRIBUTION OF CULTURE TRAITS AS A CRITERION OF AGE

Some ethnologists, as we have seen, assume that the magnitude of distribution of a culture trait is an index of its age, though few state the principle in the form in which they imply it. Thus the fact that the making of fire is known in every tribe is said to indicate its great antiquity, and the widespread use of stone implements by primitive man is considered an indication of their great age. Widely distributed stories or plots carry the same implication: "If the myth be one which encounters us in every quarter, nay in every obscure nook of the globe, we may plausibly regard it as ancient."[1] In the realm of material culture the same principle is assumed to hold: "The natural conclusion would be that the more widely distributed spur [on Eskimo harpoons] is by far the older form and the restricted screw is the more recent."[2] "In general the larger the area of distribution, the older we may judge the trait to be."[3] Certainly in many instances the age of a trait is a function of the magnitude of its distribution, yet instances to the contrary are so numerous that one must doubt the validity of using distribution as a criterion of age. In the higher cultures the opportunity for the spread of traits is greater than among primitive peoples, but the conditions are probably not essentially different, and the rapid diffusion of traits in civilization has a prototype in the slow percolation in savagery. However that may be, inference of the development of traits in the non-historical cultures must be based on the known culture development in some area, primitive or advanced, or facts cannot check fancy. In order, therefore, to test the validity of magnitude of distribution as an index to age, we selected at random the traits referred to in Chap. II, IV, IX, and XXI of James

---

[1] LANG, ANDREW, "Myth, Ritual, and Religion."

[2] WISSLER, CLARK, "Harpoons and Darts in the Stefánsson Collection," APAMNH, **14**: 443, 1916.

[3] BENEDICT, RUTH, "The Concept of the Guardian Spirit in North America," in *Memoirs of the Amer. Anthrop. Assoc.*, No. 29, p. 62, 1923.

H. Breasted, "Ancient Times" (Boston, 1916). The random selection yielded the following: Bronze, mud-brick huts, irrigation canals, phalanx, split wheat, plow, wheel, use of the horse, battering ram, coinage, concept of last judgment, cuneiform writing, town walls, market-place, settlements, roofs, metal, migrations, families, carts, business, merchants, books—in all, twenty-three. The relative distribution of the first three, bronze, mud-brick huts, and irrigation canals, does not remain constant. By about 3000 B.C. mud-brick huts and irrigation canals were more widely distributed than bronze; but by 100 B.C. the distribution of bronze over the Mediterranean and contiguous areas was greater than the distribution of mud-brick huts or irrigation canals; and a similar statement applies to the next three traits of material culture—split wheat, the plow, and the wheel. In the early centuries of the Bronze age the distribution of split wheat about the Mediterranean area, including the Swiss lake dwellings, was more extensive than that of either the plow or the wheel. Subsequently, however, the area of distribution of split wheat was less than that of either the plow or the wheel. The plow is probably older, and at one time was more widely distributed than the wheel, but by the beginning of the Christian era the wheel was more widely distributed. The next three features, namely, use of the horse, battering ram, coinage, likewise vary in relative distribution during sucessive centuries.

In the case of these traits, therefore, age is positively correlated with magnitude of distribution only at certain historical moments, and in the absence of history inference of age from magnitude of distribution is more likely to be erroneous than correct. The earliest traits have the first opportunities to spread, but later traits may outdistance them. When this occurs—and it occurs frequently—the more recent traits become the more widely distributed. Indeed, when changes are taking place, inevitably some more recent traits become more widely distributed than some older ones. The assumption that distribution is an index of age is based on the implicit assumption that all traits spread with the same rapidity and that the more widely distributed trait is therefore the older. Certainly many culture traits have a tendency to spread from place of origin to cintiguous regions, but the rates of diffusion differ greatly, due sometimes to differences in culture patterns. One culture is ready for the trait and accepts it; another is unprepared, and rejects it. There is, moreover, a specific dynamic in the respective culture traits which is reflected in the varying rates of diffusion. Agriculture, for example, may spread with greater rapidity than ceramics or basketry, canoes may be adopted with greater readiness than dog transportation, or conversely. The ghost dance religion of aboriginal North America spreads rapidly over an area in which no other trait is as widely distributed, though we know that almost all other traits in the area are older. Objection may be made that analogy with Western culture is misleading, since diffusion proceeds more rapidly in civilization than in savagery. But, with the important exception of contacts at a distance, civilization differs from savagery mainly in the acceleration of the factors which affect diffusion in the preliterate cultures. Fads spread rapidly in civilization, but they spread in savagery also. The barrier of language is greater in savagery than in civilization, but it is not insurmountable, and culture influences break through. The savage is slow to perceive the utility of a new device; in time, however, if it is not too foreign to his culture pattern, he perceives it. In civilization, likewise, receptivity varies: witness the distribution of the telephone, spreading more rapidly in America than in Europe, more rapidly in the commercial districts than in the non-commercial, more rapidly in countries in which science has made headway than in those in which it has not. If, indeed, one cannot make inferences based on known diffusion in civilization, or known diffusion in savagery, where facts can check inference, then no inferences can be made.

There has been a curious failure to appreciate the fact that the spread of a trait presupposes the existence of older traits in the areas into which the new trait travels. A trait can spread only through culture areas, and the traits which compose these respective cultures are, of necessity, older than the introduced trait; *i.e.*, they are of greater age within those areas than is the introduced trait. Thus, when tobacco spreads into new areas it is more recent there than the traits which comprise the respective cultures at the time of its introduction, and possibly it is more recent than other traits in the area from which it has come. Indeed, whenever a trait spreads rapidly this must be the case. The diffusion of a trait, therefore, implies that numerous traits which are not so widely distributed are older. To the extent that this is true, the widely distributed trait is of necessity more recent than those traits which constitute the respective cultures which it penetrates. Only on the supposition that the widely diffused trait is more persistent than those amid which it finds lodgement can it be supposed that magnitude of distribution is positively correlated with the age of the trait; and if all traits are included, probably wide distribution indicates recency rather than antiquity.

2. The Distribution of Traits of Prehistoric Culture

In his work on "Primitive Art" Professor Boas characterizes some of the reconstructions which identify magnitude of distribution with age as "untenable." The principle that the more widely distributed traits are the older is correct if properly used, he says, but it must not be used incorrectly. This seems to be equivalent to stating that it is true when it is true, and false when it is false, but gives us no inkling of when it is true and when it is false. Boas adduces the fact that the use of stone is more widely distributed than the use of metals, and suggests that other data of prehistoric archeology show a similar positive correlation of magnitude of distribution with age. He says:

The data of prehistoric archeology prove that some of these universal achievements go back to Paleolithic times. Stone implements, fire, and ornaments are found in that period. Pottery and agriculture, which are less universally distributed, appear later. Metals, the use of which is still more limited in space, are found still later. Recent attempts have been made to raise to a general principle this point of view which, with due caution, may be applied here and there. Herbert Spinden in his reconstruction of American prehistoric chronology, Alfred Kroeber in his analysis of cultural forms of the Pacific Coast, and quite recently Clark Wissler have built up, founded on this principle, a system of historic sequences that appear to me as quite untenable. That widely distributed cultural traits develop special forms in each particular area is a truism that does not require any proof. That these local developments may be arranged in a chronological series, that those of the most limited distribution are the youngest, is only partially true. It is not difficult to find phenomena that center in a certain region and dwindle down at the outskirts, but it is not true that these invariably arise on an ancient substratum. The converse is often true, that an idea emanating from a center [from the periphery?] is diffused over a wide area. Neither may the origin always be looked for in the area of the strongest development. In the same way as we find animals surviving and flourishing in regions far distant from the locality in which they developed, so cultural traits may be transferred and find their highest expression in regions far away from their origin. The bronze castings of Benin; the wood carvings of New Zealand; the bronze work of ancient Scandinavia; the giant stone work of Easter Island; the early cultural development of Ireland and its influences over Europe are examples of this kind.[1]

A comparison of the distribution of Eolithic implements with Paleolithic is scarcely apposite, for the human workmanship of the former is problematical and we know very little about their total distribution, and indeed very little about the total distribution of Paleolithic implements. With regard to Neolithic implements, however, we are on surer ground. Here the facts do not confirm the "principle." Even in the Old World, so far as the data are available, implements of Neolithic type are more widely distributed than those of Paleolithic type, and in the New World the former are universal. Thus, taking the whole of the

---

[1] BOAS, FRANZ, "Preface," "Primitive Art," Oslo, 1927.

available data, implements of Neolithic type are more widely spread than those of Paleolithic type. Copper was utilized before bronze; yet in prehistoric times bronze became more widely diffused than copper. Indeed, in most areas of the Old World in which both copper and bronze are found, bronze preceded copper, and, therefore, at an early stage in its development it was more widely distributed than the older copper. There is reason to suppose, too, that in the higher civilizations of the New World the working of copper preceded the working of bronze; yet in those portions of the New World in which this is assumed to have been the case, bronze is as widely distributed as is smelted copper; for outside of these higher cultures there was no smelting of copper in the New World. In the Old World the working of iron, which followed the molding of bronze, became more widely distributed than bronze casting. In the Old World the working of iron permeated all of the regions in which bronze had been cast, and also the entire African continent in which no bronze was worked, except in Egypt and on a small portion of the West Coast. Many parts of Asia which had never known bronze casting adopted the working of iron. In not one of these instances, then, does the alleged principle hold, or rather, in every one of them it holds in exactly reverse form, the more widely diffused trait being the younger, not the older. Many other traits of prehistoric Europe tell a similar tale. Thus, in the Magdalenian period, toward the end of Paleolithic times, there existed numerous microliths, types of implements which had appeared previously and which became common in the succeeding Azilian period, at the close of the Paleolithic. These did not become as widely distributed as the types of Neolithic implements which followed them. There existed at this time the so-called "arrow-straightener," or *baton de commandement,* which probably was not widely diffused, for it has not been found in later prehistoric Europe, and outside of the Eskimo area it is almost unknown. At this time, too, appeared the harpoon, which has diffused to so slight an extent that it has been found nowhere else in prehistoric Europe except in Denmark, Sweden and Norway, in the Epipaleolithic, and around the Mediterranean, where it was formerly used in hunting seals, probably by the ancient Egyptians. Outside of the Pacific Coast area of North America, it has been reported from less than a half dozen ethnological areas, in each of which, for any intimation to the contrary, it may have developed independently. Contemporary with it, in Magdalenian times, was the spear-thrower, and it, too, so far as is known, did not diffuse, but disappeared from prehistoric Europe, and has been found we believe, only in Australia, and in portions of the Americas.

The multi-pronged spear was used in Magdalenian times, but it, too, had a constricted distribution in the Old World, and it was absent from nearly all of the New World. Tangs were put on these implements by hacking the surface to roughen it, by end or transverse knobs, and by spurs. But the association of these three processes was not widely distributed, and is perhaps restricted to Eskimo culture. Not until Epipaleolithic and Neolithic times did the bow and arrow appear, but eventually the use of them became more widespread than the use of the spear; however, to a large extent, in contemporary preliterate culture they were concomitant, for Australia and (most of) Polynesia and Micronesia were the only large areas in which the spear was used and the bow was absent, though possibly it was once used throughout Polynesia. In Magdalenian times there was a highly developed realism in art, but this was not widely diffused; it was comparatively rare in subsequent European prehistoric art, and a comparable realism was not widely spread in the art of contemporary peoples. Masks were used, but the use of masks, so far as there is evidence, was not widely diffused through subsequent cultures in Europe, and there is no evidence that it was ever as widely diffused throughout the world as the Neolithic implements which came later. Mutilation of a finger, it is believed, was practised; but this practice appears not to have diffused over adjacent regions, and it may have developed independently in all the other regions, comparatively few, in which it is known to have existed. There was modeling, bas-relief, sculpture, perspective drawing, impressionism, composition; but no one of these traits or techniques became widely diffused, or certainly not as widely diffused as many traits which arose subsequently. In the closing phases of the Paleolithic, feather head dress was worn in Southwestern Europe, but this was of restricted ethnographical distribution, and indeed was common only in portions of the New World, where it almost certainly arose independently of Old World influences. Thus, as far as the data are available, the traits of paleolithic culture were not widely distributed in later cultures.

Diffusion of a trait involves the dimension of time, though many students treat the matter as though a given space dimension involved always the same time factor. If one assumes fairly uniform rates of diffusion and long intervals of time, and, further, that new traits arise seldom and spread slowly, then the more widely distributed traits will be the older. But the correlation implies fairly constant rates of diffusion or long time intervals. That under certain conditions the older trait will be the more widely diffused is necessarily true. Thus when only Paleolithic methods of workmanship are known only Paleolithic techniques can be diffused.

During Paleolithic times this is the case for a hundred thousand years or more, and meanwhile Paleolithic traits can travel to all cultures. The Neolithic technique originates in only one place, or certainly in only a few places, and for a time it will of necessity be less widely diffused than the older Paleolithic technique which for a hundred thousand years has had the opportunity to spread. However rapidly it spreads, it cannot at once outdistance Paleolithic techniques, and probably all existing cultures will already have adopted the latter. So, too, copper, bronze, and iron, respectively, will of necessity be of limited distribution at their inception, and they can extend their borders only gradually, but frequently a new trait travels faster than its predecessors, overtakes them, and henceforth assumes the lead in the invasion of new territory. This happened in the case of the respective metals. Here the time factors were smaller than in the stone ages, and the rates of diffusion were accelerated, because culture changes were now more rapid, and communication and trade facilitated the transmission of the new traits. Had copper been given 100,000 years to spread, it too might have gone to all mankind, and so, under similar circumstances, might bronze; but bronze spread more rapidly than copper, and iron spread more rapidly than bronze, and soon the most recent of the three metals became the most widely diffused. But even if the "principle" did hold in the pre-historic world this would be no warrant for assuming that it would hold in any other phase of the culture world, primitive or advanced, least of all outside of the sphere of material culture. Professor Boas seems to assert that the "principle" is sometimes true but not always to be trusted, good enough to believe in with caution, but not good enough to follow in practice. But the "principle" which is true if you believe it but false if you use it, seems so paradoxical as to be almost unprincipled. When and how far the alleged correlation of distribution with age exists no one, so far as we are aware, has even attempted to show. The faith is strong but the works are weak. More recently, however, Professor Boas has expressed unqualifiedly his conviction that one cannot construct from an examination of the static forms of culture the sequences which express the actual historical developments of respective traits. He says elsewhere:

Every culture is a complex growth, and, on account of the intimate, early associations of people inhabiting large areas, it is not admissible to assume that the accidental causes that modify the course of development will cancel one another and that the great mass of evidence will give us a picture of a law of the growth of culture.[1]

---

[1] Boas, Franz, "Anthropology and Modern Life," p. 209, New York, 1928.

3. The Alleged Centrifugal Spread and Centripedal Elaboration of Traits

Wissler compares the spread of a trait to the outgoing waves which ensue when a pebble is dropped into a pool of water, and states that the area of intensive development or elaboration of a trait is the place of origin and that this is approximately the geographical center of the area through which the trait has been diffused. He assumes, therefore, that the trait spreads with equal facility, or at least to an equal extent, in all directions, and asserts that the simpler forms of the traits lie on the periphery of the area of distribution and the more complex forms at or near the geographical center of the area.[1] We applied this test to the traits mentioned by Wissler in pages 150 to 157, inclusive, of "Man and Culture," in the chapter in which he discusses the relation of age to magnitude of distribution, and of elaboration of the trait to place of origin. The traits there referred to are pottery, paint, swastika, spiral, cutting off a finger, sacrifice to the sun, sacrificial blood-letting, human sacrifice, hitches, weaving instruments, age-grade societies for men, fire drill, chipping of stone, and lance. In the Old World the area of intensive ceramics has shifted from time to time, though there is probably but one area of origin. Hence as regards Old World ceramics, Wissler's method indicates the place of origin correctly only if one selects the proper century in which to identify elaboration with place of origin. By his criterion, in one century the place of origin would seem to be the Continent, in others, the Valley of the Nile, or Aegean lands. Paints, the next trait in the list, are not susceptible of historical treatment, for their origins and diffusion are not known. The diffusion of the swastika has not been a centrifugal dispersion into geographically proximate regions. It is not found in Egypt, Chaldea, Assyria, or Phœnecia, although these cultures borrowed designs liberally. It is present in Troy, whence it spread to Gaul, Scandinavia, and the British Isles. It traveled eastward into India and into all lands penetrated by Buddhism: Tibet, Mongolia, Southeast Asia, China, and Japan. In Persia it was rare and played no important rôle, but it was widespread in other Aryan lands and wherever Buddhism flourished. In the contiguous Egyptian-Semitic cultures it obtained no foothold. Perhaps the failure to find a favorable soil in the latter may be attributed to the presence in these cultures of the *crux ansata*, the Egyptian Key of Life, which is found from Persia to Libya. Possibly the *crux ansata* was already fulfilling much the same function which the swastika fulfilled in Aryan

---

[1] Wissler, Clark, "Man and Culture," New York, 1923; and "Relation of Nature to Man in Aboriginal America," New York, 1926.

and Buddhist cultures and it may, therefore, have been an indirectly repellent motive. However that may be, the ancient world is divisible into two culture zones, one of which the swastika penetrated, the other, the *crux ansata*, with but slight interpenetrations along the frontier of contact, in Cyprus, Rhodes, Asia Minor, and Libya. Certainly there was not a centrifugal radiation of the trait.

The spiral was introduced into the Aegean area by invaders who came to Thessaly from Transylvania, by way of Eastern Bulgaria and Thrace, or at least their culture spread by that route. It did not appear in Crete until early Minoan II, whence it diffused to the Aegean area. From there it traveled by the Danube route to Scandinavia, thence to Ireland, and from the Emerald Isle to Britain. Meanwhile the center of distribution was shifting to north and west, for the spiral did not travel with the same facility to east or south, although, of course, the place of origin was not shifting. The place of origin, therefore, does not remain the center of the area of distribution. The diffusion of the practice of cutting off a finger is not susceptible of historical treatment, and we pass to the next feature in the above list, sacrifice to the sun. In the Old World such sacrifice originated in Egypt or in the civilizations of Persia or India, but at a later date, when the Mithraic cult had penetrated the Roman Empire, it became as widespread in Europe as in Asia or Africa. Mithraism had only one origin, but the center of distribution shifted from century to century and therefore, by Wissler's criterion, tells a varied story, each tale contradicting the others. The center of distribution is not the place of origin, for the trait did not spread concentrically; it did not spread east or south, and it went north only after reaching the Italian peninsula. In the above instances neither the place of intensive development nor the center of distribution is an index to place of origin.

As a further check upon this principle, we again used random sampling and considered the traits described by Kroeber in Chaps. X to XIII of his "Anthropology."[1] in which he discusses the diffusion of certain traits. The principle of the arch spread about the Mediterranean, first among the ancient civilizations of that region, and later through all the regions which came under Hellenistic influence. With the spread of Roman influences through Europe the arch likewise spread. But at no time was the diffusion centrifugal. The concept of the week originated in the eastern Mediterranean area and spread into other Mediterranean cultures, and finally throughout Europe as well as far into Southern Asia, wherever Mohammedan or Buddhist influences permeated. But

---

[1] KROEBER, ALFRED L., "Anthropology," New York, 1923.

non-Mohammedan Africa was little affected, for the spread was not centrifugal. The alphabet developed in Semitic lands to the east of the Mediterranean and Phœnician traders disseminated it throughout the Mediterranean area. With the exception of China the higher civilizations adopted it but the lower cultures were not influenced, save here and there and only to a slight extent. The girls' adolescent ceremonies of the Pacific Coast, assuming that they originated on the Northwest Coast, spread south as far as the Gulf of California, and possibly even into the Southwest—if the ceremonies of the latter are not the result of influences from Mexico. But they did not spread among the Eskimo to the north and east, nor among the Plateau tribes; the diffusion was longitudinal rather than centrifugal.

Wissler points out, in a discussion of the distribution of the conical shelters typical of the Plains and the Eastern Woodland area, that the three-pole tipi is predominant near the center of the area, the four-pole tipi is to some extent interspersed with these, yet reaches wider margins of distribution to south, east, north, and west, and "conical shelters in general" are in the peripheral areas. But there is no evidence that the three-pole tipi, which predominates at the center, developed out of the types peripheral to it. It is not known that the three-pole tipi is a later development than the four-pole tipi, though the former probably possesses advantages over the latter. A similar objection applies to most of Wissler's illustrations. They do not illustrate unless one takes for granted the truth of the principle which he proposes to establish—and not always then; for some of the instances adduced by him in which the diffusion can be historically traced, do not conform with his principle.

The peyote cult, for example, began in the Rio Grande region and spread rapidly into some adjacent tribes. It did not spread in all directions, however, though the fact that Indians were then on reservations (1850–1919) would, no doubt, modify normal diffusion. Nevertheless, during the period from 1850 to 1890 it covered a region some hundreds of miles northeast and southwest but did not go a comparable distance to north, south, or west. From 1891 to 1905 it secured a footing on reservations close to those in Oklahoma where it had previously been introduced, on one far to the north, and on one far to the northwest, skipping intervening territory—though the trait could not have skipped intervening territory in aboriginal days, when there were no contacts at a distance and direct communication was limited to contiguous cultures. Its spread shows, however, that mere geographical contiguity does not insure diffusion, and that, in any case, the time element is a factor. By 1922 the peyote cult had spread through practically all of the Plains area except a corner in the northwest, but elsewhere it met with little success;

in the southwest the cultures contiguous with the region in which the peyote cult originated did not accept it.

4. CULTURE LIMITATIONS AND FACILITATIONS IN THE SPREAD OF TRAITS

The spread of a trait, therefore, has its explanation in culture rather than in mere geographical contiguity; and the fact that such is the case is further demonstrated by the variations in rate of diffusion in successive decades. Although the Kiowa adopted the peyote cult as early as 1850, before 1890 only three tribes, it appears, had adopted it. In 1890, however, three tribes adopted the cult, in 1891 two, in 1892 one, and in 1893 one. The distribution of the cult then remained stationary for a seven-year period. Not until 1900, when it came to the Shawnee reservation in Oklahoma, was it adopted in a new area. During the following year it appeared among the Winnebago of Nebraska, in 1902 among the Osage and the Ponca, in 1902 among the Northern Arapaho. In 1906 it came to the Seneca Reservation in Oklahoma and to the Omaha, there being one tribal adoption each year in the period from 1907 to 1910. There was no adoption in 1911 or in 1913, but in 1912 there was one adoption, in 1914 two, in 1915 none, in 1916 two, and in 1919 one. Thus in the 20-year period from 1890 to 1919 there were 24 adoptions, while in the 40-year period, 1850 to 1890, there were but three adoptions. This variation in rate of diffusion cannot be explained in sheer geographical terms.

The next culture trait described by Wissler is the use of the horse. Here likewise the facts contradict his thesis. As early as 1542 the horse was introduced from the region near the Gulf of Mexico or from across the Mexican border. But the trait did not spread in all directions with equal facility, nor with uniform speed. It went rapidly through the Plains area, but scarcely penetrated any region beyond, whereas a centrifugal spread would have carried the trait over most of Mexico, throughout the Southwest, into California, and well into the Southeast. Here, too, culture rather than mere geographical contiguity accounts for the diffusion. The grass dance follows similar routes of travel. It originates in the Plains area and spreads throughout that region, going into Wisconsin, the adjacent northern Minnesota area, and south into Texas. But the spread southeast-northwest is twice as extensive as the spread northeast-southwest, for the favorable soil is determined by culture and not by mere geographical proximity. Wissler significantly omits from his list the ghost dance or New World messianic religions. These do not fall into the concentric scheme which he uses as the framework for his data; indeed, they did not spread at all in some directions. Thus all that Wissler succeeds in demonstrating is: (1) a trait can spread only from the place in which it originates; (2) it can move from the place of origin only into adjacent territory, not skipping tribes along the routes of dissemination; (3) sometimes not all phases of a complex trait spread, but some may be left behind as the trait travels, so that frequently it is found in most elaborate form close to the place of origin. However, though the last-mentioned principle may be true if the trait is elaborated before it spreads, it has not been shown to be true if the trait spreads in a simple form which is elaborated subsequently. Wissler has frequently used this principle of interpretation, but, apparently, in not a single instance has he demonstrated its truth. Thus, when discussing shamanistic organizations in the Plains area, he concludes that since it is "very strong among the Pawnee and very weak among the eastern Dakota we must assume that the Pawnee are the originators."[1] But is there any justification for this inference? And can the inference be justified before the principle is established? Wissler himself emphasizes the fact that the three widely spread ceremonies in the Plains area, the grass dance, the dream dance, and the *Iruska*, or fire dance, have specific distributions which correspond, respectively, to subsidiary Plains area cultures. The grass dance is typical of the Western group: the Sarsi, Blackfoot, Gros-Ventre, Assiniboine, Crow, Hidatsa, Teton, and Arapaho; the dream dance flourishes in the north-eastern part of the area, among the Potawatomi, Menomini, Ojibway, Iowa, Winnebago, Sauk, Fox, Kickapoo, and perhaps Plains Ojibway and Plains Cree; while the *Iruska* is found in the Southeast, among the Omaha, Ponca, Oto, Osage, Iowa, Kansa, and Pawnee. Wissler says:

The most striking aspect of this distribution is its general agreement with cultural and geographical distinctions. Our western group comprises in the main the typical Plains tribes, our southeastern group is a part of the intermediate Plains group, and our northeastern, the typical Eastern Woodland group. The peculiarity of this correlation is that in each group we find a different form of the dance and that each form tends to completely cover its culture area. Of these types, the western and southeastern are much more alike than the northeastern. Thus the distinctive Central Algonkin culture seems to have modified the grass dance most. Hence, granting that the ceremony was distributed from a single center, we have what looks like pattern phenomena, for most surely the uniformity of type in each cultural group must be due to influences from within. We have, therefore, an analytic problem, to discover what specific influences were responsible for the differentiation of these types.[2]

---

[1] Wissler, Clark, "General Discussion of Shamanistic and Dancing Societies," APAMNH, 11: 860, 1916.

[2] *Ibid.*, p. 865.

. . . Notwithstanding the great uniformity in the grass dance we have a geographical grouping of minor differences and when we look a little deeper, we find evidences of pattern phenomena in that some dominant ceremonial concepts of the respective localities have been incorporated in the grass dance and have inhibited the continuance of others. It is also suggested that very great differences in the culture of two groups of people will retard diffusion, or at least tend to modify and obscure the identity of borrowed traits. Finally, we may suspect that the preceding differences in the grass dance are due to cultural differences in the tribes concerned.[1] . . . Thus we have followed the devious path of diffusion back and forth across the Plains area.[2]

Again, he says:

At the outset we found that irrespective of chronology the different forms of the ceremony correlated in a remarkable way with the culture grouping of the constituent tribes. Our subsequent analysis of its diffusion has in the main not obscured this correlation. First, we have the gross fact that, in the main, the ceremony is confined to the Plains area. Almost every tribe took it. It is true that it has found its way over the border into the fringes of two areas in very recent years, but its failure to go farther is not due to lack of time, for the older form of the ceremony followed about the same path. Why, for example, did the fire-trick complex stick to the Upper Missouri-Mississippi Basin? It is quite probable that its distribution was governed by the flora, since a plant preparation was necessary to the trick. On this point, nothing definite can be stated until the identity of the plant has been established. Yet, this could not apply to the modern form of the ceremony from which the fire trick is absent. It must be admitted, therefore, that whatever the cause, we have here the work of the same factors that produce the familiar culture area phenomenon. And, as we have previously noted, the most diverse variants of the modern ceremony are found in the west among the Shoshone and in the east among the Central Algonkin intermediate group. Again, how comes it that the Central Algonkin variant, originated by a Potawatomi, is so far removed as to be almost unrecognizable? If a mere coincidence, it is truly remarkable. It is far more likely that we have here a concrete example of what may be expected, if a trait wanders over into a culture where its pattern is a true misfit.[3]

Wissler's "principle" of centrifugal diffusion does not apply to traits of the Old World, where historical evidence is available. One may cite the relative distributions in the Old World of the symbolism attaching to the number four and that attaching to the number seven. Four was a mystic number of magical and ceremonial importance in ancient Egypt, in ancient India, among the Greeks of Hesiod's time about the eighth century B.C., in China, and in Malaysia. Presumably it represents

---

[1] *Ibid.*, pp. 867–868.

[2] *Ibid.*, p. 870.

[3] *Ibid.*, p. 872.

the diffusion through these areas of a concept which originated, or was first elaborated, in ancient Egypt. Later, there developed in Babylonia the concept of seven as a mystic number and this trait influenced all Semitic peoples, and became an important element in Jewish and Mohammedan thought. It traveled to Greece, where it overlay the older mystic concept of four, and to some extent supplemented rather than displaced it, penetrated the Arab world and European cultures, and spread through India and Malaysia. For centuries it has been a more widely diffused concept in the Old World than the concept four, although, as has been indicated, the latter is in these areas, as far as historical record is available, the older. Thus the older trait is the less widely diffused, and in neither case is the area of origin the center of the area of distribution. The explanation of the diffusion is culture and not mere geographical contiguity. The diffusion has followed the routes of Jewish, Christian, and Mohammedan influences. Similarly, the historical religions have not diffused concentrically and seldom is the place of greatest elaboration the place of origin. Buddhism traveled mainly to the east and but little to north or south as it moved eastward. Christianity spread to the west over Europe and the New World but made merely a trek across Asia, following trade routes, and scarcely influenced that continent or Africa. Mohammedanism spread through Northern Africa, India, and Southeast Asia into the Philippines, but it did not penetrate in comparable manner either Europe or Northern Asia. Protestantism spread to the north and west of Europe but not to the south and east. Methodism spread through England and Wales, and penetrated the Protestant portions of English-speaking countries across the seas, but it found little favor in Scotland and Ireland. Christian Science spread through the New England states, across the Middle West to the Pacific Coast, but it obtained comparatively few adherents in the Southern states. Presbyterianism spread through Scotland and into Protestant Ireland, but elsewhere in Great Britian and in Europe it secured no hold, although, like Methodism, it crossed the seas to Protestant lands. The diffusion of scores of other religious cults tells a similar story of geographical irregularity in spread. The difficult thing is to find an instance in which the spread through diverse culture areas has been centrifugal.

The very existence of definite culture areas is *prima facie* evidence, if not proof positive, that a culture trait seldom spreads centrifugally, for, if it did so, the boundaries of culture areas would soon disappear. And even if one admits that every new elaboration starts at the center of the area of distribution, the supposition that it spreads only to the boundaries of the culture in which it originates, implies that the explanation of the spread is not mere geographical contiguity but favorable culture soil.

CHAPTER IV

THE DIFFUSION OF CULTURE TRAITS

1. THE MIGRATION OF CULTURE TRAITS

The diffusion of traits has been prevalent in primitive cultures and in the higher civilizations. Agriculture and pottery have spread through Central, North, and South America, probably from one place of origin, and there has been a wide diffusion of these traits in the Old World. Stories built upon certain plots have a wide geographical distribution which usually is continuous or nearly so and hence implies diffusion. Even suicide is sometimes a culture trait and may spread in typical fashion. The *hara-kiri* of the Japanese is clearly a culture manifestation, as was also the so-called "Red Death," which followed in the trail of an illiterate *muzhik* by the name of Basil Volosatz, who in the latter half of the seventeenth century induced many hundred Russian peasants to commit suicide by immolation. After Peter the Great had issued the severest edicts against the practice it subsided, but it lingered on and as late as 1860 a number of people in Olonetz committed suicide in this manner. In recent years there was in the United States a mild epidemic of suicide among college students, and the phenomenon had appeared among German students more than a century previously, inspired in part, perhaps, by Goethe's "Werther." In the latter part of the eighteenth century, suicide was prevalent in English military circles, and it appears to have passed from them into French military circles, although some writers attribute the increase in suicide in France at this time to the influence of certain eighteenth-century French writers, notably, Rousseau, Montesquieu, Madam de Staël; and perhaps the French justification of suicide was a phase of the Stoic influence which marked the "back-to-nature" doctrines then prevalent in France.[1] Among many primitive peoples, too, suicide may be a culture trait, as, for example, among the Eskimo, the Trobriand Islanders, and the Maya. In other cultures, such as that of the Plains area of North America, it is absent or extremely rare.[2]

---

[1] See, for example, GUILLON, Entretiens sur le suicide, ou ouvrage philosophique opposé au courage réligieux et réfutation des principes de J. J. Rousseau, Montesquieu, Mme. de Staël, etc., en faveur du suicide," Paris, 1802.

[2] CAVAN, RUTH, "Suicide," Chicago, 1928.

2. THE SPREAD OF CULTURE TRAITS INTO ROMAN CIVILIZATION

The Romans, according to their own accounts, borrowed from Etruria much of their religion and methods of government, and from Greece their art, literature, philosophy, science, and the fundamental principles of the laws which they codified.

From many races less gifted than the Greeks and farther off than the Etruscans they adopted whatever seemed good to them: here a sword of Spanish fashion, there a Carthaginian system of rural economy, or again a Gaulish vehicle or an Oriental food-plant. Yet in all these borrowings they did not simply hand their new acquisitions upon their old attainments, but so ingrafted them that their stock, like the tree in Virgil, "marveled at new leaves and fruits not its own." Their speech was rude and uncouth; there came Greek rhetoric and Greek taste, and Cicero stood forth to rival Demosthenes and Isocrates; Virgil and Lucretius outdid all but the greatest teachers in epic and didactic poems; Horace showed that lyric poetry was yet possible, the satirists that new developments might still be looked for. The Greeks and the Etruscans taught them architecture, and the result was a new school, more grandiose than anything Europe had hitherto known. Where they could not improve, they at least preserved, and our modern scientific and philosophical vocabulary owes more to Latin than to any other single source . . . The stories of Julius Caesar learning tactics hastily from Greek manuals may not be historical, but at least accord with the practice of some officers of less genius.[1]

3. THE SPREAD OF TRAITS THROUGH MOSLEM CULTURE

Hellenistic civilization penetrated the regions conquered by Alexander. The Persian armies which invaded Mesopotamia and Syria brought back many Hellenistic traits and Hellenism flourished in the schools of Persia. Among these adopted traits was the bath, which the Persians subsequently gave to their Moslem conquerors, who disseminated it throughout the Islamic world and later introduced it among the Turks. The "Turkish bath" is a lineal descendant of the Greek bath, which passed from Persians to Moslems and from them to European peoples. The Persian soldiers returned with an admiration for Hellenistic architecture and engineering, and they brought with them captive Hellenistic architects, engineers, and craftsmen, through whose assistance Persian architects copied Hellenistic styles. Thus in the centuries preceding the diffusion of Islamism there was a wide and almost continuous spread of Hellenistic traits in science, philosophy, art, architecture, and the luxuries. After Alexander's conquest, the prevalent art *motifs* penetrated Western Asia, though in many cases they were crudely represented, and frequently they were combined with native elements. Subsequently, when

---

[1] ROSE, HERBERT J., "Primitive Culture in Italy," pp. 240–241, New York, 1927.

the native population threw off the yoke of the Umayyads, there was a revival of Hellenistic traits. In origin, therefore, Moslem art is Byzantine, though the traditions of Byzantine art were reinterpreted in the Persian setting, and after the close of the Umayyad period this new medium influenced all Moslem art. Although the Persian art which developed under the later Sasanids was derived from Byzantine models, designed mainly by craftsmen introduced about 528 by Khusraw I, Byzantine art penetrated subsequently only into Spain and, to a less degree, into North Africa. India likewise influenced Persian and East-Byzantine art and architecture, as, for example, in the horse-shoe arch, which was first used in Western Asia about 540 in the church at Dana, on the Euphrates, though here as in pre-Moslem India the horse-shoe arch is decorative rather than architectural.

Thus it appears that the real work of Islam in art and architecture lay in connecting the various portions of the Moslem world in one common life, so that Syria, Persia, Iraq, North Africa, and Spain shared the same influences, which were ultimately Greek or Graeco-Persian, the Indian element, of quite secondary importance, entering directly through Persia. Already before the outspread of Islam, Byzantine art had entirely replaced native models in Egypt, and this was largely the case in Persia as well. At most we can say that Islam evolved a quasi-Byzantine style which owed its distinctive features to the limitations of the Persian artists, but which occasionally attained a better level by the importation of Byzantine craftsmen.[1]

A similar observation applies to ceramic arts and to the illumination of manuscripts, though the prohibition in the Koran against the portrayal of animal figures, "strictly observed only in some quarters and least regarded in Persia and Spain, shifted the emphasis to vegetable forms in decoration and to geometrical patterns." In the earlier period, and also in the days of the Abbasids, the Moslems relied largely upon Greek, Persian, and, to a less degree, Coptic architects, engineers, and craftsmen; in the eighth century A.D. the Byzantine emperor sent to Cordova a mosaic worker and 320 quintals of tesserae to adorn the great mosque. In Moslem literature, science, canon law, theology, and in Arabic grammar the Persians surpassed the Arabs, and though many of the treatises were in Arabic few of the writers were Arabs.

For the most part the Arabic philosophers and scientists, historians, grammarians, theologians, and jurists were Persians, Turks, or Berbers by birth, though using the Arabic language. The fall of the Umayyads and the replacing of the Arabs by the Persians commences the golden age of Arabic literature and scholarship . . . . At the accession of the Abbasids the old

---

[1] O'LEARY, DE LACY, "Arabic Thought and Its Place in History," p. 43, London, 1922.

Arab type passes away and the intellectual guidance of the Moslem community passes into the hands of the Persians.[1]

4. THE SPREAD OF CHINESE CULTURE TRAITS

From China, following routes of trade, came traits which greatly modified European civilization; they reinforced the influences of the Renaissance and gave new direction to many aspects of Western culture, and new impetus to forces already under way. The compass led to the discovery of a New World and acquainted Europeans with many new lands; gunpowder leveled castle walls, made armed knights impotent and ridiculous, abolished feudalism, and made the common man as formidable as the man of privileged birth; paper offered a new material for the use of artists and writers, and printing made it possible to manufacture books and supply them to millions of readers. These traits originated in China and spread to Europe through the instrumentality of Arab traders and travelers. About 220 B.C. the Chinese invented the hair pen and later they replaced the earlier writing materials of bamboo and wood with silk rolls. During the first century A.D. they made from silk fiber a near-paper, although the invention of paper proper was not made until 105 A.D. The first paper, according to the Chinese source which describes it, was made of bark, hemp, old rags, or fish nets; and the earliest extant paper, which was found in a spur of the Great Wall and dates from about 150 A.D., was made out of rags. During the latter half of the third century paper was taken to Turkestan and to Niya, off the northeast border of Tibet and within striking distance of the borders of Northern India. It reached Loulan about 200 and Turfan, to the north, about 399. From Chinese Turkestan it went to Russian Turkestan, no doubt following trade routes, and was in Samarkand, north of Afghanistan, in 650. By 707 it reached Mecca, and from there it penetrated to Damascus and Cairo, arriving in the latter city by 800 or earlier. Thence Arab influence introduced it into Morocco and Spain, about 950. About 1100 it reached Constantinople, in 1102 Sicily, in 1154 Italy, in 1228 Germany, in 1309 England, and in 1322 Holland. The art of manufacturing paper followed much the same routes. Paper was manufactured in Samarkand in 757, in Bagdad in 793, in Egypt about 900, in Morocco about 1100, in Spain about 1150, in France by 1189, in Italy about 1276, in Germany in 1391, and in England in 1494. It was manufactured in Dordrecht, Holland, by 1586, and in Philadelphia about a century later, in 1690. Block printing, which began in Chinese Buddhist monasteries, spread to Japan and also westward. The earliest printed

---

[1] *Ibid.*, pp. 103–104; see also, pp. 137, 139–140, 143.

book (1016) comes from Buddhist Mongolia, and during the following century Japan printed Buddhist books; while during the thirteenth and fourteenth centuries Turfan, in Turkestan, became an important center of printing.

During these latter centuries, and possibly even earlier, block printing was taken to Egypt, and in 1289 and again in 1305 letters containing large Chinese seal impressions were sent from Persia to the King of France. By the end of the fourteenth century, block printing was initiated in Europe; the process was used to print images and to stamp playing-cards, the latter a Chinese invention which developed from dice. Block-print books, however, were not manufactured in Europe until the decade 1440–1450, and shortly thereafter block printing was supplanted by typography. The invention of movable type, about 1041–1049, is attributed to Pi Sheng. The first type was made of earthenware, set in an iron form. Later this method was improved and both type and form were made of earthenware; subsequently type was made of tin, which was perforated and held in place by a wire. The above-mentioned types, however, were not widely used, for there was no satisfactory ink. Toward the end of the thirteenth century a wooden type was employed, and its use extended to the western borders of Turkestan, where it was adopted by the vigur Turks. Metal type was invented about the close of the following century, and in 1390 the King of Korea ordered the establishment of a metal type foundry. In 1403 this foundry issued metal type, and in 1409 the first extant book printed with movable type was manufactured in Korea. A second font was produced in Korea in 1420 and a third in 1434. About 1450 Gutenberg employed movable type and during the next 50 years typography spread rapidly through Western Europe. Finally, from the Western World movable type was reintroduced into China, but it met with comparatively little success there, for China has no alphabet. Instead the Chinese use some forty thousand forms of ideographs, and block printing serves their purposes better than does type. Its adoption in Japan was facilitated when the Japanese devised an alphabet, and there is now a movement in China to adopt an alphabet which will facilitate the use of Western methods of printing with type.[1]

During the seventeenth and eighteenth centuries there was a diffusion of many Chinese traits into Europe, particularly into German-, French-, and English-speaking countries. In France the first New Year's day of the eighteenth century was ushered in with Chinese festivities, and by that time the influence of Chinese traits was considerable. About the

---

[1] WALLIS, WILSON D., and WILLEY, MALCOLM M., "Readings in Sociology," chap. II, New York, 1930.

beginning of the seventeenth century, Chinese palanquins were introduced into Europe. In a French book published in 1644 they were described as a "latest novelty," and a few years later Molière referred to them in several of his comedies. During that century, when distinctions of social rank were marked, this means of conveyance was much used, and even the order regulating the use of sedan-chairs was practically a duplicate of the Chinese regulations. From France the use of the sedan-chair spread to Germany and Austria. In France the Japanese chaise displaced the Chinese chair during the first half of the eighteenth century. In Japan the Chinese chairs were mounted on wheels and were drawn by horses. The Dutch tried, unsuccessfully, to imitate them and the first successful utilization of the device appears to have been in France. In the same century Chinese lacquer work and many Chinese designs and embroideries came into vogue. The paper strips with which the Chinese decorated the interior of houses were introduced, and shortly thereafter they were used to decorate, i.e., to cover, the entire inner walls of rooms. Although they had been imported into Europe as early as the seventeenth century, the English, about the middle of the eighteenth century, first manufactured a satisfactory and serviceable wall paper. This was decorated with landscapes in the Chinese manner. It was sold in large quantities in England, was exported to the Continent, and still does service in some old German houses. Chinese folding fans were brought to Europe early in the sixteenth century, and in the eighteenth century they played an important part in social circles. In the Rococo period, fan-academies in Paris and in London taught the elements of fan-language. The decorations on the fans show Chinese influence, as do many of the paintings of the period, particularly those of Watteau and other landscape painters. The Chinese concave roof, with long overhanging eaves, became an architectural *motif*, and this survives in many parts of Europe—in Versailles, Dresden, Potsdam, Holland, and England. The playful adoption of Chinese architectural *motifs* was wide-spread. With it began *chinoiserie*, a term suggesting pretty ornamental work.[1] The Chinese shadow-plays were introduced into Germany and from there into France. After 1767 they were known in France as *ombres chinoises*, "Chinese shadows." At first they were shown only in certain salons, but soon they became a popular amusement.

Paris had many "Chinese" social resorts. In one "Chinese Café," the service was performed by two women who wore Chinese costume, while a Chinese porter received and ushered out guests. A *rédoute chinoise* which opened in the Faubourg-Saint-Laurent in 1781 featured

---

[1] REICHWEIN, ADOLF, "China and Europe: Intellectual and Artistic Contacts in the Eighteenth Century," pp. 61–62, New York, 1925.

Chinese pageants, illuminations, and fire-works. A popular Chinese swing was attended by a Chinese man and a Chinese woman. Another amusement, possibly a forerunner of the modern merry-go-round, was the *jeu de bagne chinoise*. The Chinese baths were so popular that Cousin dedicated a poem to them—"To the Chinese, formerly called the Oriental baths, situated in the Boulevard Italien." The parks, too, showed the influence of Chinese traits.

In the midst of pavilions and grottoes the earliest pheasant-houses gleamed with the golden plumage of their Oriental denizens, while under Chinese bridges sported the first goldfish, that rare species, the production of which had cost the Chinese perhaps a thousand years of patient care, and which now, since La Pompadour had received the first specimens as a present, were becoming known in Europe. And it was quite of a piece with this bizarre, exotic notion which people had of China, that they should have taken it as the motive of their burlesque entertainments. In Paris and Vienna to begin with, and later in other courts, balls and masquerades in Chinese costume were held; and these amusements became, in the course of the century, so much the fashion, that at last the whole people came to engage in them. Even the pupils of the *Académie de France* in Rome were not to be deprived of their Chinese masquerade. In Paris these amusements soon spread to the fairs and to the boulevards, where Chinese *rédoutes* were built, and where the *Théâtre des récréations de la Chine* arose. Chinese jokes even invaded light opera and comedy. The small theaters in particular took them up, and the Italian Comedians, especially. In 1692, this company played for the first time, in the presence of the king in the *Hôtel Bourgogne*, the five-act comedy of Regnard and Dufresny, *Les Chinois*. The harlequin of this farce gave himself out as a "Chinese doctor," and the scene was laid in a Chinese cabinet.

In 1723, Nestier's troupe gave in the Faubourg-Saint-Germain *Arlequin, Barbet, Pagode et Médécin*, a Chinese piece in two acts. The scene represented the outside of the Imperial palace at Peking. At the end of this extravaganza the "King of China" pardons his children in the oracular French-Chinese phrase—"*Pardonaon, levaon, divertissaon, dansaon.*" They obey and dance, and the curtain falls.[1]

During the eighteenth century the Chinese garden came into favor in England. Previously the French garden had been popular, but Shaftesbury acknowledges the superiority of the Chinese garden, and Addison echoes his praise. "The Chinese," Addison writes in 1712, "ridicule our plantations, which are laid out by the rule and line, because they say anyone may plant trees in equal rows and uniform figures." Addison and Pope copied the Chinese style of garden, and their example was widely followed. "Old gardens disappeared, and new ones, at first scantily enough clothed, took their place."[2]

[1] *Ibid.*, pp. 67–68.
[2] *Ibid.*, p. 115.

Water painting, too, developed as a result of Chinese influence; it grew out of the need for a new rendering of landscape in keeping with the new appreciation of the beauty of unspoiled nature. John Robert Cozens (d. 1794) was the first landscape painter to employ this technique. He drew the outlines in Chinese ink, using brown and gray for the ground-tones and blue and red for the lighter shades. The ink and the colors he applied not with a pen but with a brush, and thus developed a technique which corresponded in detail with the Chinese method of landscape painting. His followers did not confine themselves to landscape painting but also depicted figures in watercolor. Though the extent of Chinese influence in the European technique of painting is difficult to determine, it is clear that such influence existed.

During the pre-Revolution period Chinese thought influenced many Europeans, among them Leibnitz and Goethe. The Chinese concept of natural rights, and the insistence upon order and good government,[1] influenced several writers of the period of the Enlightenment. Goethe speaks of the "lightness and delicacy" of Chinese outdoor life, and he ascribes to certain types of architecture an "almost super-Chinese lightness." "With them," he says, "life is clearer, purer, more moral; they everywhere appear as sensible folk, good citizens, without much passion or poetic fervor; and in this they bear a strong resemblance to my *Hermann und Dorothea,* as also to the English novels of Richardson."[2] And again: their legends "run on morality and propriety . . . But it is this strict moderation in all things which has preserved the Chinese Empire for thousands of years and will continue to preserve it.[3]"

But the most prevalent and persistent Chinese influence is represented by porcelain ware, which is now called *chinaware* or *china,* irrespective of the place of manufacture. "Among all the crafts introduced in those days from China, the treatment of porcelain easily took first place."[4] The European manufacture of porcelain began in Venice in 1470, and the Venetians are said to have acquired the art from the Arabs; but the manufacture of porcelain first attained importance in Holland, whence it passed to Germany and France. In Saxony and France it rapidly became, and has remained, a profitable enterprise. "It became of quite special importance when at last, in 1709, Böttger of Meissen succeeded in producing the first genuine European porcelain."[5]

---

[1] See below, p. 216.
[2] "Conversations with Eckermann, Oct. 31, 1827."
[3] Quoted in REICHWEIN, *op. cit.,* pp. 145–146.
[4] *Ibid.,* p. 31.
[5] *Ibid.,* p. 28.

During the early eighteenth century the use of porcelain as decorative ware had become so common that Mandeville compares the

virtues of great men to your large *China:* they make a fine Shew, and are Ornamental even to a Chimney; one would by the Bulk they appear in, and the Value that is set upon 'em, think they might be very useful, but look into a thousand of them, and you'll find nothing in them but Dust and Cobwebs.[1]

5. The Spread of Traits to, from, and within Western European Culture

Western Europe received from other areas most of the fundamental elements which characterized that culture before the beginning of the Industrial Revolution. From Babylonia came the duodecimal system which we still use in counting time on our clocks and watches, and in dividing the circle into degrees, minutes, and seconds. From Egypt came the calendrical system which the Romans improved and handed on to Northern and Western Europe. From the Greeks Western Europe learned science, the fine arts, philosophy, and poetry. Through the Arabs it obtained many Hellenistic traits, and from India, through the Arabs, the zero, and likewise many traits from China, as notably the compass, the use of gunpowder, the manufacture of paper, block printing, and probably movable type. Subsequently, as we have seen, there came into Europe many other Chinese traits, for example, tea, porcelain, or chinaware, the use of paper to cover the walls and ceilings of rooms, the overhanging gabled roof, the natural garden, such as the English, and later the French, adopted, watercolor paintings of landscapes, the use of the fan, and certain amusements, such as card playing, the merry-go-round, and others, while chess was probably an introduction from Persia. From the New World, Europe obtained tobacco, maize, chocolate, cocaine, the potato, the tomato, and other New World products; and the life or supposed life of New World peoples and other primitive folk stimulated interest in the character of non-European cultures. In the realms of religion and folklore the Near East made considerable inroads into European culture. Christianity, which centered in Jerusalem nineteen hundred years ago, spread to Rome, throughout the Roman Empire, and finally over all Europe, and eventually into all parts of the "civilized" world, and even into uncivilized portions. Contemporary with the first inroads of Christianity was the introduction of Mithraism from Persia or India by returning Roman soldiers, and its spread through a large portion of the Roman Empire. Soon thereafter, monasticism and

---

[1] Kaye, F. B., "The Fable of the Bees: Or, Private Vices, Publick Benefits. By Bernard Mandeville," vol. I, p. 168, Oxford, 1924.

asceticism, which had flourished east of the Mediterranean, moved westward and northward, and penetrated much of Europe. The folk-tales of Arabs, Persians, and Indians found their way into the repertoires of Europeans, and this phase of Eastern cultures became deeply rooted in Western folk-thought and literature. The sanctity of the king, and the union of Church and State, which the Romans encountered in the Hellenistic Empire, they introduced into the Italian peninsula, and Augustus became a god. As a result Europe accepts the divine right of kings, and in theory if not in fact the king is still the head of the Church. The existence of that tradition is due to the infiltration of Near Eastern traits. And as culture traits have poured into Western civilization, so likewise traits have radiated from it into other areas, due primarily to the explorations and colonizations of Europeans in America, Africa, Asia, and Oceania, and each outpost of Western civilization became a new center for the diffusion of European traits. Primitive peoples have been too far removed in culture pattern to absorb many of these traits, but elsewhere there has been a considerable adoption of some of them during the last half century, as notably in China and Japan. In many respects the latter country has been modernized, or "Westernized," *i.e.*, it has adopted many European traits, and so, too, has China during the present century. In these countries, as in India, an industrial revolution has set in, comparable with that which was under way in Europe a century ago. Social and political ideas, too, have penetrated many portions of the world remote from the Mother of Parliaments. Thanks to the spread of Western traits, parliaments and cabinets now flourish, or languish, in Egypt, India, Persia, China, Japan. The armies and the navies of Asiatic peoples represent the spread of European traits. The newspaper, science, the printing of books, movies, European music, and American jazz have penetrated the Asiatic world. The traits of Western culture have spread into almost all parts of the world, which in many places is taking on, at least in certain superficial respects, the cast of Western civilization. Thus, though each culture is distinctive, many traits travel from one culture to another, and history furnishes abundant examples of their diffusion.[1]

Methods of reckoning time pass from Egypt to Rome and from Rome to Western Europe. But the Gregorian calendar spread rapidly in some countries and slowly in others. In Italy it was adopted, by decree of Pope Gregory, in 1582, and Central and Western Europe soon followed suit. England and the American colonies, however, did not adopt it until 1751

---

[1] For other illustrations see WALLIS, WILSON D., and WILLEY, MALCOLM M., "Readings in Sociology," chap. II, New York, 1930.

—George Washington was not born on Feb. 22—and not until after the World War was it adopted in Russia, Greece, Turkey, and some of the smaller countries. By 1926 it had been adopted by all European countries, including those under the Greek Church, which were the last to adopt it.

Most countries, except the English-speaking ones, have adopted the metric system for everyday use or have officially taken steps to do so in the near future. In 1929 twenty-five large countries and more than fifty small ones had given up their respective original systems of weights and measures and had adopted the French metric system; and no country which has adopted it has revoked its decision. The metric system was adopted by law in France in 1795 and went into effect in 1799, but for many years it made little headway. Not until 1837 was it in general use in the retail business of France, and then the adoption was the result of a law passed that year by the French parliament. It had previously been adopted by other countries: by the Low Countries (Belgium, Holland, and Luxemburg), in 1820; by Switzerland, in some cantons, in 1822, and in all cantons by 1877. Spain accepted the metric system in 1860, Italy in 1861, Germany and Portugal in 1872, Austria in 1876, Norway in 1882, the regions now comprising Jugoslavia in 1883, Rumania in 1884, Sweden in 1889, Bulgaria in 1892, Denmark in 1912, Greece and Russia in 1922. By 1870 a large part of the scientific work of continental Europe and much of the internal trade was conducted in terms of the metric system.

Many other traits spread in similar fashion, some slowly some rapidly, some over large areas, some into only a few countries or localities. Paris styles penetrate most of the world of fashion, at least the feminine part of it, and London styles invade the masculine world from New York to Shanghai and Calcutta. Tobacco was taken to Europe where it gradually came into general use, and eventually spread over practically the entire world, reaching Asia by way of Europe, and Northwestern North America via Siberia. Political and social ideas spread through many areas. The spirit of the French eighteenth-century socio-political writers inspired the colonists of America in the struggle against England, as well as the people of France in the contest with Louis XVI. The spirit of the American Revolution reverberated through France and added strength to the movement which culminated in the French Revolution. The French Revolution echoed throughout continental Europe, first after 1789, then after 1830, and again after 1848. Military preparedness illustrates the diffusion of a trait of culture, and bolshevism has demonstrated the ability of traits of another complexion to spread.

6. The Spread of English Culture Traits to France and Virginia in the Eighteenth Century

French writers were influential in England, especially during the latter half of the eighteenth century. Some, as notably Voltaire, Montesquieu, and Saint-Simon, resided in England for a time and were much influenced by English thought and institutions; a number of English writers resided in Paris and were acquainted with France and with French thought. "There was a continual exchange of ideas between the two nations."[1] Turgot corresponded with Price, Hume, and Josiah Tucker.[2] Voltaire, says Condorcet, went to England a poet, and returned a sage. "Between 1763 and 1789 there was hardly a prominent man of letters in France who did not either visit England or mix with Englishmen; there was hardly a noble at the Court of Louis XVI of whom the same cannot be said."[3] The English nobility welcomed Helvétius in 1764, Morellet in 1772, Raynal in 1778; and Rousseau was so popular among the British aristocracy that George III pensioned him. The writers in one country were eager to make the personal acquaintance of fellow craftsmen in the other.

This reciprocal admiration of each other's brains sent Englishmen to France to study French, and Frenchmen to England to study English, and the example of a nobility [the English] which for half a century had patronized its men-of-letters was ever present to an aristocracy [the French] which was just beginning to do so.[4]

Paine states that the French National Assembly was a popular toast in England.[5] Adam Smith visited Paris in 1765, had conversations with Turgot, Voltaire, d'Alembert, Helvétius, and other economists, and doubtless was influenced by them. Priestley's enthusiasm for French ideas was so outspoken that it alienated many of his compatriots. The French Academy of Sciences made him a Foreign Associate, and the

---

[1] Delvaille, Jules, "Essai sur l'histoire de l'idée du progrès jusqu'à la fin du xviiie siècle," pp. 428, 442, Paris, 1910.

[2] Daire, Eugène, "Œuvres de Turgot," Tome II, pp. 801–811, Paris, 1844; Stephens, W. Walker, "The Life and Writings of Turgot," pp. 203–205, London, 1895; Price, Richard, "Observations on the Importance of the American Revolution, and the Means of Making It a Benefit to the World."

[3] Lockitt, C. H., "The Relations of French and English Society (1763–1783)," chap. I, pp. 1–2, London, 1920.

[4] Ibid., p. 60. For an account of the status of English writers at this time see Balfour, Arthur J., "Essays and Addresses," pp. 55–58, 3d ed., 1905.

[5] Paine, Thomas, "The Rights of Man. For the Use and Benefit of All Mankind," p. 111, London, 1795.

Convention proclaimed him one of its members and conferred upon him the title of French Citizen. When Thomas Paine, in 1792, went to France, he was elected a member of the Convention.[1] The "Preface" to his book, "The Rights of Man," bears the imprint, "Luxembourg, Paris, May 19, 1794."[2] Many Englishmen of this period might have written:

> The best of all ways
> To lengthen our lays
> Is to steal a few thoughts from the French.

Edmund Burke complained, regarding a certain London club: "The National Assembly of France has given importance to these gentlemen by adopting them; and they return the favor, by acting as a committee in England for extending the principles of the National Assembly. Henceforeward we must consider them as a kind of privileged persons; as no inconsiderable members in the diplomatic body."[3] Macaulay says, with characteristic exaggeration,

> The literature of France has been to ours [the English] that which Aaron was to Moses, the expositor of great truths which would else have perished for want of a voice to utter them with distinctness. The relation which existed between Mr. Bentham and Dumont is an exact illustration of the intellectual relations in which the two countries stand to each other. The great discoveries in physics, in metaphysics, in political science are ours. But scarcely any foreign nation except France has received them from us by direct communication. Isolated by our situation, isolated by our manners, we found truth, but we did not impart it. France has been the interpreter between England and Mankind.[4]

When the wife of the British ambassador, the Duchess of Shrewsbury, appeared at the French Court in 1714, her low coiffure was admired and soon was copied by the French ladies of fashion. The influence of English traits upon the culture of France during the pre-Revolution period was considerable, and no doubt they added impetus to the revolutionary movement; for the nobility and the intelligentsia rather than the common people inaugurated the Revolution, and it was through them that English traits influenced French life.

---

[1] DELVAILLE, op. cit., pp. 490, 492, 519, 525, 527–545.

[2] The title page of the original edition contains the following: "By Thomas Paine, Member of the French Convention; Late a Prisoner in the Luxembourg at Paris; Secretary to Congress During the American War, and Author of 'Common Sense,' etc., etc. London: Printed and Sold by Citizen Daniel Isaac Eaton, Printer and Bookseller to the Supreme Majesty of the People, at the 'Cock and Swine,' no. 74, Newgatestreet, 1795."

[3] BURKE, EDMUND, "Reflections on the Revolution in France," London, 1790.

[4] MACAULAY, THOMAS B., "Essay on Horace Walpole," quoted in ATKINSON, CHARLES M., "Jeremy Bentham: His Life and Work," pp. 93–94, London, 1905.

Furniture, wall decorations, *coiffures*, beds, everything that lent taste and beauty to the daily lives of the French passed through the same leveling, subduing process which the nobility in their enthusiasm for English forms had themselves inaugurated: the Government itself admitted that the introduction of English manufactures had become so extraordinary that unless French goods were advertised as English they had little chance of a sale, and it was to some extent through the medium of these outward and visible signs that republican notions entered into, and filled, the minds of the populace.[1]

By 1763 English cabs were introduced into Paris, and in the latter days of the old régime many were used. They must have become popular immediately, for in 1778 a thousand accidents are attributed to them, and though this may be gross exaggeration, it bespeaks their prevalence. French visitors to England were much impressed with the London clubs and with the discussion of politics which prevailed in them, and especially with their exclusion of women. In 1769 there was in Paris a *Club à l'anglaise* to which Charles Fox was invited and which stimulated him to observe that "we cannot be foolisher in point of imitation than they are." The political clubs which played an important part in revolutionary days developed in part from this borrowed English institution, which had been introduced into France early in the century, although some of the French clubs developed from the institution of the coffee house which came to Paris in the seventeenth century. "The patriotic societies in France," says an observer of the French Revolution, "found their model in England, but they abused it."[2] Card playing, betting, horseracing, dueling, and suicide were introduced, or reintroduced, from England, or were stimulated by English influence. French dragoons committed suicide à *l'anglaise*, and contemporary Frenchmen attributed the prevalence of suicide to English influence.[3] Decremps speaks, in 1789, of "that sadness which is characteristic of the English and which leads them to suicide."[4] Diderot defines an Englishman as "a man who gets out of his country to kill himself elsewhere," and in 1778 Madame du Deffand, in a letter to an English correspondent, refers to suicide as "a habit they say we get from you, this *manière de se miner.*" With the growing prevalence of betting after the English manner, there was also an increase in suicide after the English manner. Self-murder was regarded as a characteristic of the melancholy Englishman, and certainly there was an increase in "suicide after the English manner." During the same

---

[1] LOCKITT, C. H., *op. cit.*, p. 43.

[2] VON ARCHENHOLTZ, J. W., "The Jacobins, A Historical Narrative from Personal Knowledge," Hamburg, 1792; quoted in GOOCH, G. P., "Germany and the French Revolution," p. 428, London, 1920.

[3] But see above, p. 77.

[4] Quoted in HEADLAM, CECIL, "Friends That Fail Not," p. 254, London, 1902.

period there was an increase in duelling, which seems to have been inspired by the notorious political duels in England, and the English duel with pistols came into vogue in France. By 1790 a challenge and a rendezvous in the Bois de Boulogne were "quite the proper thing"; on the day set for a duel "the company was charming and of the best tone; fifty coaches awaited the scattering of some one's brains." Although at the end of the seventeenth century duelling was common in France, at least in Paris, and even many women engaged in duels, subsequent English influence seems to have stimulated it considerably and to have modified the pattern.[1]

By 1763 amateur acting was popular in England, and the vogue continued for some years. Taine says it appeared in France in 1767. Towards the end of 1769 it had become "an incredible rage"; even the Queen played in several performances. English influence brought also an improvement in the status of the actor.

In France he was excluded from the rights of citizenship and could be disinherited; he received no honors or distinctions from society, such as Garrick obtained in England. English actors and actresses went to France, and their superior status excited the envy of their fellows in Paris. Foote visited Preville; Garrick himself went in 1765, and his numerous friends opened to him the doors of all the *salons*, where alone, and surrounded by faces which almost touched his, he played the great scenes of the English theater. He is heard of at d'Holbach's, at Helvétius', and at Mademoiselle Geoffrin's, while Mole, Grimm, Mademoiselle Riccoboni, Ducis, Monnet, Suard, Le Kain, Necker and other notable literary personages are among his correspondents.[2]

Masquerades, which were popular in England as early as the time of George II and which continued in vogue under subsequent Georges, were taken to France, where they became popular and by the latter part of the century had become an established feature of French culture.

Two other traits are due largely to English influence: the practice of spending a part of the time on the country estate, and the improvement and featuring of the garden and of landscaping. Arthur Young writes of Liancour—and the statement doubtless was applicable to many French country seats—"the mode of living and the pursuits approach much more to the habits of a nobleman's house in England than would commonly be imagined." The growing French custom of spending a vacation in the country is, he says, the result of English influence:

---

[1] CAUCHEZ, "Du duel," vol. I, pp. 100–233, Paris, 1846; ZIMMERMANN, In "Gerichtssaal," 1872; "Schlaraffia Politica: Geschichte der Dichtungen vom Besten Staate," p. 171, Leipzig, 1892 (anonymous).

[2] Lockitt, *op. cit.*, pp. 57–58.

The present fashion of spending some time in the country is new; at this time of year (Sept. 16), and for many weeks past, Paris is, comparatively speaking, empty. This remarkable revolution in the French manners is certainly one of the best customs they have taken from England, and its introduction was effected the easier because assisted by the magic of Rousseau's writings.

Thus a specific culture preparedness paved the way to the innovation. A by-product was a falling off in the splendor of the Court at Versailles, and this, in turn, had significant results. "When the tradition that environed the Court with splendor had been once violated, its hold over the minds of men was gone."[1] Versailles rapidly lost its former brilliance. Several French writers of the latter half of the eighteenth century, impressed with the charm of English gardens, refer to them as modeled after the wild and uncultivated woods. "It is the English who have been able to put to advatage those falls of water, those happy charms, those delightful horrors, those caverns, those ruins, those surprise views," declares the Prince de Ligne. Voltaire claims the credit for introducing this type of garden into France. "It was I," he says, "who introduced that taste into France, and every one eagerly caught it." Montesquieu, who like Voltaire had resided in England, also adopted the English garden and sought to model his villa after the English fashion, but it was not until about 1771 that the English garden, which had been inspired by the Chinese, became popular in France. The facility with which pre-Revolution France borrowed English traits is symptomatic of the rapidity of the changes in French culture, and each is cause and effect of the other. The use of natural forms in landscaping is partly attributable to the influence of Rousseau and Linnæus, but it was stimulated by Chinese influence; the influences of these two men were stronger in France than in England, yet this type of natural garden first developed in the latter country and then spread to France. The new traits were the result of a changed attitude, and they in turn stimulated changes. Their ramifications were far reaching, and some of their implications were subtle and effective. There can be no doubt that the increased familiarity with England and the favor into which English traits had come were partly responsible for the borrowing of the English type of garden and of the other traits mentioned above; but the acculturation was consonant with changes which Rousseau, Voltaire, Montesquieu, Turgot, and other writers were advocating, and therein lies part of the explanation of the facility of the borrowing. As Ségur says, "When we were destroying in our pleasure grounds the straight walks and alleys, the symmetrical

---

[1] *Ibid.*, p. 96.

squares, the trees cut in circles and the uniform hedges, in order to transform them into English gardens, we were indicating our wish to resemble that nation in other and more essential points."[1]

Meanwhile certain French traits spread to America and to England and influenced the English settlers in the New World as well as much of the western Old World. To the colonial aristocracy in America came the gallantry, duelling, gambling, and possibly some of the subtler wit which had been traits of French culture since the days of the Grand Monarch. The dress and deportment which characterize Paris are emphasized in Northern cities and on Southern plantations, where great ladies imitate the rôles of French mistresses of salons. In the later years of the eighteenth century and during the first decades of the nineteenth the salon complex takes deep root in many parts of the United States where fashion rules. French dances are introduced and also those trivialities of lighter moments, fans, mirrors, and laces. During the second and third decades of the nineteenth century Paris dictated the changes of taste in dress, hat, bonnet, vest, perfume, and soap. The influence of French styles was responsible for the adoption of the use of the umbrella in England in the eighteenth century, although it had been known there at least as early as the tenth century. By the crowd it was detested as a "new-fangled foreign fashion," but finally it was tolerated.

In Virginia, to a greater extent than in any other colony, a close contact with England was maintained, and there English customs and ideas were deeply rooted and persistent. "Members of all classes invariably spoke of England as 'home.'" The mother country was thus referred to in business letters and in legal documents. England was designated as "home" by Virginians who had not seen England, and who did not expect to see it. When the English-born emigrant, however long he had resided in Virginia, considered the division of his estate among his heirs, he dwelt with lingering fondness upon the scenes of boyhood and early manhood, and upon kinsmen who had remained in England; and the reference to England as "home" appears most frequently in wills.

It was not simply the demands of business that, during the seventeenth century, led so many Virginians to visit England; a deep love for their old home influenced many of those who had been born there to return, whilst a natural curiosity to see what had been so often described to them, and a desire to meet kinsmen whom they had never met, prompted many of the native colonists to make the voyage. There is not a surviving county record of the century which does not contain numerous notices of an intention to go

---

[1] DE SÉGUR, COUNT L. P., "Memoirs and Recollections of Count Ségur," vol. I, pp. 130–131, London, 1825–1827; quoted in LOCKITT, op. cit., p. 99.

by the first ship to England. As early as 1632 a special license had to be obtained by any one wishing to depart before he could acquire a legal right to do so. This license seems to have been granted by the county court; and its recordation was not infrequently accompanied by that of the last testament of the person receiving it, no doubt because the voyage was looked upon as attended with extraordinary danger. This fact must have brought a strong influence to bear to discourage many to undertake such a journey; and that the perils of an ocean-crossing were so constantly defied is only another proof of the close social bonds uniting such a large number of Virginians with the Mother Country.[1]

Among the English traits which flourished in Virginia were duelling, gambling, drinking, horse-racing, dancing, theatricals, and the planting of trees and hedges about the mansion houses. The English traits which went to France went also to Virginia, and in each case intimate social contacts facilitated the migration.

There was in the South, above all in Virginia, a joyous, light-hearted, and hilarious mode of life which offered a strong contrast to the more sober hues of New England. Over wide areas the tastes and manners of English landed families were reproduced. Fox-hunting, horse-racing, circuses, gambling, cock-fighting, dancing, and drinking contests were among the frequent and reputable amusements of the time. The economy of the planting South, like its traditions, was on the side of easier and merrier ways among the upper classes. There was more leisure among masters and mistresses of slaves than among the farmers and seafaring merchants of New England who had to depend on sobriety and industry for their daily bread. There were great manor houses equipped with the luxuries that made entertainment a delight; the furnishings, plate, and good wines of the Old World . . . "Whatever goods you may send me," George Washington wrote to his factor in London, "let them be fashionable."

Like the rest of the Virginia gentry, he had a strong passion for horse-racing, and "theaters, circuses, and cock fights had an irresistible appeal for him. He was at the front at country balls in his neighborhood, in moderate drinking bouts at the tavern, and in fox-hunting parties."[2]

7. The Spread of the Tobacco Complex

Tobacco conquered all peoples of the globe without distinction, and I know of only a single trible that does not practice smoking—the poor islanders of Botel Tobago. Tobacco is more universally consumed than any other narcotic, has profoundly influenced the economy of most nations and signally affected social customs and promoted sociability. In a spirit of gratitude, Chinese and

---

[1] Bruce, Philip Alexander, "Social Life in Virginia in the Seventeenth Century," pp. 144–147, Lynchburg, Va., 1927.

[2] Beard, Charles A. and Mary R., "The Rise of American Civilization," vol. I, pp. 141–142, New York, 1927.

Japanese have bestowed on tobacco the name "herb of amiability" (ai-king ts'ao), as they explain, "on account of the affectionate feelings entertained toward one another by all classes of mankind since its use has become general."[1]

During the course of its diffusion, however, the tobacco complex underwent many changes in the various cultures into which it was introduced. Among some Indian tribes, for example, the smoking of tobacco was a semi-religious rite. Among the Crow, before a pipe was smoked it was pointed first up, then down, and then in turn to each of the cardinal points. When men smoke in a group a man takes not more than three puffs and then passes the pipe with a conventional movement to his neighbor on the left. Shoshone medicine men, when smoking during the treatment of a patient, removed their moccasins. Among the Havasupai a boy should not smoke before he had killed a coyote. Among the Cheyenne smoking was an important ceremony, and while a man smoked no one might leave the lodge. Some men when about to smoke fastened the door of the lodge so that no one might enter; and no one might stand or walk about within the lodge. These or similar regulations were not typical of Indians outside of the Plains area, and they were not taken with tobacco when it was introduced into European countries. But although these rites have not accompanied the use of tobacco in Western communities, there is in many lands a definite tobacco etiquette. In 1714 Addison writes, in the *Spectator*, of its social virtues: "Lighting a man's pipe at the same candle is looked upon among brother smokers as an overture to conversation and friendship." The same applies in English-speaking lands to this day, especially in England—though "cigarette" may be substituted for "pipe," and "match" for "candle."

The use of tobacco has spread in spite of attempts to keep it out of the culture. It has had strong opponents and vigorous defenders; yet no one can say, with confidence, why it is favored or why it is opposed. Smoking is, in part, a social custom, though it is difficult to determine why it is adopted. Once started, however,

. . . the fashion . . . involves the majority of individuals in any one group. Witness the taking of snuff in Queen Anne's day in England, and under Louis le Grand in France. One would have almost as soon come to court without stockings as without a snuff-box. Remove the social significance of tobacco, and its use would die out in a generation.[2]

---

[1] LAUFER, BERTHOLD, "The American Plant Migration," *Sci. Monthly*, **28:** 241–242, 1929.

[2] HAMILTON, A. E., "This Smoking World," p. 5, New York, 1927.

The attempt of Beau Nash in England, in 1700, to abolish smoking from good society was, indeed, partly successful for a time, during which interval English society contented itself with the taking of snuff. Despite opposition, however, smoking increased in England, and by 1702 the consumption of the weed had reached an average of two pounds per person per year.

Tobacco appears to have been introduced into New Guinea soon after the Portuguese established a factory in Amboina in 1521. In 1502 the Spanish introduced the custom of smoking into Spain, and in 1550 Francis Hernandez of Toledo brought the plant to Spain and cultivated it as a medicinal herb. In 1561 Jean Nicot took tobacco to Catherine de Medici, who learned to take snuff, and in that year the tobacco plant was cultivated in Holland. In 1599 Dutch and Portuguese traders introduced it into India, and in 1601 it was planted in Java. In 1602 the smoking of tobacco in China was reported, and in 1605 the plant was grown in Japan, though in 1612 a Chinese imperial edict prohibited the planting and the use of tobacco. In 1697 it was used in Africa by the West Coast negroes, who procured it either from the Portuguese or from the Spanish, and in 1652 Dutch settlers introduced it into South Africa. In 1586 tobacco and a pipe were taken to England and presented to Sir Walter Raleigh. He learned to smoke and introduced the custom into Ireland in 1587. In 1589 it was adopted in Italy. In England smoking spread rapidly among the upper classes; in 1596 the Bishop of London died "while sitting in his chair taking tobacco." This inadvertence on the part of the bishop inspired attempts to prove the perniciousness of the weed, and although in 1600 tobacco was mixed with incense in English churches, in that year Cobb, the anti-tobacconist, stated that, "four people have died, from tobacco within a week. One of them voided a bushel of soot." Yet in 1600 smoking was so general that it was permitted in the theaters and was usual there. In 1604 King James I published his manifesto against the use of tobacco, "a custom loathsome to the eye, hateful to the nose, harmful to the brain, dangerous to the lungs . . . resembling the Stygian smoke of the pit that is bottomless." Royal words, however, could not stay the spread of the custom. In spite of a duty of four thousand per cent., which James I imposed, imports of tobacco from the colonies increased, and it was imported likewise from Spain and Portugal until 1624, when its importation from these countries was prohibited. It invaded the universities as well as theaters, churches, and homes. In 1605 an Oxford don, Dr. Cheynell, debated, pipe in hand, with King James on the merits of the weed, and in 1615 the students of Cambridge were threatened with expulsion if they smoked in St. Mary's Church. Other countries followed suit in putting a ban upon the use of tobacco.

As stated above, in 1612 China declared against the use and the planting of tobacco, and in 1615 the Shah Abbas of Persia, fearing that smoking would result in a lowering of the birth-rate, prohibited the use of tobacco, and as a warning to offenders burned a tobacco merchant alive in the midst of his stock. Two years later, enraged that his courtiers defied the interdict, he punished offenders by compelling them to smoke camel's dung. In 1628 his grandson, Shah Sefi, sent spies through the kingdom to detect and punish smokers, and hot lead was poured down the throats of two merchants who were found selling the "infamous weed." But in 1647 Shah Abbas II, having learned to like tobacco, rescinded the laws which prohibited the use of it. By 1670 the Shah was smoking a pipe, and men and women were said to be so addicted to the use of the weed that, "to take it from them is like to take away their lives." In 1617 Jahan Geer, the Mogul emperor, decreed the death penalty for smoking or snuffing tobacco. In 1624 Pope Urban VII by interdict forbade "all persons of either sex, to take tobacco in the porches or interiors of churches, whether by chewing, smoking, or inhaling in the form of powder," and ten years later the Greek Church, averring that Noah had been intoxicated by tobacco fumes, prohibited its members the use of tobacco. Pope Benedict XIII, however, learned to smoke, and in 1724 revoked the papal bulls which prohibited the use of tobacco. In Switzerland smokers were summoned before the Council in 1635 and were fined, and in 1661 Berne legislated against tobacco on the ground that the use of it violated the Mosaic Seventh Commandment. In 1634 the Czar of Russia prohibited the use of tobacco; he prescribed whipping for the first, and execution for the second offense; and the noses of users of snuff were to be amputated. But Peter the Great smoked, and in 1700 he revoked the edicts against the use of tobacco, and leased a monopoly of it to English merchants. Then, to enrich the royal treasury, he encouraged smoking. The use of tobacco must have grown apace, for in 1743 the Empress Elizabeth ordered the confiscation of all snuffboxes which were taken to church. In 1590 Austria prohibited the use of tobacco, and in 1635 the King of France prohibited the sale of it except by apothecaries on prescription of a physician. Louis XIII, however, learned to take snuff, and in 1637 repealed all laws restricting the use of the weed. In the Southern colonies there was no restriction upon the use of tobacco. Perhaps the economic motive is accountable for the good favor into which the weed came in those portions of the New World. In 1619, and again in 1621, the Virginia colonists paid tobacco for the wives imported from England, 120 pounds per wife for the first consignment, and 150 pounds per wife for the second; the former, as befitted the heads of the F. F. V.'s, consisted of "ninety agreeable persons, young and incorrupt," whereas in the later F. F. V. shipment were "sixty maids of virtuous education, young and handsome." As late as 1723 the salaries of Virginia ministers were paid in tobacco, one Mr. Barlow receiving in that year 5,590 pounds for seventeen sermons. In New England, however, there was a different attitude toward tobacco. In 1647 the Connecticut Colony prohibited smoking in public or in company with others, although the following year the prohibition was modified to apply only to smoking in public; and in 1660 Massachusetts imposed a fine of 12 pence for smoking on Sunday within two miles of a meeting-house. Early in the present century there was much agitation in this country against the cigarette. A bill to prohibit the sale of it was introduced in Congress in 1906, and although this failed to pass, several states prohibited the sale of cigarettes, namely, Arkansas, Iowa, Indiana, Kansas, Minnesota, Nebraska, North Dakota, Oklahoma, Tennessee, Utah, Washington, and Wisconsin. The prohibition is itself an interesting example of trait diffusion, for these states constitute practically a continuous area. The basis of the antipathy probably lay in the fact that in the Middle West cigarette smoking was regarded as effeminate. All of these states have repealed the law, Kansas as recently as 1927, but in 1930 North Dakota still had a law, well honored in the breach, prohibiting smoking in the dining-room of a hotel.[1] In every state the sale of tobacco to minors is prohibited, the age limit varying from fifteen to twenty-one years. In 1877 the Methodist Episcopal Conference prohibited the use of tobacco by its ministers "without prescription by doctor," and the prohibition is still in force, although it has been much contested in recent conferences. Some other churches discourage or prohibit the use of it by members. A book entitled "What It Means to be a Mormon"[2] devotes two chapters to the topic "Cigarettes." It quotes the law of Utah which makes it a misdemeanor punishable with a fine not exceeding $100 for any person under twenty-one years of age to "buy, accept, or have in his possession any liquor, cigar, cigarette, or tobacco in any form." "To be a Mormon means to be a non-smoker," for in the revelation to Prophet Joseph Smith in 1833 there was this declaration: "And again, tobacco is not good for man, but is an herb for

---

[1] Other attitudes, embodied in legislation, may spread in similar fashion. Thus in 1920 Iowa adopted the Vigilance Committee system to deal with bank robberies. In 1925 Kansas adopted the plan, and by 1930 it had been adopted by Oklahoma, Illinois, Indiana, Michigan, Minnesota, Wisconsin, and California. With the exception of the last mentioned state these states constitute practically a continuous area. The Farmer-Labor and Non-Partisan movements suggest similar spreads, though less extensive.

[2] BENNOIN, ADAM S., Written for the Desert Sunday School Union. Published by the Desert Sunday School Union, Salt Lake City, 1917.

bruises and all sick cattle, to be used with judgment and skill." The last national prohibition of smoking appears to be that of the Emperor Menelik of Abyssinia. In 1900 he smoked a pipe, lost his dinner in consequence, and forbade his subjects to smoke. For this national self-denying ordinance he was made an honorary member of the French Anti-Tobacco Society—and a new smoking room was installed in the London Athenaeum Club.

Wars have stimulated smoking. The Thirty-Years War brought tobacco to Germany, where it was introduced in 1620 by English soldiers who had been sent to the assistance of Prince-Elector Friedrich of the Palatinate and the winter king of Bohemia. The cigar came into England after the Peninsular War and was the result of Spanish influence, as the cigarette was the result of Russian and Turkish influence. In 1856 British officers home from the Crimean War brought back cigarettes, and their example did much to restore smoking by soldiers in the open, which Queen Victoria had opposed as early as 1837, with support from the Duke of Wellington, who in 1845 prohibited smoking in mess-hall by officers of junior rank and by soldiers. General Grant, an inveterate smoker, was presented with 11,000 cigars after the capture of Fort Donelson, where he had used a cigar stump as a marshal's baton. In 1868, shortly after the Civil War, smoking compartments were installed in railway carriages in the United States and in England. In 1918 the United States Government commandeered for army use "Bull Durham" and "Duke's Mixture" tobaccos, and in the same year the Knights of Columbus sent overseas to the "boys" 1,400,000 packages of cigarettes, 5,000,000 cigars, and 4,000,000 corn-cob pipes; contemporaneously the Y. M. C. A. placed an order for 70,000,000 cigars to help win the war. In 1885 the Princess of Wales served cigarettes to women at a luncheon, and Mrs. Grover Cleveland followed suit in 1889, but not until after the World War did cigarette smoking become popular among the female sex in this country, although it was prevalent in women's clubs in England long before that time. "The World War gave initial impetus to smoking by American women, and greatly increased feminine cigarettism in England."[1] This vertical diffusion has accompanied the increased freedom of women in political, social, and economic life.[2]

---

[1] HAMILTON, A. E., "This Smoking World," p. 188, New York, 1927. Most of the facts cited above have been taken from this book. See especially chap. XIII, "A Very Condensed History of Tobacco"; the present writer's "An Introduction to Anthropology," pp. 215–216, New York, 1926; and KROEBER, A. L., "Anthropology," pp. 211–214, New York, 1923.

[2] See below, p. 115–116.

The custom of taking snuff spread to the Kafirs of South Africa, and at least as early as the middle of the last century it had become an important affair among them, though, so far as we are aware, not among any other primitive people.

Almost every individual, male and female, practices it; and Kafirs seldom meet without indulging in a concert of snuffing. The most important person is expected to supply the material, but he must be *asked* to do so; for, "should you offer snuff before it is asked for, or even give it readily when asked for (the custom is to refuse it at first and then present it) they would look upon you suspiciously; and, if they should be taken ill, think you have poisoned them. Many have been thus suspected and killed." The mode of asking differs, according to the quality of the person addressed. If he were poor, he would be solicited in plain literal language and requested to give snuff; but, if a rich man, he would have his generous instincts excited by a respectful innuendo, and it would be said to him: "What do you eat, Sir?" A rude man, who did not intend to give his snuff, answered that he eat [*sic*] food; but a polite man, who wished to reply in the negative, would say that he did not eat anything at present. When a man furnishes snuff for a party, he usually pours a large quantity into his left hand, and holds it for the others to take pinches as they may require, but without looking at them. If however he be rich and liberal, he first helps himself, and then tosses the box to his companions, that they may do the same. When a chief entertains his *ama-pakati*, the box is brought to him in a basket; he then shakes out a large quantity into the united hands of a servant, by whom it is carried round to the guests.[1]

A phase of the commercial complex of the tobacco retail business in this country was the carved wooden Indian, placed on the sidewalk in front of a tobacco store. Most of these were carved between 1830 and 1900, and each was made from a single log. Soon after the last mentioned date the police began to order them off the sidewalk, because they impeded traffic; in a few years they had disappeared, and they are now so rare that a good specimen is worth several hundred dollars. Thus a change in one phase of the culture may modify a trait complex.[2]

8. The Spread of the Coffee and the Tea Complex

The spread of coffee drinking is in many respects comparable to the spread of the use of tobacco. At various times there has been considerable opposition to it, mainly on religious or political grounds, though occasionally for reasons of health. The berry of the coffee tree was first used in

---

[1] SHOOTER, JOSEPH, "The Kafirs of Natal and the Zulu Country," pp. 223–224, London, 1857.

[2] Barber poles similarly used to stand out on the pavement, but owing to congested traffic were moved into the interior of the shop or were placed against the side of the building.

upper Abyssinia, where it was roasted, pulverized, mixed with grease, and rolled into balls to be eaten. Coffee was introduced into Arabia from Abyssinia perhaps as early as the twelfth, possibly not until the fifteenth century, and from Aden the use of it spread to other Arabian cities, notably, Mecca and Medina. The orthodox *mullahs* declared that it came under the ban of intoxicating drinks which were prohibited by the Koran, but, despite opposition, coffee drinking spread and numerous coffee houses were opened. During the first decade of the sixteenth century coffee drinking went from Aden to Cairo, where it became very popular. In 1511 the Governor of Mecca, Khaine Beg, prohibited its use as a beverage, declaring that it induced those inebriating effects which the Koran condemns; but his successor, Causin, rescinded the edict. In 1523 the chief priest, Abdallah Ibrahim, preached against the use of coffee, but opposition was futile, for the beverage was well liked and already was widely used in Arabia and Egypt. In Cairo likewise the introduction of coffee was opposed on religious grounds, though it had been introduced by dervishes from Yemen, who then resided in that city.

The Cairene opponents asserted that coffee was inebriating, and in 1523 after a denunciation of it in a sermon by Abdallah Ibrahim, there was open fighting between the defenders and the opponents of coffee. The commander of the city, Sheik Elbelet, assembled the doctors, listened patiently to their verdicts on the effects of coffee, drank a cup of it in their presence, gave each of them a cup of the beverage, and without a word dismissed them. The effect was salutary; the public peace was restored and henceforth the Cairene might drink coffee unopposed. In 1550 coffee was used in Persia, Syria, and other parts of Western Asia which had come under Arab influence. In 1554 a coffee house was opened in Constantinople by a man from Damascus, and another by a man from Aleppo. In Constantinople the introduction of coffee met with vigorous opposition. Moslem theologians discovered that when coffee is roasted it becomes a kind of coal, and the Prophet had declared that God did not intend coals to be used as food. The *mufti* sided with the theologians and closed the newly opened coffee houses. A later *mufti*, however, persuaded the theologians that coffee was not a species of coal, and the coffee houses were reopened. But the city government soon arrayed itself against the coffee houses, which they regarded as little better than nurseries of sedition. Nevertheless, though taxed they persisted, and they yielded, uncomplainingly, a goodly source of revenue, which to some extent reconciled the government to the institution. In 1717 natives from Mozambique, Portuguese East Africa, introduced coffee drinking into Madagascar, and in that and the following year it was introduced from Arabia into the islands of Bourbon and Mauritius. The first mention of coffee by a European is in a work published in 1573, written by Rauwolf, a German physician and traveler, who records the use of it in Syria, and in 1591 the plant is described in a work published in Venice, entitled "The Medicines of the Egyptians." Italian merchants were in intimate touch with Arabian and Turkish lands, and Italy was the first country in Europe to adopt the use of coffee. It was used in Venice in 1615 and in Rome in 1625. In 1644 a Frenchman brought from Constantinople coffee and the apparatus for making the beverage, and in the same year coffee was introduced at Marseilles. In 1657 Thevenot introduced it in his household in Paris, and served it to friends, and in 1660 several sacks were shipped from Alexandria to Marseilles. Before the end of the decade coffee drinking had become popular in France, and in 1670 the consumption of coffee in the household of Louis XIV cost that monarch $15,000. Coffee then sold in Paris for about $25 a pound, though by 1680 coffee drinking was common in that city. The statement that coffee was sold in Oxford in 1640 may not be trustworthy, but in 1641 a Cretan was drinking coffee in his rooms in Balliol College, and liquid coffee was sold in London by 1651. In 1653–1655 an English merchant imported coffee from Turkey. By the end of the decade it was a common beverage in London, and by 1688 it was in general use in England. In 1644 liquid coffee was sold in Holland, and after the opening of a coffee house in Amsterdam in 1666 the use of the beverage spread rapidly through the Netherlands. In 1670 it went from Holland to Germany and from Germany to Austria, though the Turks independently introduced it into Vienna in 1683, and about 1700 it went from Austria into Russia. In 1756 the use of coffee passed from Germany to Denmark and Sweden, and by 1800 it was in general use in Scandinavia. Early in the nineteenth century coffee supplanted port as the after-dinner drink in England, and the custom of taking after-dinner coffee was connected with the development of the drawing-room, and with after-dinner conversation. This marked the transfer of the coffee-house pattern to the home.

The institution of the coffee house has spread with the diffusion of the custom of coffee drinking. Coffee houses originated in Arabia and there they flourish vigorously to the present day, as they do throughout the Mediterranean area wherever Mohammedan influence is or has been potent. Natives from these regions have been the main factor in the introduction of the institution into other lands. As mentioned above, a man from Damascus and one from Aleppo introduced the institution into Constantinople in 1554. The first coffee house in Marseilles, opened in 1671, was true to Arabian type: there merchants met to play games, smoke, and talk. In 1672 an Armenian, though known by the French name Pascal, opened the first coffee house in Paris. In 1675 a

Frenchman opened the first *café*, and in a few decades there were 300 cafés in that city. In these originated some of the clubs which played an important part in later political life. In 1653–1655 a Greek servant opened a coffee tent in London, and in 1657 there were many coffee houses in that metropolis. A statute of 1663 required their licensing and in 1675 Charles II attempted to suppress them, because they were "seminaries of sedition." But there were then three thousand such establishments in London, the attempt to suppress them caused much excitement and turmoil, and a few days after its publication the edict was revoked. By 1688 coffee houses were encountered as frequently in London as in Cairo, and in the former city as in the latter they were important news centers. There, as in Paris, the intelligentsia and the literati met at coffee houses. During the seventeenth century they reached the height of their popularity. Under date of Feb. 3, 1663/4 Samuel Pepys records:

I stopped at the great Coffee-house (Will's Coffee-house), where I never was before: where [were] Dryden, the poet I knew at Cambridge, and all the wits of the town, and Harris the player, and Mr. Hoole of our college. And . . . it will be good coming thither, for there, I perceive, is very witty and pleasant discourse.

Edward Lloyd's coffee house, which is first mentioned in 1688, soon became a meeting place for merchants and shipmen, and early in the following century it was almost a small stock exchange.[1] It became the famous "Lloyd's."

The *Café Procope*, established in 1689 near the theater *Comédie Française*, became the most famous of the Parisian coffee houses. Up to the age of eighty-four Voltaire frequented it, and there, too, came some of the important figures in the French Revolution—Danton, Marat, and Robespierre. French influence introduced the French type of coffee house in New Orleans, the only American city in which it has flourished. In Virginia, New York, Massachusetts, and other colonies the English type of coffee house became an important institution, and many of these were centers of discussion in the pre-Revolution period. Burn's coffee house, the first in New York, was a favorite haunt for those who opposed the Government of George III, and many Boston coffee houses served a similar purpose.

Among the most famous was the British Coffee-house at 66 State Street, which served as headquarters for Loyalists; but later, owing to the growing

---

[1] KAYE, F. B., "The Fable of the Bees: or, Private Vices, Public Benefits. By Bernard Mandeville. With a Commentary, Critical, Historical, and Explanatory," vol. I, p. 62, Oxford, 1924.

political schism among its patrons, it became the American Coffee-house. The Bunch of Grapes, located at the southeast corner of State and Kilby Streets, was decidedly Whig in sympathies. It was here that Otis, in attempting to pull a Tory nose, received such a brutal beating as ultimately to cause the loss of his reason. The Crown Coffee-house at the head of Clark's Wharf on the north side of State Street (on the present site of the Fidelity Trust Co.), the North End Coffee-house opposite the head of Hancock's Wharf on the northwest side of North Street, the Exchange Coffee-house in Congress Square, and the Royal Exchange on State Street, were among the famous coffee houses of Boston. These coffee houses were liberally patronized by both Whigs and Tories. In some of these Coffee-house Tavern-hostelries, the British sympathizers gathered and drank toasts to King George III. In others, Yankee rebels assembled. At the Green Dragon, which was also known as Freemason's Arm, such adventurous and ardent patriots as Otis, Joseph Warren, John Adams, Cushing, Pitts, Molyneux, and Paul Revere met nightly to drink coffee and to discuss public affairs. An historical tablet at 80–86 Union Street, Boston, still marks the location of this famous coffee house.[1]

A notice which appeared in the Boston *Publick Adviser*, May 19 to 26, 1657, makes the following claims regarding the virtues of coffee: "In Bartholomew Lane on the back side of the Old Exchange, the drink called coffee, which is a very wholesom and Physical drink, having many excellent vertues, closes the Orifice of the Stomach, fortifies the heat within, helpeth the Digestion, quickneth the Spirits, maketh the heart lightsom, is good against Eye-sores, Coughs, or Colds, Rhumes, Consumptions, head-ache, Dropsie, Gout, Scurvy, Kings Evil, and many others, is to be sold both in the morning, and at three of the clock in the afternoon."[2]

In Germany and Austria, coffee houses did not play an important rôle in social or political life, although they still exist there. The dates of their introduction into the more important German cities are as follows:

Nürnberg, Regensburg, and Prag	1686
Hamburg	1687
Leipzig	1694
Danzig and Wittenberg	1700
Stuttgart	1712
Augsburg	1713
Berlin	1721
Reutlingen	1760

---

[1] CHENEY, RALPH HOLT, "Coffee," p. 233, New York, 1925.

[2] Quoted in BLEYER, WILLARD G., "Main Currents in the History of American Journalism," p. 39, New York, 1927.

Among the Greeks the coffee house still flourishes as an important center of social life, and they have introduced it into every city in this country, from the Atlantic to the Pacific, in which there is a Greek colony. During the World War the Greek coffee house was an important meeting place for political discussion, a center for either the monarchial or the republican cause, and the walls were decorated with appropriate pictures.

In coffee houses with royal sympathies, one finds the photographs of the royal family. On the walls of coffee houses with republican sympathies, one finds pictures of eminent republicans. In all Greek coffee houses, one sees pictures of Greek battle ships, usually in the process of sinking a Turkish warship, and copies of paintings which depict the historical and intellectual attainments of the Golden Age of Greece.[1]

This description of Greek coffee houses in New England applies in every detail to Greek coffee houses in California, and illustrates the persistence and diffusion of a trait complex.

During the seventeenth century chocolate became a popular drink in London and there were many well-known chocolate houses. In the latter part of the century, however, chocolate gave way to tea, and in 1702 there were only five chocolate houses in the city and only two of them were important social centers. When a chocolate house was opened in Boston in 1731 the advertisement of it described it as a place "where they [gentlemen] may Read the News, and have Chocolate, Coffee, or Tea ready made any time of the Day."[2]

Tea is first mentioned in China, the land of its origin, in the latter part of the third century, but it did not spread through North China until about the tenth century. Not until the thirteenth or the fourteenth century was it much used by the Mongols, although, probably during Mongol domination it spread to Russia and to Western Asia. It is first mentioned in European literature in 1588, when it was imported by the Portuguese from South China, before the Portuguese tea trade was taken over by the Dutch. Tea was introduced into England during the latter half of the seventeenth century. In 1664 the East India Company presented the King with two pounds of tea which, presumably, were gratefully received. In 1678 the East India Company imported nearly 5,000 pounds of tea, an amount somewhat in excess of the demand; and in 1721 the imports exceeded 1,000,000 pounds. Tea had now become a popular beverage. At first it was believed to possess medicinal properties, and this in part accounts for its early popularity;

---

[1] CHENEY, op. cit., p. 236.
[2] Boston Gazette, Sept. 13–20, 1731; quoted in BLEYER, op. cit., p. 61.

it was, in fact, probably more beneficial than the heavy chocolate which was then drunk. Many of the coffee houses of earlier days were supplanted by tea houses, and the tea garden likewise came into favor, as did chinaware, the use of which increased with the growth in the consumption of tea. Thus, to a certain extent, tea drinking fitted into the pattern of coffee drinking, although the trait brought with it several customs with which it had been associated in China.

CHAPTER V

THE ASSIMILATION OF CULTURE TRAITS

1. THE BORROWING OF CULTURE TRAITS

Man has always been subjected to and affected by outside influences. He has picked up a little here, snatched a little there, and engrafted what he has caught up on to the tree of his own ideas, with the result that its subsequent growth has become complicated or even diverted from its original tendency.

Acculturation, the utilization of fructifying culture contacts, has been a potent factor in culture change. Indeed the history of civilizations is in large part a story of acculturation. Even in the prehistoric world, as is shown by the distribution of designs and ornaments, of bronze and iron, there was culture diffusion, and when, for example, the civilization along the Nile and that along the Tigris-Euphrates mingled, each left its impress upon the other. Greece was enriched by the larger Mediterranean world. Greek culture civilized Rome, and through Rome and along Roman viaducts, reached Western Europe, and thence the New World. When two cultures come into contact, each influences the other. The influence is considerable if the contact is sympathetic and intimate, and even when it is neither sympathetic nor intimate, mutual influences are transmitted if the contact is long continued. The contact of whites with negroes in the days of slavery elicited little sympathy from the whites; yet the negro influences Southern culture and, indeed, national culture, to a considerable degree. The influences of Indian culture upon our civilization will persist when Indians are only a memory. Most culture contacts, provided they do not lead to the extermination of a people, are mutually stimulating. Acculturation, then, enlarges the boundaries of the world in which the group lives. Yet to a primitive people culture contacts depend in large part upon circumstances beyond their control. The physical environment confines the native of central Australia to desert regions and excludes him from the larger world of culture influences. It inevitably does so unless he can escape the limitations imposed by nature. Isolation tends to thwart culture development, and few peoples living apart from the influences of other cultures attain a high civilization. The Veddas of Ceylon, the Andaman Islanders, the Tasmanians, the Australians, and the Todas represent back eddies of civilization, shut off from the rest of the world. They have not lain in the path of culture diffusion—at least not when the intruding culture was sufficiently like their own to be fructifying. Not only trade but civilization as well follows the flag, and exchange of articles brings exchange of ideas. The area of contacts is the area of culture stimulus, and the civilization of a people is determined largely by its culture contacts. A broadening of the culture horizon brings corresponding enrichment to the culture. By suggestion or by counter-suggestion, by way of example or of warning, contacts add new content to a culture. When the social weather-vane veers toward another point of the compass there are new culture influences within the area of disturbance. If it is true that, "nothing moves in the world, except the blind forces of nature, that is not Greek in origin," then Greek culture is an omnipresent influence in our civilization, a force which persists beyond the geographical area of origin; and to utilize it is to be influenced by it. The converse of diffusion is borrowing, for there is a human and a social side to the spread of traits. Not only do culture areas have boundaries, but the culture soil has specific composition and fertility. The trait which in some cultures readily takes root, in others falls on stony ground, for the character and intensity of the reaction to a new trait depend largely upon the nature of the culture.

If nations actually borrow from their neighbors, they probably borrow only what they are nearly in a condition to have invented themselves. Any singular practice of one country, therefore, is seldom transferred to another, till the way be prepared by the introduction of similar circumstances. Hence our frequent complaints of the dullness or obstinacy of mankind, and of the dilatory communication of arts, from one place to another. While the Romans adopted the arts of Greece, the Thracians and Illyrians continued to behold them with indifference. Those arts were, during one period, confined to the Greek colonies, and during another, to the Roman. Even where they were spread by a visible intercourse, they were still received by independent nations with the slowness of invention. They made a progress not more rapid at Rome than they had done at Athens; and they passed to the extremities of the Roman empire, only in company with new colonies, and joined to Italian policy.[1]

With regard to the French Revolution, Mallet du Pan said, "Whoever regards this revolution as exclusively French is incapable of pronouncing judgment upon it"; and Metternich later had occasion to remark, with some bitterness, "When France has a cold all Europe

---

[1] FERGUSON, ADAM, "An Essay on the History of Civil Society," pp. 259–260, Edinburgh, 1767.

sneezes."[1] Yet the French Revolution affected England only slightly; the English "intellectuals" had acquired in large part the political rights for which Frenchmen were fighting, and in England the motive to instigate a revolution was feeble. Russia it did not affect, not because political evils were not abundant, but because the spirit of the revolution could not permeate Russian culture. That country was not prepared for the doctrines of Rousseau—its people lived too close to nature; nor for those of Voltaire: only a new order could discover the irony of the old, and in Russia there was no new order. But Prussia, and still more the South German states, were permeated with the new idealism, and there the French socio-political ideas took root. Owing to this difference in culture preparedness,

Napoleon's invasion of Spain introduced a fiercer explosion of wrath than his invasion of Prussia; but in the latter case the flame he had kindled continued to burn, while in the former, after emitting sparks of dazzling brilliance, it quickly flickered out. The difference is explained by the fact that the German mind was awake, and that the issues were formulated by an army of writers and speakers, whereas the peninsula was cut off from the intellectual movements of Europe by a barrier of ignorance and indifference more formidable than the Pyrenees. The people as a whole were wedded to their traditional beliefs and practices, and asked nothing of their neighbors but to be let alone. Such a nation could be relied on to resist attack with a passion of pride and fury; but when the danger was past it would revert to the old paths.[2]

Yet things did not "revert to the old paths." The result of the presence of French armies in Spain was a series of revolutions in that peninsula.

While the armies of France were still in possession of most of the cities of Spain, deputies and refugees from the unconquered and the conquered provinces met at Cadiz in 1812 to draw up a new constitution. They found their model in the French constitution of 1791, declared that sovereignty resided in the nation, abolished feudalism and the Inquisition and dissolved the monastic orders. In thus decreeing a revolution the legislators of Cadiz lost touch with the people; and when the dynasty was restored on the downfall of Napoleon its reforms were swept away without protest. The intellectual and moral discipline which in Germany preceded the appeal to arms had no counterpart in the peninsula. In Germany nationalism was formulated as a doctrine and took its place as a guiding principle. In Spain resistance to the invader was like a fire of straw, blazing up with bewildering rapidity and

---

[1] Quoted in Gooch, G. P., "Germany and the French Revolution," p. v, London, 1920.

[2] Gooch, G. P., "Nationalism," p. 15, New York, 1920.

falling back into ashes when the enemy was consumed in the fierce flame. Germany emerged from her martyrdom resolved to learn and to apply the lessons which had made her enemy powerful and victorious.[1]

The effects of the Napoleonic invasion were not limited to the Iberian Peninsula. They kindled in South American countries fires of nationalism which resulted in freedom from Latin European domination. The Revolution of 1830, during which Paris drove Charles X out of the country, produced great excitement in Belgium, and within a month the standard of revolt against Holland was raised in Brussels. In another two months the Provisional Government proclaimed the independence of Belgium, and announced its intention to summon a constituent assembly. The Paris July Revolution fired the nationalism of the Poles, which had smoldered fitfully since 1815, and an insurrection broke out in Warsaw, whereupon the diet proclaimed the Poles independent and entitled to choose their own ruler. The Revolution of 1848 affected peoples prepared for the doctrines of democracy but left untouched those, as notably the peoples of Eastern Europe, who were not sufficiently advanced to adopt the new ideas. Peoples too backward politically, however close geographically, were not much influenced; those politically advanced, as Great Britain and the United States, likewise were little affected, though for a different reason.

Every one is familiar with the accounts of the misery of the French people on the eve of the Revolution, the crushing exactions, feudal dues, *dimes, gabels,* church tithes, which wholly swallowed up their substance, the chronic famine and destitution which sent haggard ghosts wandering over the desolate land. It is obvious, we think, that such a state of things could not endure; it must inevitably result in rebellion. But things were just as bad at the death of Louis XIV as at that of Louis XV, and there was no rebellion.[2]

In England, however, "the eighteenth century may be said to begin with 1688,"[3] for, as Edmund Burke said, the Revolution of 1688 was "a revolution not made, but prevented." The French Revolution, which came a century later, had comparatively little influence upon English political life. Many ideas live a life of their own, independently of the minds which first shared them, but in some minds they obtain no lodgment.

In the realm of ideas, there are neither frontiers nor custom-houses; and during the latter part of the nineteenth century the principle of self-deter-

---

[1] *Ibid.,* p. 17.

[2] BRIFFAULT, ROBERT, "The Making of Humanity," p. 285, London, 1919.

[3] LASKI, HAROLD J., "Political Thought in England from Locke to Bentham," p. 7, New York, 1920.

mination, which is the essence of nationalism, spread far beyond the confines of Europe.[1] It is easier to resist armies than to resist ideas. No boundary fortresses or strategic defenses will prevent the invasion of thought.[2]

As in the case of revolutions, the origin and spread of fascism and of bolshevism are related to culture patterns. It is not accidental that bolshevism arose in Russia rather than in Scandinavia or Western Europe, nor is it accidental that it took root in Hungary but not in Austria; in Mexico but not in the United States or Canada; in Italy and Spain, but not in England, Germany, or France; in China, but not in Japan. Each was an attempt by a partially mechanized country to deal with industry by pre-industrial methods. Where men were more habituated to the problems of the industrial age neither bolshevism nor fascism could prevail. It is significant, too, that in our own country communism has found most fertile soil in those parts of the country and among those people which have had least acquaintance with the machine civilization that inspires the revolt, namely, in the suddenly industrialized Carolinas.

Hume says that the borrowing of desirable culture traits at the wrong time may be a disadvantage rather than an advantage to a culture, since it discourages the autochtonous cultivation of them—a view of which the protectionists have made use in insisting that high tariffs are necessary to enable a country to realize its best economic and industrial development. Says Hume,

Perhaps it may not be for the advantage of any nation to have the arts imported from their neighbors in too great perfection. This exstinguishes emulation, and sinks the ardor of the generous youth. So many models of Italian painting brought to England, instead of exciting our artists, is the cause of their small progress in that noble art. The same, perhaps, was the case of Rome, when it received the arts from Greece. That multitude of polite productions in the French language, dispersed all over Germany and the North, hinder these nations from cultivating their own language, and keep them still dependent on their neighbors for those elegant entertainments.[3]

Turgot says, similarly:

No art can well subsist if it does not succeed in engaging a number of men sufficient to cultivate it as a simple trade. The English have for many years spared nothing in order to acquire fine paintings, but they have not been

---

[1] GOOCH, *op. cit.*, p. 92.

[2] CHENEY, EDWARD P., "Law in History and Other Essays," p. 124, New York, 1927.

[3] HUME, DAVID, "The Rise and the Progress of the Arts and the Sciences," in "Essays, Literary, Moral, and Political," p. 79, London, 1870.

able to produce a single great painter of their own nation—the reason is that the English pay for only *good* paintings. In banishing images from their churches they have deprived of the means of living bad artists and even mediocre ones. In any trade where the worst workman cannot live or where the mediocre is not tolerably comfortable, the greater men cannot be formed.[1]

The diffusion of a trait is usually more rapid in some cultures than in others. While London merchants were leisurely discussing the possible utility of the telephone, that instrument was spreading rapidly through America, a country more disposed to try new devices. Within a few decades the civilized world adopted it, but, for obvious reasons, it did not penetrate savagery. The facility of borrowing depends upon the culture context as well as upon the nature of the new trait, for unless the culture has advanced to a certain stage adoption is not possible. In the main the telephone has gone where there is motive for its use, where it helps business or social life, where efficiency and time-saving devices have value, in short, where science, industry, and social life are sufficiently advanced to utilize it. Julius Cæsar, who is usually given the credit for the invention of the leap year, merely introduced into Rome a trait which had failed of adoption in the land of origin, namely, Egypt. In the reign of Ptolemy III, Egyptian astronomers fixed the official year at $365\frac{1}{4}$ days. This reform was embodied in the Decree of Canopus, in 238 B.C., but national conservatism prevented its adoption. Julius Cæsar employed an Egyptian astronomer, Sosigenes of Alexandria, to reform the Roman calendar, and Augustus subsequently made this calendar universal throughout the Roman Empire.

In many instances prejudice prevents the adoption of a food. For a long time Europeans would not eat the potato, because it was believed that it would cause smallpox; and as late as 1859 an American author wrote:

We are somewhat inclined to think that A. J. Davis [who is a physician by profession] is correct, when he says, "The atmosphere has had the cholera, more or less, for thirty years, and will continue to have it until there occurs a geological change in many portions of the earth; and from the atmosphere the disease has been, and is, communicated epidemically to the predisposed potato plant, and also to the human system.[2]

---

[1] TURGOT, "Universal History" (1750), transl. in STEPHENS, W. WALKER, "The Life and Writings of Turgot," p. 314, London, 1895.

[2] EMMONS, S. B., "The Spirit Land," p. 288, Philadelphia, 1859. See also the present writer's "The Prejudices of Men," *Amer. Jour. Soc.*, **34**: 804–821, 1929; and WALLIS, WILSON D., and WILLEY, MALCOLM M., "Readings in Sociology," chap. II, New York, 1930.

The adoption of a trait is sometimes facilitated by a deliberate modification of it. Thus the adoption of the Chinese game of Mah Jongg was made easy for Europeans when an Englishman substituted Western characters for the Chinese script and thus made it understandable to children and adults alike. Its sudden vogue in the United States was as suddenly terminated by the vogue of the crossword puzzle. Diffusion, therefore, is largely a matter of assimilation. Traits are not everywhere assimilated with equal facility; frequently the culture is too sophisticated, and regards the intruder as "childish," or "barbarian," or it is too naïve, and does not appreciate the value of the trait. Napoleon did not see the possibilities in Fulton's steamboat and rejected the offer of the patent. "Fulton first built a 66-foot boat on the Seine at Paris, and obtained some speed, but little attention and no success. So he returned to the great rivers of America, and in 1807 launched the *Clermont* in the Hudson, and steamed for Albany at five miles per hour."[1] Fulton and other inventors had much trouble to secure in American and European lands recognition of the importance of their inventions, but in any other land they would have had much more difficulty, and in aboriginal Australia they would have labored in vain. A trait which is too much ahead of or too much behind its time fails of adoption; and when adopted, it may not flourish full-fledged in pristine purity. Especially in the realm of the non-material, the new trait is adapted to old ones, sometimes undergoing such considerable changes as to be scarcely recognizable as its old self. It loses some old characteristics and acquires new ones, for to transmit an idea is to transmute it. As Christianity spreads through Europe, it takes on new traits with each adoption and loses some old ones. Roman law is borrowed, but is adapted to new conditions. If the trait becomes a vital phase of the culture, adoption necessitates adaption. Thus the spirit of the French Revolution is modified when it goes to new lands; it becomes acclimated to the respective national atmospheres. In Spain it is one thing, in German states something else, in Italy another expression. Each adapts the concepts to the needs of the day and place, for if the trait is to function dynamically, it must be assimilated by the culture. Occasionally, however, the introduced trait supplies the dominating and driving motive, and makes the remainder of the culture subordinate to it rather than subordinates itself to the culture. Democracy and the Industrial Revolution are illustrations. The new machine industry transforms the old life. Democracy brings a re-orientation of many phases of the culture, and bolshevism may dominate rather than be

---

[1] GILFILLAN, S. C., "Who Invented It?" *Sci. Monthly*, **25**: 530, 1927; reprinted in WALLIS, WILSON D., and WILLEY, MALCOLM M., "Readings in Sociology," chap. II, New York, 1930.

dominated. Similar phenomena are found in primitive culture. Thus the taro cult spread among the Orokaiva tribes of New Guinea with astonishing rapidity, but meanwhile the newest or most startling features of the new cult were toned down "so as to harmonize better with the existent cultural background." In keeping with this adaptability, the element in the new religion which called for the worship of the taro spirits gradually gave place to the older worship of the dead, though most other phases of the cult remained little changed. When it spread into other cultures, however, the new cult conformed to the respective culture patterns.

It has conformed to native standards of hospitality—one might say prodigality; it has given a fillip to the power of the medicine men; it has inspired the food quest with a new enthusiasm. It fits in, so to speak, with native customs and native interests. And what is more, it has never . . . been antagonistic toward existing ceremonies. If it has interfered with these cere-monies it has done so simply by replacing rather than by opposing them.[1]

2. THE VERTICAL SPREAD OF CULTURE TRAITS

Traits of culture spread not merely horizontally, *i.e*, from one locality to another, but also vertically, and penetrate different social strata in the culture area. Traits which characterize the nobility or the upper classes may be rare or absent in the bourgeoisie and the peasantry, and those shared by the intelligentsia may not be attributes of the masses. In styles of dress, for example, there is frequently a vertical spread, which usually goes from the upper classes to the lower, though sometimes in the reverse direction. Thus the dress which characterized the upper classes in both Europe and America a century and a half ago—wigs, knee-breeches, and so on—has largely been given up, save by English judges, who wear the wig, and by golfers and those who participate in English Court functions, who wear knee-breeches or plus-fours. With modifications the upper classes have adopted the style of dress which characterized the lower classes, though on ceremonial occasions they revert to the older upper-class dress. At the present time, however,

---

[1] WILLIAMS, F. E., "Orokaiva Magic," pp. 82–83, Oxford, 1928. Similarly, when the ghost dance religion spread through the Plains area of North America, it conformed with the patterns of the respective cultures. Among the Dakota, for example, it adopted many of the rites of the sun dance, notably, the use of the center pole with decorations, the use of the painted shirt, the clock-wise dance around the pole, and the vision. Among the Klamath of Oregon, it was modified into another pattern in conformity with the ceremonialism of the tribe. Practically every tribal adoption involved an adaptation to culture pattern.

especially in England, styles of dress adopted by royalty usually affect the prevalent styles in the country of the sovereign, and frequently they spread into other countries. The paint and short hair of the *demi-monde* have been adopted by conventional ladies. Bakers' bread was first used by the poorer classes and later was adopted by the well-to-do—at least this was the case in *Middletown*.[1]

In educational institutions there is a vertical as well as a horizontal spread of traits. College fraternities inspire similar if clandestine organizations in high schools, and likewise interscholastic contests, class yells, school songs, school yells, the school newspaper and the school "annual" penetrate the high schools. Another example of the horizontal spread of traits is the adoption of the circus complex in institutions of higher learning in this country. At first colleges were primarily places for study, and they were not very different from the monastic retreats in which medieval scholars found shelter. After the Civil War collegiate institutions in this country developed atheletic teams to represent them, and this was followed by the employment of coaches and professional athletes, a practice which is not yet completely defunct. Then came bleachers and finally stadiums, in which great crowds watch a performance carried on by highly selected and intensively trained teams. Meanwhile there developed various forms of student entertainment, in which frequently clownish performances were a part, or processions in which costumes figured prominently and became a part of the exhibit. During this time, too, fraternities and sororities made much headway, and in some of them the circus complex appears to be the dominating motive.

Songs, tunes, and dances likewise spread vertically. Thus negro dances, melodies, and jazz tunes have been adopted by the whites. Religious denominations utilize secular tunes in congregational and choir singing, and in sacred musical concerts. Evangelists hire assembly halls in which they advertise themselves as "making whoopee for the Lord." Between the sexes there is sometimes a vertical spread of traits. When women began to assert their independence they adopted many masculine traits, such as riding bicycles, riding astride on horseback, wearing bloomers, trousers, or knickerbockers, cutting the hair, smoking, and wearing men's-style shoes. In the colleges they took over most of the male students' complexes: athletic contests, debating societies and teams, oratorical contests, Greek letter societies. The Y. M. C. A. gave rise to a Y. W. C. A., and the Boy Scouts to the Girl Scouts and the Campfire Girls. The vertical spread of traits is a phase of the equalization

---

[1] See LYND, ROBERT S. and HELEN M., "Middletown: A Study in Contemporary American Culture," p. 155, New York, 1929.

of the sexes, which has greatly facilitated the diffusion of traits from the male to the female sex. The desire to have a boyish figure has influenced the dress, diet, and habits of girls and young women, and is, some medical authorities believe, responsible for the increase in the tuberculosis rate among them. If they are correct in this opinion, the phenomenon is a striking illustration of the unexpected reverberations of the adoption of traits.

3. DEGREES OF CULTURE SATURATION

There are differences also in the degree to which a trait permeates a culture. In some cases it is present but plays no important part in the culture, and is shared by only a few individuals. Thus matches are plentiful and ubiquitous, but diamonds, automobiles, watches, and gas furnaces are of considerably less relative frequency. When a trait is present to as great an extent as it can be utilized, the culture may be said to possess the trait to the saturation point. The telephone, for example, plays a different part in the culture of Chicago than in that of Paris, for the former is more thoroughly saturated with telephones than is the latter. The automobile plays a more important part in present-day American culture than it did a quarter of a century ago, for the automobile has more thoroughly permeated the culture. The degree of saturation is sometimes important, and should be considered when comparing cultures which possess similar traits. In 1851, for example, Horace Greely expressed the opinion that the telegraph was employed by newspapers in England "not a hundredth part" as much as in the United States; and this difference he considered related to the fact that in English newspapers news was subordinate to editorials, whereas in American newspapers the emphasis upon news was foremost.

The manner in which many objects that have commercial value have been modified seems to justify Wells' assertion that,

everything to which men continue to give thought and attention, which they make and remake in the same direction, and with a continuing desire to do as well as they can, grows beautiful inevitably. Things made by mankind under modern conditions are ugly, primarily because our social organization is ugly, because we live in an atmosphere of snatch and uncertainty, and do everything in an underbred strenuous manner. This is the misfortune of machinery, and not its fault.[1]

That the esthetic element is important in securing the acceptance of a trait is recognized increasingly in business. At first advertisements merely named or described goods, but yearly they became more artistic,

---

[1] WELLS, H. G., "A Modern Utopia," pp. 110–111, New York, n.d.

as did the articles to which they called attention. Perfumes, it is said, are sold by the attractiveness of the bottle and label rather than by the quality of the contents. Bathtubs, kitchen ranges, and automobiles have progressed from mere utility to appropriate—and sometimes to ridiculous—artistic design, for beauty, or the pretence of it, is a selling point. That is to say, the acceptance of the trait, among competing similar traits, is partly determined by the esthetic element. Types of public building, stadium, and residence lave likewise changed in keeping with this esthetic demand, which is an important element in survivals.[1]

4. The Growth, Spread, and Assimilation of the Christmas Complex

A new trait seldom travels alone. With it go other phases of the culture. With the watch goes the Babylonian duodecimal system which was in vogue in the land in which timekeeping first developed as an exact science. Maps, likewise, carry the Babylonian duodecimal subdivision of the circle into degrees, minutes, and seconds. The distances which traits travel, and also the degree to which they are elaborated, or are assimilated with others, differ greatly. Culture preparedness paves the way for a trait so that, other things being equal—though, of course, they never are—a trait originating, for example, in a French-speaking country, travels faster among French-speaking peoples than among English-speaking peoples; conversely, a trait originating in English-speaking lands travels more rapidly among English-speaking peoples than elsewhere. The facility with which a trait spreads depends largely upon the degree to which the culture is already in harmony with it and furnishes, therefore, a permeable medium. An illustration of this principle, as well as of the drive and persistence of a trait, is the celebration of Christmas. Possibly the use of the Christmas tree was introduced into Germany by Roman legions. Virgil speaks of such a tree hung with toys; and the tree displayed in the Roman *saturnalia* may be the ancestor of the Christmas tree. But although in the Elizabethan period evergreens were liberally used, especially the mistletoe, which had been a sacred plant among the Celts and the Scandinavians, the use of the Christmas tree is first mentioned in 1605, in a work written by a citizen of Strassburg. The next mention of it is in a book by another Strassburg author, published about the middle of the seventeenth century, in which the use of the tree is disparaged. In the latter half of the eighteenth century, however, the Christmas tree was apparently rather well known in Germany, for there are many references to it, and during the nineteenth century it became

---

[1] See below, pp. 125–140.

common in that country. In many parts of Germany, however, the Christmas tree was not commonly used until about the middle of the last century. The use of it was a Protestant rather than a Catholic trait, and it spread more rapidly among Protestants than among Roman Catholics. The well-to-do towns-people rather than the peasants were the first to adopt it. As late as 1855 it was not used in country districts in Old Bavaria, which is mainly Catholic, and even today it is seldom used in that part of rural Germany. In the closing years of the last century it had attained greater vogue in the Protestant north than in the Catholic south of Germany, and today it is much more prevalent in the north than in the south. In 1830 Queen Caroline introduced the Christmas tree into the Low Countries. In 1840, the Duchess Hélène of Mecklenburg introduced the Christmas tree into the Tuileries, and the Empress Eugénie approved, but for many years the French middle classes refused to adopt it. However, in 1890, a half century later, 35,000 Christmas trees were sold in Paris. The employment of the tree in England is first referred to in 1789, though its use in that country was not general before the eighteen forties. In 1840, the year in which the tree was introduced into Paris by a German, Queen Victoria and her German consort, Prince Albert, put up a family Christmas tree, and the fashion spread rapidly through England. An English woman who was nursery governess to the infant Prince of Naples, heir to the Italian throne, is said to have introduced the Christmas tree into Rome, where many of the upper-class families adopted it. The Christmas tree was first used in Denmark and in Norway about 1830. It was not introduced into Sweden proper until 1863, although the Swedish population along the coast of Finland used it as early as 1800. There is no mention of its use in Bohemia before 1862. Outside of German-speaking countries, however, the use of the tree is not general but is characteristic only of the well-to-do, whereas in North Germany every family, no matter how poor, has a Christmas tree. If a family is too poor to buy a tree one is provided by a benevolent patron or by a charity organization. The Christmas tree has not spread into Latin countries either of the Old World or of the New.

In France and in Spain at Epiphany, which marks the end of the Christmas celebration, crowds of young folk go from place to place to meet the magi. After much merriment they conclude that the magi will not appear until the following year. But the custom has not extended beyond Latin countries.

The development of the Christmas card was facilitated by the popularity of the Christmas tree in England and by the sentiments which Charles Dickens popularized. Immediately before the appearance of the Christmas card, ornamental notepaper and envelopes appeared and cards were decorated in relief, although they bore no verbal expression of the Christmas sentiment. In the forties of the last century engravers' apprentices sent to friends at Christmas-tide specimens of their work. The first Christmas card is credited to Sir Henry Cole, who in 1846 suggested to J. C. Horsley that the latter design a special form of greeting to send to friends at Christmas-tide. This suggestion bore fruit in the form of a card on which was displayed a decorative trellis covered with a grapevine that formed small panels on the right and left, in which were figures representing acts of charity. The card was reproduced in 1881 and many copies were sold. In the United States, Christmas cards were first printed in 1848. Not until 1890, however, when the so-called "calendar houses" came into existence, were Christmas cards printed in large quantities. In many parts of the country printing establishments issued Christmas cards, but the personal Christmas card did not become popular until sales agencies and companies exploited them. The Christmas card sent in 1846 was "an elaborate affair, showing two allegorical designs of clothing the naked and feeding the hungry, together with a family group of three generations, quaffing wine."[1] According to this author Christmas cards were not sold in England before 1858 or 1859, and they were not popular until 1862.

The early types were very simple: a cock-robin, or a sprig of holly or mistletoe, with a conventional greeting. Year by year they grew more artistic, until about 1883 or 1884 they reached their acme of pictorial beauty and seasonable fitness. Nothing since has surpassed a triptych in the style of early Florentine art, which was published about that time. In the center was the Holy Family, with patriarchs and prophets behind, the shepherds and magi-kings adoring in front, singing angels overhead, and in the wings the apostles and other saints, typical of the Holy Catholic Church in all the ages. Since then there has been artistic decline, art becoming more subservient to the demands of trade and the perpetual craving for novelty. The individual greeting cards have tended in the same direction. Year by year the color printers give us cards which, from a merely decorative point of view, are as beautiful as ever, but except for the lettering most of them would be just as well suited to May Day or Michaelmas.[2]

The growth of the custom of sending Christmas cards was conditioned by the development of a postal system and the existence of cheap postage. At the present time its frequency in German- and English-speaking lands is correlated with the frequency of correspondence. The peoples who conduct the largest amount of correspondence send the largest amount of

---

[1] A reproduction of it is given in CRIPPEN, T. G., "Christmas and Christmas Lore," London, 1923.

[2] CRIPPEN, T. G., "Christmas and Christmas Lore," pp. 161–162, London, 1923.

Christmas cards, but the custom has not spread through Latin countries. The sending of Christmas cards by business houses to customers has developed in the present century and largely during the last two decades. This custom has spread beyond the United States into Canada, and its adoption elsewhere may be predicted.[1] The sending of business Christmas cards is, historically, appropriate. In Italy, Germany, Russia, and many parts of the United States it has long been the custom for tradesmen to send patrons complimentary gifts at Christmas-tide. In Italy the token is recognized by the return of a small sum of money. In Maryland, and perhaps in other states, in the country districts, the stores make a present at Christmas to each customer, its value depending upon the amount of patronage. A small present of candy or of firecrackers is given to every child who goes to the store on Christmas day, and few youngsters fail to go. A custom followed by Roman pastry cooks may have suggested the Christmas card, but it is difficult to establish a historical connection. They employed poets to write verses and mottoes to accompany holiday presents of bonbons. The immediate forerunner of the present Christmas card was not very different—a small piece of cardboard to which a flower, a decoration, or an appropriate picture in colors was attached, accompanied by a printed sentiment or appropriate quotation.

The custom of kissing under the mistletoe seems not to have spread beyond English-speaking lands, though there is a roughly analogous New Year's Eve custom in Lower Austria and the Rhaetian Alps. In one form of the English and the Irish custom, the young man who kissed a girl under the mistletoe plucked a berry from the bunch, and when all were gone the privilege terminated. The custom is possibly the vestige of a license permitted at many folk festivals. The Serbian family roasts a young pig on a spit on early Christmas morning. When the pig is placed by the fire the men and boys discharge pistols or rifles. As this is the form of celebration in every household, the neighboring hills reecho to the sound of firearms, "as if persistent skirmishing were going on." In some Italian cities fireworks are set off on Christmas Eve. The booming of cannon at sunset from the Castle of St. Angelo, in Rome, announces the beginning of the Christmas season. So far as we can learn, the only other place in addition to the Southern states, in which firecrackers are used at Christmas is in Münsterthal, among the Swiss

---

[1] The writer has not succeeded in securing adequate information about this recent phase of a Christmas trait. The first Christmas cards designed solely for the use of business firms are said to have been printed in St. Paul, Minnesota, in 1913. Now practically every printer of Christmas cards in the United States carries this "line." In 1855 the London Illustrated News published the first Christmas color plates, and was the first publication to institute a Christmas number.

Protestant Zwinglians. In that valley of the Lower Engadine, a tree decked with candles, festoons, presents, and serpent-squibs is placed in church during the Christmas season. Even during the service, except during prayers, the people explode firecrackers. The source of the custom of using firecrackers in the Southern states of this country, where it has prevailed for many decades, is possibly French or Spanish influence, for the trait is found in Latin America, and it is not English.[1] Nevertheless, in the South the English form of celebration predominates. The yule log, a typical English trait, is a familiar feature, and there is much merriment and wassail. Every boy expects to find a package of firecrackers in his stocking on Christmas morning and there is an almost continuous explosion of them throughout Christmas day. But the yule log, firecrackers, and merrymaking have not played a rôle in the New England Christmas celebration. Indeed the Puritans forbade the holding of festivities on Christmas day and men were bidden to work on that day as on any other. In 1681 the Massachusetts legislature passed a law imposing a fine of five shillings upon, "whoever shall be found observing any such day as Christmas, or the like, either by forebearing labor, feasting, or any other way upon any such account." This law was repealed in 1682. Yet not until the nineteenth century did the churches in this country celebrate Christmas. The candles on the tree light the way for the Christ child. They may be a survival of the neap fires, or New Year's fires, which were kindled at about this time in pagan Europe to restore the light and heat of the mid-winter sun. In Stamboul, Greek Orthodox Christians, probably as a result of Russian influence, use the lighted Christmas tree. In modern civilization electric globes have supplanted candles, though these are appropriately in the form of candles. A recent variant is the illumination of small evergreen trees on the lawns of houses by means of electric globes attached to an extension wire. This custom now prevails in many cities, probably throughout the country. It appears not to have been practiced before 1914,[2] and presumably it has spread through the states from a single origin. The municipal Christmas tree is older, but perhaps it does not antedate the present century. It is common in the United States, but we are not aware that the trait has

---

[1] In Denmark the New Year is ushered in with the noise of firearms of every description, a practice found also in the Southern states of this country, particularly among the negroes; while in Leningrad a cannonade of a hundred shots announces the New Year. The Chinese celebrate the New Year with plentiful use of firecrackers, and there is doubtless a historical connection with similar celebrations in Western civilization. Probably its presence in the Southern states is explainable as an extension to Christmas of this phase of the New Year celebration.

[2] A tree was decorated in this fashion in Minneapolis on Christmas day, 1914.

spread into other countries. The mince pie, which is an accompaniment of the Christmas dinner in English-speaking lands, originally had a religious significance; it was oblong and represented the manger of Bethlehem. The mutton in it commemorated the flocks which the shepherds tended on the first Christmas night. The spices represented the myrrh and frankincense offered by the magi to the Christ-child. During the time of Charles II the plum pudding became a part of the Christmas dinner; it carried a flavor of pagan festivity as well as a savor of religious piety. The use of the plum pudding has spread through all English-speaking lands, but not beyond them. For centuries the singing of Christmas carols out-of-doors has been popular in Germany, France, Belgium, Holland, Russia, and England. Recently the custom has been introduced into various localities in the United States. But Christmas carols have never been a feature of the Christmas celebration in Central or Southern Europe, or in Latin America. In some countries the Christmas carol is a survival, in some it is a revival, in practically all it is a borrowed trait.

The Christmas complex is now invading Turkish Moslem families in Stamboul. Many of those who have accepted the new régime celebrate the day with the hanging of the children's stockings, the giving of presents, and the use of the tree, all for the sake of the children, who have long seen the children of neighboring Christians thus celebrate the day. The rapid intrusion of Western traits doubtless facilitates the adoption of the Christmas complex, and one may anticipate its spread throughout Turkey.

CHAPTER VI

CULTURE CHANGE AND SURVIVALS

1. THE PRIMITIVE PHILOSOPHY OF CULTURE CHANGES

To primitive thought, culture changes are cataclysmic and discontinuous; the mergings are not perceived, and successive stages appear to be abrupt transitions. In civilization, too, a similar view of culture is sometimes taken. Thus nations are said to be at peace for a period of years and then at war; but the threats of war are constantly present and the contest begins long before the outbreak of hostilities. The World War of 1914–1918 was not a fortuitous phenomenon. The absurdities, callousness, waste and destruction of life, power, and wealth, and the war insanity existed in European civilization before 1914; the war merely tore the mask and disclosed forces which had long existed.

Humans resemble red deer in some respects. Any talk of fighting seems to wake up a sort of imp in their breasts, and they bell one to the other, exactly like challenging bucks. This is noticeable even in men who consider themselves superior to privates of the line: it shows the refining influence of civilization and the march of progress.

Most culture changes are gradual rather than abrupt; the phenomenal are linked with preceding phenomena by events not less important if less startling. Although, to the undiscriminating, changes may appear to be abrupt, they are only the crests of waves: "a single ripple in the stream of human life seems at first to be merely an unrelated single ripple, but, if we look more closely we discover that in reality it is borne forward by the one great stream, of which it is the miniature image, one among the many."[1] In 1901 astronomers saw an outburst of a new star, Nova Persei, photographed some months after the flare, when it appeared as an irregular ring growing larger each night. The nebula was so large that it took months for the light to reach its outer parts. The distance of Persei from the earth was estimated at 285 light years; hence the collision which was being witnessed in 1901 had really occurred about 1616. Similarly, many of the events which we witness today are events of decades or centuries ago, the culmination of which we now view. Fre-

---

[1] REICHWEIN, ADOLF, "China and Europe: Intellectual and Artistic Contacts in the Eighteenth Century," p. 146, New York, 1925.

123

quently, therefore, a contemporary event is but the extension of an event which occurred years ago.

2. THE PULSATION OF SOCIAL LIFE

For the savage, the most important crises in individual career are birth, marriage, and death, which are also events of social importance. At the birth of an individual society acquires a new member, at marriage a new tie is introduced into social life, and at death a personality which has played a rôle in the group leaves the realm of the living. These events, therefore, have social importance. In primitive society as in civilization, "there are three times in a man's life when he is talked about,—when he is born, when he is married, and when he dies."[1] The activities of social life recur rhythmically. Festivals and fasts, ceremonies, hunting, and other food quests return with regularity. Rhythm characterizes man's physical and much of his psychological make-up, and it permeates social structure also. Although pulsation in social development, a series of crests of achievements, interpenetrates this rhythm, the power seen in great climaxes is potential in intervals of quiet, and is but summated in crises. There is a continuous though irregular development from ancient to modern times. Egyptian civilization develops in pullulations. Periods of comparative quiescence are followed by periods of heightened activity: in one century the desire for foreign conquest or for foreign goods is dominant; in another reformers demand amelioration of the status of the oppressed; now religion comes to the fore; at another time the ethical element rises to the crest of the culture wave. Other civilizations tell a similar story. The culture development of the Jews moves forward by fits and starts, as is illustrated by the period of the Major Prophets, that of the Maccabees, the struggle under Roman domination, the messianic movements of the seventeenth century, the Zionism of the last and of the present century—the tempo varies. A comparable irregularity pervades the development of Greek culture, which blossoms out suddenly in social and political life, in art, poetry, and philosophy.

Roman culture likewise develops with varying rapidity, putting into successive efforts the strength garnered in waiting intervals, reaching its climax in the Augustan period. In Western Europe there has been a similar pulsation in culture development. Each chapter is an episode of achievement, though the length of the intervals varies. Through the Dark Ages, during which, of course, there was development, come

---

[1] HAWTHORNE, NATHANIEL, "Passages from the American Note-Books," p. 190, Boston, 1883.

fitful flashes of genius, a Charlemagne and the reconstructed social and political life for which he was immediately or ultimately responsible. The socio-religious movements fostered in the monasteries; the speculations about individual (natural) rights; the renaissance of science; these and many other movements are the crests of culture waves which stir social life to its depths; and the undulations embody the continuity and the fluctuations in the drive of culture. During subsequent centuries epochs of great development are interspersed with intervals during which culture seems to be marking time. English culture is continuous from Anglo-Saxon times to the present, yet it does not proceed with equal pace through the decades, nor evenly from century to century, but moves in spurts. The pulsations in political development are most marked in the reigns of John, Edward I, the Stuarts, William III, and the Georges. Social life, especially in the case of the peasants, was deeply influenced by the Hundred-Years' War and the religious movements which accompanied the political stirrings in the times of the Stuarts and those of subsequent rulers. In France the long monotony of subjection to monarchs, broken in the orgy of the Revolution, was followed for a century with recurrent social waves. The pulsation in American development is not less definite though perhaps less extreme.

3. Survivals

Perhaps the first account of contemporary customs as indicative of the earlier historical stages of a culture is the account of the Rechabites, in *Jeremiah*, 35. This sect, which lived in Palestine, refrained from drinking wine, built no houses, but lived in tents, did not sow seed nor plant vineyards. The writer implies that these customs are survivals of conditions which formerly prevailed among the Jews generally. Thucydides adduces survivals as evidence of earlier customs. "Thucydides, notwithstanding the prejudices of his country against the name of *Barbarian*, understood that it was in the customs of barbarous nations he was to study the more ancient manners of Greece."[1] He says,

The custom of wearing weapons once prevailed all over Greece, as their houses had no manner of defence, as traveling was full of hazard, and their whole lives were passed in armour, like Barbarians. A proof of this is the continuance still in some parts of Greece of those manners, which were once with uniformity general to all. The Athenians were the first who discontinued the custom of wearing their swords, and who passed from the dissolute life into more polite and elegant manners . . . Many other arguments might

---

[1] FERGUSON, ADAM, "An Essay on the History of Civil Society," p. 121, Edinburgh, 1767.

with ease be alleged to prove that ancient Greece had forms and modes of living quite similar to those of the present Barbarian world.[1]

Plutarch explains as survivals some of the contemporary customs of the Romans. Thus he suggests that the custom of lifting the bride over the threshold may be "because their first wives were kidnaped and brought in in this manner, not of their own accord." Again, the raising of the cry *Talasio* in wedding ceremonies may be due, he suggests, to the fact that on a former occasion when

a maiden of remarkable beauty was being brought to Talasius by certain poor men of his clients, for safety's sake, to prevent any one approaching or trying to take the girl from them, these cried aloud that she was being fetched as a wife "for Talasius" (*Talasio*). So the rest of the crowd, honoring Talasius, followed with good wishes and cheers. In consequence, as the marriage was a happy one, they fell into the way of calling on the name of Talasius at other men's weddings likewise, as the Greeks call on Hymen.[2]

Tylor pointed out that many traits in our culture now without utility previously served a purpose. Civilization contains many survivals, and the meaning of some of them can be found in the simpler cultures where they still serve a useful function. Thus survivals are fragmentary records of the course of culture evolution. Some of the "adhesions" which characterize social customs he interpreted as survivals, as the persistence of old traits which no longer possess utility. Thus in some patrilocal tribes there is avoidance between the husband and the wife's people, although such avoidance is not causally associated with patrilocal residence. Such avoidance he interprets as the persistence of an earlier type of behavoir after the matrilocal residence which brought it into existence gave place to patrilocal residence.[3]

A survival is a trait of culture which persists after the reasons which called it into existence have disappeared and it no longer serves the original purpose or a comparable one. Thus, on the West Coast of Africa, the slavers in the old days trained the men of the Kru tribe to work on ships. Finding them useful allies the slavers persuaded them to adopt as a distinguishing mark a tattooed band extending from the middle of the forehead to the tip of the nose, so that they would not be enslaved by mistake.

All Kroo boys were tattooed with a broad blue Strype which extends from the top of the forehead to the nose, they all have two top centre teeth filed at

---

[1] THUCYDIDES, "History of the Peloponnesian War," bk. I., transl. by SMITH, WILLIAM, vol. I, pp. 5–6, London, 1812.

[2] ROSE, H. J., "The Roman Questions of Plutarch, a New Translation with Introductory Essays and a Running Commentary," pp. 132–133, Oxford, 1924.

[3] See above, pp. 37–39, and TYLOR, EDWARD B., "Primitive Culture."

an angle so that they could easily be known if they were captured by the slavers who would resort to all kinds of tricks to get them on board their schooners.[1]

After the suppression of the slave trade the mark was useless. But the fashion became established, and to this day, or until recently, every Kru man was thus tattooed. He has forgotten the origin and the reason for the mark, and thinks he gives an explanation when he says: "It be the fashion of the country." Our own culture contains many survivals. The little ribbon in the inner band at the back of a man's hat and the break at this point in the band are survivals of the time when all hats were of the same size and were fitted by drawing up a string and tying it in a bow at the back of the hat. On the left lapel of a man's coat is a buttonhole which now serves no purpose; formerly there was a button opposite it on the right side, so that the coat could be buttoned close to the neck, military style. These and other characteristics in dress persist after the need for them has disappeared. In social and political life likewise survivals are numerous. Our method of electing a President is largely a survival of a plan to select a group of men delegated to choose the chief executive. The existence of survivals presents a problem, for all traits do not survive; some perish with the occasion while others outlast by centuries the circumstances which elicited them. Why do some outlive the day of usefulness, while others do not? Why do survivals survive? A partial explanation is the inertia of social life, which has a tendency to persist as it is and has been; for culture tends to continue in its plane of motion until a new force gives it new trend. But this principle applies to every phase of social life and therefore it does not explain survivals, since their existence implies the non-survival of other traits. A clue to the explanation of survivals is found in the types of things which survive, most of which fall into a few classes. In dress and in conventions survivals are numerous, progressive peoples change little, and the intellectual classes are most conservative. In religion, too, survivals are common. The explanation of these survivals lies in the fact that the objective of convention is preservation of past and existing forms and formulas, and their existence is their main justification. Thus, survivals survive because they meet a real or a supposititious need, because they serve a purpose, albeit not the one for which they were designed. Many survive because of a sentimental attachment to them which is closely akin to veneration for age. Much of the past is revived in order that it may survive, and "from survival to revival is often but a step."[2] Samuel Butler remarked

---

[1] LEWIS, ETHELREDA (editor). "Trader Horn: Being the Life and Works of Alfred Aloysius Horn," p. 26, New York, 1927.

[2] MARETT, ROBERT R., "Psychology and Folk-Lore."

that when a thing is old and useless we throw it away; if it is very old, however, we set a certain store by it, and cherish it as an heirloom; if it is exceedingly old and entirely useless, we dig it up from some refuse heap and carefully preserve it in a museum along with other useless relics of the past.[1] "Only monkeyish beings could revere museums as we do and pile such heterogeneous trifles and quantities in them. Old furniture, egg-shells, watches, bits of stone . . . And next door a 'menagerie' . . . We even collect the bones of the vanquished and show them like trophies."[2] As the horse says in one of Mark Twain's stories, "the bones of my [pliocene] ancestors are held in reverence and worship, even by men. They do not leave them exposed to the weather when they find them, but carry them three thousand miles and enshrine them in their temples of learning, and worship them." Deliberately we make a museum of much of our culture, and preserve forms and ceremonies which have long since lost their original meaning, but which a sentimental attachment allows to persist. One who has lived in England or has resided in an old English university has observed many instances of the operation of this law of survivals.[3]

When the survival pertains to a deep-lying purpose it has great persistence, though it may take various garb. Belief in post-mortem existence of the soul is a case in point. The Tylorian hypothesis that animism is due to the dream philosophy of the savage fails to explain the persistence of animism after this philosophy has been dissipated. Persistent belief in the existence of the soul cannot be explained as a mere survival, for it is repeatedly reinvigorated after the original philosophy on which it was based has been abandoned, and belief in post-mortem existence is not always weakened when the dream philosophy is superseded. The dream is not unmotivated and haphazard, it is not a mere vagary of savage thought, but it is the response to a profounder motive, the reflex of a deeper philosophy which finds expression through this medium. The dream philosophy is an echo of a deep-lying purpose, of a will to live which generates a will to believe. When the will to believe is converted into a will to make believe, this is not the result of vagary, it is the response to the demand for self-preservation. The wish is father to the thought, or, in this instance, to the dream; hence the persistence and the universality of the belief in the survival of the soul. Not only is the will to live common to mankind, but all are susceptible to its illusions, and few recognize their real nature. The assumption of one's future exist-

---

[1] JONES, HENRY F., "The Note-Books of Samuel Butler, Author of 'Erewhon,' " New York, 1913.

[2] DAY, CLARENCE, "This Simian World," pp. 40–41, New York, 1921.

[3] See, for example, WELLS. J.. "The Oxford Degree Ceremony," Oxford, 1906.

ence is easy and it is difficult to imagine an end to it. It is difficult to contemplate unpleasant or undesired eventualities; conversely, building castles is an easy day-dream because one desires castles. To imagine one's self extinguished and all volitions and perceptions at an end is difficult. Hence,

. . . in his actual emotional attitude towards death, whether his own or that of his loved ones, the native [of the Trobriand Islands] is not completely guided by his belief and his mythological ideas. His intense fear of death, his strong desire to postpone it, and his deep sorrow at the departure of beloved relatives belie the optimistic creed and the easy reach of the beyond which is inherent in native customs, ideas, and ritual. After death has occurred, or at a time when death is threatening, there is no mistaking the dim division of shaking faith. In long conversations with several seriously ill natives . . . I felt, half-expressed and roughly formulated, but still unmistakable in them all, the same melancholy sorrow at the transience of life and all its good things, the same dread of the inevitable end, and the same questioning as to whether it could be staved off indefinitely or at least postponed for some little time. But again, the same people would clutch at the hope given them by their beliefs. They would screen, with the vivid texture of their myths, stories, and beliefs about the spirit world, the vast emotional void gaping beyond them.[1]

These attitudes are not peculiar to the Trobriand Islanders; they are as old and as young as human nature. Belief in survival of the soul will persist after its rational basis is discredited, and references to it in language will linger after the belief is a matter of mere historical record. The philosophy grows out of a struggle for personal survival, which persists in these rationalizations. By a like token men who have ceased to view post-mortem regions realistically, will condemn others to eternal punishment, or commend them to eternal happiness. Such is the attitude toward phases of culture which correspond in some degree, if only figuratively, to a purpose which persists. Though many of these phases are useless and their implications false, they survive because of a referential significance. It is so with the trappings of royalty, conventions, patriotic jingles, academic gowns, distinctions and formulas, phrases and pious wishes couched in language which no longer is literal but only figurative, and with linguistic form which is no longer substance but only shadow. Survivals survive because purposes survive, changing vestment but remaining at heart little altered.

> 'Tis the Past
> Contending with the Present: and in turn
> Each has the mastery.

---

[1] MALINOWSKI, BRONISLAW, "Myth in Primitive Psychology," pp. 77–78, New York, 1926.

Everyone knows what is meant by "having a horseshoe," although the time seems near at hand when few horseshoes will be made. The horseshoe has long been an emblem of good luck but the reason for the symbolism is a matter of uncertainty. It may be derived from the sacrificial importance and the sacredness which attached to the horse in Germanic lands; or from the mystic properties attributed to iron when that metal was slowly displacing bronze and became a protection against evil spirits and witches, creatures that detest new-fangled devices; its potency may be derived from the shape, which suggests the crescent of the new moon, a symbol of good portent in the early Mediterranean civilizations. All or any of these elements may have contributed to the belief that it brings good luck. However that may be, when nailed on a barn with the ends turned up it brought good luck, and when nailed with the ends turned down it repelled evil spirits. Its use in the country districts has been more wide-spread than in the cities and there it lingers on after it has disappeared from urban life. One may safely surmise that the expression "a horseshoe" will be used to signify good luck long after the shoe itself has passed out of use. Indeed, even now, this is the case. But as this use of the horseshoe was common only in Northern and Western Europe, where the horse had been sacred, so the phrase has survived only in Anglo-Saxon and Germanic cultures.

"You can catch a bird with your hand, if you first put salt on its tail," is a familiar saying, though its origin is uncertain. It probably arose from a belief in the magical properties of salt. The early Teutons believed that the swift flight of birds was due to certain powerful aerial spirits. Salt is a foe of spirits and robs them of their power. Hence it is easy to catch a bird if salt touches it. A similar belief induces the Malay to throw salt in the fire to counteract the explosions of thunder and drive away the demons who hurl the thunderbolts. Fortuna, the Roman goddess of luck and fortune, is still with us. We speak about the law-abiding nature of the universe but we believe in luck. "He was lucky," we say; "things came his way"; "how fortunate he was!" In some respects we have advanced little beyond Anaxagoras, who declares fortune a cause beyond the grasp of human reason. This philosophy of the Greeks and Romans survives in our culture.[1]

To one who sneezes the German says, *Prosit!* or *Gesundheit!*—"May all go well!" or "Your health!"—the Frenchman says *Votre santé!*—"Your health!"—and the Italian likewise expresses a pious wish that all will go well with the sneezer. These are survivals of the animistic

---

[1] See, for example, STODDARD, LOTHROP, "Luck Your Silent Partner," New York, 1929.

philosophy that a sneeze betokens the departure of the soul, which was identified with the breath, and of the belief that a charm must be pronounced to protect the threatened individual.[1] When one yawns or gapes it is polite to cover the mouth with the hand; this etiquette is a rationalized survival of the superstition that evil spirits would rush into the open mouth, and to prevent their ingress the mouth was covered with the hand.

4. Survivals in Esthetics

In the realm of esthetics survivals abound. There is a glamour about antiquity, and the old and approved carry an appeal which lends itself readily to the *motifs* of artistry. We admire the painting of old masters and the fact that they are the creations of former centuries enhances the value of pictures, statuary, mosaics, and *objets d'arts*. Until recently poetry has been a harking back to days of long ago. Marble fountains and idyllic retreats, sylvan recesses, rusticity rather than modern bathtubs, drinking fountains, plumbing, or department stores were the themes of poets, and innovators found the road a rough one. Other forms of literature tell a similar story. The themes of classical music are taken from the past. Wagner finds Siegfried a more appropriate theme then Bismarck or Moltke. Thaïs is fitter than a contemporary nun or a modern prostitute. It will be a long time, even in America, before jazz tunes supplant the old harmonies in the national anthems, even though the tune of "The Star Spangled Banner" is lifted from an old English drinking song, a bar-room ballad which would, it declares, "entwine the myrtle of Venus with Bacchus' vine," and Gregorian chants will outlive the days which called them into existence and the occasions which they fitted. Modern architecture is largely a revival of past forms, of Greek or Roman buildings, Florentine houses, French *chateaux*, English cottages. Colonial architecture is more in favor now than it was in colonial days, or in the middle of the last century. Its survival is a revival. Flemish styles come into their own long after the practical need for them has passed, and old New England houses are copied at the expense of domestic convenience.

These traits survive because they satisfy a need; they provide a temporary escape from the everyday commonplace environment and make it possible to enjoy the useless. As Mandeville observes, the sentimental appeal of survivals is partly responsible for the opposition to change.

---

[1] See the writer's article, "The Tragedy and the Romance of Sneezing," in *Sci. Monthly*, 1919, pp. 526–538.

Churches, ever since Christians have been able to Build them, resemble the Form of a Cross, with the upper end pointing toward the East; and an Architect, where there is room, and it can be conveniently done, who should neglect it, would be thought to have committed an unpardonable Fault; but it would be foolish to expect this of a Turkish Mosque or a Pagan Temple. Among the many Beneficial Laws that have been made these Hundred Years, it is not easy to name one of greater Utility, and at the same time more exempt from all Inconveniences, than that which has regulated the Dresses of the Dead.[1] Those who were old enough to take notice of things when that Act was made, and are yet alive, must remember the general Clamour that was made against it. At first nothing could be more shocking to Thousands of People than that they were to be Buried in Woollen, and the only thing that made that Law supportable was, that there was room left for People of some Fashion to indulge their Weakness without Extravagancy; considering the other Expences of Funerals where Mourning is given to several, and Rings to a great many. The Benefit that accrues to the Nation from it is so visible that nothing ever could be said in reason to condemn it, which in few Years made the Horror conceived against it lessen every Day. I observed then that Young People who had seen but few in their Coffins did the soonest strike in with the Innovation; but that those who, when the Act was made, had Buried many Friends and Relations remained averse to it the longest, and I remember many that never could be reconciled to it to their dying Day. By this time Burying in Linen being almost forgot, it is the general Opinion that nothing could be more decent than Woollen, and the present Manner of Dressing a Corps: which shews that our Liking or Disliking of things chiefly depends on Mode and Custom, and the Precept and Example of our Betters and such whom one way or other we think to be Superior to us.[2]

Owing to this appeal of the old,

the fashions of the immediately preceding generations are nearly always odious, whether in clothing or house-decoration, in philanthropy or poetry; and this means that our grandfather's day is almost as bad as our father's, since we grow up with the latter's disparagements in our ears. But throw it back one generation further, and impatience and derision give way to sentiment; we find our great-grandmother charming, whether she wear hoops or Empire high-waists, basques or even ballon sleeves—though this last is harder to believe, since these are not great-grandmother's as yet. Her furniture and her ideas are as acceptable as her styles; what was lamentable to her children has become, to her great-grandchildren, quaint. Absolving difference, which she does not live to see![3]

---

[1] Burial in "sheep's wool only" was prescribed during the reign of Charles II.
[2] MANDEVILLE, BERNARD, "The Fable of the Bees," pp. 229–230, Oxford, 1924.
[3] PHELPS, RUTH S., "Italian Silhouettes," p. 67, New York, 1924.

5. SURVIVALS IN CEREMONIALISM

If you are a favorite of royalty and the sovereign wishes to honor you, he may present you with a snuff-box. The taking of snuff passed out of Court circles about the beginning of the nineteenth century; royalty knows this but perceives no inappropriateness in the gift. Guy Fawkes' night, April Fool's day, the French *pêche d'avril*, the Christmas and the New Year's greetings and festivities, May day are continued long after the original motive is in abeyance and even after it has been forgotten. The marriage ceremony is largely a survival of empty forms which to a Roman had meaning—flowers, the bridal veil, the ring, the joining of hands, the wedding feast or marriage supper, the giving of presents, bridesmaids, and giving away the bride. The ring still is given, though the recipient no longer realizes that the custom is based on the magico-religious idea that the unending circle symbolizes eternal constancy and that the ring is efficacious in securing it. The treatment of the dead teems with survivals—the closing of the eyes and weighting of the lids by means of a piece of money laid on them (the old fare to Charon), the dressing of the corpse in fine clothes, the provision of a handsome coffin, the reluctance to substitute cremation for burial, or to permit the useless cemeteries to be made into parks or playgrounds for the living. How many know the taboo which lies back of the saying "One should speak no harm of the dead"?[1] In ceremonialism and esthetics we do not wish to be modern, if that involves renouncing survivals. We have survivals because we like them and we like them because we have them. Even when we do not like them they tend to survive, for it is hard to kill that which is already dead. Hence the persistence of the useless makes it impossible to judge human culture by purely utilitarian standards. When people do not defend a thing on grounds of utility it is futile to complain of its uselessness, it is pointless to call it a survival when they ardently wish it to survive.

In answering his own question, "Why do they [the Romans] make the month of January the beginning of the new year?" Plutarch suggests that Numa may have chosen

the natural New Year . . . It is true tnat, speaking generally, there is no end nor beginning to a circular motion, and the various New Years are fixed by custom only; but the best point at which to begin the year is after the winter solstice, when the sun ceases his forward motion and turns round to return again to us; for thus the starting point is, in a manner of speaking, natural,

---

[1] See the author's "Introduction to Anthropology," chap. XXXIV, New York, 1926.

since it increases the amount of light for us, decreases the amount of darkness, and brings nearer to us the lord and leader of all the flux of matter.[1]

New Year's day is observed as a holiday because it marks the beginning of a new year. It is an occasion for good wishes, as expressed in our "Merry Christmas and Happy New Year," for, owing to the fact that New Year's is virtually the close of the Christmas holidays, there is a tendency to merge the two celebrations. The importance of the New Year is due to the fact that the sun is starting out on a new career and a new year is beginning. What one does on that day one will do throughout the year. Hence the importance of New Year's resolutions and of "turning over a new leaf." The Seneca Indians celebrated the New Year during the early phases of the February moon. Invitations to the celebration were delivered in a formal fashion by two selected "announcers," who dressed in buffalo skins, placed crowns of braided corn leaves on their heads, and wore similar decorations on wrists and ankles. They carried large corn pounders from house to house at sunrise and at sunset and with these knocked a "joy song" at each door, which was then opened in welcome. They then, in song, proclaimed the New Year. The following day they entered each house and with long wooden oar-shaped blades stirred the ashes on the hearth-stone as they chanted an incantation designed to drive away the evil spirits or bad influences of the year that was passed. They then added new fuel to the fire or built a new fire, and besought this first fire of the New Year to come to the family and dwell by the hearth-stone. Among the Maya, if a man who was starting on a journey stumbled over one of the stones which were placed at the beginning of a road, he made an offering of a green branch to the stone, lest the entire enterprise result in misfortune. The conviction that the mistakes or successes which mark the beginning of an enterprise will characterize it throughout is found in many cultures. The belief was entertained by the Romans and was responsible for the sinister import attached to stumbling at the threshold of a house, and it is found among Hindus and Chinese. "The first year is the beginning of the whole of life to everyone," says Plato.[2] In China a sneeze on New Year's Eve is ominous for the coming year. To offset the threatened ill-fortune the sneezer must visit three families of different surname and from each beg a small tortoise-shaped cake, which he eats before midnight. During the last seven days of the old year the house is given a vigorous and thorough cleaning, this being the one occasion on which the dust is removed even from behind large pieces of furniture. In the homes of the more prosperous

[1] ROSE, H. J., *op. cit.*, p. 127.
[2] Plato, *Laws*, VI, 23.

families the walls are repapered and whitewashed and new paper is placed in the windows. On the last seven days of the year there is much bathing, washing, shaving, and general cleaning. Food is then prepared for the first day of the New Year, on which day it is not proper to use knife, scissors, or chopper, presumably lest the spirits of the dead, which are likely to be about then, should suffer injury. On this last day of the old year the people take down all the motto papers pasted by the doors, and put up new ones. Above the middle of divided doors they paste mottoes which express a wish for happiness or riches, such as, "Open the door and see joy." Over shop doors are placed such mottoes as, "Success in all affairs." Similar wishes for luck or success are pasted on the saddles of donkeys and camels, and on cart shafts and wheel-barrows. During the celebration of the New Year, in all homes except those of the poorest people, they eat a sweetmeat made of sticky rice flour, dates, and bean flour, together with sugar. There is also an abundant use of firecrackers. During the first five days of the New Year the women may not enter the house of another or even leave their own homes, but the men go out early on the first day, and on other days of the holiday, to call on friends and acquaintances and convey in person their New Year greetings and felicitations.

In many parts of Europe bonfires are lighted on New Year's Eve to "burn out the old year." In some places a lighted tar barrel is carried about the village and its embers are preserved as a charm against witchcraft. In the highlands of Scotland the outbuildings are fumigated with juniper to protect man and beast from harm during the coming year. In South Germany, Austria, and the Tyrol there is a cleansing ceremony; man and beast are "purified with sacred smoke and the holy sprinkling." In Germany, Lithuania, Greece, and Scotland it is the favorite time for divination. These practices are survivals from pagan days. The Maya began the New Year on July 16, and they celebrated the occasion in a fashion which is reminiscent of ceremonies in the Old World. During the 13 preceding days the priests and men of rank fasted and commoners cleaned their houses and painted all utensils. The temple court was purified with incense and a cord was held about it in the form of a square to exclude all evil. A new fire was built by the assistant priests, fresh incense was offered, and a feast terminated the celebration. Much importance attached to these ceremonies, for the fortune of the coming year depended to a large extent upon their proper performance. Among the Aztec the beginning of the 52-year period, which formed the larger unit in the calendar, comparable with our century, was fraught with danger, for the sun might not rise, and in that case the Tzitziminé demons would descend from heaven, destroy mankind, and bring about the end

of the world. To insure the rising of the sun on this crucial date new fire
was kindled with ceremonial firesticks. All old fires were extinguished and
the priests marched in procession to the top of a mountain, Uixachtlan,
near the present Mexico City, where they arrived just before midnight.
There the new fire was kindled on the breast of a prisoner, who was then
killed as a sacrificial offering. Torches lighted at the new fire were
carried to the chief temples in the respective cities, where an expectant
populace awaited their arrival. From the temples the fires were distributed over the cities amid universal rejoicings which hailed the commence-
ment of a new era and the deliverance of the world from destruction.
Old garments were laid aside, and all household utensils were either
broken or freshly painted in token of the new lease of life which had been
granted mankind. Similarly in the old Roman spring festival of Mars a
prominent feature was the pantomimic expulsion of the Old Year and
the induction of the New Year. Thus the motive underlying our own
celebration has been shared by many peoples. In Babylonia the gods
assembled once a year under the presidency of Marduk in the "chamber
of destinies," where they fixed the destinies of mankind for the coming
year and recorded them on the "tablets of fate." In popular Jewish
tradition God functioned at the beginning of the New Year exactly as
had Marduk, the Babylonian god.

Easter is the only movable feast in our calendar and, since it is a
shifting date, it is seldom a true anniversary of the occasion which it
celebrates. The date is determined by the Old Jewish lunar calendar, and
Easter falls on the first Sunday after the first full moon after March 21.
The twenty-first of March is the vernal equinox and the next full moon
ushers in the Jewish Passover, which formerly coincided with the Christian Easter. The date of the latter was subsequently changed so that the
two would not be celebrated at the same time, though even so, they
sometimes coincide. The celebration of Easter contains many surviving
pagan elements. The vernal equinox marks the beginning of spring and
the return of life to an earth which has long lain dormant under the cold
grip of winter. Where before was barrenness, plants and flowers spring
up, replenish the earth, and bespeak the good tidings of a renewal of
life; the resurrection of vegetable life is typified by the flowers and gar-
lands which are used in the Easter celebration. This custom, however,
is not attributable to the Demeter festivities which prevailed in Greece
and in the Roman Empire during early Christian centuries, for apparently
flowers were not used in Christian churches at Easter until after medieval
times. The name "Easter" is derived from *Eastre*, or *Ostara*, the Anglo-
Saxon goddess of spring to whom the month *Eastur-moneth*, corresponding with our April, was dedicated, and this betokens a pagan element.

The different dates for celebrating Easter in the early Eastern and Western Churches, respectively, reflect different culture influences. The Jewish Christians celebrated the Jewish festivals, though they gave them a new interpretation, and ended the fast when the Jews ended it, *i.e.*, at evening on the fourteenth day of the moon, and on the following day, irrespective of the day of the week, they began the Easter festivities. But the Gentile Christians, who had not been under the spell of Jewish culture, chose the first day of that week as the day of Resurrection, and observed the preceding Friday as the commemoration of the Crucifixion, irrespective of the day of the month. Thus the former chose the time by the day of the month or moon, the latter by the day of the week as well. Accordingly,

. . . the Western Churches kept Easter on the first day of the week, while the Eastern Churches followed the Jewish rule, and kept Easter on the fourteenth day [of the month, or moon]. St. Polycarp, the disciple of St. John the Evangelist, and bishop of Smyrna, visited Rome in 159 to confer with Anicetus, the bishop of that see, on the subject; and urged the tradition, which he had received from the apostle, of observing the fourteenth day . . . A final settlement of the dispute was one among other reasons which led Constantine to summon the Council of Nicea in 325.

The Council unanimously decided that Easter should be celebrated on Sunday, and on the same Sunday throughout the world, "that none should hereafter follow the blindness of the Jews."[1] The custom of appearing in a new dress on Easter day is old and doubtless goes back to the time when this date was considered the beginning of a New Year and one's actions were believed to influence one throughout the year. "Poor Robin," written in the latter part of the seventeenth century, advises,

> At Easter let your clothes be new,
> Or else be sure you will rue it.

Motives associated with the beginning of the New Year on Easter, *i.e.* after the vernal equinox, survive in many practices based on the belief that the light of the sun was then renewed. In many churches the candles were extinguished, were then kindled afresh from flint sparks, and the Easter wax was blessed. Neogorgus says the custom of extinguishing and rekindling fires was common among continental Roman Catholics. In some parts of Roman Catholic Ireland the people of all classes hold a high festival at midnight of Easter Eve, which they call Holy Saturday, then retire until dawn, rise to see the sun appear, and "dance in honor of the Resurrection."

---

[1] "Easter," *EB*, **8**: 829.

In Persia the New Year is celebrated at the Spring equinox, on March 21, and the celebration lasts for 13 days. Rich and poor put on new clothes, and the houses are open to all. "A town which seemed dead yesterday comes to life today. People who looked anxious yesterday, today have faces shining with gladness. The poor man of yesterday, with sordid garments, is well dressed today and the whole national life is infused with joy."[1] The Parsees distribute yellow, sky-blue, or red eggs at their spring festival which celebrates the beginning of the New Year. In the Greek churches of Asia Minor each man and woman on Easter morning gives to the priest an egg dyed red. As early as 1702 this custom was in vogue in Russia and in Siberia, where, as in Asia Minor, people carried a red egg in the hand and exchanged it for an egg carried by a friend whom one chanced to encounter. The exchange was accompanied with the greeting, "The Lord (or Christ) is risen," to which response was made, "It is so, of a truth." The Russian Easter festival, including the exchange of eggs, survives today among Russian gypsies in Chicago, and the use of the dyed egg has spread to the Malay peninsula, where it is employed in wedding ceremonies.[2] In Mesopotamia Christian children secured during the 40-day period following Easter day as many eggs as possible and dyed them red, "in memory of the blood of Christ shed as at that time of his Crucifixion"—a rationalization. Dyed eggs were sold in the market, green and yellow being favorite colors. The use of eggs at Easter seems to have come from Persia into the Greek Christian churches of Mesopotamia, thence to Russia and Siberia through the medium of Orthodox Christianity. From the Greek Church the custom was adopted by either the Roman Catholics or the Protestants and then spread through Europe.

Some local European customs, apparently of great age, indicate that the early Germans and Celts associated the hare with the emphatic change of season which came after the vernal equinox, whence the popular saying, "as mad as a March hare." It was an old custom in Swabia and Hesse to make a nest of moss, place a hare upon it, and then send the children to look for the eggs which the hare had laid. In the mountains of Saxony there is an old saying, "the Easter hare brings the Easter eggs," and in many Saxon provinces the eggs are cooked in cakes which resemble a hare. Brandt records "as ingular custom of Coleshill, in the country of Warwick, that if the young men of the town

---

[1] BAHA, ABDUL, in CHAMBERLAIN, ISABEL F., "Abdul Baha on Divine Philosophy," pp. 74–75, Boston, 1918.

[2] See WINSTEDT, R. O., "Shaman Saiva and Sufi: A Study of the Evolution of Malay Magic," p. 139, London, 1925.

can catch a hare and bring it to the parson of the parish, before 10 o'clock on Easter Monday, the parson is bound to give them a calf's head, a hundred eggs for their breakfast, and a groat in money." The importance of the hare may be attributable to the fact that hares are conspicuous at this time and are very prolific, when spring heralds the renewal of life. Possibly, too, the fact that its young are born with the eyes open may have made the hare symbolical of the phenomena of unfolding life. In regions in which the hare was not present the rabbit was substituted. When the two traits, the use of eggs and the rôle of the hare or rabbit, were brought together, they fused. The hare, or rabbit, laid the eggs. The custom of having the children hunt rabbit eggs on Easter was probably introduced into this country by the South Germans. The trait appeared in the United States at least as early as 1890, but it was not widely spread until early in the present century.

The origin of April Fool's day is a matter of uncertainty, though in our culture as in that of the Hindus it appears to be associated with the vernal equinox. During the Hindu festival of *Huli*, which celebrates the vernal equinox, "the town is thick with people running about and throwing red and yellow paint over each other. Everyone stains his face and clothes a brilliant carmine or ochre."[1] On the last day of the festival, which falls on March 31, the principal amusement is to send people on fruitless errands. In Europe April-fooling appears to have originated in France. France was the first country of Western Europe to adopt the reformed calendar which begins the year on Jan. 1 instead of on April 1. The change was established in 1564 by a decree of Charles IX. Hence the greetings, gifts, and felicitations, which had been given on the latter date, were now in order in January, and "those who disliked the change were fair butts for those wits who amused themselves by sending mock presents and paying calls of pretended ceremony on the first of April." April 1 had long been a general festival in Great Britain, but not until the beginning of the eighteenth century did April-fooling become a common custom. Outside of French and English-speaking countries it has met with little favor in Western civilization, and the "April fish" is restricted to France. The origin of the French custom of the *pêche d'avril* is uncertain, but it indicates that the recipient is a "poor fish"— an old expression in both French and English.

November 1 marks one of the great festivals of the Western Church, All Hallows' or All Saints' day, and on the following day, All Souls' day, there is a solemn commemoration of the departed. This was the Celtic New Year, and Nov. 11 was the Teutonic New Year.

---

[1] Sir Walter Raleigh, in RALEIGH, LADY, "The Letters of Sir Walter Raleigh," vol. I, pp. 55–56, New York, 1926.

The belief that the spirits of the dead returned at this time was adopted by Christianity and these days are now important in the Roman and Anglican Churches, though not in the Protestant Churches of the New World. In the New World, at least in the Protestant portions of the United States, Hallowe'en, the eve of All Hallows' day, is not a hallowed eve, though the name would indicate that it is, but a time for pranks. In the country districts gates are removed from hinges, fences are built across roads, wagons are put in hay lofts, or on the tops of barns, and general pandemonium reigns—or so it was until the automobile arrived. In the cities boys and girls go out and play pranks, upset garbage cans, ring doorbells, turn faucets, and besmear window and automobile panes with soap. The pranks which adults do on Hallowe'en in the country are, in the cities, left to the children. In some cities, however, as notably in Philadelphia and in some Ohio cities, men and women don masques and varicolored clothes and parade the streets and sidewalks.

The performance of these pranks is not an eccentricity which has developed in our culture but is a survival from the days when witches and the spirits of the dead were abroad and turned things topsy-turvy. The belief that they were abroad furnished an incentive to participate in the mischief, and the idea survives in practices which now are continued by children or adults in blissful ignorance of the concepts which underlie their Hallowe'en pranks. They do not know that the sheets and pillow cases used in their disguises clothe a survival of the belief in prowling ghosts, and they are ignorant of the death's-head significance of the jack o'lantern.

In England rowdyism characterizes not Hallowe'en but Guy Fawkes' day, which falls on Nov. 5. By name it is a commemoration of the deliverance from the "gunpowder treason plot." But the celebration cannot be explained by the historic attempt of Guy Fawkes to destroy Parliament. In Oxford and Cambridge it is the occasion for a fight between "gown" and "town." At Ludlow, in Shropshire, the local notoriety who has aroused the enmity of the people is burned in effigy along with the effigy of Guy Fawkes. At Hampstead the Guy Fawkes' fire and the procession are still an annual carnival. The burning of Guy Fawkes in effigy is probably a survival of a folk custom which centered around the spirit of vegetation. The ideas on which the custom was based faded, but the custom remained and was reinterpreted, and people used the effigy to symbolize an individual whom they regarded with aversion; in some places, Judas Iscariot; in the Catholic Tyrol, Luther; and in England, Guy Fawkes.

6. ACCULTURATION

A trait may survive as an isolated trait, but often it merges with others, so that during its survival it undergoes constant change. The celebrations described above illustrate this tendency, and it is even more strikingly exemplified in the observances of Christmas. The Christian calendar is

. . . a record of what is perhaps the most remarkable experiment in the blending of cultures on a large scale known to history; [yet] the phenomena therein exhibited have not yet been thoroughly studied from a scientific point of view. Enemies of Christianity have used the facts as a handy club with which to beat the Church, while the same facts diplomatically stated have been used by apologists as a signal witness of the triumphant and transforming power of the Christian religion. It is time we had a careful study of the facts as a means of throwing light on the mechanisms of culture mixture under conditions where unchallengeable evidence is available.[1]

There is no evidence that before the fourth century a Feast of Nativity celebrated the birth of Christ, except possibly among the Basilidians, an Eastern Christian sect. It was then celebrated on Jan. 6, though Hippolytus, a Christian Father of the third century, regarded March 28 as the day of nativity.

Finally, however, Dec. 25 won general acceptance in Christendom. In the Mithraic cult, which was the strongest rival of Christianity, Dec. 25 was celebrated as the "birthday of the unconquered sun," *dies natalis solis invicti*, or as the birthday of the "new sun," *sol novus*. Moreover, the *saturnalia*, a Roman festival, ended on Dec. 24, and thus the Church gathered into one celebration these two almost concurrent great festivals. "There can be little doubt that the Church was anxious to distract the attention of Christians from the old heathen feast days by celebrating Christian festivals on the same days."[2] When the feast commemorating the nativity of Christ was made coincident with that commemorating the heathen rites which celebrated the return of the sun, the day of creation, which was supposed to be also that of the coming of the Redeemer, was placed at the vernal equinox; but when the coming of the Redeemer was interpreted to mean not the Conception but the Nativity, the date of the latter was moved to Dec. 25, a date chosen for the feast of the "unconquered sun," since then, in the lengthening day, the triumph of light over darkness was manifest. Several early Christian writers, among them Ambrose, Augustine, and Prudentius, refer to the

---

[1] HOOKE, S. H., "New Year's Day: The Story of the Calendar," pp. 43–44, New York, 1928.

[2] LAKE, KIRSOPP, "Christmas," ERE, 3: 607.

advantage of celebrating Christmas on this pagan anniversary. Thus a hymn by Prudentius asks: *Sol jam recurrens deserit? Christusne terris nascitur, Qui lucis auget tramitem?* (Will the recurrent sun disappear? Is not Christ born on earth to increase the way of light?) Cyprian calls Christ *Sol verus* (the true sun), Ambrose, *Sol novus noster* (our new sun), and "such rhetoric was widespread."[1] Thus there was acculturation, the grafting of one religious festival upon another, or, as finally happened, the absorption of one by the other, for the Christmas celebrants adopted traits from the Roman *saturnalia* and from the Mithraic feast of the sun. With the celebration of the Nativity many other culture traits have become associated, such as the adoration of the cradle of Christ, the *praesepe*, which is celebrated in the Roman Catholic Church on Christmas Eve. Usener attributes the *praesepe* to the influence of the cult of Adonis. The cult of the cave in which the infant Adonis was born was adopted into Christianity by the Empress Helena and in 335 the Emperor Constantine richly endowed it. If the adoration of the cradle was not borrowed from heathen rites but is of early Christian origin, as Matthew, 2:11[2] and Luke, 2:7[3] seem to indicate, then it was later combined with the celebrations of the Adonis cult. One of the chief shrines of Tamuz, or Adonis, in Palestine, was at Bethlehem. "Bethlehem, which now belongs to our faith," says St. Jerome, "and is one of the most sacred places in the whole world, lay formerly under the shadow of a grove dedicated to Tammuz, that is to say, Adonis, and the very grotto where the infant Christ uttered his first cries resounded formerly with the lamentations over the lover of Aphrodite."[4]

Owing to persistent pagan influences there are many local variants of the Christmas celebration. Thus a fifteenth-century treatise states that the Bohemian Christmas customs of baking white bread, cutting and distributing apples, and wrapping fruit trees in white cloth were observed in order to insure a lucky year and a good harvest. These pagan practices had been attached to the Christmas celebration. The early Teutons believed that during the 12 days, between Christmas and Epiphany, Wodan's favorite animal, the horse, was endowed with the gift of speech and prophecy. During this holy season horses were wont to

---

[1] "Christmas," EB, **6**: 293.

[2] "And when they were come into the house, they saw the young child with Mary his mother, and fell down, and worshipped him: and when they had opened their treasures, they presented unto him gifts; gold, and frankincense, and myrrh."

[3] "And she brought forth her firstborn son, and wrapped him in swaddling clothes, and laid him in a manger."

[4] Jerome, *Epist. 58, ad Paulinum.* Quoted in Robert Briffault, *The Mothers*, vol. III, p. 97, New York, 1927.

put their heads together and confidentially impart to one another the experiences and trials of the past year. This communion of equine spirits was the sole pleasure vouchsafed these noble animals, and in a measure it atoned for their hard lot. At the present day the peasants do not harness the horses at Christmas-tide, and do not speak of them by name, but use pet epithets and circumlocutions. On Christmas night hostlers sleep in the manger, or under it, and their dreams are prophetic of events during the coming year, for in their slumbers they overhear the conversation of the horses. Thus, the method of celebrating Christmas has been influenced by culture traits already in vogue in the various areas into which Christianity was introduced. From Rome came the influence of the saturnalia, which was celebrated Dec. 17 to 24, and this contributed the "merry" element of Christmas, the celebration of which, like that of the saturnalia, continued for at least seven days. For the Romans the saturnalia was a time of joy and mirth, during which the toga was laid aside, informal dress was worn, distinctions of rank were dropped, slaves dined with their masters, were waited on by them, and enjoyed unlimited freedom of speech. Among all classes there was an exchange of gifts, the most common being wax tapers and clay dolls. The latter were given especially to children. The Christmas celebration adopted the merriment, feasting, games, giving of presents, especially to children, sweetmeats, candles, and bathing before the festival. The influence of the saturnalia persisted in the old English custom of appointing an officer, known as the "Lord of Misrule," to superintend the revels at the court and in the houses of the wealthy. In Scotland a similar official, known as the "Abbot of Unreason," was appointed until, in 1550, and Act of Parliament abolished the office. In 1644, by Act of Parliament the Puritans commanded the observance of Christmas as a fast-day rather than a feast day and forbade merriment or religious services, alleging that the celebration was a heathen festival. The suppression of festivities at Christmas was facilitated by the fact that in 1644 Christmas day fell upon the last Wednesday of the month, which the Lords and Commons had designated a day of Fast and Humiliation. But despite this favorable conjunction for initiating its celebration with solemnity and without festivity it was not possible to suppress the deeply rooted customs of the folk, who protested against the abolition of the festival. Parliament was in session every Christmas day from 1644 to 1656, and in 1644 all shops in London were closed on Christmas day. Those who opened them on Christmas day of 1646 were roundly abused, and during the following year the shopkeepers petitioned Parliament to protect them in the future. All shops were closed on Christmas day of 1647, but evergreen decorations were placed about the city, though the lord mayor and the city marshal set fire to them. In country places, notably at Canterbury, there were riots. With the Restoration the Christmas festivities were revived, though since the Puritan régime they have not been celebrated with the old abandon. A statute of Henry VII forbade card playing by apprentices except during the Christmas holidays, and many who would not indulge in games of chance on any other day of the year made an exception of Christmas. The first lines of a prologue published in a book on Christmas entitled, "Round about our Coal Fire, or Christmas Entertainment,"[1] indicate the pagan spirit which dominated the English celebration of Christmas:

> O You merry, merry souls
> Christmas is a coming,
> We shall have flowing Bowls,
> Dancing, piping, drumming.
>
> Delicate Minced Pies
> To Feast every Virgin,
> Capon and Goose likewise,
> Brawn and a Dish of Sturgeon.

In a few parts of the South of the United States the people at Christmas indulge in the capers and tricks which characterize the celebration of Hallowe'en in the North. Signs on stores are exchanged, gates are removed from hinges, ropes or wires are strung across walks to trip the unwary. This is undoubtedly a transplantation of Hallowe'en celebrations from the North, and the English method of celebration with merriment has made the transfer possible. In Northern Europe, particularly in Scandinavia, other customs became a part of the Christmas complex. At the winter solstice, the return of the sun was celebrated, and then, too, the spirits of the dead returned and were given food. Sacrifices were offered to insure a good crop during the ensuing harvest. In Denmark several of the games, rhymes, and riddles, typical of Yuletide, prognosticate the events of the coming year, such as the weather, the harvest, the matrimonial prospects of girls, fortune, misfortune, and death. These are pagan traits grafted upon Christianity and they flourish as vigorously as ever, though with modifications and ameliorations. Thus, according to a modern Danish Christmas hymn, if the angels are kindly received into the house they will prophesy and insure a good year for the seed slumbering in the fields. The Yule log customs are perhaps survivals of the belief that the spirits of the dead hovered about or visited the abodes of the living—a belief which prevailed in Greece, Rome, Iran, China, and in many primitive cultures. Ancestral spirits

---

[1] London, 1740.

were immanent in the hearth fire, and were propitiated with libations. The souls of the dead returned to their old homes at the New Year, and meat and drink were set out for them. Consequently Christmas is a family festival, a season for gatherings "round the old fireside," and a joyous time for the household.

In accordance with a pagan custom, part of the Christmas log was kept to light the fire on the following Christmas:

> Kindle the Christmas brand, and then
> Till sunne-set let it burne;
> Which quencht, then lay it up agen,
> Till Christmas next return.
> Part must be kept wherewith to teend
> The Christmas log next yeare.
> And where 'tis safely kept, the fiend
> Can do no mischiefe there.

The custom of decorating the Christmas tree with imitation apples, peaches, and pears is the objective survival of a popular belief that on Christmas Eve fruit trees blossomed and bore fruit; and so it is appropriate to serve fruit on Christmas day and to use a bowl of it as a decorative feature. There was a marvelous transformation of nature on the night of Christ's birth: the rivers turned into wine and the trees blossomed in spite of ice and snow. In England the old belief that trees blossomed at Christmas was connected with a legend about St. Joseph of Arimathea. "When the saint settled at Glastonbury he planted his staff in the earth and it put forth leaves; moreover it blossomed every Christmas Eve. Not only the original thorn at Glastonbury but trees of the same species in other parts of England had this characteristic." In 1753 when the new style was substituted for the old, i.e., the Gregorian for the Julian calendar, which made Christmas fall 12 days earlier, "folks were curious to see what the thorns would do."[1] They found that they blossomed on Jan. 5 instead of on Dec. 24, and hence concluded that the old date was the true Christmas.

Christmas gifts were originally New Year's gifts—as they still are in Roman Catholic Europe—and they date from the saturnalia. The Romans called them *strenæ*, and this word survives in the French name *étrennes*, "New Year's gifts," which has been used since at least the thirteenth century. The Greek word, *strenæ*, which appears in the Greek New Testament, is translated "delicacies." Whether or not this is the original meaning of the word, for 2,000 years the appropriate New Year's or Christmas gifts have been delicacies. As early as the seventh

---

[1] MILES, "Christmas in Ritual and Tradition," pp. 268–269, 2d ed., London, 1913.

century a church council denounced the practice of giving these presents, which they designated "diabolical New Year's gifts," and other councils denounced the custom, but, ecclesiastical denunciations notwithstanding, the practice persists to the present day. In the twelfth century the custom is reported in England. The nobility and the courtiers gave presents to the monarch, who returned presents of money or of plate, and the amount later became fixed by custom. The wardrobe accounts of Edward II indicate that he gave sumptuous presents of plate to several knights. The plan of providing presents at Christmas for the children of the poor, who otherwise would receive none, started in Berlin about the beginning of this century, and before 1908 every child in Berlin, it was said, was provided for at Christmas. This custom, initiated by a small group of women, spread through Germany and shortly thereafter through the United States. The custom of hanging up stockings on Christmas Eve was first practiced in Holland, Belgium, or northern France, and comes to us through the New York and New Jersey Dutch. Through them, too, comes "Santa Claus," "Kriss Kringle" being an old form for "Christ-child,"[1] now sometimes applied to Santa Claus. Santa Claus, however, is not of Scandinavian but of Eastern European origin, and is an instructive example of the spread and assimilation as well as survival of a culture trait. The original Santa Claus was a Greek bishop, later Saint Nicholas, the patron saint of children and sailors. The custom of giving presents to children on Saint Nicholas' day, Dec. 6, later was transferred to Christmas, and to it was moved also the rôle of the patron saint of children, Saint Nicholas, or, in the Dutch form, Santa Niklaus (whence Santa Claus). Representations of the reindeer are the result of influence from the North, from Lappland and Sweden. These animals appealed strongly to the imagination of the northern non-reindeer using peoples who had no nobler draught animals than dogs and horses. In the dead of winter no conveyance could compete with the reindeer teams mentioned in the Dutch descriptions of Santa Claus which were brought to New York and which spread from there through all of English North America and from the United States to England. In Latin America this North European celebration of Christmas is not found, for there, because of different linguistic and religious affiliations, Latin European influences are predominant. In most localities south of the Rio Grande there is no Santa Claus and children do not hang up their stockings at Christmas. However, in some Latin countries it is present in modified form. In some parts of Mexico there is a *posada*,[2] or tree, on which hang gifts which a masked

---

[1] In German, *Kris' Kind.*
[2] Literally, an "inn."

impersonator of Santa Claus bestows upon the children, making with each presentation a speech expressing good wishes for the recipient. This is a modification of an earlier practice, the posada, of carrying dolls on a pole, and selling them to children at this time of the year. The use of the Christmas tree is doubtless borrowed from this country. In Italy the rôle of Santa Claus is played by *La Benfano*, an old woman who, on the night before Epiphany, gives the children dolls, trumpets, watches, marbles, or other toys, and candy. The incentive to this practice is the fact that the Wise Men from the East brought to the Christ-child presents of gold, frankincense, and myrrh. Such, at least, is the present rationalization. In Spain, however, the custom of giving presents to children at Christmas is not prevalent. The tale that Santa Claus comes down the chimney may have had its origin in the belief that the Norse goddess Hertha descended by this route to extend her beneficent influence through the smoke arising from a fire of fir kindled in her honor. In parts of Germany, Scandinavia, and Holland on Christmas Eve the children offer up the chimney a petition to Kriss Kringle, beseeching him to fill their stockings on Christmas morning, and they may in addition voice their specific hopes. One of the latest commercializations of the Christmas complex is the formation of the United States Santa Claus Company, recently organized in Chicago, which offers to provide any home with a professional Santa Claus at Christmas, and guarantees that he will remember the names of the children, deliver the appropriate seasonal remarks, and make no mistakes in distributing the gifts. In 1927, it is said, more than a hundred orders were booked for Christmas. The next step, no doubt, will be the use of automata for this function. Though still

> . . . things are done you'd not believe
> At Madingley on Christmas eve.

Thus many elements have entered the Christmas festival, which has been celebrated in different fashion in different lands and in varying fashion, during the centuries, in the same land.

Christmas, indeed, regarded in all its aspects, is a microcosm of European religion. It reflects almost every phase of thought and feeling from crude magic and superstition to the speculative mysticism of Eckhart, from mere delight in physical indulgence to the spirituality and tenderness of St. Francis. Ascetic and bonvivant, mystic and materialist, learned and simple, noble and peasant, have found something in it on which to lay hold. It is a river into which have flowed tributaries from every side, from Oriental religion, from Greek and Roman civilization, from Celtic, Teutonic, Slav, and probably pre-Aryan, society, mingling their waters so that it is often hard to discover the faraway springs. The Reformation broke up the great medieval synthesis of paganism and Christianity, the extremer forms of Protestantism aimed at completely destroying Christmas, and the general tendency of modern civilization, with its scientific spirit, its popular education, its railways, its concentration of the people in great cities, has been to root out traditional beliefs and customs, both Christian and pagan, so that if we would seek for relics of the old things we must go to the regions of Europe that are least industrially and intellectually "advanced." Yet amongst the most sceptical and "enlightened" of moderns there is generally a large residuum of tradition. "Emotionally," it has been said, "we are hundreds of thousands of years old; rationally we are embryoes";[1] and many people who deem themselves "emancipated" are willing for once in the year to plunge into the stream of tradition, merge themselves in inherited social custom, and give way to sentiments and impressions which in their more reflective moments they spurn. Most men are ready at Christmas to put themselves into an emotional rather than a rational attitude, to drink of the springs of wonder, and return in some degree to earlier, less intellectual stages of human development, to become in fact children again . . . Each nation has fashioned its own Christmas. The English have made it a season of solid material comfort, of good fellowship and "charity," with a slight flavor of soothing religion. The modern French, sceptical and pagan, make little of Christmas, and concentrate upon the secular celebration of the *jour de l'an* [New Year's day]. For the Scandinavians Christmas is, above all, a time of sport, recreation, good living, and social gaiety in the midst of a season when little outdoor work can be done and night almost swallows up day. The Germans, sentimental and child-like, have produced a Christmas that is a very paradise for children and at which the old delight to play at being young again around the tree. For the Italians Christmas is centered upon the cult of the bambino, so fitted to their [sense of the] dramatic, their love of display, their strong parental affection. (How much of the sentiment that surrounds the *praesepio* is, though religiously heightened, akin to the delight of a child in its doll!) If the Germans may be called the industrious, sentimental children of Europe, making the most of simple things, the Italians are the lively, passionate, impulsive children, loving gay clothes and finery; and the contrast shows in their keeping of Christmas.[2]

---

[1] CLODD, E., in "Presidential Address to the Folk-Lore Society," 1894, *Flok-Lore*, **6**: 77, 1895.

[2] MILES, *op. cit.*, pp. 358–359.

CHAPTER VII

INDEPENDENT ORIGINS OF SIMILAR CULTURE TRAITS

1. DIFFUSION AND INDEPENDENT ORIGINS

Graebner and his followers attribute all close resemblances between culture traits to diffusion. But this is allotting too much weight to that factor; in addition to borrowing there is invention, and assimilation, as we have seen, involves modification. Probably in all cultures new traits arise, and there are many instances of the independent origins of similar traits. The facility of diffusion is determined by the state of preparedness of the cultures which lie within the areas of contact, and the preparedness which makes borrowing easy also makes independent origins more probable. Yet, while independent origins might account for the presence of a widely distributed trait in a few of the areas in which it is found, it could not explain its presence in all of them, nor explain the continuity in geographical distribution which usually is found when diffusion is known or is inferred as the explanation of the distribution of the trait. The marvel would be that the same trait should arise independently in numerous contiguous areas. Consequently, "the theory of independent origin of almost identical phenomena in contiguous areas can no longer be maintained and has been given up by all serious students."[1] When, however, similar traits are found in distant tribes which apparently have had no contacts, and similar traits do not bridge the intervening cultures, there is sometimes reason to suspect independent origins. Discontinuous distributions, then, may imply independent origins, though the degree of discontinuity which justifies the inference is a matter of uncertainty and varies with circumstances. Some similarities not attributed to diffusion have been explained as independent survivals. Thus, certain customs of our group which resemble those of some primitive tribes, such as elopements, or keeping secret the destination of a wedding trip, are interpreted as survivals from the time when the bride was captured and flight was necessary. Or the similarities may be explained as the result of the attainment of similar stages in culture development. This view presupposes that culture development sometimes proceeds along similar lines; that the

---

[1] BOAS, FRANZ, "Primitive Art," p. 121, Oslo, 1927.

cultures which have similar features have reached, at least in those phases, similar stages; and that the types of culture development are limited. In Australian and North American tribes, for example, there are similar methods of securing food, because the respective cultures are in the hunting and fishing stage. Thus the similarity may be the result of similar motives operating under similar circumscribing conditions; the result of similar culture environment, intentions, opportunities, and limitations. If an Australian desires fish for his noon meal, has a net, and decides to use it to catch fish, and if an Iroquois Indian wants fish for his mid-day meal, has a net, and decides to use it to secure fish, the similar needs plus similar means for satisfying them under similar limitations stimulate similar behavior in the two areas, though, to be sure, it does not follow that the two areas independently invented the net. Nevertheless, similar intentions and similar means for carrying them out account for much of the similarity of behavior. It is to some extent true that, "the same senses, the same organs, the spectacle of the same universe, have everywhere given men the same ideas, as the same needs and the same disposition have everywhere taught them the same arts,"[1] and if "similar" is substituted for "same" there is more truth in the statement. There is, indeed, some basis for Hawthorne's complaint that "men are so much alike in their nature, that they grow intolerable unless varied by their circumstances."[2]

Similarities in phases of social life do not have the same significance when they occur in contiguous areas in which there is a fundamental similarity in the cultures, as when they occur in areas widely separated geographically or in culture context. The independent formulations by Darwin and Wallace, respectively, of the theory of natural selection at a time when biologists were puzzling over the problem of evolution, was the outcome of speculations upon similar problems. The greater the similarity in the details of their findings the more remarkable it is. Yet the similarity in their views is not so remarkable as it would be if the one had been apart from European influences, and the other an educated European with a bent for biological investigation and an acquaintance with European speculations regarding evolution. Again, unless it be a case of direct or of indirect borrowing, the similarity is striking if the phenomena are separated by long periods of time. In the "Origin of Species" Darwin points out that in nearly the same way that two men have sometimes hit independently upon the same invention, so natural selection working for the good of each organism and taking advantage of analogous variations, has sometimes modified, in very nearly the same

---

[1] TURGOT.

[2] HAWTHORNE, NATHANIEL, "The Blithdale Romance," p. 174, Boston, 1880.

manner, two parts in two organic beings which owe but little of their similarity to inheritance from a common ancestor. Yet in spite of this clear assertion that probably not all anatomical similarity is the result of a common inheritance, the theory of convergence in evolution, *i.e.*, the attainment of similar structures by converging paths, usually is regarded as post-Darwinian. In 1874, however, Sir George Mivart suggested that similar structures sometimes appear independently in organisms which are not closely related phylogenetically; in 1878 Flower applied the concept of convergence to physical anthropology, and Sclater, the British zoologist, applied it to general zoology and expressed doubt whether identity of structure necessarily indicated descent from a common ancestor.[1] While divergent evolution held the field in biology, that point of view prevailed in anthropological speculation, but when biologists developed the concept of convergence, anthropologists followed suit. In 1884 Reville cited the institution of the couvade in the Old World and the New, and that of the Vestal Virgins in Rome and in Peru, as examples of what he called parallelisms. He attributed these similarities to the similar working of the human mind upon similar problems.[2] The problem of convergence in culture was treated by the American anthropologist McGee in 1889, and at greater length by Otis T. Mason in 1895. For Mason the problem of similarities in culture resolves into the question of whether the resemblances are due to chance or to the operation of similar causes. Goldenweiser showed that the possibilities of culture development and expression are limited, and that limited possibilities make similarities inevitable. If, for example, a sufficiently large number of dice with limited kinds of surfaces are shaken out of a box, resemblances will appear. This is an inevitable result of the limited number of kinds of surfaces. So with culture. If culture develops and the means of procedure are limited, there will be similarities between some phases of the respective cultures, and the degrees of similarity will depend upon the number and the range of the cultures.

The more similar two peoples are, the greater the probability that new details in their culture may also resemble each other; from seeds of the same kind very similar plants spring up[3] . . .

Human environment everywhere presents some like features, some like suggestions. The sun and moon rise and set in all lands and the stars appear;

---

[1] The views of Flower and Sclater will be found in *Proceedings of the Royal Institute*, vol. 8, 1878.

[2] REVILLE, ALBERT, "The Native Religions of Mexico and Peru," pp. 174–176 New York, 1884. For a similar interpretation of the institutions of the couvade, see KROEBER, ALFRED L., "Anthropology," p. 94, New York, 1923.

[3] WESTERMARCK, EDWARD, "Ritual and Belief in Morocco," vol. I, p. 11, London, 1926.

there is everywhere a change of seasons; everywhere injury and disease come
upon men, and men have cause to fear; everywhere they are nourished and
protected in childhood, and eat the fruits of the earth; everywhere they yearn
in desire, beget, bring forth, and nourish. Thus they receive some enlightenment, and have something of the same rude sense of the facts of life. Hence it is
that like mental processes and parallel conceptions appear everywhere.
Savage ethical notions have a general resemblance, and everywhere men
project their crude self-consciousness into the outer world, and imagine its
occurrences to be as acts of things alive. Everywhere men have worshiped the
sun and moon and their own ancestors, and have buried food and utensils with
the dead, failing to conceive of any complete cessation of bodily need and
function. Very strikingly they have everywhere used, and indeed still use,
perforce, the analogies of physical qualities and relations to help themselves to
turbid spiritual concepts . . . We may infer that, through these early
stages, confused and slowly clarifying thoughts arise from natural suggestions
—the suggestions of the human environment and of common ways of
living[1] . . .

The constituents of human nature are in the race, which in all its branches
evinces a biological unity and similar psychic processes. Human reactions to
the natural environments are analogous, and forecast the stages through
which all tribes appear to pass, insofar as they do pass. Everywhere men have
projected a crude self-consciousness into the world without, imagining the
actions of its storms and stocks and stones to be in some way as their own.
They have like thoughts of injury and disease. Religions, as well as moral codes
have common elements. Sun, moon, and ancestors have everywhere been
worshiped, and food and weapons buried with the dead. And everywhere men
have used and still must use the same physical images to indicate psychic
facts—an upright man, a crooked action.

Throughout the exhaustless tale of endeavor and manifold interrelationship
making the history of mankind, are found like traits and impulses and desires,
but, of course, with infinite differences. Out of the unspeakable welter of
conduct and interests we disentangle types or categories of intellectual and
spiritual effort. They work themselves out in distinguishable forms, which
have been mapped and schematized as science, philosophy, religion, poetry,
and art, and the various phases of the active life. They are all functions of
humanity or states of its psychic processes. They constitute human life in its
self-fulfilment. As factors of an ideal whole they are related to each other;
not as physical parts, like segments of a circle, but as interworking modes of
mental or spiritual and bodily functionings.[2]

That is why "contemporaries who belong to like social or educational
groups are apt to think and feel alike in philosophy and religion. Natur-

---

[1] TAYLOR, HENRY O., "Freedom of the Mind in History," pp. 86–87, London,
1923.

[2] TAYLOR, HENRY O., "Human Values and Verities," pp. 271–272, New York,
1928.

ally enough, having a common background, living under like conditions and usually holding uniform views upon the make-up of the world. Philosophic writings of the present day show mutual affinity, parrallel approaches to the subject, and like conceptions of the task in hand."[1]

2. EXAMPLES OF SIMILARITIES HAVING INDEPENDENT ORIGINS

As Sir James G. Frazer has said, "the sounds which the human voice can produce are strictly limited in number; and, that being so, it is probable, or rather inevitable, that many words should resemble each other in languages which have no organic or historical relation to each other. Of all the clues employed to trace the migrations of peoples, that of etymology, applied to isolated words and not to languages as a whole, is perhaps the weakest and most unsatisfactory."[2] In view of the limited means of vocal utterance, and of the large number of phonetic combinations employed, the similarities between some Hebrew syllables and those of certain American Indian languages is not surprising. With increase in the number of phonetic elements the probability that a given number of historically unrelated cultures will employ similar phonetic elements is proportionately less; but since the range of vocal utterance is limited, the greater the number of languages, the greater the probability of resemblances between some phonetic elements. That certain Arabic phonic elements resemble certain Chinook ones is, therefore, not surprising. The added similarity of a like meaning for like sounds—it does not occur in these cultures—would rule out chance as an explanation of the similarity. One writer has pointed out the similarity between some words in the Tshon language spoken in Patagonia and some in languages spoken in Australia. In many instances the words used in the two areas are strikingly alike in form and in meaning. From this similarity he infers historic contacts between these ethnological areas. But, as Professor Dixon points out, the alleged similarity is really too close to be accepted as the result of diffusion. For if the words had diffused from Australia to Patagonia they would certainly have been somewhat modified in form—not to mention other difficulties in the way of accepting the supposition of historical contacts. Professor Dixon says,

If Tshon had been found to be very remotely but still demonstrably related to the Australian languages; if the terms for similar things in each area could only with great difficulty be shown to have any resemblance, then,

---

[1] *Ibid.*, p. 126.
[2] FRAZER, SIR JAMES G., "The Belief in Immortality and the Worship of the Dead," vol. III, "The Belief among the Micronesians," p. 54, London, 1924.

paradoxically enough, the case would have been much stronger. As it is, it is literally too good to be true.[1]

Moreover, the resemblances are more specious than real, for they occur only when one American language is compared with several Australian dialects, which latter offer a large array of phonetic combinations; and "between any two languages in the world one will find a few cases of similarity depending on the doctrine of chances."[2] The larger the number of dialects chosen for comparison, the greater the probability that resemblances with some Tshon words will be found. The resemblances, therefore, do not prove historical contacts. In material culture, likewise, as Goldenweiser has shown, similarities may be anticipated in paddle blades, pottery, baskets, stone implements. A stone implement is natural, crudely shaped, well chipped, polished, or pecked. The possibilities of form are limited by the nature of the material and by the techniques.

Similar limitations in the respective environments increase the probability of similarities in things dependent upon environment. The means of transportation used in deserts resemble one another more than they resemble those used in lake districts or in mountain regions, the similarity being due to the similar limitations imposed by the respective environments. This principle, however, must be modified to the extent that the technological development of the cultures differs. Again, the wide distribution of contagious and of homeopathic magic is not attributable entirely to diffusion. The specific forms of the law of the association of ideas varies with culture and previous education, but, even so, ideas associated in time or in place or based on resemblance leave similar implications, though their specific garb may be distinctive of the culture. Civilized peoples no less than savages respond to their suggestions. Messianic religions are found in some dissatisfied tribes fretting under outside compulsions, or among the oppressed. Among a satisfied people there is no demand for change, because there is no motive for it. Dissatisfaction fosters an ardent hope for a way out of the difficulty, and the path for the messiah is cleared. People are most credulous when in dire straits, and then they grasp even at straws. In such circumstances credulity, as exhibited in these desperate attempts at self-preservation, rises with the danger.[3] The belief in the survival of the soul is universal.

---

[1] DIXON, ROLAND B., "The Building of Cultures," pp. 239–240, New York, 1928.

[2] *Ibid.*, p. 240.

[3] For examples, see the author's "Messiahs: Christian and Pagan," Boston, 1918. Similarities arise independently within the area in which the messianic concept has been diffused. And so, no doubt, with regard to many other traits which have been diffused.

The explanation of its universality is the will to live, which spills over into animistic theory of varied complexion or into reinterpretation of soul survival in terms of social survival. Similar wills generate similar beliefs. Many similarities in culture, therefore, are not accidental but are incidental to culture or psychology. Burial rites are important because the soul is influenced by the fate of the body. Practically all peoples dispose of the dead in different manner in the case of individuals of different degrees of social importance, for the social personality of the deceased does not die with the body. To it is shown the degree of respect accorded the deceased while he lived. Among many primitive peoples the corpses of women are treated differently from those of men, the corpses of children differently from those of adults. The similarity in discrimination at burial is the reflex of similar social discrimination in the respective cultures.[1] Myth making is universal, and if the similarity in the myths of widely separated tribes implies borrowing, this is because the similarity in details is greater than chance would account for. The similarity between certain Hopi and certain Mpongwe and Thonga tales, for example, is such as to imply borrowing rather than independent origins. The rôle of leopard in the Mpongwe tales parallels that of coyote in the Hopi stories. Even such details as coyote's grasping the tail of rabbit and letting go on being told that he has not rabbit's tail but some other object, have their parallels. The blowing of pepper into frog's eyes by rat (Mpongwe) is similar to the blowing of the flame and hot resin into coyote's eyes by rabbit (Hopi); and leopard lying prostrate feigning death, after sending his wife to proclaim his demise and entice rat within the danger line (Mpongwe), resembles coyote's trick when conspiring with skunk to get prairie dogs and rabbits within his reach (Hopi).[2] Here the resemblances rest in non-essential and irrelevant details, and to that extent imply borrowing, for resemblances in such details indicate borrowing rather than independent origins. The method of finding the position of a ship, by sending out a shore-sighting bird, described in the Gilgamesh epic of Sumeria, is almost identical with that described in the Old Testament account of the deluge, and these together with other details leave no doubt that the two stories have a common historical origin.[3] A similar test is used by Dawson when interpreting the implications of the resemblances between the cultures of North Italy

---

[1] For examples, see the author's "Introduction to Anthropology," chap. XXIV, New York, 1926.

[2] The account of the Hopi is based upon unpublished material obtained by the writer from a native informant. The Mpongwe tales are given by NASSAU, R. H., "Where Animals Talk," Boston, 1912.

[3] See LANGDON, S., "The Babylonian Epic of Creation," London, 1923.

and those of the Caucasus during the early Iron age: "This double series of parallels between North Italy and the Caucasus can only be satisfactorily explained by a movement of trade or migration which brought the two regions into contact, for if it was due to parallel evolution of two kindred peoples, the resemblance in points of detail could hardly be so exact."[1]

Hamilton uses this criterion with regard to types of pottery:

Types of ware and of decorative methods and motives acquire characteristics which are so remote from the obvious that their occurrence in two or more regions is generally accepted as evidence of diffusion. If the regions are not far apart, and if the coincidences are several in number, practical certainty may be reached, but the occurrence of single coincidences, at great distances apart, require to be very striking, and far removed from the probability of chance coincidence, before they can be trusted.[2]

A contemporary biblical scholar uses the criterion of similarity in details when inferring culture contacts between Egypt and Palestine. The evidence is cumulative, and the character of some items makes it clear that the Hebrews were indebted to the Egyptians for certain elements in their sacred literature. "Very striking are the resemblances between the 'Song of Songs' and the Egyptian 'love-poetry,' while some have regarded the [Egyptian] 'Dialogue of the Man-weary-of-life with his Soul' as a counterpart of Job." Here, however, the similarity does not imply borrowing.

There are too many ancient and modern parallels to the "Song of Songs" for the likenesses to prove literary connection. The literature of pessimism is likewise large, and the "Dialogue" and Job are not of the same piece, although a similar tone often appears. Both alleged parallels merely prove the general likeness between Egyptian and Hebrew modes of thinking under similar situations.[3]

Thus, though certain resemblances between passages in Hebrew and Egyptian literature are attributable to "the natural expression of human feelings under similar historical and social situations," and are "based on a similar conception of the world and on like religious presuppositions," all of the resemblances cannot be attributed to similarities in the respective historical and psychological backgrounds.

---

[1] DAWSON, CHRISTOPHER, "The Age of the Gods," p. 369, Boston, 1928.

[2] HARRISON, H. S., "Pots and Pans: The History of Ceramics," p. 81, New York, 1928.

[3] McCOWN, CHESTER C., "Hebrew and Egyptian Apocalyptic Literature," *Harvard Theol. Rev.*, **18**: 363, 1925; see the same writer's "Genesis of the Social Gospel," chap. IV, New York, 1929.

More difficult to explain is the striking resemblance between Ikhnaton's "Hymn to Aton" and Psalm 104. Although ideas analogous to those that appear in these two documents are not uncommon in other religious literatures, wherever man has risen to the conception of one great, benevolent creator and ruler in the heavens, the parallelisms between the two hymns in question, both in ideas and in their sequence, are so great as to suggest borrowing. . . . The probabilities that the Aton hymn and other features of Egyptian religion were directly borrowed by the Hebrews are greatly enhanced by the recent discovery of the translation of an Egyptian book of "admonitions" in one section of the Book of Proverbs. The publication of the "Maxims of Amen-em-ope" (Amen-em-apr), and the conclusive demonstration that it has been copied in part by the author of Proverbs 22: 17–24, are very significant events.[1]

Lang says:

An ancient identity of mental status and the working of similar mental forces at the attempt to explain the same phenomena will account, without any theory of borrowing, or transmission of myth, or of original unity of race, for the world-wide diffusion of many mythical conceptions. But this theory of the original similarity of the savage mind everywhere and in all races will scarcely account for the world-wide distribution of long and intricate mythical *plots*, of consecutive series of adroitly interwoven situations. In presence of these long romances, found among so many widely severed peoples, conjecture is, at present, almost idle. We do not know, in many instances, whether such stories were independently developed, or carried from a common center, or borrowed by one race from another, and so handed on round the world.[2]

Yet "a mythical conception which prevails from Greenland to South Africa, from Delphi to the Solomon Islands, from Brittany to the shores of Lake Superior, must have some foundation in the common elements of human nature."[3] As Turgot says, the stories of all peoples have a resemblance because there is a resemblance between the facts which they seek to explain and between the causes which they assume as a satisfactory explanation. There are differences in details because every search for truth is unique, and because imagination, though to some extent the same everywhere, does not proceed by the same steps everywhere, unless—and we would say, even if—it depends upon the same antecedents. Moreover, mythical beings are confused with historical personages, and from this confusion considerable variation develops. The sex of the gods, which often depends upon the gender of the word used in the language, varies in the mythologies of different peoples. In a

---

[1] *Ibid.*, pp. 366–367; see also p. 382.
[2] LANG, ANDREW, "Myth, Ritual, and Religion."
[3] *Ibid.*

thousand ways the details of myths may make them unique, yet without destroying their fundamental likeness. The intermingling of peoples and the trade between different groups have given birth to new myths by the failure to grasp them exactly, and misunderstood words have greatly increased the number of the myths of the ancients.[1] G. Staniland Wake's observation that what is possible in culture may be expected to occur somewhere on the earth's surface is supported by the element of relative freedom in culture and by the opportunities for varied expression. Moreover, the possible occurrence of a trait is not exhausted when it has appeared somewhere once. When the men of Barca, according to Herodotus, made a treaty with the Persians in the form, "So long as the earth whereon we stand shall abide, so long shall our covenant endure," this did not preclude the Indians of America then or centuries later making treaties under the similar formula, "So long as the sun and moon shall shine," or, "So long as the tides shall flow and the grass grow." In a review of von Hornbostel's study of pan-pipes in Brazil and in Melanesia (Solomon Islands), Sapir declares his conviction that a historical relation between the two areas is demonstrated because the instruments answer the demands of von Hornbostel's three criteria: *exact determination* (the requisite degree of exactness depending upon the nature of the culture trait), *absence of purpose* (*i.e.*, the characteristics do not inhere in the nature of the trait), and *correspondence in variability*. The *exact determination* lies in the rate of vibration, which is the same, approximately, in the instruments of both areas. The absolute pitch, which is not dependent upon the nature of the instruments, answers the test of *absence of purpose*. Since the absolute pitch is the same in the two areas there is *correspondence in variability*. Therefore, concludes Sapir,

. . . if to similarity or identity of scale is added practical identity of pitch of the homologous tones of the scales, it becomes impossible, or, at least, exceedingly difficult, to believe that they are independent in origin. And if parallel scales of practically identical pitches are found associated with musical instruments of nearly identical construction, the certainty of historical connection is indeed beyond reasonable doubt.[2]

Hence, "the pan-pipes of Melanesia and South America *are* historically connected not merely because they are pan-pipes, but because their detailed musical construction is too closely alike to be explained by convergent evolution. Here, at least, we have clear evidence of a cultural

---

[1] TURGOT, "Discours sur l'histoire universelle," in DAIRE, EUGÈNE, "Œuvres de Turgot," Tome II, p. 648, Paris, 1844.

[2] SAPIR, EDWARD, in *Current Anthropological Literature*, **2**: 69, 1913.

contact between these two parts of the world."[1] But the number of pitches in musical scales is not even theoretically infinite, and, in fact, and in practice, pitch is definitely limited. Sapir states that the number of distinguishable pitches is about five hundred, and when these are compressed within the compass of the octave there results about 70 tones, "a number that is several times larger than the number of steps in any scale so far discovered."[2] There are, indeed, limitations in pitch; and given a sufficient number of pan-pipes in various culture areas historically unrelated, it is inevitable that in some there will be the same absolute pitch—as inevitable as that some individuals will draw similar patterns if a sufficient number are given the task of drawing geometrical designs. The correspondences in absolute pitch, therefore, are not beyond the realm of probability, and investigation alone can show the degree of probability that historically unrelated pitches will be practically identical. Moreover, the probability that this instrument or a knowledge of it would travel long distances through presumably long periods of time and yet the absolute pitch be preserved, seeing that absolute pitch is an exceedingly difficult thing to appreciate, is so small that diffusion is almost ruled out. It is scarcely conceivable that appreciation of absolute pitch would be conveyed, for, by hypothesis, this does not result from the type of instrument employed. In this case, then, diffusion seems not as probable as independent origins, though only a more adequate examination of relevant date would strengthen one's conviction in the matter. Jackson finds it "altogether inconceivable that people so far apart as India and Mexico could have independently associated the conchshell with the moon and adopted it as the symbol of their Moon God, in addition to using it as a trumpet"; hence, "one may justly conclude that we have here definite proof of the transmission of an element of culture from the Old to the New World."[3] But it is not inconceivable that this association should have independent origins. Distance does not make independent origins more difficult, but, in aboriginal culture, it does make transmission of the trait from one area to the other more difficult and less probable. The shape of the conchshell may have suggested independently the association with the moon. If association of ideas could give rise to this connection in one area, it could do so in two or in three areas, quite independently of one another. It is a problem of probabilities and it can be solved tentatively when, and only when, an adequate amount of historical data are available.

---

[1] *Ibid.*, p. 72; italics in the original.

[2] *Ibid.*, p. 70.

[3] JACKSON, J. WILFRID, "Shells as Evidence of the Migrations of Early Culture," p. 55, Manchester, 1917.

W. H. R. Rivers exhibits a curious failure to appreciate the fact that from similar cultures similar traits may arise independently. In a paper in which he advances the thesis that similarities are due to diffusion, Rivers says:

> The situation is one which has an especial interest for me in that I have been led quite independently to much the same general position as that of the German school by the results of my own work in Oceania . . . With no knowledge of the work of this school, I was led by my facts to see how much, in the past, I had myself ignored considerations arising from racial mixture and the blending of cultures.[1]

Thus Rivers and Graebner, according to the former's statement, independently came to the conclusion that all striking similarities are due to diffusion; yet Rivers, apparently, did not realize that this confession was a flat denial of the principle it asserted. The inconsistency of his position is carried a point further by those who assert that all culture traits came from Egypt. So unique is the Egyptian mind that it alone invents, so alike are other minds that they accept these Egyptian traits and build them into their cultures. Yet this school denies the similarity of the human mind—except as regards a predisposition toward and attachment to Egyptian traits. Thus, in the "Preface" to the work in which he pours ridicule on "the meaningless phrase 'the similarity of the working of the human mind,'"[2] G. Elliot Smith says, regarding his own thesis: "the cumulative effect of corroboration was deliberately aimed at, by showing that many investigators employing the most varied kinds of data had independently arrived at identical conclusions and often expressed them in similar phrases." But perhaps these "similar phrases" which appear to indicate a rather remarkable "similarity of the working of the human mind," inasmuch as the conlusions were "identical" and were "independently arrived at," were also "meaningless phrases." We may leave the dilemma to Mr. Smith and company, who will doubtless trace it back to Heliopolis of ancient Egypt.

3. The Law of Probability Applied to Similarities in Culture

It seems, then, not impossible to determine the probability that similar traits will arise independently. Probability, therefore, should be the guide in inferring whether the similarities are due to borrowing or are the result of independent origins; for if there are trends in culture development a law of probability is possible. In the absence of history

---

[1] Rivers, W. H. R., "Psychology and Ethnology," p. 125, New York, 1926.
[2] Smith, Grafton Elliot, "The Migrations of Early Culture," pp. 16–17, Manchester, 1929.

the interpretation of similarities must be determined inductively from two supplementary points of view: the extent to which the trait is accidental and dispensable to the culture, or is incidental and inherent; and the number of such similarities in the cultures. With few exceptions, in the absence of history every conclusion with regard to independent origins or borrowing must be tentative. Yet we cannot agree that one must be able to trace historical transmission before one can infer that the ideas of one people are derived from those of another or are influenced by them. The similarity in the traits of two cultures may be such that borrowing must be assumed, though it is assumed only as the greater probability. A story of creation agreeing in every detail with Chap. II of Genesis could not under any circumstances be accepted as independently evolved, wherever it emanated, and whatever the testimony which vouched for its genuineness. In such a case theory would override any and all testimony of independent origins. Yet one may easily falsely attribute to diffusion a similarity really due to independent origins. If there were no history to correct us, we would say that the theory of evolution by natural selection, as formulated by Darwin and by Wallace, respectively, undoubtedly was due to diffusion. We would point to the fact that the two men lived in the same decades, were citizens of the same country, and gave expression to the idea at almost the same moment. In this case history enables us to correct the tendency to attribute the similarity to diffusion, but in the realm of primitive culture it fails us altogether. History demonstrates, however, that the culture conditions which facilitate diffusion facilitate independent origins; for convergent evolution of traits occurs with greatest frequency in those areas in which diffusion of the respective traits is most facile. In many instances, within European civilization similar ideas have been announced, or similar things invented independently at about the same period of history; but with few exceptions these convergences occur only in areas in which there has been diffusion of similar ideas or inventions which paved the way to the respective independent origins.[1]

Who invented the telegraph? Any American who has been through the eighth grade knows that it was Morse and Vail, in 1844. But there was an English commercial line seven years earlier, and the Germans credit the telegraph to Sömmering, of Munich, in 1809, and in Switzerland there was an electric telegraph in 1774, and one was proposed in Scotland, in 1753. The matter becomes rather confusing for the eighth grade. Who invented the friction match? There are so many claimants that we don't know who the devil invented it, and so have named it after Lucifer.[2] Who devised the

---

[1] Many examples are given in OGBURN, WILLIAM F., "Social Change," especially pp. 80–102, New York, 1922.

[2] This, of course, is metaphor and not etymology.

aneroid barometer? In Paris in 1848 two men, Vidi and Bourdon, each claimed it, with apparent sincerity, and different courts decided for each of them. But 152 years earlier the philosopher Leibnitz had suggested such a barometer, describing it exactly. If we should really examine the roll of honors, from Archimedes, called the inventory of the pulley, to Marconi and the much overrated Wright brothers, we should find that almost every claim is disputed, and rightly. The chief reason for this confusion of parentage is that the process of making a great invention is totally different from the common understanding about it. A great invention is not a completed product, issuing at one time from the brain of one inventor. It is a multitudinous collection of little inventions, and is a growth of centuries. Had a single inventor to make the whole, he would need more hands than a monkey, more lives than a cat and more inventive genius than Pallas, Hermes, and Loki combined. Let us illustrate this by the history of the steamship. The first stage of an invention is the beginning of a desire for it. We find the utility of the steamship perceived by Homer, who sang of the marvelous, great, black ships of the Phaeacians, which without sail or oar or crew, sped swiftly to the remotest ends of earth, bringing back merchandise. Next, paddle-wheels descend from Roman days. In the thirteenth century Roger Bacon, from his experiments with gunpowder, glimpsed the internal combustion engine, and the means of fulfilling the Homeric desire. He wrote, "Art can construct instruments of navigation such that the largest vessels, governed by a single man, will traverse rivers and seas more rapidly than if they were filled with oarsmen." A steamboat had probably been suggested by 1651, and built by 1738, and we have patents of 1729 and 1736 with descriptions. But no success was to be expected from such craft, for their engines were wretched. Watt's double-acting expansive steam engine appeared in 1782, and the next year the Marquis de Jouffroy had built a great boat, not fast enough, at Lyons. Before the end of the century steamboats had been built by many inventors, especially by Rumsey on the Potomac and Thames, by Fitch on the Delaware, who realized good speed and long commercial use, and by Evans and Miller, who in 1789 made six knots on the Firth and Clyde Canal. In 1802 on the same water Symington's *Charlotte Dundas* was a perfect success, save that she washed down the canal's banks. Presently John Stevens, of Hoboken, had speedy steam yachts on the Hudson, even with twin screws, tubular boilers and high pressure, excellent save for the damning workmanship in their motive plant. Meanwhile, Fulton, as we know from direct testimony, had been studying the plans of boats, and interviewing the designers of every one of the important previous projects, in France, England and America. So had the other inventors been studying, the steamboat evolving out of joint experience; but none were so assiduous as Fulton. In all about 30 steamboats had been built, all in those three countries, generally in the order given.[1]

---

[1] GILFILLAN, S. C., "Who Invented It?" in *Sci. Monthly*, **25**: 529–530, 1927; reprinted in WALLIS, WILSON D., and WILLEY, MALCOLM M., "Readings in Sociology," chap. II, New York, 1930.

With appropriate modifications, the statement of Stern regarding independent inventions or discoveries in medicine and anatomy are applicable to all phases of all cultures:

It is difficult to predict just when an invention or discovery will occur because all the necessary factors may exist in the cultural environment without the requisite new synthesis being made. Nevertheless, that invention is [probable] in medicine when the essential elements exist in culture, seems to be substantiated by the data derived from the many multiple inventions in the history of medicine.[1]

They grow out of a common culture base, namely, the medical science of Western civilization. But if there were similar culture bases in isolated areas there would be the same reason to anticipate independent similarities, and this holds true of every phase of culture insofar as there are similar culture bases. Thus "it often happens that an epoch-making discovery is in some mysterious way 'in the air,' and affects receptive minds independently of one another."[2] The classification of prehistoric objects on a basis of stone, bronze, and iron, appears to have been independently arrived at by Thomsen, in Copenhagen, about a century ago; by Friedrich Lisch, in Mecklenburg-Schwerin, in 1836; by Eckard a century earlier, in Brunswick, and by Mahudel in 1734. This principle of classification is adopted by Hesiod and Lucretius, but it is not probable that the above-mentioned classifiers obtained it from either of these writers. Hence,

. . . when we find a tool, weapon, ornament, custom, religious rite, or what-not, current in two widely different countries, there is absolutely no necessity to infer that there was a historical connexion between them. True, there are many reputable authorities who are assured in the conviction that such coincidences, as mere coincidences, never happen, but that they are always to be explained as the records of direct relations between the two centers—relations commercial or military, or else an actual migration from the one place to the other . . . The obvious answer to such fantasies is that even in the modern world, where intercommunication is rendered so swift and so easy, two people will often hit independently upon identical inventions or discoveries; as when Adams in England and Leverrier in France almost simultaneously discovered by calculation the unknown planet Neptune, each in ignorance of the work of the other. There is no reason to suppose that the inventor of the common safety pin was inspired by the contemplation of a bronze age fibula, though these are identical with the safety pin in prin-

---

[1] STERN, BERNHARD J., "Social Factors in Medical Progress," p. 108, New York, 1927.

[2] MACALISTER, R. A. S., "A Text-Book of European Archeology," p. 10, Cambridge, 1921.

ciple and even in detail . . . A Lower Paleolithic tool in one continent may, for aught we know, be 10,000 years older than a similar tool from another continent; the one may be the work of a man different in every respect from the maker of the other. The two have arrived at the same result because their needs were the same, their materials were the same, and the means by which they manipulated the materials to obtain their ends were the same.[1]

The minds of men are not machines which invariably grind out similar products if given similar materials, yet minds which are similar, if given similar tools and incentives, frequently arrive independently at similar results.

The problem of similarities in culture is posited by the Buddhist and his answer to it is also ours: "A man throws a perforated yoke into the sea. The winds blow it in different directions. In the same sea there is a blind tortoise, which, after the lapse of a hundred, a thousand, a hundred thousand years, rises to the surface of the water. Will the time ever come when that tortoise will so rise up that its neck shall enter the hole of the yoke?" The Buddhist answer is: "It may; but the time that would be required for the happening of this chance cannot be foretold." It cannot be foretold. The time required varies with the size of the sea, of the yoke, and of the tortoise, not to mention a thousand other factors which enter into the problem. But occasionally the unexpected must be expected. Out of the many cultures developed by men, remarkable and thoroughgoing similarities may be anticipated, even where the course of development has been an autochthonous growth and not a grafting. In every culture there is an element of freedom; yet the possibilities of expression, though almost infinite in detail, are limited in fundamental

---

[1] *Ibid.*, pp. 207–208. Compare Obermeier: "As in the present, so also in times past, the same causes under the same conditions must always produce the same effects." OBERMEIER, HUGO, "Fossil Man in Spain," p. 12, New Haven, 1924. The phraseology used in maintaining this point of view is sometimes so similar as to strengthen the case of similar independent origins, for in some cases it seems to be independently arrived at. Thus in 1917, in an article dealing with this problem, the present writer used almost the identical phraseology later employed by Macalister and Obermeier, though there is no reason to believe that either of them was acquainted with that article; and the present chapter was written before the writer had read the works of Macalister or Obermeier. Again, with all apologies to Professor Dixon for the implications, many of the points made by him in his "Building of Cultures," 1928, were independently arrived at by the present writer, who had not seen the above-mentioned work when these chapters were written. Independently we came to several similar conclusions; and so, I venture to believe, have some scores of others with regard to these problems. If this possibility did not exist there would be no laws of logic, and the agreement among the diffusionists would be sheer imitation rather than intellectual conviction. If it is the latter, our point is established, and they are confuted out of their own mouths; if it is the former, then they have merely suffered a contagion.

make-up. The nose flute is found in Fiji, New Caledonia, Formosa, the Malay Peninsula, Borneo, New Britain, New Guinea, the Philippines, and in some Melanesian islands. A similar nose flute, though made of different material, is used in the Plains area. So far as the writer is aware these are the only areas in which that form of musical instrument is used. It is probable that the nose flute of the Plains area is not derived from the Old World and that the nose flute of Oceania is not derived from the Plains area. But if such similarities occur in human history they must occur in some two areas. Having noted the two areas in which they occur we are disposed to ask, Why these two areas? But it is as reasonable to ask regarding the dice: Why in this throw did these two particular numbers turn up? The answer is: some two numbers must appear and these happen to be the two. History alone could satisfy further curiosity —if, indeed, it did not merely stimulate it anew.

Human inventiveness makes striking correspondences inevitable.[1] Thus the Malays say that the marks on a species of tree growing in the Malay Peninsula are the results of stabbings inflicted in anger by Si Jelotong. The Blackfoot say the marks on the birch tree are the gashes which Old Man, the culture hero, inflicted in a moment of anger. Probably these strikingly similar beliefs have had independent origins. Given in two unrelated areas, such as the northern Plains area of North America and the Malaysian area, a culture hero, a knife, similar markings on the bark of trees, and an interest in origins; and similar interpretations are within the realm of probability. Given a sufficiently large number of such areas and the occurrence of striking similarities approximates certainty. Many of the "explanations" of similarities in culture are, therefore, psychological rather than logical. As Heraclitus says, "If ye expect not the unexpected, ye shall not find truth, seeing that it is hard to discern and not readily accessible." And Sir Walter Raleigh remarks, "it's not the miracles that set one thinking, it's their 'undesigned coincidences.'"[2]

With David Hume,

we may, therefore, conclude, that there is no subject, in which we must proceed with more caution, than in tracing the history of the arts and sciences; lest we assign causes which never existed, and reduce what is merely contingent to stable and universal principles. Those who cultivate the sciences in any state, are always few in number: the passion, which governs them, limited: their taste and judgment delicate and easily perverted: and their application disturbed with the smallest accident. Chance, therefore, or

---

[1] See the author's "Introduction to Anthropology," pp. 466–471, New York, 1926.

[2] See RALEIGH, LADY, (editor), "The Letters of Sir Walter Raleigh," vol. I, p. 196, New York, 1926.

secret and unknown causes, must have a great influence on the rise and progress of all the . . . arts.[1]

We must, in the result of every inquiry, encounter with facts which we cannot explain; and to bear with this mortification would save us frequently a great deal of fruitless trouble.[2]

4. The Independent Origins of Similar Traits in the Old World and the New

American ethnologists have been accused by some of their British cousins of maintaining an ethnological Monroe Doctrine which denies the indebtedness of New World aboriginal culture to the Old World. As a matter of fact, however, the demonstration of Old World origins of New World civilization would be eagerly welcomed in the western hemisphere. The problem is too large to treat adequately here and we must limit ourselves to a statement of conclusions rather than attempt a full exposition of the facts from which the independence of New World development is inferred. Briefly the case is as follows: There is abundant archeological evidence that the New World was occupied several centuries before its discovery by Europeans; the original settlement of the continent could not have been by way of the Polynesian Islands, since there is evidence that they were not settled before about 600 A.D.; the infiltration of population must have been by way of the Far North, from the Siberian steppes; the culture brought by these immigrants could not have been highly developed, for they were, of necessity, hunters and fishers and not agriculturists. There is, moreover, evidence that many culture traits developed in the New World; their development is revealed in archeological strata in many parts of the continent, particularly in Mexico and Central America, which offer indisputable testimony both of long occupancy and of a long continuous culture development. That influences from the Old World would have come with the regularity and order revealed by these New World records is, to say the least, highly improbable. And, finally, with the exception of the Far North, no chain of influences from the Old World to the New is traceable. Moreover, since some traits of Maya civilization are as old as at least 100 A.D., they cannot have come to Central America *via* Polynesia. There is, then, much cumulative evidence pointing to the independence of New World culture. In the Mexican and Central American civilizations many traits display a striking resemblance to traits of the older Mediterranean civilizations. In architectural development there

---

[1] Hume, David, "The Rise and the Progress of the Arts and Sciences," in "Essays, Literary, Moral, and Political," pp. 64–65, London, 1870.

[2] Ferguson, Adam, "An Essay on the History of Civil Society," p. 51, Edinburgh, 1767.

are pyramids of sun-dried bricks, temples, and the corbeled arch, similar to that of Mycenæan civilization. In religious life there are priesthood and an approach to sacerdotalism; rites of baptism; human sacrifice; the eating of the god in sacrificial cakes; worship of the sun, which is associated with the phenomena of life; messianism, the belief in the restoration of the culture by a deity or culture hero who will return to restore the old order. There is astronomy and a calendrical system based on the solar year and on the Venus year; there is the use of a sign for zero, perhaps a full 800 years before such a sign was invented in the Old World. In applied science there are road-building, terraced irrigation, culverts, strut bridges and suspension bridges, the building of houses in stories, and the paving of streets. There is also rebus writing and the beginnings of book making. In addition to these similarities there is great diversification of cultures in the New World, and it is incredible that these respective cultures were transplanted from the Old World. In many of these areas there are traits which are found in some of the primitive cultures of Asia, Africa, or Australia, though these New World traits can scarcely have been borrowed from those various distant regions. Thus, to a certain extent, "the prehistoric peoples of America are destined to prove by their marvelous creations, particularly in the Maya countries, in Mexico and Peru, that human intellects develop on very similar lines always, however far apart geographically—which is not surprising when we reflect that from this Neolithic stage onwards every single human brain is based on the same physical pattern"[1]—and also on the same fundamental psychological pattern.

Hamilton finds it "difficult to believe that the American Indians pursued, almost step by step, and in complete independence, innumerable lines of discovery and invention which led them inevitably to so many of the same ends as those achieved by their Old World rivals. The belief," he says, "involves a form of fatalism which is a negation of scientific curiosity."[2] But the alternative seems a greater strain on credulity; for it involves the assumption that each modification recorded in archeological stratifications was introduced from the Old World *seriatim*, and that in areas geographically intermediate the evidence of transmission utterly disappeared. The alternative which he proposes has its own liberal measure of fatalism—though fatalism would seem to be beside the point. Similarly, between China and Western Europe, there are many parallels in development as well as much transmission of culture traits from the one area to the other.

---

[1] HENDERSON, KEITH, "Prehistoric Man," p. 131, New York, 1927.

[2] HARRISON, H. S., "Pots and Pans: The History of Ceramics," pp. 82–83, New York, 1928.

In China as in Europe the use of finely engraved seals began before the Christian era. In China as in Europe the desire for ornamentation led early to printing on textiles. At both ends of the world the religious impulse, reinforced in the monasteries, led to the beginnings of block printing, and in both cases the play impulse as represented by playing cards had also its part. In both China and Europe, when civilization reached the point where printing on a large scale was needed, printing came, making the diffusion of books and of education general. That it came earlier in China than in Europe, is due to the fact that China recovered more quickly from the Dark Ages and developed earlier a civilization that was ready for the diffusion of books. Finally, both China and Europe evolved elaborate and ingenious schemes for the use of movable type. That block printing finally prevailed in China, while topography prevailed in Europe is due to the difference between Chinese and European script. Given similar conditions, the two ends of the world have done similar things . . . The great outstanding fact . . . is the parallelism in the working of the human mind on the two sides of the world, a parallelism that has been manifest at every stage in the history of printing.[1]

---

[1] CARTER, THOMAS F., "The Invention of Printing in China and Its Spread Westward," pp. 184–185, New York, 1925.

Chapter VIII

CULTURE AND INDIVIDUAL INITIATIVE

1. The Continuity of Culture

In preceding chapters we have spoken of culture as though it were a phenomenon apart from individuals. This, of course, is not true in the sense that it could arise or flourish without them. But it is apart from them in the sense that an account of culture phenomena need not refer to individuals. Linguistic form and change, for example, can be described without including biographical notes, and so can many culture phenomena—such as financial organization, newspaper circulation, political programs. It does not follow that the individual plays no important part in culture phenomena, nor that, since culture development is continuous, individuals are, therefore, not responsible for the culture continuum. It does signify, however, that individuals live in a specific culture which delimits activities and supplies stimuli. Hence,

the latest efforts of human invention are but a continuation of certain devices which were practiced in the earliest ages of the world, and in the rudest state of mankind. What the savage projects, or observes, in the forest, are the steps which led nations, more advanced, from the architecture of the cottage to that of the palace, and conducted the human mind from the perceptions of sense, to the general conclusions of science.[1]

Vitruvius finds the rudiments of architecture in the form of a Scythian cottage. The armourer may find the first productions of his calling in the sling and the bow; and the shipwright of his in the canoe of the savage. Even the historian and the poet may find the original essays of their arts in the tale, and the song, which celebrate the wars, the loves, and the adventures of men in their rudest condition.[2]

The history of inventions illustrates the relation between the time and the invention, and also the fact that similar conditions and similar incentives independently give rise to similar results. So great are the restrictions upon genius that only three inventors, Archimedes, Ericsson, and Edison, are credited with more than one important invention. "Others," it has been said, "may have equaled them in genius, but not

---

[1] Ferguson, Adam, "An Essay on the History of Civil Society," p. 13, Edinburgh, 1767.

[2] *Ibid.*, p. 257.

in luck . . . The common idea that the great inventions have been dependent upon the genius of a single man, so that if the great So-and-So had died of whooping-cough all history would have been different—this idea must now appear erroneous; and it will appear absurd from our further examination into the social process and controls of invention."[1] Indeed "invention, in many ways, is the science and art of continuity of thought."[2] The chances of education or of events, Turgot says, lead to the development of men, or leave them clouded in obscurity, or they perish from want of recognition, like fruit beaten down by the wind. If Corneille had been raised in an obscure village he would have been a ploughman all his life, and if Racine had been born in Canada among the Huron, or in Europe during the eleventh century, he would not have developed his genius as he did. If Columbus and Newton had died at the age of ten, America would not have been discovered for another two centuries, and perhaps we should still be ignorant of the gravitational system which holds the earth to its orbit. Had Virgil perished in infancy we would not have had a Virgil, for there have not been two of them.[3]

Though the persons, who cultivate the sciences with such astounding success, as to attract the admiration of posterity, be always few, in all nations and all ages; it is possible but a share of the same spirit and genius must be antecedently diffused through the people among whom they arise, in order to produce, form, and cultivate, from their earliest infancy, the taste and judgment of those eminent writers. The mass cannot be altogether insipid, from which such refined spirits are extracted. "There is a God within us," says Ovid, "who breathes that divine fire, by which we are animated." Poets in all ages have advanced this claim to inspiration. There is not, however, anything supernatural in the case. Their fire is not kindled from heaven. It only runs along the earth; is caught from one breast to another; and burns brightest, where the materials are best prepared, and most happily disposed. The question, therefore, concerning the rise and progress of the arts and sciences is not altogether a question concerning the taste, genius, and spirit of a few, but concerning those of a whole people; and may, therefore, be accounted for, in some measure, by general causes and principles. I grant that a man, who should inquire, why such a particular poet, as Homer, for instance, existed, at such a place, in such a time, would throw himself headlong into chimaera, and could never treat of such a subject, without a multitude of false subtleties and refinements. He might as well pretend to give a reason, why such particular

---

[1] GILFILLAN, S. C., "Who Invented It?" in *Sci. Monthly*, **25**: 529, 534, 1927; reprinted in WALLIS, WILSON D., and WILLEY, MALCOLM M., "Readings in Sociology," chap. II, New York, 1930.

[2] LOW, A. M., "Wireless Possibilities," p. 9, New York, 1924.

[3] TURGOT, "Discours sur l'histoire universelle," in DAIRE, EUGÈNE, "Œuvres de Turgot," Tome II, pp. 645–646, Paris, 1844.

generals, as Fabius and Scipio, lived in Rome at such a time, and why Fabius came into the world before Scipio. For such incidents as these, no . . . reason can be given . . . But I am persuaded that in many cases good reasons might be given, why such a nation is more polite and learned, at a particular time, than any of its neighbors. At least, this is so curious a subject, that it were a pity to abandon it entirely, before we have found whether it be susceptible of reasoning, and can be reduced to any general principles.[1]

Indeed, "some of the greatest and most original geniuses—Shakespeare, for instance, and Molière—have distinguished themselves by the readiness with which they have made use of other men's inventions."[2] Predecessors pave the way for those who come after them. "Without Haydn we should not have the Mozart we know; without Mozart we should not have the Beethoven we know; and without Beethoven the whole musical history of the nineteenth century would have been utterly different from what it is."[3]

The development of genius, as of everything else, depends as much upon what it is now the fashion to call "environment" as upon its innate capabilities. Had Handel's lot been cast, as it might so easily have been, at some German Court; had he been organist at Hamburg, or capellmeister at Dresden, the greatest work of his life would in all probability never have been accomplished. Operas, concertos, harpsichord suites, church cantatas, and Passion music we should doubtless have had, as indeed we have them now. But "Israel," the "Messiah," "Samson," the immortal series of oratorios, secular and sacred, which gave him his peculiar and undivided glory would, so far as we can judge, never have been produced.[4]

Einstein did not enunciate the principle of relativity out of a clear sky. The way was paved by Newton, who pointed out that no observations made on the earth could demonstrate the absolute and uniform velocity of this planet, but merely its motion with regard to some star, such as the sun, assumed, for the purpose in hand, as stationary. Indeed, in 1901 and 1902 Henri Poincaré stated the relativity theory, in these words: "By means of optical and electromagnetic experiments within a system of motion, it is impossible to discover the movement of translation of the system with reference to the ether"; and,

the state of bodies and their mutual distances at any instant, as well as the velocities with which these distances vary at this same instant, will depend only on the state of those bodies and their mutual distances at the initial

---

[1] HUME, DAVID, "The Rise and the Progress of the Arts and Sciences," in "Essays, Literary, Moral, and Political," pp. 65–66, London, 1870.

[2] BALFOUR, ARTHUR J., "Essays and Addresses," p. 153, 3rd ed., Edinburgh, 1905.

[3] *Ibid.*, p. 122.

[4] *Ibid.*, p. 174.

instant and the velocities with which these distances vary at this initial instant; but they will not depend either upon the absolute initial position of the system, or upon its absolute orientation, or upon the velocities with which this absolute position and orientation varied at the initial instant.

This principle he called "the law of relativity"—*la loi de relativité*. A decade later he wrote: "It is impossible to escape the impression that the principle of relativity is a general law of nature, that one will never be able by an imaginable means to show any but relative values, and I mean by that not only the velocities of bodies with reference to the ether, but the velocities of bodies with regard to one another."[1]

Book making and printing, from the earliest stages to the latest, illustrate culture continuity. Until the second century B.C. writing was done in China, with a bamboo pen upon slips of bamboo or wood, the ink being made of lacquer from tree sap. The hair writing brush, which may have been used in China as early as the third century B.C., transformed the nature of writing materials. Silk fabrics later displaced bamboo and wood, but woven silk was too expensive and raw silk was substituted. Early in the Christian era paper was made from the bark of the mulberry tree, hemp, and various plant fibers, and from a species of grass which was converted into rags and was the beginning of the rag paper which was used for many centuries. The manufacture of paper developed rapidly in China and the material was used extensively for many purposes. To make writing easier and to facilitate the absorption of the ink the paper was treated with a coat of gypsum, later with glue or gelatine made of lichens, and subsequently with a raw dry starch flour. Improved methods of maceration produced a stronger paper, in which the fibers remained intact without causing roughness. The ancestor of the printing press is the seal from which impressions were made. Later, broken pieces of bamboo and jade, the former used somewhat like the torn Chinese laundry check of the present day, displaced seal impressions as evidence of contracts. Subsequently, seal impressions were made in wax, which was inked and then stamped on paper. The block print, first employed in printing, was merely an enlarged seal, the impression of which was stamped on paper. For successful block printing, however, a more suitable ink was needed, and the Chinese developed the lamp black which became the printer's ink. At first, sheets or rolls of silk or of paper were used. Later these were folded, like a modern railroad time-table sheet, as is still done in Buddhist China and India. Later, the sheets were printed on one side, laid in order, stitched at one edge and fastened to a

---

[1] POINCARÉ, HENRI, "The Foundations of Science," New York, 1913; see also TAYLOR, HENRY O., "Freedom of the Mind in History," chap. VI, London, 1923.

board; and thus originated the true paged book, somewhat like the modern one.

The development of playing cards shows a similar continuity. They developed from the Egyptian dice which went from the Roman Empire to China. It is probably not accidental that the transition from dice to cards took place at about the time that manuscript rolls became paged books, for it was then easier to print the surfaces of dice on flat pieces of paper, and from these arose the dominoes and playing cards, or "sheet dice," as the latter were called. The dice surfaces persisted on bone and ivory and became dominoes, while others gave rise to Mah Jongg, which was popular for a while in the United States after the World War. Thus the playing cards which reached Europe in the last quarter of the fourteenth century had developed out of Roman dice and were the forerunners of the block printing which came, probably, during the latter part of the fourteenth century, before movable type was invented there or was introduced from China. When movable type became accessible in Europe the way to book printing was made easy by the awakening intellectual life, the manufacture of a suitable material for printing, namely, paper, and the rise of arts and crafts, especially seal cutting, textile printing, and the use of the block print, which were the technological forerunners of printing. To these preparatory factors was added an external impulse, for

in all these factors the Crusades and renewed contact with the East played an important part. Europe, whose intellectual life had been largely dormant through the Dark Ages, flung herself with abandon against the older civilization of the East. The struggle affected Europe more than it did the East. Influences from Byzantium and from the Islamic world, echoes from ancient Greece preserved in the lands of the East, all surged back into Europe in a great flood. The very fact of travel, the constant meeting of new experiences, awakened all the latent powers of Christendom. It was this new life surging through the Western world that was after all the more important of the various factors in the preparation for printing . . . More important than gunpowder or plague or compass was the advance of paper. At the opening of the century paper was a fairly rare material, imported from Damascus and Spain, and being turned out in small quantities from two or three mills newly established in Italy, France, Spain, and southern Germany, and had largely displaced parchment as the writing material of all but the wealthy. It was paper that made printing worth while.[1]

A suitable material was indispensable to commercially successful printing. Gutenberg's Bible, printed on parchment, is said to have

---

[1] CARTER, THOMAS F., "The Invention of Printing in China and Its Spread Westward," pp. 152–153, New York, 1925.

required the skins of three hundred sheep. Obviously a substitute for sheepskin must be found, or books could not be printed cheaply.

Thus the individual may invent new traits, but usually the invention is merely a modification of existing traits. The way is prepared by previous accomplishments and is limited by the demands of the culture.

2. INDIVIDUAL INITIATIVE

Even in savagery initiative and originality stimulate new purposes and new concepts. Though custom and tradition control the members of each tribal group, initiative and originality occasionally modify these controls and soften their compulsions, even when the penalty for cleverness is to be accused of witchcraft. Yet though certain individuals apparently give new trend to group purposes, some sociologists resolve all individual initiative into group stimulus and describe the behavior of the individual as merely a response to group compulsion. The *Année Sociologique* school, for example, explain all originality in terms of social stimuli, describe the individual as merely an embodiment of social influences, and society as all-inclusive and all-determinative. These "pure" sociologists reject biological interpretations of society, seek within society itself the laws which govern social phenomena, and use the other sciences merely as handmaids to that end. With this position there is no quarrel, provided all the relevant data are included. But they omit some of the forces which invade the social realm. A culture is penetrated by external influences, for it is part of a larger universe; and it may be influenced by an individual, who belongs to society in a twofold capacity, participating in it, subject to its laws, yet to an extent free from its compulsions though responsive to its stimuli. Occasionally an individual exhibits the larger mind, and includes in his aims and purposes the group concepts.

"The prophet and the religious reformer, in whom a new view of life—a new revelation—becomes explicit, is perhaps the greatest of all agents of social change, even though he is himself the product of social causes and the vehicle of an ancient cultural tradition."[1] Certainly many prophets and messiahs give new trend to the religious life of the group and modify the current concepts. To describe these prophets or messiahs as but a link in the chain of social influences which join one group with another is to treat both group and individual as members of a larger group, and to do so is to make the group comparable with the individual and in effect to establish the reality of individual initiative. Often the individual maintains with the larger world relations not maintained by the group, and uniquely influences the group. Conformity with social

---

[1] DAWSON, CHRISTOPHER, "The Age of the Gods," p. xx, Boston, 1928; see KIRKPATRICK, CLIFFORD, "Religion in Human Affairs," chap. VII, New York, 1929.

demand is sometimes the result not of social compulsion but of individual choice. When, for example, he contributes of his best to the maintenance of tribal life and does this with even more zeal and satisfaction then he displays in private pursuits carried on for purely personal ends, the uniquely qualified leader is asserting individuality as well as social personality. In serving the group he satisfies the demands of self; the group may demand but it can compel only in the sense that it can impose alternatives. Social and individual self overlap, but in responding to social influences the individual does not lose individuality. He could not do so if he would, and there are strong-souled individuals who would not if they could. Individuals are controlled by society without being aware of the fact; but also, sometimes the group is led by an individual.[1] Individual initiative may fulfil the purpose of a group as well as that of an individual, but it is none the less the fulfilment of his wish if the environment is favorable. An act may be designed to save both the individual and the group, for the two aims are sometimes coordinated in one act. The individual is not enclosed by the group as a particle of air is included in a football. A better analogy would be the pack of wolves, in which there is concert between the individual members but not a closed system of influences emanating from the pack. Each wolf maintains specific relations with the outside non-wolf world, and to it as an individual may come the influence which it imparts to the pack. Concerted action may be prompted by the alarm of danger or by the signal that game has been scented, and the reaction of the pack may be the result of individual stimulus. Often the individual is ignorant of the social stimuli to which he responds, and conversely, the group unwittingly may fall under the dominant purpose of an individual. When under the spell of a messiah, for example, some groups are misled to their undoing, and are blind to rational considerations. The group obeys only when it chooses, but also the individual is compelled only when he chooses to comply, for he can accept or can reject group program.

One of the most noticeable features in Eskimo society almost everywhere is the absence of chiefs, and the Copper Eskimos are no exception. A man acquires influence by his force of character, his energy and success in hunting, or his skill in magic. As long as these last him age but increases his influence, but when they fail his prestige and authority vanish. Although there were at least half a dozen shamans in Dolphin and Union Strait, and Ikpakhuak himself professed no shamanistic powers, yet his personal dignity, his sagacity, and his prowess as a hunter won him the most prominent place among the natives of this region. He had no delegated powers, no established authority, but his counsels always carried the greatest weight and his advice was con-

---

[1] For examples, see the author's "Messiahs: Christian and Pagan," Boston, 1918.

stantly sought in all matters of importance. On my first visit to the Puivlik settlement in 1914 I carried on a little trading in the crowded dance house, and one of the natives attempted to rob me of a long machete. The rest looked on and watched the outcome. Only Ikpakhuak had the courage to interfere; he seized the man's wrist and forced him to give up the knife. Even Ikpakhuak's influence, however, could not always prevent stealing, or secure the restoration of stolen property, even among his own people . . . The shaman Uloksak, who was credited with wonderful powers of control over the world of spirits, was probably not more than 30 years of age. He was bolder and more unscrupulous than most of the Eskimos, and for a time had considerable authority among the natives around the Coppermine River; but a streak of cowardice in his nature finally brought discredit on him and destroyed much of his influence. Farther east, however, in Bathurst Inlet, there was one man, Ilatsiak, who might with justice have claimed the title of chief. His fame as a shaman had spread far and wide, and he had no rival in that sphere. The most extraordinary powers were ascribed to him—he could discover the past, foretell the future, and, more than any other shaman, control the supply of game and the elementary forces of nature. In all matters relating to everyday life his integrity was beyond question; he had never been known to abuse his influence, or divert it to his own selfish ends at the expense of his fellow countrymen. In stature he was below the mean, and he was well advanced in years—his beard, in fact, was quite white—but he was still vigorous and full of energy, and his movements quick and decided. His pleasant and open countenance wore usually a somewhat grave expression, and his manner was calm and dignified, but there was no trace of arrogance in his demeanor. Natives in his presence would recount the most wonderful tales of his shamanistic feats, and he would listen quietly, without either assenting or denying. His small black eyes were shrewd and sparkling, indicating a personality far in advance of the average Eskimo's. The natives of Bathurst Inlet seemed to obey him without question. Frequently he led them on their migrations.[1]

Of individual initiative in other fields there are abundant illustrations.

Thus the Potawatomi dream dance we know to be the creation of a single individual and the highly original Dakota songs in the grass dance must have been the work of a single composer. We may also infer that the *iruska* was likewise conceived by a single Pawnee shaman, as the origin myth asserts. Hence, this whole series of ceremonies from the ancient *beyoka* to the latest social dance is little more than the successive work of four or five highly original minds.[2]

---

[1] JENNESS, DIAMOND, "The Life of the Copper Eskimos," p. 93, *Rep. Canad. Arctic Exped.* 1913–18, Vol. XII, Ottawa, 1922.

[2] WISSLER, CLARK, "General Discussion of Shamanistic and Dancing Societies," APAMNH, **11**: 873, 1916.

In short, individuals influence all phases of culture, and the reality of their influence is consonant with the continuity of culture development. Thus, for example, in the development of English social and industrial history

there have been many sudden changes and revolutions . . . for although the main current of evolution is generally gradual it is also, at times, accentuated and hastened by sudden rapids and cataracts in its course. History, after all, is occasionally dramatic, and in the acts of the great drama men pass across the stage, who stand out head and shoulders above all their fellow actors in the permanent influence which they exercise upon the development of their time.[1]

3. THE HIERARCHY OF PERSONALITIES

Those societies and individuals are potent whose will has been embodied in thought and action which has changed, or is capable of changing, the culture. Personality is achieved by him who,

> to his native center fast,
> Shall into future fuse the past,
> And the world's flowing fates in his own mold recast.

Yet activities are not of equal value by virtue of being equally effective in achieving their respective aims. As Francis Bacon says,

The dignity of commandment is according to the dignity of the commanded: to have command over beasts, as herdsmen have, is a thing contemptible: to have commandment over children, as schoolmasters have, is a matter of small honor: to have commandment over galley slaves is a disparagement rather than an honour. Neither is the commandment of tyrants much better, over people which have put off the generosity of their minds; and therefore it was ever beholden that honors in free monarchies and commonwealths had a sweetness more than in tyrannies, because the commandment extendeth more over the wills of men, and not only over their deeds and services. And, therefore, when Virgil puteth himself forth to attribute to Augustus Caesar the best of human honours, he doth it in these words:

> *Victorque volentes*
> *Per populos dat jura, viamque affectat Olympo.*[2]

4. CULTURE CONTINUITY AND INDIVIDUAL INITIATIVE IN ART

Culture influences are effective in art as in other activities. Here as elsewhere, "a really original idea is most unusual, and the bold courage

---

[1] GIBBINS, H. DE B., "English Social Reformers," p. 1, London, 1902.

[2] "To a willing people the victor gives laws and plays the rôle of a god." BACON, FRANCIS, "Novum Organon." See further the author's article on "The Problem of Personality," *Internat. Jour. Ethics*, October, 1914.

that will make even a single experiment is rarer still." The artist con-
forms with the proprieties of time and place. The savage does not apply
to personal apparel the designs which he uses on house, canoe, basket, or
blanket, and sex and social status have distinctive appropriate designs.
A feeling of appropriateness may be essential to esthetics, but it imposes
limits upon choice of *motif*. The artist, therefore, is not absolutely but
only relatively free to introduce new elements. The Maori artist, for
example, designs new patterns, but these must conform with the traditional ones. When introducing new designs he must observe the dictates
of propriety and connive with convention. Within these limits he shows
initiative and creative genius, arranging the colors according to his
taste, as a rule avoiding a set formation, though he does not select the
fundamental colors arbitrarily. To do so would be vagary, not art. The
rafters of a Maori house are decorated with a pattern not applied to any
other portion of the house nor to any other object. When the larger
designs have been applied to the rafters, the undecorated spaces are
adorned according to the ingenuity and fancy of the artist. Sometimes he
introduces new patterns, but they must conform with the designs
already used. Culture influence, however, does not preclude unique
reaction to it by the artist. Some Arapaho women dream complex
designs, which usually appear on a cliff or a rock, though sometimes the
dream presents the work as it will appear when finished. Such dreams are
inspired by the feminine culture hero, but they presuppose a receptive
and esthetic mood in the dreamer.

To explain the existence of a design the Plains Indian resorts to
tradition, but in interpreting it he—or she—displays ingenuity. Thus
changes are introduced, if not in the objective character of the design,
at least in its subjective aspect; new emphasis is given the traditional
symbolic meaning, and the old emphasis is weakened, enhanced, or
supplemented; as a result, the Blackfoot artist entertains new standards
of esthetics. Where, as among the Arapaho and the Dakota, the designs
are the result of dreams, even if there is no new objective element, a new
psychological element is introduced, and the new intellectual and
emotional responses become part of the art complex. There is individuality in the Plains Indian's interpretation of designs, and seldom
do two individuals give identical interpretations of the same design.
Among the Arapaho there are at least ten different interpretations of
the rhomboid or diamond-shaped design. Thus the symbolism of a
design varies, though there are culture limitations to the gamut of
interpretation. Likewise the interests of individuals in a given design
differ widely. Some think primarily of the meaning, others mainly of the
appearance. "The former will probably give a coherent interpretation of

his designs if he is questioned; the symbols of the latter will have their most common conventional meaning, without much reference to each other. Young people especially are likely to think and care little about designs that they make or see."[1] Arapaho artists have individual interpretations of their respective designs. "The maker of the design has planned it with more than the usual amount of attention to its meaning, or has subsequently studied it with interest."[2] Similarly among the Cheyenne "often a woman makes a bead or quillwork design merely because she thinks it pretty, to satisfy her own idea of beauty. If asked what the design means, she may try to explain it, if she feels an explanation is expected, or she may say that she did it merely because it pleased her fancy." Though "most women still follow the old designs in their beadwork, . . . they are not held by the old traditions, and are introducing changes according to their fancy."[3] Yet notwithstanding the variety of individual interpretations there are conventional symbolisms and the interpretations fall within definite culture limits, for there are tribal limits to the significance of designs. This is inevitable, and it is inevitable also that the significance of designs should be limited by the experience of the individual, which is a partial reflection of culture stimuli, but likewise a unique reaction to them. Thus the symbol has a wide range of meanings, and these have their counterpart in a manifold of varied individual interpretations. The limits of the technique do not, however, express the limits of esthetic and intellectual experience, which are fully revealed only in the contrasting appreciations of various individuals. Whether this vacillation of interpretation is directly responsible for a modification of the character of the design can only be conjectured; there is, however, a conscious and deliberate modification of designs which is not attributable to the inaccuracies of copying. "Almost every piece of work is different from all others. There seems to be no attempt at accurate imitation, no absolute copying. An Arapaho woman may make a moccasin resembling one that she has seen and liked, but it is very seldom that she tries actually to duplicate it."[4] Usually innovations do not include ceremonial objects or those decorated with a more or less conventional tribal design, such as tents, robes, bedding, and cradles. At times there is variation in the decoration of

---

[1] KROEBER, ALFRED L., "The Arapaho," in Bulletin American Museum of Natural History, vol. 18, 1902.

[2] *Ibid.*

[3] GRINNELL, GEORGE B., "The Cheyenne Indians," vol. I, p. 168, New Haven, 1923.

[4] KROEBER, *op. cit.*

even these objects, though distinctively tribal designs differ from those used in personal ornamentation. Perhaps, however, here, as in civilization,

> No true painter ever set on canvas
> All the glorious visions he conceived.

The Apache, likewise, introduce into designs new objective as well as new psychological elements. "Even in the spirit dance, which is possibly the most solemn function in which the Apache medicine-man can engage, the head dress and kilts adhered closely enough to one pattern, but the symbolism employed by each medicine man was entirely different from that adopted by his neighbor."[1]

Of the reality of the social compulsion even when the artist is creative there is an instructive example in the drawings of one Nkwatwa, a native of Dahomey. According to Nkwatwa, the Dahomey artist when tracing geometrical designs allows the hand to wander, and does not guide it to conform with an image of a design. Indeed, however much a man may be pleased with a design, he does not attempt to copy it; that would spoil it, for the ideal in drawing is to follow momentary promptings. In corroboration of this statement, Nkwata, after drawing a design, insisted that the lines which he had drawn to fill in one of the open spaces were not as well executed as previous ones, because the latter were attempts to copy, while the former were spontaneous and unpremeditated. Yet in spite of the freedom which the artist believed himself to possess, certain tendencies governed him: "I cannot make a long regular curve—it does not feel right. I have to make a little twist in it and then I can go on. My mind makes me do it that way." There was also the feeling that spaces should be filled in with lines or designs conforming in direction and outline to the larger designs already executed. "It does not look well to have large spaces with nothing in them." The feeling for proportion subordinated individual taste to the demands of the entire design. Whether insistence on spontaneity and freedom from copying should be considered a form of social compulsion limiting individual choice we leave to a more subtle philosophy of esthetics. The artist seems unaware of the limitations which an observer of him and his work can identify, is happy in the delusion of unrestricted freedom, and believes he is making a spontaneous and undetermined creation, free from social or traditional constraints. The illusion of a spontaneous creation of new designs is complete. *Felix* (or *infelix?*) *qui potuit rerum cognoscere causas*—"Happy (or unhappy?) he who can discern the causes of things." It is commonly assumed that social

---

[1] BOURKE, JAMES G., "The Medicine-men of the Apache," *9th Ann. Rep. Bureau of Ethnol.*, p. 453, Washington, 1892.

compulsion and individual initiative, when applied to the same situation, are mutually exclusive; but both may occupy the same territory at the same moment—as a wave is the product of both horizontal and vertical forces. Conformity to the proprieties of social usage exemplifies both uniqueness and adherence to convention and illustrates both individual freedom and culture influence. They are coexistent and supplementary; the range of choice is determined by the culture medium, the specific expression is the result of individual choice and initiative. Hence, the statement, "that which, according to the history of art, impels the artist to activity, is the lively joy in the forms which life exhibits to him," is but a half-truth. The Hindu artist, for example, gives to all his work, that which he copies from other civilizations as well as that which emanates from his own, a characteristic portrayal, a touch and tone which mark it as Hindu, and these limitations have their counterpart in every civilization. The product may be new, as, for example, Cubist art, if it is not a harking back to Magdalenian times, but the artist is the connecting link which joins this new product with the prevailing forms of his age and clime, and he may give it unique expression. The intermediate steps appear in the final result. Says Sir Francis Galton,

I was staying in a country house with a very pleasant party of young and old, including persons whose education and versatility were certainly not below the social average. One evening we played at a round game, which consisted in each of us drawing as absurd a scrawl as he or she could, representing some historical event; the pictures were then shuffled and passed successively from hand to hand, everyone writing down independently their interpretation of the picture, as to what the historical event was that the artist intended to depict by the scrawl. I was astonished at the sameness of our ideas. Cases like Canute and the Waves, the Babes in the Tower, and the like, were drawn by two and even three persons at the same time, quite independently of one another, showing how narrowly we are bound by the fetters of our early education.[1]

Thus individuals unwittingly respond to the culture medium. The fact is, then, not that "art must imitate Nature,"[2] but that art must reflect the culture. The individual may not willingly submit to the decrees of fashion or to the current formulations of art and religion; but society, the court of last resort, decides whether he shall be considered right. He, however, decides whether he will accept the verdict, and he may appeal to a future society; for, as Baxter says, "Man is a free Agent

[1] GALTON, SIR FRANCIS, "Inquiries into the Human Faculty," 2d ed., Everyman's Library, London, n. d.

[2] BAXTER, RICHARD, "A Holy Commonwealth or Political Aphorisms Opening the True Principles of Government, p. 96, London, 1659.

and his Will cannot properly be compelled: If you threaten him with death, he may suffer it."[1]

The evidence, therefore, does not support Teggart's statement that "in the earlier period (that is, in primitive society), individuality did not exist. So completely was the individual subordinated to the community that art was just the repetition of tribal designs, literature the repetition of tribal songs, and religion the repetition of tribal rites."[2] Primitive man is, of course, limited by his culture pattern: but within it he frequently reacts in unique manner.[3] In civilization, too,

if the artist can carry society with him by force of the power or beauty of his creations and the force of his protestations, then he wins out; but it is, after all, only with the consent of the social group. On the other hand, however imposing and fine a man's imaginations may be to him, or to the few, still without the *visé*, the confirmation and acceptance of the social group, they disappear with the man who created them.

In art as elsewhere usually it is easier to fit the man to the age than the age to the man. The artist must heed Nietzsche's warning that to follow too closely upon the heels of truth is to be kicked in the face. Therefore,—to change the figure—let one not seek to enter the temple without undergoing the appropriate initiation. The worth of the artist must be determined, and who if not society will determine it—if not his own society, then some other group or individual? The artist's departure from the established forms may be a closer approximation to esthetics than has been attained by the group. But "no one has more need of the presence and approbation of men. He speaks because he feels their presence around him, and lives in the hope—sometimes despaired of but never relinquished—that they will come at last to understand him."[4]

5. Art as a Reflection of the Concepts of the Age and Culture

Art is a reflection of culture. Before Italian art could come into its own, it had to shake off the influences from the East which had been dominant and encompassing. In this movement the preaching of Savonarola was an important factor. He encouraged Michelangelo and other artists to renounce art for art's sake and mold art in terms of religion.

---

[1] BAXTER, RICHARD, *op. cit.*, p. 181.

[2] TEGGART, "The Processes of History," p. 86, New Haven, 1918.

[3] For examples in art, etiquette, and religion, see MEAD, MARGARET, "The Rôle of the Individual in Samoan Culture," JAI, **58**: 481–495, 1928.

[4] FAURE, ÉLIE, "History of Art," vol. I.

The introduction of printing spread learning and "made it possible for art to drop a large measure of its illustrative and narrative function and devote itself to the expression of transcendent ideas."[1] It is not surprising, then, that on every side the art reminded the individual of his religious privileges and obligations.

Fresco paintings on the walls, stained glass in every window, showed him the familiar incidents of the Old and New Testaments and, painted over the chancel arch or glowing in the West window, the awful spectacle of the Last Judgment and Hell, the literal flames and devils that were waiting for him unless by the grace of God and the good offices of Mother Church he contrived to escape into the fair fields of Paradise by way, probably, of Purgatory. Our Lord, our Lady and the saints appeared before him in lifelike images, and in one or two instances, as that of the Rood of Boxley, the illusion was strengthened by a mechanism that imparted lifelike movement to the figures. How literally these things were taken is instanced by a charming carol, in which the shepherd boy, who has just presented the little Jesus with his pipe, his tarbox, and his hat, concludes his farewell to the Holy Family with, "Farewell Joseph with thy round hat:" probably a reminiscence of Joseph's halo on a stained glass window.[2]

Religiosity as well as *chiaroscuro* characterizes a Tintoretto and a Titian; the spirit of Saint Francis of Assisi breathes in the art of Perugia and Assisi, and the piety of St. Catherine of Siena pervades the art preserved in the city in which she labored and wrought. The religious concepts of a people influence its artists, who sometimes, without intending to do so, lend their genius to a portrayal of them. Only an age in which the direst punishments were inflicted in the name of religion could inspire such paintings of punishment in hell as were produced by the Dutch painters who are represented in the Berlin and Antwerp galleries. With the passing of realism in religion, realistic portrayal of religious themes fades, and when religion becomes more symbolic, so likewise does the painting of religious themes. When the secular world invades the religious, or develops apart from it in independence, a secular art arises; hence the reaction of the present century against puritanism and Victorianism is reflected in the prevalent art. A similar statement, with appropriate modifications, applies to all cultures. If totemism is an important phase of social life, the tribe expresses its totemic concepts in art.

---

[1] STRONG, MRS. ARTHUR, "Italian Art of the Sixteenth and Seventeenth Centuries," in MARVIN, F. S., and CHILTON-BROCK, A. F., "Art and Civilization," p. 186, "Unity Series," vol. VIII, London, 1928.

[2] WINGFIELD-STRATFORD, ESMÉ, "The History of British Civilization," vol. I, pp. 350–351, London, 1928.

Thus totemism inspires the natives of Central Australia and the Indians of the Northwest Coast of North America to their finest art work. Similarly, the ceremonies which dominate the cultures in the Southwest are one of the main inspirations to its artists. The extent to which art supplements social and religious life suggests that, in the main, it is ancillary. If this is so, the artist seems to be servant and society master. The geographical distribution of types of art is further evidence that art is not haphazard but is a phase of culture. The art of a tribe is not unrelated to that of contiguous tribes, but usually resembles it more than it resembles the art of distant tribes. In a large culture area, such as the Plains area of North America, there is a prevalent type of art which is found in no other culture area. In every culture the art, taken in its entirety, is unique. One type of art prevails in Melanesia, another in Central Australia, another in Polynesia; yet in these culture areas the art of each tribe is affected by that of adjacent ones. There are art horizons as well as culture horizons, and the former are enlarged in about the proportion that the latter grow, for art is related to other phases of culture and reflects prevalent concepts and values. It is inspired by current ideas, and the limits of expression are imposed by the culture, for the artist must use a language intelligible to the group. "Even the artist, if he pleases to live, must live to please." He must get into the stream of culture influences, or he cannot swim; and usually it is easier to go with it than to stem the current. Lorado Taft has said, "The American sculptor realizes that, in order to exert an influence, his art must speak no alien tongue, but must follow the vernacular of his day and race." Yet the artist may be a transforming influence. He may have the vision and vigor to go across or contrary to the current. New motives arise in him and he may induce the group to accept his art. He may launch a new influence which radiates through the group and gives new trend to the esthetic activities of his fellows. Occasionally an individual initiates new techniques or *motifs*, which receive wide favor and acceptance. The artist is free if the group is free; and the freedom of the group is an index to his freedom.[1] To appreciate a work of art, therefore, the critic must place himself in the situation out of which the work sprang, and must understand the artist's vision; only when he perceives the world which the artist has created, and that which has created the artist, can he estimate the success of the endeavor. "The greatest works which the world has seen have not been dedicated to an unknown posterity, but have been produced to satisfy the daily needs of their age, and have, therefore, of necessity conformed to the tastes, and usually to the fashion

---

[1] See further on primitive art the author's "Introduction to Anthropology," chap. XXXVII, New York, 1926, and BOAS, FRANZ, "Primitive Art," Oslo, 1927.

and the prejudices, of the period which gave them birth."[1] Everywhere, indeed, "art responds very faithfully to the general outlook of its period. The artist is always a man of his own time."[2] Boas says regarding the cultural function of art on the Northwest Coast of North America:

This art style can be fully understood only as an integral part of the structure of Northwest Coast culture. The fundamental idea underlying the thoughts, feelings, and activities of these tribes is the value of rank which gives title to the use of privileges, most of which find expression in artistic activities or in the use of art forms. Rank with social position bestows the privilege to use certain animal figures as paintings or carvings on the house front, on totem poles, on masks and on the utensils of everyday life. Rank and social position give the right to tell certain tales referring to ancestral exploits; they determine the songs which may be sung. There are other obligations and privileges related to rank and social position, but the most outstanding feature is the intimate association between social standing and art forms. A similar relation, although not quite so intimate, prevails in the relation of religious activities and manifestations of art. It is as though the heraldic idea had taken hold of the whole life and had permeated it with the feeling that social standing must be expressed at every step by heraldry which, however, is not confined to space forms alone but extends over literary, musical, and dramatic expression. Who can tell whether the association between social standing and the use of certain animal forms,—i.e., the totemic aspect of social life,—has given the prime impetus to the art development or whether the art impetus has developed and enriched totemic life? Our observations make it seem plausible that the particular symbolic development of art would not have occurred, if the totemic ideas had been absent and that we are dealing with the gradual intrusion of ever fuller animal motives into a well-established conventionalized art. On the other hand, it seems quite certain that the exuberance of totemic form has been stimulated by the value given to the art form. We may observe among all the tribes that high chiefs claim highly specialized art forms that are built up on the general ground of totemic representation. In the South, there is clear evidence of the late exuberant development of the totemic, or perhaps better, crest idea, owing to the strong endeavor to raise by the possession of art forms the standing of the social units to which the individual belongs.[3]

These limitations do not negative the artist's originality.

Every artist works with the data of his understanding and is impelled or molded by the cast of his time. Yet though his mind be set in accepted knowledge, opinions, sentiments, he fashions his matter with a freedom commensurate with his genius . . . The sculptor, painter, poet, or composer works in freedom according to the measure of his transforming and creative genius.

---

[1] BALFOUR, ARTHUR J., *op. cit.*, p. 127.

[2] JARRETT, BEDE, "Social Theories of the Middle Ages, 1200–1500," p. 236, London, 1926.

[3] BOAS, FRANZ, *op. cit.*, pp. 280–281.

Thus the arts mirror human freedom, human nature, and humanity's checkered progress. They are the humanities *par excellence*. The tale of them passes before us, a signal and exhaustless vision. In them Greece was and still lives.[1]

The function of art is to clothe in visible form the spirit of the time, whether a spirit of rest or of unrest, of piety or impiety.

---

[1] Taylor, Henry O., "Freedom of the Mind in History," pp. 280, 282, New York, 1923.

Chapter IX

CULTURE AND ULTIMATE AUTHORITY

Preceding chapters have outlined certain social and cultural forces which normally work in cooperation, interpenetrating and causing no confusion of counsel. But social forces may conflict, and at times custom and tradition, and the demands of the individual and those of the group, are irreconcilable. The problem of ultimate authority is equivalent to the inquiry, What are the actual results? How do things work out? The issue is dramatic.

1. Ultimate Authority in Primitive Society

In the Arunta tribe of Australia, as among many primitive peoples, ultimate authority seems to reside in the traditions as these are interpreted by the elders who deliberate on tribal affairs. They discuss the traditions, are not always in agreement as to their interpretation, and probably sometimes modify them. Since ultimate authority hovers about tradition and this select assembly, only he who plays a rôle in it can deflect the current of tribal affairs. In Southeast Australia more importance attaches to the totem group, which frequently acts as a unit in affairs of importance, one group resisting the encroachments of another. Here ultimate authority appears to inhere not so much in the elders as in the totem group, but the latter must follow tradition. Among the Toda no specific group of men interprets and perpetuates the traditions. Tribal authority radiates from one of the two endogamous groups, the Tartharol or the Teivaliol, and originates in one of the component clans of these endogamous units. The formal outlines of Chilkat social structure are similar to those of the Toda, the tribe being divided into two exogamous units composed of smaller groups.[1] In the Chilkat, however, the constituent groups within the dichotomous unit comprise a hierarchy, the headman of the highest totem group being by virtue of his office head of the entire exogamous division, while the head of one of the two exogamous divisions, or phratries, is *ipso facto* tribal chief. In both tribes the chief must follow tradition and custom, though, at least among the Toda, tradition has sometimes been successfully challenged by a headman.

---

[1] Among the Chilkat the two portions of the tribes are exogamous, among the Toda they are endogamous. Only in the former tribe are the component groups totemic.

In Dahomey and in Ashantee the central figure is the king. Subordinate chiefs preside over definite territory, and under the latter are chiefs of lesser importance. In typical feudal fashion authority centers in the king, not theoretically merely as in European vestiges, but in the reality of unquestioning obedience even to his most extravagant demands. There seems to be no limit to the authority of Dahomey and Ashantee kings and none to the unwavering obedience of their subjects.

Though the New Zealand chief had considerable authority, and his person was *tabu*, his power was limited by a not infrequent assertion of group will. Ordinarily great chiefs wielded almost unlimited power over subjects, but in important matters their actions were regulated by advice from a council and they deferred to public opinion. In this primitive democracy honor could be won by men of humble descent if they possessed ability and courage. Tradition was potent, though some were able to set it aside temporarily. A man who was daring, courageous, and had military genius, though descended from slaves, might become a leader and a war chief. This rarely occurred, however, and toward such a leader the Maori did not entertain the respect which they paid to men of noble birth. Their attitude toward a successful upstart was comparable with that of the European aristocracy toward Napoleon. The lineage of a war chief might be of the nobility, but captivity tainted his name and made him a slave and chattel with reduced social personality; subsequent honors mitigated but did not remove the stigma. But if limitations involving qualifications of birth beyond the individual's control were placed upon men of merit, there was also insistence upon the possession of personal qualities in addition to royal lineage. Under rare circumstances the priestly power of a first-born prince might be lost, but more probably his temporal power would be challenged and revoked. As a rule he was supposed to receive at birth a spiritual appointment from heaven, but leadership of the people in peace or in war, and especially in war, must be confirmed by the popular opinion of tribesmen. The chief must be brave, intelligent, and generous. No coward, fool, or niggardly fellow might lead the Maori warriors. If, in consequence of a glaring physical or intellectual defect, a man was incapable of being leader and commander, by the unanimous consent of the tribe he was set aside for another, usually an uncle or a brother. The selection of a successor was made in silence, as though by a sympathetic appreciation on the part of the notables that a certain man was their choice. Since discussion of the qualifications of the chief was a breach of etiquette, they made the selection by an apparently silent understanding. The chosen man became the war chief, the director of the council, and exercised the royal privilege of veto. The warriors would not accept as leader one who was a chief merely in name.

When descent was interrupted by death of the proper heir, theoretically the succession reverted to the grandfather on the paternal side. If he was old and unable to act as leader a meeting was held in the council house for the purpose of choosing a successor. In silence the brothers of the proper heir stood up, one after another, and when the right man arose a low cough, the sign of approval, ran through the assembly.—Thus among the Maori ultimate authority seems to hover with uncertainty between tradition, personal merit, and popular approval or public opinion. The requirements for the chieftainship are fundamentally traditional and social; and virtues of a powerful leader are those required by the tribe, which has effective means of enforcing its will through a group of influential men. In the simpler Algonkian tribes there is little formal organization, though where chieftainship is recognized, fitness for office is a prerequisite. In Iroquois society a further distinction is made between fitness to conduct tribal affairs in time of peace and ability to lead the warriors. Among the Eskimo, authority hovers with uncertainty now about this individual, now about that one. A daring adventurer may awe the community and cow his enemies into subservience, but the halo of authority is as evanescent as a wandering will-o'-the-wisp. At any time the dominated community may turn the scales and suppress the upstart with heavy hand and severe penalty. Burchardt describes similar conditions among the Berbers. Upon the slightest provocation a man may kill many people with his own hands and overawe the community—until he himself is killed. Such authority cannot long maintain itself unless it has the support of tradition and the sanction of popular approval. Given these buttresses, almost anything is possible.

2. Apparent and Real Authority

The apparent authorities operative in social groups are not always the real ones, and the specious forces are sometimes not the fundamental and effective ones. Yet the power of the West African king appears to be absolute and his subjects really enthralled, although their combined strength greatly exceeds his. The subjects possess the latent power to dominate but they lack the disposition to combine and use it. The status of the slaves in the South during the last months of the Civil War was analogous. They had the power to throw off the yoke of slavery, yet they were still actually enslaved. To ask whether they did not possess freedom had they but resolved to secure it, is equivalent to asking whether the battery will not generate power if it is charged. The natives of Dahomey and the slaves of the South were exhausted batteries of social forces, not charged, or certainly undercharged, with courage and purpose. Slaves make masters no less than masters slaves. The momentum of social forces, supported by the sanctions of ancient use and wont, determines the residence of ultimate authority. "The authority even of a Southern planter over his slaves rested at bottom upon the opinion of the negroes whom he at his pleasure flogged or killed."[1] Their combined physical strength exceeded that of the planter and the whites who might stand by him. The negroes obeyed the slave owner from the opinion, whether well or ill founded, that in the long run they would have the worst of the contest, and even more from a habit of submission which, though enforced by the occasional punishment of recalcitrants, was based upon a number of sentiments, such, for example, as admiration for superior ability and courage, and gratitude for kindnesses. These constituted a prevalent moral atmosphere which cannot be identified with mere fear. "The whites, in short, ruled by virtue of the opinion, entertained by their slaves no less than by themselves, that the slave owners possessed qualities which gave them the might and even the right to be masters."[2] Only by a similar principle can one explain the fact that a few thousand English in India can control several hundred million Orientals, many of whom are their equals in intelligence, and surpass them in artistic taste and in philosophic views. Slaves of different caliber are in a correspondingly different subjection. As the temper of Berber slaves differed from that of the negroes, so the status of the former was nearer the boundary line of freedom. "Being considered as members of the family in which they resided, they assumed airs of importance superior even to those of their masters." The latter were afraid to punish or seriously reprimand them for offenses, since they could easily run away. Adult slaves carried arms, considered themselves upon a par with the best Arabs, and felt humbled only by the restriction that they might not marry Arab girls. Berber slaves showed an insolence toward masters which negro slaves did not dream of; the indignities suffered by Burchardt at their hands are without parallel in the Southern states. In medieval Egypt many rulers were born slaves and were proud of the fact, and the Maori slave could sometimes rise to chieftainship. Though such ambitions were denied slaves in the tribes on the Northwest Coast of North America, they might attain a dignified status in the tribe, acquire property, and live in comfort.

3. The Test of Ultimate Authority

Only by observing the triumph of authorities which clash, can ultimate authority be ascertained. That which overcomes, which maintains

---

[1] Dicey, A. V., "The Influence of Public Opinion upon Law in England in the Nineteenth Century."

[2] *Ibid.*

itself, is ultimate as compared with that which is dominated or check-mated. The authority which survives conflict is ultimate. An estimate of ultimate authority can be made before a conflict, but such prevision gives merely a probability. The fact that Unionism triumphed over Secession-ism in the last century does not insure a repetition of the triumph in a subsequent conflict. Indeed, owing to the growth of other motives and sentiments, the other states probably would not use force if the South seceded. Nor will an alignment of *pros* and *cons* furnish demonstration. The shrewdest anticipations are not worth the observation of events when the forces conflict under such circumstances that one must triumph over the other. The apparent authority is not always the real one and it is difficult to identify ultimate authority. An instance is the Mpongwe tribe of the Gaboon district, West Africa. Here, as in Dahomey, there are three distinct classes. The slaves have few if any rights. To a superficial observer the members of the middle class seem to enjoy all the rights accorded the nobility. Taking as our cue the progress of the people of the middle class, however, we find that ultimate authority rests not in this class but in the nobility above them. Members of this middle class have freedom, initiative, and enterprise, and many become rich. But those who acquire riches are envied by the aristocracy, and are in danger of being accused of witchcraft, of being put to death, and of having their goods confiscated for the benefit of the governing class, the aristocracy. The power of the Kafir chief is comparable with that of Dahomey and Ashantee kings. "Parents would kill their children and children their parents at his command; and so strange a hold has obedience to the king upon the mind of a Kafir, that men have been known to thank him and utter his praises while being beaten to death by his orders." When all goes well the power of a Thonga chief appears to be as absolute as that of the Dahoman king, but the conflict of purposes tells another tale. Although theoretically a Thonga chief has unlimited power and, like the King of England—also theoretically—can do no wrong, actually this power is subordinate to a higher authority, for disobeying which he is liable to suffer.[1]

A chief who wants to succeed in his government must have a good char-acter. If he imposes taxation, he must not use his wealth in a selfish way. For instance, when women bring him a *shirwalo* of a dozen pots of beer, he must give them back one or two to quench their thirst. Moreover, he must distribute most of the remaining pots to his men, who are on the *bandla* (council), always

---

[1] As Paine has remarked, "when there is a part in a government which can do no wrong, it implies, that it does *nothing*, and is only the *machine* of another power by whose direction it acts." PAINE, THOMAS, "The Rights of Man, for the Use and Bene-fit of all Mankind," p. 44, London, 1795.

ready to share with him the advantages of his position. Should he buy oxen with the product of the fines, he will be wise in slaughtering one from time to time for his counsellors and for the whole clan. A chief who is good is said to *maintain* or to *save the country*. If he does not do that he is severely criticized.[1]

Sometimes a chief is unseated and is supplanted by a man who is more amenable; indeed death may be the penalty for refusing to bow to the demands of the tribe. The Kafir chief, though his power was in many ways unlimited, and though he was regarded as above the laws, usually followed the advice of his council.

A chief who disregards the advice of the headmen of the tribe comes to be disliked and rivals appear upon the scene. These gradually gain influence and power, and a successful revolt quenches the autocratic life in darkness, when his son is placed in power, generally with the loss of the revolting clans who form themselves into an independent tribe.

Among the Zulu the chief is "the center of their thoughts and actions; with him rest their prospects and even their lives; they are entirely dependent on him and their parents for counsel and aid, not only in marrying but in every emergency." Nevertheless,

though the chief be thus theoretically absolute, in practice he is not so, being obliged to consider what effect his commands will have on the minds of his followers. Even Tshaka, one of the greatest despots who ever governed any nation, constantly kept this consideration in view, being perfectly aware that his reign would soon terminate, if he opposed the general will of his people. If then the will of the people was thus potent under the iron sway of the great Zulu king, we can imagine the position of a normal chief, and believe that it requires more than hereditary title to insure submission to his will . . . It must be acknowledged, however, that notwithstanding their democratic tendency, these people entertain great respect for authority. They are trained to it by that reverence which custom requires them to show towards their parents, and which the "men" exact from the "boys." A chief therefore who succeeded in corroborating his hereditary title, and possessed a good reputation for wisdom and courage, might acquire great influence over his followers.[2]

Even so, that influence, it appears, was never really absolute authority but was always qualified.

Similarly among the Grebo, of Sierra Leone, the power of the king, though nominally very great, in practice is considerably limited. "He dare not defy public opinion, and he is held responsible, even with his

[1] JUNOD, HENRI A., "The Life of a South African Tribe."
[2] SHOOTER, JOSEPH, "The Kafirs of Natal and the Zulu Country," pp. 97–98, London, 1857.

life, for any adversity that befalls the country." Thus "the rule of the chiefs in Africa is restricted by traditions and public opinion, frequently equivalent to a real share of the people in the government. In the kingdom of Lunda the sovereign is always attended by a body of retainers whose duty it is to prevent him from getting drunk or smoking, lest he then commit atrocities—a primitive form of constitutionalism."[1] The Winnebago chief, who is chosen from one of the Thunderbird clans, must be a man

of well-balanced temper, not easily provoked, and of good habits . . . He must be a peacemaker and love all the people of the tribe, the little children included. If he saw a man, woman, or child passing by, he was to call them in and give them food to eat, for they were his brothers and sisters. All the relatives he has are to look after his possessions and keep him well supplied, for he was supposed to give away things constantly. If any person came to borrow some object from him, he would tell the man that, since he [the borrower] was without this particular thing, to keep it and use it for all time.[2]

Among the Pomo of California the "captains" or chiefs of the local bands were governed "in the greatest measure" by public opinion. "A mightier influence than mere fear of the penal law restrained the Aztec nobility and gentry from drinking to excess; this influence was social law." For the maintenance of his authority and the enforcement of his commands the Kayan chief, of Borneo, depends upon the force of public opinion. So long as he is capable and just, public opinion supports him and brings severe moral pressure to bear upon a member of the household who is loth to submit. When certain limits of personal power are exceeded, public opinion, which holds the upper hand, checks the tyranny. There have been similar limitations upon the power of even the most arbitrary European monarchs. Although no constitution has specified sensitiveness to opinion, it is a potent arm of government which even kings cannot escape. As Demaratus assured Xerxes, "over the Spartans is a master, to wit Law, whom they fear much more even than thy men fear thee";[3] and Pericles says,

while we (in Athens) are unconstrained in our private intercourse, a spirit of reverence pervades our public acts; we are prevented from doing wrong by respect for authority and for the laws, having an especial regard to those which are ordained for the protection of the injured, and to those unwritten laws the breaking of which brings admitted shame.[4]

---

[1] HERTZ, FRIEDRICH, "Race and Civilization," pp. 246–247, New York, 1928.
[2] RADIN, PAUL, "The Winnebago Tribe," pp. 209–210, 37*th* Ann. Rep., *Bureau Amer. Ethnol.*, Washington, 1923.
[3] HERODOTUS, Bk. VII, 104.
[4] THUCYDIDES, Bk. II, 37.

In breaking away from the Church of Rome Henry VIII was able to act in an arbitrary fashion and enforce his views only because the traditional respect for the spiritual authority of a secularized papacy had already been undermined.[1] The people who are ruled are responsible for the existence of absolute monarchs. A successful autocracy implies administrative talent and a docile or a sympathetic people. If a people are not inclined to be docile no autocrat can rule them. And so, according to an old account,

the King of France, [Maximilian] was wont to declare, was a king of asses, because his subjects would bear any burden he imposed upon them; the King of Spain a king of men, since they only obeyed him in what was reasonable; the King of England a king of angels, for he commanded them but what was just and fair, whereas they on their side, obeyed him willingly and rightly. But the Emperor he called a king of kings, "because they obey us when they please."[2]

It is possible to command where most men are already obedient. But even the greatest general cannot discipline a whole army at once. It is only when the greater part of his army is with him that he can quell the mutiny of a faction.[3]

The force, which now prevails, and which is founded on fleets and armies, is plainly political, and derived from authority, the effect of established government. A man's natural force consists only in the vigor of his courage; which could never subject multitudes to the command of one. Nothing but their own consent . . . could have had that influence.[4]

The strength of government does not consist in anything *within* itself, but in the attachment of a nation, and the interest which the people feel in support-

---

[1] Compare Cheney: "As we follow the stream of English history downward toward 1527, evidences of an approaching religious struggle are visible on every hand. There was much native heresy. The influence of Luther was active at Cambridge, in London, and through the eastern countries while Henry VIII was still living happily with Catherine and writing essays in support of the pope. The monarchy was becoming constantly stronger and threatening to come into conflict with the old claims of the Church to semi-independence. Many of the monasteries were bankrupt and could have continued to exist but a little longer at best. Change was in the air; economic change, political change, intellectual change . . . I think it is safe to say that the Reformation would have occurred in England at about the time it did and about in the form it did, if Henry VIII had never seen Anne Boleyn, indeed if Henry VIII had never lived." CHENEY, EDWARD P., "Law in History and Other Essays," pp. 5–6, New York, 1927; see also WINGFIELD-STRATFORD, ESMÉ, "History of British Civilization, vol. I, pp. 337–388, London, 1928.

[2] CUST, MRS. HENRY, "Gentlemen Errant: Being the Journeys and Adventures of Four Noblemen in Europe during the Fifteenth and Sixteenth Centuries," p. 302, New York, 1909.

[3] LIPPMANN, WALTER, "A Preface to Morals," p. 318, New York, 1929.

[4] HUME, DAVID, "Of the Original Contract," in "Essays, Literary, Moral and Political," p. 271, London, 1870.

ing it. When this is lost, government is but a child in power; and though, like the old government of France, it may harass individuals for a while, it but facilitates its own fall.[1]

Opinion is potent. "A single expression, boldly conceived and uttered, will sometimes put a whole company into their proper feelings; and whole nations are acted upon in the same manner."[2] Hence as Holbach says, men, in general, fear more the judgments of men of which they are assured, than those of a God of whom they are sometimes in doubt; and hence opinion is stronger than kings and gods.[3]

The Irish brehon gave his decision, in the administration of justice, but for its enforcement he had to rely upon the pressure of public opinion. When a young Ainu is guilty of a breach of custom or of manners the old people admonish him by reciting some of the sacred verses. There is a Nandi (African) proverb to the effect that shame is not one-edged like a knife, but cuts every direction and goes deep into the heart. The Tasmanians attached much importance to shame as a factor for controlling conduct, and placed an offender on a low branch of a tree, beneath which a crowd shouted his shame and mocked him. When a Northwest Amazonian Indian ill-treated his wife, the other women composed a song in which they publicly exposed the wife-beater to ridicule. The Thompson Indians, in Northwest North America, upheld tribal standards by the threat, "People will laugh at you, will call you 'Coyote,' 'Woman,' or 'Coward.'" The Cheyenne based their discipline on the recognition that

the respect and approbation of one's fellow-men were to be desired, while their condemnation and contempt were to be dreaded. The Indian lived in public. He was constantly under the eyes of the members of his tribe, and most of his doings were known to them. As he was eager for the approval of his fellows, and greedy of their praise, so public opinion promised the reward he hoped for and threatened the punishment he feared.[4]

Thus, everywhere, shame, a feeling for the proprieties, and sensitiveness to the opinions of one's fellows, are among the potent forces which uphold and perpetuate the culture standards; and few things have more

---

[1] PAINE, THOMAS, op. cit., p. 90.

[2] Ibid., pp. 138–139.

[3] HOLBACH, PAUL H. T., "Système social, ou principes naturels de la morale et de la politique, avec un examen de l'influence du gouvernement sur les mœurs," vol. I, p. 70, Londres, 1774.

[4] GRINNELL, GEORGE B., "The Cheyenne Indians," vol. I, pp. 103–104, New Haven, 1923.

authoritative appeal.[1] To check mild and persistent misconduct the Blackfoot employ formal ridicule.

When the offender has failed to take hints and suggestions, the head men may take formal notice and decide to resort to discipline. Some evening when all are in their tipis, a head man will call out to a neighbor asking if he has observed the conduct of Mr. A. This starts a general conversation between the many tipis, in which all the grotesque and hideous features of Mr. A's acts are held up to general ridicule, amid shrieks of laughter, the grilling continuing until far into the night. The mortification of the victim is extreme and usually drives him into temporary exile, or, as formerly, upon the warpath to do desperate deeds,

and thus retrieve his social self-respect. The Fox Indian boy was restrained from unbecoming conduct by the reminder, "the people will say many things about you, though you may not know it."

In the winter of 1914–1915 a Kanghiryuak (Eskimo) woman named Keyuk taunted another woman of the same tribe with childlessness, and the latter stabbed her in the stomach with a knife and killed her. In the following year a man of the same people was sitting in his hut sharpening a knife that he had just made, when a neighbor entered and began to jeer at him, saying that he did not know how to make a knife. The owner quietly continued to sharpen his weapon until its edge was keen enough, then drove it into the jester's stomach with the remark, "Now see if I can't make a knife."[2]

There is considerable justification for Mandeville's statement that "the Passion of Shame is so general and so early discovered in all human Creatures, that no Nation can be so stupid, as to be long without observing and making use of it accordingly."[3] Ethnology corroborates this observation.

4. Cycles of Authority

No authority is always uppermost, but that which rules today may on the morrow be subordinate to some more compelling motive, for authority hovers with inconstancy over individual, group, custom, tradition, and public opinion. The Ojibwa Indians temporarily accepted the faith imposed upon them by a Shawnee prophet, but later rejected it and resumed the old life. For two or three years drunkenness was less frequent and tribal affairs were somewhat changed as a result of his influence.

---

[1] For other examples see the chapter on opinion in the author's "Introduction to Anthropology," pp. 326–334, New York, 1926.

[2] Jenness, D., "The Life of the Copper Eskimos," pp. 94–95, *Report of the Canadian Arctic Expedition*, 1913–1918, vol. XII.

[3] Mandeville, Bernard, "Fable of the Bees," pt. II, third dialogue.

But gradually the impression was obliterated; medicine bags, flints, and steels were resumed; dogs were raised, women and children beaten as before, and the Shawnee prophet was despised. At this day he is looked upon by the Indians as an imposter and a bad man.[1]

In every group there are cycles of authority. In France in 1789–1791 the Third Estate carries the day against all opposition. A faction develops within it which rules the Third Estate and its successor, the Legislative Assembly. A Robespierre secures control of this faction and of all France—to such an extent that no one is sure of his head. This reign of terror, controlled by an idea as much as by brute force, lasts until the assembly dares to rise against the lone tyrant and demand his head. Again the people triumph. A Napoleon comes upon the scene and again a nation is subject to the whim of an individual. Nor, apparently, is there an end to the story, even as there is none to a circle.

5. THE CHANNELS OF SOCIAL LIFE IN WHICH ULTIMATE AUTHORITY MUST MOVE

A common thread runs through the various cultures. In the tribes of Australia, Africa, India, North America, there are similar social and psychic activities, responses to motives which are similar though variously expressed. In all of them are sharply drawn lines of sex, and male and female have different social privileges and duties, different religious rights, a different theology, in some cases a different code of language for secret communication. In the lower cultures as in the higher the age of the individual is an index to social position and influence, as are also burial ceremonies, which everywhere reflect the social status of the deceased. In each tribe and nation some individual or group has, if not absolute, at least contingent, or temporary, social authority. When, and how much, the authority is exercised, is determined by the group, which invariably imposes limits. That culture should fall into these molds is not surprising. Social organization is indispensable to culture and its development involves the cooperation of many individuals and a continuity of effort, accretion, and readjustment which only a larger span than that of an individual life makes possible. Continuity of effort is assured only when culture is incorporated in a social organization. When external forces threaten the existence of the group, social solidarity is necessary, and centralization of authority in an individual or in a group is a prerequisite to unification. In centralized authority the social purpose can become articulate, and intentions can be brought to a focus and expressed in a manner intelligible to all. In order to apprehend its purposes and

---

[1] MOONEY, JAMES, "The Ghost-Dance Religion," 14*tb* *Ann. Rep., Bureau Amer. Ethnol.*, Washington, 1896.

profit from its counsels, social life must become articulate: hence the council and the counsellors. The application of this principle to Eskimo society is well indicated by Jenness:

The Eskimo is intolerant of anything like restraint. Every man in his eyes has the same rights and the same privileges as any other man in the community. One may be a better hunter, or a more skilful dancer, or have greater control over the spiritual world, but this does not make him more than one member of a group in which all are free and theoretically equal. In a society such as has just been outlined, without law-courts, judges, or chiefs, without laws even, save the time-honored customs handed down from one generation to another, crime can be held in check only if the majority of the people of their own accord unite in punishing the wrongdoer. Direct action of this nature, however, can rarely be taken, because there is no common council wherein the will of the people can find a voice, no spokesman to give it public expression, and no leader to translate it into action.[1]

When there is even a temporary and conditional surrender of authority to a central body, the functions of the social organism can be coordinated and the force of their concentrated efforts brought to bear on the solution of a common problem. And perhaps a coordinating authority is as necessary for social as for individual organism. As a matter of fact, in certain amorphous societies, such as the Eskimo, there is, as in the amœba, little coordination in a central authority; the more complex the organism, the greater the need for a definite center of coordination. In the more complex African cultures a coordinating authority is more insistently needed and it is correspondingly more highly developed than in the cruder cultures of that continent or in those of Australia. In the islands of the South Seas, with more complex culture and greater social differentiation, more authority inheres in chieftainship, which tends to become hereditary. But as authority becomes more highly centralized its development tends to proceed for its own sake, apart from the needs of the group and even at its expense. In the cruder cultures this authority usually is subservient to social needs and to tribal demands. In savagery, therefore, especially among tribes continually encountering foes with whom they are barely able to cope, there is readier and more consistent recognition of personal merit as a qualification for leadership than in the more advanced cultures. In Australia and in North America the small unfederated tribes demand from chiefs and leaders the qualification of personal fitness. This is less often the case in the more complex cultures of Polynesia and least of all in highly developed tribal societies, such as those of Ashantee, Dahomey, Mexico, and Peru. In the higher European societies, Rome and the inheritors of Roman institu-

---

[1] JENNESS, D., op. cit., p. 94.

tions, the office of kingship has been filled without regard to personal fitness. In these nations the culture is apparently able to take care of itself. Danger from an outside foe is not so immediately apprehended as in the small group in which every member is close to the firing line. The individual assertion, the initiative which carries the leader to a position of influence and authority at the head of the tribe, a common attribute of the simpler societies, is the fulfillment of a social demand, enforced by the harsh conditions of menace from within or from without which threaten the integrity of tribal life. The safety of civilization provides a breeding ground for satisfaction and facilitates decay. If the leader of a primitive group is inefficient he is supplanted by one who can and will lead; and even in civilization, in times of crises, if the king cannot lead his people, someone else, a general or a prime minister, will do so.

CHAPTER X

CULTURE DEVELOPMENT AND PROGRESS

1. CULTURE DEVELOPMENT AS INCREASE IN COMPLEXITY

Thomas Aquinas interprets development as proceeding from simple to complex. He says,

It is the way of nature to proceed from the simple to the complex, for we find invariably in the workings of nature that the most complex is the perfection, completion, and end of the others, as is clear in every whole in respect to its parts. The mind of man, therefore, in its artistry must no less proceed from the simple to the complex as from the imperfect to the perfect.[1]

Lamarck defines organic evolution as increase in complexity, and Herbert Spencer applies this principle to organic and social life. Its implications, however, have been grasped by many earlier writers. Compared with the Bronze and Iron ages, Hesiod's Gold and Silver ages are periods of simplicity and tranquility. Plato appeals to the principle of simplicity when he traces the origin of society to an economic stage in which each man was his own artisan for all the needs of life, before specialization led to trade, markets, and the internationalism evoked by increasing economic, social, and political complexity. Aristotle appeals to the principle of simple to complex when he interprets social evolution as development from the family to groups of families, and to village communities. The principle is accepted by Lucretius, who finds primitive social life devoid of the complexities which accompany civilization, and the concept is implicit in seventeenth and eighteenth-century philosophers who attribute the origin of society to contract. Archeology confirms the view that evolution proceeds from simple to complex. The social life of prehistoric man is not known but stone and metal implements reveal part of the story of his industrial development. The first of these stages, the eolithic, is characterized by simple forms of implements which scarcely vary in type except as accident would account for the variation. In the Early Paleolithic period the types are more numerous. During the passing of thousands of years the types of implements increase and the

---

[1] AQUINAS, THOMAS, "Commentary on the Politics of Aristotle."

techniques improve. In the Late Paleolithic period the types are more clearly demarked and are more numerous. From Paleolithic through Neolithic, the Bronze age, the Iron age, to the latest phases of the present industrial age, there is increasing complexity.[1] The unprecedented developments of the last century, the century of the engine and of electricity, have been accompanied by an increase in complexity, which is now so great that no one can master more than a small portion of the industrial field. "A wagon hath a hundred pieces (of wood)," says Hesiod,[2] with pride, of his agricultural Bronze-Iron age; he would have received with incredulity the information that a future civilization would make with ten thousand pieces, mainly of a harder metal than he knew, a self-propelling wagon which could outspeed and outdistance the swiftest birds.

Men make progress whether they will or not, says Spencer, for the cosmic process from undifferentiated homogeneity to differentiated heterogeneity goes on, and this is progress. Yet Spencer lived a simple life. He saw a complex world, but kept aloof from most of its entanglements. His statement of the principle is simple rather than complex, and it is not highly differentiated. With a simple pen he wrote his simple English, and he probably did not desire multiple differentiated hands, one for each letter of the alphabet. This biped of simple bilateral symmetry did not complain because his locomotion was much less differentiated than that of the crab or the lobster. He did not deplore the fact that man shows no tendency to develop into a centipede, a hydra, or a Janus, or to acquire as many stomachs as a camel.

As a matter of fact, development is not always from simple to complex. The devices of travel, for example, have become more complex, but traveling is simpler. The traveler takes more baggage than formerly, but conveying it is simpler than it used to be. If complexity has value it is because it simplifies the goals or the methods of reaching them, and facilitates the accomplishment of a purpose, or stimulates new purposes which afford more or deeper satisfactions. The superiority of the implements of the Upper Paleolithic over those of the Eolithic and the Lower Paleolithic lies in their greater efficiency. Bronze marks an advance over stone, iron over bronze, and steel over iron, because each new material is more efficient than the old. With these more efficient devices man attains power. Our industries are superior to those of fishers and hunters, pastoral peoples, and primitive agriculturists, because our devices are more efficient servants.

---

[1] See the author's "Introduction to Anthropology," pp. 75–98, New York, 1926.
[2] HESIOD, "Works and Days," line 456.

2. CULTURE DEVELOPMENT AS INCREASE IN POWER

Though development may bring greater complexity, the complexity is the form rather than the content, the body rather than the spirit of development. Development is the process by which latent powers reach fruition. To become an adult the child must develop from few and weak functions to many and vigorous ones. But the complexity of the adult organism does not constitute adulthood, it is merely accessory to it; and even though the organism becomes more complex, if latent powers do not function there is no progress. Complexity is a handicap if society flounders in the increasing number of phases in which it is involved or which it has evolved. No especial significance attaches to the fact that Paleolithic man evolves new types of implements. The significance lies in the fact that he makes types of implements better adapted to his purposes. Neolithic shows advance over Paleolithic man, not because the former has more implements and more activities, but because he acquires power. Ceramics, agriculture, and domestication, which come in the Neolithic period, are new sources of power. The value of complexity in culture must be judged by a like test. Civilization is not superior to primitive culture because it is more complex; its complexity is an attribute, not the essence of its superiority; it is superior in spite of its complexity. In early stages, when the economic order has not become specialized and the activities and interests of one are those of all, there is little complexity in the culture. But when specialization is under way there must be new adjustments if all demands are to be satisfied.

Increase in devices and growth in specialization enhance the power to attain objectives. To preserve these means of power new forms of social organization come into existence, and social life grows more complex. Each new trait increases the potential power of the culture. Social purposes can find more channels for expression, and new demands can be satisfied. Yet increasing complexity does not, in itself, constitute advance; it may be the outer garment of development, or the means to an end, but it is not the goal. Indeed, in many phases of social life development is from complex to simple, and to good purpose. Usually the marriage regulations in tribal culture are more complex than those in advanced civilizations, and frequently personal relationships are more involved—though this is not equivalent to more evolved. The elaborate ceremonialism of feudalism disappears when social life rests on other foundations and men have a different appreciation of position and personality. With intellectual development language grows simpler in form and in structure, for linguistic complexity is a handicap rather than an advantage. In actual vocabulary there is increase, because there is need for new words to denote new things, new relations, and new concepts. Improvement, however, does not lie in the greater complexity of language but in its more apt and effectual service. If culture develops greater complexity, this is not because men so desire, but because in their endeavor to realize their purposes they utilize many agencies. Though the phases of culture increase, we seek to simplify the culture and the scope and aim of life; our motto might be, "Seek simplicity and distrust it."[1] Complexity is a mathematical concept and cannot measure values. Civilized man possesses power undreamed of by the savage. Life is power, civilization is socialized power, and the absence of power is death and decay. Progress, therefore, implies increase in power.

3. THE TREND OF CULTURE DEVELOPMENT

The evidence for the earliest stages of man's advance consists of those material objects which have resisted the disintegrations of time. The first implements are crude, for Eolithic man is little superior to the beasts save in the ability to select from nature the useful sticks and stones. Yet this selective ability makes him a tool-using animal, and the tool-using animal develops into a tool-making animal—*homo faber*. We know something of the development of tool making through many thousands years, far back into the Pleistocene era. Progress is slow but there is improvement in stone implements from the dawn of human history to the development of a metal civilization, when man learns to hammer copper, to mold bronze, to smelt iron and fashion out of it implements which enhance his power. Throughout these long periods of time he is continually specializing, in response to developing needs, providing himself with implements better adapted to his demands, though in turn increasing his wants. Development is conditioned by the culture already attained, and there is an intimate relation between the arts of one period and those of preceding and subsequent periods. Though there are stages of accelerated improvement, the rapidity of which is a measure of the growth in interdependence and specialization, there is no break in continuity. One stage of culture does not so much give place to a later one as develop into it, and much that was of value in the past is preserved in the ensuing stage. New stone implements supplement the old; bronze and iron supplement paleoliths and neoliths and only gradually and partially supplant them. Man grows stronger by augmenting his resources, carving out a new carreer by expanding the old one. There is continuity in development, for achievement is conditioned by previous

---

[1] WHITEHEAD, A. N., "The Concept of Nature," p. 163; see also TAYLOR, HENRY O., "Freedom of the Mind in History," p. 208, London, 1923.

accomplishments, and the past and the present contain the stimuli for the future. "Every fresh addition to knowledge opens out new vistas of previously unsuspected problems. We may be certain that when more is known of the Lower Paleolithic, its history will be found to be full of complexities of which we have as yet no conception."[1] This observation applies to every phase of culture. Certain stages of development must precede certain others. The wheel must come before the wheeled vehicle; simpler types of watercraft must precede the sailboat; long voyages presuppose large vessels equipped with oars or with sails. Similarly,

. . . a discovery in medicine is not only limited by the status of knowledge in medicine, but it is dependent upon the existing knowledge in other fields . . . An analysis of any phase of medicine at any period of its history will reveal a . . . dependence upon, and limitation by, the existing knowledge in other fields.[2]

Man is not merely a conservative but a conserving animal as well, and seldom puts aside devices which have been tried and found useful. The civilization of which they are a part may be swept away and these things be lost to the world for all time or until they are rediscovered, but seldom have the useful arts, once adopted, been given up deliberately.[3] A people who have developed metallurgy do not abandon it and revert to stone culture; a people who have evolved writing do not forget it. There are exceptions, but taking human history in its entirety, so far at least as mechanical devices are concerned, man not merely learns but remembers the lessons of useful experience. In the realm of social experience this, alas, is less often the case; social advantages, unlike material advantages, are not objectified, and seldom are they obvious to those who share them.

4. Unconscious Motives May Promote Culture Development

Usually the forces which stimulate culture development are not understood by those who respond to them. The motive of self-preservation may be exhibited by the group, whereas the individual who rises to the occasion may be ignorant of the more fundamental motives which prompt his response, for he is inclined to interpret the significance of events according as they serve or thwart his purposes. Hence he thinks

---

[1] Macalister, R. A. S., "A Text-book of European Archæology," p. 348, Cambridge, 1921.

[2] Stern, Bernhard J., "Social Factors in Medical Progress," pp. 106–107, New York, 1927.

[3] See, however, "The Disappearance of Useful Arts," in Rivers, William H. R., "Psychology and Ethnology," pp. 190–210, New York, 1926; and Dixon, Roland B., "The Building of Cultures," pp. 147–149, New York, 1928.

that he freely fights for defense of country, rather than is subtly impelled by social influences. Influences external to the individual do not interest him until they are incorporated in his conscious motives. He then is interested in the fact that they are his motives; and their externality appears to him largely accidental. Culture development is largely a matter of knowing how rather than knowing about, and the group may act intelligently even when but vaguely aware of the circumstances which motivate it. It stumbles along its path, maintaining an acquired momentum, seeking points of least resistance, but guided by no charted course or compass. Although members of the group are only dimly conscious of their path and of their purpose, and culture development consists more in knowing how than in knowing about, the latter plays a larger part in human history when man understands himself both as individual and as a carrier of culture. For to know about is incipiently to know how; and such knowledge, if not the open door to progress, is at least the key which will unlock the door, the open sesame if there is one.

5. SPECIALIZATION, FRICTION, AND INTEGRATION

Many phases of civilization seem like,

> A tale told by an idiot,
> Full of sound and fury—signifying nothing.

The story of civilization leaves one guessing at the *motif* and wondering whether it embodies a rational plot. Scientific knowledge forges ahead but develops conditions, such as those exhibited in the industrial stage, which are worse than those of previous decades. Poison gas and high explosives give greater power for evil than had hitherto been achieved. Advance bring specialization, and specialization causes frictions which in turn necessitate a new integration of old forces. Then come further specialization, new frictions, and a new integration to solve the new problems. It is a never-ending series of mistakes and corrections followed by further mistakes. Whether the spectacle arouses optimism or pessimism depends upon the part of the circle which arrests attention; but attention should not be limited to any one of these phases, for each one of them is consequent upon the others. Specialization develops new power and also new potential evil; the clash of powers leads to antagonisms, the friction which puts the brake on progress. Integration releases the brake by a redistribution of power, and a focusing upon new ends recognized as common. At this point man raises the question of the value of his culture and of the reality of progress. Social forces play a relatively independent part, though they may conflict with the economic régime at many points. With every thrust into new fields new conflicts arise, for a phase of culture developed to the full may impede the development of other phases unless there is deliberate and determined effort to prevent this result. Development of economic power, for example, may occasion conflicts with other phases of culture, and necessitate readjustments. The gregariousness which protects the individual when social development is feeble may later become a tyrant. There arise problems of adjustment of individual demand to social demand, and of class to class. Indeed, in civilization, the individual, once the center of his world, as man was once the center of the universe, now seems precariously on the periphery. Man controls nature but not human nature. Satisfaction of demands at one point leaves them unsatisfied at others, and while man makes gains along some lines he loses ground at others. To attain power he must attend to one thing at a time, but to retain power he must attend to all the means of salvation, for they are interdependent; and, apparently, he "cannot focus all good things at the same time."[1] A way out of this dilemma he has not found; and not until he finds it will development be equivalent to progress. As man attains a fuller knowledge of his world it becomes larger in meanings as well as in spatial dimension. Copernicus, Giordano Bruno, Galileo give him a new knowledge of the universe and of his position in it, as Darwin, Wallace, Huxley give him a new realization of his place in the animal kingdom. History, anthropology, prehistoric archeology pave the way to a new conception of the place of contemporary life in the larger scheme of human culture. Man can no longer be content to see the world in relation to himself, he must also see himself in relation to the world of which he is a part. Only through awareness of the forces with which he deals can he learn to command.

> Without the truth there is no knowing,
> Without the way there is no going.[2]

Only when man learns the course of culture development can he control it. He cannot wisely deflect a tendency until he wisely detects it.

> The will to learn bringeth of learning growth;
> Learning makes insight grow, and by insight
> We know the Good; known Good brings bliss along.

In many respects man seems the victim rather than the hero of the drama of culture change. The progress of Western civilization has brought not only modern science and internationalism but also a World War. The Industrial Revolution brought comforts to many and misery to more. Man has acquired power, but meanwhile many lives and many goods have been snuffed out. New values have been gained, but old ones have been lost; and we are not yet able to assess the results.

---

[1] WELLS, HERBERT G., "A Modern Utopia," pp. 233, 235, New York, n. d.
[2] Á KEMPIS, THOMAS, "Imitation of Christ."

PART II
THEORIES OF PROGRESS

INTRODUCTION

At certain periods of history men have shown increased interest in the progress of their species, culture, or group. Usually these have been times of storm and stress in which old ideals were being challenged. Among the Greeks the interest in progress was stimulated by the introduction of new ideas from other cultures, and again by the threat of Persian conquest. Thus progress is the concern of Hesiod, whose father moved from the islands of the Ægean to the mainland when Greek culture was undergoing radical changes. Subsequently it is the concern of Plato, who has behind him the lessons of the Persian and the Peloponnesian wars, and about him the challenge of other systems of life unlike the Athenian. The interest in progress is reflected in the speculations of the Stoics, who orient themselves in the larger world of humanity and in that of physical nature, and are ambitious to be not merely citizens of a city but cosmopolitans in a world of men and in a universe of suns and planets. It is implicit as well as explicit in the thought of Lucretius, who seeks the rationale of life in a comprehensive scheme of evolution comprising matter and men, and it is a problem of the poets Virgil and Ovid. The interest in progress comes to the fore again when the Renaissance directs attention to the accomplishments of former centuries and men wonder whether contemporaries are capable of duplicating the achievements of the ancients. Interest in progress revives in the eighteenth century during the period preceding the French Revolution and in the days following the Revolutions of 1848. It waxes again at the close of the last and in the early years of the present century, particularly during the decade following the outbreak of the World War. The problem of progress remains one of the insistent questions of the present day and deserves a clearer answer than has yet been offered. Both external influences and changes within the culture focus attention upon the problem. An industrial revolution in England stimulated More to write the "Utopia," and the Industrial Revolution of the last century and a half inspired many European writers whose works now interest alert Orientals who find their respective civilizations in the toils and coils of a comparable industrial revolution.[1]

---

[1] See, for examples, WALLIS, WILSON D., and WILLEY, MALCOLM M., "Reading in Sociology," chap. II, New York, 1930.

CHAPTER XI

THE PROBLEM OF PROGRESS

1. CULTURE CHANGES

All phases of culture change. In some cases the change is merely evolution; in some it constitutes progress. In the former case the changes are cumulative; in the latter, they secure greater values. A proper arrangement of culture changes in a time perspective would rectify much social philosophy. Since that has not been achieved, the time perspective may be disregarded, and the data of culture arranged in a perspective of values, based on the significance of culture changes. Does every culture swing like a pendulum from low to high and back again to low, as history indicates was the case with all previous civilizations? If so, in what direction is contemporary civilization moving? We usually assume that Western civilization makes progress, for progress seems fundamental to our culture; but is this assumption correct, or are we on a treadmill of futile repetition? Our scientific achievements, already unparalleled, increase with an acceleration born of genius and application. In all fields knowledge grows. Industry, as represented by both capital and labor, attains organization and power not realized before. Facts of this order touch the imagination and appeal to us as demonstration of progress. But do these really constitute progress, or have we failed to grasp the significance of these culture changes? Bacon assures us that man will rise by conquering nature, and assuredly in recent years man has made marvelous conquests. He now knows the universe more intimately than formerly men knew the earth, or, indeed, their own locality. The stars have become closer acquaintances than were mountain systems or continents to his forebears, for now knowledge as well as imagination encompasses the stellar spaces. The immediate environment he has analyzed with unprecedented thoroughness. He knows much about natural laws and physical bodies, and is familiar with their behavior as entities and as chemical compounds. He knows organism and mind more intimately than did his ancestors. He thinks in social terms and applies new knowledge to social problems. Yet despite these achievements there is reason to pause and inquire whether on the whole he is better off; for in many instances the specious advance is not progress. The simple savage, for example, has no better weapon of

210

offense or defense than an unadorned war club. Some peoples have improved the efficiency of the war club by increasing the weight at one end and by providing protuberances and edges. The war club evolved into spear, then into bow and arrow, and after these came firearms. Firearms have been perfected until a machine gun is more efficient than a host of clubs and bows and arrows. Whereas formerly men could knock one another on the head and kill only one at a time, now, thanks to "civilized" devices, they can kill by scores and hundreds. Does this evolution constitute progress? Man has developed not only in material resources but also in knowledge; yet knowledge as well as material things can be employed destructively. In modern warfare, for example, even opinion is drafted, and history and psychology, as well as physics and chemistry, are utilized as destructive devices.[1]

2. Adaptation to Culture Changes

Contemporaries point with pride to advance in medical skill. It is fortunate that medicine advances, for advance in civilization has been accompanied by a host of bodily ills of which savagery is innocent. Savagery has little medical skill and little disease; we have ample measure of both; but, all things considered, does this indicate progress? Civilized man has many comforts; but increase in comforts and advantages is not equivalent to enhancement of life. Some animals languish in captivity and die an early death, and man is only partially adapted to domestication. Human nature changes slowly. Man builds habitations and finds that he cannot live happily in them. In the case of many a primitive tribe the price for the gifts of Western civilization is extermination. And indeed adaptation to the demands of culture is one of civilized man's problems, for while he makes progress at one point he may lose ground at some other. The Industrial Revolution is an illustration. Man regarded more efficient machines as necessarily an increment to his happiness; but he had not fathomed their significance. Soon he had occasion to ponder the fact that machines do not work of themselves, but work for men only when men work for them. Man must serve the machine or it will not serve him. Thus the Industrial Revolution solved one problem and added a thousand others which still plague us. Indeed certain phases of civiliza-

---

[1] See, for example, Lasswell, Harold D., "Propaganda Technique in the World War," p. 222, New York, 1927. "Propaganda," Professor Lasswell says, "is the new dynamic of society, for power is subdivided and diffused, and more can be won by illusion than by coercion. It has all the prestige of the new and provokes all the animosity of the baffled. To illuminate the mechanisms of propaganda is to reveal the secret springs of social action, and to expose to the most searching criticism our prevailing dogmas of sovereignty, of democracy, of honesty, and of the sanctity of individual opinion."

tion seem to advance faster than the capabilities of the men who inherit them. More adequate means of salvation are at our disposal, but do we control them for our good? This is the crux of the problem. Our environment is more richly endowed, but are we richer? Our life is reembodied in new surroundings, but is it reensouled in them? We have found a new world, but have we found ourselves in this new world? Is improvement in the conditions of life equivalent to improvement in life, or must there be more than opportunity if the potentiality of progress is to become a reality?

If the significance of the changes which have taken place in human culture from Paleolithic times to contemporary civilization can be expressed in a single word, that word is *power*. "Man never acknowledged Superiority without Power."[1] Man has gained power in almost every phase of culture: power to understand, control, and predict. In almost all phases of life, the savage, compared with the civilized man, is as puny and weak as the new-born child compared with the adult. But power means possibilities for evil as well as for good. It means that man holds in one hand salvation, and in the other, destruction. Savagery cannot cause a tithe of the misery of which civilization is capable. In four short years savagery could not have left the heritage of distrust, misery, economic ruin, and intellectual and spiritual disaster which was bequeathed to Western civilization by Western civilization during the period 1914 to 1918. With every accretion of power man is capable of more evil than before; and "when civilization degenerates, it falls lower than barbarism can ever reach; for the latter can only become a beast, while the former lapses into a devil."[2] Man needs, then, not merely resources, but ability to use them to good purpose; not merely power to do something, but a willingness and a readiness to accomplish something worth while; not merely power to meet an immediate situation, but ability to meet larger and more remote situations in and through the immediate one. In present achievements man has outdone and almost has undone himself. If the powers which he develops are not coordinated and utilized for the enhancement of life, he suffers from rather than is benefited by them.

Mere knowledge, therefore, does not insure progress, and an understanding of nature and of human nature does not insure salvation; for the more the sinner knows, the more he can sin. The value of knowledge depends upon the manner in which it is utilized, the ends it serves, and the means used in attaining them; for means are not detached from the end but are a part of it, and in choosing means man is also choosing

---

[1] MANDEVILLE, BERNARD, "Fable of the Bees," remark P.

[2] SCHILLER, "Briefe," vol. III, p. 411; quoted in GOOCH, G. P., "Germany and the French Revolution," p. 220, London, 1920.

ends, for he is choosing one course and rejecting others. Merely to will the good is not sufficient, for the will which does not reckon with the social environment is futile. A man cannot be merely a physicist, for the world in which he lives is not composed of mere mass and motion; he cannot be merely a historian, for he must reckon also with the demands of the present. Preceding generations bequeathed us our problems; we pass them on little altered; and the world we inherit and that which we, in turn, bequeath is a jumble of inconsistencies. Man possesses ample resources, but what they contribute to human worth and to human values we do not know, and seldom do we care. Yet man's discovery of his misery, his knowledge of the futility of his efforts, and his appreciation of the inadequacy of the ends which he pursues, are occasion for congratulation. The discovery of weakness is a step toward the attainment of power. Only the conscience sensitive to injustice is alive to justice. Man alone possesses this conscience and he alone has the power and the disposition, if occasional and half-hearted, to use it.

3. Culture and Values

Some paths are circular, and those who pursue them may merely repeat previous circumambulations. Civilization, it may be, is headed into a blind alley, or perchance it has already completed that portion of its path which can be called upward. Or, again, it is possible that culture, which is external to the individual at birth and must be acquired, may be developing faster than the capacities of the men who seek to profit by their civilization. Hence it is possible that individuals are no better off despite the fact that their civilization is richer. A man values the traits of his own culture above those of others; he is accommodated to them and takes their values for granted; but values cannot be ascertained by a count of the opinions of individuals. The spokesmen of progress whose views deserve attention must represent something more than the culture of a given period or that of a given group. In this matter an exception cannot be made of Western civilization, for it is merely one of many cultures. There are, however, common qualities in all civilizations, and on this common ground their respective protagonists must meet, or there is no establishing of credit, and none are bound to accept the conclusions of others; for when conclusions have validity only in those cultures in which they are enunciated, they are merely a reflection of culture psychology, interesting as such, but otherwise inconclusive. In estimating values all cultures, therefore, must be included, and they must be estimated on a plane where comparison is possible. To judge otherwise is merely to voice a culture prepossession and prejudice.

We must, therefore, not merely view civilization from the perspective of values, but also view values from the perspective of cultures. To the extent to which values depend upon the culture in which they are expressed, their importance is not absolute but merely relative; and in many cases the chief significance attaching to a judgment of value derives from the fact that it reflects the emphasis inspired by a given culture.[1] Moreover, "the distance which separates the victor from the victim is often no greater than the breadth of a hair."

---

[1] See the author's article, "The Prejudices of Men," in *Amer. Jour. Sociol.*, **34**: 804–821, 1929.

CHAPTER XII

CONCEPTS OF PROGRESS IN THE OLDER CIVILIZATIONS

1. EARLY CONCEPTS OF PROGRESS

Among savages there is little speculation regarding progress, though many primitive cosmogonies explain the origin of death and evil. The Kafirs, of South Africa, say that after the creation of mankind a chameleon was sent to men to tell them that they were to live forever, and a lizard was dispatched with the message that they were to die. The chameleon tarried by the way to eat berries, and the lizard arrived first and delivered the message of death. Thus mankind became mortal. For the Hopi death was not part of the original plan of human life on earth, but was due to malign magic. "The Cheyennes have a tradition of a Golden age when war was unknown and universal peace prevailed. All strangers met in friendship and parted on good terms. Such a far-off time, when hostile encounters were unknown, is told of by many of the tribes of the northern plains."[1] The Northern Iroquois say that "when the world was first made, men-beings did not know that they must die some time. In those days everyone was happy and neither men, women, nor children were afraid of anything. They did not think of anything but doing what pleased them."[2]

Generally savages have no prevision of the remote future. The Mortlock Islanders of Micronesia, however, describe the end of the world. There will come a day when men will cease to honor Luk, their god, will offer no sacrifices to him, but will wage wars and commit sins. Then the Lord of the World will destroy them. He will send Thopulap, the thunder; Ainiar, the whirlwind, who turns everything upside down; Atupuase, who throws down the trees; Lifau faunemai, who hugs sea and land; and Lisea piro, who hurls great rocks from the sea upon the land. Then everything will go to wrack and ruin; only the gods above will survive these calamities.

A Taoist Chinese account states that originally man obeyed the Heavens. Neither disease nor death visited him, and by instinct he

---

[1] GRINNELL, GEORGE B., "The Cheyenne Indians: Their History and Ways of Life," vol. II, p. 1, New Haven, 1923.

[2] PARKER, ARTHUR C., "The Code of Handsome Lake," in N. Y. State Museum Bull. No. 163, p. 105, 1912.

was wholly good and spiritual. The immoderate desire to be wise, or, according to Lao-tze, to eat, brought ruin to mankind. A follower of Lao-tze (604–532 B.C.), Kwang-tze, said: "In the age of perfect virtue men attached no value to wisdom . . . They were upright and correct, without knowing that to do so was Righteousness: they loved one another, without knowing that to do so was Benevolence: they were honest and leal-hearted, without knowing that to be so was Good Faith." Later, however, "the manners of the people, from being good and simple, became bad and mean."

Confucius taught that intelligent freedom of conduct is attained by conforming the will with the way of Heaven. The conception is similar to the Stoic idea that virtue consists in following nature. He sought to restore the social and religious laws which, he believed, prevailed in the ancient Chinese Empire before it fell into the turmoil which characterized it in his day, when it suffered from the misrule of many princes. These principles, if incorporated in political and social practice, would insure proper ties between ruler and people, within the family, and throughout society.

What Heaven has conferred is called the Nature; and accordance with this Nature is called the Path; the regulation of the Path is called Instruction. The path may not be left for an instant . . . On this account the superior man does not wait till he sees things, to be cautious, nor till he hears things, to be apprehensive . . . While there are no stirrings of pleasure, anger, sorrow, or joy, the mind is in a state of equilibrium. When these feelings have been stirred, and they act in due degree, there ensues a state of harmony. Equilibrium is the great root, and Harmony is the universal Path. Let the states of Equilibrium and Harmony exist in perfection, and a happy order will prevail throughout heaven and earth, and all things will flourish . . . What has Man in common with Heaven? His intelligent nature. Conformity with this nature gives the rule of action.

This doctrine bears a striking resemblance to Stoic philosophy.[1] Mu Ti, probably a younger contemporary of Confucius, is a utilitarian. "The existing state of things [is] far from ideal because everybody esteems his own self above others. One should love all others as one's own self, each nation should respect others as it respects itself, the sovereign should love his subjects as he loves himself"—in short, everybody should love everybody else without stint, i.e., to the degree that one loves oneself.

Similar ideas are current in the early Mediterranean civilizations. Either men independently reach similar conclusions with regard to these problems, or there has been a wide diffusion of these concepts. Certain

_____
[1] See below, chap. XIV.

similarities in the respective accounts, and the culture contacts in these areas, suggest that many of them have a common historical source. Yet men independently come to similar conclusions with regard to similar problems, and in the realm of speculation independent origins supplement diffusion.

2. HINDU, BUDDHIST, AND JAIN CONCEPTS OF PROGRESS

The early Hindu account of human progress describes a first age, a Golden age, the *krytayuga*, in which all was well with man. The duration of life was 4,000 years, there were no quarrels and no wars, virtue reigned unchallenged, and caste and religious prescriptions were obeyed. The desires of men were fulfilled upon the mere wish. The people had no houses, for the climate was balmy, and the earth spontaneously produced delicious foods, though animals and plants had not yet arrived. The first population consisted of 1,000 pairs of twins. At the end of 4,000 years each pair of twins procreated a pair of twins who were exact duplicates of the parents.[1] Perfection reigned, and human life was maintained in its pristine condition without distinction between good and evil. A change in climatic conditions marks the end of the *krytayuga*. For the first time rain falls and trees grow which produce honey and other good things that supply the needs of the people. In the ensuing age, the *tetrayuga*, the twinning propensities of mankind are greatly curtailed, and men and women become like those of today. They experience the discomforts of cold and heat, and, to secure comfort, they build houses. Also they quarrel about the control, *i.e.*, the ownership, of the miraculous trees. As if in spite, the trees disappear and give place to herbs. Trade begins, personal property comes into existence, and the latter gives rise to social distinctions and to problems consequent thereon, from which the earth has not since been free—a *motif* in European thought from the time of the Greeks to the present. During this epoch Brahma establishes the four castes and the four *asramas* and assigns to each caste and priestly order its specific functions. At the end of the last age, the *kaliyuga*, the heat of the sun will become so intense that it will set the three worlds on fire and consume them. Finally, enormous clouds will appear, it will rain for hundreds of years, and the earth will be deluged with the waters from heaven. The four *yugas*, or ages, which total 12,000 years, become successively shorter in duration and man degenerates with increasing rapidity.

---

[1] A Mohammedan Malay charm which reflects Hindu influence refers to Eve as bearing twins, until she had borne 44 children. The children were wedded, handsome with handsome and plain with plain.

The *Mahabharata* assigns four ages to the endless world cycle, each characterized by a specific color. The first age is the color of Vishnu, white or light, for then right has full sway and there is no death, sickness, pain, pride, dislike, strife, exhaustion, emnity, fear, jealousy, or wickedness. Men live in peace and each attends to his own affairs. In the second age Vishnu becomes red, and though men are dutiful and industrious, right loses a fourth of its power. In the third age Vishnu is yellow and right retains only half its original power among men. Death appears and those who do wrong suffer sickness and pain. In the fourth age there remains only a fourth of the original power of righteousness, which dwindles rapidly. Vishnu becomes black, and diseases, plagues, anger, pettinesses, accidents, cares, hunger, and fear prevail. The ages then run the gamut in inverse order, until right and happiness again prevail. Another Hindu story states that a world tree, or tree of knowledge, reached to heaven. In its pride it resolved to spread its branches over the earth and bring all men under them to protect them and prevent their separation one from another. Brahma, however, cut off its branches and cast them upon the earth. They sprang up as *Wata* trees and caused the differences in belief, speech, and customs, which now prevail and which have dispersed men over the earth. A Brahmanical theory of the four ages divides them into the Golden, Silver, Bronze, and Iron ages. Men are now in the Iron age of the first Intermediate Period of the Period of Stability. From centenarians—100 years is the maximum age attained in this period— man will decline in longevity to the uppermost limit of 10 years of life. When this stage shall have been reached, human destiny will realize the worst. The majority of human beings will succumb to hunger, epidemics, and the sword. Finally, when the majority are dead, those who survive will be "converted," and again the duration of life will increase. A new intermediate age will then begin and the eternal cycle will resume. Nowhere in Hindu thought is there much incentive to progress.

The religious philosophers of India, viewing the world of nature through the disaffection of their introspection felt no impulse to study it. Contemplating its phenomena, they investigated none of them, deeming them but as *Maya*— delusion and temptation. So they gained no real knowledge of the world they lived in. Phenomenal life was to them but bondage to unreality. Their goal was liberation, [and] beyond this liberation lay the blessed Absolute or Nirvana . . . Guided by [the Upanishads] the enlightened soul might gain knowledge and clarity of purpose enabling it to dissolve desire and disentangle itself and its true goal of the Absolute from the illusions of the world.[1]

The idea of cyclical changes is further elaborated in Buddhism. A Buddhist account states that when the Great Period begins, the first

---

[1] TAYLOR, HENRY O., "Freedom of the Mind in History," p. 93, London, 1923.

portion of which is the Destructive age, the length of human life is 80,000 years. Then comes gradual moral deterioration and a corresponding decrease in the span of life. In the third period, the Period of Duration, the average length of life decreases to 10 years, but later increases to 80,000 years.

But Buddhist philosophy contains the concept of progress. Gautama taught that there was a cause for the wickedness of the world and that there was likewise reason to hope for its regeneration. Sensuous experience does not yield absolute happiness, and this is well, for unmitigated happiness offers no spur to higher ideals. Conversely, if life were all pain, men could only despair. The mingling of pleasure and pain is a hindrance to spiritual progress but makes its attainment possible. The highest progress will be realized beyond, rather than in, human experience. "Whereas everything born, brought into being, and organized, contains within itself the inherent necessity of dissolution, how can it be possible that such a being should not be discovered? Decay is inherent in all component things."[1]

The Jains divide all time into 12 periods, nearly half of which have already transpired. The second half is a repetition in inverse order of the first. In the first age men lived an inexpressibly long time—three *palyas*—and attained a stature of approximately six miles. They were born as twins and when mature they procreated twins who became their successors. Ten varieties of miraculous trees furnished all that the heart could desire. The earth was sweet as sugar, the water as exhilarating as wine. This condition lasted for three ages, though in each succeeding period the length of life decreased, as did also the stature of men. The trees supplied needs more slowly, hence less adequately. Then, to insure the fulfilment of needs, individuals appropriated the trees as personal property. Then, too, one man, the first patriarch, was appointed to maintain order among his fellows. In the fifth and the sixth ages life will decrease to 16 years, the stature of men will shrink to a cubit, and the pendulum of the ages will then swing back.

The problem of length of days intrigues Hindu, Buddhist, Jain, Hebrew, Greek, primitive man, and many a Bernard Shaw. Poor mundane man, whose life is but a flitting phantom in the stream of change, must not be denied the boon of length of days, for only once is the drama of this world unrolled before his eyes, and, however bitterly he complains, he is loth to leave the earthly scene.[2]

---

[1] "Book of the Great Decease, Bk V, 38; quoted in TAYLOR, HENRY O., "Ancient Ideals," vol. I, p. 98, New York, 1900.

[2] See, for example, EYCLESHYMER, A. C., "Growing Old and the Search for an Elixir of Life," in *Sci. Monthly*, **26**: 400–411, 1928.

A Lama version states that the first men attained the age of 60,000 years. They were invisibly nourished and could raise themselves to the heavens when they wished. During this first period of the world all men were born twice. A thousand gods abode in heaven. But, unluckily for men, the earth, at last, produced a honey-sweet substance, of which one did taste and give to his companions. As a result of imbibing this drink men lost the power to rise from the earth, lost, too, their great size and their wisdom, and henceforth were compelled to eat the products of soil and toil. This is apparently a variant of the *Tantra* account that,

. . . originally the earth was uninhabited. In those times the inhabitants of *Abbaswara*, one of the heavenly mansions, used frequently to visit the earth, and thence speedily return. It happened at length that when a few of these beings, who though half male, half female, through the innocence of their minds had never noticed their distinction of sex, came as usual to the earth, Adi Buddha suddenly created in them so violent a longing to eat, that they ate some of the earth, which had the taste of almonds; and by eating it they lost their power of flying back to heaven, and so they remained on the earth. They were now constrained to eat the fruits of the earth for sustenance.[1]

A Sinhalese (Ceylon) account states that the Brahmas lived in perfect happiness in the higher regions of the air until,

. . . one of them beholding the earth said to himself, What thing is this? and with one of his fingers having touched the earth, he put it to the tip of his tongue, and perceived the same to be deliciously sweet; from that time all the Brahmas ate of the sweet earth for the space of 60,000 years. In the meantime, having coveted in their hearts the enjoyment of this earth, they began to say to one another, this part is mine and that is thine; and so fixing boundaries to their respective shares, divided the earth between them. On account of the Brahmas having been guilty of covetousness, the earth lost its sweetness, and then brought forth a kind of mushroom.[2]

This the Brahmas coveted and divided, but they were deprived of it also. They tasted one food after another, until their nature was transformed, they ceased to be spiritual beings, became human, developed wicked propensities, and eventually lost every vestige of their ancient glory.

3. Iranian Concepts of Progress

In early Persian literature, men are described as originally humble of heart, pure in thought, word, and deed. But Ahriman, the evil spirit,

---

[1] Hodgson, "Buddhism," p. 63.

[2] Baring-Gould, S., "Legends of the Patriarchs and Prophets and Other Old Testament Characters from Various Sources," p. 37, New York, n. d.

tempted them to drink goat's milk and to eat the fruit which he had brought them.

Then the Div, the liar, grown more bold, presented himself a second time, and brought with him fruit of which they ate; and of a hundred excellencies they before possessed, they now retained not one. And after 30 days and nights they found a white and fat sheep, and they cut off its left ear; and they fired a tree, and with their breath raised the fire to a flame; and they burned part of the branches of that tree, then of the tree *khorma*, and afterwards of the myrtle; and they roasted the sheep, and divided it into three portions: and of the two which they did not eat, one was carried to heaven by the bird *Kehrkas*. Afterwards they feasted on the flesh of a dog, and they clothed themselves in its skin. They gave themselves up to the chase, and with the furs of wild beasts they covered their bodies. And Meschia and Meschiane digged a hole in the earth and they found iron, and the iron they beat with a stone; and they made for themselves an axe, and they struck at the roots of a tree, and they felled the tree and arranged its branches into a hut; and to God they gave no thanks; and the Divs took heart. And Meschia and Meschiane became enemies, and struck and wounded each other and separated; then from out of the place of darkness the chief of the Divs was heard to cry aloud: O man, worship the Divs! And the Div of Hate sat upon the throne. And Meschia approached and drew milk from the bull, and sprinkled it toward the north, and the Divs became strong. But during fifty winters, Meschia and Meschiane lived apart; and after that time they met, and Meschiane bare twins.[1]

The *Dinkart*, a Zoroastrian compilation of the ninth century A.D., describes four periods: a Golden, a Silver, a Bronze, and an Iron age. In the last the villains are in authority, goodness and virtue decay, and honor and wisdom disappear from the land of Iran. In Hushetar's millennium the enclosure will be opened which Yima made to house a chosen host of men, animals, plants, and fires, in order to insure their preservation during the coming harsh winters. A thousand years after Hushetar, a second son of Zarathustra will be born, Ukhshyatnemah, who, when thirty years of age, will confer with the archangels. He will inaugurate the last millennium. When it has passed, the third miraculous son of Zarathustra will be born, though, more frequently, this third expected restorer of religion is called *Saoshyant*, i.e., "savior," "helper." The time preceding the coming of the three restorers of faith will be marked by misery and impiety, but after their advent the final conflict will open the way to eternal bliss. Old age will not bring feebleness, life will lengthen, and humility and peace will prevail throughout the earth. At the end of the world, men will not need food and they will cast no shadow, that is, presumably, they will have neither material needs nor

---

[1] *Ibid.*, pp. 38–39.

material embodiment. To have originated faith in the significance and purpose of history, it has been said, was "Zarathustra's greatest gift to mankind."[1] But since all the Mediterranean cultures shared this faith, the Iranian contribution is not unique, and, indeed, may have been borrowed from Babylonia.[2]

4. BABYLONIAN CONCEPTS OF PROGRESS

In one of the earliest of their myths the Babylonians describe evil as inherent in human nature, for man was made from the blood of Kingu, the god who "caused the strife, led the rebellion, and brought on the battle" which well nigh resulted in the destruction of the gods. Here as in other early Mediterranean civilizations, there is a sense of the prevalence of evil in the world and in human society; the struggle against it constitutes the tragedy of human existence. The Babylonian version of the Sumerian epic of Gilgamesh, which dates from the twenty-first century B.C., is dominated by a sense of bitter frustration, and declares that the gods have cheated man of the gift of life. "When the gods first made man, they allotted to him death, and life they held in their own keeping." In spite of the labors of the hero, fate denies him the one boon which he asks: "that mine eyes may continue to see the light of the sun."

Later Babylonian thought describes a succession of metal ages, representing them as Gold, Silver, Copper (or Bronze), and Iron, and associating them with the heavenly bodies. The Golden age is the age of Saturn; the Copper (or Bronze) age that of Istar-Venus. The Iron age, the end of evil times, precedes the destruction of the world. It is a time of cursing, tribulation, and a reversal of the natural order. "Then will clear become dull, the pure dirty, the lands will fall into confusion, prayers will not be heard, the signs of the prophets will become unfavorable." The ruler will not obey the commands of the gods. "Under his rule the one will devour the other, the people will sell their children for gold, the husband will desert the wife, the wife her husband, the mother will bolt the door against her daughter."[3] Dire distress will precede the flood which will sweep over the earth. Hope of salvation reposes in the king, who will restore the rule of the gods on earth. Hammurapi (about 2350 B.C.), like other Babylonian rulers, was a descendant of the gods, and their representative on earth. The belief prevailed that he would inaugurate a golden age of peace, and after his death his return was expected.[4]

---

[1] SÖDERBLOM, NATHAN, "Ages of the World (Iranian)," in ERE.

[2] See the author's "Messiahs: Christian and Pagan," chap. I, Boston, 1918.

[3] There is a similar strain in Hesiod and in the New Testament; see, below, p. 233, and Matthew, **10**: 34–38.

[4] See the author's "Messiahs: Christain and Pagan," pp. 15–16, 18, Boston, 1918.

5. EGYPTIAN CONCEPTS OF PROGRESS

The early literature of Egypt describes the rule of divine beings on earth when the men of old "listened to the gods," and attained the "honor of great age." A more perfect condition prevailed in primeval times, yet rebellion, deceit, and wickedness of all kinds appeared among gods and men, even when the gods ruled. The hope for a restoration of the rule of the gods became an anticipation. Thus, in a document which is as old as 1500 B.C. and may be much older, Ipuwer, after picturing the calamities which have come to the land, declares:

He bringeth coolness upon that which is hot. It is said he is the herdsman of mankind. No evil is in his heart. When his herds are few, he passes the day to gather them together, their hearts being on fire. Would that he had perceived their nature in the first generation of mankind; then he would have repressed evil, he would have stretched forth his arm against it; he would have destroyed their seed and their inheritance. Where is he to-day? Is he sleeping? Behold his might is seen.

The prophecy has been interpreted as heralding a coming prince who will rescue his people, heal them of their affliction, and restore Egypt to her former place of prestige and power. Possibly, however, it refers to the god Re, who will return to earth, perhaps in the person of a future king, and restore peace and prosperity.[1]

An Egyptian myth recorded by Diodorus Siculus states that Osiris lived with his sister Isis, who was also his wife, in Nysa, or Paradise, then located in Arabia. Nysa, a steep island mountain, accessible from only one side, was surrounded by the stream Triton. Beautiful flowers adorned it, and trees laden with pleasant fruits and watered by sweet streams. Within its confines dwelt the deathless ones. There Osiris found the vine, and Isis, wheat, the one to furnish drink to men, the other, food. There, too, they built a golden temple, and lived in unalloyed happiness until Osiris became possessed of a desire to discover the water of immortality. To search for this he left Nysa, and finally was slain by Typhon.

6. THE HEBREW CONCEPT OF SOCIAL PROGRESS

The original condition of man is described in Genesis. The etiological element is prominent, but many phases of the account reflect a background of speculation on man's progress in the past and on his capacity for future progress. Man was created peaceable and sociable and was placed in a favorable environment. Nature was made for man and was to be his servant. The stars and the moon were hung in the heavens to give him light by night, the sun to give him light by day. Plants and

---

[1] See the author's "Messiahs: Christian and Pagan," pp. 16–18, Boston, 1918.

animals were created to serve his needs; and man was made lord of the
world, and given command over the beasts. Into this paradise came
the Creator, august and forbidding, yet anthropomorphic, walking in the
garden in the cool of the envening, discoursing with the Adam whom he
had created, seeing his work and calling it good. For Adam, God had a
measure of fellow-feeling, as indeed he well might have, for Adam was
created in God's image, and God desired to make Adam's lot a happy one.
Hence the advent of woman. But Paradise was encompassed with dangers.
Potential evils lurked within its bounds. The highway of happiness was
not free from pitfalls which, though labeled, were enticing and aroused a
curiosity which must be satisfied. Man was told not to taste of the fruit
of the tree of the knowledge of good and evil, but the serpent tempted
Eve, and Eve tempted Adam.[1]

The Christian Fathers were inclined to interpret the story of Creation,
like much of Genesis, allegorically. Origen, for example, says:

What man of sense will suppose that the first and second and the third
day and the evening and the morning existed without a sun, or moon and
stars? Who is so foolish as to believe that God, like a husbandman, planted a
garden in Eden and placed in it a tree of life, that might be seen and touched,
so that one who tasted of the fruits by his bodily lips obtained life?[2]

Tertullian gave an esoteric interpretation to the fig leaves.[3] St.
Augustine interpreted Eden as the life of the blessed and the four rivers
as the four virtues; though he also refers to Eden as the Church and the
four rivers as the four Gospels. Richard Baxter explains the Genesis
account as follows:

At his first Creation man was subjected to none but God: though it was
provided in Nature, that there should have been Government and Subjection

---

[1] "Certain Rabbis say that Adam ate only on compulsion, that he refused but
Eve 'took of the tree,'—that is, broke a branch and 'gave it him,' with the stick.

"According to the Talmudic book, 'Emek Hammelech,' Eve, on eating the
fruit, felt in herself the poison of *Jezer bara,* or original sin, and resolved that Adam
should not be without it also; she made him eat and then forced the fruit on the
animals, that they might all, without exception, fall under the same condemnation,
and become subject to death. But the bird *Chol*—that is, the Phœnix—would not be
deceived, but flew away and would not eat. And now the Phœnix, says the Rabbi
Joden after the Rabbi Simeon, lives a thousand years, then shrivels up till it is the
size of an egg, and then from himself he emerges young and beautiful again."—
BARING-GOULD, S., *op. cit.,* p. 45.

[2] ORIGEN, "De Princip.," IV, 1, 7–16.

[3] TERTULLIAN, "De Pall.," p. 13; see HALLIDAY, W. R., "The Pagan Background
of Early Christianity," pp. 206–207, Liverpool, 1925; and LIPPMANN, WALTER,
"A Preface to Morals," p. 37, New York, 1929.

though man had continued innocent: but that would have been only a Paternal assisting Government for our good, having nothing in it that is penal, or any way evil. When God immediate Ruled, and man obeyed, all went right: Had this continued, the world had not felt those fractures and wounds, nor been troubled with rapines, wars, or confusion, as it is. God being most perfectly Wise and Just, could not err in Commanding: Man was innocent and able to obey, but free and mutable: and so was tempted from his Obedience. Satan by disobedience having overthrown himself, did know it was the way to overthrow man. God could not be corrupted, nor tempted to unwise or unrighteous Government: And if neither King nor subject were corrupted, the Kingdom could not have decayed. But Satan knew which was the weakest link in the chain: Man was frail, though holy; and not confirmed yet, though upright: and therefore defectible. The attempt of breaking his rank, and forsaking his due subjection, was the Devil's fall: and by the same way he assaulted man, inciting in him a desire to be as God, and then provoking him to seek it by disobeying God: A Foolish means to an impossible or impious end. The breach being thus made between man and his universal King, the joynts of holy order were loosed, and a breach was made also between man and himself, and man and the inferiour creatures, and enmity and confusion took possession in the world. The creatures Rebell against their Master turned Rebell: His own passions and appetite Rebell against his Reason: and the seeds of all the Confusions that have followed in the world, were sown within us. As the enmity between the woman's and the Serpent's seed being propagated to posterity, is the great quarrel of the world, so all those vices in which the Malignant enmity doth consist, are propagated and by custom receive an increase.[1]

When man acquired knowledge he lost his pristine innocence, and knowledge encompassed his fall. The immediate cause of the fall was disobedience, but the acquisition of knowledge was at the root of it. The Hebrew writer exhibits the subtle discernment that he who lacks understanding lacks responsibility. Man was punished by being excluded from this happy paradise and from frequent direct communion with God, and was condemned to earn his living by the sweat of his brow, *i.e.*, by agriculture. Work was an evil. The leisure of Paradise was bliss and work was a curse and a nuisance; now he who would eat must work. Nor did Adam's descendants fare well. Abel and Cain followed different occupations; Cain was a hunter and a tiller of the soil, and Abel a keeper of flocks. When God looked with favor upon the offerings of Abel and rejected those of Cain, Cain's jealousy turned to murder. And it was doubtless in part because the one was a keeper of flocks and the other a hunter and an agriculturist that it chanced, as they were in the fields, that Cain killed Abel. Or did this merely symbolize the struggle of agricultural with pastoral life, of settled abode with nomadism?

---

[1] BAXTER, RICHARD, "A Holy Commonwealth," pp. 200–201, London, 1659.

Perhaps there is some basis for the version in the Jewish Book of Jasher of this first quarrel:

One day the flock of Abel ran over the ground Cain had been ploughing; Cain rushed furiously upon him and bade him leave the spot. "Not," said Abel, "till you have paid me for the skins of my sheep and the wool of their fleeces used for your clothing." Then Cain took the coulter from his plough, and with it slew his brother.[1]

Apparently many Israelites had never become reconciled to settled abode. Their earliest written documents reflect the view that only the nomadic life was blessed by Jahweh. He rejects the offerings of Cain, the farmer, and accepts those of Abel, the keeper of flocks. When Adam was driven from Paradise and was punished he was not given sheep to tend, but the soil to till. The patriarchs were nomads or half-nomads, and the glamour of their day hung over the writers of the traditions of the Chosen People. The curse is upon the tiller of the soil; the first farmer was the first sinner, and the second farmer, Cain, was the first murderer. The descendants of the accursed farmer Cain built the first cities and invented the instruments and the arts of civilization, and the wickedness of his descendants brought the flood. The cities of the plain were destroyed, and Lot, a nomad who had been enticed by their wickedness and glitter, lost his wife and escaped only with his life.[2]

During successive generations things went from bad to worse. A primitive peace was followed by bickerings, jealousies, antagonisms, and hardships. Man refused to follow the dictates of God, failed to obey the behests of the higher spirit, we would say. Finally the Deity decided that the experiment with man was a failure and that he would destroy him so that he would no longer encumber the earth and be a reproach to his Creator. Yet God softened his heart and decided to let live Noah and his family, and two members of each species of animals.[3] But henceforth men would not achieve the ripe old age of their forebears. Adam had attained an age of 930 years; Seth lived to be 912;

---

[1] The Rabbi Menachem, however, ingeniously argues that the cause of the quarrel was a dispute as to whether a certain word was written *zizit* or *zizis* in the "Parascha." Some Jewish accounts attribute the quarrel to a dispute over a sister who was desired as wife, and others allege it was a dispute about ownership of the ground—or of the habitable earth.

[2] I have followed here the interpretation of CHESTER C. McCOWN in his "Genesis of the Social Gospel," pp. 136–138. Professor McCown appears to have been among the first to appreciate the significance of these chapters in Genesis as a record of speculations about progress; see also McFAYDEN, in *Hibbert Jour.*, **19**: 702–711, 1921.

[3] Similarly, the Egyptian god Re, incensed at the refractory character of men, ordered the goddess Sechet to destroy the human race, but later repented and spared it.

Enos attained the age of 905; Cainan was 910 years of age; Mahalaleel was 895; Jared was 962; Enoch was 365; Methusalah was 969; Lamech was 777; and Noah reached the age of 950, a duration of life exceeded by only two of his ancestors—Jared and Methusalah. God decided that in the future the limit of man's life would be 120 years, and later three-score years and ten was made the usual limit, which few would exceed. And so it remains today. Yet "death did not first strike Adam, the first sinful man, nor Cain, the first hypocrite, but Abel, the innocent and righteous."

From Noah the human experiment started again, and this second Adam became the ancestor of post-diluvial humanity. But again, difficulties developed, for man was wayward. Instead of adapting himself to the requirements of God, he sought to protect himself from God's just wrath by building a tower which would reach to the heavens and be a place of refuge in the event of another flood. Men tried to escape the penalty of their iniquities rather than to uproot them; and for this presumption they were punished by being compelled to speak mutually unintelligible tongues. The ensuing inability to understand one another was fertile soil for dissension. The story of the tower of Babel, suggests Chesterton,

might be interpreted in many ways—religiously, as meaning that spiritual insolence starts all human separations; irreligiously, as meaning that the inhuman heavens grudge man his magnificent dream; or merely satirically as suggesting that all attempts to reach a higher agreement always end in more disagreement than there was before . . . But when all was said, the symbol would remain that a plain tower, as straight as a sword, as simple as a lily, did nevertheless produce the deepest divisions that have been known among men. . . . For whatever reason, what is said to have happened to the people of Shinak has precisely and practically happened to us.[1]

To diversity of languages were added racial distinctions, and the earth was sown with the seeds of disharmony which have since brought forth fruit abundantly. Henceforth the story is not about mankind, but about the Hebrews, the Chosen People, whom God favored and exalted above all others. The tribal point of view prevailed, for Jahweh was a tribal god. Not until a later time, during the days of the Major Prophets, was Jahweh regarded as the only God, as the Jehovah who controlled other nations as well as Israel. He used them as a scourge for Israel, for he was not interested in them for their own sakes, but only as instruments to the greater good of his Chosen People. During the period of Old

---

[1] CHESTERTON, GILBERT K., "Utopia of Usurers and other Essays," pp. 174–175, New York, 1917. On the importance of language as a social bond, see MARETT, ROBERT R., "Anthropology," EB, 2: 44, 14th ed., 1929.

Testament history, therefore, the religious conception underwent considerable development. At first God dealt merely with individuals; then he took under his care families; after the family, the kin group; finally, the nation. The post-exilic prophets coveted better things for Israel, and preached a doctrine of national regeneration. By straying from the path of righteousness Israel had fallen; by forsaking evil and following righteousness, salvation would be achieved. Their hope for progress did not include other nations; for about the salvation of other peoples the Hebrews troubled themselves not at all. Consequently, the early Christians, who were Jews, were not receptive to the message that the new religion should not be limited to the Chosen People but should include all humanity, irrespective of race or nationality; and even at the present day neither Jews nor Christians desire to have all other races on an equal footing either on earth or in heaven.[1] The messianic idea, which arose after the Babylonian captivity, or earlier, some have considered the highest exemplification of the idea of progress; yet, from one point of view, it is the despair of progress, the hope that God will intervene miraculously because man unassisted cannot achieve salvation. The messianic aspiration which has permeated Jewish thought for 2,500 years still survives among the orthodox.[2]

7. Mohammedan Concepts of Progress

A Mohammedan version of the Fall, which is obviously of Jewish or Christian inspiration, explains the matter in this wise:

Before the Fall, wheat grew to a tree with leaves like emeralds. The ears were red as rubies and the grains white as snow, sweet as honey, and fragrant as musk. Eve ate one of the grains and found it more delicious than anything she had hitherto tasted, so she gave a second grain to Adam. Adam resisted at first, according to some authorities for a whole hour, but an hour in Paradise was 80 years of our earthly reckoning. But when he saw that Eve remained well and cheerful, he yielded to her persuasions, and ate of the second grain which Eve had offered him daily, three times a day, during the hour of 80 years. Thereupon all Adam's heaven-given raiment fell from him, his crown slipped off his head, his rings dropped from his fingers, his silken garments glided like

---

[1] "We give up our own immortality sooner than believe that all the hosts of Hottentots and Australians that have been, and shall ever be, should share it with us in *sæcula sæculorum*. Life is a good thing on a reasonably copious scale; but the very heavens themselves, and the cosmic times and spaces, would stand aghast, we think, at the notion of preserving eternally such an ever-swelling plethora and glut of it . . . Our culture has humanized us . . . but we cannot yet conceive them as our comrades in the field of heaven."—James, William, "Human Immortality: Two Supposed Objections to the Doctrine," pp. 70–73, London, 1906.

[2] See the author's "Messiahs: Christian and Pagan," chap. I, Boston, 1918.

water from his shoulders, and he and Eve were naked and unadorned, and their fallen garments reproached them with the words, "Great is your misfortune; long will be your sorrows; we were created to adorn those who serve God; farewell till the resurrection!"

The throne recoiled from them and exclaimed, "Depart from me, ye disobedient ones!" The horse Meimun, which Adam sought to mount, plunged and refused to allow him to touch it, saying, "How hast thou kept God's covenant?" All the inhabitants of Paradise turned their backs on the pair, and prayed God to remove the man and the woman from the midst of them. God himself addressed Adam with a voice of thunder, saying, "Did not I forbid thee to touch of this fruit, and caution thee against the subtlety of thy foe, Eblis?" Adam and Eve tried to fly these reproaches, but the branches of the tree Talh caught Adam, and Eve entangled herself in her long hair. "From the wrath of God there is no escape," cried a voice from the tree Tahl; "obey the commandment of God." "Depart from Paradise," then spake God, "thou Adam, thy wife, and the animals which led you into sin. The earth shall be your abode; in the sweat of thy brow shalt thou find food; the produce of earth shall cause envy and contention; Eve (Hava) shall be afflicted with a variety of strange affections, and shall bring forth offspring in pain. The peacock shall lose its melodious voice, and the serpent its feet; dark and noisome shall be the den in which the serpent shall dwell, dust shall be its meat, and its destruction shall be a meritorious work. Eblis shall be cast into the torments of hell." Our parents were then driven out of Paradise, and one leaf alone was given to each, wherewith to hide their nakedness. Adam was expelled through the Gate of Repentance, that he might know that through it alone could Paradise be regained; Eve was banished through the gate of grace; the peacock and the serpent through that of Wrath, and Eblis through the Gate of Damnation. Adam fell into the island Serendib (Ceylon), Eve at Jedda, the Serpent into the desert of Sahara, the peacock into Persia, and Eblis into the river Eila. Tabari says that when the forbidden wheat had entered the belly of Adam and Eve, all the skin came off, except from the ends of the fingers. Now this skin had been pink and horny, so that they had been invulnerable in Paradise, and they were left naked and with a tender skin which could easily be lacerated; but as often as Adam and Eve looked on their fingernails, they remembered what skin they had worn in Eden.

Tabari also says that four trees pitying the shame of Adam and Eve, the Peacock, and the Serpent, in being driven naked out of Paradise, bowed their branches and gave each a leaf.[1]

---

[1] BARING-GOULD, S., *op. cit.*, 43–45.

Chapter XIII

GREEK THEORIES OF PROGRESS

1. Homer

The "Agon," which in its present form does not antedate the second century A.D., attributes to Homer the statement, "Never to be born at all is best for mortal men, and if born to pass as soon as may be the gates of Hades." But this is apocryphal. There is in the "Odyssey," however, an account of the Elysian plain and also of the Phæacians, dear to the immortals, whose banquets the gods visited in person. The golden palace of Alcinous, in which the leaders of the Phæacians eat and drink to their content, stands gleaming like the sun, while without are various kinds of trees which bear never-failing fruits. Their large black marvelous ships speed smoothly and swiftly, without oar, sail, or crew, to the remotest ends of the earth, and bring back highly valued merchandise. Olympus, the abode of the gods, is without wind, rain, or snow, the sun eternally bright, the skies cloudless. Homer describes also an island on which hunger and disease are unknown and goods are abundant. To it Apollo and Artemis remove men by an easy death when old age encroaches. The king of the island is compared with the immortal gods. Menelaus is told that he will not die in Argos: the gods will transport him to the Elysian plain at the ends of the earth, where men have an easy life, for Ocean sends up the breezes of Zephyrus to soften the climate, and there is no rain, snow, or cold. The "Odyssey" speaks also of

an island called Syria, as you may have heard, over above Ortygia where are the turning places of the sun [that is, where the sun turns back from its setting in the west]. It is not very thickly peopled, but a good land, rich in herds and flocks and wine and corn. No death is there nor sickness for mortals; but when people grow old, silver-bowed Apollo comes and slays them with his painless arrows. In the island there are two cities, and all the land is divided between them.[1]

2. Hesiod

Many of the ideas in Genesis are probably primitive elements which had long been current among the people. Some of them were placed in

---

[1] "Odyssey," 15, 404ff. This *motif* reappears in later Greek writing; see below, p. 261.

writing in the ninth century B.C., practically in the form now preserved in the Bible. Probably the "Works and Days" and the "Theogony" of Hesiod were written in the eighth century B.C. Like the writers of Genesis, Hesiod was much interested in human progress. Work was no evil, but war was the worst calamity known to man. In fact, work was a blessing rather than an evil, and poverty was better than riches. "Work is no reproach; the reproach is idleness." Yet elsewhere Hesiod appears to regard work as a necessary evil, which increased in the successive epochs through which the human race passed. He does not, like the writer of Job, ponder pessimistically the problem, Why does the evildoer flourish while the upright and the holy are afflicted? but declares that the gods punish vice and reward virtue, especially justice. Man, however, is not an entirely free agent. The will of Zeus is unescapable and the fates hold in store harsh circumstances which man must face. Responsibility for the evils in the world is laid not upon man but upon the gods. Originally the human race was happy, but Pandora brought to earth blessings mixed with evil, and released envy, which destroyed much of the prevailing beneficence. Thereafter, the lot of man would have been unendurable, but for the retention of hope, which has remained to alleviate his sad plight. Through the tangled mesh of encompassing evils hope beckons him to a happier future. In the "Works and Days" Hesiod describes a first and Golden age, in which all men lived happily and enjoyed great length of life without the feebleness which now accompanies old age. In the next period, the Silver age, life was long but old age was accompanied by feebleness, though only late in life did it creep upon one. This was followed, in turn, by the Bronze age, the Heroic age, the Iron age. As one age followed another, man lost many desirable traits, and in the later metal age learned the arts of war. Strife became more prevalent, and war degraded men to a lower plane.

But the story deserves telling in more detail and in Hesiod's own words. The men of the first period, then, the men of the Golden age,

lived like gods without sorrow of heart, remote and free from toil and grief: miserable age rested not on them; but with legs and arms never failing they made merry with feasting beyond the reach of all evils. When they died, it was as though they were overcome with sleep, and they had all good things; for the fruitful earth unforced bare them fruit abundantly and without stint. They dwelt in ease and peace upon their lands with many good things, rich in flocks and loved by the blessed gods.

The men of this age became the benign spirits which still roam the earth. They "are kindly, delivering from harm, and guardians of mortal men." Then the gods on Olympus made another race of men, like the Golden race neither in body nor in spirit. A child was brought up at his good mother's side an hundred years, in utter simplicity, playing like a child in his own home. But when they were fully grown and were come to the full measure of their prime, they lived only a little time and that in sorrow because of their foolishness, for they could not keep from sinning and from wronging one another, nor would they serve the immortals, nor sacrifice on the holy altars of the blessed ones as it is right for men to do wherever they dwell.

Because they had little religious piety they were thrust aside to make room for the next generation of men and became the blessed spirits of the underworld, spirits of the second order. Then came the Bronze race, sprung from ash trees [a race terrifying because of their ashen spear shafts]. These Bronze-age men were inferior to those of the Silver age, though they were fearsome and strong. They loved war and deeds of violence. "They ate no bread, but were hard of heart like adamant, fearful men. Great was their strength and unconquerable the arms which grew from their shoulders on their strong limbs. Their armor was of bronze, and their houses of bronze, and of bronze were their implements: there was no black iron." But their ferocity was suicidal. "These were destroyed by their own hands and passed to the dank houses of chill Hades, and left no name: terrible though they were, black death seized them, and they left the bright light of the sun." The fourth generation of men was nobler and more righteous,

a god-like race of heroes, who are called demi-gods, the race before our own, throughout the boundless earth. Grim war and dread battle destroyed a part of them . . . But to the others father Zeus, the son of Chronos, gave a living and an abode apart from men, and made them dwell at the ends of earth. And they live untouched by sorrow in the islands of the blessed along the shore of deep-swirling Ocean, happy heroes for whom the grain-giving earth bears honey-sweet fruit flourishing thrice a year, far from the deathless gods, and Chronos rules over them.

Now, most hopeful and most tragic of all, comes the fifth type, the present race of men.

For now truly is a race of iron, and men never rest from labor and sorrow by day, and from perishing by night; and the gods shall lay sore trouble upon them. But, notwithstanding, even these shall have some good mingled with their evils. And Zeus will destroy this race of mortal men also when they have gray hair on the temples at their birth.[1] The father will not agree with his

---

[1] Premising a degeneration of the race which will proceed until, at last, even a newborn child will show the marks of old age, and men will be old at birth. This suggests Hindu influence; see above, p. 219.

children, nor the children with their father, nor the guest with his host, nor comrade with comrade; nor will brother be dear to brother as aforetime. Men will dishonor their parents as they grow quickly old, and will carp at them, chiding them with bitter words, hard-hearted they, not knowing the fear of the gods.[1] They will not repay their aged parents the cost of their nurture, for might shall be their right; and one man will sack another's city. There will be no favor for the man who keeps his oath nor for the just nor for the good; but rather men will praise the evildoer and his violent dealing. Strength will be right and reverence will cease to be; and the wicked will hurt the worthy man, speaking false words against him, and will swear an oath upon them. Envy, foul-mouthed, delighting in evil, with scowling face will go along with wretched men one and all. And then Aidos and Nemesis,[2] with their sweet forms wrapped in white robes, will go from the wide-pathed earth and forsake mankind to join the company of the deathless gods: and bitter sorrows will be left for mortal men, and there will be no help against evil.

Hesiod's closing strain is the antithesis of Browning's "All's well with the world," but he does not utterly despair of the times. Though they are bad enough, they might be worse and they can be improved. Man must counter fate by making the best of the world in which he lives. Industry, economy, thrift, the homely virtues, will lighten the lot of the individual and make him glad to live among men. And so the old rhyme:

> Next came old Hesiod, teaching us husbandry,
> Ploughing and sowing and rural affairs,
> Rural economy, rural astronomy,
> Homely morality, labor, and thrift.

Hesiod, therefore, has a concept of progress, else he could not compare the worth of life in the past with that in the present; and although he asserts that his civilization is not superior to that of the past, he does not dismiss the possibility of progress. Rather, in his advices to farmers and to citizens, he implies that progress beyond the achievements of contemporary life is a possibility and that the power to attain it lies with those whose will is equal to the task.

---

[1] Compare Matthew, 10: 34–36: "Think not that I am come to send peace upon earth: I came not to send peace, but a sword. For I am come to set a man at variance against his father, and the daughter against her mother, and the daughter-in-law against here mother-in-law. And a man's foes shall be they of his own household."

[2] *Nemesis* is righteous indignation, especially that aroused by the sight of the wicked enjoying an undeserved prosperity; while *aidos* is a quality of reverence or shame, akin to a feeling of propriety, which restrains men from committing wrong. *Aidos* has been defined as "shame at all things shameful and reverence for all things to be revered." TAYLOR, HENRY O., "Human Values and Verities," p. 239, New York, 1928.

3. Theognis and Anacreon

Theognis, an impoverished squire who lived in Megara, between Corinth and Athens, wrote in the third quarter of the sixth century B.C. his "Elegies and Proverbs," wherein he laments:

It is not for nothing, Plutus, that mortals do honor thee most, for of truth thou bearest distress with ease. For, verily, it is fitting for the bettermost to have wealth indeed, but poverty is proper for a mean man to bear. Many dunces have riches. Others, though harassed by severe poverty, seek what is noble, but impossibilities of working lie beside both. The one is impeded by want of riches, the other, by want of intellect. For to the multitude of men there is this virtue only, namely, to be rich, but of the rest I wot there is no use. Nay, then 'tis right that all should lay up this maxim, that wealth has the most power among all.

Anacreon, a poet of the second half of this century, disparages wealth:

> What avails ingenuous worth,
> Sprightly wit or noble birth?
> All these virtues useless prove,
> Gold alone engages love.
> May he be completely cursed
> Who the sleeping mischief first
> Wak'd to life:
> Gold creates in brethern strife,
> Gold destroys the parent's life;
> Gold produces civil jars,
> Murders, massacres and wars.
> But the worst effect of gold,
> Love, alas, is bought and sold.[1]

4. Pre-Socratic Speculation

The pre-Socratic philosophers merely touched the fringes of the problem of progress and their treatment of it is only incidental. According to Heraclitus most men live like the beasts, reveling in mud and, like worms, eating earth. They are born, bring forth their young, and die without any higher end in life than the continuation of themselves and their kind. The things for which the masses strive, the wise man despises as worthless and perishable. Yet he does not follow his own caprice, but the common law is his standard. He avoids most of all presumption, the overstepping of the bounds set for the individual and for human nature. In thus subjecting himself to the order of the whole he attains that satisfaction which Heraclitus considers the highest end of life. He who will can be happy. To criticize the world

---

[1] Quoted in Beer, Max, "Social Struggles in Antiquity," pp. 58–59, Boston, n. d.

order is absurd; it is as it ought to be and men must adapt themselves to it. The character of a man resides in his dæmon, and as with individuals so with State and community. Law is the basis of society and a nation must fight for its laws as for its walls. The sovereignty of law is infringed whether an individual or the masses rule arbitrarily. Heraclitus counsels concord as indispensable to the State and champions individual freedom, but despises democracy because it rejects the best men and will not tolerate preeminent greatness. *Panta rhei*—all things are in flux, but Heraclitus does not suggest that these incessant changes promise progress.

Empedocles accepts the view that things are in a continual flux, but emphasizes the importance of the emotions of love and hate. In the original condition of society all were happy, food was abundant, and Venus reigned—to man's great felicity. Later, however, enmity and war expelled love. Eventually men will be more like the gods, indeed, their souls will become godlike. Although man degenerated in the past, there will be progress in the future; but Empedocles paints no clear picture of the paradise which awaits mankind.

Happiness, declares Democritus, is attained only through labor, but misery comes unsought. Yet all the means to happiness are available to man and he alone is responsible if he fails to use them properly. The gods give man only good, but human folly turns it into evil. Character is determined by conduct. Happiness consists in utilizing and contenting oneself with the things one has. Life is short, shabby, and exposed to many vicissitudes. The man who recognizes this fact is satisfied with moderate possessions and is content and happy if he secures the necessities of life. The things really needed are easily acquired; discontent is inspired by imaginary wants. The Sophists, the last of an old school and the founders of a new, developed a philosophy of relativity in social and ethical standards. Distinctions are not rooted in the nature of things, but exist only in the mind; good and evil are relative to person, place, and time. "Nothing is either good or bad, but thinking makes it so." In themselves, institutions are neither good nor bad; the same institutions may be good in one age and to one people, and bad in another age and to another people. The Sophists challenged the assumption that the Greeks were superior to all other peoples. Their views provided a larger international culture perspective, and a broader basis for social theory. Greek civilization, they believed, was superior only when measured by Greek standards. Relativity raised the question of the validity of Greek norms, and stimulated a consideration of the actual and potential assets of the various cultures, such as Plato gives in the "Republic" and the "Laws," and Aristotle in the "Politics." The Stoics carried the doctrines of the Sophists to their logical conclusion, though the times furnished the inspiration.

Colonization, by its formation of new States with new laws, and reflection on the variety of customs in different tribes and peoples, seemed to make it doubtful if there was any absolute law in regard to human affairs. The Persian wars gave an impulse to freedom of thought by increasing both national and individual self-consciousness, a self-consciousness which first appears in the philosophy of Protagoras and Gorgias. Protagoras transferred his gaze from external nature to man, and declared that "man is the measure of all things," while Gorgias claimed that as a knowledge of nature is impossible, we ought to concentrate our attention on human affairs. It is man, subsequent Sophists went on to say, who in his own interest establishes the State and human institutions generally.[1]

The inference that laws and institutions exist, not by nature, but merely by convention, was inevitable. Current moral ideas are not divine ordinances; on the contrary, they are opposed to the ideal code of morality. The source of law is the individual's desire for pleasure and satisfaction. "Justice is the interest of the stronger."[2]

5. PLATO

In the "Politicus"[3] Plato (427–347 B.C.) refers to an early stage of the human race in which a divine king or demi-urge presided over men, managing everything for them, keeping them happy, and amply endowing them with the goods of this world. The universe, too, was under the direction of his guiding hand. Subsequently, however, that guidance was withdrawn from nature and from society, and men were compelled to accept human kings. This necessity reduced them to a state of misery, which, however, was alleviated by various gifts from the gods—fire from Prometheus, the arts from Hephæstus and Athene, plants and seeds from Demeter. Yet man's lot was filled with hardship and his path beset with difficulties. It remained for him, by selecting a suitable king, and by devising proper social machinery, so to reconstruct his world that these evils would be minimized. Plato, probably as a result of Hindu influence, describes four epochs of human history. The first age preceded the reign of Chronos, the second was synchronous with his reign, the third is the present age of Zeus during which the world moves of its own impetus, and the fourth age is yet to come. During the reign of Chronos, when God was at the helm, the universe

---

[1] WATSON, JOHN, "The State in Peace and War," p. 4, Glasgow, 1919.
[2] PLATO, "Republic."
[3] Sometimes called the "Statesman."

had a motion opposite to that of the present.[1] The age of all creatures came to a halt and then they grew younger and more tender. The hoary locks of the aged resumed their youthful light hue, the roughened cheeks of the bearded became smooth with youth, and men returned to the springtime of life. Their bodies diminished in size until they were no larger than those of new-born babes, and finally they faded away. Then from the earth the dead rose to live again.[2] This we know from our first forefathers who flourished immediately after the end of the first period and remembered these things. Lesser divinities, or dæmons, presided over affairs on earth, and there was neither savagery nor war; there was neither government nor marriage, and creatures were not begotten after their kind, for all came up from the underworld to live again on earth. In a later work, the "Republic," Plato turns attention to the reorganization of society and pictures the ideal city-state. The evils of the present city-state are excluded, and new factors of progress are introduced. The "Republic" is the first attempt[3] to set up, if only in words, an ideal State which man can fashion, thus controlling his social destiny. The ideal society described in the "Republic" is an amplification of the individual. As the individual is composed of three elements, emotion, will, and knowledge, so the State will have three classes: the workers, the warriors and guardians, and the rulers. The rulers will be philosophers, for they are capable of doing the best for the State. Children will be assigned to one of these respective classes according to their abilities, rather than according to birth or preference. In order that the favoritism and nepotism so rife in the Athens of Plato's day may find no place here, there will be communism in wives and children, and parents will not know their children, nor children their parents. Property is limited to a certain multiple of a fixed minimum amount. The inequalities of property, and the avarice and ambition which lead to the pursuit of riches are excluded. Plato pays much attention to education, and maps out a course of instruction to cover the periods from about two years of age to over thirty. Only those who prove themselves qualified will continue with the education designed to fit the élite to become rulers. The rulers need more education than any one else, and, accordingly, more is

---

[1] Doubtless the Hindu reversed cycle; see above, p. 217.

[2] Compare the belief of the Trobriand Islanders: "When a spirit becomes tired of constant rejuvenation, after he has led a long existence 'underneath,' as the natives call it, he may want to come back to life again. And then he leaps far back in age, and becomes a small, unborn infant." MALINOWSKI, BRONISLAW, "The Father in Primitive Psychology," pp. 30–31, New York, 1927.

[3] I.e., the first of those which have been preserved. Aristotle refers to several earlier or contemporary ones, but the treatises have been lost.

prescribed for them. Gymnastics play an important rôle, as do music and poetry, and military training is essential.

In his final work, the "Laws," Plato returns to the problems of the ideal society. Basic principles are revealed in the stages through which society has passed. The few individuals who survived the flood began anew the achievement of civilization. These remnants of the human race gathered on the top of a hill, for the waters had not subsided from the lowlands. Cattle were few and flocks small. The survivors had forgotten all knowledge of the metals, and practiced only weaving, pottery making, and the simpler handicrafts which preceded the metals. Gradually they acquired the lost arts, made progress in them, and established communities. Then came conflicts of interests and a need for laws to modify the customs and practices, not always harmonious, which had been adopted by the various groups before contact with one another. Originally man had been innocent of both the virtues and the vices which characterize later social life.

In the "Laws," as in the "Republic," Plato models the ideal community after the Spartan system, although he criticizes the Cretan assumption that war is the natural condition of man and the supreme end of the State; an assumption upon which the scheme of Spartan education is based. In his natural condition, man is an enemy to fellowman, and to himself. Thus there are foes to combat within as well as without the State. Laws must be framed to meet the needs of the individual, encourage virtue, and check vice. The "Laws" apportions the citizens into four classes. "Friends have all things in common"; hence the members of the commonwealth, being brothers, should share equally in one another's property. Yet the "Laws" makes concessions to the conservatism of human nature, and allows moderate wealth. Since gold and silver give rise to inequalities, they will be excluded, and iron will serve as money—an idea borrowed, no doubt, from Sparta. The community must be maintained intact. It will consist of 5,040[1] householders, or citizens, together with their families and slaves. The population will be kept down by prudential restraint, supplemented by advice from the elders to the young, postponement of the age of marriage, emigration and the establishment of colonies, and the adoption of sons by the childless, who, without increasing the number of citizens, will thus become the heads of households. The optimism which pervades the "Republic" is not found in the "Laws." Plato assesses human nature anew and does not exalt it.

---

[1] A mystic number, the product of 1, 2, 3, 4, 5, 6, 7—seven being a mystic number; see above, p. 76.

With the growing conservatism of age, Plato in the "Laws" clipped those wings of his imagination which had borne him aloft in the "Republic" into the blue. In his later work he took a lower flight, and hovered much nearer to Greek earth and Greek usage than when he had surveyed the whole world from the empyrean heights of pure idealism.[1]

The society described in the "Republic" is the best if only men knew it; but since they will not acknowledge the truth, let them receive less than the best. Yet Plato does not abandon ideals. Even though an ideal is unrealizable it is a guide or a goal, and better a goal worth striving for, though unattainable, than aimless wanderings amid ways which are less than the best. He is aware of the dangers which lurk in the acquisition of political power by individuals. Even in the happy days of mankind when all good things were abundant and spontaneous, "Chronos knew what we ourselves were declaring, that no human nature invested with supreme power is able to order human affairs and not overflow with insolence and wrong." So reflecting, the gods appointed as the rulers over men, not men but demigods, even as men do not trust sheep to rule over sheep, nor cattle over cattle, but themselves undertake this duty. The demigods protected men, established peace, reverence, order, and justice, and kept the respective tribes of men happy and united. Human rule inaugurated dissension, disorder, injustice, and revolt.[2]

In the "Republic" and the "Laws," Plato's imagination soars above the commonplace and transcends many of the traditional and contemporary limitations. But though Plato escapes much of the current superstition and bias, he does not transcend all the limitations of the day, some of which are the result of false inductions. One of these limitations is apparent in his division of the mind into will, emotion, and reason, watertight compartments conceived of as distinct entities, now one, now the other, presiding over the assemblage of mental states. Plato's analogy of individual and State, then, cannot be accepted. The State may be a personality, but it is on a different plane from that of the individual. There is no thorough-going parallelism of interests, activities, purposes, or functions. A State is not a magnified individual and an individual is not a miniature State. Group and individual are vastly different, and they

---

[1] FRAZER, SIR JAMES G., "The Cursing of Venizelos," *New Europe*, **2**: No. 19, 1917, and *Folklore*, **28**: 133–140, 1917; reprinted in WALLIS, WILSON D. and WILLEY, MALCOLM M., "Readings in Sociology," pp. 140–144, New York, 1930.

[2] Compare Wells: "Certainly there is no race so superior as to be trusted with human charges. The true answer to Aristotle's plea for slavery, that there are 'natural slaves,' lies in the fact that there are no 'natural' masters. Power is no more to be committed to men without discipline and restriction than alcohol." WELLS, HERBERT G., "A Modern Utopia," p. 337, New York, 1905; see below, p. 364.

achieve different ends.[1] The commonwealth is fixed rather than flexible; it is adamant though it should be plastic and susceptible of taking on new form and content from time to time, for history shows that no established form of social life is best for all time.[2] Plato's republic is static rather than dynamic, and there is no provision for expansion—either in numbers, function, purpose, or component elements. Moreover, his ideal commonwealth is not oriented in the larger social world. There is no attempt to provide for relations with other States, save incidentally, or to assess contributions from them or duties owing to them. Plato's thought has little reference to the larger international world, except to insist that no foreigners be admitted, for they would introduce exotic customs and laws, and these would produce frictions. Thus Plato makes the part larger than the whole, and so reverses the relations which hold in nature and in history. The error is more easily excused in a man of his day than in one of ours; but it is none the less a shortsightedness. In brief, the "Republic" ignores the larger social and political world. The State is cast in Athenian molds and no provision is made for extraneous influences. That Athens was not and could not be apart to itself Plato seems not to have realized. Yet he points out that man may rid himself of present ills by constructing a new social order, one based on reason, where all important activities are subordinate to a comprehensive plan which would enhance the State and exalt its citizens; and he is one of those who, to use a phrase of Pericles, "rule our spirits from their urns."

Plato's sketches of the ideal community were specifically directed against what struck him and his contemporaries as the most serious problems of the day. They were inspired by distress at the turn affairs were taking and not merely by desire to round out a theoretical system. They were protesting specifically against a large and growing society in which social distinctions were breaking down, against the loss of common interests among the citizens in a State where a new insistence on private property was conflicting with the old allegiance to State, an insistence which extended to wives and children as well as other forms of property, and most important of all they were protesting against the growing confusion between the life of the State as a whole and the economic interest of its various individuals. If it was written for all time and mankind it was at any rate directed against a particular time and people.[3]

---

[1] See the chapters on "Society and the Individual" and "The Group as an Entity" in the author's "Introduction to Sociology," New York, 1928.

[2] This point is emphasized by Herbert G. Wells in "A Modern Utopia," New York, 1905; and in many of his later books.

[3] COPELAND, EDITH A., "The Institutional Setting of Plato's Republic," *Internat. Jour. Ethics*, **34**: 237, 1923–24.

6. Aristotle

Plato's disciple, Aristotle (384–322), turns to the problem of an ideal commonwealth and develops his conceptions in a work, left incomplete, known as the "Politics," or "Politicus." His method of procedure reflects his philosophy and ethics, which are inductive and functional. The meaning of an act lies in the purpose it serves and the end for which it exists. The whole is larger than the part and the part must be defined in terms of the whole, not the whole in terms of the parts. The meaning of the State, therefore, lies in its function, which is the enhancement of the life of the individual. The State exists for the sake of the individual; hence the ideal State will insure the citizens an ideal life. The elements of Statehood inhere in the individual, for man is a political animal. The social urge, which is innate in the individual, is the actuating cause of group life, and hence the State precedes the individual and the family. In all civilizations, however, the family is fundamental and represents the very beginning of society. It is patriarchal; under the authority of the father there is specialization in work and in social function. When the group increases in size until some families must remove to other localities, it is no longer economically complete, and exchange of articles begins. Thus the roots of social life and trade are in the family rather than in individual differences. The "Politics" contains a critical account of utopias which have been suggested or attempted. Before one describes the ideal city-state, one should know both the speculation regarding it and the attempts to realize it; otherwise one may repeat what has been said by others, or may recommend a plan which experiment has proved futile. Aristotle has a trenchant criticism of Plato, and rejects the communism recommended by Socrates in the "Republic." Socrates' defense of it contains a contradiction. When to the question, "Whose is this?" all can reply either "Yours," or "Mine," the harmony is only formal and verbal. For if all own a thing it is not owned by each; whereas ownership by each is the token of property. Socrates, therefore, confuses *all* with *each*. Nor is communism in wives and children feasible. Resemblance between parents and children is deeply rooted in nature and is so characteristic of human beings that it will be noticed. Hence kinship ties will be formed, however stringently the laws forbid them; for the ties of family affection are deep and abiding. Favoritism and nepotism would, therefore, have as much opportunity to flourish in the communistic State advocated by Plato as in any other. Plato aims at unity and succeeds only too well. In the "Republic" there is too much of it; to make life worthwhile there must be diversity and a little looseness of ends. The analogy with the individual is false, for the State is not an amplification of the individual. Aristotle criticizes the communism of Phaleas of Chalcedon because it presupposes equalization not of property but of desire. Not to possess but to want the same things is true communism. Phaleas' system, moreover, provides only for internal welfare and not for relations with other States. Hence the State proposed by him may be internally perfect but it is weak and incapable of resisting the extraneous currents which it must encounter. Hippodamus of Miletus proposed a system of rewards for those who discover something useful for the State; but Aristotle, apparently not convinced of its merits, hedges on this provision, and neither accepts nor rejects the principle. Since happiness, or well-being, is the highest good, the attainment of it by the citizens is the highest goal of the state. Education, then, must insure happiness. To insure happiness or well-being the citizens must be proficient in music and poetry, for the sense of rhythm, symmetry, balance, and proportion will fit the soul for a harmonious and well-rounded life. To be happy one must dwell in a State which provides the conditions on which happiness depend, and the ideal State will secure these conditions.

7. Sparta

The Spartan régime influenced both Plato and Aristotle, and many have considered it the highest political and social organization achieved in the ancient civilizations. The law-giver of the Spartans was Lycurgus, a figure probably partly historical and certainly partly mythical. Though there are many scattered references to the Spartan scheme, the only account which attempts a measure of completeness is that of Plutarch, from whose pages we take the following details. The ideal of Lycurgus was a self-sufficient community containing no internally disrupting forces. Disruptions were caused by jealousies and rivalries, resulting from inequalities in power or in property, or from the pursuit of wealth. Two kings, a senate, and the people participated in the government, and each was a check upon the others. Thus prerogatives, stripped of extravagant pretensions, would not occasion envy nor be a source of danger to the State. In order to remove the social inequalities arising from the unequal distribution of wealth, determined to root out the evils of insolence, envy, avarice, luxury, and those distempers of a State still more inveterate and fatal, namely, poverty and riches, Lycurgus annulled the old divisions of land and parceled it out anew, so that there would be equality in possessions and in standards of living.

Hence, if they were ambitious of distinction they might seek it in virtue, as no other difference was left between them but that which arises from the dishonor of base actions and the praise of good ones.

Yet, in spite of equality in property, by means of money men could maintain many inequalities, for they could purchase luxuries and "movables." But Lycurgus perceived that inequality in private wealth could be countered by debasing the coinage. Here Plutarch makes a shrewd observation on the economic function of money.

First he stopped the currency of gold and silver coin, and ordered that they should make use of iron money only, then to a great quantity and weight of this he assigned but a small value; so that to lay up 10 minae, a whole room was required, and to remove it, nothing less than a yoke of oxen. When this became current, many kinds of injustice ceased in Lacedaemon. Who would steal or take a bribe, who would defraud or rob, when he could not conceal the booty; when he could neither be dignified by the possession of it, nor served by its use?

Furthermore, since iron money was not current in other parts of Greece the Spartans could not purchase foreign wares and curios. As a matter of fact, Sparta was still using the coinage of the early Iron age, and the observations are the rationalizations of Plutarch, but the results of the use of such a coinage probably are correctly stated. Later, the introduction of the precious coins, says Plutarch, brought ruin to the Spartan State.

The first symptoms of corruption and distempers in their commonwealth appeared at the time when the Spartans had entirely destroyed the Athenian power, and begun to bring gold and silver into Lacedaemonia. When the love of money made its way into Sparta, and brought avarice and meanness in its train, on the one hand, and, on the other, profusion, effeminacy and luxury, that State soon deviated from its original virtue, and sank into contempt till the reign of Agis and Leonidas. Men of fortune now extended their landed estates without bounds, not scrupling to exclude the right heirs, and property quickly coming into a few hands, the rest of the people were poor and miserable. There remained not above seven hundred of the old Spartan families, of which perhaps one hundred had estates in land. The rest of the city was filled with an insignificant rabble without property or honor, who had neither heart nor spirit to defend their country against wars abroad, and who were always watching an opportunity for changes and revolutions at home.

Lycurgus excluded the luxuries as debasing; this he accomplished by introducing a practically useless coinage. On the other hand, he stimulated the useful arts because they contributed to the permanent and greater good of all the people. "Hence it was, that excellent workmanship was shown in their useful and necessary furniture, as beds, chairs, and tables." Houses likewise were of simple construction, that they might not harbor luxury and effeminacy. An ordinance levelled against magnificence and display prescribed that the ceilings of houses be wrought with no tool but the axe, the doors with nothing but the saw. "Indeed, no man could be so absurd as to bring into a dwelling so homely and simple, bedsteads with silver feet, purple coverlets, golden cups, and a train of expense that follows these: but all would necessarily have the bed suitable to the room, the coverlet to the bed and the rest of utensils and furniture to that."

Another phase of Spartan equality was the custom of dining at public tables.[1] Here all ate together of the same meat, and partook only of foods designated by law. Men might not eat at home upon expensive couches and tables, nor command the services of butchers and cooks and fatten in private like voracious animals.

For so not only their manners would be corrupted, but their bodies disordered; abandoned to all manner of sensuality and dissoluteness, they would require long sleep, warm baths, and the same indulgence as in perpetual sickness. To effect this was certainly very great; but it was greater still, to secure riches from rapine and from envy, as Theophrastus expresses it, or rather by their eating in common, and by the frugality of their table, to take from riches their very being. For what use or enjoyment of them, what peculiar display of magnificence could there be, where the poor man went to the same refreshment with the rich?

About fifteen were seated at a table. Each man contributed monthly a bushel of meal, eight gallons of wine, five pounds of cheese, two pounds and a half of figs, and a little money for the purchase of meat and fish. The father might not decide whether the child born to him should be allowed to live, but the infant was carried to a place called "Lesche," where it was examined by the oldest men of the tribe. If strong and well proportioned it was allowed to live, but if weak or deformed it was killed. From infancy much attention was given the child's development. Nurses, selected with care, taught the children to have no fear of the dark, or of being alone, and to banish ill-humor and crying. At an early age the lads were enrolled in companies, where they lived in common, and took gymnastics, military training, and recreations, together. The lad who excelled in conduct and courage was selected as the captain of the company. The boys were not educated in intellectual matters, but they acquired stamina and learned to endure hardships without complaining. Their beds were of rough reeds from the banks of the river Eurotas; these they gathered with their own hands without the assistance

---

[1] These were also an institution in Crete, and among the Essenes.

of knives; in winter, as a protection against the cold, they were permitted to add a little thistledown.

To prevent the introduction of foreign manners and customs which might be out of keeping with their own, Lycurgus permitted to go abroad into other countries only a selected number of those who wished to travel. For a similar reason, foreigners might not enter Sparta unless they had acceptable reasons for coming.

For along with foreigners come new subjects of discourse; new discourses produce new opinions; and from these there necessarily spring new passions and desires, which, like discords in music, would disturb the established government. He, therefore, thought it more expedient for the city to keep out of it corrupt customs and manners, than even to prevent the introduction of a pestilence.

As Plutarch observes, the system was well calculated to produce valor but not to promote justice. The treatment of the Helots, the State slaves, was often inhuman, deceptive, and cowardly; and there was little valor in the attitude toward the customs and standards of other peoples. Against arms they were valiant, but not against opinion. For protection they depended upon isolation, insulation, and arms. Holbach says,

Those Spartan virtues which have been so much lauded are those of veritable savages, homicides, destroyers, well conceived for rendering a people savage, unjust, unsociable. Does one find a shadow of equity, of well-doing, or decency in the customs established by Lycurgus? Did not that famous legislator propose to keep his people in a state of war and thus perpetuate their brutal ferocity? The Spartans were merely monks inspired with political fanaticism.[1]

Sparta tried to stabilize herself, and her history suggests an antithesis to the Frenchman's aphorism—the more it is the same thing, the more it changes. Every generation saw Sparta more out of tune with the real world.[2]

Yet some features of the Spartan system have been a stimulus to social reformers from the days of Plato to the present. Perhaps, as Ferguson suggests,

we may easily account for the censures bestowed on the government of Sparta, by those who considered it merely on the side of its forms. It was not calculated to prevent the practice of crimes, by balancing against each other the selfish and partial dispositions of men; but to inspire the virtues of the soul, to procure innocence by the absence of criminal inclinations and to derive its

---

[1] HOLBACH, PAUL H. T., "Système social, ou principes naturels de la morale et de la politique, avec un examen de l'influence du gouvernement sur les mœurs," p. 40, Londres, 1774.

[2] GLOVER, T. R., "Democracy in the Ancient World," p. 23, New York, 1927.

internal peace from the indifference of its members to the ordinary motives of strife and disorder . . . What affinity of consequence can be found between a state whose sole object was virtue, and another whose principal object was wealth; between a people whose associated kings, being lodged in the same cottage, had no fortune but their daily food; and a commercial republic, in which a proper estate was required as a necessary qualification for the higher offices of state?[1]

---

[1] FERGUSON, ADAM, "An Essay on the History of Civil Society," pp. 245–246, Edinburgh, 1767.

CHAPTER XIV

STOIC AND EPICUREAN CONCEPTS OF PROGRESS

1. Introduction

The Hesiodic legend of the Golden age persists in Greek thought, although in the fourth century the writers of comedy ridicule it. Thus, in the "Amphyktyonen" Telekleides calls up an ancient legendary king of Athens, Amphyktyon, who returns from the nether-world to bring a promise of peace and happiness to Athenian citizens—and laughter to an audience. His description is a caricature of the Golden age:

Above all, peace reigned in the land every day, like air and water. The earth did not yield fear nor sorrow, but good things in abundance. Purple wine foamed in the brooks. Fishes followed men into their houses, fried themselves on the pans, laid themselves on the table, and mounted the splendid plates. Soup streamed through the town, and roasted legs of mutton danced; sauce trickles down from the eaves; the hungry may tarry a while and fill themselves with good things. Lard cakes are despised. And the men were a strong race, like giants sprung from the earth.[1]

The world was changing. Even in the age of Pericles, Athens was in the center of the world, and the world was demonstrably one world, not the old collection of odd and dislocated spots where you could live alone; you would never live alone or be let alone again. Syracuse, Carthage, the Black Sea, Egypt, Susa—it is all one world; even Corcyra was in it, in spite of the Corcyraean fancy for being neutrals, standing outside the world.[2]

Before the end of the third century B.C. a reconstruction of the city-state along the lines suggested by Plato or Aristotle had become obviously impossible. Political changes of far-reaching significance had passed over Greece and the Eastern Mediterranean, and the localism, isolation, and apparent self-sufficiency of the city-state had disappeared. Alexander, to whom Aristotle had been tutor, brought under one rule all the Greek autonomies, and amalgamated into one empire those little city-states and territories which, to their respective selves, had seemed self-sufficient because they had enjoyed political independence and comparative isolation.

---

[1] Quoted in BEER, MAX, "Social Struggles in Antiquity," p. 109, Boston, n. d.
[2] GLOVER, T. R., "Democracy in the Ancient World," p. 53, New York, 1927.

Philosophical speculations paved the way to larger conceptions. With a fine contempt for the times and its conventions the Sophists spurned the idea that virtue resided in custom, law, or morality, and declared that these were but episodes in the history of peoples, accidental, not inherent. An act which was right in Athens might be wrong in Corinth or in Thebes, and conversely. Freedom consisted largely in escape from convention.[1] This view prepared the way for a new and more significant interpretation of culture. If convention and custom were episodical, guiding principles must be found for the individual and society. The Stoics developed a cosmopolitanism of which up to this time men had taken no thought; and the way to the Stoic conception was prepared when "Alexander united the whole civilized world for the first time under a single head and gave to it a common language and culture . . . by breaking down the barriers which racial and lingual divisions had hitherto set up between different nations of the earth."[2] "Live as on a mountain," said a later Stoic, Marcus Aurelius, "for whether it be here or there, matters not, provided that, wherever a man lives, he lives as a citizen of the world-city."

2. THE STOICS

The founder of Stoicism, Zeno of Citium (350–260 B.C.), born in Cyprus, of Semitic descent, had imbibed the ideas which, in the Eastern Mediterranean area, were upsetting the established conventions and convictions. Probably he was familiar with some of the books later included in the Old Testament, whence came, perhaps, his *Logos* doctrine and his concept of an all-pervading God of the universe—for hylozoism was linked with cosmopolitanism. Indeed in the third century B.C. the first five books of the Old Testament, the Pentateuch, were translated into the Greek Septuagint.

The time of [Zeno's] coming . . . was a time when landmarks had collapsed, and human life was left, as it seemed, without a guide. The average man in Greece in the fifth century B.C. had two main guides and sanctions for his conduct of life: the welfare of his city and the laws and traditions of his ancestors. First the city, and next the traditional religion; and in the fourth century both of these had fallen. Devotion to the city or community produced a religion of public service. The city represented a high ideal, and it represented supreme power. By 329 B.C. the supreme power had been overthrown. Athens, and all independent Greek cities, had fallen before the overwhelming force of the great military monarchies of Alexander and his generals. The high

---

[1] See above, p 235.

[2] LEGGE, F., "Forerunners and Rivals of Christianity Being Studies in Religious History from 330 B.C. to 330 A.D.," p. 26, Cambridge, 1915.

ideal at the same time was seen to be narrow. The community to which a man should devote himself, if he should devote himself at all, must surely be something larger than one of these walled cities set upon separate hills. Thus the city, as a guide of life, had proved wanting . . . Thus the work that lay before the generation of 320 B.C. was twofold. They had to rebuild a new public spirit, devoted not to the city but to something greater; and they had to rebuild a religion or philosophy which should be a safe guide in the threatening chaos . . . Zeno girded himself to this task. Two questions lay before him—how to live and what to believe. His real interest was in the first, but it could not be answered without first facing the second. For, if we do not know what is true or untrue, real or unreal, we cannot form any reliable rules about conduct or anything else.[1]

In his "Republic," written in the first half of the third century B.C., Zeno attains a breadth of perspective long unrivaled. He describes a universal State, with one government and one manner of life for all mankind, in which there are no nationalities and no geographical or racial discriminations. The distinction between Greek and barbarian disappears, and the bond of human brotherhood unites all men in one commonwealth. The "Republic" of Zeno, probably inspired by the "Republic" of Plato, which it aspired to supersede, is known only through fragments preserved in the writings of others. The author describes the perfect State, and is ambitious to complete the unfinished work of Alexander. This ideal State includes the whole world, and its citizens say, not, "I am of Athens," or, "I am of Sidon," but, "I am a citizen of the world." Its laws are prescribed by nature, not by convention. There are no images of the gods and no temples, for these are derogatory to the Deity. There are no sacrifices, for God is not pleased by such offerings; nor law-courts, for in a State in which the citizens do one another no wrong they are not needed; nor statues, since the virtues of the citizens are sufficient adornment for the State; nor gymnasiums, for in them the youth merely waste time in useless exercise. The people are not divided into classes, as in Plato's "Republic," for all, rather than only a small class, possess wisdom. Men and women dress alike, and do not shamefacedly hide any part of the body. Women are members of the community, and there is no control over one woman by one man, though the wise man has wife and children. The conception of progress as an indefinite improvement the Stoics reject. The universe is composed of many primary elements which in different combinations produce various sequences of events, though these are of a limited number of types. Law prevails everywhere, "chance" being but a word for ignorance of cause. This world of limited possibilities consists of predetermined cycles. Death and decay are a part of the

---

[1] MURRAY, SIR GILBERT, "Tradition and Progress," pp. 90–91, New York, 1922.

scheme of nature, and are as inevitable as life and growth, for decadence is as necessary and natural as development. Into the contract for youth and development are written degeneration and the feebleness of old age, and the price paid for life is death. So let it be, for so it inevitably will be. Change is incessant and universal but of necessity it runs through fixed cycles. There is a passage up and down, repeated upon a grand scale as well as upon a small one, through the whole of history, always the same dramas, the selfsame scenes reproduced: the courts of Hadrian, Antoninus, Philip, Alexander, Crœsus; the same stock rôles, with merely a change of actors. Man, then, must find his place in nature, and since nature cannot be altered, it is futile to complain about it. Let one accept the inevitable cheerfully, for accept it one must. Life must be ordered according to nature, and one must not complain because nature does not bend to one's whims; for the personal will which ignores or goes counter to the will of the universe is merely whim. Virtue, then, consists in conformity with nature and her laws.

There is no value independently of the external world, but in order to have value, a thing must either be in harmony with nature or be the means of procuring something which is. All objects, then, that are in accordance with nature, are relatively choice-worthy on their own account, while their opposites have negative value and call for rejection. The primary duty is that the creature should maintain itself in its natural constitution; next, that it should cleave to all that is in harmony with nature and spurn all that is not; and when once this principle of choice and of rejection has been arrived at, the next stage is choice, conditioned by inchoate duty; next, such a choice is exercised continuously; finally, it is rendered unwaveringly and in thorough agreement with nature; and at that stage the conception of what good really is begins to dawn within us and be understood. Man's earliest attraction is to those things which are conformable with nature, but as soon as he has laid hold of general ideas or notions and has seen the regular order and harmony of conduct, he then values that harmony far higher than all the objects for which he had felt the earliest affection and he is led to the reasoned conclusion that herein consists the supreme human good.[1]

If a man cannot conform with nature it is possibly better that he end his life, and so escape a problem which he cannot solve.[2] But "live according to Nature, and Life itself is happiness. The Kingdom of Heaven is within you—here and now. You have but to accept it and live

---

[1] CICERO.

[2] Hawthorne is sympathetic with this sentiment. "Has not the world come to an awfully sophisticated pass, when, after a certain degree of acquaintance with it, we cannot even put ourselves to death in whole-hearted simplicity?" HAWTHORNE, NATHANIEL, "The Blithdale Romance," p. 269, Boston, 1880.

with it—not obscure it by striving and hating and looking in the wrong place."[1]

The hymn to Zeus, by the Stoic, Cleanthes, of Assos, embodies a conception of law and justice which is reminiscent of the loftiest tone of the Hebrew prophets:

> Most glorious God, invoked by many names,
> O Zeus, eternally omnipotent,
> The Lord of nature, ruling all by law,
> Hail! For all men may speak to thee unblamed;
> From thee we spring, with reasoned speech endowed
> Alone of tribes that live and creep on earth.
> Thee will I hymn, and ever sing thy power.
> Thee all this cosmos, circling round the earth,
> Obeys, and willingly is ruled by thee.
> Thou holdest in unconquerable hands
> So grand a minister, the double-edged,
> The burning, ever living thunderbolt;
> For 'neath its strokes, all things in nature awed,
> Shudder; and thou therewith directest wise
> The universal reason, which through all
> Roams, mingling with the lights both great and small . . .
> The great supreme, all-penetrating king.
> Nor without thee, O God, is any work
> Performed on earth or sea, or in the vault
> Ethereal and divine, save whatso'er
> The wicked do through folly of their own.
> But thou canst perfect make e'en monstrous things,
> And order the disordered; things not dear
> Are dear to thee: for into one thou so
> Hast harmonized the whole, the good and ill,
> That one eternal reason dwells in all;
> From which the wicked flee, ill-fated men,
> Who, longing ever to obtain the good,
> Nor see nor hear God's universal law,
> Obeying which they might achieve a life
> Worthy, enriched with mind; but they in haste
> Forsaking good, seek each some different ill.
> For glory some arouse the eager strife;
> And some, disordered, turn to gain; and some
> Pursue, ungoverned, bodily delights.
> But Zeus, all bounteous, wrapt in sable cloud,
> Thou ruler of the thunder, oh! redeem
> Mankind from mournful ignorance. Do thou
> Dispel, O Father, from our souls this fault,
> And grant that we attain that wisdom high
> On which relying thou dost rule the world
> With Justice; so that, honored thus by thee,

---

[1] MURRAY, SIR GILBERT, op. cit., p. 85.

> Thee we in turn may honor, and may hymn
> Unceasingly thy works, as doth beseem
> A mortal, since nor men nor gods can know
> A grander honor than to greatly hymn
> The universal and eternal law.

The value of the Stoic conception lies principally in the view of nature as an ordered and orderly system in which the individual has a definite and proper place, and in the insistence that he find and fill it. But he who refuses to conform his will with nature may make nature conform with his will, and Stoicism disregards the fact that sometimes revolt against nature changes it. The conception that indefinite progress is not possible may be a damper to adventurous spirits, and a comfort only to those who say that the evils of the times, inasmuch as they are inevitable, the fated working out of the processes of cosmic history, should not occasion worry. It has a flavor of the philosophy expressed in the lines:

> The toad beneath the harrow knows
> Exactly where each tooth-point goes.
> The butterfly beside the road
> Preaches contentment to that toad.

Yet some of the Stoics, for example, Seneca (3 B.C.–65 A.D.) and Marcus Aurelius, urge the improvement of the present state of man. This can be accomplished through rational conformity with nature. Though in a sense fatalists, they believe in limited progress. Seneca predicts that men will seek novelty by traveling through the air and under the sea, will force their way into the frigid climes of the poles, and will penetrate the humid forests of the tropics. From these follies they can be saved only by submission to the will of the Deity, or by a sense of humor which sees the absurdity of taking so much trouble for so small a gain. Nature, the permanent rather than the ephemeral, says Seneca, is the guide of life. Slavery is but a relative term, some men who are called free being more truly enslaved than are some who are called slaves. Slaves are of the same nature as masters. He accepts the theory of a previous Golden age and the subsequent fall of man through avarice and vice. Before covetousness distracted society and introduced poverty,

the social virtues had remained pure and inviolate, for men ceased to possess all things when they began to call anything their own. The first men and their immediate descendants followed nature, pure and uncorrupt. When, however, vices crept in, kings were obliged to show their authority and enact penal laws. How happy was the primitive age when the bounties of nature lay in common and were used promiscuously![1]

---

[1] SENECA, "Letters," 90.

Avarice and luxury introduced discord and incited men to prey upon their fellows. Originally, then, men lived together in peace and happiness, possessed all things in common, were innocent of private property, accepted nature as their guide, and chose the best and wisest men as rulers. The rulers directed their fellows for the latter's own good; they commanded wisely and justly and were willingly obeyed. Eventually, however, avarice entered, and as a result of the desire for personal possessions men ceased to own all things in common. The rulers grew dissatisfied with paternalistic rule, the lust for authority seized them, and the kingship of the wise gave place to tyranny. It became necessary to restrain and control the rulers by laws. Though the defects of human nature made political institutions necessary they are not a part of ideal progress. Recognition of his original sin constitutes the first step in man's salvation, and only through knowledge of his errors can he proceed aright. Their thought resembles that of Spinoza, who said,

The heaviest burden that men can lay upon us is not that they persecute us with hatred and scorn, but it is by the planting of hatred and scorn in our souls. That is what does not let us breathe freely or see clearly.

There is not anything in this world, perhaps, that is more talked of, and less understood, than the business of a happy life [said Cicero].

It is every man's wish and design; and yet not one of a thousand knows wherein that happiness consists. We live, however, in a blind and eager pursuit of it; and the more haste we make in a wrong way, the farther we are from our journey's end. The true felicity of life is to be free from perturbations; to understand our duties toward God and man; to enjoy the present, without any anxious dependence upon the future. Not to amuse ourselves with either hopes or fears, but to rest satisfied with what we have, which is abundantly sufficient; for he that is so, wants nothing. The great blessings of mankind are within us, and within our reach; but we shut our eyes, and like people in the dark, we fall foul upon the very thing we search for, without finding it. "Tranquility is a certain quality of mind, which no condition of fortune can either exalt or depress." Nothing can make it less; for it is the state of human perfection: it raises us as high as we can go, and makes every man his own supporter; whereas he that is borne up by anything else, may fall. He that judges aright, and perseveres in it, enjoys a perpetual calm: he takes a true prospect of things; he observes an order, a measure, a decorum in all his actions: he has a benevolence in his nature; he squares his life according to reason; he draws to himself love and admiration. [Cicero.]

Cicero regards men as equal in nature, capacity, and rights, a view which the Hellenism of Alexander's empire made plausible to the cultured world of Greece and Rome. Some men have been depraved by custom and must be governed by others. Since man is naturally inclined to social life, political life is an organic growth and not a mere mechanical arrangement. Nature, the highest guide, is fully revealed only in social life. Man differs from the other animals in analyzing the past and forecasting the future, whereas the beasts perceive only the present.[1]

The problem of progress is posited by Epictetus, but he answers it solely in terms of individual values, not in social language. The individual makes progress when he learns the ways of nature and submits cheerfully to the inevitable:

> It is one to me that they come or go
> If I have myself and the drive of my will.[2]

Progress consists in "learning what to seek and what to shun, that you may neither be disappointed of the one nor incur the other; in practicing how to pursue and how to avoid, that you may not be liable to fail; in practicing intellectual assent and doubt, that you may not be liable to be deceived. These are the first and most necessary things." Progress lies in attitude rather than in accomplishment:

How you exert those powers, how you manage your desires and aversions, your intentions and purposes, how you meet events—whether in accordance with nature's laws or contrary to them. If in accordance, give me evidence of that, and I will say you improve; if the contrary, you may go your way . . . Where, then, is progress? If any of you, withdrawing himself from externals, turns to his own will, to train, and perfect, and render it conformable with nature—noble, free, unrestrained, unhindered, faithful, humble;—if he has learned, too, that whoever desires or shuns things beyond his own power can neither be faithful nor free, but must necessarily take his chance with them, must necessarily, too, be subject to others, to such as can procure or prevent what he desires or shuns; if, rising in the morning, he observes and keeps to these rules; bathes regularly, eats frugally, and to every subject of action applies the same fixed principles—if a racer to racing, if an orator to oratory—this is he who truly makes progress; this is he who truly has not labored in vain. The only real thing to study is how to rid life of lamentation, and complaint, and *Alas!* and *I am undone*, and misfortune and failure. What your own aims are, it is your business to consider. Those things are not false on which true prosperity and peace depend . . .

We must act in life as when starting on a voyage. What is it possible for me to do? To select the captain and the crew, the season and the day. Then, perhaps, a storm bursts upon us. Well! but what does it matter to me any more? because all that was mine to do has been already done; the problem is now another's, namely, the captain's. But the ship is actually sinking. What have I to do then?

---

[1] MOMMSEN, however, has described Cicero as "a statesman without insight, foresight, or backsight"—*Ohne Einsicht, Ansicht und Absicht.*

[2] TEASDALE, SARA, "Dark of the Moon," New York, 1926.

Why, simply the only thing I can—drown—without terror or screaming or accusing God, but knowing that what is born must also perish.

For I am no eternal, but a man—a fragment of the whole, just as an hour is of the day; like the hour, then, I must arrive, as an hour pass away. What does it matter therefore how I pass away, whether by drowning, or by a fever? For pass I must—in this, or some other way.

Remember that thou art an actor in a play, of such a kind as the manager may choose—with a short part, if he assigns you a short part, or a long one, if he shall choose a long; if he wishes you to act the part of a beggar, see that you act the part naturally; if the part of a cripple, of a magistrate, of a private person, see that you act each gracefully. For this is your duty, to act well the part that is given to you; but to select the part, belongs to another.

Hesiod's thought is echoed in Ovid, who describes the Gold, Silver, Bronze, and Iron ages. In the Bronze age men are fierce in disposition and prone to fight, but there are no criminals. In the Iron age selfishness and greed prevail, for scruple and fidelity have given place to insidious plots and open violence, and men sail the seas seeking fortune. The land, which formerly was common property, is now measured off by the surveyor and is appropriated bit by bit. The earth is forced to bear crops, men dig from her depths gold and iron to incite themselves and their fellows to evil, and war brings death and destruction. The guest is not safe in the house of his host, and even the bonds of kinship are ignored. The sense of duty vanishes and the Virgin Astræa, the last of the celestials, departs the earth and leaves it reeking with blood. Virgil's "Sibylline Oracles" likewise speaks of ages, though the names of the metals are not attached to them. A flood destroys the fifth race of giants and then, in the sixth age, comes the Golden age of blessedness, followed by the race of titans who war against Olympus. During the reign of Saturn communism prevails:

> No fences parted fields nor marks nor bounds
> Divided acres of litigous grounds,
> But all was common.[1]

The Stoics, inspired by the Hesiodic account, came to the conclusion that advance in the arts of civilization had been purchased at the expense of the character, health, and happiness of the individual.

When we consider the Stoic argument by which this conclusion was made to yield the theory that the Golden age of the past was the ideal simple life of the past, we perceive that it was founded on two assumptions. The first is that this conclusion, that advance in the arts is at the expense of the individual, is a truth of universal application, and not to be modified. The second is that

---

[1] VIRGIL, "Georgics," I, 125–128.

the twin process to which it refers has operated continuously, and will go on doing so. The Stoics could make these assumptions without hesitation, since both of them followed, inevitably, from the cyclic theory of the ages to which this school of philosophers gave its enthusiastic support.[1]

A certain coldness in the Stoic detachment makes that philosophy repellent, but there is also a note of grandeur.

If you see a man undismayed by dangers, untouched by passion, happy in adversity, placid in the tempests of life, viewing the human scene as from an eminence, and rising to a level with the gods, shall you entertain for such a person no veneration? Shall you not say [continues Seneca], this is an object greater and more exalted than can be believed to exist in that little body which he occupies? Divine influences descend on him. The superior, moderate mind, which rises above all external things as of smaller consequence, and despises both what we fear, and what we desire, is actuated by celestial energy . . . It holds intercourse with mortals yet clings to its heavenly course.

If one cannot counter evils, one can at least keep oneself above them:

> But we have lived enough to know
> That what we never have remains;
> It is the things we have that go.[2]

The Stoics rejected the theory of progressive degeneration, strictly interpreted. The principal cause of the downfall of man was greed and selfishness. These drove him to war, suggested the first ship, inspired him to explore the earth for treasures better hid, devised the vexations of the law, and brought the injustices of wealth and poverty; through crime and self-indulgence they brought sorrow, disease, and all the ills the flesh is heir to. Thus man shortened his life, brought upon himself anxiety, dyspepsia, and a bad conscience, and made marriage a failure and children a burden.

Though the Stoic believed that the Divine spark was immanent in all men, in some it flickered but feebly. His view of mankind as a whole was pessimistic; from past history he drew no hopes for the future, and he cherished no illusions as to the moral progress of the ages. True that moral values do not correspond with material or social distinctions, but they have, nevertheless, their own different gradation. The ruck of men are incapable of rising far above the brute. Ages have differed, not in viciousness so much as in the forms which vice has assumed. The simple age of primitive man was less wicked, for the possibilities of wickedness have developed with the increasing luxury and complexity of civilization . . . It is hardly to be called more virtuous, for virtue depends upon moral choice and cannot be predicated of ignorance or of

---

[1] SMITH, KIRBY FLOWER, "Ages of the World (Greek and Roman)," ERE.
[2] TEASDALE, SARA, in "American Poetry," p. 91, New York, 1922.

lack of opportunity. There is, therefore, individual moral progress; but general standards have not altered for the better, nay rather, in practice, with the growing complexity of civilization, they have degenerated.[1]

But the Stoics do not entirely despair of progress. Seneca declares that nature will always reveal new secrets to those who seek them, though her mysteries are unfolded to successive generations only gradually; we may fancy ourselves initiated into truth, but we are only at the threshold of the temple. Pliny, too, would have us "trust that the ages go on incessantly improving," and Florus compares the progress of Roman civilization to the development of the individual. The latter says in his "Epitome of Roman History,"

If any one will consider the Roman people as if it were a man, and observe its entire course, how it began, how it grew up, how it reached a certain youthful bloom, and how it has since, as it were, been growing old, he will find it to have four degrees and stages.

But, unlike the individual, a State is capable of renewing its youth.

From Caesar Augustus to our own age is a period of little less than 200 years, in which through the inactivity of the Caesars the nation has, as it were, grown old and feeble, except that now under the sway of Trajan it raises its arms, and, contrary to the expectation of all, the old age of the empire, as if youth were restored to it, flourishes with new vigor.[2]

Under the influence of the Stoics, Roman legalists developed the concepts of *jus gentium*, law which is primitive, universal, rational, and equitable; and *jus naturale*, law which is instinctive and general. Slavery is founded in the *jus gentium*, and is not compatible with the *jus naturale*. *Jus civile*, or civil law, which expresses the perpetual principles of justice and goodness, is derived from the will of the people.

A conception of natural justice . . . could not fail to spring up in the minds of Roman jurists educated in a Stoical philosophy which had so much to say of human reason existing among all men. The idea of a *naturalis ratio* [natural reason] was in the air, and these jurists began to treat the *jus gentium* and the *jus naturale* as identical. Thus, rules conceived as belonging to the *jus gentium* or the *jus naturale*, and representing rational principles, impressed themselves upon the development of the *jus civile*. The jurists applied them effectively to broaden and rationalize the whole Roman law. Judge and jurist learned when to disregard the formal requirements of the older and stricter Roman law, and found the way to recognize what was just and expedient.

---

[1] HALLIDAY, W. R., "The Pagan Background of Early Christianity," pp. 137–138, Liverpool, 1925.

[2] Quoted in FLINT, ROBERT, "History of the Philosophy of History," p. 95.

So the demands of *aequitas*, equity, were met, which is a progressive and discriminating legal justice.[1]

The Stoic attitude may be summed up as, "We can indeed do as we like, but we are compelled to like what we must do." The importance of the Stoic attitude toward the trivialities of life has, however, only recently been appreciated.

As we live longer in the world we see that the bothers, the teasings, and the bad temper, brought about by trifles, place more trouble and divisions between people than do serious things. It is deplorable to see so many quarrels, and so many people made unhappy actually on account of mere nothings.[2]

There is, we fear, some point to Marquis' fable regarding the Hindu sage who sat him down on the banks of the Ganges to contemplate for 70 years the promise of the millennium, when, "just as he arrived at the solution and was putting it into verse, a mosquito stung him and he forgot it again at once."[3] If we are Stoics,

. . . we learn that there are more things in heaven and earth than we dreamed of in our immature philosophy, that there are many choices and that none is absolute, that beyond the mountains, as the Chinese say, there are people also. The obviously pleasant or unpleasant thus becomes less obviously what we felt it was before our knowledge of it became complicated by anticipation and memory . . . They are absorbed into a larger experience in which the rewards are a sustained and more even enjoyment, and serenity in the presence of inescapable evil. In place of a world, where like children we are ministered to by a solicitous mother, the understanding introduces us into a world where delight is reserved for those who can appreciate the meaning and purpose of things outside ourselves, and can make these meanings and purposes their own.[4]

3. THE EPICUREANS

The view of the Stoics and of Aristotle that man is naturally inclined to society is the antithesis of the view of Carneades and the Epicureans. The latter consider man by nature solitary, and not inclined toward the society of his fellows, into which he is driven by the need for mutual protection. Epicurus, the founder of the school known as the Epicureans, is interested in the problem of progress, but instead of indulging in idealism, after the manner of Plato, he proposes the use of experiment.

[1] TAYLOR, HENRY O., "Freedom of the Mind in History," p. 71, London, 1923.

[2] TURGOT, "On Some Social Questions, Including the Education of the Young." Addressed to Madame de Graffigny (1751). Transl. in STEPHENS, W. WALKER, "The Life and Writings of Turgot," pp. 199–200, London, 1895.

[3] MARQUIS, DON, "The Almost Perfect State," p. 166, New York, 1927.

[4] LIPPMANN, WALTER, "A Preface to Morals," p. 183, New York, 1929.

Man will obtain freedom by substituting knowledge for superstition— the truth will make him free. Knowledge, or wisdom, brings quietude and well-being. By obeying the laws of nature, and keeping step with progress in the natural world, man, too, makes progress. The doctrine of Epicurus is further developed by Lucretius, a Roman philosopher of the first century B.C. Like Plato he attempts to separate the necessary and fundamental from the accidental and superficial and thus give a logical basis to his account of culture development. Had he been familiar with the ethnographical evidence he could have written a volume on social evolution as convincing as any that we now have. He represents the prevailing tone of the thoughtful men of his day, who "had begun to realize the fact of human progress, but envisaged it, as was natural in a first view, mainly on the external side, and, above all, had no conception of its infinite possibilities."[1] Lucretius describes man as starting on the level of the brute and slowly acquiring through the ages a knowledge of the use of wood and stone as materials for tools, of the working of bronze, then of iron, shaping his career by gradually modifying it. By observing nature and by profiting from her suggestions man makes progress. Lucretius is the first to use the word "progress" in the modern sense, as well as the first to utilize consistently the conception of culture as a continuous evolution. Yet progress is not an unmixed blessing, for with the goods of civilization go also its evils. In his primitive condition man suffered from the attacks of wild beasts and from his ignorance of medicines. But he was not poisoned, save accidentally, either by his own hand or by that of others—a jibe at the Stoics. Neither did he suffer from shipwreck, nor from the luxuries and vices which accompany wealth. Like Hesiod, Lucretius is aware that progress brings in its train evils of such magnitude that they seem almost to nullify the goods of civilization.

Men desire to be famous and powerful, in order that their life may rest on a firm foundation and they may be able by their wealth to lead a tranquil life; but in vain, since in their struggle to mount up to the highest dignities they render their path one full of danger; and even if they reach it, yet envy, like a thunderbolt, sometimes strikes and dashes men down from the highest point with ignominy into noisome Tartarus, since the highest summits and those elevated above the level of other things are mostly blasted by envy as by a thunderbolt; so that far better is it to obey in peace and quiet than to wish to rule with power supreme and be master of kingdoms. Therefore let men wear themselves out to no purpose and sweat drops of blood, as they struggle on along the road to ambition after things from hearsay rather than their own apprehension.

---

[1] MARVIN, FRANCIS S., "Progress and History."

The primitive condition out of which civilized man has developed was in some ways more ideal than ours, in some ways more wretched.

The race of men in the fields was much hardier, as beseemed it to be, since the hard earth had produced it; and built on a groundwork of powerful sinews throughout the frame of flesh; not rightly to be disabled by heat or cold or strange kinds of food or any malady of body. And during the revolution of many lusters of the sun throughout heaven they led a life after the roving fashion of wild beasts.

It was a life of healthy animal contentment.

Never with loud wailings would they call for daylight and the sun, wandering terror-stricken over the fields in the shadows of night, but silent and buried in sleep they would wait, till the sun with rosy torch carried light into heaven; for accustomed as they were from childhood always to see darkness and light begotten time about, never could any wonder come over them, nor any misgiving that never-ending night would cover the earth and the light of the sun be withdrawn for evermore. But what gave them trouble was rather the races of wild beasts which would often render repose fatal to the poor wretches. And driven from their homes they would fly from their rocky shelter on the approach of a foaming boar or a strong lion, and in the dead of night they would surrender in terror to their savage guests their sleeping places strewn with leaves. Nor then much more than now would the races of mortal men leave the sweet light of ebbing life. For then this one or that one of them would be seized, and torn open by their teeth would furnish to the wild beasts a living food, and would fill with his moaning woods and mountains and forests as he looked on his living flesh buried in the grave.

Yet, all things considered, these primitive men were perhaps not worse off than the civilized Romans.

More and more every day men who excelled in intellect and were of vigorous understanding, would kindly show them how to exchange their former way of living for new methods. Kings began to build towns and lay out a citadel as a place of strength and of refuge for themselves, and divided cattle and lands and gave to each man in proportion to his personal beauty and strength and intellect; for beauty and vigorous strength were most esteemed. Afterwards [now come man's woes] wealth was discovered and gold found out, which soon robbed of their honors strong and beautiful alike. For men, however valiant and beautiful of person, generally follow in the train of the richest man.

False ambition caused man's downfall. "But were a man to order his life by the rules of true reason, a frugal subsistence joined to a contented mind is for him great riches; for never is there lack of a little."[1] The

---

[1] LUCRETIUS, "On the Nature of Things," bk. V, English trans. by Munro.

Epicureans believed that the development of civilization had been accompanied by degeneration in man himself, though they did not consider this principle universally applicable. Every advance in civilization was in some respects unfavorable to the individual, and in some ways favorable. As Horace said:

> When men first crept from out earth's womb, like worms,
> Dumb speechless creatures, with scarce human forms,
> With nails or doubled fists they used to fight
> For acorns or for sleeping-holes at night;
> Clubs followed next; at last to arms they came,
> Which growing practice taught them how to frame,
> Till words and names were found, wherewith to mould
> The sounds they uttered, and their thoughts unfold;
> Thenforth they left off fighting, and began
> To build them cities, guarding man from man,
> And set up laws as barriers against strife
> That threatened person, property, or wife.[1]

4. UTOPIAN LANDS

The Alexandrian conquests brought the Greeks into contact with distant peoples and acquainted them with many foreign customs; and these contacts stimulated imaginative accounts by poets and self-proclaimed historians. Thus Theopompos of Chios (born 377/6 B.C.), the first historian of Philip of Macedon, speaks of a land at the farthest bounds of the earth, whose inhabitants attain an unheard-of stature and have a double span of life. In this distant isle are many cities and two countries; the inhabitants of one of these countries are cheerful, friendly, and without sickness or pain, while in the other there is never-ending strife. The Meroper inhabit several large cities. Outside of their territory is a place called *Anostos*, "Never-ending," like an abyss, neither dark nor light, but pervaded by a turbid red vapor. Two rivers flow around it, the river Pleasure and the river Sorrow, and singular trees stand on the banks. He who eats of the fruit of the trees along the stream of sorrow breaks into tears, spends the remainder of his life weeping, and in sorrow dies. But he who eats of the fruit of the trees along the river Pleasure, forgoes all that he previously held dear, and the things which he formerly loved are forgotten. He becomes younger and the stages of life through which he has passed he lives through again in inverse order. The old return to manhood, then to youth, to childhood, to prenatal existence, and finally vanish into nothingness.—Here, beyond doubt, is Hindu influence.[2] In the "Aigyptiaka" Hecataios of

---

[1] CONINGTON, "The Satires, Epistles and Ars Poetica of Horace," p. 21, London, 1904.

[2] See above, p. 217.

Abdera gives a description of an island, Helixoia, lying far to the north in the ocean, on which the inhabitants live a long happy life and enjoy plenty the year round. All the people are priests of Apollo. Every nineteenth year this god comes to them, playing the zither, dancing, and accompanied by singing swans. The people are vegetarians. At the end of 1,000 years the inhabitants are overcome with illness, and drown themselves in the sea.

In the "Sacred Inscription" Euhemeros describes a land far to the east, near India, in which there live a happy people who possess all goods in common. They are divided into three castes, and religion plays a large part in their life. Iambulos (about 200 B.C.?) describes a land in the southern seas to which he, a merchant's son, was carried captive. In this large island day and night are as one, there are sweet waters and rivers of oil and wine, and everywhere rare plants and fruits abound. The inhabitants are remarkably alike. With their two-pronged tongues they can speak all languages and can imitate the calls of birds. They do not succumb to illness, and live to the age of 150 years. Those who become physically deformed or who suffer illness must take their own lives. But death is made easy by lying on a certain plant which induces sleep followed by death. The inhabitants revere all celestial bodies, especially the sun. The people are divided into groups of four hundred, over whom an elder presides and rules like a king. In the common tasks they relieve one another by taking turns, first at fishing, then at handicrafts, and so on. Wives and children are held in common, and a mother does not know her own child. They pursue knowledge, especially the science of astronomy. Their alphabet is composed of seven signs, and they write from below up. On this island Iambulos lived seven years, then returned to Hellas by way of India and Persia. But who Iambulos was we do not know; indeed, we know neither his country, nor, with certainty, the period in which he wrote. He appears to have been a member of the Stoic school, many of whose ideas he has incorporated, and he shows familiarity with Plato's "Republic." The island to which he refers is possibly Ceylon.

Chapter XV

THEORIES OF PROGRESS IN CHRISTIAN COUNTRIES BEFORE THE EIGHTEENTH CENTURY

1. Early Christian Concepts of Progress

Christian thought gave a new trend to the concept of progress. The Jewish controversies over political issues did not interest the early Christians, and the attempt to involve Jesus in them did not succeed: "Render unto Cæsar the things that are Cæsar's." About the political oppression from which the Jews suffered, Jesus had nothing to say, nor had early Christian writers. "Servants obey your masters," is the Pauline injunction.

It does not seem to have been the intention of Christianity to abolish the distinctions of rank, or to alter the civil rights of mankind which were already established. There is no precept of the gospel by which the authority of the master is in any respect restrained or limited; but, on the contrary, there are several passages from which it may be inferred that the slaves, even after they embraced the Christian religion, were not absolved from any part of the duties formerly incumbent upon them.[1]

There is no incitement to revolt, no hint that there are claims of native land or need for social reconstruction. Passages in Acts II, IV, and V, however, imply that property was held in common among the early Christians, at least in the community at Jerusalem, a fact familiar to early Christian writers, accepted by the Church Fathers, and referred to by Campanella and Sir Thomas More. This early Christian communism may have been suggested by the practices of the Essenes, a Jewish sect some four thousand strong, dwelling mainly in the wilderness of Judea, but probably established also in colonies throughout Palestine. The Essenes practised an almost absolute communism. About 70 A.D. Philo of Alexandria writes,

No one had his private house, but shared his dwelling with all, and, living as they did in colonies, they threw open their doors to any of their sect who came their way. They had a common storehouse, common expenditures, com-

---

[1] Millar, John, "Observations Concerning the Distinction of Ranks in Society," pp. 287–288, London, 1773.

mon garments, common food eaten in *syssitia*.[1] They dwelt in the villages and avoided the towns on account of the licentiousness which was customary among the inhabitants. Many of them carried on agriculture, others pursued peaceful avocations, and in this wise employed themselves and their neighbors. They accumulated neither silver nor gold, nor did they acquire lands in order to procure large incomes for themselves; but they toiled merely to secure the necessary means for supporting life. Thus they are practically the only men who possess no property, not because of the mischance of fortune, but because they do not strive after riches, and yet they are, in truth, the richest of all, as they count as riches contentment and the absence of needs. You will not find among them artificers of arrows, javelins, swords, helmets, breast-plates and shields, nor any who are engaged in the construction of implements of war, or generally anything which pertains to war. Commerce, liquor, manufacturing, and seafaring have never entered their heads, for they desire to avoid all things that give rise to covetousness. There are also no slaves among them. All are free and work for each other. They despise rulers and governors because they are ungodly in abolishing an institution of nature, which, like a mother, creates and nourishes all as true and loving brothers, a relationship which is destroyed by triumphant cunning and avarice, which have put alienation in place of trustfulness and hatred in place of love. The Essenes are taught the principles of godliness, holiness, and righteousness in the government of the house and the community, in the knowledge of what is good and what is evil, and they accept as their three moral conceptions or principles, love of God, of virtue, and of mankind. The manifestations of love of mankind are benevolence, equity, and community in goods, which cannot be praised too highly. We may add something about the latter. First of all, none has a house which does not belong to all. In addition to the fact that they dwell together socially, every house is open to comrades who come from a distance. Also the storehouse and the provisions contained therein belong to all, as well as the articles of clothing; likewise the eatables are available to those who do not observe the common meal times. And generally the condition of dwelling, eating and living together socially has, among no other race, been carried to such a high degree of perfection as among these men. For they do not keep for themselves what they have earned during the day, but put it together and offer it for general consumption. The sick and aged are treated with the greatest care and gentleness. Even the most cruel rulers and proconsuls were unable to do them harm. On the contrary, they quailed before the unsullied virtue of these men, met them in a friendly spirit, as such as had the right to make their own laws and were free by nature; they commended their meals in common and their most praiseworthy institution of holding goods in common, which was the most striking proof of a full and happy life.[2]

---

[1] *I.e.*, common meals; see "Essenes," ERE; and the author's "Introduction to Sociology," p. 58, New York, 1928.

[2] Quoted in BEER, MAX, "Social Struggles in Antiquity," pp. 46–48, Boston, n. d.

"They despise wealth," says Josephus, "and the common life they practise is marvelous. Thus, it is impossible to find among them any one who wishes to distinguish himself by property. For it is a law that those who are admitted into this sect transfer their property to the order. Consequently there is neither privation and poverty, nor superfluity and luxury."[1] Similarly in the Jerusalem Christian community described in Acts,

all that believed were together, and had all things common; and sold their possessions and goods, and parted them to all, as every man had need . . . Neither said any of them that aught of the things which he possessed was his own: but they had all things common.[2]

Early Christianity placed little value on the possession of property, regarded it as a handicap rather than a means to salvation, and advocated emancipation from political and economic oppressions by rising above their compulsions. What one owned and what political allegiance one owed were unimportant. Through help from a Divine power, and by humility and self-abnegation, men would solve worldly problems and obtain salvation. The early Christians were too much preoccupied with the next world to construct redemptive schemes for this one, and they believed that an imminent universal conflagration would consume all terrestrial things.[3] Why, then, should they be concerned about social progress? Though eventually Christianity gave new emphasis to the problem of progress, the underlying ideas were drawn from contemporary thought, and its philosophy was built on a Jewish background of patriarchs, prophets, kings, and kingdoms. Like the Stoics, the Christians acknowledged the common origin and kinship of all mankind, and regarded slaves as of like nature with masters. The injunction of St. Paul, "Render to all their dues; tribute to whom tribute is due; custom to whom custom, fear to whom fear; honor to whom honor,"[4] contains no threat against the established order. The early Christian ideal of communism persisted for centuries, and found its greatest embodiment in monasticism; and during the first three centuries of Christianity the

---

[1] Quoted in BEER, MAX, op. cit., pp. 48–49.

[2] Acts, 2: 32, 44–45; see also Acts 4: 33–37, and 5: 1–11.

[3] "For this we say unto you by the word of the Lord, that we which are alive and remain unto the coming of the Lord shall not prevent them which are asleep. For the Lord himself shall descend from heaven with a shout, with the voice of the archangel, and with the trump of God: and the dead in Christ shall rise first. When we which are alive and remain shall be caught up together with them in the clouds, to meet the Lord in the air: and so shall we ever be with the Lord." I Thessalonians, 4: 15–17. In Stoic thought a conflagration marks the end of the great cycle and the beginning of its repetition.

[4] Romans, 13: 7.

communistic idea dominated many Christian communities. Although the laws and institutions of the Roman Empire were passively obeyed, most Christians regarded them as unjust. Greek and Latin Church Fathers adhered, at least in theory, to anti-government and communistic doctrines, condemned the institution of private property, and denied the claims of the State to obedience, military service, and patriotism. They championed asceticism and communism and bequeathed a tradition hostile to Mammon and to the supremacy of economic, worldly, private, and State interests. The description in Acts of the primitive Jerusalem community kept alive the longing for a communal and communistic life, and furnished the model for the Church Fathers and for all earnest Christians, although during the first century the ideal was transfused with millennial expectations, and with certain Hellenic-Roman, particularly Stoic, influences.

The Church Fathers were the custodians of this religious, ethical and philosophical knowledge, and all of them were partly hostile to mammon, and partly inclined towards communism. At least in theory they regarded the communistic way of living as virtuous, and as the ideal of a Christian.

Barnabas, the first of the Church Fathers, in the "Epistle to the Christians," written during the first third of the second century, exhorts the Christian, "to communicate in all things with thy neighbour; thou shalt not call things thine own; for if ye are partakers in common of things that are incorruptible, how much more should ye be of those things which are perishable." Justin the Martyr, who wrote about the middle of the second century, bases his plea on the Gospels[1] and in his "Apology" (I, 14, 15) declares, "We who loved the path to riches and possessions above any other now produce what we have in common, and give to everyone who needs." Clement of Alexandria, who wrote during the last quarter of the second and the first quarter of the third century, and was strongly influenced by Stoic ideas, declares: "Let it then be granted that good things are the property only of good men, and Christians are good. Accordingly good things are possessed by Christians alone. But what is possession? Not he who has and keeps, but he who gives away, is rich." ("Pædog.," III, 6). "Lust of money is the citadel of sin." In these opinions he is supported by Origen (died 254).

Tertullian, a contemporary of Clement of Alexandria, and the son of a Roman captain who had been stationed at Carthage, is an implacable opponent of Roman Imperial power, and declares the acceptance of a position in a heathen State incompatible with the duties of a Chris-

---

[1] Matthew **5**: 42, 45; **6**: 19, 20, 25, 31; Mark **8**: 36; Luke **6**: 34; **9**: 25; **12**: 22, 31, 34.

tian: "There is no agreement between the divine and the human sacrament, the standard of Christ and the standard of the devil, the camp of light and the camp of darkness" ("Idolatry," Chap. 19). He denounces both patriotism and statesmanship. In 197 he writes: "But as those in whom all ardor in the pursuit of glory and honor is dead, we have no pressing inducement to take part in your public meetings, nor is there aught more entirely foreign to us than politics. We acknowledge one all-embracing commonwealth: the world." ("Apology," Chap. 38.) Again, in this same work, which is a defence of Christians, he says:

Only those are brothers who are good men. But on this very account perhaps we are regarded as having less claim to be held true brothers that no tragedy makes a noise about our brotherhood, or that the family possessions which generally divide brotherhood among you create fraternal bonds among us. One in mind and soul, we do not hesitate to share our earthly goods with one another. All things are common among us but our wives.

Cyprian, a contemporary of Origen, says apropos of the primitive Jerusalem community:

All that comes from God is for our common enjoyment, and from His benefits and gifts none is excluded, so that the whole human race may share equally in God's munificence . . . For whatsoever is of God is in our using common, nor is any man shut out from His bounties and gifts, to the end the whole human race may equally enjoy God's goodness and bounty. In which example of equality the earthly possessor who shares his gains and his fruits with the brotherhood, free and just in his voluntary bounties, is imitator of God the Father.

Cyprian, too, denounces attachment to property: "You are captive and slave of your money. You are fast in the chains and bonds of covetousness; you whom Christ had once loosened, again are become bound." Lactantius, writing in the early fourth century, is much influenced by Plato's "Republic." He considers economic communism feasible, if its disciples revere God as the source of wisdom and religion, but he opposes communism in wives. Like Plato, he would fain see the present age revert to the happy conditions of the age of Saturn, that primeval time when righteousness prevailed, the earth was the common possession of all, and men lived a common life ("Epitome," 35 to 38). In the "Homilies," Basilius the Great (died 379) complains: "Nothing withstands the power of wealth, and everything bows before its tyranny . . . Are ye not thieves and robbers? The bread thou hast belongs to the hungry, the mantle thou wearest belongs to the ill-clad, the shoes thou hast on belong to the unshod, the silver thou hast heaped up belongs to the needy. Thou doest injury to as many men as thou couldst give to." He advocates communal ownership:

We who are gifted with reason show ourselves to be more cruel than the irrational animals. The latter make use of the natural products of the earth as common things. The herds of sheep feed on one and the same pasture. Horses browse all together on one and the same meadow. But we make things to be our own which are common, and possess all that belongs to the community . . . Let us imitate the Hellenes and their mode of living, which was full of humanity. There are people among them with the excellent habit of all citizens assembling in one building around a table for meals in common.

Gregory Nazianzen accepts the doctrines of communism and natural rights which characterize the Church teaching of his time. Freedom and serfdom, poverty and riches, are the result of departure from the primitive condition, the consequence of greed, envy, discord, and sin. "But thou, O Christ, lookest upon the original freedom, and not upon the subsequent separation, supportest with all thy strength Nature, honorest the original freedom, and consolest poverty." In a sermon delivered in Constantinople in 400, Chrysostom (died 407) recommends communistic experiments, and extols the primitive Christian community in Jerusalem:

For they did not give in part and in part reserve, nor yet in giving all gave it as their own, and they lived moreover in great abundance. They removed all inequality from among them, and made a goodly order. But to show that it is the living separately that is expensive and causes poverty, let there be a house in which are contained children and the wife and the man. Let the one work at her wool, the other bring his earnings from his outdoor occupation. Now tell me in which way would these spend most, by taking their meals together and occupying one house, or by living separately? Of course, by living separately; for if the ten children must live apart they would need ten several rooms, ten tables, ten attendants, and the income otherwise in proportion. Is it not for this very reason that where there is a great number of slaves they have all one table, that the expense may not be so great? For so it is division always makes diminution, concord and agreement make increase. The dwellers in the monasteries live just as the faithful did. Now did ever any of these die of hunger? It seems people are now more afraid of this than of falling into a boundless and bottomless deep. But if we did make actual trial of this, then indeed would we boldly venture upon this plan.

Ambrose (died 397) regards private property as sinful and as originating in sin.

Nature provides everything for all to have in common. God has, in fact, created all things, so that enjoyment may be common to all and the earth may be the common possession of all. Nature therefore creates the right to communism, but coercion makes of it the right to private property . . . Our Lord God has willed that this earth should be the common possession of all mankind, and its produce be shared by all, but covetousness has divided up this right of possession.[1]

Augustine (354–430), a disciple of Ambrose, is inclined to accept the theory of communism:

Consider this, beloved, that on account of private possessions exist lawsuits, enmities, discords, wars among men, riotous dissensions against one another, offences, sins, iniquities, murders. On account of what? On account of what we each possess. Let us, therefore, brethren, abstain from the possession of private property or from the love of it if we may not from its possession[2] . . . For we have many superfluities if we keep nothing but what is necessary. Find out how much He hath given thee, and take of that what is enough. All other things which remain as superfluities are the necessaries of others. The superfluities of the rich are the necessaries of the poor. Seek what is enough for God's sake, not what is sufficient for your greediness.[3]

In the fourth and fifth centuries, while Ambrose and Augustine were giving expression to these views, landworkers in North Africa were engaged in a struggle for common ownership, or, at least, for freedom, equality of possessions, and social and political equality. The leaders of this rural labor movement, known as the Circumcellion, united with the Donatists, who were originally merely a religious or reform group within the Church, led by Bishop Donatia, who gave his name to the order. The Donatists opposed abuses in the Church hierarchy, particularly the domination by priests, and advocated reforms within the Church. The rural proletarians, held in subjection by the powerful landlords, joined the Donatists. The Circumcellionists resorted to force, but combination of Church and State, aided by Roman exploitation, finally defeated the agricultural proletarians. In 411, St. Augustine wrote against the Donatists and Circumcellionists, declared that only the just were entitled to possess property and that, since the Donatists and Circumcellionists had defied civil and ecclesiastical authority, they had forfeited their rights to property. In the fourth century, when Christianity became a buttress of the State, communism was confined mainly to the cloisters and to heretical sects, but during the middle ages and in modern times, with every rebellion communistic and chiliastic aspirations revived. The rules of the Benedictine Order, drawn up in 529 by its founder, Benedict of Nursia (480–543), contain elements which bear a striking similarity to some of the measures advocated by both earlier and later

---

[1] "De Nabuthe," chap. I, 2; "Expositio in Lucam," chap. XII, 15, 22, 23.

[2] "Commentary to Psalm CXXXI."

[3] "Commentary to Psalm CXLVII: 12"; see BEER, MAX, "Social Struggles in Antiquity," pp. 197–209.

writers of utopias. They deal with problems which confronted Plato and
Aristotle: the problems of work, family life, and the right to leave the
community. The Benedictine rules prescribed that the monastic community should perform, as far as possible, all labor necessary to its existence
and wants. Its members, the monks, might not marry, and they might
not leave the community. The Christian monastic order began in Syria
and in North Africa, where communistic traditions were strong, and it is
almost certain that its early organization and ideals are historically
related to those championed by the Greeks and the Essenes and to those
practised in the early Jerusalem Christian community.

St. Augustine's "City of God" is the first noteworthy attempt
by a Christian writer to solve for all men and for all time the problem
of social progress. It was written (about 413–429) after Alaric's sack
of Rome, which occurred in 410. The writer is much concerned over the
fall of the greatest civilization of historical times. He reviews the history
of Rome, estimates the significance of the various phases of her development, and deprecates her gods and her religion. The "City of God"
reflects many Stoic conceptions, and acknowledges obligations to
Seneca and Cicero. St. Augustine urges the need for a commonwealth
in which all men, united under the reign of God, are subject to His
laws. Parts of the work imply that this commonwealth will exist on
earth, though some passages imply that it will be realized only in
heaven. "That heavenly State," he says,

while in pilgrimage on earth, calls its citizens from all races and its pilgrim
company is gathered from men of every tongue: for it cares not for diversity
in manners, laws, or administration, by which peace on earth is acquired or
maintained. None of these are abolished or destroyed, but they are kept and
followed. For the diversity of different tribes tends to the single end of earthly
peace if it does not hinder the religion which teaches the service of the only
true God.

The City of God, then, is a universal commonwealth which unites
all men in the bonds of the Christian religion. Present difficulties will
disappear in this commonwealth, which is under a single temporal and
spiritual authority. St. Augustine has the cosmopolitanism of the Stoics
but not their charity. In addition to the apology for the Christian religion
and the assertion that it has not been responsible for the fall of Rome, a
calamity which even the Christians must regret, there is a description
of the civilizations of the past, and the first philosophy of history, an
attempt to assess the contributions which the respective historical
cultures have made to human civilization. The human race is a single
species, for all men are descended from Adam, and consequently all are
bound together by ties of kinship. God has introduced order throughout

nature and chance does not exist. Man is endowed with a capacity for progress and is stimulated, now by necessity, now by inventiveness, to devise the arts and sciences. He has made remarkable advancement in weaving, building, agriculture, navigation, pottery, painting, sculpture, in destroying and in healing fellow-man, in arousing and in satisfying appetite, in communicating thought and feeling, in music and in musical instruments, in measuring and in numbering, in a knowledge of the stars and other phases of nature, and in philosophic discrimination.

Dante declares that the proper aim of the human race, taken in its entirety, is to stimulate the understanding to its fullest development in speculation and in action. Peace is a prerequisite to progress. As the individual, by rest and quiet, becomes perfect in wisdom and prudence, so the human race applies itself most freely and easily to its proper work when peace and tranquility prevail. These are secured only by submission to a common authority; without it wars and conflicts will continue. Only in a universal empire can equal justice to all be insured and the freedoms of men be preserved. Therefore, "cities, nations, and kingdoms should be governed by a rule common to them all, with a view to their peace." In vein similar to that of Dante, St. Thomas Aquinas (1227–1274) asserts that the proper function of mankind is to develop and diversify human interests and activities. No doubt he would consider the complexity of civilization an evidence of superiority over savagery. He rejects communism on the ground that its success presupposes perfect men. It may have existed in the remote Golden age, for then all was peaceful, there was no strife among men, and no disaffection. As men are now constituted, however, private property is more natural, though it is incumbent upon the rich to give alms to the poor. Inequalities in property are the result of inequalities in the productiveness of labor. Political organization does not remove human vices, but it is the most appropriate form in which men can live together.

Marsiglio of Padua shares Aristotle's conviction that the ultimate purpose of the State is to secure for its citizens not merely life but a good life; and any lesser aim is unworthy. Men who are not bereft of reason, or otherwise perverted, naturally strive for a complete and satisfying life, but their passions deflect them from this natural and rational end. They are liable to suffering, they may be destroyed by the powers of nature, and therefore they need various arts to ward off impending ills. Men must establish civil communities to secure the good and escape the evil. If the community is not united by rules of justice, dissension and strife will disrupt it. Laws which insure justice guarantee a rational government, and the State must be able to use force against those who threaten its existence. The function of government is to restrain dangerous transgressors and those who harass the community, either from within or from without. Organized society exists to provide a good life and to transmit to subsequent generations the things necessary to the attainment of well-being. To accomplish these purposes, there must be different ranks or offices, each contributing something which man needs for the realization of the good life; to secure this end law is necessary. Strongly suggestive of Lucretius is the view of Mariana, a Spanish Jesuit, that originally nature supplied all man's needs, and that, in this primitive state, vices were unknown. Since private property did not exist, there was no cheating, lying, avarice, or ambition. Man's superiority lay in the fact that his wants were greater than those of the beasts. His weakness as an individual led to the need of association and so to social life, through which he was elevated to his present lofty estate.

In 1305–1307 Petrus de Bosco (Pierre du Bois, 1250 or 1260 to 1321)· published a work entitled "De Recuperatione Terra Sancte," ("On Regaining the Holy Land"), called forth by the contest between Church and State during the time of King Philip and Boniface VIII. He advocated the reconquest of Palestine and the establishment of a World State. There was to be an organization of European States, with representatives in a council at Toulouse which would maintain eternal peace. Clashes of interest which might threaten war would be dealt with through an international court of arbitration. The highest court, that of last resort, would be the Papacy. It would be a department, or bureau, of peace, but would have no temporal power. If a prince started a war his property would be confiscated and he would be exiled to the Holy Land; thus, its Christian population would be increased. To those who assisted in punishing and transporting princes who had started a war, full indulgence would be granted. When peace had been established among all Catholics they could easily conquer the Holy Land. This is the first formulation by a European of a league of nations—more than 600 years before there was an effort to put such a plan into effect in the Old World. In the New World, however, the Iroquois league of Five Nations was formed about 1570, and in 1722 the Tuscarora were admitted, thus making the Six Nations, as the English called the federation. The Delaware, although of another stock (Algonkian), and the Tutelo, of Siouian stock, were almost given this coveted honor.

The confederation functioned as an asylum for almost any nation, and even fragments of tribes which had once been the most bitter enemies of the Iroquois, like the Erie and Huron, were received into the fold. Peace and unification were the two avowed purposes animating the league and these are best illustrated by what might be called the three fundamental laws of the realm: first, that though a chief die his office shall not perish with him; second, that no personal revenge was to be taken individually for the murder of any member in the league but that the whole matter was to be referred to a general council; and thirdly, that the elaborate and ruinous mourning ceremonies which prevailed should be reduced to one simple rite in which a few individuals, delegated to represent the whole league, were to address words of comfort to the bereaved. All these provisions suggest definitely that the Iroquois ... sought refuge and a haven of rest from the spirit of war ... in a political assembly and in the league. That the breaking up of such a league meant practically the destruction of the nation, is not to be wondered at and we can enter into the feelings of the litany in which its weakening was deplored.[1]

Ibn Khaldun (1332–1408), an Arab philosopher, like Florus regards an empire as having a life analogous to that of an individual. Usually it lasts only three generations, *i.e.*, about a hundred and twenty years. In such an empire the first generation is characterized by tribal spirit and the men are hardy and militant, like nomads. The second generation is self-indulgent and loses force and courage, for it has acquired power and wealth and leads a sedentary life. In the third generation the fighting qualities deteriorate further and the empire cannot resist the attacks of outside foes. A change in one phase of social life affects all phases, and the sentiments of any one group penetrate the entire political unit.

John Wycliffe (died 1384) accepted the teachings of the Stoics regarding *jus naturale*.[2] In the earliest social life communism and innocence prevailed and there was neither private property nor civil law. Man fell, however, and then laws become necessary. John Ball, who was active in the peasant revolt of the fourteenth century, was likewise an avowed communist. In the early condition of man there were no class distinctions. "When Adam delved and Eve span, Who was then the gentleman?" "My good people," he said, "My good people, things

---

[1] RADIN, PAUL, "The Story of the American Indian," pp. 282–283, New York 1927. See also "Iroquois," in "Handbook of the American Indians," vol. I, Washington, 1907. "When the Europeans made their first settlements in America, six such nations had formed a league, had their amphyctiones or states-general, and, by the firmness of their union, and the ability of their councils, had obtained an ascendant from the mouth of the St. Laurence to that of the Mississippi. They appeared to understand the objects of the confederacy, as well as those of the separate nation; they studied a balance of power; the statesman of one country watched the designs and proceedings of another; and occasionally threw the weight of his tribe into a different scale. They had their alliances and their treaties, which, like the nations of Europe, they maintained, or they broke, upon reasons of state; and remained at peace from a sense of necessity or expediency, and went to war upon any emergence of provocation or jealousy." FERGUSON, ADAM, "An Essay on the History of Civil Society," pp. 130–131, Edinburgh, 1787.

[2] See above, p. 257.

cannot go well in England, nor ever will, until all goods are held in common, and until there will be neither serfs nor gentlemen, and we shall be equal. For what reason have they, whom we call lords, got the best of us? How did they deserve it?"[1] Similarly Jack Cade is reported by Shakespeare as saying in the Kentish rebellion of 1449: "And henceforth all things shall be in common," "Away, burn all the records of the realm; my mouth shall be the parliament of England."[2]

Savonarola (1452–1498) declared that government is necessary, since man is a social animal and must live with his fellows. Despotism is the best form of government if the despot is benevolent and upright, but it is the worst if he is harsh and corrupt. Despotism prevails in the warmer regions where ambition is lacking, and also in the northern latitudes where the intellect is weak. In Italy, however, where blood and intellect commingle, men do not submit patiently to the rule of one man. Each would fain be head and ruler of others, and from this ambition discords arise. Hence, at least in Italy, and especially in Florence, government by many is better than government by one. Unless the government is well balanced, however, one faction will come into control and will persecute the members of other factions.

In 1462 the Czech king, George von Podiebrad, sought to unify the Christian nations into one parliament and to create an international militia as a means of defense against any disturber of the international peace. The pope, however, laid a ban on him, and other sovereigns gave no heed of his advice.

2. Sir Thomas More's "Utopia"

In the beginning of the sixteenth century two important tendencies were dominant in Europe. One was the conservatism of the Church and the enlarging, not to say encroaching, theories of the theologians, the compass of whose thought was growing in volume rather than in quality. The other was the spirit of the Renaissance, fostered by the discovery of new continents and civilizations and by the development of the arts and sciences.

These currents met in the personality of a remarkable young man, Sir Thomas More, who in 1515–1516, when thirty-seven years of age, wrote the "Utopia." Yet already his knowledge of men and affairs was broad, and his learning as inclusive as the culture of his day permitted; no contemporary save Erasmus was his peer in the "New Learning."

---

[1] Froissart, "Collection des chroniques," vol. VIII, p. 106; quoted in Laidler, Harry W., "A History of Socialist Thought," p. 25, New York, 1927.

[2] Shakespeare, "Henry VI," pt. II, act 4, scene 7; quoted in Laidler, op. cit.

He had held important political positions and had earned the respect of his monarch, Henry VIII. No other, perhaps, who was tempted by such high position and royal honors, resisted so successfully their seductiveness. Erasmus says,

He had been thrust more than once into an embassy, in the conduct of which he has shown a great ability; and King Henry in consequence would never rest until he dragged him into Court. "Dragged him," I say, and with reason; for no one was ever more ambitious of being admitted into a Court, than he was anxious to escape it. But as this excellent monarch was resolved to pack his household with learned, serious, intelligent, and honest men, he especially insisted upon having More among them—with whom he is on such terms of intimacy that he cannot bear to let him go. If serious affairs are in hand, no one gives wiser counsel; if it pleases the King to relax his mind with agreeable conversation, no man is better company. Difficult questions are often arising, which require a grave and prudent judge; and these questions are resolved by More in such a way that both sides are satisfied. And yet no one has ever induced him to accept a present. What a blessing it would be for the world, if magistrates like More were everywhere put in office by sovereigns! Meanwhile there is no assumption of superiority. In the midst of so great a pressure of business he remembers his humble friends and from time to time he returns to his beloved studies. Whatever authority he derives from his rank, and whatever influence he enjoys by the favor of a powerful sovereign are employed in the service of the public, or in that of his friends. It has always been part of his character to be most obliging to everybody, and marvelously ready with his sympathy; and this disposition is more conspicuous than ever. now that his power of doing good is greater.[1]

The "Utopia" has deservedly given its name to all schemes of ideal society. No other has been more clear cut, more imaginative, or more realistic. It is a castle in the air, but, at least by More's interpretation, one with foundations in the possibilities of human nature. His treatise begins with observations about the ancient peoples, in an endeavor to learn from their experience and profit from their fate. Standing armies overturned and ruined the civilizations of Rome, Carthage, Assyria, and many other nations and cities. Peace is the normal condition, war is abnormal. Those, moreover, who devote themselves to the profession of arms do not make better soldiers than do untrained men, for the latter fight with admirable valor when the occasion demands; "and it seems very unreasonable, that for the prospect of a war, which you need never have but when you please, you should maintain so many idle men, as will always disturb you in time of peace, which is ever to be more

---

[1] Letter from Erasmus to Ulrich von Hutten; quoted in KAUTSKY, KARL, "Thomas More and His Utopia, with a Historical Introduction," p. 92, London, 1927.

considered than war." It is the first vigorous argument against the maintenance of a standing army. The times are awry and call for remedies. Grazing has commandeered the soil previously devoted to agriculture, and the former tenants are ousted by the rich proprietors. The poor, forced to move, are destitute. They are poverty-stricken and must steal in order to maintain life; and for thefts to which they are driven by circumstances beyond their control, they are hanged from the gibbet. Aside from the fact that they are not responsible for the circumstances which force them into crime, the punishment is too severe, for the severity of a punishment is not a measure of its efficacy in preventing crime. "Extreme justice [*i.e.*, extreme punishment] is an extreme injury." Such offenders should be fined, not hanged. And "if you suffer your people to be ill-educated, and their manners to be corrupted from their infancy, and then punish them for those crimes to which their first education disposed them, what else is to be concluded from this, but that you first make thieves and then punish them?" After these observations on the evils of the times, More describes Utopia, an island in the Atlantic, the waters of which touch the shores of many remarkable lands. The work reflects the influence of Plato's "Republic" and More's references to Plato show that he consciously had this work in mind. Utopia comprises 54 cities,[1] distant about 24 miles from one another, large and well built, all having the same manners, customs, and laws. The number of families in a city is limited to six thousand. A city has jurisdiction over the adjacent territory, to a distance of about 20 miles—an idea undoubtedly suggested by the territorial control exercised by the Greek city-states. Each city is surrounded by a wall and has straight streets 20 feet wide—when More wrote city streets were narrow, winding thoroughfares. The houses are so much alike that the appearance of one side of a street resembles that of a single house. At the back of each house is a garden. This is the first description of the model workmen's city, in which there are uniformity of plan, simplicity, neatness, and gardens. The people dwell by turns in the country districts and in the city, only part of the population exchanging places in any one year, so that there are always some older inhabitants to advise the new. The government embodies a balance of power, and thus prevents the rulers from intriguing against the people. In order to provide time for deliberation and for the emotions to cool, hasty legislation is not permitted. Every man has a trade, which usually passes from father to son; but a man who shows especial aptitude in some other pursuit than that of his father may

---

[1] The number was probably unconsciously suggested by Plato's number of citizens, 5,040; see above, p. 238.

follow it. In the "Preface" to the "Utopia," More declares that England's evils would be greatly decreased if all worked and there were no idle class; in Utopia, therefore, every man must work; there are no drones. Six hours constitute the working day. When the day's work is over and supper has been eaten, the people spend their leisure in some pleasant diversion, out of doors or in the dining halls. Amusement and entertainment are furnished, and there are intellectual pursuits for those who wish them.

More follows Aristotle rather than Plato in making the family the central unit in social life. Each family group is composed of not less than ten and not more than sixteen individuals. The oldest member of the family group is its head; husbands command wives, children obey parents, and the younger obey the older.[1] There are two slaves in each family. They do the laborious work and that which is untoward in its effects, such as killing the cattle, for this would spoil the kindly disposition of the citizens and weaken their pity; and these are among their most valuable qualities. Though the difficult and sordid work is done by slaves, the women prepare and cook the meat and serve the meals. A man who wishes to travel abroad must obtain permission, secure a passport, and return within a specified time. The Utopians use iron in place of gold and silver. They thus diminish the love of wealth and break down the false preference for precious metals which other peoples value because of their scarcity and not in proportion to their utility, and they thus avoid a perversity which elsewhere leads to much evil. Jewels they find, diamonds and carbuncles, but these are regarded as mere baubles which please children; adults who use them lower themselves to the status of infants. All education is in their own tongue, and no other language is needed. For them, as for the Epicureans, a virtuous life is a life according to nature. This brings the highest pleasures, keeps the mind free from passion, and inculcates cheerfulness.

They infer that a man ought to advance the welfare and comfort of the rest of mankind, there being no virtue more proper and peculiar to our nature than to ease the miseries of others, to free from trouble and anxiety, in furnishing them with the comforts of life, in which pleasure consists.

Although "no man can be bound to look after the good of another more than his own," he should not prefer his own good to that of another. This is an anticipation of utilitarianism: pleasure is the highest goal, and the pleasure of others is as important as one's own.[2] Unlike Bentham,

---

[1] Exactly as in the early historical civilizations; see the author's "Introduction to Sociology," part I, New York, 1928.

[2] See below, p. 335.

however, More emphasizes the differences in the qualities of pleasures. Hunting especially is deprecated and only butchers kill game. One must not secure pleasure at the expense of others, not even of the brutes. The killing of a hare should excite pity rather than joy. Men share the pleasures of sense with animals, and such enjoyments, therefore, are not above the animal level. Since, however, the pleasures of the mind yield peculiar delights they should be cultivated. Here, too, More is an exponent of Epicureanism.[1] Stoic influence, however, appears in the statement that the Utopians

. . . define virtue thus, that it is a living according to nature, and think that we are made by God for that end; they believe that man then follows the dictates of nature when he pursues or avoids things according to the direction of reason . . . Reason directs us to keep our minds as free from passion and as cheerful as we can, and that we should consider ourselves as bound by the ties of good nature and humanity to use our utmost endeavors to help forward the happiness of other persons . . . But of all pleasures, they esteem those to be most valuable that lie in the mind; the chief of which arises out of true virtue, and the witness of a good conscience. They account health the chief pleasure that belongs to the body; for they think that the pleasure of eating and drinking, and all the other delights of sense, are only so far desirable as they give or maintain health . . . They think, therefore, none of those pleasures are to be valued any further than as they are necessary; yet they rejoice in them, and with due gratitude acknowledge the tenderness of the great author of nature, who has planted in us appetites, by which those things that are necessary for our preservation are likewise made pleasant to us.[2]

There are no lawyers among the Utopians for the laws are so simple and straightforward that all understand them; they need no interpretation and occasion no haggling.

All laws are promulgated for this end, that every man may know his duty; and therefore the plainest and most obvious sense of the words is that which ought to be put upon them, since a more refined exposition cannot be easily comprehended, and would only serve to make the laws become useless to the greater part of mankind, and especially to those who need most the direction of them: for it is all one, not to make a law at all, or to couch it in such terms that without a quick apprehension, and much study, a man cannot find out the true meaning of it; since the generality of mankind are both so dull, and so

---

[1] See above, p. 258.

[2] This last-mentioned phase of pleasure, its survival value, was emphasized by HERBERT SPENCER in his "Data of Ethics."

much employed in their several trades, that they have neither the leisure nor the capacity requisite for such an inquiry.[1]

In the conduct of war the Utopians have many novel methods. Wives follow husbands into the fray and assist them unto the death, but when possible mercenaries are employed. Victory is not pressed, lest the foe become more obstinate. Prisoners are well treated and, seeing this, prefer comfortable imprisonment to risk of death from continuing the fight. In order to encourage flight, enemies are not pursued.

The individual is allowed great latitude in religion. Here, for the first time, is an outspoken plea for freedom of worship: "there are several sorts of religions, not only in different parts of the island, but even in every town." Yet all believe in a Supreme Being, Mithras, who made and governs the world. One of their oldest laws provides that no man shall be punished on account of his religion.

Every man might be of what religion he pleased, and might endeavor to draw others to it by the force of argument, and by amicable and modest ways, but without bitterness against those of other opinions; but that he ought to use no other force but that of persuasion, and was neither to mix with it reproaches nor violence; and such as did otherwise were to be condemned to banishment or to slavery—

---

[1] See also Harrington, below, p. 288. Perhaps More's own experiences stimulated these remarks. His father had been a lawyer and More had been compelled, against his own wishes, to prepare for the legal profession. "For remote as that profession is from true learning," writes Erasmus, "those who become masters of it have the highest rank and reputation among their countrymen; and it is difficult to find any readier way to acquire fortune and honor. Indeed, a considerable part of the nobility of that island [England] has had its origin in this profession, in which it is said that no one can be perfect, unless he has toiled at it for many years. It was natural that in his younger days our friend's [that is, More's] genius, born of better things, should shrink from this study." Letter from Erasmus to Ulrich von Hutten; quoted in KAUTSKY, KARL, *op. cit.*, p. 89. See JARRETT, BEDE, "Mediæval Socialism," chap. V, (London, n.d.) regarding the role of lawyers in medieval times. In the early American colonies, too, lawyers were unpopular. In 1641 the Massachusetts Body of Liberties provided that every litigant might plead his own case and might pay counsel "noe fee or reward for his paines." In the early days of the Maryland colony a local chronicler gave thanks that there were no lawyers in the colony. See, BEARD, CHARLES A. and MARY R., "The Rise of American Civilization," vol. I, pp. 100–101, New York, 1927. Hugh Brackenridge, a Pennsylvania lawyer, wrote early in the nineteenth century: "They (the lawyers) have so much jargon that the devil himself cannot understand them. Their whole object is to get money; and, provided they can pick the pocket of half a joe, they care little about the person that consults them ... This thing of the law has been well said to be a bottomless pit." BRACKENRIDGE, HUGH, "Model Chivalry"; quoted in BEARD, CHARLES A. and MARY R., *op. cit.*, vol. I, p. 474.

a rather severe penalty for those who interfered with religious freedom. In the interest of religion itself tolerance is needed. Indeed, perhaps all religions come from God, who inspires men in different manner. Is it not foolish as well as indecent to threaten and terrify another in order to make him believe that which to him does not appear to be true?

And supposing that only one religion was really true, and the rest false, [the founder of Utopia] imagined that the native force of truth would at last break forth and shine bright, if supported only by the strength of argument, and attended to with a gentle and unprejudiced mind; while, on the other hand, if such debates were carried on with violence and tumults, as the most wicked are always the most obstinate, so the best and most holy religion might be choked with superstition, as corn is with briars and thorns; he therefore left men wholly to their liberty, that they might be free to believe as they should see cause; only he made a solemn and severe law against such as should so far degenerate from the dignity of human nature as to think that our souls died with our bodies, or that the world was governed by chance, without a wise overruling Providence.

Those who do not believe that after death a different fate awaits the good and the wicked cannot be held to any standard of conduct on earth, and are not to be trusted by their fellows; hence they are not raised to any high estate or office, but are despised.[1] Kautsky remarks of this passage,

These discussions, so far as they relate to the toleration of all creeds, are more suggestive of the age of "Enlightenment" than of the Reformation, more in harmony with the age in which "Nathan the Wise" was written than the age in which Calvin burnt Servetus, immediately before the bloodiest wars of religion that the world has ever seen, and they seem to us all the more generous as not coming from an unbeliever, who actually stood above religions, but from a profoundly religious spirit, a man who found in religion the sole medium which his age offered for giving expression to his enthusiastic love of mankind, for whom irreligiosity was synonymous with lack of common sense. The materialism of the sixteenth century arose, in fact, not among the exploited, but among the exploiting classes. Those who disbelieved in God and immortality were popes and cardinals, princes and courtiers; their contempt for religion was concomitant with their contempt for the people. This must be borne in mind, in order to understand why More excluded materialists as common egoists from the political administration.[2]

---

[1] Compare Harrington, below, p. 288. Mandeville, too, thinks that "without the Belief of another World, a Man is under no Obligation for his Sincerity in this: His very Oath is no Type upon him." MANDEVILLE, BERNARD, "Fables of the Bees," pt. II, sixth dialogue, London, 1723.

[2] KAUTSKY, KARL, *op. cit.*, p. 240.

Money is the root of all evil. Abolish it and with it go, "frauds, thefts, robberies, quarrels, tumults, contentions, seditions, murders, treacheries, and witchcrafts . . . Men's fears, solicitudes, cares, labors, and watchings, would all perish in the same moment with the value of money: even poverty itself, for the relief of which money seems most necessary, would fall." Take away pride, which accompanies inequalities, and another source of evil is removed. When society is protected against foes within, it is invulnerable. In Utopia men live happily;

. . . for, having rooted out of the minds of their people all the seeds both of ambition and faction, there is no danger of any commotion at home; which alone has been the ruin of many States, that seemed otherwise to be well secure, but as long as they live in peace at home, and are governed by such good laws, the envy of all their neighboring princes, who have often though in vain attempted their ruin, will never be able to put their State into any commotion or disorder.

Thus were the idealisms of Lycurgus, Plato, Zeno, and Epicurus interpreted to sixteenth-century Europe by one who was steeped in the thought of the past, yet modern in his sympathies and outlook.

3. CAMPANELLA'S "CITY OF THE SUN"[1]

Campanella, a Spanish Jesuit, a contemporary of Bacon, constructs his ideal commonwealth as a city, built on a high hill, which rises from an extensive plain and is so located that it can be easily defended. Its natural defense is strengthened by concentric ramparts, so that if some were taken, the remaining fortifications would be ample defense. Much attention is given to preparation for defensive, but not for offensive, warfare. Defense is insured by military training, by the armor which is provided against the day of need, and by the attention paid to tactics and strategy. The inhabitants of the City of the Sun utilize extensively the resources of nature. The impending weather is foretold. There is knowledge of the whole world, including geographical features and products, the cultivation of plants, the breeding of animals, and the development of new varieties. Nor is interest in physical types limited to plants and beasts. Human matings must be so arranged as to insure the best offspring. The inhabitants laugh at us who exhibit a studious care for our breeds of horses and dogs and leave to chance the breeding

---

[1] In late Roman days and through the Middle Ages the term "Sun State" referred to a communistic establishment. See BEER, MAX, *op. cit.*, p. 154, and KINGSLEY, CHARLES, "Hypatia."

of human beings.[1] A prerequisite to good citizenship is physical fitness,
which insures the health and strength without which one cannot perform
the tasks incumbent upon all members of the commonwealth. There is
communism in wives, and in all possessions. This was the case among
the early Christians—as the Church Fathers pointed out, though some
of them did not believe that the early Christians extended their communism to wives.[2] The apportionment of property is left to the magistrates, but

. . . arts and honors and pleasures are common, and are held in such a manner,
that no one can appropriate anything to himself . . . They say that all private
property is acquired and improved for the reason that each one of us by himself
has his own house and wife and children. From this self-love springs. For when
we raise a son to riches and dignities, and leave an heir to much wealth, we
become either ready to grasp at the property of the State, if in any case fear
should be removed from the power which belongs to riches and rank; or
avaricious, crafty, and hypocritical, if any one is of slender purse, little strength,
and mean ancestry. But when we have taken away self-love, there remains
only love for the State.

The argument is almost identical with that of Plato.

Work is not ignoble. "They laugh at us in that we consider our
workmen ignoble." Here Hesiod rather than Genesis is the guide. More
reduces the hours of work to six, Campanella to four. Since all work, and
work efficiently, four hours of labor suffice; the remainder of the time is
spent in leisure and in improving body and mind. The attainment of old
age is insured by simple living and by proper care of the body, and after
the age of seventy there is a rejuvenescence. Many live to the age of a
hundred and some to the age of two hundred, though imagination has
not yet compassed the hundreds of years which Bernard Shaw would
assign to human beings in the three hundred and twentieth century
A.D., or thereabouts.

An undercurrent of cosmopolitanism runs through the work and
appears in many specific statements. The Heliopolitans know the physical geography of the world and the history of all peoples. "There are
tablets setting forth for every separate country the customs both public
and private, the laws, the origins and the powers of the inhabitants; and
the alphabets the different people use can be seen above that of the City

---

[1] *Ac irrident nos qui generationi canum et equorum studiosam nauamus curam,
humanam vero negligimus.* P. 149 of the Folio edition. See "Schlaraffia Politica.
Geschichte der Dichtungen vom Besten Staate," pp. 78–79, Leipzig, 1892. Campanella had some weird ideas of insuring eugenic measures by precautions based on
astronomical observations.

[2] See above, pp. 266–270.

of the Sun." The great ruler, Hon, "or, as we should call him Metaphysics," must know the histories of nations, their customs, sacrifices, laws, and forms of government, whether republics or monarchies. "He must also know the names of the lawgivers and the inventors in science, and the laws and the history of the earth and the heavenly bodies. They think it also necessary that he should understand all the mechanical arts, the physical sciences, astrology and mathematics." Other nations may have some customs which are better than those of the inhabitants of the City of the Sun, and these should be adopted. Since the manner of life in that city eventually will be accepted by all peoples, its citizens should acquire as soon as possible every useful and good trait.

Here, then, as in St. Augustine and in Dante, is the conception of all men living under one form of government. The City of the Sun selects the best and orients itself in the larger world of which it is a part. Government is conducted with a consciousness of this world orientation, and the ruler lives in a world atmosphere.

The closing words of the book express belief in progress. We are on the threshold of great achievements which will come with unprecedented rapidity. "Oh, if you knew what our astrologers say of the coming age, and of our age, that has in it more history within a hundred years than all the world had in four thousand years before! Of the wonderful invention of printing and guns, and the use of the magnet! . . . " Following which is the caution: "Ah, well! God gives all in His good time. They astrologize too much."

As early as 1586 the Jesuits acquired land in Paraguay, and between 1601 and 1615 large tracts came under their control. Here they planned among the Indians a system of life comparable with that advocated by Campanella in the City of the Sun. There was to be a city of not less than 2,500 and not more than 7,000 inhabitants and no one was to be domiciled on the surrounding territory. The territory under control was to be encircled by a wall. All capital, including even the draught cattle, was owned communally, and no child in the State belonged to one individual more than to another. The community flourished for some decades but in 1768 practically all of the Jesuits in Paraguay were deported and the church-state came to an end. Every vestige of it was destroyed and soon the site of the community was again covered by the forest.[1]

4. Bacon's "New Atlantis"

The "New Atlantis," by Francis Bacon, was published (1617 or 1623) a century after the composition of More's "Utopia." The author died

---

[1] See LAIDLER, HARRY W., "A History of Socialist Thought;" "Schlaraffia Politica"; and GOTHEIN, EBERHARD, "Reformation und Gegenreformation."

before it was completed, and left no intimation of the further course of his thought. He refers to Plato and Aristotle by name, and there is one unmistakable reference to More's "Utopia." Yet without these specific references it would be evident that Bacon was acquainted with these utopias. He was a profoundly learned man, steeped in the classical lore of his day, and was well informed in contemporary literature, for he had taken all knowledge to be his province. New Atlantis is a remote island in the South Seas, possessing traditions of a former union with the New World and of earlier Jewish influence. Some nineteen hundred years previously Salomon [Solomon] was the king. Like the Greeks—Lycurgus, Plato, Aristotle—the New Atlanteans excluded foreigners, "doubting novelties and conmixture of manners." It is true that this policy of isolation as practiced by China has not been beneficial to that country; yet the case here is different, for they are always ready to harbor strangers cast upon their shores. But Bacon fails to show that the policy of isolation would be more advantageous in another land than it had been in China, where isolation had been a handicap, cutting off the fructifying influences of the Western world. Aristotle's influence appears in the importance assigned to the family. The eldest male is the head of the family group. When a man has 30 surviving descendants over three years of age he is made the hero of an important public festival or feast. Problems of over-population do not trouble the author of "New Atlantis."

The point of departure in Bacon's "New Atlantis," and the unique contribution up to this time of his utopia, is the scientific and mechanical advance which the people have made and the methods which they have devised for the further conquest of nature through knowledge of her laws.[1] Mines are sunk into the earth to extract the ores; towers a half-mile high are erected to facilitate the study of atmospheric conditions, heavenly bodies, and celestial manifestations—eclipses, meteors, and other phenomena—to enable men to forecast the weather, and to increase knowledge. There are experiments with porcelains and cements, and with composts and soils which will make the earth fruitful. There is grafting and the production of new varieties of plants, selective breeding of animals, and the production of new breeds. Experiment and observation penetrate every corner of nature. Much of the twentieth-century world is adumbrated in the "New Atlantis"—airplanes, submarines, telescopes, microscopes.[2] Boards of experts summate the results of the experiments and tabulate them so that they can be readily found, and others give particular attention to possible means of utilizing them. In this respect

---

[1] His contemporary, Campanella, likewise stresses the promise of science. See above, p. 281.

[2] See also above, p. 252.

the New Atlanteans are in advance of us. The concept that science will remake the world attracted other seventeenth-century scholars. "Posterity will find many things that are now but rumors, verified into practical realities," writes Granville in 1661. A voyage to the South Seas, even one to the moon will be no more strange than one to America. Men will buy wings for flight and will talk to distant friends as easily as they correspond by letter. The old will be made young, and the desert will be converted into a paradise. Science will bring utopia. Descartes said:

We shall be able to find an art, by which, knowing the force and action of fire, water, air, stars, the heavens, and all other objects, as clearly as we know the various trades of our artisans, we may be able to employ them in the same way for their appropriate uses, and make ourselves the masters and possessors of nature. And this will not be solely for the pleasure of enjoying with ease and by ingenious devices all the good things of the world, but principally for the preservation and improvement of human health, which is both the foundation of all the goods and the means of strengthening and quickening the spirit itself.

5. ANDREÆ'S "CHRISTIANOPOLIS"

"Christianopolis," published by Johann Valentin Andreæ in 1619, appeared about the time of the "New Atlantis" (which was published in 1617 or in 1623), and the two works have much in common. In this utopia, located somewhere in the wide Atlantic, the form of commonwealth is the city. There are public storehouses, adjoining which are seven mills and as many bakeries, also meat shops and provision chambers. The men who do the rough work are gentle and refined. "The government is administered in a way so advantageous in all respects that the people can enjoy all these privileges with a pleasure that is decent and need not be concealed." The houses, which have plain and simple furniture, contain only three rooms, and the cooking is done in common bakeries. There is specialization in industry, and each does the thing for which he is especially fitted. Manual labor is conducted in a prescribed manner; all manufactured articles are brought to a public booth, from which each workman receives out of the stores the things needed for the tasks of the ensuing week. The entire city is a single workshop and harbors all crafts. Those in charge of the activities are stationed in the smaller towers at the corners of the wall; they know in advance, and in detail, what is to be made, and this information they impart to the mechanics. If the supply of material in the work booth is sufficient, the workmen are permitted to use it as they wish, to give play to inventive talent. No one is richer than another. No individual has money and no one needs it, though there is a public treasury. Superiority is attained by ability and genius, the highest respect being paid to morals and piety. In the short working day as much is accomplished as during the long day in other places, for it is disgraceful to take more rest or leisure than is allowed. Since, in other places, it requires 10 workers to support one idler, it is plausible that where all work there is leisure for all, and the manner of working is such that men seem to benefit rather than harm their bodies. Moreover, where there is no slavery, manual labor is not irksome and does not weigh down or weaken. "And who will doubt that where God is favorable, all things are done with greater force and zeal, more easily and more accurately than where against the wishes and favor of God, a mass of useless buildings is heaped up?"

6. Hartlib's "Kingdom of Macaria"

In the utopian "Kingdom of Macaria," described by Hartlib in 1641, the government is conducted by a Great Council, consisting of five committees which deal, respectively, with agriculture, fishing, trade by land and by sea, and plantations. Through it the State supervises every branch of production. No individual is allowed to hold more land than he can utilize intensively. For retaining inadequately utilized land the individual incurs a penalty, which doubles each year, and if he is incorrigible, the lands are forfeited to the community. Hartlib believed his plan would be adopted by England and eventually by the entire world.

7. Samuel Gott's "Nova Solyma"[1]

In 1648 Samuel Gott, who had taken his degree at Cambridge University in 1632, published "Nova Solyma," a work dealing primarily with education in the ideal city, which is located somewhere near Jerusalem. New Jerusalem is doubtless the suggestion for Nova Solyma, and the influence of much of the "Nova Solyma" is probably traceable to Andreæ's "Christianopolis."

The education of children begins as soon as they can stand and walk, which they are taught to do gracefully and firmly. The training of the body as well as of the mind is emphasized, and,

we try every method we can to make our children healthy and robust and natural in their bodies, nor do we put aside those methods which breeders are so careful about with their dogs and horses, as we hold it a great personal matter for every parent.[2]

---

[1] This work, published anonymously, Begley erroneously attributed to John Milton.

[2] Bk. I, chap. I.

In order to learn the essentials of government and statecraft it is necessary to study the history of past civilizations. Instruction is conducted in the language of the respective peoples. Specialization begins, as soon as the individual is ready for it, in the field in which he displays the greatest talent, interest, and ability. An important and honorable position in the commonwealth is assigned to teachers.

There are doctors and inspectors of education, authorities who can be consulted on educational problems, and there are extension lectures: "public discourses held frequently in all parts of the land, not only of a religious nature, but on ethics, the family life, and such topics . . . If anyone is gifted with abilities out of the common it looks after him and helps his career. Nor is anyone with natural endowments of a higher order allowed to remain unnoticed and neglected from the obscurity of his birth, as is so often the case elsewhere." Special endeavors are expended upon the less gifted, also,

that they may be able at least to rise to the full height of their capacity and in due course fitly perform their duties to the State. In point of fact, when we, as teachers, look for the highest results and greatest pleasure from our work, we find that it is not so much the very talented that satisfy us, for these, by their shortcomings in other matters, often cause far more trouble and offense than do those pupils of less ability, but greater goodness of disposition.[1]

8. Winstanley

In "The Law of Freedom" (1652) Gerrard Winstanley advocates a communistic utopia.

There shall be no buying and selling of the earth, nor of the fruits thereof . . . If any man or family want corn or other provisions, they may go to the storehouse, and fetch without money. If they want a horse to ride, they may go into the fields in summer or to the common stables in winter, and receive one from the keepers, and when the journey is performed, bring him back . . . As every one works to advance the common stock, so every one shall have free use of any commodity in the storehouse for his pleasure and comfortable liveli-hood, without buying or selling or restraint from anybody.[2]

"The Law of Freedom" is dedicated to "All the Nations of the Earth," and in the new society proposed by Winstanley there is neither buying nor selling, for bargaining fosters deception, and from deception springs oppression. With the disappearance of buying and selling, there will be an end to lawyers. One man may not be richer than another, for riches enable men to oppress their fellows and to foment war. Moreover,

---

[1] *Ibid.*

[2] WINSTANLEY, GERRARD, "The Law of Freedom," pp. 74–75, 1652; quoted in LAIDLER, HARRY W., "A History of Socialist Thought," pp. 49–50, New York, 1927.

riches cannot be obtained by honest means. A man cannot become wealthy by his unaided efforts, and those who assist him are entitled to a share of the results of their joint exertions.

9. HARRINGTON'S "OCEANA"

The "Oceana" of James Harrington (1611–1677), published in 1659 during Cromwell's rule, deals exclusively with political problems. He contrasts Plato with Hobbes, and believes the ancients conceived society as an empire of laws in contrast with the moderns, who conceive it as an empire of men. The government of Oceana is controlled by a series of checks and balances, for Harrington, like Polybius and Cicero, is convinced that without checks a government will run to extremes. It is modeled to some extent after the government of Venice under the doges. Aristocracy is the best form; indeed, it is inevitable, for inequality rather than equality is the outstanding characteristic of human beings. In any group of 20 men, at least six have a deep interest in problems of government. Being interested, they discuss politics, inform themselves more fully in this field, and develop keener judgments than do the others. Their fellows, accordingly, soon acknowledge that these men are peculiarly able to pass judgment on political matters. It thus becomes obvious that any wisdom in political affairs is the wisdom of the few. But the wisdom of the few seldom is equivalent to the interest of the many, and herein lies the difficulty of government by an aristocracy. In a representative form of government there is, moreover, the further difficulty that the governing body both makes the alternatives and chooses among them. Yet justice for all cannot be guaranteed unless all are equally able to determine the alternatives. The laws should be few and comprehensible to all, and they should not permit of quibbling nor require expert interpretation.[1] There should be freedom of conscience and religion, yet this does not apply to the Jew or the agnostic.[2]

The "Oceana" reviews the theories of predecessors and assesses the value of their respective contributions to political speculation. The author, however, ignores the problem of the extent to which the system enunciated by a thinker may be adapted to his time and culture, yet ill-fitted to other cultures and other times. It remains for subsequent writers to exploit the concept of relativity in the realm of social phenomena, though the Sophists had clearly grasped it.[3]

Since the author feels that there is no reason why a commonwealth should not be as immortal as the stars in heaven, no efforts are to be spared that the

---

[1] Compare Sir Thomas More, above, p. 278.

[2] Compare More, above, p. 280.

[3] See above, p. 235.

methods by which this is to be attained may be put in force. True government resting on persuasion, weekly classes for the explanation of the constitution are to be held, and a thousand officials are to traverse the country to give the people their first lessons in the mysteries of the ballot, a familiarity more essential to be acquired, since all elections, local as well as general, are conducted on this principle.[1]

No individual may own land the income from which exceeds £2,000 a year. The religious life of the nation, and the maintenance of religious freedom, is entrusted to the control of a national council of religion. There is religious toleration, and there is no political disqualification because of religious belief. Baxter, too, believes that

> Men's consciences are not under the inspection or cognizance of the magistrate. He that will be an infidel, must have liberty of conscience to damn himself and then to torment himself whether the magistrate will or no: But if he have liberty to infect and seduce others, the magistrate shall answer for it.[2]

The "History of Severambe," by Vairasse (or Vayrasse), published in Paris in 1677, two decades after the appearance of Harrington's "Oceana," is in lighter vein, and reflects the prevailing French classicism. The verse is interspersed with comment upon matters of contemporary interest and with references to classical literature. In Severambe the dead are cremated, and here, 200 years before their appearance in Europe, large crematories are erected. The natives have evolved a simple grammatical structure for their language, which incorporates the elements of European languages. It may be regarded as a prototype of Volapük. Thus the paradigm for love is:

MASCULINE	FEMININE	NEUTER
ermana	*ermane*	*ermano*
ermanach	*ermanech*	*ermanoch*
ermanas	*ermanes*	*ermanos*
ermanan	*ermanen*	*ermanon*
ermananchi	*ermanenchi*	*ermanonchi*
ermanansi	*ermanensi*	*ermanonsi*

Their poetry is metrical, but without rhyme, and a child, an unlettered man, or a peasant, can speak extemporaneously in rhyme.

"The Adventures of Jacques Sadeur in the Discovery of Southern Lands," written by Foigny, a Frenchman, in 1676, gives an account of a happy folk in the South Seas, where communism prevails and frolic

---

[1] GOOCH, G. P., "The History of English Democratic Ideas in the Seventeenth Century," p. 293, Cambridge, 1898.

[2] BAXTER, RICHARD, "A Holy Commonwealth," p. 278, London, 1659.

and fun reign. Political authority, clothing, and families do not exist.
The fact that each individual is both male and female makes the ideal
State possible. Ideal existence is easily attained by reason of a mere
physiological change! The author is poking fun at utopian writers who
would have us believe that this or that trivial modification of human nature would bring social perfection.

In the "Kingdom of Ophir," written by Werner Happel, and published in 1699, the author bewails the fact that his is the day of gold and
silver. When they jingle, men dance. Gold! Gold has its own subtle
craft: it conquers the invincible, and accomplishes the impossible; it
makes the wise foolish, and the foolish wise. So it was in the time of
the king Solomon, and so it is in the year 1699. Ophir is an intensely
religious land. The churches are small schools, the schools are small
churches. The professors in the universities are diligent, and competition
keeps them alert. Theologians give lectures on exegesis and ethics. The
lectures on law are concerned with its meaning and not with its formulas.
The crown prince travels through the land to study the status of the
inhabitants. There is careful observation of living conditions and an
accurate record of them is kept, such as we now include under statistics.[1]

Fénelon's "Telemachus" has been called "a book for the world," and
"one of the finest examples of the literature of the seventeenth century.[2]"
It was written between 1693 and 1697 and was published in 1699. It is a
long satire on the politics and person of Louis XIV, though it pretends
to be a continuation of the fourth book of the "Odyssey," and to relate
the adventures of Telemachus, the son of Odysseus and Penelope.
During the decade following its publication its popularity was exceeded
only by that of the Bible and Thomas à Kempis' "Imitation of Christ."
It was soon translated into all European languages, including Latin
and Greek, in verse and in prose.[3]

10. Spinoza and Cornelius

Spinoza believes that men naturally pursue happiness and that
poor judgment alone causes them to err when choosing the means of

---

[1] The "Telemachus," by Fénelon, published in 1699, also advocates obtaining
and systematizing information in a manner which we would now refer to as statistics.
These recommendations by a French and a German writer, respectively, appear to be
the first advocacy of securing comprehensive statistical information.

[2] Stehle, Bruno, "Fenelon, Die Erlebnisse des Telemach," "Vorwort," Münster,
1892.

[3] See, for example, Voltaire, "Siècle de Louis XIV," chap. XXXII. Voltaire
refers to the "Telemachus" as "an indirect criticism of the government of Louis
XIV."

attaining it. A bad action, therefore, indicates inadequate knowledge. To improve a man, then, one must give him a reason to change his opinions. A society which by its laws provides a motive for industry, enterprise, honesty, and thrift, supplies to its citizens adequate reasons for regarding these qualities as beneficial. The thief can be converted into an honest tradesman if convinced that the skill which he displays in depriving another of his money can be employed to his own greater advantage in other ways. To be angry or indignant with the evil-doer is useless; one must remove the causes which lead to wrong-doing. A better social environment, more suitable conditions of labor, and a higher type of family life are needed. The end of the State is to make men free, i.e., to induce them to live according to reason. This it can do only by prescribing and enforcing certain courses of conduct; hence the supreme importance of law, which is indispensable to social life.

A fellow-countryman of Spinoza, the Dutchman Peter Cornelius, proposed a "Way to the Peace and Settlement of these Nations, to make the poor in these and other nations happy." Established governments should come to an end, and Christendom should become a World State under one government. To hasten this day individuals should form joint-stock associations in which they would live together, although each might retain possession of his property. Each "little commonwealth" thus organized would function as a single household. From among their number the members would elect a governor, whose term would be one year, but who might be reelected. Only "honest and rational" people who were masters of a trade or occupation would be admitted to the association as members, and those who proved themselves unfit would be expelled. Those to whom admission was denied might be employed by the association, and might be admitted to it when they had attained a specified standard of good conduct and efficiency. Thus the vices arising from riches, poverty, inequality, exploitation, or other causes would vanish. The pamphlets issued by Cornelius were written in English and the author shows familiarity with English political and social conditions. Such speculations were not common in the Low Countries at this time, and they were probably the result of English influence.

Cornelius was probably influenced by a pamphlet bearing the title, "A Colledge of Industry," issued in the latter part of the century by John Bellers, which outlines a reconstruction of society. Groups of individuals will form "Colledges of Industry," which will be associations producing and consuming in common. He later declared that such associations were intended only for those in want, and subsequently advocated cooperative production as a means of ameliorating the state of the poor and abolishing poverty.

The title of Bellers' first work indicates the emphasis of his thought: "Proposals for Raising a Colledge of Industry of all Useful Trades and Husbandry, with Profit for the Rich, a Plentiful Living for the Poor, and a Good Education for Youth Which will be Advantage to the Government by the Increase of the People, and their Riches. By John Bellers, Motto, Industry Brings Plenty. The Sluggard shall be cloathed with Rags. He that will not Work, Shall not Eat." London, 1696. Bellers finds it "as much more charity to put the poor in a way to live by honest labour, than to maintain them idle; as it would be to set a man's broken leg, that he might go himself, rather than always to carry him," a doctrine which did not become a commonplace among social workers until the twentieth century. Instruction is vocational and the association is self-supporting.

CHAPTER XVI

CONCEPTS OF PROGRESS IN FRENCH THOUGHT BEFORE THE NINETEENTH CENTURY

1. BODIN

By the sixteenth century European thought was emerging from the bondage of classicism. The ideals of the moderns are well represented in French writers, particularly in Jean Bodin, a social philosopher of the sixteenth century, and in Perrault and Fontenelle. Bodin divides human history into three periods, represented by the successive dominance of the Southeastern, the Mediterranean, and the Northern nations. The first period, which lasted about 2,000 years, is marked by development in religion, the second excels in practical sagacity, and the third is characterized by warfare and inventive skill. The theory of a Golden age and of subsequent human degeneration is discredited by the fact that the powers of nature remain uniform and that they do not in one century produce types of men and conditions which they do not duplicate in another. Unlike Machiavelli, he does not imply that human nature is immutable, but merely that natural capacities are permanent. Since primitive times, however, culture has developed to such an extent that, if the so-called "Golden age" could be recalled and compared with our own, we should find it an age of iron rather than one of gold. In this respect he reflects the views of Lucretius. Civilization, which is dependent upon the wills of men, is in constant flux. Every day appear new laws, customs, secular and religious institutions, and errors. Throughout these shifting scenes, cultures rise and fall with wave-like undulations. This does not imply that the human race has been degenerating; for, if this were the case, it would long since have reached the depths of iniquity and vice. On the contrary, throughout these oscillations man makes progress. The mythical Gold and Silver ages are tinseled misnomers for times when men lived no better than the beasts. From that state they have slowly risen to the culture of today which is characterized by manners and a rational social order.[1] The comparison of modern with ancient times is in optimistic vein. Knowledge, letters, and arts have their vicissitudes; they rise, develop, and flourish, then

---

[1] A thoroughly Lucretian view; see above, p. 259.

languish and die. The long fallow period, initiated by the fall of Roman civilization, was followed by a revival of knowledge and by an intellectual productivity which no other age has excelled. The scientific discoveries of the ancients deserve much praise; but the moderns have thrown additional light on phenomena which the ancients had explained, and their discoveries are of equal or greater importance. To find great accomplishments in various phases of civilization, said Perrault, it is not necessary to turn to the age of Pericles; inexhaustible possibilities of achievement are represented by the accomplishments of seventeenth-century scholars and artists. The human race is eternal and its potentiality has not been exhausted in any civilization. Humanity has passed through the stages of infancy and youth, is at present in its maturity, and will not decline.[1] Perrault compares developments in the seventeenth century with the growth of an individual, the century having its infancy, childhood, adulthood, and, in the last quarter, its decline. Similarly, the stages in the development of the respective arts are comparable with those in the life of an individual. Nature is immutable. The dispositions of animals do not change. The lions of the African desert are as ferocious now as they were in the days of Ptolemy and Strabo. But the dispositions of men change, and, unlike the beasts, man is capable of making indefinite progress. Therefore, since nature is constant in gifts of mind as well as of body, contemporary man can duplicate the feats of the ancients:

> A former les esprits comme à former les corps,
> La Nature en tout temps fait les mêsme efforts,
> Son êstre est immuable, et cette force aisée,
> Dont elle produit tout, ne s'est point epusée.[2]

The Italian philosopher Vico (1668–1744) was much influenced by Bodin, although his thought is similar to that of the Stoics. Everywhere men are essentially the same, though their characteristics differ in details; hence nations, which are composed of men, are fundamentally alike and pass through similar stages of development. Any individual, therefore, might remark to another, "I am a man like you," and the history of any nation is reflected in that of any other, although the development of one nation is not influenced by that of another. Each nation passes through three stages—a view which Herodotus learned from the Egyptians and Varro adopted. These three stages are, respectively, the ages of the gods, of heroes, and of men. The motives which guide historical development hover about a sense of the interdependence

---

[1] FLINT, ROBERT, "History of the Philosophy of History," p. 214, Edinburgh, 1893.

[2] PERRAULT, "Le siècle de Louis le Grand."

of the sexes and reverence for the dead, the latter being the result of belief in a future life. These motives are essential to the maintenance of society and to its progress. They unite one generation with another, link the past with the present, and make men optimistic regarding the future.

2. FONTENELLE

A writer of the seventeenth century, Fontenelle, like Bodin, assumes constancy in the forces of nature, and denies that the ancients were superior to the moderns. The ancients did not have larger brains than the moderns, hence they could not have had greater mental capacity. Mankind will have no old age, will never degenerate, but will always be capable of repeating the successes of youth. In conceiving of progress as extending indefinitely into the future, and as being necessary and certain, Fontenelle goes beyond Bodin. Progress does not depend on chance or on an unpredictable non-human will, and mankind has sufficient potentiality of progress. Science will progress and knowledge will increase. Had their positions in history been reversed, the men of antiquity would be the progressive moderns, and the moderns would not have advanced beyond the position attained by the men of antiquity; historic opportunity explains the difference between their respective achievements. A necessary order underlies the stages of progress. The progress of a science, for example, depends upon the advance already made by related sciences; not until they have attained a certain fruition can it come into its own: "it has to await its turn to burst its shell."

3. SAINT-PIERRE

The Abbé de Saint-Pierre elaborated the concept that humanity progresses by a summation of achievements. The individual grows old, his powers wane, his abilities degenerate; but with the passing of generations, humanity's capacity for wisdom and happiness increases. Humanity will have a long progressive life, since civilization is now in its infancy. Saint-Pierre does not inquire to what extent human destinies are contingent upon the fate of this planet or upon that of the solar system of which our planet is a part. He does, however, think in larger terms than race or nation, and offers a plan which will insure progress. An association of nations will bring eternal peace—an idea which Rousseau and Kant subsequently exploit. Saint-Pierre specifies nineteen states or sovereigns as members of this congress which would represent the republic of Europe, namely, the emperor of the Holy Roman Empire, the Russian emperor, the kings, respectively, of France, Spain, England, Denmark, Portugal, Prussia, Naples, Sardinia, Rome (the pope), Sweden, Poland, the elector of Savoy and his associates, the elector of the Palatinate and his associates, the ecclesiastical electors and their associates, the republic of Venice and its associates, and a voting unit consisting of the republic of Genoa, the duke of Modena, and the duke of Parma. The five articles to which they would subscribe provided that the contracting sovereigns would establish an eternal alliance; specified the membership of the diet or congress; guaranteed to each member the existing possessions, territory, and government as provided in the fundamental laws of the respective lands; specified that a refractory member should be under a ban and be proscribed as a common public enemy if it (1) failed to conform with the decisions of the congress, (2) made preparation for war, (3) negotiated treaties contrary to the provisions of the confederation, or (4) used armed force to resist the congress or to attack a member State. The fifth article provided that, with the approval of the court, a majority vote might make regulations which were deemed advantageous for the European Republic, and, by a unanimous vote, might change the five fundamental articles of confederation. These provisions have many points in common with the covenant of the League of Nations drafted at Versailles in 1919. Saint-Pierre's "Projet" also provided for arbitration in case of the outbreak of hostilities between States; disarmament was proposed as a prelude to establishing perpetual peace in Europe.

4. PRE-REVOLUTION WRITERS

Pre-Revolution writers inquire into the significance of contemporary events and suggest remedies for the miseries and calamities of the day. Voltaire comments on the times in biting satire and ridicules many of the prevailing customs and beliefs. His irony, destructive in form, paves the way to constructive thought. It deals a death blow to old conventions, and dispels old chimeras and delusions. Voltaire finds the times rapidly changing for the better. In the age of Louis XIV men acquired more enlightened information than all the preceding ages could boast. Compared with the period of Henry IV and Huguenot persecutions, "Government is stronger everywhere and morals have improved." Different times have different appropriate needs; we must "get out of our grooves and study the rest of the world."

Montesquieu seeks an understanding of contemporary life through a comparative study of the laws and institutions of other peoples, thus placing in new perspective those of his own land and time. Men will no longer think in the narrow confines of the now and here, but will see contemporary institutions and events from a larger perspective.

In his letter concerning the Abbé de Saint-Pierre's plan for perpetual peace Rousseau points out that, with the exception of Turkey, Europe is already united in a society. It remains only to acknowledge the common bond and establish a machinery to strengthen and perpetuate existing ties. No nation makes war without promise of help from some other. When all are united in a firm bond, offensive alliances, and therefore war, will be impossible. Rousseau depicts the earlier life according to nature once followed by man and now abandoned. Wheat and iron have civilized man and have ruined him. The power which gave him control over nature brought also war, economic exploitation, and control over his fellows. The artificialities of life are responsible for the miseries created by civilization. Man can escape them by returning to that simple life according to nature which is his birthright, though civilization has denied him its enjoyment. He held a higher opinion of the savage than was entertained by our contemporary who wrote: "For the noble savage, when you meet him in real life, is not impressively noble; he usually has a stomach ache and is ready to trade his kingdom for a bottle of gin, and will barter his nobility for a box of pills."[1]

In "Letters from a Peruvian Lady," Madame de Graffigny gives an account of Peruvian civilization and then, by implication as well as directly, of European civilization, not always to the glorification of the latter. The French have genius, but their manner of life leaves much to be desired, and their charms should not blind one to their faults. Luxury saps energy which might be turned to better things, and privileges of birth and wealth procure advantages to the disregard of merit. "Happy the nation which has only nature as its guide, truth as its principle, and virtue as its possession."[2]

5. HOLBACH

At the beginning of his career, says Holbach, man subsists on acorns, and disputes with the beasts for his sustenance, but eventually he measures the heavens. After he has tilled and planted, he invents geometry. To protect himself against the cold, he covers his body with the hides of the beasts which he has killed; and in a few centuries he wears gold brocade. A cave, the trunk of a tree, constitute his first habitations, but eventually he becomes an architect and builds palaces. Increasing needs stimulate industry and he is compelled to bend his genius to work;

---

[1] HEADLAM, CECIL, "Friends That Fail Not; Light Essays Concerning Books," p. 88, London, 1902.

[2] "*Heureuse la nation qui n'a que la nature pour guide, la vérité pour principe et la vertue pour mobile*"; in De Graffigny, "Lettres d' une Peruvienne," vol. II, p. 46, Nouvelle édition, Paris, 1775.

thanks to the concatenations of human knowledge, he discovers, step
by step, the sciences and the arts. Much which does not serve his needs
satisfies his curiosity, which is incessant and never satiated. And so,
after measuring the fields, he surveys the firmament and unveils the laws
that govern heavenly bodies which the unaided eye cannot discern.
Under his hand the tree is transformed into an architectural column, the
cave into a palace, the wild grass into a lawn, the rough and fetid skin
into a magnificent robe. Through all these various steps, however distant
one from another, he is guided by his nature, which incessantly inspires
him to improve his lot and make it a source of greater pleasure. After
having been deprived for a long time of opportunity for reflection, he
commences to ponder; after having suffered for a long time from errant
ignorance, he cultivates the mind; after having strayed afar in the darkness of superstition, he searches for truth, which he uncovers with difficulty; and finally he finds the remedies for his misfortunes.

The savage has been represented as a happier being than civilized
man. But in what does his good fortune consist, and what, indeed, is a
savage? He is a vigorous child, deprived of resources, experience, reason,
and industry, suffering incessantly from famine and misery, compelled to
struggle constantly with the beasts, knowing no other virtue than temer-
ity. He is passionate, inconsiderate, cruel, vindictive, unjust, impatient
of restraint, taking no thought for the morrow, continually exposed to
the danger of becoming a victim either of his own peculiar folly or of the
ferocity and stupidity of those who are like himself. The life of the savage,
the state of nature described by jaded speculators, the Golden age lauded
by the poets, are in reality merely states of misery, imbecility, irrationality. In the importance which he attributes to climate as a factor that
influences human institutions, Montesquieu, says Holbach, goes beyond
the facts. Although climate influences men, in a fashion, very markedly,
and has modified many of their customs and opinions, it is not the most
important influence. Despotism flourishes equally well on the burning
sands of Libya and in the frigid forests of the North, in the fertile plains
of Hindustan and in the deserts of Scythia. In a warm land, in which
the sun furnishes warmth, food is abundant, and cultivation of the soil
is not necessary, the enervated inhabitant will be, one imagines, weak,
lazy, effeminate, and largely free from the fate which compels the robust
inhabitant of a mountainous or an inhospitable land to work; yet the
wandering Arab has eluded the yoke of slavery, though for centuries he
has been the neighbor of Persian, Egyptian, and Moor, and the climate
of Arabia does not differ markedly from that of Chaldea, Assyria, or
Morocco. The indomitable Tartar inhabits a region no more favorable
than the habitat of the Siberian; yet he is as inured to exertion, and as

little inclined to be a slave as are the Russian, the Japanese, and the Turk. Despite an unfavorable climate, the Tartars face death courageously. By nature man is neither good nor evil. He continually pursues his welfare, and employs all the faculties to obtain pleasure or to avert pain. The emotions, an essential inherent element in the species, and characteristic of sensitive creatures, are reducible to desire for welfare and aversion to misfortune. The emotions, therefore, are necessary, though in themselves they are neither good nor bad, and occasion neither admiration nor blame; what they become depends upon how they are utilized; they are useful and estimable when they secure our real welfare and the welfare of our fellows; they are rational when they adopt means designed to satisfy the need at which they aim. But the power of circumstance is great. Through it one can fashion man at will. As Seneca says, "You are wrong if you suppose that our vices are born with us; they are imposed upon us." The greatest criminal would have become a good man if he had been born of virtuous parents, had been disciplined wisely, and in his youth had associated with the virtuous. The great man whose virtues we admire would have been merely a brigand, a robber, an assassin, if he had associated only with brigands, robbers, and assassins. The abject courtier, who in the court of the despot becomes an intriguer, in Athens or in Rome would have become a noble and upright citizen. The effeminate Sybarite would in Sparta have been a courageous warrior. If Newton had been born among the Tartars or among the Arabs, he would have been merely a savage vagabond. No one does wrong wilfully. The sinner is a bad calculator, the dupe of ignorance, imprudence, and prejudice; in proportion as intelligence grows one learns to calculate correctly and to prefer the greater sum of good to the less. Holbach states clearly the utilitarian calculus which is usually attributed to the invention of Bentham.[1] But, unlike Bentham, he realizes that

every man who thinks holds the judgment in suspense, because he must judge of such a large number of complicated circumstances that it is practically impossible to distinguish the good from the bad, the true from the false, the useful from the useless.[2]

Truth consists in conforming ideas with the nature of things; it interests men only because it enables them to ascertain what actually exists, *i.e.*, the real qualities of things, and the connection of cause and effect. Such knowledge, which is identical with reason, and can be

---

[1] See below, p. 335.

[2] HOLBACH, PAUL, H. T., "Système social, ou principes naturels de la morale et de la politique, avec un examen de l'influence du gouvernement sur les mœurs," vol. I, pp. 1–100; vol. III, pp. 6–7, London, 1774.

acquired only through experience, enables one to distinguish the useful from the useless, reality from appearance, and the well-being which is real and enduring from the pleasure which is fugitive and evanescent. Truth, therefore, is indispensable to human welfare. Man needs it in order to identify the roads which lead to happiness. That which men like they wish to be true, says St. Augustine.[1] We do not like things because they are true, says M. Nicole, but we believe thay are true because we like them. But, says Holbach, no man is a sinner by preference. He succumbs to evil only when he entertains false ideas of well-being, utility, and his highest interests. The ideas which lead him to commit evil are the result of ignorance, inexperience, prejudice, or vicious tendencies. Injustice, fraud, debauchery, fanaticism, and false zeal have only relative and momentary utility; nevertheless, such things are rightly abhorrent to the rational man, because they lead to the ruin of society, and to the destruction of those who would profit by them.

Men grow better when they search for truth, cultivate reason, and assess experience. They must know the dangers of vice and the advantages of virtue. This knowledge is the objective of ethics. To increase happiness it is necessary to distinguish between things which make for good and those which make for evil. The object of every government is to induce its citizens to practice the rules of ethics, *i.e.*, the art of living well (*de bien vivre*) among their fellows.[2] Virtue consists in rendering others happy by increasing or insuring their welfare, and consequently all recognize the utility of ethics. Like the physical sciences, the science of morality should be based on facts, *i.e.*, on experience. The ancient philosophers, like many modern ones, appear to have relied on nothing more stable than inspiration and imagination; but experience is the only master whose lessons do not deceive and whose authority contributes to the love of wisdom. To keep the eyes of men fixed on the heavens while they walk on the earth is to invite a repetition of the imprudence of the ancient philosopher who, his eyes glued to the stars, tumbled into a ditch. Morality is one, and it should be the same for all the inhabitants of the globe. If, as Turgot says, man is everywhere the same, if he has everywhere the same nature, tendencies, and desires, then the study of man and of his relations with his fellows will reveal his obligations to himself and to others. The savage and the civilized, the White, the Red, the Black, the Indian, the European, the Chinese, the Frenchman, the Negro, and the Lapp, have the same nature: the differences between them are merely

---

[1] *Hoc quod amant volunt esse veritatem.*

[2] "Ethics is the art of living together humanely." Dole, F., "The Ethics of Progress or the Theory and Practice by Which Civilization Proceeds," p. 266, New York, 1909.

modifications of the same human nature, produced by climate, government, education, opinion, and other influences which impinge upon them. Men differ merely in their conception of welfare and in the choice of means. A morality based on evidence and on experience should make clear to princes and subjects, great and small, rich and poor, that happiness, public or private, of necessity lies in abiding by the obligations which it imposes. No people, empire, or individual can be truly and assuredly happy without virtue.

6. TURGOT

Turgot points out that the phenomena of nature, held in the grip of natural law, are delimited by a circle of recurrent changes which must remain forever the same. All returns to life, all perishes again; and in these successive generations, in which vegetables and animals reproduce their kind, time merely brings back the image of the past. The succession of men, on the contrary, gives rise to continual variations. Reason, freedom, the passions, produce new events. All epochs are bound together by ties of cause and effect. Speech and writing enable men to store ideas and impart them to others. Thus is accumulated a common treasure, which each generation transmits to its successor, and the discoveries of each succeeding generation augment the culture heritage. The human race is a living whole, which, like each individual in it, has its infancy and its growth. There is a sameness in human nature and therefore similar circumstances bring similar reactions. Thus,

the actual state of the universe, by presenting at the same moment on the earth all the shades of barbarism and civilization, discloses to us as in a single glance the monuments, the footprints of all the steps of the human mind, the measure of the whole track along which it has passed, the history of all the ages.

The human mind makes progress in knowledge. "Its history is the history of the growth and spread of science and the arts. Its advance is increased enlightenment of the understanding." From Adam and Eve to Louis XIV, the record of progress is the chronicle of the ever-increasing additions to the sum of human knowledge, which becomes more accurate as well as more ample. The chief instrument in this enlightenment is the occasional appearance of a lofty and superior intelligence; for, though human character contains everywhere the same principle, some men are endowed with more talent than are others. "Circumstances develop these superior talents, or leave them buried in obscurity; and from the infinite variety of these circumstances springs the inequality among nations." Agriculture precedes a high development of civilization. It brings a surplus of means of subsistence which allows men of higher capacity the leisure necessary for the acquisition of knowledge.[1] When the sciences are well under way—and the art of writing accelerates their development—each assists the others by reflecting light upon related fields. Though they tend to develop apart from one another in virtual independence, they will be brought together in a common synthesis, "because that mutual dependence of all truth is discovered, which, while it links them one to another, throws light on one by another."[2]

The rate of progress varies according to circumstance and talent. A happy arrangement in the cortices of the brain, more or less retentiveness or sensitiveness in the organs of sense and in the faculty of memory, and different degrees of vitality in the blood, probably constitute the unique differences among men for which nature is entirely responsible. Their mentalities display innate inequalities of power and quality, the cause of which is not known and never can be known. All other differences are attributable to education, which is the resultant of all the sensations received and all the ideas conceived. All elements of the environment contribute to it, and parental teaching and formal instruction constitute but a minor portion of such determinative influences. The innate

---

[1] "From leisure, in a good moral and intellectual atmosphere, come experiments, come philosophy and the new departures. In any modern Utopia there must be many leisurely people. We are all too obsessed in the real world by the strenuous ideal, by the idea that the vehement incessant fool is the only righteous man. Nothing done in a hurry, nothing done under strain, is really well done. A State where all are working hard, where none go to and fro, easily and freely, loses touch with the purpose of freedom."—WELLS, HERBERT G., "A Modern Utopia," p. 154, New York, n.d. Montesquieu said that civilization presupposes leisure.

[2] Baxter complained: "We parcel Arts and Sciences into fragments, according to the straitness of our capacities, and are not so pansophicall as *uno intuitu* to see the whole; and therefore we have not the perfect knowledge of any part." BAXTER, RICHARD, "A Holy Commonwealth, or Political Aphorisms, Opening the True Principles of Government," p. 493, London, 1659. But this view, while old, is remarkably modern. "As the sciences advance and extend their inquiries, they interlace with one another, and render mutual aid. It is still more significant of their unity that, as each science pushes its research back to the causes or foundations of its subjects of inquiry, it tends to merge with other sciences. Today, for instance, only superficially, for convenience's sake, would a line be drawn between physics (including mechanics) and chemistry. And historically the line of great names—Boyle, Priestley, Lavoisier, Cavendish, Faraday, Dalton, to mention some of the most revered—which appear in any history of chemistry, would also be included in a history of physics. These two sciences dealing with what still is masked under the name of inorganic nature, have become the bases of the biological sciences, which treat of the phenomena of living things. For example, 'general physiology' is now based on physics and chemistry. One might even say that it largely is physics and chemistry."—TAYLOR, HENRY O., "Freedom of the Mind in History," pp. 261–262, London, 1923.

capacities of primitive and of civilized peoples do not differ; they are essentially the same in all places and at all times. In every culture genius is as rare as a gold mine.

Progress, although inevitable, is interrupted by the decadence of cultures and by untoward events and revolutions. Its course varies greatly from one culture to another. Men who live in isolation from other cultures and have no trade with other peoples have attained little advance. Consequently, those small groups which are dependent upon the chase have about the same culture, the same arts, weapons, and customs. In such cultures genius is not spurred by greater needs. When men break the narrow confines of the primary needs they develop greater capacities, and their natural inequalities emphasize the inherited culture differences. Men are first hunters, then keepers of flocks or herds. In the first stage families are necessarily somewhat isolated, for to support life a large territory is required. Men have no settled abode, and they move with little impedimenta from one place to another. Domestication makes a higher civilization possible, for pastoral peoples have a more assured and a more abundant food supply. Turgot rejects as premature and exaggerated Montesquieu's explanation of progress in terms of climatic factors, for peoples living under the same climatic conditions differ, and those living under climatic conditions which have little in common have similar characters and mental traits. The spirit and the despotism of Oriental peoples are born of barbarism combined with favorable circumstances; similar to them are the ancient Gauls and Germans, and the Iroquois who dwell in the harsh climate of Canada. Physical conditions, therefore, are not the prime factors which contribute to the shaping of mind and character. Their influence cannot be estimated until culture factors are weighted and these and other factors have been proven inadequate.[1]

"We little know the power of education." One of the reasons for its frequent failure lies in the fact that we content ourselves with giving rules, whereas we should create habits. Nature has sown in all hearts the seeds of all the virtues, and they merely require development. A skilful education can make the majority of men virtuous, but progress cannot be rapid; man trails along slowly step by step. Parents must be taught the necessity of providing their children a proper education, and also the

---

[1] For similar interpretations see the present writer's "Introduction to Anthropology," chaps. VII and XLI, New York, 1926; his "Introduction to Sociology," chap. IX, New York, 1928; the article on "Geographical Environment and Culture," in the *Journal of Social Forces*, 4: 702–708, 1926; DIXON, ROLAND B., "The Building of Cultures," chap. I, New York, 1928; and WALLIS and WILLEY, "Readings in Sociology," chap. III, New York, 1930.

necessity of adequate methods of imparting it. "Each generation will learn a little from the preceding one, and thus books will become the preceptors of nations."[1]

7. CONDORCET

In France the successor to Bodin, Fontenelle, Saint-Pierre, and Turgot, is Condorcet, whose "Historical View of the Progress of the Human Mind," written in the period following the outbreak of the French Revolution, and published posthumously in that century during Jacobin rule, interprets culture development and progress. The psychological equipment of man consists in the ability to receive sensations, distinguish objects in an outer world, remember, and rationalize the data of experience. Words facilitate recognition of objects and man combines ideas not associated in original experience. With some experiences are associated pain; with others, pleasure. Thanks to this association, he learns what to strive for as well as what to avoid—an idea subsequently elaborated by Herbert Spencer. To the historian who observes men from an ample perspective of time and space, culture is continuous from one generation to another. This culture continuity constitutes the potentiality of progress. The achievements of a given time or place depend upon predecessors, and the present determines the future. The continuity of development in human history does not imply fatalism, but, thanks to the historical perspective, the trend of development can be ascertained, although there are no limits to the perfectibility of man. The development of culture is frequently retarded, but its field is as large as the globe, and the only absolute limits are the life and power of humanity. It always progresses and never retrogresses.

Analysis of the intellectual and moral nature of man reveals the beginnings of social life. The family, the first stage in social organization, is the outcome of the mutual dependence of parent and child, and of the need for protection and the desire to bestow it—an interdependence enforced by the conditions of survival—and mutual aid is a factor in the struggle for existence. The identity of interests among members of different families welds them into one group. A chief is needed to coordinate authority and insure adequate protection, and hence executive power develops as a specific social function. Knowledge increases but soon becomes the peculiar possession of one class which thus obtains a tyranny that it has continuously exercised.

---

[1] TURGOT, "On Some Social Questions, Including the Education of the Young. Addressed to Madame de Graffigny" (1751); transl. in STEPHENS, WALKER W., "The Life and Writings of Turgot," p. 202, London, 1895.

Humanity has passed through nine stages or epochs and is now in the tenth epoch. In the first, men are united in small groups or tribes. The second epoch is the pastoral stage. This insures a more dependable diet, and places men above the contingencies of the chase. There results a life more sedentary, involving less fatigue and offering opportunities more favorable to the development of clothing. Inequalities in wealth arise, and the power of the chief increases proportionately.

With the development of the agricultural stage, in the third epoch, life becomes more disparate and distraught, and is characterized by invasions, conquests, and the establishment and the overthrow of empires. The hazards of social life offset the dependability of the food supply, and progress is not an unmixed good. The fourth epoch comprises the period from Greek civilization to specialization in the sciences, about the time of Alexander. The fifth epoch includes the progress of the sciences to their decadence; the sixth includes the decadence of learning, from the downfall of the Roman Empire to the contact with Arab civilization during the Crusades; the seventh comprises the progress of the sciences after their rejuvenation following the Crusades until the invention of printing; the eighth epoch extends from the invention of printing to the time of Descartes, when philosophy and the sciences throw off the yoke of authority;[1] the ninth epoch comprises the time from Descartes to the establishment of the French Republic; and the tenth epoch is the time remaining, comprising the future progress of the human mind. This falls into three fields: the removal of the inequalities among nations; the development of equality within the nation; and the substantial improvement of the individual. Inequalities among nations will disappear when European countries abandon commercial monopolies, treacherous practices, mischievous and extravagant proselyting, and the sanguinary contempt for those of another color or creed.

Vast countries, now a prey to barbarism and violence, will present in one region numerous populations only waiting to receive the means and the instruments of civilization from us, and as soon as they find brothers in the Europeans, will joyfully become their friends and pupils; and in another region, nations enslaved under the yoke of despots or conquerors, crying aloud for so many ages for liberators. In yet other regions, it is true, there are tribes almost savage, cut off by the harshness of their climate from a perfected civilization, or else conquering hordes, ignorant of every law but violence and every trade but brigandage. The progress of these last two peoples will naturally be more tardy, and attended by greater storm and convulsion. It is possible even, that

[1] See TAYLOR, HENRY O., "Freedom of the Mind in History," pp. 154–164, London, 1923.

reduced in number, in proportion as they see themselves repulsed by civilized nations, they will end by insensibly disappearing.[1]

There are three primary inequalities within a community: inequality in wealth; inequality of condition between the man whose means of subsistence are both assured and transmissible, and him whose means depend upon the length of his working life; and inequality of instruction. Inequalities in wealth will decrease when artificial restrictions and advantages are removed from fiscal or other legal arrangements by which property is acquired or accumulated. A change in this direction is indicated by the tendency for public opinion to banish an avaricious or mercenary spirit from marriage. Inequality between assured and precarious incomes will be radically modified by the utilization of the calculus of probabilities to determine the expectation of life. The extension of annuities and insurance will benefit many individuals, and society at large, by putting an end to the periodical ruin of a large number of families, which is a constant source of misery and degradation. Another means to the same end will be found in the discovery, by the principle of probabilities, of some other equally solid basis for credit in lieu of large capital, and of a means for rendering the progress of industry and the activity of commerce more independent of the existence of great capitalists. An approximation to equality of instruction, even for those who can spare only a few of their early years and in later life only a few hours of leisure for study, will be achieved by an improved selection of subjects, and by better methods of teaching. Men will profit from a more extensive use of scientific devices, which will make the land more productive and supply food sufficient for all. A forward step will be taken when women participate in social life on the same plane as men. Laws and institutions will be modified in keeping with individual and collective interests. When hereditary and dynastic rights disappear, wars will become less frequent. Learning will be facilitated by the institution of a universal language and by improvement in methods of teaching; the sciences will be comprehended and taught in their inherent relations; then, knowledge will be liberalized and will become a common possession. Advance in medicine will bring wholesome food and healthy living conditions, life will be greatly prolonged, transmissible diseases will decrease in virulence and will disappear.

May we then not hope for the arrival of a time when death will cease to be anything but the effect either of extraordinary accidents, or of the destruction, ever slower and slower, of the vital forces? May we not believe that the duration of the interval between birth and this destruction has no assignable term?

---

[1] MORLEY, JOHN, "Condorcet."

Man will never become immortal, but is it a mere chimera to hold that the term fixed to his years is slowly and perpetually receding further and further from the moment at which his existence begins?[1]

Morelly's revision of society provided for its reorganization along three fundamental lines: there was to be no private property except in things necessary for the individual's daily comfort; the citizen was a public servant and the State would supply his needs; he would contribute to the general welfare to the extent that his powers, talents, and the age made this possible. The State was composed of families, tribes, and garden cities, each respective unit of the same size. In the city was a public square about which were grouped "uniform and agreeable" shops and assembly halls. The residential sections were of the same character throughout, and in them the streets were parallel or crossed at right angles. A tribe occupied one quarter of the city and each family had a commodious convenient house exactly like that of its neighbors near or distant. The workshops were placed on the outskirts of the city, and here there were also special houses for the agricultural workers, as well as a public hospital, a workhouse, and a prison. Beyond lay the "burial field," a strongly fortified place in which were incarcerated those who were "civilly dead." All business transactions were in communal possessions, and durable goods, housed in public stores, were rationed and distributed daily to the citizenry. Nevertheless, citizens might exchange their surplus of agricultural products in the public square. Young men between the ages of twenty-one and twenty-five were compelled to assist in agricultural work in the fields close to the city.

8. Post-Revolution Writers

Jacques Henri Bernardhin de Saint-Pierre (1737–1814), inspired by Rousseau, proposes to dispense with books and rely on nature. To him nature speaks a language not current among modern nations, and one which neither time nor people can alter. The plants of field and prairie will be his history and his journal. Thanks to the books of travelers, he becomes acquainted with all parts of the world. Of modern books these alone interest him, for they introduce him to other forms of social life and permit converse, almost at first hand, with nature.

The "Arcadia" pictures a life of classic simplicity, in which all moves with ease and grace amid rustic bowers and simple beauty in a blessed land which seems far removed from contemporary civilization.

---

[1] Diannyère, "Esquisse d'un tableau historique des progrès de l'esprit humain. Ouvrage posthume de Condorcet," p. 291, nouvelle édition, Paris, 1797.

We hear the quiet splash of comforting fountains, the gurgle of bubbling springs, the footsteps of fawns and sibyls, and the rustle of leaves in a quiet retreat undisturbed by the clamor of the busy work-a-day world. Shepherds play their pipes and nymphs dance on the green to the rhythm of the music. Esthetic activities predominate, beauty fills every crevice, happiness lingers idly in every niche. The dying echoes of St. Pierre's "Arcadia" come more than a century later from a Paris pastor, Charles Wagner, in the "Simple Life." But the simple life has given place to the strenuous life, as existence has become more complex.[1]

In the "Preface" to "Literature Considered in Its Relation to Social Institutions,"[2] Madame de Staël defends the thesis of the indefinite perfectibility of the human race, which must be distinguished from the perfectibility of the human spirit. Man's endowment may not change, but his social equipment changes. The proof of indefinite perfectibility is found in science, albeit those who refuse to accept indefinite progress deny that progress in science implies human progress. But the inherent connection between science and other phases of life shows that it must do so. Science abolishes superstition, the foe of enlightened progress, and it is intimately bound up with the ideas that interpenetrate political and social life. The invention of the mariner's compass made possible the discovery of a new world, and that discovery altered the political and social complexion of Europe. Science brought printing, and behold the social and political transformations which it entailed! Should man some day succeed in his attempts at aerial navigation, many readjustments of social life would be necessary.[3] The fact that nations make progress in civilization is demonstrated by many examples, especially Russia and the United States. Humanity is thereby advanced, as also whenever a class, whether of slaves or of peasants, improves its status. In literature, especially, there is evidence of progress; and Madame de Staël describes the development of literature in ancient and modern times, as a reflection of intellectual and ethical development.

---

[1] Quoted from the author's "Introduction to Sociology," pp. 413–414, New York, 1928.

[2] First ed., 1800.

[3] See Tissander, "La navigation aërienne," Paris, 1886, and "Histoire des ballons," Paris, 1887.

Chapter XVII

EIGHTEENTH CENTURY THEORIES OF PROGRESS IN ENGLISH AND IN GERMAN THOUGHT

1. Concepts of Progress in English Writers

Mandeville, whose name indicates French extraction,[1] says that the achievement which is attributed to the invention or the genius of an individual would be impossible without the long unconscious cooperation of a number of generations. It is so, for example, in language and in religion. Society, similarly, is the result of continuous human manipulation, and, indeed, is an artificial product, a veritable work of art. Man is not capable of indefinite progress, for human nature will remain forever essentially what is has been through thousands of years, and however long the world may endure, human nature will not change. The purpose of his work, "The Fable of the Bees," Mandeville says, is

to shew the Vileness of the Ingredients that all together compose the wholesome Mixture of Political Wisdom, by the help of which so beautiful a Machine is rais'd from the most contemptible Branches. For the main Design of the Fable (as it is briefly explain'd in the Moral) is to shew the Impossibility of enjoying all the most elegant Comforts of Life that are to be met with in an industrious, wealthy, and powerful Nation, and at the same time be bless'd with all the Virtue and Innocence that can be wish'd for in a Golden Age; from thence to expose the Unreasonableness and Folly of those, that desirous of being an opulent and flourishing People, and wonderfully greedy after all the Benefits they can receive as such, are yet always murmuring at and exclaiming against those vices and Inconveniences, that from the Beginning of the World to this present Day, have been inseparable from all Kingdoms and States that ever were fam'd for Strength, Riches, and Politeness . . . If mankind could be cured of the Failings they are Naturally guilty of, they would cease to be capable of being rais'd into such vast, potent and polite Societies, as they have been under the several great Commonwealths and Monarchies that have flourished since the Creation.

Mandeville follows Plato, in attributing great importance to the division of labor:

---

[1] Mandeville was born in Holland, and matriculated at the University of Leiden. After taking his degree there he went to London "to learn the language," and, liking the country, made England his home.

Man, as I have hinted before, naturally loves to imitate what he sees others do, which is the reason that savage People all do the same thing: This hinders them from meliorating their Condition, though they are always wishing for it: But if one will wholly apply himself to the making of Bows and Arrows, whilst another provides Food, a third builds Huts, a fourth makes Garments, and a fifth Utensils, they not only become useful to one another, but the Callings and Employments themselves will in the same Number of Years recieve much greater Improvements, than if all had been promiscuously follow'd by every one of the Five. The truth of this is in nothing so conspicuous, as it is in Watch-making, which is come to a higher degree of Perfection, than it would have been arrived at yet, if the whole had always remain'd the Employment of one Person; and I am persuaded, that even the Plenty we have of Clocks and Watches, as well as the Exactness and Beauty they may be made of, are chiefly owing to the Division that has been made of that Art into many Branches.[1]

Mandeville, and not Benjamin Franklin, appears to have been the first English writer to appreciate the significance of the struggle for existence and its relation to the fecundity of species.

We see in Ponds, that, where Pikes are suffer'd to be, no other Fish shall ever encrease in Number. But in Rivers, and all Waters near any Land, there are amphibious Fowls, and many sorts of them, that live mostly upon Fish: Of these Water-Fowls in many Places there are prodigious Quantities. Besides these, there are Otters, Beavers, and many other Creatures that live upon Fish. In Brooks and shallow Waters, the Hearn and Bittern will have their Share: What is taken off by them, perhaps, is but little but the young Fry, and the Spawn that one of pair of Swans are able to consume in one Year, would very well serve to stock a considerable River. So they are but eat, it is no matter what eats them, either their own Species or another: What I would prove, is that Nature produces no extraordinary Numbers of any Species, but she has contriv'd Means answerable to destroy them. The Variety of Insects, in the several Parts of the World, would be incredible to any one, that has not examin'd into this matter; and the different Beauties to be observ'd in them is infinite: But neither the Beauty nor the Variety of 'em are more surprizing, than the Industry of Nature in the Multiplicity of her Contrivances to kill them; and if the Care and Vigilance of all other Animals, in destroying them, were to cease at once, in two Years time the greatest part of the Earth which is ours now would be theirs, and in many Countries Insects would be the only Inhabitants.[2]

To George Turnbull, a contemporary of Mandeville, human intelligence is in itself sufficient evidence that man will make progress. By using his intelligence man obtains power over both physical nature and human nature. The sciences are interrelated, and logic, which makes

---

[1] MANDEVILLE, BERNARD, "The Fable of the Bees," vol. II, p. 284, Oxford, 1924.
[2] *Op. cit.*, vol. II, pp. 248–249, Oxford, 1924.

the interrelation clear, is a means to power. But progress is possible only when man adopts the means to secure it, and this involves a proper direction of human will. Society is essential to human welfare, for only in society can man develop his emotional nature or his personality. Social life is the true end of human endeavor.

David Hartley, like Turnbull, emphasizes the interdependences of the sciences. "All these branches of knowledge are very much involved in each other; so that it is impossible to make any considerable progress in any one, without the assistance of most or all the rest." He compares the State with the individual; the former, like the latter, is capable of improvement and development.

Hume believes that the proper conduct of society involves such complex tasks that

no human genius, however comprehensive, is able, by the mere dint of reason and reflection, to effect it. The judgments of many must unite in this work: experience must guide their labor: time must bring it to perfection; and the feeling of inconveniences must correct the mistakes, which they inevitably fall into, in their first trials and experiments . . . Law, the source of all security and happiness, arises late in any government, and is the slow product of order and liberty.

Once gained, however, the constituents of progress are not easily lost, for each useful culture trait tends to persist.

When it has once taken root, it is a hardy plant, which will scarcely ever perish through the ill culture of men, or the rigor of the seasons . . . What is profitable to every mortal, and in common life, when once discovered, can scarcely fall into oblivion, but by the total subversion of society, and by such furious inundations of barbarous invaders, as obliterate all memory of former arts and civility.

Yet in the same essay he says, with apparent inconsistency, "when the arts and sciences come to perfection in any State, from that moment they naturally or rather necessarily decline, and seldom or never revive in that nation, where they formerly flourished"; for "no advantages in this world are pure and unmixed."[1]

To Adam Ferguson the superiority of modern over ancient culture inheres in the development of science, the discoveries of voyagers who have penetrated to every part of the globe, the amelioration of the means of obtaining a living, attainment of security of life, development of commerce, and division of labor. These have evolved from more primitive elements. The plans, reflections, and observations of the savage

---

[1] HUME, DAVID, "The Rise and the Progress of the Arts and Sciences," in "Essays, Literary, Moral, and Political," pp. 71–72, 75, 78, London, 1870.

in the forests are the first steps in civilization. From the hut comes the palace, and from the crude perceptions of sense come the laws of science. Human progress is intermittent, but "it is impossible to ascertain [its] limits."[1] Yet men do not foresee the consequences of their acts, least of all those which lead to changes in the culture.

Mankind, in following the present sense of their minds, in striving to remove inconveniences, or to gain apparent and continuous advantages, arrive at ends which even their imagaination could not anticipate, and pass on, like other animals, in the track of their nature, without perceiving its end. He who first said, "I will appropriate this field; I will leave it to my heirs," did not perceive that he was laying the foundation of civil laws and political establishments. He who first ranged himself under a leader, did not perceive that he was setting the example of a permanent subordination, under the pretence of which, the rapacious were to seize his possessions, and the arrogant to lay claim to his service. Men, in general, are sufficiently disposed to occupy themselves in forming projects and schemes; but he who would scheme and project for others, will find an opponent in every person who is disposed to scheme for himself. Like the winds, that come we know not whence, and blow whithersoever they list, the forms of society are derived from an obscure and distant origin; they arise, long before the date of philosophy, from the instincts, not from the speculations, of men. The crowd of mankind are directed in their establishments and measures, by the circumstances in which they are placed; and seldom are turned from their way, to follow the plan of any single projector. Every step and every movement of the multitude, even in what are termed enlightened ages, are made with equal blindness to the future; and nations stumble upon establishments, which are indeed the result of human action, but not the execution of any human design. If Cromwell said, "That a man never mounts higher, than when he knows not whither he is going"; it may with more reason be affirmed of communities, that they admit of the greatest revolutions where no change is intended, and that the most refined politicians do not always know whither they are leading the state by their projects.[2]

Ferguson, like Perrault, Turgot, and Holbach, compares man with nature and the beasts. Throughout the animal kindgom the individual develops from infancy to maturity, but, as Mandeville had pointed out, this period of development was longer in the case of man than in that of any other animal.[3]

---

[1] FERGUSON, ADAM, "Institutes of Moral Philosophy," pt. IV, chap. III, sec. 3, Edinburgh, 1773.

[2] *Ibid.*, pp. 186–187.

[2] Anaximander (611–547 B.C.), a Greek philosopher of the Ionian school, had pointed out that man's ability to advance or, as we would say, his educability, was in large part due to the long period of helplessness after birth—a view which Fiske popularized in the latter half of the nineteenth century. See OSBORN, HENRY F., "Man Rises to Parnassus," pp. 4–5, Princeton, 1927.

Not only the individual advances from infancy to manhood, but the species itself from rudeness to civilization. Hence the supposed departure of mankind from the state of their nature, hence our conjectures and different opinions of what man must have been in the first age of his being.

Whether the Golden age existed of which poets have sung and about which historians and moralists have written, or whether mankind has risen from humbler estate,

the first state of nature must have borne no resemblance to what men have exhibited in any subsequent period; historical monuments, even of the earliest date, are to be considered as novelties; and the most common establishments of human society are to be classed among the incroachments which fraud, oppression, or a busy invention, have made upon the reign of nature, by which the chief of our grievances or blessings were equally withheld.

In the interpretation of human life man shows curious predilections.

He admits, that his knowledge of the material system of the world consists in a collection of facts, or at most, in general tenets derived from particular observations and experiments. It is only in what relates to himself, and in matters the most important, and the most easily known, that he substitutes hypothesis instead of reality, and confounds the provinces of imagination and reason, of poetry and science.

The character of man as he now exists, and the character of the realm of nature and of animal life to the extent that his happiness depends upon them, are deserving of study; but

general principles relating to this, or any other subject, are useful only so far as they are founded on just observation, and lead to the knowledge of important consequences, or so far as they enable us to act with success when we would apply either the intellectual or the physical powers of nature, to the great purposes of human life.[1]

The drive toward improvement is rooted deep in human nature.

We speak of art as distinguished from nature; but art itself is natural to man. He is in some measure the artificer of his own frame, as well as his fortune, and is destined, from the first age of his being, to invent and contrive. He applies the same talents to a variety of purposes, and acts nearly the same part in very different scenes. He would be always improving on his subject, and he carries this intention wherever he moves, through the streets of the populous city, or the wilds of the forest. While he appears equally fitted to every condition, he is upon this account unable to settle in any.

Though he is obstinate and fickle, and descries innovations, he is never sated with novelties.

---

[1] FERGUSON, ADAM, "An Essay on the History of Civil Society," pp. 2–4, Edinburgh, 1767.

He is perpetually busied in reformations, and is continually wedded to his errors. If he dwell in a cave, he would improve it into a cottage; if he has already built, he would still build to a greater extent. But he does not propose to make rapid and hasty transitions; his steps are progressive and slow; and his force, like the power of a spring, silently presses on every resistance; an effect is sometimes produced before the cause is perceived; and with all his talent for projects, his work is often accomplished before the plan is devised. It appears, perhaps, equally difficult to retard or to quicken his pace; if the projector complain he is tardy, the moralist thinks him unstable; and whether his motions be rapid or slow, the scenes of human affairs perpetually change in his management: his emblem is a passing stream, not a stagnating pool. We may desire to direct his love of improvement to its proper object, we may wish for stability of conduct; but we mistake human nature, if we wish for a termination of labor, or a scene of repose.[1]

The apparent differences in innate capacities may be due to differences in circumstance and in interest.

Persons who are occupied with different subjects, who act in different scenes, generally appear to have different talents, or at least to have the same faculties variously formed, and suited to different purposes. The peculiar genius of nations, as well as of individuals, may in this manner arise from the state of their fortunes.[2]

Ferguson, following Montesquieu, is impressed with the influence of climatic factors. The highest civilization has been achieved in the temperate climes, rather than in the extremes of heat or cold, and this fact "sufficiently declares either a distinguished advantage of situation, or a natural superiority of mind." In the torrid zone of the New World, however, there were "mere arts of mechanism and manufacture," while in the comparable climate of India manufacturing flourished. In the latter region the "vertical sun" ripens a mild disposition.

The sun, it seems, which ripens the pine-apple and the tamarind, inspires a degree of mildness that can even assuage the rigours of despotical government.[3] But under the extremes of heat or of cold, the active range of human soul appears to be limited; and men are of inferior importance, either as friends, or as enemies. In the one extreme, they are dull and slow, moderate in their desires, regular and pacific in their manner of life; in the other, they are feverish in their passions, weak in their judgments, and addicted by temperament to animal pleasure. In both the heart is mercenary, and makes important concessions for childish bribes: in both the spirit is prepared for servitude: in

---

[1] *Ibid.*, pp. 9–10.

[2] *Ibid.*, pp. 38–39.

[3] *Ibid.*, pt. III, sec. 1.

the one it is subdued by fear of the future; in the other is not roused even by its sense of the present.[1]

He admits, however, that "we are still unable to explain the manner in which climate may affect the temperament, or foster the genius, of its inhabitants," but suggests that climatic conditions may affect the organism, and thus indirectly the mind of man.[2]

Adam Smith attributes the recent impetus of civilization to the invention of printing, the discovery of America, and the finding of the passage to India by way of the Cape of Good Hope. These geographical discoveries brought an extension of commerce which, in turn, stimulated the division of labor that is the basis of all economic progress. He deplores economic rivalries between nations; economically the world is a unit, and the civilized world will one day become a single workshop and a single market. This interdependence of peoples will bring universal peace and abolish enmity between nations.

Richard Price calls attention to the fact that culture changes incessantly. In a given epoch different cultures prevail in the respective nations, and a phase which is a benefit to one may have malign consequences for another. Like the Sophists he emphasizes the relativity of moral values.[3] Yet morality, though relative, may increase. Intelligence is capable of indefinite development, and there is a mutual influence between it and morality. Indeed every step in the discovery of truth is accompanied by a higher morality. There is unlimited scope for improvement; therefore, infinite advance is possible.

Reason as well as tradition and revelation, lead us to expect that a more improved and happy state of human affairs will take place before the consummation of all things. The world has hitherto been gradually improving. Light and knowledge have been gaining ground, and human life *at present*, compared with what it once was, is much the same as a youth approaching manhood, compared with an infant. Such are the natures of things that this progress must continue. During particular intervals it may be interrupted, but it cannot be destroyed. Every present advance prepares the way for further advances; and a single experiment or discovery may sometimes give rise to so many more as suddenly to raise the species higher, and to resemble the effects of opening a new sense, or of the fall of a spark on a train that springs a mine. For this reason, mankind may at last arrive at degrees of improvement which we cannot now even suspect to be possible.[4]

---

[1] *Ibid.*, pt. III, sec. 1, p. 171.

[2] *Ibid.*, p. 180.

[3] See above, p. 235.

[4] PRICE, RICHARD, "Observations on the Importance of the American Revolution, and the Means of Making It a Benefit to the World," pp. 3–4, London, 1794. The

After pointing out that the greatest danger the United States faces is war not with a foreign country, but between the states themselves, Price continues with some observations which are remarkably like those of Kant:

When a dispute arises among *individuals* in a State, an appeal is made to a *court* of law; that is, to the wisdom and justice of the State. The court decides. The losing party aquiesces; or, if he does not, the power of the State *forces* him to submission; and thus the effects of contention are supprest, and peace is maintained.—In a way similar to this, peace may be maintained between any number of confederated States; and I can almost imagine, that it is not impossible but that by some such means *universal* peace may some time or other be produced, and all war excluded from the world.—Why may we not hope to see this begun in America?[1]

Price is a champion of unrestricted freedom of religious belief and discussion, which he would apply,

to all points of faith, however sacred they may be deemed. Nothing reasonable can suffer by discussion. All doctrines *really* sacred must be clear and incapable of being opposed with success. If civil authority interposes, it will be to support some misconception or abuse of them. That immoral tendency of doctrines which has been urged as a reason against allowing the public discussion of them, may be either *avowed* and direct, or only a consequence with which they are charged. If it is *avowed* and direct, such doctrines certainly will not spread. The principles rooted in human nature will resist them; and the advocates of them will be soon disgraced. If, on the contrary, it is only a *consequence* with which a doctrine is charged, it should be considered how apt all parties are to charge the doctrines they oppose with bad tendencies. It is well known that *Calvinists* and *Arminians, Trinitarians,* and *Socinians, Fatalists* and *Free-willers,* are continually exclaiming against one another's opinions as dangerous and licentious. Even Christianity itself could not, at its first introduction, escape this accusation. The professors of it were considered Atheists, because they opposed Pagan idolatry; and their religion was on this account reckoned a destructive and pernicious enthusiasm. If, therefore, the rulers of a State are to prohibit the propagation of all doctrines in which they apprehend immoral tendencies, an opening will be made, as I have before observed, for every species of persecution. There will be no doctrine, however true or important, the avowal of which will not in some country or other be subjected to civil penalties.[2]

---

dedication page contains the following: "*To the Free and United States of America, the Following Observations are Humbly Offered, as a Last Testimony of the Good-will of the Author.*"

[1] *Ibid.,* pp. 14–15.
[2] *Ibid.,* pp. 29–31.

Like several French and German contemporaries, Price is an optimistic advocate of education.

Nothing is more necessary than the establishment of a wise and liberal plan of *education*. It is impossible properly to represent the importance of this. So much is left by the author of nature to depend on the turn given to the mind in early life and the impressions then made, that I have often thought there may be a *secret* remaining to be discovered in education, which will cause future generations to grow up virtuous and happy, and accelerate human improvement to a greater degree than can at present be imagined.

But little hope lies in the conventional routine education.

The end of education is to direct the powers of the mind in unfolding themselves; and to assist them in gaining their just bent and force. And, in order to accomplish this, its business should be to teach *how* to think, rather than *what* to think; or to lead into the best way of searching for truth, rather than to instruct in truth itself.—As for the latter, who is qualified for it? There are many indeed who are eager to undertake this office. All parties and sects think they have discovered truth, and that they alone are its advocates and friends. But the very different and inconsistent accounts they give of it demonstrate they are utter strangers to it; and that it is better to teach *nothing*, than to teach what they hold out for truth. The greater their confidence, the greater is the reason for distrusting them. We generally see the warmest zeal, where the object of it is the greatest nonsense. Such observations have a particular tendency to shew that education ought to be an initiation into candour, rather than into any systems of faith; and that it should form a habit of cool and patient investigation, rather than an attachment to any opinions.[1]

This better system of education "supposes, however, an *improved* state of mankind; and when once it has taken place, it will quicken the progress of improvement."[2] Like Fontenelle and Condorcet Price places no limits upon the possibilities of human achievement.

Who could have thought, in the first ages of the world, that mankind would acquire the power of determining the distances and magnitudes of the sun and planets?—Who, even at the beginning of this century, would have thought that in a few years they would acquire the power of subjecting to their wills the dreadful force of lightening, and of flying in aerostatic machines?—The last of these powers, though so long undiscovered, is only an easy application of a power always known and familiar. Many similar discoveries may remain to be made, which will give new directions to human affairs; and it may not perhaps be too extravagant to imagine that (should civil government throw no obstacles in the way) the progress of improvement will not cease till

---

[1] *Ibid.*, pp. 50–51.
[2] *Ibid.*, p. 56.

it has excluded from the earth, not only *vice* and *war*, but even *death* itself, and restored that *paradisiacal* state, which, according to the *Mosaic* history, preceded our present state.[1]

In "A Vindication of Natural Society" (1756) Edmund Burke follows Aristotle in supposing the family the original unit of social life. The ills of life have come with civilization.

> Our inheritances are become a prize for disputation; and disputes and litigations are become an inheritance . . . Consider the ravages committed in the bowels of all commonwealths by ambition, by avarice, envy, fraud, open injustice, and pretended friendship; vices which could draw little support from a society.

The ills of society seem to increase with the necessity for social life, and man becomes the greatest enemy of man.

2. PRIESTLEY

In "An Essay on the First Principles of Government," published in 1768, Joseph Priestley speaks optimistically of progress, though claiming "no greater liberties than becomes a philosopher, a man, and an Englishman."[2] The goal of human striving is happiness. Man is more capable of attaining this than are the beasts, for he can compass past and future as well as present, and his span of the present is greater than any other animal can claim. Education enables one to profit from the pursuits of former generations. In the future, therefore, men will be much better off than they are today, for education will give them a great advantage over the men of the eighteenth century.

The great instrument in the hand of divine providence, of this progress of the species toward perfection, is *society*, and consequently *government*. In a state of nature the powers of a single man are dissipated by an attention to a multiplicity of objects. The employments of all are similar.

In civilization, however, there is specialization of tasks and of interests, so that "the powers of all have their full effect: and hence arise improvements in all the conveniences of life, and in every branch of knowledge."[3] Priestley wishes to "see things *in a progress* to a better state, and no obstructions thrown in the way of reformation"; and he is confident that this will be the case. "In spite of all the fetters we can lay upon the human mind, notwithstanding all possible discouragements

---

[1] *Ibid.*, p. 110.

[2] PRIESTLEY, JOSEPH, "An Essay on the First Principles of Government," p. v, London, 1768.

[3] *Ibid.*, pp. 5–7.

in the way of free inquiry, knowledge of all kinds, and religious knowledge among the rest, will increase. The wisdom of one generation will ever be the folly in the next." Yet

the great misfortune is, that the progress of knowledge is chiefly among the thinking few. The bulk of mankind, being educated in a reverence for established modes of thinking and acting, in consequence of their being established, will not hear of a reformation proceeding even so far as they could really wish, lest in time, it should go farther than they could wish, and the end be worse than the beginning.[1] . . . However, such is the progress of knowledge, and the enlargement of the human mind, that, in future time, notwithstanding all possible obstructions thrown in the way of human genius, men of great and exalted views will undoubtedly arise, who will see through and detest our narrow politics.[2]

Like many of his French contemporaries[3] Priestley believes in the possibility of indefinite progress. There may be limits to the possible improvements of the arts, such as painting, music, and poetry, but it is inconceivable that there are limits to the possibilities of human reason. The events which have contributed most toward modern progress, are the discovery of gunpowder, the discovery of America, the extension of European commerce, and the capture of Constantinople by the Turks. The changes which these events have brought have made the human race more happy and our corner of the globe a paradise in comparison with what it formerly was. Many considerations justify the hope that a state of happiness awaits humanity, for government, the principal instrument in the progress of the human species, becomes more just and efficient.

3. JOHN MILLAR

In the "Preface" to his "Observations Concerning the Distinctions of Ranks in Society,"[4] John Millar gives the following apology for the comparative study of peoples:

Those who have examined the manners and customs of nations have had chiefly two objects in view. By observing the systems of law established in different parts of the world, and by remarking the consequences with which they are attended, men have endeavored to reap advantage from the experience of others, and to make a selection of those institutions and modes of government which appear the most worthy of being adopted. To investigate the causes of different usages, hath also been esteemed an useful as well as

---

[1] This sounds like a text for EDMUND BURKE's "Reflections on the French Revolution."

[2] Priestley, op. cit., pp. 144, 147, 187.

[3] See above, chap. XVI.

[4] London, 1773.

an entertaining speculation. When we contemplate the amazing diversity in the manners of different countries, and even of the same country at different periods; when we survey the distinctions of national characters, and the singular customs that have prevailed; we are led to discover the various dispositions and sentiments with which man is endowed, the various powers and faculties which he is capable of exerting. When at the same time we consider how much the character of individuals is influenced by their education, their professions, and their peculiar circumstances, we are enabled, in some measure, to account for the behavior of different nations. From the situation of a people in different ages and countries, they are presented with particular views of expediency; they form peculiar maxims, and are induced to cultivate and acquire a variety of talents and habits. Man is everywhere the same; and we must necessarily conclude, that the untutored Indian and the civilized European have acted upon the same principles.

Thus, by real experiments, not by abstracted metaphysical theories, human nature is unfolded; the general laws of our constitution are laid open; and history is rendered subservient to moral philosophy and jurisprudence. The manners and customs of a people may be regarded as the most authentic record of their opinions, concerning what is right or wrong, what is praiseworthy or blameable, what is expedient or hurtful. In perusing such records, however, the utmost caution is necessary; and we must carefully attend to the circumstances in which they were framed, in order to ascertain the evidence which they afford, or to discern the conclusions that may be drawn from them. As the regulations of every country may have their peculiar advantages, so they are commonly tinctured with all the prejudices and erroneous judgments of the inhabitants. It is therefore by a comparison only of the ideas and the practice of different nations, that we can arrive at the knowledge of those rules of conduct, which, independent of all positive institutions, are consistent with propriety, and agreeable to the sense of justice.

Only by acquaintance with the "ideas and the practice of different nations" can we learn those common rules of justice which should be observed by all governments. Moreover,

to know the laws already established, to discern the causes from which they have arisen, and the means by which they were introduced; this preliminary step is essentially requisite, in order to determine upon what occasions they ought to be altered or abolished. The institutions of a country, how imperfect soever and defective they may seem, are commonly suited to the state of the people by whom they have been embraced; and therefore, in most cases, they are only susceptible of those gentle improvements, which proceed from a gradual reformation of the manners, and are accompanied with a correspondent change in the condition of society. In every system of law or government, the different parts have an intimate connection with each other. As it is dangerous to tamper with the machine, unless we are previously acquainted with the several wheels and springs of which it is composed; so there is reason to fear, that the violent alteration of any single part may destroy the regularity of its movements, and produce the utmost disorder and confusion . . ·

Man differs remarkably from other animals in that wonderful capacity for the improvement of his faculties with which he is endowed. Never satisfied with any particular attainment, he is continually impelled by his desires from the pursuit of one object to that of another; and his activity is called forth in the prosecution of the several arts which render his situation more easy and agreeable. This progress however is slow and gradual; at the same time that, from the uniformity of the human constitutions, it is accompanied with similar appearances in different parts of the world. When agriculture has created abundance of provisions, people extend their views to other circumstances of smaller importance. They endeavor to be clothed and lodged, as well as maintained, in a more comfortable manner; and they engage in such occupations as are calculated for these useful purposes. By the application of their labor to a variety of objects, commodities of different kinds are produced. These are exchanged for one another, according to the demand of different individuals; and thus manufactures, together with commerce, are at length introduced into a country. [But] the first attention of a people is directed to the acquisition of the mere necessaries of life, and to the exercise of those occupations which are most immediately requisite for subsistence. According as they are successful in these pursuits, they feel a gradual increase of their wants, and are excited with fresh vigor and activity to search for the means of supplying them. The advancement of the more useful arts is followed by the cultivation of those which are subservient to pleasure and entertainment. Mankind, in proportion to the progress they have made in multiplying the conveniences of their situation, become more refined in their taste, and luxurious in their manner of living. Exempted from labor, and placed in great affluence, they endeavor to improve their enjoyments, and become addicted to all those amusements and diversions which tend to occupy their minds, and to relieve them from languor and weariness, the effects of idleness and dissipation.

Millar is the first to call attention in some detail to the influence on social life of culture change. Indeed this theme runs throughout his work. In the section devoted specifically to "the changes produced in the government of a people by their progress in civilization and refinement", he says, "the advancement of a people in civilization, and in the arts of life, is attended with various alterations in the state of the individuals, and in the whole constitution of their government."[1]

4. Paine

Thomas Paine's "Rights of Man" contains a perfervid plea for the recognition of the right of each generation to determine its own policies.

---

[1] Pp. 82–83, 95–96, 228.

Every age, and generation, must be as free to act for itself, in all cases, as the ages and generations that preceded it. The vanity and presumption of governing *beyond* the grave, is the most preposterous and insolent of all tyrannies. Man has no property in Man—neither has any generation a property in the generations that are to follow . . . Every generation *is*, and *must* be competent to all the purposes which its occasions require. It is the living, and not the dead, that are to be accommodated . . . The circumstances of the world are continually changing, and the opinions of men change also; and, as government is for the *living*, and not for the *dead*, it is the living only that have any right in it. That which may be thought right, and be found convenient in one age, may be thought wrong, and found inconvenient, in another . . . Man, considered as man, is all of *one degree*, and consequently all men are born equal, and with equal natural rights. Natural rights are those which appertain to man in right of his *existence*. Of this kind are all the *intellectual* rights, or rights of the *mind;* and also, all those rights of acting, as an individual, for his own comfort and happiness, which are not injurious to the natural rights of others. Civil rights are those which appertain to man, in right of his being a member of society. Every civil right has, for its foundation, some natural right preexisting in the individual, but to which his individual power is not, in all cases, sufficiently competent. Of this kind are all those which relate to *security* and *protection*.

Paine is an ardent advocate of freedom of conscience and of religion.

As to what are called National Religions, we may, with as much propriety, talk of National Gods. It is either political craft, or the remains of the Pagan system, when every nation had its separate and particular deity. It is an erroneous principle, that the operations of the mind, as well as the acts of the body, are subject to the coercion of the laws. Our rulers have authority over such natural rights only as we have submitted to them. The rights of conscience we never submitted—we could not submit. We are answerable for them to our God.

The legitimate powers of government extend to such acts only as are injurious to others. But it does me no injury for my neighbor to say, there are twenty gods, or no god:—It neither picks my pocket, nor breaks my leg. If it be said that his testimony, in a court of justice, cannot be relied on—reject it then, and be the stigma on him. Constraint may make him worse, by making him a hypocrite, but it will never make him a truer man. It may fix him obstinately in his errors, but will never cure them. Reason, and free enquiry are the only and effectual agents against error. Give a loose [*sic*] to them, they will support the true religion, by bringing every false one to their tribunal, to the test of their investigation: they are the natural enemies of error, and of error only. Had not the Roman government permitted free enquiry, christianity could never have been introduced. Had not free enquiry been indulged at the era of the reformation, the corruptions of christianity could not have been purged away. If it be restrained now, the present corruptions will be protected, and new ones encouraged. Was the government to prescribe to us our medicine and diet, our bodies would be in such keeping as our souls are now. Thus, in France, the emetic was once forbidden as a medicine, and the potato as an article of food.[1] Government is just as infallible too, when it fixes systems in physics. Galileo was sent to the inquisition for affirming that the earth was a sphere—the government had declared it to be as flat as a trencher; and Galileo was obliged to abjure his error. This error, however, at length prevailed—the earth became a globe—and Descartes declared that it was whirled round its axis by a vortex. The government in which he lived was wise enough to see that this was no question of civil jurisdiction, or we should all have been involved, by authority, in vortices. In fact, the vortices have been exploded, and the Newtonian principle of gravitation is now more firmly established on the basis of reason, than it would be were the government to step in, and make it an article of necessary faith.

Reason and experiment have been indulged, and error has fled before them. It is error alone which needs the support of government. Truth can stand by itself. Subject opinion to coercion—whom will you make your inqusitors?—fallible men—men governed by bad passions, by private as well as public reasons. And why subject it to coercion?—to produce uniformity. But is uniformity of opinion desirable?—no more than of face and stature. Introduce the bed of Procrustes then—and, as there is danger that the large men may beat the small, make us all of a size by lopping the former, and stretching the latter. Difference of opinion is advantageous in religion. The several sects perform the office of a *censor morum* over each other. Is uniformity attainable? Millions of innocent men, women, and children, since the introduction of christianity, have been burnt, tortured, fined, imprisoned; yet we have not advanced one inch towards uniformity. What has been the effect of coercion?—to make one half the world fools, and the other half hypocrites. To support roguery and error all over the earth. Let us reflect that it is inhabited by a thousand millions of people: that these profess, probably, a thousand different systems of religion: that ours is but one of that thousand. That if there be but one right, and ours that one, we should wish to see the nine hundred and ninety-nine wandering sects gathered into the fold of truth. But against such a majority we cannot effect this by force. Reason and persuasion are the only practicable instruments . . . It is time enough for the rightful purposes of civil government for its officers to interfere when principles break out into overt acts against peace and good order.[2] And, finally, . . . truth is great, and will prevail if left to herself; . . . she is the proper and sufficient antagonist to error, and has nothing to fear from the conflict, unless by human interposition, disarmed of her natural weapons, free argument and debate— errors ceasing to be dangerous when it is permitted freely to contradict them. Therefore no man should be compelled to frequent or support any religious worship place, or ministry whatsoever, nor should be enforced, restrained, molested, or burthened, in his body or goods; nor should otherwise suffer on

---

[1] Turgot induced the French to use it as food. (Note by W. D. W.).

[2] This is also Richard Price's conviction. (Note by W. D. W.).

account of his religious opinions or belief; but that all men should be free to profess, and by argument to maintain their opinions in matters of religion, and that the same ought in nowise to diminish, enlarge, or affect their civil capacities.[1]

Like Kant and Price, Paine would fain see the abolition of war, which he considers utterly silly and one of the greatest handicaps to human development. This, he believes, could be effected by an alliance between England, France, and the United States, to which Holland could later be made a party, and the alliance might lead to a limitation of armaments.

It is, I think, certain, that if the fleets of England, France, and Holland, were confederated, they could propose, with effect, a limitation to, and a general dismantling of all the navies in Europe, to a certain proportion to be agreed upon.

First, that no new ship of war shall be built by any power in Europe, themselves included. Secondly, that all the navies, now in existence, shall be put back, suppose, to one-tenth of their present force. This will save to France and England at least two millions sterling annually to each and their relative force be in the same proportion as it is now. If men will permit themselves to think as rational beings ought to think, nothing can appear more ridiculous and absurd, exclusive of all moral reflections, than to be at the expense of building navies, filling them with men, and then hauling them into the ocean, to try which can sink each other fastest. Peace, which costs nothing, is attended with infinitely more advantage, than any victory with all its expense.[2]

5. GIBBON

In a section entitled "General Observations on the Fall of the Roman Empire in the West," appended to Chap. XXXVIII of "The Decline and Fall of the Roman Empire," Gibbon gives an interpretation of progress. He looks upon Europe not as an aggregate of countries, but as one great community in which the various peoples have attained approximately the same degree of culture. They have common interests which should unite them, if necessary, against the rest of the world, especially the realms of savagery. The savage is naked in body and mind, destitute of laws, arts, ideas, "and almost of language." From this abject condition man has gradually risen to command the animals, cultivate the earth, traverse the oceans, and measure the heavens. Progress in the improvement and exercise of mental and physical faculties has been irregular, slow in the early stages, but increasing with accelerated velocity; ages of laborious ascent have been followed by a

---

[1] PAINE, THOMAS, "The Rights of Man. For the Use and Benefit of all Mankind," chap. II, London, 1795.
[2] *Ibid.*, pp. 147–148.

rapid downfall; and all countries have experienced the vicissitudes of light and darkness. But the history of the last four thousand years enlarges our hope and diminishes our apprehension; we cannot determine to what extent the human race will advance, but no people, unless the face of nature is changed, will lapse into their original barbarism. The progress of civilization can be described under three aspects: improvement of the individual, of laws and institutions, and of group life as an agency capable of perpetuating the instruments of advance.

Since the first discovery of the arts, war, commerce, and religious zeal have diffused, among the savages of the Old and New World, those inestimable gifts; they have been successively propagated; they can never be lost. We may therefore acquiesce in the pleasing conclusion that every age of the world has increased, and still increases, the real wealth, the happiness, the knowledge, and perhaps the virtue, of the human race.

6. CONCEPTS OF PROGRESS IN GERMAN WRITERS: JACOB DANIEL WEGELEN[1]

Wegelen pictures "natural" man as devoid of inspiration, passively submissive to the laws of physical and animal life, incapable of conceiving anything better than his own condition, moved by imagination but not by judgment. When, later, reason enters, changes are introduced into the culture in accordance with rational dictates. Reason is much influenced by the prevalent habits of thought and feeling. In each community the conflict of parties and opinions produces a consensus of opinion which influences the conduct of all members of the community and shapes its development. The spirit of its constitution determines the character of a nation; and in many respects particular causes are conditioned, directed, and controlled by general ones.

7. ISAAK ISELIN[2]

Isaak Iselin's "Philosophical Conjectures on the History of Humanity" ("Philosophische Mutmassungen über die Geschichte der Menschheit"), published in 1764, contains much which is similar to the thought of Condorcet, though the latter probably was not acquainted with this work. In the original state of man, he says, there was no property, decency, duty, speech, or sense. In the second state—Iselin, like Condorcet, thinks in terms of epochs—man came to recognize distinctions where before there was only confusion, to have a few comparatively steady feelings, to appreciate, dimly, general notions, and to use the

---

[1] 1721–1791.
[2] 1728–1782.

faltering beginnings of human speech. The next state, the simplest form of culture, is that of nomad shepherds; the people have rudimentary notions of truth, justice, chastity, domesticity; language is further developed, and they claim a larger measure of happiness than their predecessors enjoyed. The third stage is followed by one of two others which lead in opposite directions: Either man succumbs to barbarism, giving way to a natural tendency, or he develops a civilization. The history of civilization falls into the three epochs of oriental, classical, and modern. Those peoples who in the pastoral stage were tempted to plunder, destroy, or enslave their more prosperous neighbors, brought to an end the state of nature and degenerated to the status of savagery which is now widespread.

8. Mendelssohn and Lessing

Moses Mendelssohn was the first able modern apologist of the Jewish people. His thesis attracted Lessing, who vigorously championed his views regarding the Jews and later collaborated with him in important publications. Mendelssohn's interest in the Jewish people gave rise to his reflections regarding human progress. Since he could not believe the Jews had achieved the acme of human progress, and could not regard their present condition as one for which they were entirely responsible, or as casting discredit upon them, it remained to reconcile his admiration for the Jews with his interpretation of the course of human progress. These motives, though not conscious or deliberate, were the undercurrents which determined the flow of his thought and the drift of his arguments. In the "Jerusalem" Mendelssohn advances the thesis that man is essentially incapable of permanent progress, and is destined to lose from time to time the several successive footholds gained by long persistent effort, and suddenly, or slowly, slide back into the less desirable condition from which he has temporarily risen. The human race, viewed as a whole, makes oscillations backward and forward and has never taken a few steps forward without soon sliding back with double rapidity to its former state. Man, the individual, advances, but mankind, as a whole, moves up and down between fixed limits, maintaining through all periods of history about the same stage of morality, religion and irreligion, virtue and vice, happiness and misery. This vacillation cannot be inconsistent with the purposes of Providence, and it must, therefore, be part of the Divine Plan.

From this view Lessing dissents. All "races," *i.e.,* culture groups, pass through the stages of infancy and childhood. The Hebrews of Old Testament times were in the period of infancy, in the primer stage, and divine revelation was adapted to that status. When a race progresses it receives revelations better fitted to its more mature condition; for as the individual increases in knowledge and in stature, so does the race. There is, indeed, a close analogy between the development of the individual and that of the race. "What education is for the individual, revelation is for the whole race. Education is revelation that affects the individual; revelation is education which has affected and still affects the race." Moreover, the individual, in the course of his development, passes through the stages through which the race has passed. As there is a prospect of better times for the individual, so there is a brighter future in store for the human race, which eventually will reach its acme of purity and clarification. The education of the race, like that of the individual, has a goal, for education implies an objective; and the prospect of better things in store is a spur to both individual and race. "What art succeeds in doing for the individual, shall nature not succeed in doing for the whole?" Temporary setbacks should not be disheartening.

Pursue thy secret path, everlasting Providence, only let me not, because thou art hidden, despair of thee. Let me not despair of thee even if thy steps appear to me to retreat. It is not true that the shortest line is always straight. Thou hast upon thine eternal way so huge a burden, thou hast so many asides to take.

To the progress of the race each individual can make unique contributions.

9. IMMANUEL KANT

Kant revolted from Mendelssohn's inference that the vacillation in human progress shown by the rise and fall of cultures is part of the purpose of Providence. If, said he, in "Natural Principles of the Political Order," it is a spectacle worthy of a divinity

to see a virtuous man struggling with adversities and temptation, and yet holding his ground against them, it is a spectacle most unworthy—I will not say of a divinity, but even of the commonest well-disposed man—to see the human race making a few steps upward in virtue from one period to another, and soon thereafter falling down again as deep into vice and misery as before. To gaze for a short while upon this tragedy may be moving and instructive; but the curtain must at last be let fall upon it. For when prolonged in this manner it becomes a farce; and, although the actors may not become weary, being fools, yet the spectator will become tired of it, having enough in one or two acts to infer that this play which comes never to an end is but an eternal repetition of the same thing.

Since the sameness in such a drama makes it a bore, Kant prefers to think of it as an effort to attain somthing higher.[1] Accordingly, the assumption is made that the human race is continually advancing, and that its progress, although interrupted, will never cease. Kant is so firm in this faith that he does not attempt to prove the assumption, but says the burden of proof lies on those who deny its validity. This, however, is not an answer to Mendelssohn's argument. Elsewhere, following Leibnitz and Lessing, Kant advocates education as the means of perfecting human nature and insuring the future happiness of the human race.

In the "Anthropology," Kant declares,

Man must and can be the creator of his own fortune; but whether he will be, cannot be predicted *a priori* from his endowments, but only from experience and history, which furnish us with sufficient evidence to justify our hope in his continued progress towards the better. So that we need not despair, but can hasten the approach to this goal (each according to his ability), by whatever prudence and moral foresight we possess.

In the essay on "The Idea of a Universal History on a Cosmo-Political Plan" he asserts that man is both egotistic and altruistic, social and anti-social. From man's desire to advance his own interests and also to live in society comes the possibility of progress. The possibilities of individual progress are limited, but the continuity of efforts through successive generations makes indefinite progress possible. Human progress is interrupted by the destructive and disruptive forces of war, but war can be abolished if the nations of Europe will unite in a federation.

Visionary as this idea may seem, and as such laughed at in the Abbé de Saint-Pierre and in Rousseau (possibly because they deemed it too near its accomplishment),—it is notwithstanding the inevitable resource and mode of escape under that pressure of evil which nations reciprocally inflict; and, hard as it may be to realize such an idea, States must of necessity be driven at last to the very resolution to which the savage man of nature was driven with equal reluctance—*viz.*, to sacrifice brutal liberty, and to seek peace and security in a civil constitution founded upon law.

10. HERDER'S "PHILOSOPHY OF HISTORY"

Herder's "Philosophy of History," published in the latter part of the eighteenth century, is an attempt to orient man in the universe and to

---

[1] An eminent physicist of our century expresses a similar prejudice: "I would feel more content that the universe should accomplish some great scheme of evolution and, having achieved whatever may be achieved, lapse back into chaotic changelessness, than that its purpose should be banalised by continual repetition. I am an Evolutionist, not a Multiplicationist. It seems rather stupid to keep doing the same thing over and over again."—EDDINGTON, A. S., "The Nature of the Physical World," p. 86, New York, 1929.

discover the trend and the meaning of culture development. Man is an inhabitant of the universe and should be adjusted to his environment, and Herder's account of man's orientation begins with a description of the world as one of the planets in the solar system, intermediate in distance from the sun. The earth has passed through many "revolutions," i.e., it has undergone a long evolution. It carries a great variety of organizations and of organisms, and the plants are a part of its life. The animal kingdom stands at the threshold of human history, but man is the central figure of the animal world. There follows a description of the flora, and a more detailed account of the fauna; and the similarity between the anatomical structure of man and that of other animals is indicated. Man's structure resembles most that of the apes, especially the anthropoids; and Herder's comparison of man with the anthropoid apes is apt and correct. Animals which walk with head erect have greater wisdom than those which carry the head low; witness the apes, and, among the quadrupeds, the elephant, an animal renowned for its wisdom. By holding his head aloft man has been able to think above the other beasts.[1] Herder considers the erect posture one of the most important advantages which man possesses over the other primates.[2] Man's adaptability to climatic conditions has advanced beyond that of other animals. Modesty, which first developed in woman, resulted in the use of clothing, and this enabled man to adapt himself to the harshness of cold climates. Indeed, among the animals, scarce one, save the dog, is able to live in such varied climates as is man. By his ingenuity, also, man demonstrates his superiority over the apes. The apes are imitators of many human actions: they can be taught to sit at table and to eat food with knife and fork, much as a man does, but beyond imitation they do not go. They gather around a fire and hover there as long as the embers glow; but it does not occur to them to keep the fire going by adding fuel.[3] The possession of speech and reason establishes man's superiority over the brute crea-

---

[1] A view advanced by Plato. In commenting on the importance of the upright posture WEULE, ("The Culture of Barbarians: A Glimpse into the Beginnings of the Human Mind," p. 42, London, 1926) says: "It is strange, however, that apes with their head upright have not developed within historical times a language and a mind that brings them near even to the most savage and primitive human creature. And why, may we ask, have giraffes and camels not developed a language and a higher intellect? Their heads are elevated enough, lofty, and not dragged downwards as with other quadrupeds. Birds also have their heads upright. But apart from the chattering of a parrot they have not acquired a language, nor has their intelligence developed far beyond the intelligence of a silly goose."

[2] See the author's "Introduction to Anthropology," pp. 26–27, New York, 1926.

[3] An observation usually credited to Schopenhauer. But Schopenhauer ("Die Welt als Wille und Vorstellung") undoubtedly took the idea from Herder.

tion. His knowledge, it is true, is not that of the angels; it belongs to the plane of humanity, not to that of celestial creatures, yet the divine spark of reason makes man a god on earth. He is adapted primarily to the cultivation of humanism and religion.

Climate, though important, is not all-determining. It does not develop culture, but may negate it; it is a limiting condition rather than directive or positively determining. Herder acknowledges obligations to Montesquieu, but shows no acquaintance with Bodin. Savages are not essentially different from civilized men. Biologically, mankind is a unit; the races constitute varieties, not species, in the animal kingdom. The endowments of the savage do not differ from those of civilized man; the deaf and dumb tribes described by Diodorus are mythical. The differences between savagery and civilization are merely matters of culture and enlightenment; there is no gulf between them, but only degrees of difference. Mankind, therefore, constitutes one species; for all men have the same intellectual endowment and the same biological composition. Herder shares the cosmopolitanism of the Stoics, and he arrives at it by similar, though not identical, inductions. Through tradition and the organization of the crafts man summates his achievements, and these become for successive generations stepping-stones to higher things. Culture is dynamic and its possibilities are limitless. The philosophy of history is the attempt to discover the traditions which have been useful and have made progress possible, and a philosophy of history may itself become a useful tradition. Tradition is dependent upon language, which is one of the most important human acquisitions, and reason without language is but a utopian concept. Speech clarifies thought and gives it expression and effectual play; the soul is revealed only in language. Language is to the race what character is to the individual: it enables the race to maintain the position it has gained and to move forward. The impartial observer sees in the march of humanity an oscillation, for humanity does not always move forward. At times it loses ground, but, all things considered, both individuals and States make progress.

Herder's cosmopolitanism is a common strain in the writings of many German contemporaries, but it is rare during the next century, when nationalism is developing under the stimulus of Fichte, Hegel, and other ardent patriots. There is, however a reverberation of it in Humboldt, who declares:

Whilst we maintain the unity of the human species, we at the same time repel the depressing assumption of superior and inferior races of men . . . There are nations more susceptible of cultivation, more highly civilized, more ennobled by mental cultivation, than others, but none in themselves nobler than others. All are in like degree designed for freedom—a freedom which, in the ruder conditions of society, belongs only to the individual, but which, in social states enjoying political institutions, appertains as a right to the whole body of the community . . . If we would indicate an idea which, throughout the whole course of history, has ever more and more widely extended its empire, or which, more than any other, testifies to the much contested, and still more decidedly misunderstood perfectibility of the whole human race, it is that of establishing our common humanity—without reference to religion, nation, or color, as one fraternity, one great community, fitted for the attainment of one object, the unrestrained development of the psychical powers . . . This is the ultimate and highest aim of society, identical with the direction implanted by nature in the mind of man towards the indefinite extension of his existence. He regards the earth in all its limits, and the heavens so far as his eye can scan their bright and starry depths, as inwardly his own, given to him as the objects of his contemplation, and as a field for the development of his energies . . . Thus deeply rooted in the innermost nature of man, and even enjoined upon him by his highest tendencies, the recognition of the bond of humanity becomes one of the noblest leading principles in the history of mankind.[1]

11. SCHILLER

Kant's ideas of progress are further elaborated by the poet J. C. F. Schiller, in his "Letters upon the Æsthetic Education of Man." Schiller finds it unworthy to live out of one's own time and day and for another generation. One must not scorn the customs and manners of one's generation, but must heed the voice of the epoch, and conform with its tastes and requirements.

Man starts his career no better endowed by nature than are the other animals, but he does not remain where nature has placed him. He solves his problems and rises above physical compulsion to the plane of moral law. As a moral being, he cannot rest satisfied with the political condition which he finds forced upon him rather than chosen by him, and it would be occasion for regret if he were satisfied with it. By free spontaneous action man shakes off the initial blind law of necessity. By nature man is selfish and violent, and directs his energies to the destruction rather than to the preservation of society. He must shape his moral character; it cannot be made by legislation, for the individual is a free agent. The antagonisms inherent in individuals are essential to the progress of the race. Often the development of a particular culture goes to its absolute limit, and no further progress is possible until failure in this blind alley is recognized and an experiment is made along some other line. As Paine said, "it appears as if the tide of mental faculties flowed as far as it could in certain channels, and then forsook its course, and arose

---

[1] HUMBOLDT, "Cosmos," vol. I, p. 368, Bohn's ed.

in others."[1] The civilization achieved by the Greeks, for example, was the highest of which they were capable. To have continued their progress in culture, they would have been compelled to renounce their whole civilization and begin anew. For mankind, however, it could not stop there; intelligence must pass beyond feeling and intuition, and lead to clearer knowledge. The manifold aptitudes of man develop only through opposition. Antagonism and rivalry can enhance culture, though they are merely instruments; but while antagonism lasts, man is only on the road to culture, and does not possess it.

But can it be true that man has to neglect himself for any end whatever? Can nature snatch from us, for any end whatever, the perfection which is prescribed to us by the aim of reason? It must be false that the perfecting of particular faculties renders the sacrifice of their totality necessary; and even if the law of nature had imperiously this tendency, we must have the power to reform by a superior art this totality of our being.

Specialization is necessary, but it must not mar personality, which demands the development of all the faculties.

---

[1] PAINE, THOMAS, "The Rights of Man, for the Use and Benefit of all Mankind," p. 72, London, 1795.

Chapter XVIII

THEORIES OF PROGRESS IN THE NINETEENTH AND TWENTIETH CENTURIES

1. Saint-Simon

The successor to Saint-Pierre, Turgot, and Condorcet is Saint-Simon, who, in collaboration with Augustin Thierry, published in 1814 an essay on the reorganization of European society, which bore the subtitle: "The means of uniting the various nations of Europe into a political body, and at the same time preserving the national independence of each." No wonder Napoleon declared him "simply a fool." A hereditary king and a parliament would preside over this federation. The parliament would compose differences between nations which otherwise might eventuate in war, and would initiate and supervise works of great public utility, such as connecting the Danube with the Rhine and the latter with the Baltic. It would regulate European education, provide a code of morals, and supervise the emigration of Europeans into all parts of the world. Eventually the nations of Europe will realize that questions of general interest should predominate over merely national ones. The misery which oppresses society will then diminish, the troubles which menace its peace will disappear, and wars will cease. Poets place the Golden age at the beginning of human history, amid the ignorance and barbarity of early times, but it would be more rational to relegate the Iron age to that period. The Golden age of the human race is not in the past but in the future, and its potentiality lies in the perfectibility of society. Our fathers have not seen it, but if we make ready the way our children will behold it. In a later work, Saint-Simon advocates a reorganization of society into two classes, the intellectual and the industrial, the former to advance knowledge of the laws of nature, the latter to apply them. Thus all mankind will be engaged in promoting industry, theoretical or applied. His motto was, "Everything by Industry, Everything for Industry."

Capitalists, proprietors of land, and beggars are merely robbers. Lawyers, too, are essentially robbers, for they produce nothing; as a body they are obstructive; they adhere obstinately to traditions which are obsolete, and they resist every movement for reform. Agriculturists and manufacturers combined will form an industrial community in which will be centered the power at present exercised by the government and the legal profession. Christianity has served a useful purpose by raising moral standards but its utility has long ceased, its supernaturalism must be rejected, and henceforth morality must be placed on a positivistic basic. Society will be organized so as to insure the greatest possible production, and politics will become merely the science of production. The most important as well as the most difficult problem in politics is to ascertain what distribution of property will bring the greatest freedom and wealth to society.

2. COMTE AND POSITIVISM

*Auguste Comte, who wrote in the second quarter of the nineteenth century, is the founder of Positivism, the religion of humanity. Comte, the first to use the term "altruism," describes the spread of moral sentiment from the family group, to which, originally, it had been limited, to the local group, the tribe, and the nation. Humanity is the ultimate goal. Religion develops from fetishism to astrology, polytheism, monotheism. It conflicts with science, but ultimately the two must be reconciled. Peace is becoming the normal, and war the abnormal condition, in contradistinction with earlier times when war was the normal condition, and peace but an interval for rest. In politics the emphasis is shifting from natural rights to duties, and there is a growing tendency to judge conduct by social standards. Like Pascal, who declared that "the whole succession of men during the course of so many centuries should be considered as one man, ever living and continually learning," and like Saint-Simon, whose disciple he was, Comte regards the human race as a unity, a great organism with a continuous life. It has its own characteristic development, in which the component parts are integrated. The thought and life of each individual depends upon this all-embracing humanity, and these differ at various stages of human development, for every man is the child of his civilization and time.

As a theory and a program of progress two criticisms seem apt. Humanity, it has been said, is not a worthy object of worship. The Eskimo, the Bashi-Bazouks, the crude Australians, the Veddas, the Andamanese, arouse in us no feelings of worshipful reverence. Man demands, even if he does not deserve, a more exalted ideal. The critics of Positivism are not inspired by contemplating the spectacle of mankind bowing down to worship itself.[1] Comte, however, would have men worship not so much actual humanity as potential humanity; not man

---

[1] See, for example, below, p. 350.

as he is, but man as he should be. Comte does not define the goal of humanity, but he says it will be attained by following a calendar of "saints" composed of the great minds of the past; his selection of saints, however, shows that cool reason was sometimes far in the offing when Comtean sentiment was steersman.

3. The Utilitarians

Social and philosophical thought in the nineteenth century was stimulated by the work of Jeremy Bentham, the so-called "father of utilitarianism."[1] The criterion of progress used by Bentham, the greatest good of the greatest number, in which each counts as one and not more than one—the greatest good meaning pleasure—was not new. It is adumbrated by earlier British moralists, in particular, Shaftesbury and Hutcheson, and is clearly expressed in More's "Utopia." More recognizes a distinction in kinds of pleasure, for they are not of equal worth; whereas Bentham considers one as desirable as another—"push-pin is as good as poetry"[2]—provided it yields as much pleasure. Bentham believes pleasures are cumulative and may constitute a sum of greatest happiness. His hedonistic calculus is now discarded, though many psychologists recognize that pleasures differ in intensity as well as in quality. It is difficult to believe that pleasures can be summated, although one line of conduct may yield more pleasure than does another.

---

[1] Holbach is more deserving of this title. See above, p. 299. Bentham states that he had seen the phrase, "the greatest happiness of the greatest number," in Priestley, as early as the year 1764. This is probably a mistake as to date, for Priestley's "Essay on Government" was first published in 1768. In it the phrase occurs, "the good and happiness of the members, that is the majority of the members, of any State, is the great standard by which everything relating to that State must finally be determined." Later he attributes his inspiration to Montesquieu, Barrington, Beccaria, and Helvétius, especially the last. See ATKINSON, CHARLES M., "Jeremy Bentham, His Life and Work," Chap. II, London, 1905. The term utilitarianism may have been suggested by a passage in Ferguson: "This term interest which commonly implies little more than our regard to property, is sometimes put for utility in general, and this for happiness; insomuch that, under these ambiguities, it is not surprising we are unable to determine, whether interest is the only motive of human action, and the standard by which to distinguish our good from our ill."—FERGUSON, ADAM, "An Essay on the History of Civil Society," p. 22, Edinburgh, 1767. And again, "Hence the rule by which men commonly judge of external actions, is taken from the supposed influence of such actions on the general good. To abstain from harm, is the great law of natural justice; to diffuse happiness is the law of morality; and when we censure the conferring a favour on one or a few at the expence of many, we refer to public utility, as the great object at which the actions of men should be aimed."—*Ibid.*, p. 56.

[2] Bentham's definition of poetry was "a method of printing in which the lines do not reach the usual margin of the page."

However that may be, Bentham, acquainted with many of the leading parliamentarians of the day, directly or indirectly exerted more influence on legislation than did any other man of his time. He opposed class legislation and the tendency to regard party or local interests as tantamount to public interest. Yet in his letter of acceptance of the title of "Citizen of France," addressed to the French Minister of the Interior, Bentham insists that this new obligation shall not in any way impair his duties to his native country.

If unfortunately I were forced to choose between incompatible obligations imposed by the two positions, my sad choice, I must own, must fall on the earlier and stronger claim . . . Passions and prejudices divide men; great principles unite them. Faithful to these—as true as they are simple—I would think myself a bad citizen were I not, though a royalist in London, a republican in Paris. I should deem it a fair consequence of my being a royalist in London that I should become a republican in Paris. Thus doing, I should alike respect the rights and follow the example of my sovereign who, while an Anglican in England, is a Presbyterian in Scotland, and a Lutheran in Hanover.[1]

He urged legislation to ameliorate conditions among prisoners, and advocated some excellent prison reforms and also some oddities. Education likewise engaged his attention. He was not deceived by the patter about natural rights which had been the theme of French writers and of his compatriot Tom Paine, and had been given official sanction in the famous French "Declaration of Rights." For him,

natural rights is simple nonsense—nonsense upon stilts. But this rhetorical nonsense ends in the old strain of mischievous nonsense: for immediately a list of these pretended natural rights is given, and those are so expressed as to present to view legal rights.

He, it appears, was the first to perceive clearly that "natural rights is simple nonsense"; and the concept persisted for a long time as "learned nonsense"—indeed it still persists.

James Mill said a man must not seek his own happiness at the expense of that of others. He advocated a control by the House of Commons over the House of Lords which is practically identical with that now exercised. He urged an extension of the suffrage to include all whose interests were not represented by those already possessing it, such as children, whose interests were represented by parents, and wives, whose interests were represented by husbands. Pleasures, said John Stuart Mill, are not of the same value; some possess more worth and dignity than do others. Better be a Socrates dissatisfied than a fool satisfied.

---

[1] Quoted in ATKINSON, CHARLES M., *op. cit.*, p. 101.

Push-pin is not as good as poetry. Some pleasures, however intense or perdurable they may be, men should not seek, for they degrade rather than dignify human life. Men must live on a plane of human dignity, whether pleasure or pain is involved. He advocated extension of the suffrage to women, and championed the cause of freedom of thought and speech. Although he believed in the greatest good of the greatest number, he saw the danger of tyranny by the majority, and advocated proportional representation, so that minorities might have a voice in the government. In "Representative Government" Mill discussed the relation of order to progress, a problem which he recognized as prominent in the French thought of the preceding half century. The two essentials in government are order and progress, order being the regulation of society, and so a means of preserving its values, and progress consisting in improving the existing forms. Without order, progress is impossible, although the former can exist without the latter. The form of government must not make it difficult for society to take the next step in its development, and the value of the form of a political organization depends upon the advance which a people has made. The autocracy found in savagery and in the lower cultures may be the form of political life best adapted to this stage of culture, even if unfitted to a more advanced civilization. Similarly, slavery, which we justly condemn in a modern State, may be justifiable in those lower societies which have had to depend upon force in order to secure the labor on which civilization is built. There is an almost infinite gradation of cultures from our own down to the lowest savagery; similarly, we may think of more advanced societies filling up the vista of the future, though we cannot know the extent of that vista. Almost invariably the fall of civilizations has been due to the failure of the political order to facilitate the next stage of progress; hence the deterioration and degeneration so familiar to the student of civilizations. Early Mediterranean civilizations were not static, but were progressive. Progress is best exemplified by the Greeks and, after them, by the Hebrews. The Bible, read as a collection of books, rather than, mistakenly, as one book, reveals the successive stages of progress in Hebrew civilization.

Mill considers progress innate in human nature, or at least in culture. Government should adapt itself to changing needs, and thus facilitate the next step in progress. The Greeks, he says, generally thought of progress as a postponement of the degeneration which they considered inevitable, an assumption which Mill believes contrary to fact; but even if they were correct, there would still be a motive to postpone the evil day as long as possible and to make the best of the opportunities which precede ruin, for the inevitability of future calamity does not justify neglect of present opportunities. Men struggle for life, and the fulness of life, although they know that eventually death will overtake them. In the "System of Logic" Mill returns to the problem of progress, and searches for the historical and scientific basis of the concept. The achievements of one generation depend upon the accomplishments of the preceding generation and influence those that follow. Either culture continuity is cyclical, involving a repetition after a certain series of changes have occurred, or there is progress, in an ascending if not in a straight line. Progress is not synonomous with improvement, nor with the tendency toward it. Possibly the laws of human nature make setbacks a necessary part of progress, but taken in their entirety the changes may represent improvement, even though some of them do not. The general course of history, though not all of it, is a record of progress. There is a progressive change in the character of the human race and in the circumstances which man controls. In each age the principal social phenomena differ from those of the immediately preceding age, and they differ even more from those of an earlier age. Mill does not define the criterion of progress, though in the essay on "Utilitarianism" he expresses confidence in the great possibilities of human progress, since man is a "progressive being." Most of the major positive evils are removable, and if human affairs continue to improve, these evils will be reduced. By the wisdom of society, supplemented by the good sense and providence of individuals, poverty can be eradicated, disease reduced to a minimum, and human life greatly prolonged. Intelligent and generous minds will gladly cooperate in a program which will increase the happiness and satisfactions of human life. The nineteenth century, he says, has witnessed a partial fulfilment of these aims, in which intelligent and generous men willingly cooperate.

4. ROBERT OWEN

One of the most dramatic and engaging personalities of the first half of the nineteenth century was Robert Owen, manufacturer, philanthropist, reformer, idealist, visionary, and man of affairs. In his factory at New Lanark, Scotland, he instituted many of the reforms which he advocated, and he considered his fortune not too high a price for his zeal. As early as 1817 he pointed out the evils, many of them unanticipated, which the factory system had brought. That the immediate effects of manufacture and trade had been an augmentation of the wealth of the empire, there could be no doubt; yet "these important results . . . great as they really are, have not been obtained without accompanying evils of such a magnitude as to raise a doubt whether the latter do not preponderate over the former." Previously, legislators recognized merely the national wealth which manufacturing has brought; it is now time to recognize that "the political and moral effects . . . well deserve to occupy the best faculties of the greatest and wisest statesmen."[1] A list of the fundamental reforms which Owen urged upon Parliament is sufficient commentary upon existing evils. These proposed measures were:

1st. To limit the regular hours of labour in mills of machinery to 12 per day, including one hour and a half for meals. 2nd. To prevent children from being employed in mills of machinery until they shall be 10 years old, or that they shall not be employed more than 6 hours per day until they shall be 12 years old. 3rd. That children of either sex shall not be admitted into any manufactory—after a time to be named—until they can read and write in an useful manner, understand the first four rules of arithmetic, and the girls be likewise competent to sew their common garments of clothing.[2]

Confident that character is molded by circumstance, and that proper laws will bring the proper circumstances, he turned attention to remedial legislation and to the means for securing it. He was convinced that world conditions must be changed before proper local conditions could be secured, and he believed that the opinion of the forward-looking people of civilized nations should be mobilized. Accordingly, under his instigation and direction, a "Congress of the Advanced Minds of the World" met in London in 1857 to consider the needed reforms and the means of inducing peoples and legislatures to adopt them. The name of the congress was unfortunate, and one may smile at the implications; but there is something admirable in the activities of this old man of eighty-six, who, still vigorous in mind and spirit, closes a half century of active work with the attempt to mobilize enlightened opinion in order to effect much needed reforms. His recognition of the potency of public opinion and of the power of circumstance contains a remarkably modern note, as witness these paragraphs from the opening address to the congress:

Let the present irrationally conducted newspapers throughout Europe and America, be rationally conducted for one year, and the inhabitants of these continents would have their minds opened; their angry feelings calmed; they would become conscious of the glaring folly of their past and present proceedings; they would have new feelings of kindness created for them towards their fellow men; they would in reality learn to love their neighbors as themselves, and to have genuine charity for all of their race. But this is not a change to be effected by any class, or sect, or party; it cannot be concocted in secrecy, or by any conspiracy, or by any one nation; it must be accomplished at once, by a simultaneous change of the principle on which

---

[1] OWEN, ROBERT, "Observations on the Effect of the Manufacturing System," etc., pp. 3–5, 2d ed., London, 1817.

[2] Ibid., p. 11.

society has been hitherto founded, and at once by the authorities of the civilized world. And, now, by the adoption of wise measures, it may be so accomplished speedily.[1]

5. W. Cooke Taylor's "The Natural History of Society"

W. Cooke Taylor, a British clergyman, surveys human society in its various manifestations, seeks an understanding of the source of the superiority of one culture over another, of civilization over savagery, of Greek over barbarian, of modern times over ancient, and searches for the qualities which contribute most toward genuine progress. The continuous progress manifested by one culture, he says, is conspicuously lacking in another, while some cultures show progress in the past but not in the present. In the latter class are the stagnant civilizations of the East. Savages belong to a class apart, for they show no progress in the past and promise none for the future. "The primary element of civilization, according to the common sense of mankind, is progress, not from one place to another, but from one condition to another, and always in advance." But—and this is characteristic of civilization—every advance leaves the horizon of future accomplishment as remote as it had been. If humanity attained perfection, the condition could not be called a civilization: "Who has ever dreamed of speaking of the civilization of the kingdom of heaven!" Capacity for civilization inheres in the human race; barbarism is not a state of nature, and there is no reason to assume that it is the primary condition of man. The inferiority of barbarous tribes is manifest in many ways, especially in their physical aptitudes. Savages have keener sense perceptions than have civilized men, but these are handicaps rather than assets, for they chain them to the world of sense. Biologically they are on a lower plane, for they cannot withstand the diseases which afflict the civilized. Their language, also, is weak; it has too many discriminations in vocabulary, and is deficient in abstract and generic terms. For example, they specify various species of trees, but they have no generic word for tree. In the position of woman and in family life civilization has advanced beyond savagery. The communism alleged to be prevalent in the earlier societies does not indicate that this is the natural condition of man. Ownership begins as soon as the individual appropriates something, *i.e.*, as soon as he draws breath, and it continues as long as he lives. Savages own individually their bows and arrows, spears and hunting implements, and the game which they take; but Taylor says nothing about their ownership of land. In civilization, the increasing complexity of life makes crime possible where previously it

[1] *Ibid.*, p. 142.

had been impossible. Where paper has not been invented there can be no forgery, and pickpockets cannot flourish in a society in which people go naked. The number of criminals, therefore, is not an index of the amount of criminality.

Thus viewed, the official returns which have been published and which seem to prove an increase in the number and variety of crimes, are far from being discouraging: they do not justify the feelings of apprehension, with which the progress of humanity is so often viewed, nor the cry of alarm that is so often raised; they do indeed hold out motives for continued exertion and increased energy—for measures of prevention and vigilance—not to stop the progress of degradation, but to accelerate the advance of amelioration.

Without law and order, ideas of right and wrong, and considerable social complexity, abundant crime is not possible. Only an utterly depraved society has no crimes, and the progress of a people depends upon its choice of crimes as much as upon its choice of virtues; the one is the counterpart to the other. Progress makes more crimes possible, but it should not make criminals more common. After labeling the roads which are not to be traveled, society must see to it that the traffic does not go that way; for the prohibitions are useless if too many disregard them. In personal security, civilization is likewise far in advance of savagery, and anarchy is not a proper goal. Society does not so much create rights or obligations as recognize those which are inherent in human association. Liberty and law are not opposing principles but are correlative. If no obligation exists there is no right. In barbarism, where each may do as he pleases, a man may at any time be deprived of his catch, or even of his life; for this possibility is a necessary result of absolute liberty of action. Thus, civilization is necessary, not merely to the enjoyment, but even to the possession of freedom.

Liberty arises out of the development of society; it is indeed a natural principle, but then it is a principle which requires both sanction and protection. Like property, it has been acknowledged, in some form, from the earliest ages; as civilization advanced, it became more clearly defined, more distinctly recognized in the various spheres of human activity and enterprise, spheres which could not have existed or been maintained without civilization.

Otherwise, to do as one pleases implies the power to make others do as one pleases. "That condition of society must be most accordant with nature in which human rights are most fully developed, and best protected." Intertribal relations are on a low plane, for in savagery warfare is the natural state. It is rooted in the instinct of revenge, which is frequently displayed between members of the same tribe, and coupled with it are ferocity and cruelty. In civilized life war sometimes promotes progress; but this is not true of savagery, where the motive is always weak. "In savage warfare, passion is arrayed against passion, and it is quite indifferent who shall be the gainer; in civilized contests, idea is opposed to idea, and in the long run the victory must be on the side of humanity." In civilization war will ultimately be supplanted by discussion and reason, and nations will resort to arbitration rather than arms.

As regards poverty, civilization is not more unfortunate than is savagery. There is, to be sure, more poverty in civilization; but this is because our standards are higher. Those whom we regard as indigent would, in other societies, and in early centuries, have been considered affluent. The highland chief who thought his son pampered because, when sleeping in the snow, he rolled some of it into a ball for a pillow, had a standard of luxury different from ours. So had the Greeks, when they esteemed the Persians effeminate because, in cold weather, they wore gloves. Poverty is prevalent among civilized peoples, but they are meeting it in a rational manner and are attempting to eliminate rather than merely to alleviate it.[1]

---

[1] Mandeville, likewise, emphasizes the relativity of standards of comfort. "If," says he in the "Fables of the Bees," "everything is to be Luxury (as in strictness it ought) that is not immediately necessary to make Man subsist as he is a living Creature, there is nothing else to be found in the World, no not even among the naked Savages; of which it is not probable that there are any but what by this time have made some Improvements upon their former manner of Living; and either in the Preparation of their Eatables, the ordering of their Huts, or otherwise, added something to what once sufficed them . . . When People tell us that they only desire to keep themselves sweet and clean, there is no understanding what they would be at; if they made use of these Words in their genuine proper literal Sense, they might soon be satisfy'd without much cost or trouble, if they did not want Water: But these two little Adjectives are so comprehensive, especially in the Dialect of some Ladies, that no body can guess how far they may be stretcht. The Comforts of Life are likewise so various and extensive, that no body can tell what People mean by them, except he knows what sort of Life they lead . . . People may go to Church together, and be all of one Mind as much as they please, I am apt to believe that when they pray for their daily Bread, the Bishop includes several things in that Petition which the Sexton does not think on." And compare the lines, "The very Poor liv'd better than the Rich before." See the author's "Introduction to Sociology," chap. XXVII, New York, 1928. Compare also the description of the Numidian savage, in Addison's "Cato":

> "Coarse are his meals, the fortune of the chase,
> Amid the running stream he slakes his thirst,
> Toils all the day, and at the approach of night,
> On the first friendly bank he throws him down,
> Or rests his head upon a rock till morn;
> And if the following day he chance to find
> A new repast or an untasted spring,
> Blesses his stars, and thinks it's luxury."

The customs characteristic of savagery discredit those cultures. Their dances are lewd or are merely a celebration of military exploits. Their orators employ metaphors and substitute sound for sense.[1] Superstition in regard to disease is rife, and the magical efficacy of the curse is an accepted dictum. The difference between savagery and civilization is largely a difference between knowledge and ignorance. Yet new knowledge involves new adjustments and causes inconvenience to some, and "the complaints of those who suffer are always far louder than the gratulations of those who are benefited." It is easier for the civilized man to become a savage than for the savage to become a civilized man. The former has only to throw aside the arts and knowledge acquired by exertion and retained through effort; whereas the savage has the double task of laying aside old ideas and customs and adopting new ones. Hence the reluctance with which fishing and hunting peoples adopt pastoral life—as witness Siberian tribes—and the indisposition of a pastoral people to adopt agriculture. Was it not necessary for Parliament to pass laws forbidding the Irish peasants to hook the plough to the tails of horses, or to burn the oats in the straw to save themselves the labor of threshing it? In the history of inventions and devices nothing deserves more attention than the tendency of some of these to stop suddenly in their progress at the moment when they seem to be approaching fruition. The Romans blocked out the letters of the alphabet but did not put the blocks together, and the printing press was not invented until centuries later.[2] Practically all inventions are the response to a conscious demand, the creation of necessity, though there is also borrowing from other peoples. In this manner Taylor, a poor anthropologist it must be confessed, explains the presence of the boomerang in Australia, an implement, he says, known elsewhere only in ancient Greece and Egypt and exhibiting in those civilizations more ingenuity than can be credited to the Australians—a wrong comparison. So, too, the fishing nets of the Maori are beyond the skill of that people, for they were not known to Britain until introduced in the Christian era—another wrong statement.[3] The arts develop with equal pace in various lines, but they may degen-

---

[1] Taylor forbears comparison with contemporary political orators. Compare Headlam: "Eloquence, the noblest form of imposture, is usually introduced to obscure the evidence."—HEADLAM, CECIL, "Friends That Fail Not," p. 265, London, 1902.

[2] And then the idea was borrowed from China, as was also block printing. See CARTER, T. F., "The Invention of Printing in China and Its Spread Westward," New York, 1925; and above, p. 81.

[3] The elder Pliny states that the Britains made cords out of marsh reeds "and with these they make nets for catching fish." Taylor shows no familiarity with these early accounts.

erate in one line when others do not simultaneously fall into abeyance. Savages have developed the useless arts, particularly music and musical instruments, to a disproportionate extent. Even the invention of their useful arts they generally attribute to inspiration from a god, and do not claim the credit for themselves. Evidences of lost civilizations are abundant. The mounds of the Mississippi Valley and the ruins of Central America proclaim them, and history records the fall of Mediterranean civilizations. Savagery, therefore, is not the pristine condition of man, who, by nature, is not even a savage. Then follows an analysis of the ancient civilizations—Hebrew, Egyptian, Babylonian, Assyrian, Persian, Phœnician, Carthaginian, Greek, Roman, early Christian, medieval, and modern. The downfall of Egyptian civilization was the result of the immutability enforced by the theocracy and the caste system. Such a rigid system was not adjusted to the new influences which came with new contacts, and, a part of the machinery being dislocated, the whole system broke down.

In conclusion, the author reviews the progress in the sciences and arts since the rise of Arab civilization, and grapples with, but fails to solve, the problems raised by the Industrial Revolution. He outlines the hardships of the workers and describes the beastly conditions in which they live. A solution will be found. He would not, like Ruskin and Morris, abolish the factories, but he would alleviate the harsh conditions which they have imposed upon great masses of men. The "Natural History" closes with a crescendo of faith in the ultimate outcome of humanity's experiment, and with a thought suggestive of Dove's insistence on proper "credence."[1] Everything which directs public attention to existing conditions of society has a tendency to suggest the correction of social evil and the advancement of social good. But he differs from Dove in the efficacy which he assigns to the arts: "Impressed with the belief, he joins from his heart in the wish and anticipation of Hope's own bard—

> 'Come, bright Improvement! on the car of Time,
> And rule the spacious world from clime to clime;
> Thy handmaid arts shall every wild explore,
> Trace every wave, and culture every shore.'"

Inventions and mechanical devices, we are assured, will solve the problem of progress. Yet the inability to use these devices, without being misused by them, has given rise to the problems consequent upon the Industrial Revolution. There seems no justification for Taylor's closing note of optimism, unless it is that he has come to the brink of despair: There is no good in us; therefore, let us hope for the best.

---

[1] See below, p. 345.

6. Dove's "Theory of Human Progression"

In 1850 Patrick Edward Dove (1815–1873), a Scotchman, published "The Theory of Human Progression",[1] which attracted the attention of the followers of Henry George, but which, like the writings of the latter, goes much further in its philosophy than the mere advocacy of the single tax, a theory which both men held. Dove regards politics as the supreme science, since it treats of the relations between men. It defines liberty, the condition in which man uses his powers without the interference of another, and freedom, a condition in which interference by others is altogether removed. Freedom of speech is the great turning-point of liberty. Law introduces artificial restraints, as, for example, when it restricts the right to hunt and fish, a right which, originally, all men possessed, irrespective of occupancy of the land. Human welfare is the supreme objective of politics. The factory system, the outgrowth of the Industrial Revolution, is a blot upon civilization, a "monstrous sytem of misdirected intention, based on a blasphemy against man's spiritual nature." The natural and mechanical sciences have now far outstripped the social sciences. The latter, however, are destined to improve, and will achieve in human affairs greater wonders than have been produced in the realm of matter. Britain needs not more railroads, larger orders for cotton, new lords, mercantile or economic change, but social change—new and equitable social arrangements. There must be a change in credence, *i.e.*, in point of view, conviction, social conscience, and social consciousness. Men's minds have been dominated by the ideals of the papacy, of feudalism, and of the aristocratic classes which had their inception in feudalism. Now they are swayed by the ideals of the industrial era. None of these ideals is satisfying, albeit each in a measure was suited to the needs of the day which elicited it. But systems outlive their usefulness and become a drag upon progress. Feudalism, though based on false principles, was nevertheless organization, and as long as this was genuine and spontaneous, the feudal system was the true and living expression of a need. The leader was a lion-heart who could dare and do, and he was followed because he possessed the qualities of leadership. When, however, the feudal system was transplanted from the field to the court its *raison d'être* was gone. Its privileges became hereditary, but since neither courage nor skill is hereditary, hereditary warriors are mere mummies. So it is with all social forces which persist by inertia rather than in response to actual needs. With advance in credence the social system will advance. If men learn to think aright and to see their real

---

[1] Reissued, New York, 1910.

needs and their real rights, social systems will inevitably be adapted to
the new credence.

Change of action comes from change of credence, and change of credence
comes from theoretical speculation. If there were no theories there would be
no change . . . Man is a rational and a moral being, and his rational and
moral nature must ultimately prevail to determine the arrangements of
society.

7. C. S. Henry's "Social Welfare and Human Progress"

About the middle of the last century a remarkably able statement
of the problem of progress was given by an American theologian, C. S.
Henry, in "Social Welfare and Human Progress." The idea of perfection
has given rise to utopias from the days of the Greeks to the present.
Crimes and follies are the mistakes and perversions of human progress
rather than its negation. There is an almost continuous striving toward
a better social order. Yet the ideal is not realized, for with every
augmentation of good there is an increase of evil. In those places—
London, Paris, New York—and in those centuries—the eighteenth, nineteenth (and, we might now add, the twentieth)—in which most good has
accrued to human life, most evil and suffering exist and offset the total
good. The picture does not correspond with one's ideal world. The
spectacle of such a civilization spread over the globe would not satisfy
the wise and good man who contemplates the present and considers the
prospects of the future; indeed the development of such a civilization in
the same line would result in an intensification of all the irrational
aspects it now presents. Human progress implies the progress not only
of individuals, but also of social units, particularly of nations. In community life there has been little advance. Extension of commercial
relations does not guarantee peace, though it tends to secure it. The
conquests of science will of themselves not bring progress, for they will
not make men "wiser, better, or happier, nor society more rational,
nor better off in any element in which the true well-being of society
consists."

"Unless permeated and actuated by higher influences, the widest
diffusion of knowledge will only make society less wise and less happily
off in all that constitutes its rational perfection and true welfare."[1]

---

[1] This is likewise the conclusion of Professor Hayes: "Mere literacy does not
make humans humane or critical or even intelligent; and in literate nationalities, the
majority of boys and girls, who do not pass beyond the earlier grades of elementary
schooling, acquire only sufficient mastery of the art of reading to render them gullible
victims of penny dreadfuls, graphics, newspaper headlines, advertising posters, movie
captions, and in general the cheaper sort of journalism which is apt to reek with

Neither the theoretcal possibility of the social perfection of the human race; nor the necessity and universality of the idea and of the impulse to realize it; nor the actual progress of civilization; nor any advancement of science, or widest diffusion of knowledge, contain in themselves any certain warrant that this perfection of society will be realized, or perpetually approached, in the lifetime of humanity. Elements of evil, causes of disaster, perilous possibilities of defeat, lie in the very constitution of civilization.

8. George Harris' "Civilization Considered as a Science"

In "Civilization Considered as a Science, in Relation to Its Essence, Its Elements, and Its End,"[1] the author points out that man is distinguished from the animals by the possession of higher faculties, and by the ability to make progress. The animals remain on one level, whereas man pushes forward to new types of life and embarks on new forms of activity. The point of view of the author is Stoic in its cosmopolitanism rather than Platonic or Aristotelian. The cause of civilization is the cause of all mankind and not that exclusively of any one land, culture, or century. Its principles apply to no one race exclusively but to all peoples alike. The potentiality of progress inheres in every culture, though it may be exemplified at a given historical period by some peoples more than by others; to assert that any people is absolutely unfitted and incapacitated for civilization is, however, unphilosophical, and the supposition is controverted by human nature. At one time the peoples of Great Britain, Greece, and Rome were as unfitted for civilization, and as far from attaining it, as are the tribes in the interior of Africa at the present day. Let the centuries tell their story: no one people has throughout the ages been the carrier of civilization or the herald of progress. Nations, like individuals, have distinguishing characteristics, and periods of growth, maturity, old age, and death. Civilization raises the level of intelligence— which is low in savagery—and this in turn raises the plane of civilization. Appreciation of wants and attempts to satisfy them are the great levers of progress. Whatever produces a want, or occasions the perception

---

nationalism."—Hayes, Carlton J. H., "Essays On Nationalism," p. 87, New York, 1926. However, as Lowie says, "being illiterate is not in itself a safeguard against folly."—Lowie, Robert H., *Are We Civilized?* 166, New York, 1929. Compare Plato: "For an ignorance of all things is by no means a dreadful thing nor slippery, nor yet the greatest evil; but much skill and great learning united to an improper education, is a calamity much greater than these."—Laws, bk. VII, I. 21.

[1] First published in 1861, and issued in a second edition in 1872. Our account is based on the second edition, more particularly on the first and last parts of the book, entitled, respectively, "The Real Nature and Essence of Civilization," and "The End Resulting from the Complete Establishment of Civilization."

of it, promotes civilization, whether in the individual or in the State. Consciousness of a want stimulates exertion, exertion brings progress, and progress advances civilization. An individual who has no wants remains inactive, and similarly in the case of a State. The great steps in progress in recent centuries are represented by printing, gunpowder, steam, and the compass. Each invention has been elicited by a definite need, in order to supplement a power already achieved. "In many cases, indeed, the main result of any new discovery, or the development of a new element or principle in any science, is to counteract that of some other; and this is essentially so in the science of civilization."

The fulfilment of civilization then, implies the effective union and cooperation of its component elements; and the success of one civilization depends to some extent upon that of all. As the civilization of a nation is effected only through the application and cooperation of all its component elements, so the civilization of the world will be effected only by the cooperation of civilized nations, each of which, it may be, differs widely from every other in character, condition, and pursuits. But each civilization influences all others and eventually the world will be unified and civilized.

Optimism pervades the author's view of the future of civilization. Its vices and diseases can thrive, it is true, only in civilization; but this is not because of the superiority of savagery, but rather because the soil of savagery is too barren to produce any vegetation at all. Weeds are more apt to spring up in fertile than in stony ground, but this does not imply that the earth should not be cultivated. If the civilization of the ancient world, with its great advance in art and in the cultivation of the intellect, were combined with the scientific achievements of the present—and this could be done—the result would be a culture which would surpass both past and contemporary civilizations. Hitherto men have not had proper charts and pilots, but there is now a prospect of attaining those blissful shores which they have long in vain attempted to gain. The peaks and even the outlines of the Promised Land are discernible.

9. CROZIER'S "CIVILIZATION AND PROGRESS"

While Darwin and Spencer were preoccupying the attention of English readers, John Beattie Crozier published "Civilization and Progress",[1] an attempt to estimate the value of the different approaches to the problem of progress and to analyze the principles and movements on which European progress is based. Neither history, philosophy, psychology, nor

---

[1] Third ed., revised and enlarged, 1892.

supernaturalism supplies the needed foundations. History, both descriptive and philosophical, is inadequate, because it is determined by the point of view of the historian. It may account for the present but it does not explain it; it may describe antecedents, but, as description, it cannot identify efficient causes. It is important to know, not the manner in which institutions have developed, but their effects, and history does not give this information. It cannot direct imagination in the choice of ideals, reason in deciding upon action, or conscience in the realm of duty and action. Only insight into present conditions can achieve these things. History has meaning only when it appeals to present conditions. The past must be interpreted in the light of the present and its causes assessed on the basis of the forces known to be efficient causes at the present time. Hence history, so far as it is useful, is merely a projection of the present into the past.[1] Metaphysics and philosophy are merely a bandying with words, a refined analysis without any constructive synthesis. Psychology stops with analysis, and yields neither qualitative results nor an enlightening account of causes. Supernaturalism also fails to explain; it is, in fact, a despair of explanation. By nature men are not fitted for civilization, for they are egoistic, antagonistic, self-centered, and self-controlled. How, then, out of chaos bring order—how from a universe of knaves secure common honesty? By social pressure on the moral nature of each individual and by the general conscience of the community. *All* can provide protection against *each*. Previous writers have selected one factor or element of human nature as essential, whereas in estimating progress all factors and all elements must be included. Human nature in its entirety, and not merely one aspect of it, must be considered. The end of progress has been regarded sometimes as the perfection of society, sometimes as the perfection of the individual. As between these two ideals the latter is of paramount value. Society and the State exist for the individual. This principle must be the guiding thread. The watchword of the one is order, of the other, progress; the motto of the one is despotism, of the other, liberty.

The one would tighten the bonds that keep man dependent on and subservient to man; the other would relax them. The one preaches a religion of social duty; the other, of individual expansion and enlargement . . . *The elevation and expansion of the individual is the goal of civilization, the true aim of Government, as it is the end to which Nature works.*

Throughout nature all creatures strive to fulfil the law of their being, "to secure the free and unimpeded play of every power and native im-

---

[1] See the present writer's "History and Psychology," in Ogburn, W. F., and Goldenweiser, A. A., (editors), "The Social Sciences and Their Interrelations," chap. XVIII, New York, 1927.

pulse, and to make for themselves room to expand to the full compass of their being." The beasts and men alike struggle for this much desired end—

the contests in which they are engaged being but a way of determining who is to be leader, and who follower; who master, and who servant; who to follow the impulses of his own genius, the dictates of his own conscience, and who to obey the mandates of another, and bear stamped on his soul the impress of an alien personality. This deep-rooted desire in the heart of every man to be his own master, this never-ceasing struggle to rise to successive positions of less and less dependence, are hints that *the elevation and expansion of the individual mind,* is the end that Nature has at heart.

From the fact that this purpose is inherent in nature we may infer that it is fundamental also in government and in civilization. But in making this transition Crozier confuses ideal with fact, and desires with desirability, *i.e.,* with their value for personality.

Crozier finds little solace in the political philosophy of Comte. Humanity is not a goal toward which men should strive, if this implies the subordination of individual aims to those of mankind. Carlyle's hero worship comes nearer the heart of the matter. But Carlyle leaves out of the reckoning the fact that ideals change with the times and that the man who is a hero to one age may be unimportant to another. Carlyle, moreover, does not present a hierarchy of heroes or of great men, but offers examples which are kaleidoscopic rather than panoramic, for no one age accepts all of them as great heroes. One may worship individual assertion and independence of thought and action, but not the individual, and least of all can mankind worship itself, as Comte would have it do. All for all is a shabbier ideal than each for each. Neither is each for all an adequate ideal.

It is impossible so to irradiate Humanity by any halo of pleasing fictions as to make it an object of worship. Who could worship, for example, the Esquimaux, the Fijian, the Bashi-Bazouk, the Digger Indian, the base and groveling Oriental and slave? Who has ever done so, or pretended to do so? And if we cannot worship the individual, why the tribe? If not the tribe, why a number of tribes, or nations, or even the human race at large?

Thus Crozier rejects entirely the Comtean Positivism.

Constructively Crozier has little to offer. His "equalization of conditions" implies a tendency for one social movement to elicit its supplementary corrective, but he gives no criterion for assessing the resultant. The four great factors in civilization are religion proper, material and social conditions, religion in the rôle of philosophy, and the natural and the psychological sciences. He voices a vague faith that the times will be able to satisfy their own peculiar needs and that each evil will be countered with a corrective.

The civilization of any given epoch, then, is the *immediate* result of the material and social conditions of that epoch, and images and reflects them. If religious philosophies were to have their own way entirely, they would, by consecrating these material and social relationships, perpetuate them unchanged to all time.

But material and social conditions are constantly changing and improving, and civilization is ever advancing. There must, therefore, be in society a dynamic and active force which is responsible for this advance; some impetus, initiative, and self-evolved power which is not the mere reflex of the material and social surroundings, but which, while breaking down the old religious philosophies, brings these conditions to a higher point of development. Otherwise men, like the lower animals, would tread the same monotonous round forever. An idealism which has not yet been realized in this world, but which cannot rest until it has formed the world after its image, constitutes the dynamic power which communicates the impulse, sets the ball rolling, and initiates a new departure in civilization and progress. This ideal is building up the new civilization which lies more or less concealed under the old, and which, when the old has decayed and fallen to pieces, will take its place. Though many-sided, the ideal may be summed up as the love of beauty, right, and truth.

Crozier's interpretation may be compared with that of Winwood Reade, who closes his survey of human history with the observation that

now knowledge, freedom, and prosperity are covering the earth; for three centuries past human virtue has been steadily increasing, and mankind is prepared to receive a higher faith. But in order to build we must first destroy . . . In each generation the human race has been tortured that their children might profit by their woes. Our own prosperity is founded on the agonies of the past. Is it therefore unjust that we also should suffer for the benefit of those who are to come? Famine, pestilence, and war are no longer essential for the advancement of the human race. But a season of mental anguish is at hand, and through this we must pass in order that our posterity may rise.[1]

This continuous progress is made possible by intellectual tradition. "Men die, and the ideas which they call gods die too; yet death is not destruction, but only a kind of change. Those strange ethereal secretions of the brain, those wondrously distilled thoughts of ours—do they ever really die? They are embodied into words; and from these words, spoken

---

[1] READE, WINWOOD, "The Martyrdom of Man," pp. 542–544, 20th edition, London, 1912.

or written, new thoughts are born within the brains of those who listen or who read."[1]

The progress which has been achieved by the human race, says Reade, is due predominantly to a few things: to mental effort and the desire of men to obtain distinction through recognition by their fellows; to religion and its incentives to conduct; to inequalities of conditions, which have been a stimulus to the less fortunate, or have permitted the more fortunate to exploit the labors of others, who by nature are indolent.

10. RUSKIN AND MORRIS

A reaction to the optimism which followed the Industrial Revolution is marked in the writings of John Ruskin, artist and humanist, who attempted to arouse the world of letters and that of political economy to a realization of the disastrous consequences of *laissez-faire*. Three of his shorter works, "The Political Economy of Art," "Unto This Last," and "Essays on Political Economy" undertake this critical and constructive task. Ruskin speaks with conviction, and with a better understanding of the fundamental principles than his contemporaries realized. He points out that real wealth implies social and political weal; that wealth means properly those things which contribute to human welfare, and not those which enrich one individual at the expense of another.

William Morris, a kindred spirit, in "News from Nowhere; or, an Epoch of Rest," depicts a utopia in which all is well with man because all is well with his social world. Like Ruskin, Morris deprecates the factory system and advocates a return to the handicrafts. In this land of Nowhere

. . . we live amid beauty without any fear of becoming effeminate; we have plenty to do, and on the whole enjoy doing it . . . England was once a country of clearings among the woods and wastes with a few towns interspersed, which were fortresses for the feudal army, markets for the folk, gathering places for the craftsmen. It then became a country of huge and foul workshops and fouler gambling dens, surrounded by ill-kept, poverty-stricken farms, pillaged by the masters of workshops. It is now a garden, where nothing is wasted, and nothing is spoiled, with the necessary dwellings, sheds, and workshops scattered up and down the country, all trim and neat and pretty. For indeed, we should be too much ashamed of ourselves if we allowed the making of goods, even on a large scale, to carry with it the appearance of desolation and misery.[2]

11. H. G. WELLS

In his earlier writings H. G. Wells accepts the Baconian prescription of science as the panacea for human ills. He depicts with insight and

---

[1] *Ibid.*, p. 496.
[2] MORRIS, WILLIAM, "News from Nowhere," pp. 100–101, Boston, 1891.

imagination scientific inventions which will strew the path of man with roses; where once he went to his toil with muscles weary from the work of the previous day he will now accomplish all by the aid of electricity, or by the power inherent in the atom which some day will be utilized. Yet the novelist was scarcely in mid-career before he perceived that a Baconian utopia will not solve the problems of human life, least of all those bequeathed by the Industrial Revolution. In 1908 he published "New Worlds for Old: A Plain Account of Modern Socialism," in which he turns to other sources for a solution of man's difficulties. The solution consists of more regulation by society of the conditions under which individuals live, particularly by alleviating the lot of the lowly and insuring advantages to those who, under the existing scheme, cannot cope with circumstances. In the main, the remedies which he offers are those advocated by the socialists. Before proceeding with a detailed account of these evils and of the potential remedies, Wells turns aside to discuss progress. The times are bad enough, but they are better than preceding centuries. Courage lurks in every dark corner of human history and man struggles toward better things. The underlying unity is the good will. The good will as well as lust, hunger, avarice, vanity, and fear are among the motives of mankind. Taking mankind in the aggregate, this good will of the race is dynamic.

In spite of all the confusions and thwartings of life, the halts and resiliences and the counterstrokes of fate, it is manifest that in the long run human life becomes broader than it was, gentler than it was, finer and deeper. On the whole—and now-a-days almost steadily—things *get better*. There is a secular amelioration of life, and it is brought about by Good Will working through the efforts of men.

Those who dispute this inference are, mainly, those who idealize the past, who select only a portion of it and ignore its untoward tendencies. When, for example, they exalt the age of the Antonines, they forget the misery and degradation which were the lot of most of the citizenry. Comparison should include all elements of the respective civilizations.

Such a comparison justifies the conviction that the world is now a better place for the common man, the spectacle wider, richer, deeper, and charged with more hope and promise. Think, for example, of the growing multitude of those who may travel freely about the world, and who may read, think, and speak freely! Think of the unprecedented numbers of well-ordered homes and the cared-for, wholesome, questioning children! In the aggregate, in philosophy, literature, architecture, painting, scientific research, engineering, mechanical invention, state-craft, humanitarianism, and valiant deeds, the last 30 years of man's endeavors compare favorably with any other 30-year period in history. Improvement presupposes effort; things get better because men, intending that they shall, endeavor to improve them; progress is a reality because, in spite of evil temper, blundering, vanity, indolence, and base desire, men respond to and display good will. The measure of progress in a generation is the degree to which children improve upon their parents physically, mentally, and in social coordination and opportunity. Nothing else suffices, if in these respects the good will fails.

In the closing chapters of the "Outline of History" Wells grapples anew with the problem of progress. At every period of history the individual desires progress. Although all individuals pass through similar phases of development, there is everywhere the beckoning beam of hope. Yet nothing so much upsets the fond anticipations of the individual as a disturbance in the larger world of social relations. "Our lives, we see with a growing certitude, are fretted and shadowed and spoiled because there is as yet no worldwide law, no certain justice." These, however, are attainable and they are within the reach of a larger number of men today than has been the case at any previous time. The hope for the new day is the morning beam which betokens its coming. "To be aware of a need is to be half-way toward its satisfaction." This stir toward a new order is called "unrest," but in reality it is hope. Among the tendencies which make an adequate world control necessary are the following:

1. The increasing destructiveness and intolerableness of war waged with the new powers of science. 2. The inevitable fusion of the world's economic affairs into one system, leading necessarily, it would seem, to some common control of currency, and demanding safe and uninterrupted communications, and a free movement of goods and people by sea and land throughout the whole world. The satisfaction of these needs will require a world control of very considerable authority and powers of enforcement. 3. The need, because of the increasing mobility of peoples, of effectual controls of health everywhere. 4. The urgent need of some equalization of labor conditions, and of a minimum standard of life throughout the world. This seems to carry with it, as a necessary corollary, the establishment of some minimum of education for everyone. 5. The impossibility of developing the enormous benefits of flying without a world control of the airways.

In spite of nationalism and race antagonisms, the next great struggle in history will involve the attempt to establish a world control. In the age of world control there will be a common religion, universal education, and no armies, navies, unemployed, rich, or poor; there will be world organization of scientific research, plentiful free literature of criticism and discussion, a political organization in touch with and responsive to the general thought of the educated whole population; economic enterprises will utilize science for the exploitation of natural wealth for the common good; common political methods will prevail and a common currency will be guarded against the contrivances and manipulations of clever and dishonest men.

This world order will emancipate individual enterprise and provide an outlet for individual energies which our present scheme makes impossible; then human adventure will begin. "Hitherto man has been living in a slum amidst quarrels, revenges, vanities, shams and taints, hot desires, and urgent appetites. He has scarcely tasted sweet air yet and the great freedoms of the world that science has enlarged for him." The weaving of mankind into one community does not imply a monotonous or a homogeneous community, but rather the reverse—"the welcome and the adequate utilization of distinctive quality in an atmosphere of understanding. It is the almost universal bad manners of the present age which makes race intolerable to race." Every phase of life is capable of improvement through intelligent collective effort. By believing in the approaching day we hasten its realization. Without this hope there can be no assurance of better times. Indeed the future may bring calamities which will make those of the past comparatively insignificant. These disasters, though "unnecessary," are "unavoidable." Man can escape them if he will; but will he? The future is a race between education and catastrophe. Men follow a false gleam, are led into disaster, and collapse amid the slaughter of generations. Clumsily or smoothly, however, the world progresses and will progress. Nor is there in this progress any pause. Into it will be injected new struggles on vaster designs. Yet men will search for knowledge and power and continue to live for the new occasions which hope makes possible. Through increased knowledge man will attain greater power.

Gathered together at last under the leadership of man, the student-teacher of the universe, unified, disciplined, armed with the secret powers of the atom and with knowledge as yet beyond dreaming, Life, forever dying to be born afresh, forever young and eager, will presently stand upon this earth as upon a footstool, and stretch out its realm amidst the stars.

—Or will man kick the footstool out from under him and collapse amidst the ruin of a world which he has made and can unmake? "Who knows whether their worn-out race will not already have fulfilled its destiny, and whether other beings will not rise upon the ashes and ruins of what once was man and his genius?"[1]

---

[1] FRANCE, ANATOLE, "The Revolt of the Angels."

In "The Salvaging of Civilization," Wells returns to the problems treated at the close of the "Outline of History." The antagonisms consequent upon nationalism can be removed only in a World State. The World State would have power to enforce its decisions, and there would be no war for there would be no extraneous foe. In preparation for life in this state, men must learn to think in common terms. They need a bible of civilization containing within brief compass the best contemporary thought dealing with the important problems of human life. It should give in the concepts of modern science an account of the origin of the world, of life, and of man. History should emphasize the common human attributes rather than, as at present, the national and local differences. Science gives man a power unprecedented, which he can utilize to inaugurate a happier era than the world has known. But will he do so? Wells does not predict what man will do, but tells us what man can do if he will. The world we desire would be ours today,

if we could but turn the minds of men to realize that it is here for the having. These things can be done. This finer world is within reach . . . But whether we are to stop this folly of international struggle, this moral and mental childishness of patriotic aggressions, this continual bloodshed and squalor, and start out for a world of adult sanity in ten years, or in twenty years, or a hundred years, or never, is more than I can say.[1]

"The World of William Clissold" contains a further insistence that man must prepare for life in a World State. By a knowledge of nature and of man in his historical and contemporary aspects, men must orient themselves in the world of reality and thus learn to live more abundantly.

12. Biological Concepts of Progress

The earlier evolutionists were concerned not with progress but with change. The Greek evolutionists describe it as a development from simple to complex, or as the results of admixture of the primal elements, such as earth, air, water, fire, heat, though Anaxagoras pictures it as due in large part to the chance association of forms already at large that united fortuitously into combinations which proved valuable, and which, therefore, were preserved. Darwin's detailed examination of the evidence for evolution turned men's thoughts anew to this problem. He says little about progress but describes the processes of change and the presumed origins of species. The followers of Darwin, however, were not slow to apply to human life, individual and social, his doctrine of struggle for existence and survival of the fittest. According to Nietzsche, the individual should ride ruthlessly over conventions and the established

---

[1] Press despatch from the Washington Disarmament Conference, Dec. 20, 1921.

moralities in order to become the superman which evolution promises. Historians and political scientists applied, or misapplied, Darwinism to the State, insisting that war brings progress, and that suppression of the struggle for existence is followed by degeneration and survival of the weak.

Not until Huxley delivered his Romanes Lecture[1] did the scientific world receive from one of its recognized leaders a critical statement of the fundamental ethical issues at stake and an interpretation of the social significance of natural selection. Huxley shows that survival of the fittest means only the fittest to survive, *i.e.*, those who are best adapted to their environment, means, in fact, merely survival of the survivors. It has no ethical connotation. On the contrary, much of human endeavor is directed toward combatting rather than forwarding the cosmic process, *i.e.*, toward fitting as many as possible to survive. We endeavor not to foster, but to eliminate the tiger element in man. Ethics, therefore, implies an attempt to combat natural selection.

Herbert Spencer, working to a large extent independently of the Darwinian school, and, in fact, actually anticipating Darwin in an account of evolution, inquires into the conditions underlying progress. This consists of development from simple to complex, from homogeneity to heterogeneity. Such is the story of evolution, and it is also its meaning. Change is identified with progress. Evolution is progress, and it is inevitable, whether we desire it or not.

Heterogeneity is still increasing. It will be seen that as in each event of today, so from the beginning, the decomposition of every expended force into several forces has been perpetually producing a higher complication; that the increase of heterogeneity so brought about is still going on, and must continue to go on; and that thus progress is not an accident, not a thing within human control, but a beneficient necessity.

A more barren conception of progress can scarcely be imagined.

In opposition to the Darwinian view of evolution as an accumulation of blind variations, is the thought of Lamarck, who saw in it a response to the striving of the organism. Giraffes grow long necks because they want to eat the higher foliage, and cranes, in order to have a deep reach. In the last quarter of the nineteenth century Edward Carpenter, in an essay on "Exfoliation,"[2] returns to the Lamarckian conception, and describes evolution as the unfolding of potentialities inherent in the organism, and as due to effort. This view he elaborates in the "Art of Creation."

---

[1] "Evolution and Ethics," 1893.
[2] Published in his "Civilization: Its Cause and Cure."

At about the same time Samuel Butler championed Lamarckianism, pointing out the impossibility of accepting blind chance as an explanation of the variations which are perpetuated in species. The purposes which these serve are so well coordinated and are so selectively cumulative that we must assume they arise in response to a need of the organism. Heredity is purpose embodied in organic memory. The twentieth century exponent of these views is Bergson, whose "Creative Evolution" roused European thought anew to their importance. The *élan vital*, the vital urge, the straining toward the goal, is the source of the organism's achievement. Inspired by these ideas Bernard Shaw wrote "Back to Methuselah," a dramatic and imaginative account of the achievements of man in a future age after he has willed the right things with due continuous persistence, until in the prenatal stage the individual passes through those phases of development which are now taken with slow and halting steps during infancy and adolescence.[1] The doctrine of emergent evolution, now accepted by some of the leading biologists, emphasizes the appearance in the animal kingdom, from time to time, of new and unpredictable elements which can be assessed only after the fact and cannot be foretold. This doctrine is almost the antithesis of mechanistic interpretation, for it insists that thought and purpose make a difference, and that the idealisms of men are causative factors in the world of nature, for a man with an idea behaves differently from a man without one and he modifies circumstances differently.

---

[1] A view anticipated in part by Taoism; according to one account Lao-tze was seventy years of age when he was born.

Chapter XIX

UTOPIAS IN THE NINETEENTH AND TWENTIETH CENTURIES

1. Cabet and Lytton

The most popular utopia of the period of the Bourbon Restoration is Cabet's "Voyage to Icarie," which is mainly a continuation of the ideas contained in Morelly's socialistic schemes. Cabet introduces efficiency and improvement in methods of labor, which is a dominating ideal during much of the nineteenth century. The material conditions of life are greatly improved, but Icarie contains no essentially new element. The title page of the "Voyage to Icarie," which outlines the social philosophy of the author, is reproduced below.

Bulwer-Lytton's "The Coming Race" reflects Bacon's ideal. Science has advanced and electricity has practically eliminated labor. The weapons of destruction are so effective that warfare is abolished because it threatens the destruction of all concerned. There is no crime and there are no criminal courts. Poverty is unknown, but there is no communism. Government is in the hands of one man, or of a few men. Women have come into their own. They are larger than men and have greater physical

FRATERNITÉ

Tous Pour Chacun		Chacun Pour Tous
Solidarité	*Amour*	*Éducation*
Égalité—Liberté	*Justice*	*Intelligence—Raison*
Eligibilité	*Secours Mutuel*	*Moralité*
Unité	*Assurance Universelle*	*Ordre*
Paix	*Organisation Du Travail*	*Union*
	Machines Au Profit De Tous	
	Augmentation De La Production	
	Répartition Équitable Des Produits	
	Suppression De La Misère	
	Améliorations Croissantes	
Premier Droit	*Mariage Et Famille*	Premier Devoir
Vivre	*Progrès Continuel*	Travailler
	Abondance	
	Arts	
À chacun		De chacun
suivant ses besoins		suivant ses forces

BONHEUR COMMUN

359

FRATERNITY

ALL FOR EACH		EACH FOR ALL
Solidarity	Benevolence	Education
Equality—Liberty	Justice	Intelligence—Reason
Opportunity	Mutual Assistance	Morality
Unity	General Security	Order
Peace	Organization of Labor	Union
	Machinery for the Profit of All	
	Increase of Production	
	Equitable Distribution of Profits	
	Suppression of Misery	
	Belief in Progress	
The First Right,	Marriage and the Family	The First Duty,
to Live	Continuous Progress	to Work
	Abundance	
	The Arts	
To each		From each
according to his needs		according to his ability

THE COMMON WELFARE

power. Their wishes are not countered, least of all those of unmarried daughters. The young women woo the men, and the latter never take the initiative in matrimonial ventures. Individuals show the benefits of inherited acquired characteristics. "The Coming Race" is an adumbration of Bernard Shaw's "Back to Methuselah," of which it is in many respects a prototype.

2. EDWARD BELLAMY'S "LOOKING BACKWARD"

Edward Bellamy's "Looking Backward" enjoyed an immediate popularity which has been accorded few utopias. In the decade following its publication in 1887, millions of copies were sold in England and America, and it was translated into many foreign languages—German, French, Russian, Italian, Arabic, Bulgarian, Japanese, and other tongues. The author compares contemporary society with a stage coach. In the coach are those who have not paid for a seat but to whom it has been given, usually by father or grandfather. A portion of society does not ride in the coach but pulls it. Sometimes those who ride look down with pity on those who trudge through the mire, many of whom, unable to stand the strain, break down and are run over, or are abandoned by the wayside. In the main, however, indifference prevails. Occasionally, one of those who ride is forced to descend to the place of those who pull, and occasionally one who has been pulling climbs up and takes a seat, but, in the main, the original arrangement is little altered.[1] The society

---

[1] The comparison with the stage-coach was probably suggested by a passage in Robert Owen: "Man so circumstanced sees all around him hurrying forward, at

of the year 2000, whence the title "Looking Backward," is described as the logical development of trends already observable in Bellamy's day, the result not of revolution, bloodshed, or anarchy, but of social forces which have long been operative. Real property and industrial enterprises belong to the State; credit slips are issued, but there is no money; all between the ages of twenty-one and forty-five work in an industrial army. All receive the same remuneration and they may spend as they like. Some built fine houses, some buy books, some indulge in music, though, in the main, music is furnished by excellent musicians and is transmitted to private houses by telephone—the first forecast of the radio—and some spend their money in travel. Crime is practically unknown, for the motives to commit theft have gone, and with them have disappeared the incentives to commit crimes which, directly or indirectly, depend upon the system of private property and the unequal distribution of opportunities. People aim at cooperation and mutual enrichment rather than at competition and opposition. But fundamentally human nature has not changed; and special incentives in the form of prizes and advantages are required to call out the best endeavors of the average man.

The army of industry is an army, not alone by virtue of its perfect organization, but by reason also of the ardor of self-devotion which animates its members. But as you used to supplement the motives of patriotism with the love of glory, in order to stimulate the valor of your soldiers, so do we. Based, as our industrial system is, on the principle of requiring the same unit of effort from every man, that is, the best he can do, you will see that the means by which we spur the workers to do their best must be a very essential part of our scheme. With us, diligence in the national service is the sole and certain way to public repute, social distinction, and official power. The value of a man's services to society fixes his rank in it. Compared with the effect of our social arrangements in impelling men to be zealous in business, we deem the object lesson of biting poverty and wanton luxury, on which you depended, a device as weak and uncertain as it was barbaric. The lust of honor, even in your sordid day, notoriously impelled men to more desperate efforts than the love of money could.

Even the ironical Anatole France indulges for a moment in utopian revery. In the year 2270 there will be a federation of the States of Europe, for aeronautics will have made peoples very close to one another, and boundary lines will then have little significance. Already, too, republics

a mail-coach speed, to acquire individual wealth, regardless of him, his comforts, his wants, or even his sufferings, except by way of a degrading parish charity, fitted only to steel the heart of man against his fellows, or to form the tyrant and the slave." OWEN, ROBERT, "Observations on the Effect of the Manufactured System, etc.," p. 10, London, 1817.

will have been formed in Germany, Austria, and other countries, and the people will have come into their own. Collectivism will have displaced the older individualistic capitalism which was responsible for the proletariat and for the downfall of capitalism. Science will have displaced history as the main interest of men, and nationalism will have reached its climax. There is no limit to man's capacity for progress, and these men of the future will excel us as much as we excel the pithecoid creatures which once roamed the Siwalik hills.

3. HERTZKA'S "FREELAND"

In 1889 Theodor Hertzka, an Austrian economist of the first ability, completed his "Freeland," in which he pictures a society in Central Africa organized in accordance with that economist's ideas of social and economic justice. In the "Preface" to the work the author points out that one of the present economic problems is associated with the phenomenon of overproduction, and that

protective duties, cartels and trusts, guild agitations, strikes—all these are but the desperate resistance offered by the classes engaged in production to the inexorable consequences of the apparently so absurd, but none the less real, phenomenon that increasing facility in the production of wealth brings ruin and misery in its train.

The solution of the social problem which he offers he regards as "the very solution of the economic problem which the science of political economy has been incessantly seeking from its first rise down to the present day." As yet, however, we have not been able to answer the question, "Why do we not become richer in proportion to our increasing capacity for producing wealth?" His answer is:

Because wealth does not consist in what can be produced, but in what is actually produced; the actual production, however, depends not merely upon the amount of productive power, but also upon the extent of what is required, not merely upon the possible supply, but also upon the possible demand: the current social arrangements, however, prevent the demand from increasing to the same extent as the productive capacity. In other words: We do not produce that wealth which our present capacity makes it possible for us to produce, but only so much as we have use for; and this use depends, not upon our capacity of producing, but upon our capacity for consuming . . . I perceived that capitalism stops the growth of wealth, not—as Marx has it—by stimulating "production for the market," but by preventing the consumption of the surplus product; and that interest, though not unjust, will nevertheless in a condition of economic justice become superfluous and objectless . . . If interest can be dispensed with without introducing communistic control in its stead, then there no longer stands any positive obstacle in the way of establishment of the free social order.

In concluding his account of "Freeland" Hertzka declares that his scheme is practicable and that it can be realized as soon as men desire to realize it.

For this book is not the idle creation of an uncontrolled imagination, but the outcome of earnest, sober reflection, and of profound scientific investigation. All that I have described as really happening *might* happen if men were found who, convinced as I am of the untenability of existing conditions, determined to act instead of merely complaining. Thoughtlessness and inaction are, in truth, at present the only props of the existing economic and social order. What was formerly necessary, and therefore inevitable, has become injurious and superfluous; there is no longer anything to compel us to endure the misery of an obsolete system; there is nothing but our own folly to prevent us from enjoying that happiness and abundance which the existing means of civilization are capable of providing for us.

So said the writer of Genesis; it was the conclusion of Confucius; the observation of Plato; and the lament of H. G. Wells.

4. "The Great Analysis"

In 1912 appeared anonymously a small book entitled "The Great Analysis," which deserves attention for its close and ordered argument, and for its sane and penetrating view. The "Preface" is written by Sir Gilbery Murray, who presumably is the author. "The Great Analysis" points out that the world is rapidly becoming a unit. We are in a chaotic state of mind regarding world problems, though we are at the threshold of times when a world order must be achieved or active disorder will result. Such a world order may be a benefaction, or it may prove a calamity;

the best way to avert the latter alternative is assuredly to study, from a planetary point of view, the conditions and potentialities of life for the crew of sentient creatures who have somehow been marooned on this island in space. The human intellect, organizing, order-bringing, must enlarge itself so as to embrace, in one great conspectus, the problem, not of a parish, or of a nation, but of the pendent globe.

Already men possess the seeds of knowledge out of which may grow a living system which provides an understanding of the problems of life, society, nation, race, class, and individual. A selected, rather than an elected, group of individuals who understand these respective phases might be gathered into an international college from which they would give to the world, from time to time, the results of their findings. This task involves not only the accumulation of data but also an insight into the drift, meaning, and solution of problems of individual and national life.

And while this College of Sociology is working toward a largely planned and rational order, it does actually fulfil the great function of keeping peace between antagonistic creeds, traditions, and interests, by playing the part of an external, impartial intelligence, superior to petty animosities, and studying, sincerely though no doubt fallibly, the welfare of all.

The world needs a rational self-consciousness, "to act as a great fly-wheel, absorbing and equalizing all irregular and excessive movements in individual parts of the machine." The student of practical politics cannot supply this, for he is so deeply immersed in the trivial details of immediate problems that he does not see their wider bearings or envisage the underlying principles. Principles rather than policies will save mankind; the one is for the occasion only, the other is for many occasions and possesses an adaptability which tolerates the modifications necessary to meet new needs.

The future at which the most far-sighted aims is only a slightly reformed present ("reformed," sometimes, in a retrograde sense) which is to be, as Euclid says, produced to infinity. Mankind is always to be animated by the same stupidities and cupidities, the same traditions and superstitions. The idea that the future must be something immeasurably vaster, and may be something immeasurably wiser, than this groping, elbowing, snarling present of ours, has never dawned upon the political mind; much less the idea of fixing the view on a saner, nobler, not too distant future, and going forth to meet it. The typical diplomatist-politician lives from hand to mouth, on a set of ideas so old that it is high time they went to the public analyst, who should report as to whether they are still fit for human food.

In this world order there should be a universal language, either an artificial one, or one of those which are now spoken and written. The mooted problems of race can be solved only when there is more knowledge than ethnologists now possess regarding the respective advantages of mixed and pure races.

In "A Modern Utopia" Wells proposes to start with society as it is and to construct utopia for such men and women as are here, who will live in a world similar to the present one. It will, therefore, not be perfection, but it will be a great improvement upon our present world.

Cooperative planning will take the place of the haphazard local or individual activities on which we are now dependent. There will be inequalities of wealth, but they will not be so marked as those which now prevail.

There will be a class of *samurai*, an aristocracy of talent and high moral character. They will transmit the social tradition and initiate most of the reform movements. No society can be considered the best for all time. Utopia must be conceived dynamically, not statically. All things change; and so it will ever be.

5. THE CONTRIBUTIONS OF UTOPIAS

How shall one assess the contributions of utopias? Plato's remarks about the *"Republic"* are applicable to most of them—

. . . the city we have been founding, built in words—for I do not think it is anywhere on earth. No, but in heaven perhaps there is laid up the plan of it, which he who desires may behold, and, beholding, may set his own house in order. But whether such an one exists, or ever will exist in fact is no matter; for he will live after the manner of that city, having nothing to do with any other.[1]

Some, like Sophocles, will reply, "Truly, I fear, 'tis best to spend our lives keeping established laws";[2] for to some, utopia is but

> Blank misgivings of a creature
> Moving about in worlds not realized.

But so are all new conceptions, whether of nature or of human nature. The indestructibility of matter, relativity, the uniformity of nature, the universality of natural law—are these not, after all, merely points of view, working principles, or postulates, which have been justified by their usefulness—until discarded as useless? Even the belief that water is composed of hydrogen and oxygen remains in the main a postulate rather than an empirical finding, for most of the water of the globe has not been analyzed. By practical knowledge, it has been said, men usually mean "their knowledge of the details necessary for the conduct of their own particular business."[3] But practical, too, is he who sees his interests in larger perspective, and takes advantage, in advance, of hints to which others are blind or deaf. Perhaps in all great enterprises the idea, the plan, or architechtonic, precedes the realization; and this is true of accomplishments in the natural sciences no less than in the social. Hawthorne, contemplating the failure of the Brook Farm experiment, could say:

The better life! Possibly, it would hardly look so now; it is enough if it looked so then. The greatest obstacle to being heroic is the doubt whether one may not be going to prove one's self a fool; the truest heroism is, to resist the doubt; and the profoundest wisdom to know when it ought to be resisted, and

---

[1] PLATO, "Republic," bk. IX, line 592A.
[2] SOPHOCLES, "Antigone," bk. V.
[3] BALFOUR, ARTHUR J., "Essays and Addresses," p. 236, 3d ed., Edinburgh, 1905.

when to be obeyed. Yet, after all, let us acknowledge it wiser, if not more saga-
cious, to follow out one's day dream to its natural consummation, although,
if the vision have been worth the having, it is certain never to be consummated
otherwise than by a failure. And what of that? Its airiest fragments, impalpable
as they may be, will possess a value that lurks not in the most ponderous
realities of any practicable scheme.[1]

Ideas are as potent as things, and are fruitful when planted in proper
soil. The dreams of Plato, the unrealized World State of the Stoics, the
devotion to science pictured by Campanella and by Bacon, the religious
toleration advocated by More, Harrington, and by numerous writers
in the latter half of the eighteenth century, have born fruit, although
they have been merely a portion of the contributing causes.

Indeed, the very detachment of the dreamer of utopia is one of the
most valuable elements in his thought. His shortcomings, compared with
those of the "practical" reformer, are his virtues, for he aims at comprehensive reforms, and he is, therefore, the practical reformer with long
range view. Who, in the ancient world, gave such intelligent criticisms of
the times, and such stimulating ideas of reform, as did Plato and Aristotle,
Zeno and Epicurus? Who has written more intelligently of social life
than Sir Thomas More, or, among contemporaries, than H. G. Wells?
Moreover, this long line of utopias is itself evidence of man's impulse
toward progress:

> *Es reden und träumen die Menschen viel*
> *Von besseren günstigen Tagen,*
> *Nach einem glücklichen, goldenen Ziel,*
> *Sieht man sie rennen und jagen.*
> *Die Welt wird alt und wird wieder jung,*
> *Und der Mensch hofft immer Verbesserung.*
> ....
> *Und was die innere Stimme spricht,*
> *Das täuscht die hoffende Seele nicht.*[2]

---

[1] HAWTHORNE, NATHANIEL, "The Blithdale Romance," pp. 17–18, Boston, 1880.
[2] SCHILLER, "Hoffnung," 1797.

> Much do men talk, and dream,
> Of better days to come—
> After that happy golden age
> Of the hunt and the chase.
> The world grows old, and young again,
> But the hope for improvement abides.
> ....
> And the inner voice
> Does not deceive the hopeful soul.

Nor have these dreams been wholly vain, but something has been gained from those,

> Who, rowing hard against the stream,
> Saw distant Gates of Eden gleam
> And did not dream it was a dream.

One who spent a busy and fruitful life in the most practical of professions, the study and treatment of disease, could say, near the end of his career:

Nothing in life is more glaring than the contrast between possibilities and the actualities, between the ideal and the real. By the ordinary mortal, idealists are regarded as vague dreamers, striving after the impossible; but in the history of the world how often have they gradually molded to their will conditions the most adverse and hopeless! They alone furnish the *Geist* that finally animates the entire body and makes possible reforms and even revolutions. Imponderable, impalpable, more often part of the moral than of the intellectual equipment, are the subtle qualities so hard to define, yet so potent in everyday life, by which these fervent souls keep alive in us the reality of the ideal.[1]

And one of the great physicists of our day declares: "We are all alike stumblingly pursuing an ideal beyond our reach. In science we sometimes have convictions as to the right solution of a problem which we cherish but cannot justify; we are influenced by some innate sense of the fitness of things."[2]

The character of utopian thought is various, but there are similar interests in many of the utopias and the solutions have much in common. Nearly all are concerned with the problem of the equitable distribution of property, and most of them solve the problem of inequalities by abolishing private property, or by limiting it to a few indispensable things. Such is the attitude of Plato, Campanella, More, Cabet, Bellamy, Hertzka, and other utopians, though some, as notably Aristotle and Wells, reject communism. Many are concerned with the conditions and kinds of work. Plato is not alone in his insistence that the special aptitudes of individuals should determine their rôles as workers, for More, Bellamy, and others pay homage to individual aptitudes. With the exception of Plato and Aristotle, however, nearly all believe every member of utopia should be a worker. Money is a matter of much concern and usually is regarded as inseparably bound up with the prob-

---

[1] Osler, Sir William, "Æquimitas with other Addresses to Medical Students, Nurses, and Practitioners of Medicine," pp. 448–449, Philadelphia, 1925.

[2] Eddington, A. S., "The Nature of the Physical World," p. 337, New York, 1929.

lem of property. Nearly all utopians dispense with it, although Bellamy introduces credit slips which are a recognition of the purchasing power of labor, and several writers, like More, use it only in dealing with foreign States. The problem of military defense of the community is seldom dealt with by utopian writers, who are inclined to place utopia in some distant region of the world where warfare is not a contingency. Plato and Campanella, however, give due attention to it, and even More recognizes that war is a possibility. Nevertheless, no writer of utopia, Plato, perhaps, excepted, regards war as a normal condition of States. Many have adopted More's suggestion that the laws should be so simple that any citizen could understand them. But Plato (in the "Laws") is almost alone in supposing that the laws are of fundamental importance. Crime, too, they tend to disregard, assuming that it will not exist, or will be so infrequent as to constitute no major problem. Most of them have paid little attention to religion, although many utopians have insisted that there should be complete freedom of religious belief, or at least merely the requirement of adherence to a minimum religious creed. Since the establishment of Protestantism, however, most writers of utopia, whether Protestant or not, have taken freedom of worship for granted.

Esthetic values have been almost entirely neglected. Even Plato seems little concerned with the cultivation of art in his ideal State, and until the time of Wells the writers of utopia devoted little attention to it. The descriptions which they give of the buildings and the life in utopia show no appreciation of the fine arts, no attention to painting, architecture, music, poetry, ritual, or ceremony. Almost without exception life in utopia is drab, and is lived amid surroundings which are mean and monotonous, if not sordid. Almost uniformly, too, adventure and novelty are eliminated. The community runs as though by a time-piece, with all the cogs in place, everybody doing the expected. Dreams and romance have no place. The dwellers in utopia do not write novels, they have no adventures, and the community makes no history.

Yet many of the policies which the authors of utopias have advocated either have come to pass, or are part of the program of social reform today. Nowhere has there been such an intelligent and persistent dealing with the problem of the position of woman. In this respect Plato is more modern than the writers of the last century, and indeed than those of today, and in subsequent utopias woman has been practically on a plane of equality with man. None of them assign woman a less important position than she then occupied. Many advocate maximum hours of labor which approximate modern ideals. More reduces them to six, Campanella to four, Morelly and Cabet to eight. The writers of utopias are the first to appreciate the problem of leisure and to make provision for a satisfactory manner of spending it. More and Bellamy deal at some length with this problem. Here they have been ahead of other social reformers, most of whom have assumed that all the needs of workers would be met by shortening the hours of labor and by increasing wages. From the time of Plato and Aristotle the utopians have also been foremost in dealing with the problem of education. There are excellent observations on education in Campanella, More, Andreae, Gott, and Happel, and education has been one of the major interests of the ablest of modern utopians, Wells. The educational theories of the writers of utopia are more constructive than those of contemporary educationalists. They show insight, imagination, appreciation of fundamental problems, and transcend the pettiness of the pedagogue. But perhaps the most important contribution of writers of utopia transcends their specific social programs. It lies in the objectivity with which they analyze contemporary life, laying bare, by contrast, its stupidities and shortcomings, and in the implied suggestions for a better order. How this might be brought about was, for them, not so important as an account of the changes which were needed and the reasons for desiring them. Their value, in short, consists not so much in introducing us to utopia, as in acquainting us with our own civilization by giving us an intellectual standpoint from which to view it in new perspective. That they have contributed both to an understanding of contemporary culture and to the motives for reconstructing it there can be no doubt, for many of their ideas have insinuated themselves into the social philosophy of contemporaries and successors, who are influenced whether they know it or not, and often whether they wish it or not. They have been a leaven and a ferment in the hard cake of custom and conservatism. And though utopia is but a dream—"*aber auch das Träumen ist bisweilen schön!*"[1]—How passing sweet the dream!— With some justification might these builders of utopias declare:

> We are the music-makers
> And we are the dreamers of dreams
> Wandering by lone sea-breakers
> And sitting by desolate streams;
> World-losers and world-forsakers,
> On whom the pale moon gleams:
> Yet we are the movers and shakers
> Of the world for ever, it seems.

Perhaps, as Mandeville says, "one of the greatest Reasons why so few People understand themselves, is, that most Writers are always teaching Men what they should be, and hardly ever trouble their Heads

---

[1] BÜCHER, KARL, "Die Wirtschaft der Naturvölker," p. 47, Dresden, 1893.

with telling them what they really are."[1] Admitting this, is it not useless to tell them what they are, unless there is some implication of what they should be? For if no "should be" is implied, why be concerned with what they are?

6. INVERTED UTOPIAS: JOSEPH HALL'S "OTHER-AND-SAME WORLD"

Joseph Hall's "Other-and-Same World" was published in 1607, about the time of the composition of the "New Atlantis" and the "City of the Sun." This "ideal world" is divided into regions which correspond with man's chief weaknesses or vices. Its "utopianism," therefore, consists in showing what man should not do. Probably, however, this does not exhaust the purpose of the writer. It is a satire on the prevailing practices of the day which the author caricatures by disclosing them in their baldness, ironically describing as purposeful and valuable those traits which men exhibit but which, perchance, they are ashamed to acknowledge and are not so base as to attempt to justify.

This inverted utopia lies out at sea, south of the equator, somewhere in the broad Atlantic. In *Crapula*, one of the regions into which it is divided, there is no money, but values are estimated in terms of commodities: two sparrows are a starling, two starlings a fieldfare, two fieldfares a hen, two hens a goose, two geese a lamb, two lambs a kid, two kids a goat, two goats a cow, and so on. The soil is too fertile and the heavens too serene. The inhabitants suffer from economic overproduction and languish from overeating. The test of a man's virtue is the amount he eats, and high position in the State is meted out to those who have capacious abdomens.—One wonders whether Hall was a dyspeptic who soured on diet, or a temperate man who abhorred gluttony.

The streets are of smooth marble; not for beauty, but in order that the inhabitants will not have to lift their feet, and the dignitaries of State receive no jolts as their chairs are pushed along the thoroughfares. In some provinces of this strange land the people specialize in drinking, the greatest sin being to return a cup partly drained. In another province the men wait on the women at table and do the servile work about the house. If a man survives his wife he is forthwith married to her maid. *Moronia*, or "Foolsland," is the vastest, the most uncultivated, and the most populous of all these provinces. In winter, when there is little heat, the people keep their clothing open so that the scant heat may the more easily penetrate, and in summer they wear heavy garment to keep out the heat. "They shave their heads, either because they remember that they were born bald, or to allay the heat of the brain, or because the

---

[1] MANDEVILLE, "Introduction," "An Enquiry into the Origin of Moral Virtue."

hair comes between the brain and heaven, and checks the freedom of the mind in going heavenward." At the end of the account Hall proposes no moral, but merely remarks: "These men, these manners, these cities I have seen, have marveled at, have laughed at, and at last, broken by the toils of so great a journey have returned to my own land, *Perigrinus, Quondam Academicus*"—once but a poor academic, now a traveled man.

7. Mark Twain's "The Mysterious Stranger"

A picture of human progress is painted by Mark Twain in "The Mysterious Stranger." The angel, Satan, close kin to that better known Prince of the Lower Realms, reveals the story of human progress, beginning with the Garden of Eden, the crime of Cain, the devastation wrought by the flood, Noah and Lot in drunkenness and debauchery, Sodom and Gomorrah, and the "attempt to discover two or three respectable persons there."

Next came the Hebraic wars, and we saw the victims massacre the survivors and their cattle, and save the young girls and distribute them around.

Next we had Jael; and saw her slip into the tent and drive the nail into the temple of her sleeping guest.

Next we had Egyptian wars, Greek wars, Roman wars, hideous drenchings of the earth with blood; and we saw the treacheries of the Romans toward the Carthaginians, and the sickening spectacle of the massacre of those brave people. Also we saw Caesar invade Britain—"not that those barbarians had done him any harm, but because he wanted to confer the blessings of civilization upon their widows and orphans."

Next Christianity was born. Then ages of Europe passed in review before us, and we saw Christianity and Civilization march hand in hand through those ages, "leaving famine and death and desolation in their wake, and other signs of the progress of the human race," as Satan observed.

And always we had wars, and more wars, and still other wars—all over Europe, all over the world. "Sometimes in the private interest of royal families," Satan said, "sometimes to crush a weak nation; but never a war started by the aggressor for any clean purpose—there is no such war in the history of the race."

"Now," said Satan, "you have seen your progress down to the present, and you must confess that it is wonderful—in its way. We must now exhibit the future."

He showed us slaughters more terrible in their destruction of life, more devastating in their engines of war, than any we had seen.

"You perceive," he said, "that you have made continual progress. Cain did his murder with a club; the Hebrews did their murders with javelins and swords; the Greeks and Romans added protective armor and the fine arts of military organization and generalship; the Christian has added guns and gunpowder; a few centuries from now he will have so greatly improved the deadly effectiveness of his weapons of slaughter that all men will confess that without Christian civilization war must have remained a poor and trifling thing to the end of time."

Then he began to laugh in the most unfeeling way, and make fun of the human race, although he knew that what he had been saying shamed us and wounded us. No one but an angel could have acted so; but suffering is nothing to them; they do not know what it is, except by hearsay.

Satan laughed his unkind laugh to a finish; then he said: "It is a remarkable progress. In five or six thousand years five or six high civilizations have risen, flourished, commanded the wonder of the world, then faded out and disappeared; and not one of them except the latest ever invented any sweeping and adequate way to kill people. They all did their best—to kill being the chiefest ambition of the human race and the earliest incident in its history— but only the Christian civilization has scored a triumph to be proud of. Two or three centuries from now it will be recognized that all the competent killers are Christians; then the pagan world will go to school to the Christian—not to acquire his religion, but his guns. The Turk and the Chinaman will buy those to kill missionaries and converts with."

By this time his theater was at work again, and before our eyes nation after nation drifted by, during two or three centuries, a mighty procession, an endless procession, raging, struggling, wallowing, through seas of blood, smothered in battle-smoke through which the flags glinted and the red jets from the cannon darted; and always we heard the thunder of the guns and the cries of the dying.

"And what does it amount to?" said Satan, with his evil chuckle. "Nothing at all. You gain nothing; you always come out where you went in. For a million years the race has gone on monotonously propagating itself and monotonously reperforming this dull nonsense—to what end? No wisdom can guess! Who gets a profit out of it? Nobody but a parcel of usurping little monarchs and nobilities who despise you; would feel defiled if you touched them; would shut the door in your face if you proposed to call; whom you slave for, fight for, die for, and are not ashamed of it, but proud; whose existence is a perpetual insult to you and you are afraid to resent it; who are mendicants supported by your alms, yet assume toward you the airs of benefactor toward beggar; who address you in the language of master to slave, and are answered in the language of slave to master; who are worshiped by you with your mouth, while in your heart—if you have one—you despise yourselves for it. The first man was a hypocrite and a coward, qualities which have not yet failed in his line; it is the foundation upon which all civilizations have been built. Drink to their perpetuation! Drink to their augmentation!

It is a sweeping indictment of what Mark Twain elsewhere calls the "damned human race," and the indictment is justified. But only man is capable of making such an indictment, and his nobility lies in the ability thus to indict himself.

8. Havelock Ellis' "The Nineteenth Century: an Utopian Retrospect"

"The Nineteenth Century" is not a utopia but a condemnation, largely by implication, of the last century, a time which was tolerable to the men who lived in it, partly because they did not really understand it, partly because their imaginations were so limited by the conditions amid which they lived that the larger world of possibilities was not discovered. The life of the better-to-do classes was known, that of scholars, poets, scientists, and men of means, but not the lives of the average man and woman, nor the conditions amid which they lived. The average man lived amid filth, ignorance, dullness, and lack of amibition. Christianity was adopted by the fighting classes of Northern Europe. If Jesus was the son of God, Carnage was his daughter. "They were closely connected—the Bible and shoddy clothes—by which they meant clothes that were so bad and ugly, or so unnecessary, that no one would put them on except under the stress of extreme poverty, or at the point of the bayonet." Thus militarism, Christianity, and commercialism worked together in the service of the State.

The nominal adoption of Christianity had nothing to do with love or hate, but was dependent on various facts, of which race and tradition were among the most important. We can see that in operation at the time when the Christianity of the West split up into two factions, Catholic and Protestant, the first appealing above all to the sensory, the second to the emotional aptitudes.

The Roman Catholic ritual was a great and prolonged drama, while Protestantism offered an emotional spur to action. Those who were susceptible to beauty and drama chose Catholicism; those who were indifferent to beauty, and loved only some violent stimulus to action, chose Protestantism. "It was largely a matter of racial esthetics; but they took it very solemnly, killed one another very copiously, and when they no longer dared to do that, were never tired of thinking evil of one another."

9. Communism and Socialism

Communism is not a recent doctrine but an old one revived. It was practiced in Sparta by the Dorians, who possibly continued there an early form of social life discarded by other Greek cities before historical times. The Spartan scheme influenced Plato and Aristotle and, through them and Plutarch, many Christian writers. The Essenes practiced communism in Palestine and possibly these communities inspired the communism of the primitive Christian Church. However that may be, the early Christian Church in Jerusalem was communistic:

Neither was there any among them that lacked: for as many as were possessors of lands and houses sold them, and brought the prices of the things that were sold, And laid them down at the apostles' feet; and distribution was made unto every man according as he had need.[1]

But whether Ananias and his conniving wife were punished with death because they failed to give all their possessions to the community, or because of their deceit, is not clear. The context implies, however, that death would not have been meted out to them if the deception had not concerned an important matter. The Waldensians, a sect which arose in the south of France in the latter half of the twelfth century, were communistic, as were also the Apostolicans, a sect founded at Alzano, near Parma, about 1260. The latter lived in the greatest poverty, no one was allowed provisions for the following day, or a house, or anything that was comfortable and convenient. Every man who joined the community was required to give all his property to it. In France, the sect survived until the middle of the fourteenth century. It was communistic, was composed chiefly of weavers, and its aim was to reestablish the apostolic manner of life. In the Netherlands and in Germany communism developed among the Beghards, who likewise were mostly weavers. In England, the Lollards, a medieval communistic group, were established in Norfolk, the center of the woolen industry, and in the thirteenth century a communistic order of weavers, the Weaving Friars, flourished in Bruges. In the fourteenth century the society known as the Fraternity of Life in Common was founded in the Netherlands. About twenty of these Friars lived together in one house, and shared money and food in common. Applicants were admitted to membership only after a year's probation. During this period the novice relinquished his property for the common use and underwent many hardships. "Woe to him who, living in the community, sought his own interests, or said that anything was his." Early in the fifteenth century the communistic order of Taborites was established in Tabor, Bohemia. Its members, too, appear to have been weavers, for the order owes its origin to one Pytel, a rich manufacturer and merchant, who employed a number of journeymen weavers. The later as well as the original members of the community were probably weavers. Forty-two thousand persons, it is said, participated in a communistic gathering held in Tabor on July 22, 1419, and there must, therefore, have been a wide dissemination of communistic ideas at this time.

---

[1] Acts, IV.

In Moravia, a communistic organization known as the Moravian Brethren, organized in the early part of the sixteenth century, flourished until crushed by an outside force nearly a hundred years later. The community was composed of "households," *Haushaben*, which were scattered throughout Moravia. During its greatest prosperity there were seventy of these. There were from 400 to 600 individuals in the average "household," and as many as two thousand in the largest of them. In a "household" there was

. . . but one kitchen, one bakehouse, one brewhouse, one school, one room for women in child-bed, one room in which the mothers and the children were with each other, and so on. In such a household there was one who was host and householder, who purchased all the wheat, wine, wool, hemp, salt, cattle and every necessity, out of the money of all the trades and all the incomes, and divided it according to the several needs of all in the house; food for the children, the lying-in women and all other people being brought into one room, the eating-room. Sisters were appointed for the sick, who carried them their food and waited on them. The very old were placed apart; and to them somewhat more was allowed than to the young and wealthy, but to all a sufficiency was granted according to their several wants and the wealth of the community.[1]

The Anabaptists were communistic, and when Münster fell into their hands in 1534 private property in gold, silver, and money was abolished. The prophets, preachers, and council

. . . came to an agreement, and decreed that all possessions should be in common; each one should bring forward his money, gold, and silver, and this was finally done. The money served to defray the expenses of intercourse between the town and the outer world, and especially the sending out of agitators, as well as proselyting among the mercenaries.[2]

As an effective force, Christian communism came to an end in Europe with the fall of the Anabaptists in 1535, although some sects, like the Mennonites, have survived to the present day, and many communistic communities have been founded in various Christian lands, especially in the United States. But the backgrounds of modern communism lie more directly in the writings of Rousseau, with his picture of the original state of mankind, in those of Morelly, whose "Code de la Nature" (1755) holds institutions responsible for man's ills, and in those of Babeuf, whose

---

[1] EHRENPREIS, ANDREAS, "A Circular Letter: Concerning Brotherly Communion, which is the highest precept of Love," 1650; quoted in KAUTSKY, KARL, "Communism in Central Europe in the Time of the Reformation," pp. 203–204, London, 1897.

[2] *Ibid.*, p. 257. See the present writer's "Messiahs: Christian and Pagan," pp. 156–158, Boston, 1918.

"Secte des Égaux" (1796) was a plea for economic and social equality. Saint-Simon, writing in the period 1820–1832, urged the abolition of bequests, Fourier (1772–1837) proposed the reorganization of all mankind in a phalanx system, and Owen introduced practical reforms in the factory system. Proudhon insisted that all property is robbery, and Karl Marx and Engels urged a union of workers against capitalists.[1] The nineteenth century communist movement was mainly an attempt to benefit one class, and called forth the famous lines from the "Corn Law Rhymer":

> What is a Communist? One that hath yearnings
> For equal division of unequal earnings.
> Idler or bungler, or both, he is willing
> To fork out his penny and pocket your shilling.

Many socialistic or communistic communities have been organized in the last century, more than a hundred of them in this country, some of which still exist. Most of them have failed, though the causes of failure are various. R. Bruce Taylor, who has made a careful study of them, attributes failure to one or more of the following causes: (1) disruption of the family; (2) surrender of individual liberty; (3) loss of the young people of the best sort; (4) lack of opportunity for culture; (5) economic weakness, arising from, (a) increased idleness, (b) lack of thrift, (c) small capital, and its inefficiency.

In 1928 there were thirty agricultural communistic communities of Jews in Palestine, in the land which harbored the Essenes 2,000 years ago. Meals are eaten in common. Women work with the men in field, shop, and kitchen, except during the months immediately preceding or following child-birth. The mother cares for her child until it is weaned; it is then turned over to nurses and teachers in the children's house, which is maintained by the community. Children and parents are together on the Sabbath, and "there appears to be no lack of parental or filial love." The mothers are said to be the "most emphatic in their approval of the cooperative rearing of children."[2] The most famous of utopian schemes attempted in the New World is the Brook Farm experiment at Roxbury, Massachusetts, organized by philanthropists, where Emerson, Thoreau, and Hawthorne lived for a while, and which all, before as well as after its abandonment, declared a failure. Emerson said that physical and intellectual pursuits could not be combined, and Hawthorne came to the same conclusion. "Is it," he complains, "a praiseworthy matter that I have

---

[1] See the author's "Introduction to Sociology," pp. 68–75, New York, 1928.

[2] BERNSTEIN, PHILIP S., "Where Communism Is Real," *The Nation*, **126**: 588–589, 1928.

spent five golden months in providing food for cows and horses?"[1] In "The Blithdale Romance" Hawthorne describes his disillusionment.

What, in the name of common-sense, had I to do with any better society than I had always lived in? It had satisfied me well enough . . . Was it better to hoe, to mow, to toil and moil amidst the accumulations of a barnyard; to be the chambermaid of two yoke of oxen and a dozen cows; to eat salt beef, and earn it with the sweat of my brow, and thereby take the tough morsel out of some wretch's mouth, into whose vocation I had thrust myself? . . . Intellectual activity is incompatible with any large amount of bodily exercise. The yeoman and the scholar—the yeoman and the man of finest moral culture, though not the man of sturdiest sense and integrity—are two distinct individuals, and can never be welded into one substance.[2]

---

[1] HAWTHORNE, NATHANIEL, "Passages from the American Note-books," p. 235, Boston, 1883.

[2] HAWTHORNE, NATHANIEL, "The Blithdale Romance," pp. 18, 52, 80, Boston, 1880.

PART III
THE CRITERIA OF PROGRESS

INTRODUCTION

If civilization exemplifies progress, a comparison with savagery should disclose the important advances which have been made. To those who, like Rousseau, consider the savage superior to the civilized man, the comparison should indicate the extent to which contemporary civilization has departed from the path of progress. Back of comparisons, however, lie criteria, otherwise the comparisons are futile, indeed, meaningless. A criterion of progress implies a theory of values, for without a standard of values there can be no judgment regarding progress. A theory of value must take cognizance of needs, but the things which men choose are not necessarily the things which have most value. Men interpret their needs variously, but the criterion of progress must be objective. The dynamic of culture development is apparent when human history is viewed in ample time perspective. It then becomes clear that man has developed from helplessness to independence, from weakness to power. Yet there can be no surety of progress in the future. The gains already made may facilitate further progress, but also they contain the seeds of ruin and disaster. Men can make progress if they will, but they alone can guide the will, and the good will is indispensable not only to further progress, but even to the retention of the good which has been wrung from obstinate nature and from an even more obstinate human nature.

CHAPTER XX

VALUES IN CIVILIZATION AND IN SAVAGERY

Primitive culture is not so static as is commonly supposed. Even in savagery culture changes, though it keeps within certain channels. Variations are common, and, upon closer acquaintance, the supposed uniformity of individuals disappears. On the other hand, the warp of the culture pattern of civilization does not differ markedly from that of savagery. There are similar basic drives, similar profound influences, similar insistent needs. Everywhere man is made in much the same pattern; and though individual and group assume a varied aspect from clime to clime and from century to century, the moving forces in civilization and in savagery are alike in principle and design. Human nature in essence is much the same the world over and frequently uses similar devices to achieve similar purposes.[1]

Anyone who has lived with primitive tribes, who has shared their joys and sorrows, their privations and their luxuries, who sees in them not solely subjects of study to be examined like a cell under the microscope, but feeling and thinking human beings, will agree that there is no such thing as a "primitive mind," a "magical" or "prelogical" way of thinking, but that each individual in "primitive" society is a man, a woman, a child of the same kind, of the same way of thinking, feeling and acting as man, woman, or child in our own society.[2]

But if stages of progress can be found they should be evident in the contrasts between savagery and civilization, wherein, if common opinion is accepted, the worst and the best, respectively, or the least and the most, of human life have been realized.

1. THE SUCCESSFUL APPLICATION OF THE CONCEPT OF CAUSATION

A phase of the alleged superiority of civilization over savagery lies in the more successful application of the concept of causation. Primitive man believes physical forces respond to his will and his magic,

---

[1] See, for example, the author's "Introduction to Anthropology," especially "Part V" and "Conclusion," New York, 1926; "Introduction to Sociology," pt. I, New York, 1928; and, with WILLEY, MALCOLM M., "Readings in Sociology," chap. I, New York, 1930.

[2] BOAS, FRANZ, "Primitive Art," p. 2, Oslo, 1927.

and that nature is not inexorable, whereas civilized man acknowledges their inevitableness and by understanding and obeying nature commands her. The savage, presumptuous of power and ignorant of limitations, believes himself a magically directive force, while civilized man, bowing before external forces of which he finds himself an integral portion, rises, through knowledge of his weakness, to command. The latter has learned that knowledge is no less an awareness of limitations than of possibilities; he works "by wit and not by witchcraft";[1] and the portal to the kingdom of science bears the superscription "Humility." Yet of what value are the instruments men have molded if they lack the will and the imagination to wield them for their good? Civilized man possesses more accurate concepts of causation than does the savage, but what is the answer to the query of the poet?—

> ....True is it Nature hides
> Her treasures less and less.—Man now presides
> In power where once he trembled in his weakness;
> Science advances with gigantic strides;
> But are we aught enriched in love and meakness,
> Aught dost thou see, bright Star, of pure and wise
> More than in humbler times graced human story?[2]

Control of natural forces does not in itself bring progress, for it is merely ability to direct physical forces. Granted that men shall have increased their power of influencing nature and of harnessing her to their service; that they shall have found new routes and new methods for traveling round the globe; that they shall have mounted nearer to the outer limits of the shell of the earth's atmosphere; that they shall know infinitely more about the earth and the solar system; that they shall have increased a thousandfold their knowledge of the stellar universe and shall have gained new planetary acquaintances; they will not necessarily be nobler or happier, but only possessed of greater power which may be directed either to their enhancement or to their undoing; for every conquest opens the way to a new struggle. The superiority of the civilized man over the savage has been attributed also to the greater appreciation by the former of the value of change as contrasted with the savage's appreciation of the value of conservatism. "A pure love of change, acting according to some law of contrast as yet imperfectly understood, especially characterizes civilized man."[3] His superiority has been found also in his superior foresight. This "foresight," however, is an acquired way of doing things, and so is merely a matter of social inheritance, and, indeed,

---

[1] Sir William Osler.
[2] Wordsworth.
[3] Galton, Sir Francis, "Inquiries into the Human Faculty."

a culture trait. Moreover, civilized man, it appears, has "foresight" for his undoing as well as for his enhancement. Wherever European influences penetrate the world of savagery, savages reform by drinking brandy instead of eating one another—"this is the only new custom which our active minds have been quite successful in imposing; it does not mark a great step in advance." Yet may not a civilization which degrades all it touches be superior to all others? "Armed with science, one can rise above all one's fellows."[1] but, also, one can destroy oneself and others. The issue raised by the poet is not met by those who insist that in the successful application of the concept of causation lies the superiority of civilization; this may increase the potentiality of progress but in itself it is not progress and does not insure it.

2. The Greater Range and More Inclusive Character of Civilization

In knowledge, power, social unity, and organization, civilized man has advanced beyond the savage. The knowledge of civilized man so greatly exceeds that of the savage that the latter seems, by comparison, as naked in mind as in body. "The modern compared with the primitive is immeasurably more powerful, more knowing both of himself and all other beings, more united as a world-being and conscious of this being and of the universe in which it moves."[2] Civilization brings within its purview the world of savagery to a degree that surpasses the savage's comprehension of civilization. The ability of civilization to cope with savagery in the physical, intellectual, and moral realms is greater than the ability of savagery to cope with civilization. Though the larger and more inclusive system may not, *per se*, be higher, it is potentially an element of progress. The genius is the most indebted man, and civilization displays the qualities of genius in being heir to all the ages. Yet it is dangerous to be an heir, for civilization inherits not only the rationality of preceding millennia, but their madness also. Though it is heir to a great estate it may, as a matter of fact, profit little by the inheritance; nevertheless, in its claim to the succession, and in the larger opportunities thus offered, it possesses a superiority over savagery, for potential advantages are assets whether or not their cash value is realized. The intensive and far-reaching specialization in modern society, the comparative ease with which society changes its program in the light of new duties and new developments—thanks to inherited knowledge of facts and theories which assist in eternal readjustment and readaptation—are increasing

---

[1] Pasteur, Louis.
[2] Marvin, Francis S., "Progress and History."

its potentiality and adding to the accumulated wealth of values which now far exceeds that of savagery.

3. The Fuller and Freer Development of Individuality in Civilization

In civilization some individuals attain a freedom from group psychology not found in savagery, and the attainment of individuality is a step along the path of progress. An understanding of group psychology, since it reveals the nature of the environment in which the individual must realize his potentialities, is an avenue to individual freedom. This comparative freedom, if it exists, may bring progress, but it does not necessarily do so. An individual of the crowd may or may not be superior to one in isolation; neither or both may be

> Reaping a harvest of wise purposes,
> Sown in the fruitful furrows of his mind.

The freedom of the individual from group control may be a test of the comparative value of life within a given culture, but it is not a test of the value of life in different cultures. We are raised above our fellows because we stand on the shoulders of those who have preceded us, and not because our stature is greater. This elevation increases our advantages but it does not make us intrinsically greater:

> Pygmies are pygmies still though perched on Alps;
> And pyramids are pyramids in vales.

Kant insisted that in the interplay of social and individualistic factors lies the potentiality of progress. The unsocial sociability of men, the twofold tendency to accept culture and also to resist it, stimulates progress. Without these unsocial qualities men might have lived a quiet life, but they would not have made progress. "All their talents would have forever remained hidden in their germ. As gentle as the sheep they tended such men would hardly have won for their existence a higher worth than belonged to their domesticated cattle."[1] Such tendencies, though untoward, increase the content of group life, for they stimulate thought and action, and variety is essential to fruitful motivation.

The progress of civilization has consisted in the attainment of greater liberty, the unsuccessful effort of man to free himself from the restraints by which he finds himself surrounded—restraints of physical environment, restraints from his fellows, restraints of ignorance. He has progressed in civilization as he has conquered nature, established social order, and gained knowledge. With the conquest of nature has come leisure, order has given

---

[1] Kant, Immanuel, "On the Natural Principles of the Political Order."

security, knowledge makes culture possible. Leisure, security, and culture are the ideals of civilization. But as yet these blessings are very imperfectly possessed, and very unequally distributed so far as possessed. Leisure is the possession only of the idle rich and the idle poor; security is the possession of any only in a relative degree; culture is possible only to the favored few. No liberty is worth having that does not bestow all three upon all.[1]

4. REWARD OF PERSONAL MERIT LAGS BEHIND SOCIAL DEVELOPMENT

The readiness to reward personal merit does not keep pace with social development. Goethe's reflection on the course of institutions—"Reason turns to nonsense, and benefit to nuisance"—is not totally inapt as a summary of the tendencies in civilization. There is some truth in Chateaubriand's allegation that "every institution goes through three stages—utility, privilege, and abuse." Personal worth, it is true, is recognized in our social choices, for even the grafter or the boss possesses fitness as a party "machine" man and a distributor of spoils, but he is not fulfilling social demands. In the complexity of modern society the worth of the candidate is not a matter of common knowledge, whereas in primitive society every member of the group is personally acquainted with him. But even when this difference is taken into account, the fact remains that civilization is comparatively unconcerned about the fitness of its leaders. In many of the lowly cultures the stress of conflict demands fitness for office as a condition of the survival of the tribe in competition with surrounding tribes, especially when the latter have efficient leaders; in the comparative security of the higher cultures there is not this immediate and constant pressure. A modern municipality can survive in spite of inefficient mayor and councilmen, but a tribe with inefficient leaders in war, and weak counsellors in peace, will perish. A modern community is not disrupted by the parasite of graft and nepotism, but undue influence and patronage would soon weaken a savage tribe and shatter its solidarity. Whether or not each people has as good a government as it deserves, it assuredly has as good a government as the conditions of survival demand; inefficiency can be tolerated only when efficiency is not a prerequisite to survival. It may be that "it is in the selection of officials that democracy has everywhere conspicuously failed," but only comparatively recently could democracy afford to fail in such an enterprise. In time of war, when national existence is endangered, merit comes to the fore and is rewarded, or the nation perishes. When, however, security is assured, other motives may dominate. "When no enemy appears from abroad, they have leisure for private feuds, and employ that

[1] VEDDER, HENRY C., "Socialism and the Ethics of Jesus," pp. 271–272, New York, 1912.

courage in their dissensions at home, which, in time of war, is employed in defense of their country."[1] Only in the more highly evolved political groups is there a tendency to make appointments to high office with little regard to the merit of the candidate. As the culture becomes secure against disaster from without, social demands weaken. Unremitting external pressure tends to purge the tribe or nation of corruption, and supplies an incentive to reward the qualities which insure group survival. Even the democratic Athenians did not choose their military generals by lot, although all other officials were so chosen—"No! where life is concerned, you want an expert leader."[2]

Primitive society is appreciative of individual merit and rewards it. Among the Maori, for example, any man who is not a slave may acquire power and influence and become a chief. In the simpler cultures the son does not invariably succeed his father in the chieftainship; whether he does so depends upon personal fitness. Savagery places a higher value upon personal fitness than does civilization, and more frequently selects its leader on the basis of merit.

> Among the Arabs there were no distinctions, traditional or natural, except the unconscious power given a famous sheik by virtue of his accomplishment; and they taught me that no man could be their leader except he ate the ranks' food, wore their clothes, lived level with them, and yet appeared better in himself.[3]

As Turgot points out, in a small group the entire political unit is under the eyes of each individual. Each participates immediately in the benefits of the society and no one can reap any great advantage from oppression, but each must take account of the others. The absence of wealth makes bribery impossible. There are no "masses," and an approach to equality prevails; the "kings" cannot live apart from the people, and the people are of necessity the ruler's guard and court.

5. THE ATTAINMENT OF COMFORT AS THE GOAL OF PROGRESS

H. S. Williams[4] gives the following résumé of the motives and methods by which progress has been attained: Man struggles for the greatest degree of comfort attainable with the least expenditure of energy. The pursuit of the ideal of comfort has been the ultimate impelling force in human nature, and has urged man forward. The only change which

---

[1] FERGUSON, ADAM, "An Essay on the History of Civil Society," p. 159, Edinburgh, 1767.

[2] GLOVER, T. R., "Democracy in the Ancient World," p. 57, New York, 1927.

[3] LAWRENCE, T. E., "Revolt in the Desert," p. 50, New York, 1927.

[4] "Civilization," EB.

pre-history and history reveal lies in the interpretation of the ideal, and in the estimate of the things most worth the purchase price of toil and self-denial. In a progressive civilization a given effort produces a larger measure of average individual comfort. The industrial urge is the most powerful factor in civilization, and the economic interpretation of history is the most searching. Civilized man has a marvelous range of comforts. To savages and barbarians our present-day "necessities" are undreamed-of luxuries. The important lines of future progress will be: the organic improvement of the race through wise application of the laws of heredity; a decrease of international jealousies and therefore of war and its unto-ward effects; an ever increasing movement toward the industrial and economic unification of the world. These lines will converge in greater comfort. Franz Boas has somewhere said that the civilized man labors most of all for comfort; but Boas does not confuse the attainment of it with progress.

Indeed, the attainment of comfort is not equivalent to progress. Nirvana is at best merely anaesthesia. If comfort were the goal of human progress it would be a misfortune to attain it, since the attainment would remove the motive for progress and convert the goal into comfortable retrospect. Comfort may be attained through progress but comfort is not progress, neither is its absence the negation of progress. If comfort is the goal of evolution, then evolution culminated in the clam many ages ago.

6. INCREASE IN HAPPINESS

Increase in happiness in the development from savagery to civiliza-tion is not demonstrable if happiness means mere pleasure. In the abandon of savage life there is an element of unrestrained pleasure. Only in the sense that the adult is happier than the child is the civilized man happier than the savage. For all our luxuries we are not of necessity, and often not in fact, any happier; sometimes less so, for the luxuries of yesterday become the necessities of today and the fear of losing them on the morrow counterbalances the pleasure derived from their posses-sion. By the test of pleasure, the laggard who basks in the ruins of West Indian plantations lives on a high plane. If pleasure is the test the gammon of savagery is as good as the poetry of civilization, and the former may be more abundant. "We are always happy," said a Hawaiian woman, "we never grieve long about anything. We have no cares, the days are too short." Melville wrote regarding the valley of the Typees, in the Marquesas,

In this secluded abode of happiness there were no cross old women, no cruel step-dames, no withered spinsters, no love-sick maidens, no sour old bachelors, no inattentive husbands, no melancholy young men, no blubbering youngsters, and no squalling brats. All was mirth, fun, and high good humor. Blue devils, hypochondria, and doleful dumps went and hid themselves among the nooks and crannies of the rocks. Here you would see a parcel of children frolicking together the live-long day, and no quarreling, no contention among them. The same number in our own land could not have played together for the space of an hour without biting or scratching one another. There you might have seen a throng of young females, not filled with envyings of each other's charms, not displaying the ridiculous affectations of gentility, nor yet moving in whalebone corsets, like so many automatons, but free, inartificially happy, and unconstrained.[1]

Admit exaggeration—enough truth remains. "Humanity weeps over the ruin . . . inflicted upon them by their European civilizers. Thrice happy are they who, inhabiting some yet undiscovered island in the midst of the ocean, have never been brought into contaminating contact with the white man."[2] Another writer says of the natives of the Sibutu Islands, the most southerly extension of the Philippines:

life in a village like Sibutu flows on evenly without rush or worry and demonstrates that much of our alleged progress and complex civilization is either unnecessary or else leads nowhere. There are no factories or stores, hotels or restaurants, streets or roads, newspapers or movies, telephones or radio, police or clergy, lawyers or prostitutes or any of the other concomitants of modern city life, some of which are necessary to any considerable group of people, but others are certainly not. There is no booze problem, for the Koran forbids alcoholics and Mohammedans apparently live more closely after their religious precepts than do Christians.[3]

7. Difficulties Inherent in Comparing the Worth of Life in Civilization with Life in Savagery

How shall we rate in terms of our culture that atmosphere where all is one gigantic dream, a fairy tale in which imagination is reality and the commonplace does not exist?

Teach the Hindoo the earth goes round the sun. It may be so; but in his heart there echoes some scrap of ancient poetry, where every sun descends behind the western hill. Would you blame him for choosing to err with Kalidas and Walniki, rather than to go right with some elementary manual of geography? For him the dream is the reality; and the spell is the language in which these things are written; who does not know the language cannot understand the spell.[4]

---

[1] Melville, Herman, "Typee," pp. 132–133, 154–155, New York, 1923.
[2] *Ibid.*, p. 13.
[3] Herre, Albert W., "The Sibutu Islands," *Sci. Monthly*, **28**: 315, 1929.
[4] Bain, F. W., "A Digit of the Moon."

"We have not the reverent feeling for the rainbow that the savage has, because we know how it is made"; and perhaps we have "lost as much as we gained by prying into that matter."[1] What can one say to the Dakota Indian who returns to his tribe with the declaration, "I have tried civilization for 40 years, and it is not worth the trouble?"[2] Is the Sioux to be taken at his word when he says that civilized life is but a painted landscape, thin and veneered, while his is in closer touch with reality? Does P. Lacombe decide the issue when he points out that many savages, after trying civilization, have been disgusted with it, and many civilized people who have come into close contact with "savagery" prefer the latter? If such examples are not to the point, neither are instances to the contrary. Statistics of personal preferences cannot determine the values of the respective cultures.

Most travelers (e.g., the English explorers from Parry to M'Clintock) are a unit in characterizing the Eskimo's conditions of life as "wretched." What most of these writers say is that the Eskimo are wretched; what they really mean is that they suppose an Englishman would be wretched if he had to live as the Eskimo live. In this latter they may be right . . . But whether or not an Englishman could live comfortably in a snowhouse on seal meat is beside the question.[3]

We are generally at a loss to conceive how mankind can submit under customs and manners extremely different from our own; and we are apt to exaggerate the misery in a situation to which we are not accustomed. But every age hath its consolations, as well as its sufferings.[4]

Many warriors who have returned to civil life prefer the military régime, and many civilians who have entered military life prefer the latter. But this establishes merely the fact of personal preferences. One must ask, preference for what reason and with what justification? To accept the testimonies of individuals at face value is to attempt to arrive at truth by counting noses. To discount the argument is, however, not to discredit the conclusion.

We seldom understand the appeal which life has for the savage because we do not appreciate his interests. Yet interest is largely responsible for the pleasures and values of life. Francis Bacon observes,

This must be remembered, that there be many of great account in their countries and provinces, which, when they are come up to the seat of the

---

[1] MARK TWAIN.

[2] EASTMAN, CHARLES.

[3] STEFÁNSSON, VILHJÁLMUR, "The Stefánsson-Anderson Arctic Expedition of the American Museum: Preliminary Ethnological Report," APAMNH, 14: 129, 1914.

[4] FERGUSON, ADAM, op. cit., p. 161.

estate, are but of mean rank and scarcely regarded; so these arts, being here placed with the principal and supreme sciences, seem petty things; yet to such as have chosen them to spend their labors and studies in them, they seem great matters.[1]

It is so in the world of the savage. Interest elevates the trivial into the important; or, perhaps we should say, that which claims one's interest is thereby made important and raised above the trivial.[2]

8. Are the Defects of Civilization Incidental or Inherent?

As compared with savagery, civilization seems to have not only its growing pains, but its constitutional ailments, its vestigial remainders and horrid reminders. Many of the ills of the body social develop only in civilization and are its peculiar inheritance. They seem inherent in the highest cultures, growing as they grow, parasites which flourish best where the best flourishes. The cruder Australian and Tasmanian cultures are innocent of the human sacrifice which is found in Polynesia. In the primitive African tribes it is unknown; in the more highly developed cultures of Ashantee and Dahomey it flourishes. In the Americas it is not found among the more lowly cultures, but the highly developed peoples of Central America, the Aztecs, with their pyramids, their astronomical and calendrical knowledge approximating in accuracy that of pre-Columbian Europe, workers in copper and gold, tore the bleeding heart from the living victim and held it up, palpitating, before the worshipers. They had, indeed, in intervals of peace, developed the killing of men with "real virtuosity," as an admirer of their civilization describes it.

First, there was the ordinary sacrifice. The victim was stretched on the sacrificial stone while five priests held his arms, legs, and head. The sacificial priest opened his breast with a stone knife and, placing his hand in the wound, tore out the heart, which was then held to the lips of the god or offered directly to the sun. In many instances this sacrifice took place at the top of the temple-pyramid and the body of the victim was thrown down the steps to be carried away and dismembered. Second, there was the sacrifice by decapitation; third, that by flaying; fourth, that by shooting. The captive, in the latter case, was tied to a scaffold and arrows were discharged at him. Finally there was the well-known gladiatorial sacrifice, an unusually dramatic rite.[3]

---

[1] Bacon, Francis, "Novum Organon."

[2] The values pertaining to different planes of interest are discussed in the next chapter.

[3] Radin, Paul, "The Story of the American Indian," pp. 91–92, New York, 1927; see also Mandeville, Bernard, "Fable of the Bees," pt. II, sixth dialogue, London, 1723.

In one form of the Mexican human sacrifice the living victim was cast into a huge brazier, and before death brought a welcome relief, was dragged out with hooks so that the heart might be torn out in the customary manner. Many children were sacrificed to the rain god, and if they wept while on the way to the place of sacrifice, this was a good omen, for their tears portended a plentiful fall of rain. The Chibcha, of Colombia, another highly developed culture, practiced human sacrifice, and the blood of the victim was devoured by the grateful sun. In some instances the priests chose as the victim a boy of fifteen who had been carefully educated in the priests' seminary; he was placed on a special altar and killed with spear thrusts. No lowly culture has developed human sacrifice with such elaboration and finesse. Only a sophisticated civilization can do so, whether in the Old World or the New.

In the highly evolved Central American and adjacent Andean cultures, if anywhere in savagery,[1] syphilis had begun the ravages which have since been perpetuated and distributed by civilized peoples, who have carried it, along with a host of other ills, into the remotest corners of the globe. The incidence of slavery tells a similar story. There is no slavery in Australia, whereas in Polynesia it is abundant. It does not exist in the cruder cultures of Africa, but it is found in the higher cultures of the West Coast, in Dahomey and Ashantee. In North America, the simpler Algonkian cultures were scarcely acquainted with the institution, while in the more complex Northern Iroquois and Northwest Coast cultures it reached its consummation. In the Old World, "slave labor vitiates all ancient life; it is the common cancer of every form of government."[2] It did not exist in early Hebrew civilization but came with the later higher culture.

The goods of civilization seem always to ally themselves with proportionate evils. Civilization evolves standards of chastity unknown to savagery; it evolves, also, with every advance to higher personal worth, a degradation and bestiality unknown to savagery. Legalized slavery passes, but leaves in its wake other social and industrial evils which in some respects are more malign and insidious. Civilization learns the secrets of diseases and evolves methods of treatment in comparison with which the remedies of savages deserve only pity or derision. But, we must add, our superior remedies merely counter easily acquired and hardly lost diseases with which savages have little acquaintance until introduced

---

[1] See WILLIAMS, HERBERT U., RICE, JOHN P., and LACAYO, JOSEPH R., "The American Origin of Syphilis: with Citations from Early Spanish Authors," *Arch. Dermatol. and Syphilol.*, **16**: 683–696, 1927.

[2] GLOVER, T. R., "Democracy in the Ancient World," p. 73, New York, 1927.

to them by civilization.[1] We have diphtheria and the cure for it; the savage has neither the disease nor the cure. Advance in other branches of science comes, like that in medicine, largely in response to civilized man's needs. A problem solved poses a new one. Are these needs plus their [partial] fulfilment preferable to the absence of both? Each advance satisfies a want and, in satisfying it, opens the way to a new and unsatisfied one. Our sciences and achievements, therefore, create new needs as well as satisfy old ones. Much of our progress seems like going to things as bad, though bad in a different way. Competition turns from food to thought, yet remains none the less competition, whether it aims at filling the empty stomach or the empty head. Savagery, however, is more easily discredited, for it is naïve and grotesque; whereas civilization hides untoward tendencies and pretends they do not exist. Savagery kills outright; civilization murders slowly and insidiously, sacrificing the health, happiness, and moral possibilities of one class that another may have luxury or learning. Savagery has the appearance of being brutal, because it acts openly and directly; civilization conceals its evils, as though hidden cancer were less offensive than impertinent wen. But is it not more insidious and inimical? Ultimately civilization may profit from these inflictions, but the lesson reminds one of the African proverb: "Eat this thing, and then you will know what you have died of." We may be better off, but are we better? We have more of the comforts of life, but are we more comfortable? Our life has been reembodied in new surroundings, but has it been reensouled in them? When an individual becomes better in this and worse in that; more philanthropic with stolen wealth; more honest in dealings with friends, less honest in those with the public; kinder to some and harsher to others; readier to lend a helping hand, and to take unfair advantage—does he become better or worse? Similar inconsistent developments are found in civilization; and in treating such problems it is easy to confuse truth with emotional satisfaction.

The contrasts in civilization seem tragic fulfilment of Nietzsche's assurance:

That the superman may not lack his dragon, the superdragon that is worthy of him, there must still much warmth glow on most virgin forests! Out of your wild cats must tigers have evolved, and out of your poison-toads, crocodiles; for the good hunter shall have a good hunt.[2]

---

[1] As a result of the influx of traders and missionaries into the region of the Coppermine Eskimo, "famine looms less in the foreground, but in its place European diseases are threatening the health of the communities and bid fair to rival all other causes in their effect on the death-rate."—JENNESS, DIAMOND, "The Life of the Coppermine Eskimo," in *Rep. Canad. Arctic Exped.* 1913–18, **12**: 43, Ottawa, 1922.

[2] NIETZSCHE, FRIEDRICH, "Thus Spake Zarathustra."

Thus spake Zarathustra. Civilization, Nietzsche suggests, must pass through greater ills in order to build upon them, if only by the suggestion of contrast, to greater heights. Advance in ethical ideas is often accompanied by degeneration in other phases of the culture. Whether this correlation is accidental or inherent it is difficult to say; but it furnishes a fitting application of Wells' "Theory of the Perpetual Discomfort of Humanity." Crime calls forth new laws and new laws increase the possibility if not the actuality of crime. Perhaps, without crime, social progress is not possible, the nature of crime being, of course, a matter of constant reinterpretation. Measured by the frequency of crime, Iceland is a model country, but it does not follow that it has the highest civilization. Kant's remark that in the present condition of mankind the luck of States grows in proportion to the misery of man, accords with the testimony of history. The height of the slave system in antiquity was synchronous with the highest development of ancient civilization. Greece and Rome, with their aristocracy and their slavery, are examples; to which, until recently, could be added almost all European countries, with their well-born aristocracy and their miserable peasantry, organized in a despotism which made for efficiency in the international world of statecraft.

It is an incontestible truth, that there is more havoc made in one year by men, of men, than has been made by all the lions, tigers, panthers, ounces, leopards, hyenas, rhinoceroses, elephants, bears, and wolves, upon their several species, since the beginning of the world; though these agree ill enough with each other, and have a much greater proportion of rage and fury in their composition than we have. But with respect to you, ye legislators, ye civilisers of mankind! ye Orpheuses, Moses, Minoses, Solons, Theseuses, Lycurguses, Numas! with respect to you be it spoken, your regulations have done more mischief in cold blood, than all the rage of the fiercest animals in their greatest terrours, or furies, has ever done, or ever could do! These evils are not accidental. Whoever will take the pains to consider the nature of society, will find that they result directly from its constitution. For as *subordination*, or in other words, the reciprocation of tyranny, and slavery, is requisite to support these societies, the interest, the ambition, the malice, or the revenge, nay even the whim and caprice of one ruling man among them, is enough to arm all the rest, without any private views of their own, to the worst and blackest purposes; and what is at once lamentable, and ridiculous, these wretches engage under those banners with a fury greater than if they were animated by revenge for their own proper wrongs.[1] [Thus man] mars his legacy of gold by binding it

---

[1] BURKE, EDMUND, "A Vindication of Natural Society: Or, A View of the Miseries and Evils arising to Mankind from every Species of Artificial Society. In a Letter to Lord——By a Late Noble Writer," 1756, in "The Works of the Right Honourable Edmund Burke," vol. I, pp. 31–32, London, 1803.

up inextricably with a heritage of dross. Posterity learns to chip a stone knife *and to* chop off a finger joint with it in mourning or prayer. Firearms shoot down game *and* human beings. Rulers elaborate law for large states *and* devise torture chambers. Biologists study heredity *and* try to tinker with human beings. The result is largely to nullify the good achieved. As if life were not an inexhaustible source of ills, man gratuitously adds to the load. The struggle is no longer merely one of adaptation to Nature, but largely with "the strolls that infest our hearts and brains." Is the game worth the candle? Our chimpanzee may inherit nothing in the way of tools, dress, or hut to aid and shield him; but neither is he summoned to trial for bewitching a fellow ape or sacrificed as a messenger to the ancestors of an anthropoid chief. If he falls short of the species Wise Man (*Homo sapiens*), he has escaped membership in the variety Dunce (*insipiens*) to which all known forms of *Homo* naturally belong.[1]

9. THE INDUSTRIAL SYSTEM

Those who point with pride to our industrial system may reflect upon this observation by Kant: Either man must work or others must work for him; and the work others do for him robs them of their happiness to the degree that it exalts his. In spite of this do the advantages in civilization offset the handicaps in savagery? The answer, suggests Lacombe, depends upon the position of the individual with reference to the industrial system. By virtue of the possession of a franc, even so small a sum, I have advantages not possessed by the man who lived in the Middle Ages. For example, I can go 20 kilometers in a few minutes. But I must have the franc. As my francs increase, so do my advantages, to the extent that they are dependent upon the economic organization of society. Thus the superiority of modern times over medieval is not unconditional, but varies with the resources of the individual.

The problem is not whether certain conditions are better than certain others of former times, but whether the whole of life at the present time is better than the whole of it in former times. Civilization is a living whole, and when estimating its values one must include all phases. The values of industrialism, as Ruskin insisted, must be expressed in social and cultural terms, in those of the arts, the moralities, and character. Socrates says that physical enervation weakens the soul, and that the demands which the mechanical arts make on the time of those employed in them leaves the workers little leisure to devote to the claims of State or self. Can the contemporary Socrates pronounce a different judgment,

---

[1] LOWIE, ROBERT H., "Are We Civilized?" pp. 293–294, New York, 1929; italics in the original.

or must he admit that in our civilization machinery controls man? Yet perhaps,

the simplification of machine movements renders it possible for the worker to change his work from time to time, bringing into play a number of muscles and nerves whose harmonious activity will impart vitality just as unproductive gymnastics do today. Successively engaged in the most diverse occupations, he will then become a free man. And the simultaneous preoccupation with the sciences, which will come with a shorter working day, will restore intellectual meaning to his work, by disclosing its connection with the totality of technical and economic processes and their roots.

At the present time, however,

. . . only a few easily learned movements in connection with supervising the machinery or the chemical processes are left to the hand worker. This vacuity and simplicity of manual labor is to-day one of the most important causes of its degrading tendency.[1]

---

[1] KAUTSKY, KARL, "Thomas More and His 'Utopia,' With a Historical Introduction," pp. 206–207, London, 1927.

CHAPTER XXI

PROGRESS AND VALUE

1. PROGRESS AS THE FULFILMENT OF NEEDS

The "true benefit" of a nation, said Ruskin, consists in "extinguishing a want—in living with as few wants as possible." "To have no wants at all is, to my mind, an attribute of godhead; to have as few as possible, the nearest approach to godhead"—is attributed to Socrates. Epictetus asks,

Where, then, is progress? If any of you, withdrawing himself from externals, turns to his own will to exercise it and to improve it by labor, so as to make it conformable with nature, elevated, free, unrestrained, unimpeded, faithful, modest; and if he has learned that he who desires or avoids the things which are not in his power can be neither faithful nor free, but of necessity must be changed with them and be tossed about with them as in a tempest, and of necessity must subject himself to others who have the power to procure or prevent what he desires or would avoid; finally, if, when he rises in the morning, he observes and keeps these rules, bathes as a man of fidelity, eats as a modest man; in like manner, if in every matter that occurs he works out his chief principles as the runner does with reference to his running, and the trainer of the voice with reference to the voice—this is the man who truly makes progress—this is the man who has not traveled in vain.

Though there is continual change everywhere, says Marcus Aurelius, it runs through cycles and does not escape their confines. There are repetitions upon a grand scale as well as upon a small one, through the whole of history: the same dramas, the same scenes; the courts of Hadrian, Antoninus, Philip, Alexander, Crœsus; the same rôles, merely with change of actors. The antithesis to this view is found in Lessing, who, like Lucretius, regards humanity as pursuing an upward path.

Thanks to the researches of historian and ethnographer we have a more intimate and extensive knowledge of cultures than could be claimed by our predecessors, and we know vastly more about man and his environment; but can we answer the questions of Lessing, Mendelssohn, and Kant with regard to the progress of mankind? Was Rousseau justified in depicting savages as leading a natural life in which they fulfil their capacities as human beings? If we agree with him that iron and wheat have civilized man and have ruined him, shall we have civilization and ruin, or savagery and safety? Is the Taoist correct in his teaching that the perfect man does nothing, the greatest sage originates nothing? Or is there a profounder solution from the socialist Ferdinand Lassalle, who answers the question, "What is the greatest misfortune for a people?" with the words: "To have no wants, to be *lazzarone* sprawling in the sun.—But to have the greatest number of needs, and to satisfy them honestly, is the virtue of today."

2. Progress Presupposes Achievement

The number of needs may not be an index of progress, but progress implies the satisfaction of needs. Progress presupposes achievement, and achievement involves the overcoming of obstacles. As Ecclesiastes says, a living dog is better than a dead lion: "The living know that they shall die, but the dead know not anything, neither have they any more reward." Man, Pascal observes, is but a thinking reed, and the most miserable of creatures; yet awareness of his misery demonstrates his superiority over trees and animals. Others identify progress with satiety. "Briefly, therefore," writes Sir Thomas Browne, in a vein which contrasts with that of Pascal, "where the soul hath the full measure and complement of happiness; where the boundless appetite of that spirit remains completely satisfied that it can neither desire addition nor alteration, that, I think, is truly heaven." Such is the oyster's kingdom of heaven— satiety desiring neither addition nor alteration. Man, indeed, is noble because he refuses to subside into the environment, and rejects a shellfish heaven. The clam

. . . developed a bivalve shell and burrowed in the mud. He thus gained almost complete protection from his enemies, abundant food, rapid increase in numbers, and nearly unchanging surroundings. Having once adapted himself to the mud, further development was entirely useless. The shell hampered or prevented locomotion, made most of the senses unnecessary, stopped the development of muscle and nerve, made further progress impossible. Amid all the changes of the vast geological periods the clam has slumbered peacefully in inexpressible comfort.[1]

By overcoming obstacles man has risen; when he ceases to struggle he will be a spirit kindred to the clam, in similar congenial environment. "Progressive races have created necessities, setting them continually higher through ability to attain them. If a stagnant existence with least effort is the ideal, then man is not the dominant ideal. It is the cow."[2]

"To be happy is to be pleas'd," says Mandeville, "and the less Notion a Man has of a better way of Living, the more content he'll be with

---

[1] Tyler, John M.

[2] East, Edward M., "Heredity and Human Affairs," p. 192, New York, 1927.

his own."[1] But to the extent that he is content he will have no desire to improve his condition; for, "when a man is perfectly content with the state he is in . . . what industry, what action, what will is there left, but to continue in it?"[2] The better ideal is that of Voltaire, who hopes that death will find him planting his cabbages. It is exemplified again in the gentleman described by R. L. Stevenson, who is not convinced that he should leave off shaving simply because within ten minutes he will be dynamited into eternity. Death is always more or less proximate, and moving it closer does not tinge the value of a purpose which is realizable; for, after all, only those who are alive run the risk of dying. The astronomers tell us that in a million million years the earth will become uninhabitable; but it does not follow that it will also "be more purposeless when the human race knows that within a measurable space of time it must face extinction, and the eternal destruction of all its hopes, endeavors, and achievements."[3] While life remains, purpose remains, and the wills of men can be directed toward the realization of their purposes within whatever bounds fate prescribes.

3. PROGRESS PRESUPPOSES THE REALIZATION OF PURPOSES

Progress must be estimated in terms of the purposes of a group or those of an individual. These operate in a world which, whether social, individual, or physical, is one not of uniform tendencies and fixed relations, but a flux of conditions which demand incessant adaptation in order to meet them at their best, cope successfully with the situation, and insure the fulfilment of purposes; for the life of an individual is an arena of conflicting purposes. When one purpose clashes with another and only one of them survives, does this eventuality betoken progress or retrogression? An answer implies a standard which will measure the value of conflicting purposes. The elimination of both purposes is a gain only if it results in the realization of a more desirable one. But how shall we know that the survivor, for the sake of which the others have perished, is preferable to either or both of them? When the conflicting purposes give place to a third one which secures the objectives of the others, the new purpose embodies progress.

There are many examples of such progress. The conflict of purposes may be due to the fact that the individual misinterprets his real wants: It is not those particular foods chosen by him which he really wants, but

---

[1] MANDEVILLE, BERNARD, "An Essay on Charity and Charity-Schools," in "Fable of the Bees."

[2] LOCKE, JOHN, "Essay Concerning the Human Understanding, vol. II, p. xxi, 3d ed. of Fraser, 1894.

[3] JEANS, SIR JAMES, "The Universe Around Us," p. 326, New York, 1929.

foods which satisfy the cravings of appetite and the demands of the body; not friendship with these particular people, but friendship with those who reciprocate with comradeship, understanding, and sympathy.

[Hence,] the words of a statesman prove to have value because they express not the desires of the moment but the conditions under which desires can actually be adjusted to reality. His projects are policies which lay down an ordered plan of action in which all the elements affected will, after they have had some experience with it, find it profitable to cooperate. His laws register what the people really desire when they have clarified their wants. His laws have force because they mobilize the energies which alone can make laws effective. It is not necessary, nor is it profitable, that a statesmanlike policy will win such assent when it is first proposed. Nor is it necessary for the statesman to wait until he has won complete assent. There are many things which people cannot understand until they have lived with them for a while. Often, therefore, the great statesman is bound to act boldly in advance of his constituents. When he does this he stakes his judgment as to what the people will in the end find to be good against what the people happen ardently to desire. This capacity to act upon the hidden realities of a situation in spite of appearances is the essence of statesmanship. It consists in giving people not what they want but what they will learn to want. It requires the courage which is possible only in a mind that is detached from the agitations of the moment. It requires the insight which comes only from an objective and discerning knowledge of the facts, and a high and imperturbable disinterestedness.[1]

4. DOES THE CIVILIZED MAN REALIZE HIS PURPOSES MORE FULLY THAN DOES THE SAVAGE?

When we attempt to ascertain whether the civilized man realizes his purposes more fully than does the savage, we are prone to underestimate here and overestimate there. If our culture fulfils more needs it also creates more, whereas the needs of the savage are as simple as their fulfilment. Moreover, we easily misinterpret the life of savages, for we do not comprehend its inner aspects and we do not grasp the meaning which it has for those who participate in it. In the main, it seems, the savage accomplishes the tasks which he undertakes, is satisfied, and finds little contradiction in his needs or in the demands of the culture. So far as success means getting what one wants and being satisfied with it, the savage achieves no small measure of success. Yet the slave and the menial, the sluggard and the incompetent, may get what they want and be satisfied—or think they are. Nevertheless, whatever value the savage attaches to his culture, his social, economic, and intellectual environment is simpler and less ample than that of civilization. There is correspondingly less opportunity for individual

---

[1] LIPPMANN, WALTER, "A Preface to Morals," p. 283, New York, 1929.

effort and enterprise suited to the peculiarities of individual demand, supposing the idiosyncracies of individual savages as great as those of civilized folk. Civilization has greater amplitude, changes more rapidly, widens its horizons with greater facility, and provides more opportunities for self-realization. In civilization, therefore, the potentialities of life, at least for some, are greater than in the comparatively static culture of the savage.

5. Mere Pleasure Is Not an Adequate Test

Pleasure is not a test of the superiority of civilization. To pass from comfortable adjustment in a familiar environment to a misfit in a new one may be painful; but if the change is the fulfilment of potentialities it is progress. Civilization is in pain and travail, but if this suffering brings a fuller realization of human purposes, civilization is coming, though through agony, into its own, and into a realm superior to that of savagery. "Do I then strive after happiness?" asks Nietzsche's superman, "I strive after my work." Progress implies a struggle for remoter goods through the utilization of present ones. Man's ability to experience grief, pain, and distress is a token of his nobility. Appreciation of a discord implies a standard of value. Unless pessimism has an optimistic element as its background it is futile to indulge in it. Only those who allow themselves to sink into a purely passive state are thoroughgoing pessimists, for only then are they ignorant of their pessimism, and not sufficiently optimistic to attach value to it.

6. Pleasure as the Realization of Purpose

A pleasure implies a larger system of which it is a part, though this larger system cannot be experienced in a moment. One cannot, in a moment, hear or appreciate an opera, a play, or a book. Moreover, the experience of pleasure does not imply an awareness of it as pleasure. On the contrary, the experience of it is to a large extent independent of the consciousness of it as pleasure. If it is "known" too insistently, it changes countenance, much as an inside becomes an outside as soon as one pulls it out to look at it. The pleasure which is truly and not falsely pleasure, reality and not illusion, is part of a larger pleasure, namely, the realization of purposes. Acquaintance with purposes, therefore, will disclose the nature of pleasure, and a better understanding of purposes will give a better insight into pleasure. Not sheer pleasure, but a satisfying human dignity, is the chief aim in life, and he who attains it achieves happiness; for happiness consists in hopefully and cheerfully fulfilling one's real purposes. In this sense progress is getting what one wants and not being satisfied with it; for certainly "one would like to draw from success something better than the mere pleasure of succeeding."[1]

7. UTILITARIANISM AS A TEST OF PROGRESS

Ethics is the search for satisfactory standards of conduct. It is difficult to orient oneself in a world in which there are as many standards as standard bearers, and one seeks a criterion by which to measure all standards. If pleasure is the ideal, then, said the early hedonists, it is easily recognized, for each man knows his own pleasure, though in order to recognize a pleasure it is necessary to occupy the unique position of the individual who experiences it. Yet almost at the beginning of hedonistic speculation there were attempts to discriminate among pleasures, some being considered more desirable than others, and there were also attempts to instruct others regarding the nature of the greatest pleasure, rather than to leave the discovery to each individual. But the hedonistic philosophy scarcely advanced beyond the speculations of the Greeks and Romans. The eighteenth-century theological hedonists considered posthumous pleasure preferable to all others because there was more of it; the utilitarians said that each should prefer the pleasure of all to his individual pleasure; and the psychological hedonists declared the choice of pleasure inevitable. But these views did not supply a norm of pleasure. In recent speculation about the value of pleasure a twofold standard is proposed: pleasure and an ideal status. Thus John Stuart Mill insists that poetry is better than push-pin and Socrates is better than a fool, irrespective of the element of pleasure. Sidgwick, Rashdall, and Everett[2] consider pleasure the ideal. But the problem as posited by these writers cannot be solved. It is solvable if pleasure, experience, and activity are brought into the same category and made transposable, but a solution is not possible if pleasure is interpreted as a unique subjective experience. The concept of pleasure, therefore, must be in terms which admit of comparison and evaluation. It is fruitless to allege that pleasure is merely pleasure and that it can be recognized only by the individual experiencing it, though in a sense, this is true—as it is true of the perception of a star, a picture, or an intellectual process; and it is possible to ascertain whether the experience which the individual interprets as pleasure is or is not actually such. His judgment about the character of his experience may be wrong. He may be mistaken in his judgment about his own pleasure, for the immediacy of the experience is not a guarantee of the truth of the inference about it. In short, the experient is not an infall-

---

[1] BRYCE, JAMES (Viscount).

[2] EVERETT, WALTER, "Moral Values," New York, 1918.

ible judge of whether or not he is experiencing pleasure. The hedonistic
paradox is a partial recognition that experience and the judgment about
it are not identical, for pleasure is likely to disappear when a man consciously strives for it, or when he introspects in order to discover whether
he is experiencing it. The "paradox"—which is not peculiar to hedonism
—arises from the fact that two processes are confused in thought, namely,
the experience of pleasure, and the consciousness that the experience is
pleasure. As it is not essential to greatness that a man be conscious of his
greatness, nor to philanthropy that the donor be conscious of his philanthropy, so it is not essential to the reality of pleasure that the experient
be aware of the fact that the experience is pleasure. If the pleasure is
long-continued, and involves many phases of life, the experient is probably not conscious of it as pleasure.[1] One may think one is enjoying pleasure when one is not remotely near it—as is the case, for example, with
the hilarious but feeble drunkard. Seldom does he who judges self judge
best. Of the existence and nature of pleasure, then, the experient is
not the sole judge, and his judgment is not necessarily correct. Tentatively, pleasure may be defined as the doing of a thing for its own sake.
It may be objected that by this principle debaucheries are justified, at
least are pleasures, when done for their own sake. Perhaps they are such
to the extent that they are isolated bits of experience, or are self-complete, but if the experience is part of a larger one, if the day is part of a
year, there remains the problem of whether it is pleasure if viewed as
part of this more inclusive whole, and that inquiry must be answered
empirically.

As there are false estimates of things which should be done for their
own sake, so there are false as well as true views of pleasure. True
pleasure, then, is not so much that which is done for its own sake, as
that which, all things considered, should be done for its own sake.
The traditional hedonistic controversy is futile, because it assumes
that pleasure is an ineffable something known only to the experient and
that he alone can pass judgment upon it, since one who does not share a
secret cannot know its value.   But secrets are meaningless until they
are shared and if one is to know that pleasures exist they must be something more than hidden treasures. The individual who imparts to others

---

[1] Mandeville appears to have been the first to appreciate this general position.
In the course of his observations on memory he says: "A mother, when her Son is
thirty years old, has more Reason to know that he is the same whom she brought
into the World, than himself; and such a one, who daily minds her Son, and remembers the Alterations of his Features from time to time, is more certain of him that he
was not chang'd in the Cradle, than she can be of herself."—MANDEVILLE, BERNARD,
"Fable of the Bees," pt. II, fourth dialogue, London, 1723.

a knowledge of his pleasures makes this knowledge common property, and the world is then able to pronounce him happy. Otherwise one cannot know that an experience constitutes pleasure. The mirage is none the less a mirage because it is alluring, and it is no less false if it simulates pleasure than if it simulates a landscape. To define pleasure as that which should be done for its own sake implies that men do not always choose that which is pleasurable, and that they can correct false judgments. It is wise to enjoy the day for its own sake, but it is wiser to enjoy it also as part of the year. Life is a unity, not a sum of discrete elements; when making a choice, the individual chooses not merely an act, but one totality rather than another. The ill-spent day deflects the realization of a life program in one direction, the well-spent day, in another. A happy life is a continuum of purposes, the fulfilment of which remains incomplete. As the Mu'tazilite, Bishr b. Mu'tamir said, "in dealing with actions and their moral values we have to consider not only one agent and one object, but often a series, the act being transmitted from one to the other so that each of the intervening objects becomes the agent to the next object."[1] The belief that one is experiencing pleasure is, therefore, not necessarily correct; the validity of the judgment can be determined only in the light of values. When these are understood the experience previously adjudged a pleasure must sometimes, in the light of larger knowledge, be reinterpreted as no pleasure at all. It may be merely a light-hearted way of experiencing pain.

This view may seem monstrous to those who insist that pleasure is what it is at the time it is experienced and independently of whether it came at the wrong time, or was accepted in the wrong way, with painful rather than pleasurable results. One may inquire, derisively, if a house was not a house, though now it has collapsed in a heap of ruins upon the head of the occupant. If we state the problem so as to bring it within the realm of purpose, we may answer with some confidence: If we define a house as a habitation fit to live in, or as one which adds happiness to the occupant, then, indeed, the structure was not really a house; subsequent events show the falsity of the earlier judgment. The structure was complete but not the human life to whose purposes it had reference, and so the meaning of the former, so far as it concerned the occupant, could not be determined until his purposes were known and had been realized or thwarted. An experience is no less liable than is a dwelling to be estimated as pleasurable when actually it is painful and disastrous.

---

[1] O'LEARY, DE LACY, "Arabic Thought and Its Place in History," p. 127, London, 1922.

8. Value in Individual and in Social Life

Value refers to purpose, and that which does not affect purpose is neither valuable nor harmful. The smothering of a purpose cannot, as such, contribute value; for value pertains to the fulfilment of purpose. Schopenhauer's pessimism does not solve the problem of value but gives it up in despair. The solution would be simple if men had a single purpose or if their purposes were continuous and mutually supplementary. Human life, however, is not a sum of simple and supplementary purposes, but an inextricable complexity of purposes, which are sometimes mutually helpful, sometimes antagonistic and ultimately irreconcilable. Every individual embodies numerous purposes, which make his life a veritable battlefield and graveyard of warring or defeated desires. But desires may have allies, for there is cooperation as well as antagonism among them. In the ideal alliance each ally secures its end without obstructing the others; while securing its own objectives, it paves the way to the fulfilment of theirs as well. Cooperation is progress, for it facilitates the realization of purposes. The harmonizing of purposes, and the things and activities which facilitate it, constitute value. Since, however, purposes differ from one individual to another, is it possible to compare harmonies which embody different purposes, or which stress differently the constituent elements in the harmony? An overtone, a *timbre*, imparts unique values to the respective purposes embodied in different individuals. But this does not preclude profitable comparison of purposes. However various the purposes, however unique their setting, they belong to a limited number of types; for individuals embody similar purposes. Values, says Höffding, depend on the motives which prompt one in estimating existence. The motive may be merely a momentary need, which is soon pressed into the background by another need; or it may lie in a ceaseless striving, in response to the instinct of self-preservation. It may be conditioned by man as an isolated being, in which case it is stamped with an individualistic or even egoistic character, or it may arise because a man cannot separate his weal and woe from the great web of events in which he feels himself a member of a large group of men, a partaker in wide and common interests. The values which an individual desires to conserve are those which he regards as the highest. These vary among men who live under different historical and cultural conditions. The Greenlander's belief in the conservation of values differs widely from the Greek's, and the Hindu's from the Christian's. The egoist and the voluptuary, as well as the ethical idealist or he whose life is spent in the worship of the beautiful, have their heavens, though these are very different.[1] Yet even in such contrasting cultures as those

---

[1] HÖFFDING, HARALD, "The Philosophy of Religion."

of the Eskimo and the European the spheres of purposes are not mutually exclusive, but intersect, and purposes common to individuals can be compared on the basis of the values which they contribute. In all cultures men strive for things common to their needs: for home, knowledge, bodily sustenance, privileges, and advantages which bring pleasure and satisfaction. In every individual there are the elements of human nature, and every community contains the elements of internationalism.

Experience endured or experience desired or experience feared . . . are everywhere intrinsically the same. Men endure birth and growth and labor and grief and death. They desire food and fortune, love and joy, adventure and peace. They fear loneliness and poverty and frustration, accident and torment, premature annihilation or life drawn out too long. The special or local conditions in which they live . . . are merely an idiom . . . The important human experiences fall into simple patterns.[1]

Progress, it has been said, is a matter of faith, not an object of knowledge, and the conviction of one need not be accepted by another. But if the test is not objective, how shall one distinguish whim from wisdom? "Life is a school," says Charles Reade, "and the lesson ne'er done; we put down one fault and take up another, and so go blundering here and blundering there, till we blunder into our graves, and there's an end of us."[2] Harmonization of purposes seems to leave open as large an issue as that which it solves. Many and diverse purposes characterize humanity, and they are not of equal value.

If, however, purposes are not of equal value, harmonization of some is more desirable than harmonization of others. In one group of purposes a greater harmonization may be possible than in another, but progress may occur at any point. The concrete situation, however, presents the greatest difficulty.

Morality, duty, I know. But how hard to discover what is duty. I assure you that for three-quarters of my time I do not know where duty lies. It is like the hedgehog that belonged to our English governess at Joinville; we used to spend the whole evening looking for it under the furniture; and when we found it, it was time to go to bed.[3]

The weary soul pursues life's problems persistently, and in the end lies down, a weary soul, the solution only begun. For the solution which does not in turn give rise to new problems is unworthy of the effort. "It

---

[1] VAN DOREN, CARL, "Literature," in BEARD, CHARLES A. (editor), "Whither Mankind," p. 401, New York, 1928.

[2] READE, CHARLES, "The Cloister and the Hearth."

[3] FRANCE, ANATOLE.

is only in fiction that conclusions are final," and solutions will always bring new problems—

> There is always a land of Beyond
> A vision to seek, a beckoning peak,
> A farness that never will fail;
> And, try how we will, unattainable still.

Pleasure lies in the zest of overcoming. He who finds it there need not be a weary soul, for he conquers even in the moment of defeat. What matters it then if no social "problem" is really "solved," if even as it is "solved" it reappears in some new form? We may accept contentedly the assurance that "emancipation carries in its carpet-bag no panacea but a fresh pack of problems."

Man's aim is to culminate, but it is the saddest thing in the world to feel that we have accomplished it.[1] Even in rational knowledge the principle of truth lies in the desire to know, the striding on of thought, rather than in any particular fact ascertained, which further knowledge may *unascertain*.[2]

9. The Interpretation of Purposes

If men do not know what they want, and think they want a certain thing when, as a matter of fact, they want not it but something else, how can they know what they really do want? In most cases, not until after the choosing, and luckily if then. Where the alternatives are marriage for life or celibacy for life, one cannot try both. Perhaps the individual is not more capable of judging their respective worths after having tried one of them. Nevertheless a calculus based on the deflection and the fulfilment of the purposes of individuals who have tried the one or the other may yield an index to their respective values, provided the data are at hand and the understanding of them is thorough and intimate. The inquiring individual will then subsume his own case under the others and interpret it objectively. The pathway of individual welfare is found by scrutinizing the highway of individual welfares; for the individual is member of a class, and only by virtue of belonging to it and yet transcending it does life have significance and satisfaction. The values of life are discovered by applying an objective standard, else there are data for comparison but no standard, things to be measured, but no measuring stick. Value must be put into individual purposes before it can be gotten out of them. The measuring of purposes by purposes may seem a circular procedure, as, indeed, it is. But a standard

---

[1] MEREDITH, GEORGE.

[2] TAYLOR, HENRY O., "Human Values and Verities," pp. 201–202, New York, 1928.

of values in which purposes are compared in terms of realization and
harmonization is as legitimate as comparing lengths in terms of length—
and no less inevitable; for the value of a purpose can be measured only
by a standard derived from the world of purpose. Höffding finds the
conservation of values furthered in a living by realities rather than, like
Heegard, in a living by possibilities. But this is not a real antinomy.
Possibilities are phases of the realities, rooted in ideals rather than in
the accepted traditions. The real cannot be greater than the possible,
and the possible comprises nothing which falls without the realm of
the real. The Abbé Cotin—"Nature has more ways of making things
than we have of knowing them"—and Shakespeare—"There are more
things in Heaven and earth than we have dreamed of in our philosophy"
—speak figuratively. The things opposed are supplementary, each a
counterpart to the other. So with our half-realized purposes and aims:
the ideal is only a phase of the real, and what should be is merely an
emphasis upon what is. How, indeed, can the value of a purpose be estimated save in terms of some existing one? How can man rise above himself, after the manner of Nietzsche's superman, except by the fuller play
of an existing purpose exalted at the expense of others, which thus
become "stepping-stones to higher things?" The motive to rise above
oneself means that a thwarted purpose is seeking a path to fuller realization.

For there is not a Man in the World, educated in Society, who, if he could
compass it by wishing, would not have something added to, taken from, or
alter'd in his Person, Possessions, Circumstances, or any part of the Society
he belongs to. This is what is not to be perceiv'd in any Creature but Man;
whose great Industry in supplying what he calls his Wants, could never have
been known so well as it is, if it had not been for the Unreasonableness, as
well as Multiplicity, of his Desires.[1]

The ideal is but a certain emphasis upon the real, and the "beyond"
is what Boutroux calls a "beyond that is within." "As soon as we
study humanity with care, we find that a common trait characterizes
all its longings, all its perceptions: the pursuit of something, not only
different, but superior—the endeavor to outstrip itself." To outstrip
itself, however, is to make itself the victor. Such victory is possible
in a realm of competing purposes in which the hierarchy is in the form-
ative stage. Here, as elsewhere, the hidden forces are partly revealed,
for nothing can be called concealed that is not, in part, already revealed.
Hence, as Goethe says, "man must hold fast to the belief that the incom-

---

[1] MANDEVILLE, BERNARD, "Fable of the Bees," pt. II, fourth dialogue, London,
1723.

prehensible is comprehensible"; for an unknowable affirmed is an unknowable in some way known. "Life exists in the possible as well as in the actual: the must and the maybe are equally valid."[1]

"Ideals are not hallucinations. They are not a collection of pretty and casual preferences. Ideals are an imaginative understanding of that which is desirable in that which is possible."[2]

---

[1] MUMFORD, LEWIS, "The Golden Day," p. 118, New York, 1926.
[2] LIPPMANN, WALTER, "A Preface to Morals," pp. 258–259, New York, 1929.

Chapter XXII

A TIME PERSPECTIVE OF CULTURE CHANGES

1. The Larger Time Perspective

"The history of society is a history not of centuries but of ages,"[1] and we may, for the moment, seek larger vistas and briefly survey man's culture development. Probably human culture has existed for 240,000 years. If we reduce this period to a scale of 12 hours, so that each hour represents 20,000 years and each minute $333\frac{1}{3}$ years, we find that during the first $11\frac{1}{2}$ hours man lived in a Stone-age preliterate culture. Twenty minutes ago the earliest vestiges of Egyptian and Babylonian civilization appear; Greek literature, philosophy, and science flourished 7 minutes ago. A minute ago Lord Bacon wrote the "Advancement of Learning" and the "New Atlantis," and less than a half minute has elapsed since man invented the steam engine.[2] If we take half of this time interval, assuming that the Stone age was well under way 120,000 years ago, and plot human history on a scale of 6 inches, allotting 20,000 years to an inch, we find that 5 of the 6 inches are occupied by the Paleolithic, or Old Stone age. The Lower Paleolithic occupies much the greater part of the Old Stone age, approximately four-fifths of it. The more advanced culture of the Upper Paleolithic fills a much shorter interval than that of the Lower Paleolithic, and gives place to the Neolithic about 10,000 years ago. In 3,000 years Neolithic man learns to work copper, in another 2,000 years bronze, proceeding in another thousand years to the working of iron, the metal on which modern civilization is built. He improves the working of iron, engages in engineering enterprises, and embarks on the career of applied science which blossoms into the civilization of the present age. If these millennia of human culture are reduced to a scale of one hour, man has spent about 55 minutes in the Paleolithic culture; 5 minutes ago he embarked upon the Neolithic culture, the cultivation of plants, the domestication of animals, the making of pottery, weaving, and the use of the bow and arrow; $3\frac{1}{2}$ minutes ago he began the working of copper; $2\frac{1}{2}$ minutes ago he began to mold bronze; 2 minutes ago he learned to smelt iron; one-fourth of a

---

[1] SOULE, GEORGE.
[2] Adapted from ROBINSON, JAMES HARVEY, "The New History."

minute ago he learned printing; 5 seconds ago the Industrial Revolution began; 3½ seconds ago he learned to apply electricity; and the time he has had automobiles is less than the intervals between the ticks of a watch, *i.e.*, less than one second. To those who take a microscopic view of human history contemporary civilization looms large, but to those who go aeroplaning through the millennia of human history our modern culture is brief.[1]

	Lower Paleolithic	118,000 B.C. - 20,000 B.C.
	Upper Paleolithic	20,000 B.C. - 8,000 B.C.
	←Neolithic	8,000 B.C. - 5,000 B.C.
	←Copper	5,000 B.C. - 3,000 B.C.
	Bronze	3,000 B.C. - 2,000 B.C.
	Iron	2,000 B.C. - 2,000 A.D.

2. THE LARGER PHASES OF CULTURE DEVELOPMENT

In this larger perspective certain phases of culture development are of primary significance. One is the *acceleration in development*. The long interval of the Lower Paleolithic contrasts with the shorter period of the Upper Paleolithic, while the Neolithic abbreviates the preceding period of culture by tens of thousands of years; the Copper and the Bronze age are progressively shorter; and since the introduction of iron, culture has speeded up in unprecedented manner. At first man proceeded with slow and halting steps. As culture developed, the pace of progress

---

[1] For other illustrations of these time intervals see JENKS, A. E., "Pre-History Chart," Nystrom, Chicago, 1927; and the author's "Introduction to Anthropology," pp. 88–90, New York, 1926.

increased rapidly, and man achieved vastly more during the last 10,000 years than during the preceding 100,000 years.

In a few thousands of centuries profound essential changes have been brought about. From being a prowler, man has become a hunter, a hunter in packs, and in the last hundred centuries or so he has taken to agriculture, become the first of the mammals to be economic as well as social, and developed societies on such a scale as life has never known before, not even among the termites and ants and bees. This process still goes on with if anything an increasing rapidity. No living species except such as have passed under catastrophic circumstances toward extinction has ever been under so violent a drive of change as man. The violence of the drive is even more conspicuous when it is measured against the length and scope of man's individual life. In my own lifetime his usual food, his range of activity, his rate of reproduction and the spirit in which he reproduces, his average length of life, his prevalent diseases, his habitations, and his coverings have changed. No animal species has ever yet survived such rapid and comprehensive changes.[1]

The first steps in civilization were slow and halting. Man has been on the earth 500,000 years. It required some two or three hundred thousand years to improve the crude Eolithic stone implements with which he worked, and 100,000 years or more to fashion a Paleolithic implement into a Neolithic one. In a much shorter time he learned to utilize that malleable metal, copper; after a still shorter interval he learned to mold bronze, and then to smelt iron. As compared with the Stone age the Metal age is a thing not of yesterday but of today. Within this Metal-age day of human history man has advanced in unprecedented manner, taking each new stride with faster pace, for acculturation brings acceleration in culture development. When new influences enrich the culture, his horizon is enlarged, his environment amplified, his power enhanced. At the present time man has levers and leverage to move the world as he will. But culture development has been marked by acceleration only in those areas in which there has been acculturation. The unprecedented powers of civilized man are, therefore, a heritage as well as a development. Civilization has them because they have been given it, though they would not have been given it had it not been able to adopt and adapt them. Bronze was 1,000 years in permeating the continent of Europe, iron hundreds of years, platinum only a little over 50 years, and radium less than five, while the radio spread over North America in a few months. Until about 1750 transportation in the British Isles differed little from that which prevailed in the time of William the Conqueror.

---

[1] WELLS, H. G., "The World of William Clissold: A Novel at a New Angle," vol. II, p. 548, New York, 1926.

It moved by the same means and at about the same speed. Habitations were only slightly more luxurious.

The Renaissance, the only period in English history of transforming power [comparable with that of the Industrial Revolution] had left the outward aspects of the Isles practically untouched . . . George II enjoyed practically the same comforts as Henry II, Chaucer as Addison. Their clothing was made in the same manner, their houses lighted by the same means.[1]

The significant changes have come within a century. In most respects the daily routine of life with which Webster and Lincoln were familiar did not differ from that with which George Washington and Benjamin Franklin were acquainted. There is not the profound contrast between them which distinguishes the times of Lincoln from those of today. "If Lincoln were to return now and walk about [the capitol] he would be surprised and bewildered by the things he would see."[2] Of the nineteenth century, Balfour says:

No century has seen so great a change in our intellectual apprehension of the world in which we live. If we could construct an imaginary conversation between a man of science who lived a century ago and one who lived two centuries ago—say between Priestley, who died in 1804, and Hooke, who died in 1703—we should, I think, represent the interlocutors as addressing one another, so to speak, on equal terms. Though discoveries which have subsequently proved to be of the most far-reaching importance had been made in the interval, these had as yet affected no great revolution in general modes of thought. Indeed it may be suspected that the earlier philosopher would have been in some respects nearer to the moderns than the later. But leap over another hundred years, and imagine Priestly conversing with any of the gentlemen who have promised to take part in the proceedings we are inaugurating today,[3] and a very different state of affairs would then present itself . . . It is not too much to say that for us in the year nineteen hundred the world, considered as a pageant slowly unrolling itself through the ages, is a wholly different world from that which presented itself to the imagination of our grandfathers a hundred years ago; I am not even sure that it would be too much to say that in this particular we differ more from them than they differed from the Babylonians.[4]

---

[1] NEFF, EMORY, "Carlyle and Mill: Mystic and Utilitarian," p. 47, New York, 1924.

[2] SCHLESINGER, ARTHUR M., "New Viewpoints in American History," p. 247, New York, 1923.

[3] "Inaugural Address," "Cambridge University Local Lectures," delivered on Aug. 2, 1900.

[4] BALFOUR, ARTHUR J., "The Nineteenth Century," in "Essays and Addresses," pp. 326–329, 3d ed., Edinburgh, 1905.

In the year 1927–1928 the United States Patent Office issued 118,000 patents, 35 per cent more than the number issued in the preceding year. In the sciences the development is so rapid that few of the older men can hold the pace. Many of the important developments in physics in recent years have been carried forward by men under 35 years of age, and one physicist has said that only the younger physicists have minds sufficiently plastic to absorb the new ideas and make the new contributions. An eminent physiologist who gave the opening address at the Thirteenth International Physiological Congress, held at Harvard University in the summer of 1929, said, apropos of the development of physiology:

It is extremely gratifying from a general point of view to see how even the most advanced ideas and methods of physics and chemistry are inspiring the work of a few of our colleagues. I use the words "from a general point of view" on purpose, because for my own part the fact shows me that development is taking place along lines where I cannot follow and I believe we have to admit that with the rate at which advance is now taking place in the sciences the useful span of life in the front line of research is likely to be cut short for many of us, because our view-points and even our methods become antiquated.[1]

Progress is made possible by the fact that *culture is cumulative*. Man did not abandon the earlier culture but improved it. He developed beyond the Stone age rather than out of it, adding to an earlier culture new devices and new knowledge. The Metal ages did not displace stone but added other materials of which Stone-age man had been ignorant. The significance of the present age as compared with the Stone ages is not that we are out of the latter but rather that we have added the metals to the stone used by Paleolithic and Neolithic man. There is also *increase in complexity*. Man's early culture was as simple as it was crude. It exhibited few divergences, departed little from stereotyped pattern, was as simple in design and outline as in composition. Throughout the Metal age, culture has grown more complex, until now its complexity distinguishes our age from previous ones as definitively as does any other characteristic. Even more significant is the *increase in power* which has accompanied increase in complexity, acceleration, and the cumulative nature of culture. In the earliest Stone ages, man was using simple and not very efficient means for the accomplishment of his purposes. In the Neolithic age he increased his control over nature, not so much through new techniques in working stone implements as in control of the food supply through the domestication of animals, the cultivation of plants, and the invention of the bow and arrow. Metal has increased man's

---

[1] KROGH, AUGUST, "The Progress of Physiology," *Science*, **70**: 201, 1929.

power more than has any other material, and every scientific achievement, every improvement in technology, has further increased it. Compared with modern man, the cave man was as deficient in power as he
was simple in culture, as inefficient as he was uninformed. With civilization, to use a phrase of Dante, man's will is transformed into power;
power is the daily bread of our civilization.

A *drive toward specialization* almost invariably accompanies acceleration, increase in power, and growth in complexity. Early man—
witness the simplest cultures of contemporary savagery—was not a
specialist, unless he may be called a specialist in all phases of culture.
All were workers in stone, all were hunters, all were fishers. With the
onset of the Metal cultures and the more complex economic and industrial life, specialization was given impetus. It was under way with a
compulsion born of necessity which has not abated but rather has
increased until our age is characterized by specialization as much as
by power; for "people grow expert by specializing."[1]

3. ADJUSTMENT AND READJUSTMENT

Specialization introduces new problems, because it brings a *necessity
of adjustment and readjustment* which does not arise in the earlier unspe-
cialized cultures. The specialist becomes dependent upon the remainder
of the group; this is not the case when all men are specialists in all
things—or none in anything. The specialist flourishes only when there
is demand for his goods, and only when he shares in benefits which he
does not directly create. Unless readjustment is made after each step
in specialization, some individuals are less fortunate than previously.
New situations are created which are not foreseen by those who in
part create them, and divergent interests give rise to friction and
maladjustment. Since these are a drag on the culture, and to that
extent detract from its human value, readjustments become necessary
and "there must be a new world, if there is to be any world at all."[2]
As a result of maladjustments it becomes necessary to make progress
in a new field, in that of social and cultural readjustment, and to apply
knowledge to problems essentially new. Yet man seldom has new intellectual devices for new situations. He has replaced flint knives, clubs,
and slings by the elaborate implements and weapons of the present day,
but, in the main, he is still content with a social philosophy inherited

---

[1] LOWIE, ROBERT H., "Are We Civilized?" p. 43, New York, 1929.

[2] CARLYLE, THOMAS. And similarly Osler, with regard to the post-war world.
See OSLER, SIR WILLIAM, "The Old Humanities and the New Science," New York,
1920; and SISSON, EDWARD O., "Educating for Freedom," New York, 1925.

from the Stone age.[1] Previously his efforts have been directed to improving old devices. Confronted with a novel situation he is unable to cope with it in any essentially new manner. He dodges new problems rather than faces them, turning attention to the old and familiar rather than coming to grips with the new and strange; and he is not conscious of the cause of the friction. Yet the drag is there, and when conflicts obtrude there must be harmonization of efforts and purposes if there is to be progress. The need for harmonization solicits but does not always elicit adjustments, for history offers few suggestions to help men on a path which has not been trod. It is futile to turn to precedent when the problems are unprecedented. Appeal to tradition is vain, for tradition cannot dispel the perplexities of new problems. Harmonization is especially difficult, since no sooner do men effect harmony at one point than new frictions develop at another. From one point of view culture development is like a stream which grows in volume as it moves from the source and builds up its bed until the waters break over the banks. Men reinforce the inadequate banks with levees, but the higher bed gives higher reach to the waters, the new danger is more threatening, and stronger and higher levees are needed.

This is part of the price men pay for the coveted augmentation of the culture which they demand at whatever cost. Yet, apparently, man finds a way out of his dilemma when he persistently seeks one. To the potentialities inherent in a spirit of determination coupled with insistent and patient striving, no limits can be placed. Only time, opportunity, determination, and the requisite effort and will are necessary to insure salvation. Meanwhile, man is in danger of losing some of the valuable traits of culture which he has inherited. There is no more assurance of progress now than there was when the problems were simple and his attention was less diverted by disturbing forces. These now impinge multitudinously. An apparently trivial matter to which he pays little heed may prove his undoing; he must give attention to all the means of salvation in order to preserve any one of them, for in the complexity of culture there is also an interdependence; and it is necessary to do all things well in order to preserve balance. A loose stone in the foundation undermines the superstructure, if not immediately, then by slow processes which, in the end, bring disaster. "As one half of one's Life can put the other in the Grave,"[2] so a portion of the culture can destroy all of it.

---

[1] But see below, p. 426.

[2] MANDEVILLE, BERNARD, "The Fable of the Bees," pt. II, sixth dialogue, London, 1723.

4. THE ENLARGING WORLD

Another aspect of progress is *the enlarging world* in which it takes place. In the earlier stages of culture, man's life is bounded by a narrowly restricted horizon. Primitive man does not look far abroad; tribal life is encircled by a narrow horizon. With advance in the arts and sciences the culture horizon is enlarged, and intellectual life expands in the larger and freer atmosphere. Contacts with other tribes enlarge the culture horizon, bring new ideas, and acquaint tribesmen with devices hitherto unknown. A larger culture horizon brings new stimulus to Hebrew, Babylonian, Egyptian, Greek, Roman. The story of advance in these respective cultures is closely related to that of expanding horizons. An enlarging horizon brings new contacts and new traits, and these make culture readjustments necessary. Witness the conflicts within Jewish civilization when new influences enter. When the strange mingles with the familiar, stress and strain mark the struggle to amalgamate the new with the old. When the culture embraces new points of view, the difficulties are proportionate to the potential advantages. Yet

. . . the fact that we can think and act in connection with many different races, or at least with our own race in many different lands, is a step onwards in what may be called civilization . . . There is a certain breadth of vision which is by no means unpractical in the conception of the English State as "that new Venice whose streets are the oceans."[1]

At the present day every State is a World State, for its culture horizon encompasses the globe.

---

[1] BURNS, C. DELISLE, "Political Ideals, Their Nature and Development," p. 212, Oxford, 1915.

Chapter XXIII

A PERSPECTIVE OF CULTURE ACHIEVEMENTS

1. Primitive Culture

A complete account of culture achievements would include the fields of ethnology and history, and the task would be stupendous; for "the multiplicity of forms . . . which different societies offer to our view, is almost infinite."[1] In the case of the primitive cultures alone the task would exceed the erudition of any ethnologist, since there are many thousand primitive cultures, and each is to some extent distinctive; there are, in addition, many historical civilizations. Human culture, therefore, is too multifarious to comprehend in detail, but it may be possible to select traits which to some extent are typical of the respective cultures.

The preliterate cultures, comprising practically all of the savage or primitive and many of the so-called "barbarian" cultures, may be divided into those of hunters and fishers, keepers of herds or flocks, and agriculturists. In the main, the culture of hunters and fishers is on a different plane from that of agriculturists. They are dependent upon game and therefore they cannot live in large social units, neither, in the main, can they have settled abode. There is little incentive to acquire any large amount of goods, since they are difficult to move.

The improvement of agriculture produceth a greater abundance of the necessaries of life; and excites, in the better sort of people, more attention to those pleasures and refinements of which their situation admits, and to which they are prompted by their natural appetites. We may observe also that it gives rise to property in land, the most valuable and permanent species of wealth; by the unequal distribution of which a greater disproportion is made in the fortune and rank of individuals, and the causes of jealousy and of dissensions between the members of different families are increased and multiplied.[2] [Perhaps] it is the first and indispensable condition of human progress that a people shall be married to a single land: that they shall wander no more from one region to another, but remain fixed and faithful to their

---

[1] Ferguson, Adam, "An Essay on the History of Civil Society," p. 97, Edinburgh, 1767.

[2] Millar, John, "Observations Concerning the Distinction of Ranks in Society," pp. 59–60, London, 1773.

418

soil. Then if the Earth-wife be fruitful, she will bear them children by hundreds and thousands; and then, Calamity will come and teach them by torture to invent.[1]

In the hunting and fishing areas of the Northwest Coast of North America, where there is a regular and assured supply of food, due to the salmon runs, settled abode is feasible, and there is an elaboration of culture traits comparable with that of many agricultural areas—large houses, villages, slavery, trade, money, high finance, elaborate art, cult of ancestors, considerable political development, social hierarchies, and prestige of chieftainship, which is hereditary. Many agricultural communities are less elaborately developed than those of some hunters and fishers, but in its entirety the agricultural stage represents additions to, or amplifications of, the traits characteristic of the more primitive economic stage. Of necessity, the agriculturist is a man of settled abode. In the agricultural stage village communities are established and property rights receive more attention. There is frequently a high development of priesthood, religious rites, and ceremonialism; chieftainship is strengthened and more attention is paid to individual rights, which become more numerous and are more easily infringed. Warfare becomes a community enterprise, and replaces the sallies of marauding or avenging parties, which are typical of hunters and fishers. In the preliterate cultures, as compared with modern industrialism, much attention is paid to esthetic values. Almost everywhere in primitive society the individual has skill in some esthetic pursuit and devotes an appreciable proportion of his time to the beautifying of objects or of person, and to ceremonialism. In most tribes ceremonialism plays an important rôle, and in many cultures social values are thus dramatically expressed. Ceremonial organizations abound in the Plains area of North America and they are an outstanding feature in the culture of the Southwest. So, too, in Australia, Melanesia, and many parts of Africa, ceremonialism is a pronounced feature of the culture. The savage loves action, drama, and display, and he glories in ceremonies, both as participant and as observer. One is impressed also with the all-roundness of the savage. He recounts the origin of the world, the sun, and the stars; he relates the story of the creation of plants, animals, and men, of the origin of death and of sin, and of his tribe, clan, gens, or totem group. He is acquainted with the larger constellations and with many of the stars and planets. He knows the physical features of his environment, its fauna and flora, and has an intimate knowledge of the characteristics and habits of the animals within his habitat. He participates in the

---

[1] READE, WINWOOD, "The Martyrdom of Man," p. 5, 20th ed., London, 1912.

religious, economic, technological, esthetic, ceremonial, and social phases of his culture to an extent seldom seen in our civilization. All of his personality functions dynamically, and he participates in all phases of the culture. There is also an element of abandon for which the savage may be envied. Perhaps there will be no food on the morrow; but if he is not hungry today the pangs of the morrow cause no present pain. He may be attacked by foes, but until they appear, this prospect does not harass him. He lives for the moment, and the passing moment is not spoiled by past sorrows or imminent miseries.

Capable of a great variety of arts, yet dependent on none in particular for the preservation of his being; to whatever length he has carried his artifice, there he seems to enjoy the conveniences that suit his nature, and to have found the condition to which he is destined. The tree which an American, on the banks of the Oroonoko, has chosen to climb for the retreat, and the lodgement of his family, is to him a convenient dwelling. The sopha, the vaulted dome, and the colonade, do not more effectually content their native inhabitant.[1]

Worries and irritations are—always comparatively speaking—absent. He has no frayed nerves, no fear that his child will be stupid or go wrong, no apprehension that he will lose his job or be unable to meet payments, no fear that a revolution will overthrow the government. Why, indeed, should he not be happy? There is little envy, and there is little occasion for it. All share alike, the opportunities of one are those of all, the tasks and hardships, the reliefs and rewards, are the same for all. There are no irritating inequalities of wealth and position. Primitive society is a democratic society in which there is equality of opportunity, the sharing of a common lot, reflection upon a common traditional background, and the anticipation of a common fate. (All of which, of course, must be qualified.) It is only partially true, therefore, that "we must not imagine them as hesitating and simple philosophers, seeking the why and wherefore of existence, digging beneath the effects and discovering the causes, and often the wrong causes, of what they experienced. They did not face life with questions, they fought it with desires."[2]

2. ORIENTAL CULTURES

In the early historical civilizations some culture values are gained, but also some are lost. Life has greater surety than in the non-agricultural preliterate cultures, and there is considerable extension of the culture area and of the area of political control. Laws are formalized,

---

[1] FERGUSON, ADAM, op. cit., pp. 11–12.
[2] LANGDON-DAVIES, JOHN, "A Short History of Women," p. 79, New York, 1927.

elaborated, and enforced and there is greater centralization of authority. The historical cultures of the Far East—China, Japan, Persia, India— are aggregates of kinship groups which practice ancestor worship and are intent upon maintaining the *status quo*. Innovations are frowned upon, if, indeed, they are conceived. Children must follow in the footsteps of parents who, in turn, follow the example of ancestors. The living serve the dead, and if the ways of the fathers are faithfully followed, the dead serve the living, but punish them if the sacred traditions are not adhered to. There is no drive toward change, and the changes which come are imperceptible or are contested with an overwhelming weight of accrued conservatism. In the early Mediterranean civilizations of the Near East—Babylonia and Egypt—there is a stronger drive toward change. The kin group becomes a State, the State becomes an Empire. The priesthood waxes strong and so does the kingship. Laws are elaborated, science is born, art and technology develop. The metals are adopted, and also the horse and the chariot. War is carried into outlying districts, and conquest becomes a profession and at times almost an obsession. Trade brings articles from contiguous cultures and even from distant regions. By the sluggish rivers of Mesopotamia and Egypt civilization forges ahead with a rapidity unknown in the Far East. As early as the eighteenth century B.C. there are ardent social and political reformers, and also blatant calamity howlers. The culture has become self-conscious, and so rapid and so radical have been the changes that already there are vivid pictures of a Golden age in the past when men lived with the gods and the gods with men. But we know more about the origins and development of the arts, crafts, and the religion and social life of early Egypt than did the learned priests of that land.

3. Greek Culture

Meanwhile another distinctive culture pattern, that of Greek civilization, was being woven on the shores of the Aegean, and was destined to influence not merely proximate regions but many parts of the world distant in time and space. The Greeks deserve the title of "scientific ancestors of us all," for they developed the concept of a unified world of interdependent parts, its phenomena subject to natural laws. Not only did they conceive a world of unity and order, but also they perceived that one field of scientific investigation shades into another, "as, for instance, when they noticed that the lowest kinds of animals were scarcely distinguishable from plants";[1] and they regarded

---

[1] Taylor, Henry O., "Freedom of the Mind in History," p. 257, London, 1923.

the life of the individual as likewise a unity which should exemplify order and harmony. It has been said that

Most of us are fractions of a man—decimals, I fear, at that; we do one thing and do it in a lame way because we do it in a dull spirit of unawareness, irresponsive to the world's wonder and variety. Not so the Greek, nor the Athenian! "You Greeks are always children—young in your souls," says Plato's old Egyptian. The world was an integer, not a mass of segments, for them a whole to be grasped and understood; life was an integer, to be lived, not bisected.[1]

To the Athenians harmony and balance were essential to beauty, and beauty was a prerequisite to the good life. They regarded human life and its activities as a unit, and believed this unified existence should be framed in the symmetry which characterizes art. They tested democracy to its utmost, and even resorted to the drawing of lots for office, that no preference might be shown one man over another. Freedom of mind and body they valued more highly than did any other peoples, and their thought ranged the universe of discourse with abandon and daring which has never been exceeded or excelled.

Compare our inventions, our material civilization, our stores of accumulated knowledge, with those of the age of Aeschylus or Aristotle or St. Francis, and the comparison is absurd. Our superiority is beyond question and beyond measure. But compare any chosen poet of our age with Aeschylus, any philosopher with Aristotle, any saintly preacher with St. Francis, and the result is totally different. I do not wish to argue that we have fallen below the standard of those past ages; but it is clear that we are not definitely above them. The things of the spirit depend on will, on effort, on aspiration, on the quality of the individual soul; and not on discoveries and material advances which can be accumulated and added up . . . There are many elements in the work of Homer and Aeschylus which are obsolete and even worthless, but there is no surpassing their essential poetry.[2]

They developed the fundamentals of present-day civilization in everything except the applied arts, in which their ablest men were little interested. Modern philosophy, psychology, ethics, history, political, science, art, architecture, and poetry have their roots in Athenian civilization. Yet the autonomous city-states which shared a common Greek culture could not unite, and seldom could they cooperate. They were jealous of one another, competed and fought among themselves, and finally fell a common prey to a foreign conqueror. The fundamental unity of Greek civilization was acknowledged by some of Athens'

---

[1] GLOVER, T. R., "Democracy in the Ancient World," p. 66, New York, 1927.
[2] MURRAY, SIR GILBERT, "Tradition and Progress," pp. 20–21, New York, 1922.

citizenry—by Socrates, Isocrates, and Aristotle; and Herodotus pointed out that the Greeks were in reality one people because they shared a common language, a common religion, common customs, and common traditions. But little heed was given this sentiment. Some, indeed, appreciated the fact that other cultures were not to be spurned as "barbarian," and urged a world unity, a society of men bound together by the ties of a common human nature with common endowments and common potentialities. But those who shared these views were too few and too detached from current thought and events to deflect national destiny.

4. Roman and Arabian Cultures

Meanwhile, the culture which had entrenched on the banks of the Tiber, in the peninsula to the west, is already at the doors of Greek civilization, which succumbs to the more powerful Roman. Latin-Roman culture concentrates upon political development and military conquest. Organization and discipline are highly developed—courage, hardihood, law, obedience, political craft. The Roman has a bent for practical affairs. Roads are mainly for military purposes; bridges and aqueducts, enduring and sometimes artistic, and even amusements, are of a military cast—the gladiatorial contest and the chariot race, so different from the Greek's ideal of the athlete competing for the crown of wild olive, or to perfect the body and make it a fit habitation for the well-balanced mind. Individual values, so precious to the Athenian, are subordinated to the demands of the State, and there is much catering to the populace. On the ruins of preceding Mediterranean civilizations grows Arabian civilization, an amalgam of Greek, Roman, Persian, and other influences superimposed upon a primitive culture as old as any of these, and representing in some respects traits as ancient as those of Babylonian and Egyptian civilizations. It is, indeed, a meeting point of many cultures, but the culture integrations are new, however old the component elements. The religion is the gift of a nomad fanatic, the art and architecture are indebted to Greece, Persia, and Babylonia. The agricultural skill is the bequest of Mesopotamia and Egypt, though food products have been gathered liberally from the larger Mediterranean area. Arabian civilization is heir to Hellenistic civilization, which had flourished in many cities within its provinces, and is now reinterpreted and in some respects elaborated. Through it, primarily, the torch is handed on to Western Europe, which learns astronomy, mathematics, medicine, anatomy, agriculture, trade, and navigation from Arabian civilization.

5. Western Culture

The culture which develops in Northern and Western Europe after the fall of Rome is likewise an amalgam. It incorporates Greek, Roman, and Arabian traits, and utilizes New World products, for example, tobacco, maize, cacao, the potato. Greek and Roman influences persist, mainly in the monasteries, but the Arabs in Spain, and the Crusaders in Arabian lands—using *Arab* and *Arabian* in their cultural and not in their geographical connotations—were the medium of much Arabian influence. With the discovery of the New World and of other new lands there was a spurt in culture development, though this had, to some extent, already come and would have come without these discoveries. The contributions made by Western civilization are difficult to assess, because it is many-sided and contains elements which are likewise traits of other cultures. It has excelled in the development and application of science, and in the extension of the scientific method into new fields.

In art, architecture, poetry, philosophy, history, drama, and comedy, the Greeks seem not far removed from ourselves, and the accomplishments in these respective fields are interesting for their own sake. Plato's philosophy raises problems which are still pertinent, Greek art and architecture command our admiration, and Greek literature and history are read for their inherent value. But this is not true to comparable extent of Greek medicine, biology, geography, astronomy, or applied science. In scientific knowledge and its application to material things, Western civilization has no peer; since the middle of the eighteenth century science, pure and applied, and technology have been the dominating interest. The increasing size of the culture unit, the greater area and the greater population, plus the greater opportunities for the spread of a new device, have brought rewards to inventors which would have been impossible in any earlier century or in any other culture, and the stimulus to improve mechanical devices has been unprecedented. There have been also an unprecedented interest in scientific and mechanical devices for their own sake, and a drive toward their improvement which, in many cases, has operated independently of rewards. Many inventors have sought no reward and have devoted themselves wholeheartedly to their work without the prospect of profits. The above mentioned factors do not wholly account for the character of the culture drive in Western civilization, for different ideals have guided it at different periods, and in different localities, but they indicate some of the motives which have fostered it, once under way. From the time of St. Augustine to that of Sir Thomas More, for example, religion was the dominant motive in the centers of intellectual activity. During these centuries scarcely any important movement was without the tinge of religion, and most activities were dominated by the religious attitude. The fourteenth century has been called

. . . the early dawn of the modern world. It is a century that sings with the birdsong of new life. Chaucer sang that new life in England in all its freshness; Dante had given it a richer deeper note in Italy. All over Europe the cathedral builders were reaching their triumph. In Florence and in Flanders art was waking from its thousand years' sleep. In religion the century began with the simplicity and beauty of the early followers of St. Francis. It closed with the deep moral earnestness of Wyclif, Savonarola, and Huss. Ecclesiastical religion was in captivity at Avignon; the religion of the spirit was breaking free. Europe had been to the East in the Crusades and had come back ready for new things. Travel inspired her; the germs of a thousand ideas were suggested to her. But Europe with her newly awakened creative genius did not merely copy. She used rather the impulses that had been suggested to her to rear a structure all her own.[1]

In the fifteenth century there is another great spurt in development.

The discovery of American in 1492, enlarging the sphere of human imagination and teasing out the spirit of adventure; the capture of Constantinople by the Turks in 1453 and the consequent dissemination of fugitive knowledge from the libraries and studies of the Eastern capital; the Reformation, freeing men from religious inertia when in 1517 Luther nailed up his theses, which vitalized even where they destroyed; the decay of the great secular empire, paving the way for the new loyalties of nationalism and dynasticism; the last break-down of feudalism and its adjuncts, paving the way for the new loyalties of capitalism and labor; the deposition of the earth from its usurped throne in the center of the universe, resulting in the diminished grandeur of earth's chief parasite, man; the popular use of great inventions, such as the mariner's compass, of printing, of paper, of gunpowder; all these great events, crowded into what was virtually a moment of time, altered in a very few years, the sea, the sky and the earth, the universe about men, and with equal force, the universe within their minds and souls.[2]

During the Renaissance, artistic and literary impulses come to the fore, mainly in religious guise, but with fuller and freer esthetic expression, first in the cities of Italy, later in those of Northern and Western Europe. Then, too, philosophic interest awakens, and from the early seventeenth to the latter part of the eighteenth century there is a notable development in philosophic insight and methods. Concurrently there is

---

[1] CARTER, THOMAS F., "The Invention of Printing in China and Its Spread Westward," p. 150, New York, 1925.

[2] LANGDON-DAVIES, JOHN, op. cit., pp. 302–303.

a new and heightened interest in social and political structure, in nationality, and in science. These interests have grown apace up to the present, and there have been notable almost continuous advances in these several lines. Now one, now the other, of these trends of development may have been in the ascendant, but, if so, the ascendancy was temporary. For example, the period called the Industrial Revolution was also a period of social and political revolutions, and a period of political and scientific development. Comparison of things which have no common denominator is difficult, yet perhaps social and political theories have changed as much since 1760 as have industrial and technological organization, and perhaps present-day science, social, biological, or natural, differs from that of the eighteenth century as much as do means of transportation or methods of manufacture. It is not true that we merely attempt to adapt ourselves to technological changes; there is a comparable independence in the social and political realms, and we attempt also to adapt technological devices to the new social and political philosophies. Once under way, both science and speculation build on the old, amplify themselves, and mortgage the future. Nevertheless, taken in its entirety, Western culture is at loose ends. A worker in one phase may know nothing of other phases, indeed may regard them as beyond his province, however pertinent the one may be to the other. For example,

No one who knows the small-minded cynicism of our plutocracy, its secrecy, its gambling spirit, its contempt of conscience, can doubt that the artist-advertiser will often be assisting enterprises over which he will have no moral control, and of which he could feel no moral approval. He will be working to spread quack medicine, queer investment . . . And to this base ingenuity he will have to bend the proudest and purest of the virtues of the intellect, the power to attract his brethren, and the noble duty of praise.[1]

The physician cures the wounds of the soldier and considers the political situation which is responsible for them as no concern of physicians. Nations tax themselves millions for the support of armies and navies to fight one another, and, until recently, they have spent not one cent on devising means to make this eventuality improbable. By money and credit a locality or an individual may be exploited to accomplish ends of which they are ignorant and which, actually, they may abhor. Most citizens do not know what is being done by their government or to what alternatives the activities of a Foreign Office are committing them; they do not comprehend the educational policies which are sup-

---

[1] CHESTERTON, GILBERT K., "Utopias of Userers and Other Essays," pp. 7–8, New York, 1917.

ported by the community; they do not know the roots of the economic and social order in which they live, and they are ignorant of the manner in which it functions. "Specialize and conquer," is the motto of the day, but there appears to be no unified command, and little cooperation. Few know what they are conquering, if anything, or what is conquering them.

CHAPTER XXIV

CONCLUSION

1. THE NATURE OF PROGRESS

Progress consists in performing a function with greater ease or with greater proficiency or efficiency, and in doing something desirable. The test of desirability is more difficult to apply than that of efficiency, for that which is desired may not be desirable, and that which is wanted may satisfy no actual need. The desirability of a thing depends, moreover, upon contingencies which ramify indefinitely. That which is desirable, all things considered, is the final test of progress. But all things cannot be considered. No one, therefore, can know what is really most desirable. Yet it may be possible, although an element of error intrudes, to discover the more desirable.

It is only by treating the matter in its whole length and breadth, and by developing in their natural order all the principles involved, that we can determine what is the best; for it is always with the *best* that we must concern ourselves in theory. To neglect this research, under the pretext that the best is not practicable in existing circumstances, is attempting to solve two questions at one operation; it is to miss the advantage of placing the questions in the simplicity that can alone render them susceptible of demonstration; it is to throw ourselves without a clue into an inextricable labyrinth, or rather it is to shut our eyes wilfully to the light, by placing ourselves in the impossibility of finding it.[1]

Where the issue is uncertain, the more desirable can be ascertained, at least provisionally, by including more relevant data, and thus men can make progress in understanding progress. Progress, however, is not synonomous with evolution. Whether a series of changes which illustrates evolution illustrates progress also can be ascertained only by reference to a larger system and by considering the effect of these changes upon human life and purposes. By way of illustration let us recur to the story of the development of weapons. Men begin with a stick or a stone, and the arm is the only instrument of propulsion. The spear thrower sends the implement farther, but its range is outdistanced

---

[1] TURGOT, "Sur les impositions," 1764; transl. in STEPHENS, W. WALKER, "The Life and Writings of Turgot," p. 309, London, 1895.

by the bow-shot arrow. Thus, in the evolution of weapons, the bow-using American Indians had advanced beyond the spear-throwing Australians. The Romans devised siege engines and vessels with banks of oars; no implements or craft of primitive man could cope with these contrivances. Then came liquid fire, and mechanical devices for throwing it; finally, cannon and explosives, which vanquished all other weapons. But the development of weapons is not the whole story. Superior strategy and better defense offset the initial benefit of the bowman's greater range; the more penetrable arrow encounters a less penetrable material, for shields of wood, skin, or metal make it difficult for the wielder of the bow and arrow to reap the initial advantage. Explosives shatter defensive walls, but earthworks, sandbags, and steel ramparts make it more difficult for the marksman to do more than score useless hits. The first use of poison gas is terrifying and efficacious; but masks afford protection to the wary, and possibly some new gas will neutralize the most deadly vapors. Throughout human history each improvement in destructive devices has been followed by improvement in defensive devices which to some extent offset the advantages of the innovator, so that no one profits, and perhaps all lose. If, therefore, the evolution of weapons is viewed in its larger setting and not merely as improvement in the technique of taking or of defending lives or property, the problem of progress takes on new complexion. Men have not necessarily made progress because they can shoot at one another with high explosives at a distance of 20 miles rather than throw stones at one another at a distance of 100 paces as, perhaps, did Stone-age men. When the improved fire-arms are possessed by the enemy also, the resulting advantage is not obvious; and

. . . in war it is rare that all the learning is on one side. Samuel Champlain with his French fire-arms gave the Hurons their most complete victory over the Iroquois. The Iroquois realized at once the value of the gun, and for a century and a half French Canada had cause to regret that Champlain had ever used his fire-arms in Indian wars, for Dutch and English could supply similar weapons to savages who never forgave the first wrong.[1]

Man has developed more effective techniques for fighting, but each new device with which he can kill is also a new device with which he can be killed. If being blown to atoms is preferable to having one's skull smashed, perhaps the evolution of weapons betokens progress. If being able to kill and be killed by scores and hundreds is preferable to killing and being killed one at a time, then, too, men may have gained. But to ascertain whether a so-called "improvement" is progress, one must inquire beyond the process itself and learn whether it serves human

---

[1] GLOVER, T. R., "Democracy in the Ancient World," p. 107, New York, 1927.

purposes better under the new conditions than did the old device under the old conditions. More efficient weapons may be merely weapons with which to fight more dangerous foes, and they may be relatively no more efficient under the new conditions than were the old under more primitive conditions. The real need is not more efficient weapons, but a culture in which weapons are superfluous; and abolition of the presumed need for them would be a further step in progress than any new type of weapon has brought or can bring.

By his ability to control a fluctuating environment, by improved tools, weapons, and mechanical devices, man acquires greater power. He learns to control and even to create a sustaining environment. The cultivation of plants and the domestication of animals are followed by industrialism and applied science. These later stages are superimposed upon the earlier and supplement rather than supplant them. So far as power is concerned, Western civilization is the highest attainment of culture, and the key to power is knowledge. Man increases the amount and range of knowledge, organizes it, and makes transfer from one field to another feasible and fruitful. When cooperation supplements knowledge there is greater efficiency. Increase in power, however, does not always connote progress, although progress implies increase in power. The increased ferocity of the tiger may enhance its immediate power to destroy, but it also stimulates in men additional incentives to destroy it. The nitroglycerine which can destroy enemies is, in their hands, a weapon of comparable destructive power, and it is "a singular fact, that, when man is a brute, he is the most sensual and loathsome of all brutes."[1] Often the device which man uses to increase his power proves to be a boomerang. Slaves may be an immediate advantage to the master, but in the long run enslavement of others is also enslavement of self. Again, the power which man develops may redound to the good of some but not of all. The Industrial Revolution brings increments of power, but the benefits are for the few, and the many pay heavily for them. Civilization is an interdependent whole, yet the accretion of power which affects the various elements of the culture differently may bring progress to only a portion of the culture.

Nowhere is it truer than in science that one generation shall labor and another shall enter into the fruits of its labors. In the middle eighties of the last century, a chemist prepared dichloroethylsulfide. In 1918 every one called it by a simpler name—"mustard gas." What an unfortunate example! And yet how few are the examples of the achievements of science which are wholly without unfortunate aspects if we look at the full possibilities. The industry

---

[1] HAWTHORNE, NATHANIEL, "Passages from the American Note-Books," p. 34 Boston, 1883.

which grasps the nitrogen from the air and with its fertilizers multiplies the yield of our vast acreage may tomorrow send forth the munitions which will strew those same fields with human wreckage. The radio may fill the night with music or it may turn back the page of science and teach the multitudes that the earth is flat. The telegraph may one day spread joy with the news that the income tax has been reduced half of one per centum, and next day sorrow at the news that families will be split asunder in each petty nation in order that their individual coinage may be made safe for their monied classes. The same reproducing device which may lift our souls to the heights of a grand symphony may also cause us to respond once more to the pulse of primitive strains. The food which science has given us is better and more varied than that of kings of yesteryear, but this very blessing has given us many a sleepless night, and 'twould be a happy bargain if we could trade our teeth for theirs. The automobile may be a pleasure and a business necessity, but little permanent value can it offer to the group or the individual if its acquirement by easy-payment plans obligates the future to decreasing currency values and forced increased production. The mortgaging of homes to satisfy the cravings of a world on pleasure bent may reduce us to a new form of wandering tribes, the very wealthy migrating from one palatial residence to another, the poor journeying in worn-our vehicles from one place of short employment to another. The morning paper gives us news from all corners of the earth of war, pestilence, and famine; the murders, suicides, and robberies; the sorrows and intrigues of the world are laid before us at breakfast and the evening paper adds the daring daylight holdups. And so on, examples showing the pleasant results and likewise the equally unpleasant consequences and dangers of applied science could be added without end.[1]

Benjamin Franklin said,

It is impossible to imagine the height to which may be carried in a thousand years the power of man over matter. We may perhaps learn to deprive large masses of their gravity and give them absolute levity for the sake of easy transport. Agriculture may diminish its labor and double its produce, all diseases may by sure means be prevented or cured, not excepting that of old age, and our lives lengthened at pleasure even beyond the antediluvian standard. O that moral science were in a fair way of improvement, that men would cease to be wolves to one another, and that human beings would at length learn what they now improperly call humanity.

Franklin appreciated the potentialities of science and also its limitations.

Science is a good old barn-door fowl; build her a hen-roost, and she will lay you eggs, and golden eggs. Give your money to science, for there is an evil side

[1] Lucasse, Walter W., "Progress and the Sciences," in *Sci. Monthly*, **25**: 214–215, 1927; reprinted in Wallis, Wilson D., and Willey, Malcolm M., "Readings in Sociology," New York, 1930.

to every other kind of almsgiving . . . It is science that will redeem man's hope of Paradise.[1]

But more precisely it is science which enables man to attain a finer paradise or to create a fiercer hell than was possible in a prescientific age. Science, it is true, may create Paradise; but it was in Paradise that man fell. Indeed, practically every power which is capable of increasing the good is capable also of increasing the evil, for nothing automatically effects a good purpose. The sun which returns with the dawn and provides the conditions under which life can bestir anew provides also the conditions under which evil designs can be carried out. The light which assists the hunter brings greater danger to the hunted. If achievement in one phase of culture necessarily brought improvement in other phases the issues would be simple. But progress along one line sometimes leads to maladjustments elsewhere; a step forward at one point may shift the center of gravity and necessitate readjustments in other phases of the culture. The development of the automobile, for example, works hardship upon the horse-trader, and the mechanic supplants the smith. It makes new demands upon the department of highways and even upon highwaymen. It affects social life in many ways. The neighborhood church becomes a different institution, the rural community is expanded, the bounds of municipal influence are extended. The possibilities of crime are increased and crimes as well, while new situations are introduced into the lives of the young. In short, every phase of the culture is affected by the presence of the automobile.

The culture may become more diverse, but the parts remain interdependent; and if gains in one phase of the culture are not to be offset by losses in another, then with every new device, idea, or knowledge, there must be a new integration, a new evaluation, and a new orientation of the culture. Where perfection prevails there can, of course, be no progress; yet one of the threats inherent in progress is the fact that the higher man climbs the further he can fall. As Sir Thomas More said when assuming his duties as Lord Chancellor, "the higher the post of honor the greater the fall,"[2] and *facilis est descensus Averni*—the road to hell is easy. For now, at last, "man has a greater power for evil against his fellow-man than the devils have."[3] The fall of a highly developed culture is, therefore, a greater calamity than the fall of a crude one. But the fact that degeneration has been a common character-

---

[1] MOORE, GEORGE, *Modern Painting*, Carra ed., **19**: 113–114, 1923.

[2] Quoted in KAUTSKY, KARL, "Thomas More and His 'Utopia,' with a Historical Introduction," p. 155, London, 1927.

[3] GOTT, SAMUEL, "Nova Solyma," bk. II, chap. VI.

istic of cultures, if not a universal one, does not imply that there has been no progress. As the death of individuals paves the way to progress within the culture, so, it may be, the death of cultures paves the way to progress in human civilization. There is some justification for the philosophy implicit in a Greenland Eskimo account of the creation, which says that the first woman, who had been created out of the thumb of the first man, Kallak, brought death into the world and justified it thus: "Let us die to make room for our successors."[1] As a matter of fact, however, human culture, like the human race, does not die. The early historical civilizations disintegrate, but they are succeeded by others which pass on the torch. Babylonia falls, but Assyria, Persia, Greece come upon the world stage. As a nation and a world power the Hebrews fail, but their contributions to religion and ethics are a heritage of later civilizations. Greece falls a prey to internal strife and barbarian invasions, but Hellenistic civilization becomes widespread, and other cultures are benefited, Western Europe, finally, most of all. Chaldea influences Assyria, Ionian Greece contributes culture traits to Persia, Athenian civilization transforms the Dorian.

Athens mounts to the peak of history at the hour when the moors of Brittany were being covered with their dull flowers of stone; Rome comes to reap them; Rome goes down in the flood that rolls from the North; then the rhythm quickens—great peoples grow up on the cadavers of great peoples.[2]

Something has been lost, but much has been gained. With cultures as with individuals there is not only decay and death but also birth and new life. Yet whether the new total is a gain over the old is not easily determined, for civilization acquires new evils as well as new goods.

Cultures are humanity's diverse experiments, and out of them, possibly, will come a civilization superior to all predecessors. Throughout them all runs a thread of something fundamentally human—

> Our deeds still travel with us from afar,
> And what we have been makes us what we are.

The present can utilize the past, and with increase in the number of culture traits there is a more rapid and a more fructifying oscillation of interacting culture influences. The traits of the culture develop in interrelation, and each is responsive to change in any part of the culture. When permanent abode supplants nomadism there is usually a strengthening and a localization of the family circle. The house becomes the

---

[1] CRANTZ, "Histoire von Grönland," vol. I, p. 262, Leipzig, 1770.

[2] FAURE, ÉLIE, "History of Art," vol. I; Turgot ("Universal History") uses almost the same phraseology.

"castle" only when it is a place of permanent abode. Mrs. Benedict says,

> It is . . . an ultimate fact of human nature that man builds up his culture out of disparate elements, combining and recombining them; and until we have abandoned the superstition that the result is an organism functionally interrelated, we shall be unable to see our cultural life objectively, or to control its manifestations.[1]

The result may not be an organism, and certainly is not such if biological analogy is meant; but assuredly the culture traits are functionally interrelated, or their continued existence in the culture would be most precarious. In this functional interrelation lies the significance of new traits, for the culture is soon busily "combining and recombining them." Each new trait is a stimulus or a challenge to others. Hence, "for no idea of historical importance can a clear and unique line of descent be established. Suggestions and influences always cross one another and mix."[2] Trade routes are means of intercommunication as well as channels for the exchange of articles. New agricultural appliances suggest new mechanical devices in other phases of culture, and these, in turn, react upon agriculture. Performances in war challenge the ability of the story-teller, and mythology and folklore are enriched. The greater the number of radiating influences, the richer the culture content. Specialization brings a new focusing of attention and the development of keener instruments of control. Knowledge gained in one sphere is transferred to others and becomes a stimulus in many lines of thought.

Enlargement of the culture horizon, therefore, increases the possibilities of progress. For primitive man, limited to the territory of the tribe for means of subsistence, inspiration, and effort, the world is small. When, through trade or other contact, tribal barriers break down, the culture world is enlarged. When the geographical horizon expands the mental horizon enlarges. With the growth of the mathematical and the astronomical sciences the sky is no longer a covering vault, but a step into infinite stellar spaces. The center of interest shifts from the individual or the tribe to the larger universe of which man is now aware. It no longer is obvious that all things were made for man, but the world is now merely one of several planets in a solar system which is one of many solar systems, and man is but one of the many animals on the earth. Inspired by Nicholas of Cusa, and by the timidly enunciated

[1] BENEDICT, RUTH F., "The Concept of the Guardian Spirit in North America," *Memoirs Amer. Anthrop. Assoc.*, No. 29, pp. 84–85, 1923.

[2] REICHWEIN, ADOLF, "China and Europe: Intellectual and Artistic Contacts in the Eighteenth Century," p. 102, New York, 1925.

hypothesis of Copernicus, the imagination of Bruno "outsoared the solar system and the sphere of the fixed stars, and went flying through an infinite universe of endless worlds."[1] Previously, man has seen everything from his own point of view, self-centered; now he views himself and his culture from many objective points of view. A new intellectual orientation reveals a new world with new meaning, and life is correspondingly enriched—sometimes through the discovery of its poverty. Yet "the further we go, the more distant the goal," for the solution of a problem poses new problems; and complete realization of every purpose would bring a state of satiety of which the oyster is a fair, if pale, representative. The reward is in the race that is run, not in the prize. Progress consists in harmonizing rather than in achieving complete harmony; those who have finished a task have undertaken no great one. Value lies in the achievement of harmony, but no final end is attained if the end is worthy of supreme effort. Value, in short, involves the possibility of a conflict of purposes, and achieving rather than completing ends is its characteristic. In the realm of mind the same test applies. Intellectual progress involves the ability to break down old habits and systems of thought, and with loss of ability to do this degeneration sets in. A closed system in philosophy, education, or any other field cripples development. The value of a possession, then, is measured by its contribution to the realization of a purpose. Completion of a purpose, unless it is part of an unrealized purpose, results in the inertness of petrifaction. Only things of eternal value are worthy of effort; and upon human potentiality no limit can be placed. Perhaps men will always sail a troubled sea; but were there no breeze to make it such there would be none to move their barques onward.

Professor Cheney finds that during the period of recorded history culture has developed as if "some inexorable necessity" were controlling "the progress of human affairs." Historical development, he says, is not the result of the voluntary action of individuals or of groups of individuals, it is not due to chance, but it is guided by law. Men play the parts assigned to them and they do not write the play. He specifies the following six phases of this alleged law of development:

1. *Continuity.*—All developments arise from preceding conditions.

2. *Impermanence of cultures.*—Cultures languish and die because they do not accommodate themselves to the changing demands of the times. Conservatism, therefore, tends to effect its own destruction and the death and disappearance of the culture which it obstinately upholds.

3. *Interdependence of individuals, classes, tribes, and nations.*—Among units which are interdependent one does not progress or retrograde without affecting

---

[1] Taylor, Henry O. "Freedom of the Mind in History," p. 152, London, 1923.

the others. No portion of mankind has progressed at the expense of another, but all have fallen or risen together.

4. *A tendency toward the development of democracy.*—Considered in its entirety, democracy has justified itself as the best form of government yet devised.

5. *The necessity of free consent.*—Individuals and groups can be only temporarily, not permanently, compelled.

6. *Progress in the moral sphere.*—Moral influences have grown and have become more widely diffused than material influences.

Cheney does not conceive these changes as merely a summary of what has taken place, but as "natural laws, which we must accept whether we want to or not, whose workings we cannot obviate, however much we may thwart them to our own failure or disadvantage; laws to be accepted and reckoned with as much as the laws of gravitation, or of chemical affinity, or of organic evolution, or of human psychology."[1] Waiving the question of the correctness of this summary of the changes which have characterized the period of recorded history, the conclusion is based on a misconception of the nature of law. The culture changes in Western civilization, or in all historical civilizations taken in their totality, constitute a unique event in a unique culture world. The thing which has been has never been before, and there is no basis for the induction that it will be again, or that it will persist.

The whole civilization of each particular race, whether of the Herero of South-West Africa, the Hottentots, or the different Bantu tribes, ought to be regarded as a single and unique occurrence in the course of historical events and in the intellectual happenings of society.[2]

Physics and chemistry discover laws only when they consider their respective data distributively, not when they consider them collectively; neither the universe as a whole, nor the solar system as a unique concourse of matter, furnishes laws for physics or for chemistry, or even for astronomy. To the extent that a thing or an event is unique, there can be no inference that it will occur again, and none that its occurrence was inevitable, unless one define inevitable as that which has happened, rather than as that which could not have been otherwise. Men can always make progress, but there can be no guarantee that they will always do so.

As our expectations of limitless progress for the race cannot depend upon the blind operation of the laws of heredity, so neither can they depend upon

---

[1] CHENEY, EDWARD F., "Law in History," in *Amer. Hist. Rev.*, **29**: 231–248, 1924; and "Law in History," chap. I, New York, 1927.

[2] THURNWALD, RICHARD, "The Social Problems of Africa," in *Africa*, **2**: 134, 1929.

the deliberate action of national governments. Such examination as we can make of the changes which have taken place during the relatively minute fraction of history with respect to which we have fairly full information, shows that they have been caused by a multitude of variations, often extremely small, made in their surroundings by individuals whose objects, though not necessarily selfish, have often had no intentional reference to the advancement of the community at large. But we have no scientific ground for suspecting that the stimulus to these individual efforts must necessarily continue; we know of no law by which, if they do continue, they must needs be coordinated for a common purpose or pressed into the service of the common good. We cannot estimate their remoter consequences; neither can we tell how they will act and react upon one another, nor how they will in the long run affect morality, religion, and other fundamental elements of human society. The future of the race is thus encompassed with darkness; no faculty of calculation that we possess, no instrument that we are likely to invent, will enable us to map out its course, or penetrate the secret of its destiny. It is easy, no doubt, to find in the clouds which obscure our path what shapes we please: to see in them the promise of some millennial paradise, or the threat of endless and unmeaning travel through waste and perilous places. But in such visions the wise man will put but little confidence: content, in a sober and cautious spirit, with a full consciousness of his feeble powers of foresight, and the narrow limits of his activity, to deal as they arise with the problems of his own generation.[1]

2. Is Culture Development Predictable?

To what extent can the course of culture development be predicted? Some of our inventions have been called inevitable and the fact that in many instances the same device has been invented, or the same idea arrived at independently, is interpreted by some students of culture as implying inevitability. The concurrence, however, does not show that the invention was inevitable, but merely that, given certain conditions, it was probable, for the concurrence implies that if the invention had not been achieved when it actually was, it would probably have been achieved at some other time or times by some other person or persons. This observation applies not merely to things which, as a matter of fact, have been invented independently, but also to others which, invented and diffused, make independent invention impossible or superfluous. No doubt certain inventions can be predicted, provided certain persistent conditions of culture are assumed. Thus one can predict with high probability that specific cures will be found for certain diseases which now receive indirect medical treatment; for example, one may anticipate, let us say, a specific cure for tuberculosis.

---

[1] BALFOUR, ARTHUR J., "A Fragment on Progress," in "Essays and Addresses," pp. 278–280, 3d ed., Edinburgh, 1905.

But the possibility of prediction implies that the culture which possesses the appropriate base of science, technology, and medical knowledge, will retain possession of this heritage and even add to it. It implies also that tuberculosis will continue its ravages, and that there will be a desire to salvage rather than to eliminate the susceptible carriers of the germ. We may admit that all of these presuppositions are probable, but assuredly they are germane to the problem.

The ability to predict implies, also, specific potentialities in culture development; otherwise, a forecast could not be made. Negatively, therefore, one can predict a great many things about culture development. Thus one can be sure that until the necessary preliminary culture stages have been reached, by either invention or borrowing, certain other stages will not be attained. No culture, for example, can have a high industrial development until it achieves a certain stage in science and technology; it cannot have a complicated financial organization until it has money or a credit system; it cannot have machinery until it has the wheel, nor telephones until it utilizes electricity and the metals.[1] But the prediction of positive accomplishments is much more difficult. The Greeks, for example, possessed the necessary equipment for great advances in experimental science. They used observation and classification, and their ability in detached and abstract thought was of a high order.

They did, in fact, experiment in the social sciences, but they did not carry experimentation into the natural or the biological sciences. Had they achieved experimental results in these fields we would, no doubt, point to these as precisely the results to be anticipated. Certainly the character of Greek civilization could not have been predicted.

The possibility of predicting culture development implies that the predicted development is inherent in the culture already achieved. The ability to predict a specific for tuberculosis implies that a method and purpose capable of yielding that result have already been achieved and need only be continued and refined. That, for example, all men will some

---

[1]This has been pointed out by Professor Usher: "The technological changes that have become conspicuous in the last 50 years are merely the completion of tendencies that have been significantly evident since the time of Leonardo da Vinci. They represent the accumulated result of two elements that were then more largely than ever before brought to bear upon technology: the first of these new factors was an organized body of scientific knowledge based deliberately upon experimentation; the second was a quickened imaginative perception of the consequences and potentialities implicit in single abstract principles. . . . In every case, the specific act of innovation completes a pattern or configuration that was previously felt to be incomplete." Usher, Abbot P., "A History of Mechanical Inventions," pp. 21–22, New York, 1929.

day be happy is an eventuality which one would not predict with much assurance, for no culture possesses a technique which carries this potentiality. Indeed, the prediction of an invention or a discovery implies that there is a drive toward invention or discovery, or a desire to rationalize and utilize experience and observation. Cultures appear to differ in the amount and quality of this drive. Thus Hindu culture, compared with Western culture, has been conspicuously lacking in it; and a culture, like Melanesian, may seem to lose whatever culture drive it once possessed and to lapse into inertness and listlessness. Unless, therefore, one presupposes the specific drive the prediction of inventions will likely outrun the facts.

In at least one phase of culture, prediction is incomparably hazardous, namely, in esthetics. Here, too, there are limitations, as, for example, the necessity of achieving certain technical controls of material, whether in music, sculpture, painting, or drawing. But a prediction of positive achievement is difficult and hazardous. Indeed, the artistic achievements of peoples, aside from the limitations referred to, appear to have been largely independent of other culture achievements, and to have been unpredictable. The superb realism of the Magdalenian artist, the artistic achievements of the Greeks, the art of the Renaissance, are examples of achievements which were not predictable. In literature the same is true. None of the great literary productions were predictable, not the "Iliad," the "Odyssey," the "Æneid," the "Divine Comedy," the "Pilgrim's Progress," or any other great literary work. The artistic product, it is true, is related to the culture, and in a certain sense is its outcome; but it is a psychological rather than a logical outcome of the culture, and only after the event is it amenable to the formula of prediction. A similar observation applies to fashion, and perhaps to the whole realm of esthetics.[1]

3. Progress and Culture

The word "progress," was first used in the modern sense by Lucretius, a Roman writer of the first century B.C. It means literally "going ahead," its contrary being "retrogression," "going backward." Lucretius believed that in the main the evolution of human society exemplified progress, although he recognized that some phases of it were not improvement. Considering social evolution in its broad sweep, he says in effect, man has made progress, but here and there he has retrogressed, or has stagnated, rather than progressed.

---

[1] For the suggestion regarding the difficulty or impossibility of predicting in the realm of art and fashion I am indebted to W. Allen Wallis.

Though no comparable view of evolutionary progress is found in the civilizations which antedate Lucretius, most of them entertained the concept of progress. They believed the highest good had been realized in the earliest stages of man's life, in the fabulous paradise or elysium in which men lived before they embarked upon social and political evolution. They, therefore, viewed the reattainment of an earlier status as progress. A harking back to an earlier status was, to be sure, retrogression in the sense that it was a retracing of a course traversed in pain and sorrow, but it was progress, so at least they thought, in the sense that it was the way to the attainment of the better life. Thus even those writers who bemoan the passing of better times have a concept of progress, otherwise they could not depict man as degenerating.

Contemporaries have attached various meanings to progress. To some it means merely the continuation of processes already under way. The term may connote mere continuance of a movement, force, or activity, or merely an increase in the momentum of a phase of social life. Thus a nation is said to make progress in, for example, manufacturing, road building, imperialism, if these activities are carried on with increasing success. But this concept is inadequate, for quantitative or linear dimensions cannot measure progress. Many a town or city boasts of "progress" in population, meaning that the number of inhabitants is increasing; but whether the increase in number of inhabitants really indicates progress depends upon various circumstances. Or one says that a community makes progress in wealth, meaning that the valuation of taxable property or of bank clearings is increasing; but this, too, must be interpreted in human terms before one can ascertain whether this indicates progress. A mere quantitative increase does not necessarily betoken progress. If men are no better off there is no progress, there are merely more men who are no better off; and if dollars increase but human weal is no greater, then, too, there is no progress. Some use the term "progress" to indicate approach toward a goal explicit or implicit. Progress, no doubt, implies a goal, and, indeed, more than a mere goal. A disease may be said to be moving toward a goal, but to the extent that it is attaining its culmination the patient is not making, but is failing to make progress; he makes progress if he thwarts the disease. Progress, then, implies at least a desirable goal and this means more than a desired one. It means a goal which embodies a desirable end and one which, in the long run, brings satisfaction. A desirable goal presupposes a choice of goals, a choice made with discrimination and a knowledge of means as well as of ends; and choice, in turn, involves evaluation. There must be also a weighing of means, for in choosing the goal one is also choosing the means to it; and when a man or a culture chooses wrongly, "life and the consequences of the wrong may not ask as to intent," but merely demand the penalty. Progress, then, implies the choice of a desirable goal and the utilization of adequate means for attaining it; and the highest progress involves the choice of the most desirable goal and the best means of attaining it. But interpretations of conditions underlying progress have varied widely.

Some have regarded progress as resting in the hands of fate, destiny, or inevitable historical forces. Everywhere man struggles with nature, and in every culture he strives to improve his lot. Even in the remotest periods of prehistory there was the endeavor to conquer the hazards of nature and to accumulate good. Early Stone-age man improved the crude stone implements of predecessors and each generation, or at least each millennium, added something to the achievements of predecessors. Thus he who struggled with circumstance helped to bring the modern age. Yet some regard retrogressions as inevitable. Man struggles with fate but he does not always plan wisely or execute efficiently. Set-backs are indeed real, but they need not occasion discouragement. The pessimist, however, is always with us, he is almost a culture phenomenon:

> My grandpa notes the world's worn cogs,
> And says we're going to the dogs.
> His grand-dad, in his house of logs,
> Swore things were going to the dogs;
> His dad, among the Flemish bogs,
> Vowed things were going to the dogs;
> The caveman in his bearskin togs
> Said things were going to the dogs;
> But this is what I wish to state—
> Those dogs have had one awful wait!

Given things as they were, we are assured, events could not have been otherwise, and men could not have acted differently. We may admire the torch-bearers of the Renaissance, but granted the opportunity, the response to the inspiration was inevitable. The Industrial Revolution might have come earlier or later, but come it must; and given things as they were a century ago, a Civil War in this country was inevitable. The World War, similarly, grew out of antecedent conditions; it might have come earlier or later, but come it must. With regard to the invention of mechanical devices a similar conclusion is drawn. But for a happy concourse of events and personalities the radio might not have been invented for another decade, but invented it would be, once man had advanced to a certain point in science and ambition. Thus inventions, we are told, are inevitable, once culture has attained a certain status of accumulated science and technology. In support of this position attention is called to the fact that certain discoveries and inventions can be predicted with a slight margin of error.

Perhaps there is no general progress, but only progress in certain fields of activity. However that may be, progress in one line is not an isolated phenomenon, but implies progress in related lines. Progress in technology, for example, has been preceded, accompanied, and followed by progress in trade, science, specialization, and an assured, *i.e.*, a dependable, interdependence, without which any considerable specialization is impossible. Thus the Industrial Revolution has been intimately bound up with advance in trade, science, technology, a credit system, and internationalism, and advance in any one of these has always to some extent depended upon advance in the others. Hence social progress, however strictly interpreted, involves progress in some larger sense, as, for example, in political life; and this, in turn, is bound up with economic and industrial organization, technological development, and with communication and the dissemination of information. A change in any one of these may have far-reaching effects in the social world, as witness events which followed the development of the printing-press, the railroad, the telephone, the telegraph, the radio, the airplane. Thus the problem of progress is many-sided, and it becomes increasingly difficult to fathom as civilization becomes more complex. Social life, for example, is a phase of a specific civilization, and it is therefore dependent upon a specific culture. But, as history testifies, civilizations rise and fall. Must, then, every civilization, after a certain period of development, fall and pass off the stage? If such be the case, what limits does this necessity impose upon the possibilities of social progress? In addition to the apparently limited life of a civilization, there may be within a given civilization certain specific limitations upon progress. Greek civilization, for example, seemed capable of making great progress in literature and the fine arts. but it was weak in national and international politics, and in the domain of technology, and perhaps it was destined to make no notable achievements in other domains. Another possible limitation upon progress arises from the fact, if fact it be, that along with the seeds of good are sown the seeds of evil, so that in any culture which is advancing there is a contest between the forces which make for progress and those which tend to thwart it. Witness the increase in crime, disease, and war which have been the invariable accompaniments of progress. A primitive culture is comparatively free from these untoward tendencies, but a developing civilization must cope with them at every step. If these are necessary evils, then, it seems, a bane is inherent in progress. Indeed perhaps progress is necessarily dangerous. Consider, for example, the development of transportation. With the canoe and the dug-out there are few dangers; the sail-boat is a step in advance, but it brings added dangers, and the steamboat intensifies these in a thousand ways—think of the *Titanic* disaster. In the ox-cart we travel slowly but safely; in the horse-drawn vehicle we make more rapid progress but encounter greater dangers from steed and speed; in the automobile we hurl our bodies through space with locomotive velocity, and there is greater danger of hurling them straight to heaven or hell; in the airplane we fly faster than the swiftest birds, but the danger from a summersault or a nose-spin is greater than the danger from a hurtling automobile. Do these dangers typify a tendency which is inherent in progress? Certainly they are an accompaniment of many phases of it. Internationalism has grown, but it has brought a larger number of possible and indeed of actual entanglements. The larger the number of nations with which we have relations, the greater the possibilities of friction and enmity. Meanwhile war itself becomes fraught with greater danger to all participants. In using instrumentalities we become dependent upon them and to that extent place our fate beyond our immediate control. The Erewhonians discovered this danger and they therefore rigorously excluded all machines from their civilization. Is there not a grain of realistic truth in the ironic fancy of Samuel Butler? Are we not annually more dependent upon our machines? And is it not true that we work for them as well as they for us?

Finally, there is the possibility that a civilization, particularly our civilization, may become so complex that men cannot solve its problems. With all our boasted ingenuity and science we are almost fundamentally ignorant of the character of our civilization and of its trends. Although human presumption knows few bounds, no one presumes to understand contemporary civilization. At most, one claims but small knowledge of a small field. We do not know where we are going; neither do we know that we are on our way. If there is a desirable goal somewhere in the future, then, alas, we may be far out of our way. We have given tremendous impetus to our culture and have specialized and intensified it in many ways; now our problem is to keep up with it, and little time is left us to inquire whither it leads. Nor can one be confident that the most leisurely inquiry would make us much the wiser; for the course of culture is difficult to predict. The goal, if there is one, seems to be somewhere the other side of nowhere.

In the future, no doubt, men will have a better understanding of cultures. They will know more about the development, diffusion, and assimilation of culture traits. Guided by this knowledge it will be possible to build the culture, to fashion and refashion it, in ways more rational. The vista is one of illimitable possibilities. But culture development has not removed the problems of progress, and it will not remove them in the future. On the contrary, it will augment them. During the first quarter of the twentieth century, for example, culture development, due to the rapid invention and diffusion of traits, proceeded at an amazing pace. Yet life and events in the Western world during that period do not suggest utopia. World-wide trade, increase in literacy, and the new powers which have been developed, have carried the seeds of evil, and some malign genius of affairs has sowed them broadcast amid all peoples. Even a change which in itself is desirable may bring unforeseen distress.

Now, as a century ago, the increased efficiency of machines results in much misery; to this factor must be attributed much of the unemployment which affects millions in every industrialized country. In addition to enforced leisure it has, of course, brought much voluntary leisure. By the middle of the last century, it has been estimated, the average man in this country was utilizing the equivalent of about $2\frac{1}{2}$ slave power; and by 1923 the average man was utilizing the equivalent of the power of more than 160 slaves. The exactness of the comparison may be doubted, but the essential difference is indisputable. But how do men utilize the newly acquired advantages? How do they employ the increased leisure which the Industrial Revolution has made possible, and how do they utilize the new instruments of power? Men must adapt themselves to the new culture, and they cannot do this by merely developing the culture, i.e., by merely intensifying or augmenting it. Men are not automatically made greater by the ampler world in which they live. There is still need for the philosophy of Confucius, the Stoics, More, Campanella, Rousseau, and Owen.

Culture is a group problem, but life and living are individual and are personality problems, and only the individual can solve them. Personal relations, the art of living, the harmony of the soul, as the Greeks called it, which after all involves more than hormones, are persistent problems, and they must be faced by every individual, for in the last event not culture, but man, is the measure of all things. What he gets out of culture depends as much upon what he brings to it in receptivity and attitude as upon culture itself. To many an Eskimo life is richer and more significant, existence happier and more satisfying, than to many who live in Western civilization.

The Invention of Iron, the working of the Oar into a Metal, must contribute very much to the completing of Society; because Men can have no tools nor Agriculture without it. Iron is certainly very useful; but Shells and Flints, and hardening of Wood by Fire, are Substitutes, that Men make a Shift with; if they can but have Peace, live in Quiet, and enjoy the Fruits of their Labour.[1]

The test of the value of a culture is the extent to which it enriches individual existence; and the test of the individual is the extent to which he utilizes the potentialities of culture and personality. To neglect either is to miss the larger opportunities. Singer has said that "the measure of man's cooperation with man in the conquest of nature measures progress."[2] We would amplify the statement as follows: The measure of man's cooperation with man in the conquest of nature and of human nature, and in the building of a more satisfying culture, is the measure of progress. We should be "pretty well vers'd in the Defects of Mankind"; but also, we should be acquainted with "the Excellences of Human Nature."[3]

4. WHY DO MEN HOPE FOR PROGRESS?

Why do men hope for and believe in a better future for their species, race, nation, class, or group? Why are they concerned with the problem of progress? What difference could it make to a Condorcet, a Turgot, a Saint-Simon, whether the civilization of Europe, or that of the human race, goes to pot? Why could they not say, as Louis XV is purported to have said, that the little world about them would outlast their day, and be content with that assurance? Why should an H. G. Wells be concerned with the problem of a world society in the next century? Doubtless he does not expect to outlive the present century. Many do not care about these matters, but many do care. We may be disposed to justify the interest, after the manner of Havelock Ellis, by recalling that all we are we owe to the past, to our culture heritage, and by concluding that we should, therefore, strive to transmit the best of this heritage unimpaired. Yet it is difficult to justify on logical grounds the "therefore" of this proposition. If we owe all to the past, why not repay all to the past? The debt would seem owing to the creditor, not to an age which may be debtor to us. As the Irishman complained, "What has posterity ever done for me?"

The explanation of the interest in and concern about the future of one's culture must lie elsewhere. The reason, probably, derives from the fact that the future is but the prolongation of the present, the continuation by generations now unborn of plans and promises which they will

---

[1] MANDEVILLE, BERNARD, "Fable of the Bees," pt. II, sixth dialogue, London, 1723.

[2] SINGER, EDGAR A., "Modern Thinkers and Present Problems," p. 279, New York, 1923.

[3] Mandeville, op. cit.

inherit from the present generation and its predecessors. The question, Why are men interested in the future fate of their group or culture? is, therefore, equivalent to the question, Why are they interested in their group or their culture? And this, in turn, is almost equivalent to the question, Why are they interested in the world in which they live? or, Why are they interested in anything? The significance of present tendencies cannot be fully grasped until their outcome is known. The significance of the events of the year 1913, for example, cannot be estimated apart from their sequel, namely, the events of 1914 to 1918, of 1918 to 1930, and of subsequent years. Logically, and psychologically, it is as reasonable for men in 1913 to be concerned with events of the next decade as with those of their present decade. Only the man who in 1940 can look back upon 1930 will be able to see it in its historical setting, and then, of course, not so clearly as can the man of 1950; nevertheless, the intelligent man of 1930 must envisage contemporary events as forerunners of future events. If he has no interest in the outcome of contemporary events the compass of his intellectual interests is small. To the extent that he is rational, he will wish to see a rational development of his culture and a rational solution of human problems, whether they pertain to his culture or to another. Perhaps, as he peers into the future, he will not despair. In less than a billion years we have developed from something like the amœba to the thing we call man, and during the next few million years men may make great advances. If they dare to challenge all things, they will make great ventures, and if they must die fighting, it will be an open-eyed death.[1]

5. The Difficulties of Social Experimentation

The difficulties which confront the social engineer exceed those which challenge the natural scientist, the physician, the surgeon, or the experimental biologist. Two notable contributors to our knowledge of nutrition have said that through the ages philosophers have given attention to the problems of nutrition and proper food, and, they add, "the growth of knowledge in this field, like that in all other fields of science, was the result of experimental verification of philosophical speculation."[2] With regard to social life, too, there has been through the ages much speculation by philosophers, but there has been no comparable amount of experimentation.

It is not easy to induce men to make or to submit to social experimentation. Some communities, indeed, have engaged in radical experimenta-

---

[1] See Muller, H. J., "The Method of Evolution," *Sci. Monthly*, **29**: 505, 1929.

[2] McCollum, E. V., and Simmonds, Nina, "The Story of the Discovery of Vitamins," in "Chemistry in Medicine," p. 112, New York, 1929.

tion, but these have been comparatively small and they have been compelled to function in the midst of a world very different in complexion and usually hostile or at least unsympathetic. Hence neither their success nor their failure could be considered a conclusive experiment. The lesson, moreover, is difficult to draw, because the success of a social program depends in part upon the attitude toward it. The effect of drugs or of foods is little influenced by the attitude of the patient, but the success or failure of a social experiment may depend mainly upon the attitude taken toward it by the people who are immediately affected by it. Prohibition is a case in point.

If the people wish prohibition to succeed it will succeed; if they are determined that it shall not succeed, then it is foreordained to fail. And so with many, perhaps with all, social programs. To ascertain experimentally the roads which lead to progress in social relations is, therefore, a well-nigh hopeless procedure. Often, indeed, the people who vociferously laud scientific method and the value of experiment, are little inclined to favor, much less to further, social experimentation. They are willing to experiment with anything except social life. While that attitude prevails and there is no disposition to accept the findings of those who have given most study and thought to these matters, there is little reason to hope that the progress of the social sciences will be comparable with that of the biological or the natural sciences. As Dove said, we need a new credence; not credulity, but an open-mindedness on social as on other problems. For the most part, we do not worship things because they are sacred, but they are sacred because we worship them. Collectively, individuals can fashion their world as they will. Men have as satisfying a social life as they deserve; when they deserve better it will be theirs for the asking and the taking. Only those who really desire a more satisfying world deserve it; others will not achieve it, nor will it mean much to them if they inherit it. Even those who inherit must learn that "No thorns go as deep as a rose's."

References For Further Reading

INTRODUCTION[1]

BERNARD, LUTHER L.: "The Interdependence of Factors Basic to the Evolution of Culture," *Amer. Jour. Sociol.*, **32**: No. 2, 1926.

GOLDENWEISER, ALEXANDER A.: "History, Psychology, and Culture," *Jour. Phil., Psych., and Sci. Method*, vol. 15.

KROEBER, ALFRED L.: "Subhuman Culture Beginnings," *Quart. Rev. Biol.*, **3**: 325–342, 1928.

———: "The Superorganic," AA, **19**: 163–219, 1917; reprinted by the Sociological Press.

MALINOWSKI, BRONISLAW: "Sex and Repression in Savage Society," New York, 1927.

RIVERS, W. H. R.: "Survival in Sociology," *Sociol. Rev.*, **6**: 293–305.

STERN, BERNHARD J.: "Concerning the Distinction between the Social and the Cultural," *Social Forces*, **8**: 264–271, 1929.

CHAPTER I

ABEL, THEODORE: "Is a Cultural Sociology Possible?" *Amer. Jour. Sociol.*, **35**: 739–752, 1930.

ASWELL, EDWARD C.: "Student Suicide," *Forum*, **77**: 699–703, 1927.

BOAS, FRANZ: "Anthropology and Modern Life," chaps. VII, IX, New York, 1928.

BURGESS, ERNEST W.: "The Cultural Approach to the Study of Personality," *Mental Hygiene*, **14**: 307-325, 1930.

BYRD, RICHARD E.: "Wings: The Future of Aviation," in "The Drift of Civilization," pp. 95–100, New York, 1929.

CARTER, THOMAS F.: "The Invention of Printing in China and Its Spread Westward," New York, 1925.

CASE, CLARENCE M.: "The Culture Concept in Social Science," *Jour. Appl. Sociol.*, 1924.

———: "Culture as a Distinctive Human Trait," *Amer. Jour. Sociol.*, **32**: 906–920, 1927.

CHAFFEE, GRACE E.: "The Isolated Religious Sect as an Object for Social Research," *Amer. Jour. Sociol.*, **35**: 618–630, 1930.

CHAPIN, F. STUART: "Cultural Change," New York, 1928.

CHASE, STUART: "A Billion Wild Horses," *Tech. Rev.*, 1929.

CHILDE, VERNON G.: "The Dawn of European Civilization," New York, 1925.

---

[1] The following abbreviations are used: AA, "American Anthropologist," new series.

APAMNH, "Anthropological Papers of the American Museum of Natural History."

EB, "Encyclopædia Britannica" (11th edition unless specified).

ERE, "Hastings' Encyclopædia of Religion and Ethics."

JAI, *Journal of the [Royal] Anthropological Institute of Great Britain and Ireland* ("Royal" after 1907).

UC, "University of California Publications in American Archaeology and Ethnology."

COUNTS, GEORGE S.: "School and Society in Chicago," New York, 1929.

DAVIDSON, DANIEL S.: "The Chronological Aspects of Certain Australian Social Institutions as Inferred from Geographical Distribution," chap. I, Philadelphia, 1928.

DIXON, ROLAND B.: "The Building of Cultures," New York, 1928.

FOLSOM, JOSEPH K.: "Culture and Social Progress," chap. II, New York, 1928.

GAUS, JOHN M.: "Great Britain: A Study in Civic Loyalty," chap. XIV, Chicago, 1929.

GILLETTE, JOHN M.: "Extent of Personal Vocabularies and Cultural Control," Sci. Montbly, 29: 451–457, 1929.

HART, HORNELL: "The Science of Social Relations: An Introduction to Sociology," chap. IX, New York, 1927.

HART, HORNELL, and PAUTZER, ADELE: "Have Subhuman Animals Culture?" Amer. Jour. Sociol., p. 30, 1925.

HEADLAM-MORLEY, J. W.: "The Cultural Unity of Western Europe" in CARTER, E. H. (editor), "The New Past and Other Essays on the Development of Civilization," Oxford, 1925.

HERSKOVITS, MELVILLE J.: "Acculturation and the American Negro," Southw. Polit. and Soc. Sci. Quart., 8: 211ff, 1927.

———: "Social Pattern: A Methodological Study," Social Forces, 4: 57–69, 1925.

KAEMPFFERT, WALDEMAR: "The Age of Superpower," N. Y. Times Mag., Sept. 22, 1929.

———: "The Light of Edison's Lamp," Survey Graphic, 16: 13–16, 58–59, 1929.

KROEBER, ALFRED L.: "The Anthropological Attitude," Amer. Merc., 13: 460–469, 1925; reprinted in WALLIS, WILSON D., and WILLEY, MALCOLM M., "Readings in Sociology," chap. I, New York, 1930.

LAUFER, BERTHOLD: "Sino-Iranica," Chicago, 1919.

LITTLE, ARTHUR D.: "The Hand Writing on the Wall," Boston, 1928.

LOW, A. M.: "Wireless Possibilities," New York, 1924.

LOWIE, ROBERT H.: "Culture and Ethnology," chap. I, New York, 1917.

———: "Are We Civilized?" New York, 1929.

———: "American Indian Cultures," American Mercury, 20: 362-366, 1930.

LYND, ROBERT S. and HELEN M.: "Middletown, A Study in Contemporary American Culture," New York, 1929.

MALINOWSKI, BRONISLAW: "Sex and Repression in Savage Society," pt. 4, New York, 1927.

———: "Crime and Custom in Savage Society," New York, 1926.

———: "Instincts and Culture," Nature, 1924.

———: "Argonauts of the Western Pacific," London, 1922.

MARETT, ROBERT R.: "Anthropology," EB, 2: 44–46, 14th ed., 1929.

McCOWN, CHESTER C.: "The Genesis of the Social Gospel," chaps. IV, XII, New York, 1929.

MULLER, H. J.: "The Method of Evolution," Sci. Montbly, 29: 481–505, 1929.

O'BRIEN, EDWARD J.: "Dance of the Machines," New York, 1929.

O'LEARY, DE LACY: "Arabic Thought and Its Place in History," London, 1922.

RADIN, PAUL: "The Story of the American Indian," New York, 1927.

RANDALL, JOHN H.: "Our Changing Civilization," New York, 1929.

RUSSELL, OLAND D.: "Suicide in Japan," American Mercury, 20: 341–344, 1930.

"Social Anthropology," EB, 14th ed., 1929.

SPECK, F. G.: "Culture Problems in Northeast North America," Proc. Amer. Phil. Soc., 63: 272–311, 1926.

SPENGLER, OSWALD: "The Decline of the West," Engl. transl., New York, 1926, 1928.

SPIER, LESLIE: "Problems Arising from the Culture Position of the Havasupai," AA, 31: 213–222, 1929.

SPROWLS, JESSE W.: "Social Psychology Interpreted," chaps. VII, VIII, Baltimore, 1927.

STORCK, JOHN: "Man and Civilization," chap. II, New York, 1927.

THURNWALD, RICHARD: "Die Auswirkung der Technik auf das soziale Leben und die Geistesverfassung so wie das Problem des Fortschritts," Mitteil. d. anthrop. Ges. Wien, 57: 24–32, 1927.

TYLOR, EDWARD B.: "Primitive Culture," vol. I, chap. I, London, 1889.

WALLIS, WILSON D.: "An Introduction to Anthropology," chap. XXXVIII, New York, 1926.

———: "An Introduction to Sociology," Pt. I, and chaps. X, XXXII, New York, 1928.

———: "Missionary Enterprise from the Point of View of an Anthropologist," Amer. Jour. Theol., 19: 268–274, 1915.

———: "Mental Patterns in Relation to Culture," Jour. Abnor. Psych. and Social Psych., 19: 179–184, 1924.

———: "Beliefs and Tales of the Canadian Dakota," Jour. Amer. Folklore, 36: 36–101, 1923.

WALLIS, WILSON D., and WILLEY, MALCOLM M.: "Readings in Sociology," New York, 1930.

WATERMAN, THOMAS T.: "Culture Horizons in the Southwest," AA, 31: 367–400, 1929.

WILLEY, MALCOLM M.: "The Culture Approach in Sociology," in DAVIS, JEROME and BARNES, HARRY E., and others, "Introduction to Sociology," pp. 516–586, New York, 1927; and in "Readings in Sociology," (by the same editors), pp. 607–716, New York, 1927.

WILLEY, "The Validity of the Culture Concept," Amer. Jour. Sociol., 35: 204–219, 1929.

WILLEY, MALCOLM M. and HERSKOVITZ, MELVILLE J., "The Cultural Approach to Sociology," Amer. Jour. Sociol., 29: 196–199, 1923.

———: "Psychology and Culture," Psych. Bull., 24: 253–283, 1927.

WISSLER, CLARK: "Man and Culture," New York, 1923.

———: "Psychology," "Handbook of American Indians," vol. II, pp. 311–313, Washington, 1910; reprinted in WALLIS and WILLEY, op. cit.

———: "An Introduction to Social Anthropology," chaps. XVII–XX, New York, 1929.

———: "The American Indian," New York, 1922.

———: "Relation of Nature to Man in Aboriginal America," New York, 1926.

———: "The Culture-Area Concept in Social Anthropology," Amer. Jour. Sociol., 32: 881–891, 1927.

———: "The Culture-Area Concept as a Research Lead," Ibid., 33: 894–900, 1928.

WOOD, MARGARET W.: "Latinizing the Turkish Alphabet," Amer. Jour. Sociol., 35: 194–203, 1929.

YOUNG, KIMBALL: "A Story of the Rise of a Social Taboo," Sci. Monthly, 26: 449–453, 1928; reprinted in WALLIS and WILLEY, op. cit.

CHAPTER II

BROWN, A. R.: "The Methods of Ethnology and Social Anthropology," So. African Jour. Sci., 20: 124–147, 1923.

CANNEY, MAURICE A.: "Givers of Life," chaps. I, II, London, 1923.

CZEKANOWSKI, JAN: "Verwandschaftsbeziehungen der Zentral-Afrikanischen Pygmäen," Korrespondenzbl. d. deutsch. Ges. f. Anthropol., Ethnol. und Urgeschichte, 41: 107, 1910.

CZEKANOWSKI, "Objective Kriterien in der Ethnologie," *Ibid.*, **42**: 71–74, 1911.

DIXON, ROLAND B.: "Review of WISSLER'S 'Relation of Nature to Man in Aboriginal America,'" AA, **29**: 326–332, 1927.

———: "The Building of Cultures," New York, 1928.

DIXON, ROLAND B., and SWANTON, JOHN: "Primitive American History," AA, **16**: 376–412, 1914; and *ibid*, **17**: 588–600, 1915.

ELLWOOD, CHARLES A.: "Primitive Concepts and the Origin of Cultural Patterns," *Amer. Jour. Sociol.*, **33**: 1–13, 1927.

———: "Cultural Evolution: A Study of Social Origins and Development," New York, 1927.

GOLDENWEISER, ALEXANDER A.: "The Heuristic Value of Traditional Records," AA, **17**: 763–764, 1915.

HARTLAND, E. SIDNEY: "On the Evidential Value of the Historical Traditions of the Baganda and Bushongo," *Folklore*, **25**: 428–456, 1914.

HOBHOUSE, LEONARD T., WHEELER, G. C., and GINSBERG, M.: "The Social Institutions and Material Culture of Primitive Peoples," "University of London Publications in Economics," London, 1915.

HODGE, F. W.: "The First Discovered City of Cibola," AA, **8**: 142–152, 1895.

JOYCE, THOMAS A.: "Mexican Archæology," chaps. I, XIV, London, 1914.

KASTEN, A.: "Gesundheitsstatistik und Soziologie," *Jahrb. f. Nationalökonomie und Statistik*, **126**: 417*ff*, 1927.

KELLER, ALBERT G.: "Societal Evolution," in LULL, R. S., "Evolution of Man," chap. IV New Haven, 1922.

KROEBER, ALFRED L.: "Anthropology," New York, 1923.

KROEBER, "Review of BOAS, FRANZ, 'Primitive Art,'" AA, **31**: 138–140, 1929.

LAUFER, BERTHOLD: "Methods in the Study of Domestications," *Sci. Monthly*, **25**: 251–255, 1927.

LOWIE, ROBERT H.: "Primitive Society," chap. V, New York, 1925.

CHAPTER III

DAVIDSON, DANIEL S.: "The Chronological Aspects of Certain Australian Social Institutions as Inferred from Geographical Distribution," Philadelphia, 1928.

DAWSON, CHRISTOPHER: "The Age of the Gods: A Study in the Origins of Culture in Prehistoric Europe and the Ancient East," Boston, 1928.

DECHELETTE, JOSEPH: "Manuel d'archéologie préhistorique, celtique et gallo-romaine," vol. II, pp. 453–469, Paris, 1910.

HANDY, E. S. CRAIGHILL: "Probable Sources of Polynesian Culture," *Proc. Third Pan-Pacific Sci. Congr.*, Tokyo, 1926, **2**: 2459–2468, 1928.

KIRKPATRICK, CLIFFORD: "Religion in Human Affairs," pp. 165–166, New York, 1929.

KROEBER, ALFRED L.: "American Culture and the Northwest Coast," AA, **25**: 1–21, 1923.

LOWIE ROBERT H.: "Plains Indians Age-societies: Historical and Comparative Summary," APAMNH, **11**: 881–992, 1916.

———: "Oral Tradition and History," AA, **17**: 597–599, 1915.

———: in *Jour. Amer. Folklore*, **30**: 161–167, 1917.

MASON, J. ALDEN: "Some Unusual Spear-throwers of Ancient America," *Museum Jour.*, **19**: 290–324, 1928.

WISSLER, CLARK: "An Introduction to Social Anthropology," chap. XVIII, New York, 1929.

MAYO-SMITH: "Statistics and Sociology," New York, 1895.

OGBURN, WILLIAM F., and GOLDEN-WEISER, ALEXANDER A., (editors) "The Social Sciences and Their Interrelations," chaps. X, XV, XX, XXIII, XXX, New York, 1927.

RADIN, PAUL: "The Story of the American Indian," chap. I, New York, 1927.

——: "A Grammar of the Wappo Language," UC, **27**: 16, 1929.

——: "History of Ethnological Theories," AA, **31**: 9–33, 1929.

RIVERS, WILLIAM H. R.: "Psychology and Ethnology," New York, 1926.

SAPIR, EDWARD: "Time Perspective in Aboriginal American Culture: A Study in Method," *Canadian Geological Survey, Museum Bull.*, Anthropol. ser., Ottawa, 1916.

SPINDEN, HERBERT J.: "The Origin and Distribution of Agriculture in America," *Proc. 19th Int. Cong. Americ.*, Washington, 1915, pp. 269–276.

STEWARD, JULIAN H.: Irrigation without Agriculture," *Papers of the Michigan Academy of Science, Arts and Letters.* **12**: 149–156, 1930.

THURNWALD, RICHARD: "Die Probleme einer empirischen Soziologie," *Zeitschr. f. Völkerpsychol. und Soziol.*, **3**: 257–273, 1927.

TYLOR, EDWARD B.: "On a Method of Investigating the Development of Institutions," JAI, **18**: 245–269, 1889; reprinted in KROEBER, A. L., and WATERMAN, T. T., "Source Book of Anthropology," pp. 321–342, Berkeley, 1920.

WALLIS, WILSON D.: "The Problems of an Empirical Sociology," *Social Forces*, **7**: 46–49, 1928.

——: "Der Einfluss der Geistesform auf Methode und Theorie," *Zeitschr. f. Völkerpsychol. und Soziol.*, **6**: 10–21, 1930.

——: "Probability and the Diffusion of Culture Traits," AA, **30**, 94–106, 1928.

WALLIS, "Psychological and Statistical Interpretations of Culture," *Amer. Jour. Sociol.*, 1917.

——: "An Introduction to Sociology," pp. 395–397, New York, 1927.

——: "An Introduction to Anthropology," chap. XXXIX, New York. 1926.

——: "The New Cults of Pythagoreans and Procrusteans," *Pedag. Seminar*, 1927.

——: "Review of RIVERS 'Psychology and Ethnology,'" *Psychol. Bull.*, 1927.

WISSLER, CLARK: "The American Indian," 2nd ed., New York, 1922.

——: "Man and Culture," pp. 66–71, New York, 1923.

——: "Relation of Nature to Man in Aboriginal America," New York, 1926.

CHAPTER IV

D'ALVIELLA, GOBLET: "The Migration of Symbols," London, 1894.

APPERSON, G. L.: "The Social History of Smoking," London, 1914.

ASHTON, JOHN: "Social Life in the Reign of Queen Anne, Taken from Original Sources," vol. I, chap. XVIII, London, 1882.

BALFOUR, HENRY, "The Geographical Study of Folklore," *Folklore*, **35**: 16–25, 1924.

BLACKMAR, FRANK W.: "The Diffusion of Culture," *Journal of Applied Sociology*," II: 503–509.

BOAS, FRANZ: "Migrations of Asiatic Races and Cultures to North America," *Sci. Monthly*, **28**: 110–117, 1929.

BOTSFORD, JAY B.: "English Society in the Eighteenth Century as Influenced from Oversea," New York, 1924.

CALKINS, ERNEST E.: "Beauty, the New Business Tool," *Atl. Monthly*, **140**: 145–156, 1927.

CANNEY, MAURICE A.: "Givers of Life and Their Significance in Mythology, chap. III, London, 1923.

CARTER, THOMAS F.: "The Invention of Printing in China and Its Spread Westward," New York, 1925.

CHENEY, RALPH H.: "Coffee, a Monograph on the Economic Species of the Genus Coffea L," Plate 44, and Appendix B, New York, 1925.

CHINNERY, E. W. P., and HADDON, A. C.: "Five New Religious Cults in British New Guinea," *Hibbert Journal*, **15**: 448–463, 1927.

"Coffee," EB, 14th ed., 1929.

"Coffee," "Rees' Cyclopædia."

COOPER, J. M.: "Culture Diffusion and Culture Areas of Southern South America," 21ᵉ Congrès Internationale des Americanistes, Göteburg, 1925.

"Culture Contact, Psychology of," EB, new vol. I, pp. 769–771, 13th ed., 1926.

DAWSON, CHRISTOPHER: "The Age of the Gods," Boston, 1928.

DECREMPS: "Advice to Frenchmen Who Go to England," Amsterdam, 1789.

DE KOVEN, ANNA: "Horace Walpole and Madame du Deffand. An Eighteenth Century Friendship," New York, 1929.

DIXON, ROLAND B.: "The Building of Cultures," New York, 1928.

DUSHKIND, CHARLES: "Tobacco Manual," New York, 1928. (Published by the Tobacco Merchants Association of the United States, 5 Beekman St., New York.)

EDKINS, JOSEPH: "The Early Spread of Religious Ideas, Especially in the Far East," London, 1893.

FÄY, BERNARD: "L'esprit révolutionaire en France et aux États-Unis à la fin du xviiie siècle," Paris, 1925.

GARDINER, EDWARD: "The Trials of Tobacco," London, 1600.

GEORGE, M. DOROTHY: "London Life in the XVIIIth Century," pp. 306–307, New York, 1925.

GLOVER, T. R.: "The Conflict of Religions in the Early Roman Empire," London, 1909.

GIBBIN, H. DE B.: "English Social Reformers," pp. 73–74, 95, London, 1902.

GOOCH, G. P.: "Nationalism," New York, 1920.

———: "English Democratic Ideas in the Seventeenth Century," pp. 305–313, 2nd ed., Cambridge, 1927.

GRAEBNER, F.: "Methode der Ethnologie," Heidelberg, 1911.

HAMILTON, A. E.: "This Smoking World," New York, 1927.

HARRIS, RENDEL: "Traces of Ancient Egypt in the Mediterranean," "Woodbrooke Essays," No. 1, Cambridge, 1927.

HEADLAM, CECIL: "Friends That Fall Not: Light Essays Concerning Books," chaps. IX, XI, London, 1902.

HETTNER, A.: "Der Sang der Kultur über die Erde," Berlin, Leipzig, 1929.

HOOKE, S. H.: "Diffusion with a Difference," AA, **29**: 615–624, 1927.

HEWARD, E. V.: " St. Nicotine, or the Peace Pipe," London, 1909.

HOPKINS, E. WASHBURN: "The Origin and Evolution of Religion," chap. XII, New Haven, 1923.

JONES, HOWARD M.: "America and French Culture 1750–1848," Chapel Hill, N. C., 1927.

KROEBER, ALFRED L.: "Anthropology," New York, 1923.

———: "The History of Philippine Civilization as Reflected in Religious Nomenclature," APAMNH, **19**: 39–67, 1918.

———: "Arrow Release Distributions," UC, **23**: 283–296, 1927.

LAUFER, BERTHOLD: "The American Plant Migration," *Sci. Monthly*, **28**: 239–251, 1929.

LEVIN, RUBEN: "Look at Canada, Mayor Thompson," *Plain Talk*, 1928.

LOCKITT, C. H.: "The Relations of French and English Society (1763–1793)," London, 1920.

LOEB, E. M.: "The Blood Sacrifice Complex," *Mem. Amer. Anthrop. Assoc.*, No. 30, 1923.

LOWIE, ROBERT H.: "Are We Civilized?" chap. V, New York, 1929.

MACKENZIE, DONALD A.: "Ancient Man in Britain," chap. XVII, London, 1923.

———: "The Migration of Symbols and Their Relations to Beliefs and Customs," New York, 1926.

MAIGRON, LOUIS: "Le Romantisme et les Mœurs: Essai d'étude historique et sociale," pp. 312–350, Paris, 1910.

MALINOWSKI, BRONISLAW: "The Life of Culture," *Forum*, **76**: 178–185, 1926.

MARETT, ROBERT R.: "Foreword," in MURPHY, JOHN, "Primitive Man, His Essential Quest," pp. 7–11, Oxford, 1927.

———: "The Diffusion of Culture," Cambridge, 1927.

MERRILL, E. D.: "Tobacco in New Guinea," AA, **32**: 101–105, 1930.

MOORE, EDWARD C.: "The Spread of Christianity in the Modern World," Chicago, 1922.

OGBURN, WILLIAM F., and GOLDENWEISER, ALEXANDER A. (editors): "The Social Sciences and Their Interrelations," chaps. VII, IX, New York, 1927.

O'LEARY, DE LACY: "Arabic Thought and Its Place in History," London, 1922.

PARSONS, ELSIE: "The Laguna Migration to Isleta," AA, **30**: 602–613, 1928.

PERRY, W. J.: "The Children of the Sun," London, 1923.

———: "The Diffusion of Civilization," in CARTER, E. H., (editor), "The New Past and Other Essays on the Development of Civilization," chap. III, Oxford, 1925.

———: "The Growth of Civilization," New York, n.d.

PETTAZZONI, R.: "The Chain of Arrows: The Diffusion of a Mythical Motive," *Folklore*, **35**: 151–165, 1924.

PRICE, MAURICE T.: "Christian Missions and Oriental Civilizations: A Study of Culture Contacts," Shanghai, 1924.

REES, J. AUBREY: "Tea in England," *Contemp. Rev.*, No. 747: 361–365, 1928.

REPPLIER, AGNES: "Collective Unreason," *Atl. Monthly*, **140**: 768–775, 1927.

RENAUD, E. B.: "Prehistoric Female Figurines from America and the Old World," *Sci. Monthly*, **28**: 507–512, 1929.

RINE, ALFRED: "The Consumption of Tobacco since 1600," *Econ. Jour.*, Economic History series, No. 1, 1926.

RIVERS, W. H. R.: "Psychology and Ethnology," New York, 1926.

RUSSELL, MICHAEL, "Nubia and Abyssinia," pp. 435–436, Edinburgh, 1833.

SAPIR, EDWARD, "Time Perspective in Aboriginal American Culture," Ottawa, 1916.

SCOTT, LEONARD D.: "The History of Paper Making," *Minn. Techno-Log*, **9**: 220–221, 238, 242, 1929.

SMITH, G. ELLIOT: "The Migrations of Culture," Manchester, 1918.

———: "The Diffusion of Culture," *Forum*, **76**: 171–177, 1926.

——— and others: "Culture: The Diffusion Controversy," New York, 1927.

———: "Human History," chaps. XII–XV, New York, 1929.

SPIER, LESLIE: "The Sun Dance of the Plains Indians: Its Development and Diffusion," APAMNH, **16**: 453–527, 1921.

STANGER, HERMANN: "Tabak und Kultur," Dresden, 1922.

STEINMETZ, ANDREW: "Tobacco," London, 1857.

STERN, BERNHARD J.: "Social Factors in Medical Progress," New York, 1927.

———: "Should We Be Vaccinated: A Survey of the Controversy in Its Historical and Scientific Aspects," New York, 1927.

TARDE, GABRIEL: "The Laws of Imitation," Engl. transl., New York, 1903.

"Tea," EB, 14th ed., 1929.

"Tobacco," EB, 14th ed., 1929.

"Tobacco Talk and Smoker's Gossip," London, 1886 (anonymous).

"Traité théorique et pratique du culottage des pipes" (anonymous).

TYLOR, EDWARD B.: "On the Diffusion of Mythical Beliefs as Evidence in the History of Culture," "Report British Association for the Advancement of Science," p. 774, 1894.

VIERKANDT, ALFRED: "Die Stetigkeit im Kulturwandel," Leipzig, 1908.

WALLIS, WILSON D.: "An Introduction to Anthropology," chap. XXXIX, New York, 1926.

———: "Probability and the Diffusion of Culture," AA, 30: 94–106, 1928.

———: "An Introduction to Sociology," pp. 213–216, and chap. XXXII, New York, 1928.

WILLIAMS, F. E.: "Orokaiva Magic," pp. 16–30, London, 1928.

WISSLER, CLARK: "The American Indian," 2nd ed., New York, 1922.

———: "Distribution of Moccasin Decorations among the Plains Indians," APAMNH, 29: 5–23, 1927.

———: "Costumes of the Plains Indians," APAMNH, 17: 45–91, 1915.

———: "Structural Basis of the Decoration of Costumes among the Plains Indians," ibid., pp. 99–114, 1916.

———: "Introduction to Social Anthropology," New York, 1929.

WRIGHT, CHARLES, and FAYLE, C. ERNEST: "A History of Lloyd's, from the Founding of Lloyd's Coffee House to the Present Day," New York, 1928.

CHAPTER V

BARTLETT, FREDERICK C.: "Psychology and Primitive Culture," Cambridge, 1923.

FIRTH, RAYMOND: "Primitive Economics of the New Zealand Maori," chap. XIV, New York, 1929.

KIRKPATRICK, CLIFFORD: "Religion in Human Affairs," chap. VI, New York, 1929.

LEGGE, F.: "Forerunners and Rivals of Christianity," Cambridge, 1915.

"Mah Jongg," EB, 14th ed., 1929.

MEEK, THEOPHILE J.: "The Interpenetration of Cultures as Illustrated by the Character of the Old Testament Literature," Jour. Relig., 7: 244–262, 1927; reprinted in WALLIS, WILSON D., and WILLEY, MALCOLM M., "Readings in Sociology," chap. II, New York, 1930.

RADIN, PAUL: "A Sketch of the Peyote Cult of the Winnebago," Jour. Relig. Psych., 7: 1–22, 1914.

———: "The Winnebago Tribe." 37th Annual Report, Bureau of American Ethnology, Washington, 1923.

SCHERMERHORN, W. D.: "Syncreticism in the Early Christian Period and in Present-day India," Jour. Relig., 4: 464–467, 1924; reprinted in WALLIS and WILLEY, op. cit.

CHAPTER VI

Culture Changes and Survivals

ARMYTAGE, PEREY: "By the Clock of St. James," London, 1927.

BENTLEY, ARTHUR F.: "Relativity in Man and Society," pp. 184–185, New York, 1926.

BOUGLÉ, C.: "The Evolution of Values," pp. 80–87, Engl. transl., New York, 1926.

CHAPIN, F. STUART: "A Theory of Synchronous Culture Cycles," *Social Forces*, **3**: 596–604, 1925.

CHAPIN, "Culture Change," New York, 1928.

CROOKE, W.: "The Interpretation of Survivals," *Folklore*, **30**: 132–133, 1919.

EASTMAN, GEORGE and NICHOL, FRANCIS D.: "The Thirteen-Month Calendar," *Forum*, **84**: 14–22, 1930.

EDGELL, G. H.: "The American Architecture of Today," New York, 1928.

GAUS, JOHN M.: "Great Britain: A Study of Civic Loyalty," chap. III, Chicago, 1929.

GUIGNEBERT, CHARLES: "Christianity Past and Present," New York, 1928.

HOCART, A. M.: "Kingship," Oxford, 1927.

"Horseshoes," *Folklore*, **31**: 233–234, 1920.

KENNELLY, ARTHUR E.: "Vestiges of Premetric Weights and Measures Persisting in Metric System Europe 1926–1927," New York, 1928.

LAWRENCE, ROBERT M.: "The Magic of the Horse-shoe with Other Folk-lore Notes," Boston, 1899.

MACDONOUGH, MICHAEL: "The Pageant of Parliament," London, 1921.

MARETT, ROBERT R.: "Psychology and Folk-Lore," London, 1920.

———: "The Interpretation of Survivals," *Quart. Rev.*, 1919.

———: "The Transvaluation of Culture," *Folklore*, **29**: 15–33, 1918.

"Material Culture," EB, 14th ed., 1929.

MCDANIEL, WALTON B.: "Roman Private Life and Its Survivals," Boston, 1924.

MEEK, THEOPHILE J.: "The Interpenetration of Cultures as Illustrated by the Character of the Old Testament Literature," *Jour. Relig.*, **7**: 244–262, 1927; reprinted in WALLIS, WILSON D., and WILLEY, MALCOLM M., "Readings in Sociology," New York, 1930.

MERZ, CHARLES: "The Great American Bandwagon," chaps. III, IX, New York, 1928.

MIELZINER, M.: "The Jewish Law of Marriage and Divorce in Ancient and Modern Times," New York, 1901.

MUNRO, WILLIAM B.: "Modern Science and Politics," *Yale Rev.*, **16**: 723–738, 1927.

MYERS, JOHN L.: "Cycles in History," New York, 1930.

———: "Oxford in the Making," *Amer. Oxonian*, **15**: 40–60, 1928.

OSBORN, HENRY F.: "Man Rises to Parnassus," pp. 134–136, Princeton, 1927.

PASCOE, CHARLES E.: "The Pageant and Ceremony of the Coronation of Their Majesties King Edward the Seventh and Queen Alexandra," New York, 1902.

PETRIE, WILLIAM FLINDERS: "The Revolutions of Civilization," New York, 1912.

SHARP, EVELYN: "Here We Go Round: The Story of the Dance," New York, 1928.

SOROKIN, PITIRIM A.: "A Survey of the Cyclical Conceptions of Social and Historical Process," *Social Forces*, **6**: 28–40, 1927.

SPENGLER, OSWALD: "The Decline of the West," Engl. transl., New York, 1926, 1928.

STODDARD, LOTHROP: "Luck Your Silent Partner," New York, 1929.

TYLOR, EDWARD B.: "Primitive Culture," New York, 1924.

———: "The Study of Custom," *Macmillan's Mag.*, p. 465, 1882.

VAN GENNEP, ARNOLD: "Rites des passages," Paris, 1908.

WALLIS, WILSON D.: "The Tragedy and the Romance of Sneezing," *Sci. Monthly*, pp. 526–538, 1919.

———: "An Introduction to Sociology," p. 42, New York, 1928.

WEBSTER, HUTTON: "Primitive Secret Societies," New York, 1908.

WELLS, J.: "The Oxford Degree Ceremony," Oxford, 1906.

WINSTED, R. O.: "Shaman Saiva and Sufi: A Study of the Evolution of Malay Magic," London, 1925.

WISSLER, CLARK: "An Introduction to Social Anthropology," pp. 218–220, New York, 1929.

——: "The Conflict and Survival of Cultures." In Murchison, Carl (editor), "The Foundations of Experimental Psychology," 786–808, Worcester, 1929.

WOOLEY, R. M.: "Coronation Rites," Cambridge, 1915.

Calendrical Celebrations

"All-Fools' day," ERE.

"April-Fools' day," EB, **2**: 231.

ASHTON, JOHN: "A Rite Merrie Christmasse!!! The Story of Christtide," London, n. d.

BRAND, JOHN: "Observations on the Popular Antiquities of Great Britain: Chiefly Illustrating the Origin of Our Vulgar and Provincial Customs, Ceremonies, and Superstitions," London, 1877.

BREWSTER, H. P.: "Saints and Festivals of the Christian Church," New York, 1904.

BRIFFAULT, ROBERT, "The Mothers," vol. III, pp. 101–103, New York, 1927.

CHAMBERLAIN, ISABEL F.: "Adbul Baha on Divine Philosophy," pp. 74–75, Boston, 1918.

CHASE, STUART: "Play," in BEARD, CHARLES A. (editor), "Whither Mankind," p. 351, New York, 1928.

"Christmas," EB.

"Christmas Candles," *Folklore*, **28**: 106–107, 1917.

CONVERSE, HARRIET M.: "The Seneca New-year Ceremony, and Other Customs," *Indian Notes*, **7**: 69–89, 1930.

CORMACK, J. G., MRS.: "Chinese Birthday, Wedding, Funeral, and Other Customs," chap. IX, 2nd ed., Peking, 1923.

COSGRAVE, LLOYD M.: "Christmas Clubs," *Quart. Jour. Econ.*, pp. 732–739, 1926–27.

COUZENS, REGINALD C.: "The Stories of the Months and Days," London, 1922.

CRIPPEN, T. G.: "Christmas and Christmas Lore," London, 1923.

EARLE, ALICE M.: "Customs and Fashions in Old New England," chap. IX, New York, 1894.

"Easter," EB, ERE, "New International Encyclopædia."

EICHLER, LILLIAN: "The Customs of Mankind with Notes on Modern Etiquette and the Newest Trend in Entertainment," chap. XIV, New York, 1924.

FRAZER, JAMES G.: "The Worship of Nature," vol. I, pp. 502–528, New York, 1926.

——: "Adonis, Attis, Osiris," vol. I, pp. 302–305, New York, 1906.

GRAINGER, A.: "Permanent Values in Chinese Festivals," *Chinese Recorder*, **49** (2): 732–736, 1918.

HAZLITT, W. CAREW: "Brand's Popular Antiquities of Great Britain, Faiths and Folklore, etc.," London, 1905.

HERVEY, THOMAS K.: "The Book of Christmas Descriptive of the Customs, Ceremonies, Traditions, Superstitions, Fun, Feeling, and Festivities of the Christmas Season," Boston, 1888.

HILLARD, KATHERINE: "The Easter Hare," *Atl. Monthly*, **65**: 665–670, 1890.

HONE, WILLIAM: "The Every-day Book, and Table Book: Everlasting Calendar of Popular Amusements, Sports, Pastimes, Ceremonies, Manners, Customs, and Events, Incident to Each of the Three Hundred and Sixty-five Days, etc.," London, 1826.

HOOKE, S. H.: "New Year's Day: The Story of the Calendar," New York, 1928.

IGLEHART, FANNY C. G.: "Christmas in Old Mexico," privately printed, n. d.

——: "The Tradition of Guadalupe and Christmas in Old Mexico," privately printed, n. d.

KELLY, WALTER K.: "Curiosities of Indo-European Tradition and Folk-Lore," London, 1863.

KNOWLSON, T. S.: "The Origins of Popular Superstitions and Customs," London, n. d.

LAKE, KIRSOPP: "Christmas," ERE, 3: 601–608.

LECHE, WILHELM: "Der Mensch, sein Ursprung und seine Entwicklung in gemeinverständlicher Darstellung," pp. 223–228, Jena, 1911.

LEHMANN, EDWARD: "Christmas Customs," ERE, 3: 608–610.

London Illustrated News, 175: 901, Nov. 23, 1929.

MACKENZIE, DONALD A.: "Easter Eggs in Scotland," Folklore, 28: 450, 1917.

MAYLAM, PERCY: "The Wooden Horse, an East Kent Christmas Custom," Canterbury, 1909.

McCown, CHESTER C.: "The Genesis of the Social Gospel," pp. 329–330, New York, 1929.

MEANS, P. B.: "New Year's in Sumatra," Amer. Oxonian, 15: 161–165, 1928.

MEEK, THEOPHILE J.: "The Interpenetration of Cultures as Illustrated by the Character of the Old Testament Literature," Jour. Relig., 7: 244–262, 1927.

MILES, CLEMENT: "Christmas in Ritual and Tradition Christian and Pagan," 2nd ed., London, 1913.

PETROVITCH, WOISLAV M.: "Hero Tales and Legends of the Serbians," pp. 46–51, New York, 1914.

PHILPOT, J. H., MRS.: "The Sacred Tree, or the Tree in Religion and Myth," London, 1897.

PRINGLE, MARY P., and URANN, CLARA A.: "Yule-tide in Many Lands," Boston, 1916.

RICE, SUSAN T., and SCHAUFFLER, ROBERT H.: "Easter, Its History, Celebration, Spirit, and Significance as Related in Prose and Verse," New York, 1924.

RIETSCHEL, GEORGE: "Weihnachten in Kirche, Kunst und Volksleben," Leipzig, 1902.

ROBERTSON, WILLIAM: "Historical Essays in Connexion with the Land, the Church, etc., pp. 72–87, Edinburgh, 1878.

"Round about our Coal Fire, or Christmas Entertainments: Wherein is described Abundance of Fiddle-Faddle-Stuff, Raw-heads, Bloody-bones, Buggy-bows, and such like Horrible Bodies, Eating, Drinking, Kissing, and other Diversions; Witches, Conjurers, and their merry Pranks; Fairies, Spectres, Ghosts, and Apparitions; A Right Merry Tale:—The Story of Jack Spriggins and the Enchanted Bean; Curious Memoirs of Old Father Christmas," London, 1740; republished by Field and Tuer, London, n. d.

SALEMAN, F. L.: "Merry Christmas," Athenaeum, No. 4678: 1393–1394, 1919.

SANDYS, WILLIAM: "Christmastide, Its History, Festivities, and Carols," London, n. d.

SCHAUFFLER, ROBERT H.: "Christmas: Its Origin, Celebration and Significance as Related in Prose and Verse," New York, 1925.

SMITH, ELVA S., and HAZELTINE, ALICE I.: "Christmas in Legend and Story," Boston, n. d.

SPERLINGII, OTTHONIS: "De Nomine et Festo Juel Septentrionalium Tam Antiquorum Quam Hodiernorum Dissertatio," Havniæ, n. d.

STEWART, JANE A.: "The Christmas Book," Philadelphia, 1908.

TILLE, ALEXANDER: "Die Geschichte der deutshen Weihnacht," Leipzig, n. d.

"Trees and Plants," ERE, 12: 454–456.

WALN, NORA: "The Coming of 'China New Year,'" Atl. Monthly, 137: 88–93, 1926.

WEIGALL, ARTHUR: "Wanderings in Anglo-Saxon Britain," chap. VI, London, n. d.

CHAPTER VII

ANDREE, RICHARD: "Ethnographische Parallelen und Vergleiche," Leipzig, 1889.

"Asceticism (Introductory)," "Assimilation," ERE.

BARTLETT, F. C.: "Psychology and Primitive Culture," chaps. VI–VII, Cambridge, 1923.

———: "Social Constructiveness," Brit. Jour. Psych., 18: 388–391, 1928.

BEVAN, EDWYN: "Stoics and Sceptics," pp. 77–81, Oxford, 1913.

BEWER, JULIUS A.: "Ancient Babylonian Parallels to the Prophecies of Haggai," Amer. Jour. Semitic Lang. and Liter., 35: 128–133, 1919.

BOAS, FRANZ: "Classification of American Languages," AA, 22: 367–376, 1920.

———: "The Development of Folk-Tales and Myth," Sci. Monthly, 2: 335–343.

———: "The Methods of Ethnology," AA, 22: 311–321, 1920.

———: "Limitations of the Comparative Methods of Anthropology," Science, New Series, 4: 901–908, 1896.

———: "Review of Graebner's 'Methode der Ethnologie,'" Science, p. 343, 1911.

BRIFFAULT, ROBERT: "The Making of Humanity," pt. I, chap. VI, pp. 88–101, London, 1919.

BUTLER, SAMUEL: "Unconscious Memory," chap. I, London, 1880.

CARTER, THOMAS F.: "The Invention of Printing in China and Its Spread Westward," pp. 184–185, New York, 1925.

COOLEY, CHARLES H.: "Social Process," chap. I, New York, 1922.

DIXON, ROLAND B.: "The Building of Cultures," New York, 1928.

DURARBIER, GEORGES: "Chinese Originators," Living Age, 317: 33–37, 1923.

EINSTEIN, LEWIS: "Tudor Ideals," pt. II, chap. VII, New York, 1921.

FREEMAN, E. A.: "History of Federal Government," chap. XI, 2nd ed., 1893.

FRIEDERICI, GEORG, "In der vorkolumbischen Verbindung der Südseevölker mit Amerika," Anthropos, 24: 441–488, 1929.

GILFILLAN, S. C.: "Who Invented It?" Sci. Monthly, 25: 529–534, 1927; reprinted in WALLIS, WILSON D., and WILLEY, MALCOLM M., "Readings in Sociology," New York, 1930.

GOLDENWEISER, ALEXANDER A.: "Early Civilization," New York, 1922.

———: "The Principle of Limited Possibilities," Jour. Amer. Folk-Lore, p. 26, 1913.

———: "Diffusion vs. Independent Origin: A Rejoinder to Professor G. Elliot Smith," Science, New Series 44: 531–533, 1916.

GRAEBNER, F.: "Methode der Ethnologie," Heidelberg, 1911.

HAEBERLIN, H. K.: "The Idea of Fertilization in the Culture of the Pueblo Indians," Mem. Amer. Anthrop. Assoc., 3: 1–55, 1916.

HARTLAND, E. SIDNEY: "Ritual and Belief," p. 268, London, 1914.

HARRISON, H. S.: "Inventions," Man, 26: nos. 74, 101; 27: no. 28, 1926–27.

———: "Pots and Pans," chap. IX, New York, 1928.

———: "Material Culture," EB, 14th ed., 1929.

HEADLAM, CECIL: "Friends That Fail Not," chap. I, London, 1902.

HELD, F. E.: "Christianopolis," chap. III, New York, 1916.

HENDERSON, KEITH: "Prehistoric Man," pp. 250–253, New York, 1927.

HOBHOUSE, LEONARD T.: "Sociology," ERE.

HOCART, A. M.: "Kingship," chap. I, Oxford, 1927.

———: "The Convergence of Customs," Folk-Lore, 34: 224–232, 1923.

HOLMES, W. H.: "Handbook of Aboriginal American Antiquities," Smithsonian Institution, Bureau of American Ethnology, Bull. 60, pt. I, chap. IV, Washington, 1919.

HOOKE, S. H.: "New Year's Day: The Story of the Calendar," chap. X, New York, 1928.

HORNBOSTEL, VON: "Über ein akustisches Kriterium für Kulturzusammenhänge," Zeitschr. f. Ethnol., pp. 601–615, 1911.

———: "Über einige Panpfeifen aus Nordwest-Brazilien," in KOCH-GRÜNBERG, T., "Zwei Jahre bei den Indianern Nordwest-Braziliens, vol. II, pp. 378–391, Stuttgart, 1923.

IHERING, RUDOLPH VON: "The Evolution of the Aryan," bk. IV, New York, 1897.

JENKS, J. W., and LAUCK, W. J.: "The Immigration Problem," chap. XV, pp. 284–318, New York, 1926.

JOYCE, THOMAS A.: "Mexican Archæology: An Introduction to the Archæology of the Mexican and Mayan Civilizations of Pre-Spanish America," London, 1914.

KEIMER, LUDWIG: "The Wisdom of Amen-Em-Ope and the Proverbs of Solomon," Amer. Jour. Semitic Lang. and Liter., 42: 8–21, 1926.

KORZYBSKI, ALFRED: "The Manhood of Humanity," New York, 1921.

KROEBER, ALFRED L.: "Anthropology," chaps. V, VIII–IX, New York, 1923.

KROEBER, ALFRED L., and HOLT, CATHERINE: "Masks and Moieties as a Culture Complex," JAI, 50: 452–460, 1920.

LANG, ANDREW: "Myth, Ritual, and Religion," vol. I, chap. II, New York, 1913.

LAUFER, BERTHOLD: "The Eskimo Screw as a Culture-Historical Problem," AA, 17: 396–406, 1915.

LOWIE, ROBERT H.: "On the Principle of Convergence in Ethnology," Jour. Amer. Folk-Lore, 25: 24–42, 1912.

———: "Survivals and the Historical Method," Amer. Jour. Sociol., 23: 529–535, 1918.

LULL, RICHARD S.: "Organic Evolution," pp. 687–691, New York, 1917.

MacDOUGALL, WILLIAM: "Social Psychology," chap. XV, 14th ed., Boston, 1921.

MacLEOD, WILLIAM C.: "On the Diffusion of Central American Culture to Coastal British Columbia and Alaska," Anthropos, 24: 417–441, 1929.

———: "On the Southeast Asiatic Origins of American Culture," AA, 31: 554–560, 1929.

MARETT, ROBERT R.: "Psychology and Folk-Lore," chap. I, London, 1920.

MARVIN, FRANCIS S. (editor), "Western Races and the World," chaps. III, IV, The Unity Series, V, New York, 1922.

MASON, OTIS T.: "Similarities in Culture," AA, vol. 8, 1896.

McGEE, W. J.: "Anthropology and Its Larger Problems," Science, 21: 780–783, 1905.

———: "The Trend of Human Progress," AA, vol. 1, 1889.

MEANS, PHILIP A.: "Racial Factors in Democracy," chap. V, Boston, 1918.

———: "Some Objections to Mr. Elliot Smith's Theory," Science, 44: 533–534, 1916.

"Monasticism," ERE, 8: 783.

MORE, PAUL E.: "Hellenistic Philosophies," pp. 127–129, Princeton, 1923.

OGBURN, WILLIAM F.: "Social Change," pt. II, New York, 1922.

RADIN, PAUL: "Literary Aspects of North American Mythology," Ottawa, 1915.

RENAUD, E. B.: "Prehistoric Female Figurines from America and the Old World," *Sci. Montbly*, **28**: 507–512, 1929.

RIVERS, WILLIAM H. R.: "Psychology and Ethnology," pp. 141–150, New York, 1926.

RIVET, P.: "Relations commerciales précolombiennes entre l'Océanie et l'Amérique," in KOPPERS, W. (editor), "Festschrift Publication d'hommage offerte au P. W. Schmidt," pp. 583–609, Wien, 1928.

———: "Migration Australienne en Amérique," *Proc. Pan-Pacific Sci. Congr.*, *Tokyo*, 1926, **2**: 2354–2356, Tokyo, 1928.

ROSS, EDWARD A.: "Principles of Sociology," chaps. XIX–XX, New York, 1920.

SAPIR, EDWARD: "Review of VON HORNBOSTEL," Über ein akustisches Kriterium für Kulturzusammenhänge," *Current Anthrop. Liter.*, **2**: 69–72, 1913.

———: "Language," chap. IX, New York, 1921.

SCHRIEKE, B.: "The Evolution of Culture in the Pacific in Relation to the Theories of the 'Kulturhistorische' and 'Manchester' Schools of Social Anthropology," *Proc. Third Pan-Pacific Sci. Congr.*, *Tokyo*, 1926, **2**: 2423–2441, Tokyo, 1928.

SMITH, GRAFTON ELLIOT: "The Origin of the Pre-Columbian Civilization of America," *Science*, **44**: 190–195, 1916.

———: "Elephants and Ethnologists," New York, 1924.

———: "In the Beginning," New York, 1927.

———: "The Diffusion of Culture," New York, 1929.

SMITH, GRAFTON ELLIOT, MALINOWSKI, BRONISLAW, SPINDEN, HERBERT J., and GOLDENWEISER, ALEXANDER A.: "Culture: The Diffusion Controversy," New York, 1927.

SMITH, STEVENSON, and GUTHRIE, EDWIN R.: "General Psychology," chap. VII, New York, 1921.

SMITH, WILLIAM C.: "Cultural Diffusion," *Jour. Appl. Sociol.*, **7**: 123–129.

SPENCER, HERBERT: "Principles of Sociology," vol. I, pt. II, chap. III, New York, 1914.

STERN, BERNHARD J.: "Social Factors in Medical Progress," pp. 108–127, New York, 1927.

STEWARD, JULIAN H.: "Diffusion and Independent Invention: A Critique of Logic," AA, **31**: 491–495, 1929.

TAYLOR, HENRY O.: "Ancient Ideals," vol. I, chap. I, New York, 1900.

THOMPSON, L. ERIC: "The Elephant Heads in the Waldeck Manuscripts," *Sci. Montbly*, **25**: 392–398, 1927.

THURNWALD, RICHARD: Review of W. Schmidt and W. Koppers, in *Deutsche Literaturzeitung*, Heft 39, pp. 1907–1916, 1927.

WALLIS, WILSON D.: "The Animistic Hypothesis," AA, **21**: 292–295, 1919.

———: "Australian Social Organization," *ibid.*, **19**: 109–129, 1917.

———: "Similarities in Culture," *ibid.*, **19**: 41–54, 1917.

———: "Review of R. H. Nassau, 'Where Animals Talk,'" in *Current Anthrop. Liter.*, **1**: 206–208, 1912.

WESTERMARCK, EDWARD: "The History of Human Marriage," vol. I, "Introduction," 5th ed., New York, 1922.

———: "Marriage Ceremonies in Morocco," pp. 7–9, London, 1914.

WEULE, KARL: "The Culture of Barbarians: A Glimpse into the Beginnings of the Human Mind," pp. 9–23, London, 1926.

"Who Invented the Steamboat?" Editorial in *The Nation*, **124**: 659–660, 1927.

Wissler, Clark: "Man and Culture," chap. VI, New York, 1923.

Zimmern, Alfred E.: "Greek Commonwealth," chap. VIII, 2nd ed., Oxford, 1915.

CHAPTER VIII

Adams, James T.: "Historic Determinism and the Individual," *Atl. Monthly*, **134**: 510–519, 1924.

Adamson, John E.: "The Theory of Education in Plato's Republic," chap. IX, pp. 166–169, London, 1903.

Baldwin, J. Mark: "Social and Ethical Interpretation in Mental Development," chap. XVI, pp. 569–572, New York, 1902.

———: "The Individual and Society," Boston, 1911.

Balfour, Arthur J.: "Essays and Addresses," pp. 127–174. 3rd ed., Edinburgh, 1905.

Beard, Charles A. and Mary: "History and Culture," *Sat. Rev. Liter.*, **6**: 101–102, 1929.

Boas, Franz: "Primitive Art," Cambridge, 1928. (Oslo, 1927.)

Briffault, Robert: "The Making of Humanity," chap. IV, pp. 63–68, London, 1919.

Brinton, Daniel G.: "The Basis of Social Relations," chap. II, pp. 23–45, New York, 1902.

Bryce, James: "The American Commonwealth," vol. I, chap. XXVI, New York, 1927.

Bushell, S. W.: "Chinese Art," London, 1906.

Catt, Carrie C.: "The Menangkabaur," *Harper's Monthly Mag.*, 1914.

Chancellor, W. E.: "Educational Sociology," chap. II, pp. 14–23, New York, 1919.

Chatterton-Hill, George: "The Sociological Value of Christianity," London, 1912.

———: "Heredity and Selection in Sociology," pt. II, chap. I, London, 1907.

Cheney, Edward P.: "Law in History and Other Essays," New York, 1927.

Clow, F. R.: "Principles of Sociology," chap. VIII, pp. 210–214, New York, 1920.

Cooke, George W.: "The Social Evolution of Religion," chap. II, sec. 1, Boston, 1920.

Cooley, Charles H.: "Human Nature and the Social Order," chap. I, p. 13, New York, 1922.

Durkheim, Émile: "Elementary Forms of the Religious Life," London, 1915.

"Ethics (Australian)," ERE.

Garinei, Michele: "La Funzione dell' Individuo Nelle Collettivita Umane," Florence, 1897.

Gettell, R. B.: "Problems in Political Evolution," chap. II, Boston, 1914.

Gehlke, Charles E.: "Émile Durkheim's Contributions to Sociological Theory," New York, 1915.

Hamilton, Sir William: "Lectures on Metaphysics and Logic," vol. I, Lecture V, London, 1859.

Hetherington, H. J. W., and Muirhead, J. H.: "Social Purpose," chap. VIII, pp. 164–168, New York, 1918.

Hose, Charles, and McDougall, William: "Pagan Tribes of Borneo," London, 1912.

Huxley, Thomas H.: "Evolution and Ethics," (Romanes lecture), New York, 1902.

James, William: "The Will to Believe and Other Essays in Popular Philosophy," Chapter on "Great Men and Their Environment," New York, 1912.

———: "Varieties of Religious Experience," New York, 1925.

Jarrett, Bede: "Social Theories of the Middle Ages, 1200–1500," chap. IX, London, 1926.

Kirkpatrick, Clifford: "Religion in Human Affairs," pp. 178–221, New York, 1929.

KROEBER, ALFRED L.: "The Arapaho," Bull. American Museum of Natural History, vol. 18, 1902.

LIPPMANN, WALTER: "A Preface to Morals," pp. 94–111, New York, 1929.

LOWIE, ROBERT H.: "Primitive Society," chaps. XIII, XIV, New York, 1920.

———: "Individual Differences and Primitive Culture," in KOPPERS, W. (editor), "Festschr. Publication d'-hommage offerte au P. W. Schmidt, pp. 495–500, Wien, 1928.

MACHIAVELLI, NICCOLO: "The Prince," chap. VI, New York, 1906.

MACIVER, R. M.: "Elements of Social Science," chap. VII, sec. I, pp. 149–153; sec. IV, pp. 174–179, London, 1921.

MEAD, MARGARET: "The Rôle of the Individual in Samoan Culture," JAI, 58: 481–495, 1929.

MONTESQUIEU, CHARLES L.: "The Spirit of the Laws," bk. 19, chap. III, New York, 1900.

RADIN, PAUL: "Crashing Thunder: The Autobiography of an American Indian," New York, 1926.

"Religion," sec. 13, ERE.

"Report of the Cambridge Anthropological Expedition to Torres Straits," vol. VI, Cambridge, 1901.

RINK, H.: "Tales and Traditions of the Eskimo," London, 1875.

ROTHENSTEIN, WILLIAM: "Some Desultory Remarks on Art and Civilization," in CARTER, E. H. (editor), "The New Past and Other Essays on the Development of Civilization," chap. XI, Oxford, 1925.

SPIER, LESLIE: "The Sun Dance of the Plains Indians: Its Development and Diffusion," APAMNH, 16: 459–522, 1921.

STERN, BERNHARD J.: "Social Factors in Medical Progress," pt. II, New York, 1927.

"Symbolism," ERE.

TAYLOR, HENRY O.: "Freedom of the Mind in History," chap. VII, London, 1923.

"Technique in Art," EB, 14 ed., 1929.

WALEY, ARTHUR: "An Introduction to the Study of Chinese Painting," London, 1923.

WALLIS, WILSON D.: "Ethical Aspects of Chilkat Culture," Amer. Jour. Psych., 1918.

———: "Individual Initiative and Social Compulsion," AA, 17: 647–665, 1915.

———: "An Introduction to Sociology," pp. 422–423, New York, 1928.

———: "Durkheim's View of Religion," Jour. Relig. Psych., 7: 252–267, 1914.

———: "Messiahs: Christian and Pagan," chap. IX, Boston, 1918.

———: "An Introduction to Anthropology," chap. XXXVII, New York, 1926.

———: "The Problem of Personality," Internat. Jour. Ethics, 1914.

WEBB, CLEMENT C. J.: "Group Theories of Religion and the Individual," New York, 1916.

WEBSTER, HUTTON: "Primitive Individual Ascendancy," Publ. Amer. Sociol. Soc., 12: 46–60, 1917.

WEEKS, JOHN H.: "Among the Primitive Bakongo," London, 1914.

WISSLER, CLARK: "Material Culture of the Blackfoot Indians," APAMNH, vol. 5, 1910.

———: "Psychology," in "Handbook of American Indians," vol. II, pp. 311–313, Washington, 1910.

CHAPTER IX

ADAMS, HENRY: "The Education of Henry Adams," chap. XXVIII, Boston, 1918.

BACON, FRANCIS: "Essayes or Counsels, Civill and Morall," chaps. XXIX, XL, New York, 1909.

BAUDRILLART, HENRI J. L.: "Jean Bodin et son temps," chap. IX, pp. 296–302, Paris, 1853.

BOAS, FRANZ: "Eskimo of Baffin Land and Hudson Bay," Bull. American Museum of Natural History, vol. IV, New York, 1901.

BRYCE, JAMES: "The American Commonwealth," vol. I, chap. XXXVI, New York, 1927.

———: "Studies in History and Jurisprudence," Chapter on "Sovereignty," New York, 1901.

BURTON, THEODORE E.: "Modern Political Tendencies," pp. 15–20, Princeton, 1919.

CLEMENS, SAMUEL L.: "A Connecticut Yankee at the Court of King Arthur," chap. XIII, New York, 1925.

CRONKHEITE, LEONARD W.: "American Idealism," Amer. Oxonian, 10: 332–345, 1923.

DICEY, A. V.: "The Relation between Law and Public Opinion in England during the Nineteenth Century," New York, 1908.

ENDLE, SIDNEY: "The Kacharis," London, 1911.

ERSKINE, J. E.: "Journal of a Cruise Among the Islands of the Western Pacific," London, 1853.

FIRTH, RAYMOND: "Primitive Economics of the New Zealand Maori," pp. 117ff. New York, 1929.

FRAZER, JAMES G.: "Belief in Immortality and Worship of the Dead," vol. I, London, 1913.

GALTON, SIR FRANCIS: "Probability, the Foundation of Eugenics," Section on "Influence of Collective Truths upon Individual Conduct," in "Herbert Spencer Lectures, 1904–1914," Lecture III, Oxford, 1917.

HALDANE, VISCOUNT: "Higher Nationality, a Study in Law and Ethics," International Conciliation Leaflet, No. 72.

HERBERT, ANDERON: "The Voluntaryist Creed," In "Herbert Spencer Lectures, 1904–1914," Lecture II, Oxford, 1917.

JOHNSTON, SIR HARRY H.: "British Central Africa," London, 1898.

JUNOD, HENRI A.: "The Life of a South African Tribe," vol. I, London, 1912.

KELLY, EDMOND: "Government or Human Evolution," vol. I, pp. 264–273, New York, 1901.

KIDD, BENJAMIN: "The Science of Power," chap. IX, New York, 1918.

"King (Greek and Roman)", sec. 8, ERE.

"Labour," EB, 14th ed., 1929.

LANE-POOLE, STANLEY: "Cairo," Mediæval Town Series, London, 1892.

LASKI, HAROLD J.: "Authority in the Modern State," New Haven, 1919.

LAUBER, ALMON W.: "Indian Slavery in Colonial Times within the Present Limits of the United States," New York, 1913.

LE BON, GUSTAVE: "Psychology of Peoples," New York, 1898.

LOWELL, A. LAWRENCE: "Public Opinion and Popular Government," New York, 1926.

LOWIE, ROBERT H.: "Societies of the Crow Indians," APAMNH, vol. 21, 1922.

———: "Are We Civilized?" chaps. XV, XVI, New York, 1929.

MACDONALD, "The Damara of South Africa," JAI, vol. 19.

MILLIGAN, ROBERT H.: "Fetish Folk of West Africa," New York, 1912.

NELSON, EDWARD W.: "Eskimo about Behring Strait," 18th Ann. Rept., Bureau of American Ethnology.

"Report of the Cambridge Anthropological Expedition to the Torres Straits," vols. V–VI, Cambridge, 1901.

RITCHIE: "Conception of Sovereignty," in "Annals of American Academy of Political Science," vol. I.

RIVERS, W. H. R.: "The Todas," New York, 1906.

SCHUYLER, ROBERT L.: "History and Public Opinion," Educ. Rev., 1918.

SELIGMANN, C. G.: "Melanesians of British New Guinea," Cambridge, 1910.

SHORTLAND, EDWARD: "Traditions and Superstitions of the New Zealanders," London, 1856.

TREGEAR, EDWARD: "The Maori Race," Wanganui, 1904.

TREMEARNE, ARTHUR J. N.: "The Tailed Headhunters of Nigeria," London, 1912.

TURNER, GEORGE: "Samoa," London, 1884.

TYLOR, EDWARD B.: "Anthropology," chap. XVI, London, 1881.

WALLAS, GRAHAM: "Our Social Heritage," chap. XX, New Haven, 1921.

WALLIS, WILSON D.: "Ethical Aspects of Chilkat Culture," Amer. Jour. Psych., 29: 66–80, 1918.

——: "An Introduction to Sociology," pp. 190–194, New York, 1927.

WEST, WILLIS M.: "The Modern World," sec. 86, Boston, 1924.

WILLIAMS, JOHN M.: "Foundations of Social Science," chaps. I, II, New York, 1920.

WILLOUGHBY, WESTEL W.: "The Nature of the State," chaps. IX–X, pp. 181–275, New York, 1903.

WISSLER, CLARK: "Medicine Bundles of the Blackfoot," APAMNH, vol. 5, 1910.

——: "An Introduction to Social Anthropology," pp. 130–136, New York, 1929.

YOUNG, KIMBALL: "Source Book for Social Psychology," chaps. XXV–XXVII, New York, 1927.

CHAPTER X

Culture Development as Increase in Complexity and as Increase in Power.

BROWNELL, BAKER: "The New Universe," pp. 176–181, New York, 1926.

CARMICHAEL, R. D.: "On the Character of Primitive Human Progress," Sci. Monthly, 12: 54–61, 1921.

CRAWFORD, O. G. S.: "Man and His Past," chap. I, Oxford, 1921.

FERRERO, GUGLIELMO: "Europe's Fatal Hour," chap. VII, New York, 1918.

HUXLEY, JULIAN S.: "Essays of a Biologist," London, 1923.

——: "Progress Shown in Evolution," in MASON, FRANCES (editor), "Creation by Evolution," pp. 327–339, New York, 1928.

KIDD, BENJAMIN: "The Science of Power," New York, 1918.

MACIVER, R. M.: "Community," bk. III, chap. I, London, 1920.

MARVIN, FRANCIS S., "Recent Developments in European Thought," pp. 86–92, New York, 1920.

MORGAN, C. LLOYD: "Mind in Evolution," in MASON, FRANCES (editor), "Creation by Evolution," pp. 340–354, New York, 1928.

PITKIN, WALTER B.: "The New Testament of Science," Century Mag., p. 114, 1927.

RITCHIE, DAVID G.: "Natural Rights," chap. V, pp. 111–114, 3rd ed., London, 1916.

RUSSELL, BERTRAND: "Icarus, or the Future of Science," New York, 1925.

SLOSSON, EDWIN E.: "Creative Chemistry," chap. I, New York, 1921.

SPENCER, HERBERT: "The Data of Ethics," New York, 1890.

WEBER, LOUIS: "Le rhythme du progrès," chap. II, pp. 27–53, Paris, 1913.

Development and Progress

ADAMS, HENRY: "The Education of Henry Adams," chaps. XXXIV, XXXV, Boston, 1918.

ALEXANDER, H. B.: "Justice and Progress," Jour. Phil., Psych. and Sci. Method, 12: 207–212, 1915.

ARRHENIUS, S.: "The Life of the Universe," "Preface," New York, 1909.

"Asia" (History), EB.

BERGSON, HENRI L.: "Creative Evolution," New York, 1911.

BOODIN, J. E.: "The Unity of Civilization," Internat. Jour. Ethics, 1920.

BRIFFAULT, ROBERT: "The Making of Humanity," pt. I, chap. V; pt. II, chap. II, London, 1919.

BUCKLE, HENRY T.: "History of Civilization in England," chaps. I–IV, New York, 1913.

BUTLER, SAMUEL: "Alps and Sanctuaries," chap. V, London, 1920.

CARPENTER, EDWARD: "Civilisation: Its Cause and Cure," chapter on "Exfoliation," New York, 1921.

CONKLIN, EDWIN G.: "The Direction of Human Evolution," pp. 69–99, New York, 1921.

————: "The Rate of Evolution," *Sci. Monthly*, **10**: 600–602.

COOLEY, CHARLES H.: "Social Process," chap. III, New York, 1922.

DEALEY, JAMES Q.: "The Development of the State," chap. XV, New York, 1909.

DELBERT, PHILIP: "Social Evolution," London, 1891.

DOW, GROVE S.: "An Introduction to Principles of Sociology," chap. XI, Waco, 1919.

ELY, RICHARD T.: "Studies in the Evolution of Industrial Society," chaps. IV–VI, New York, 1903.

FISKE, JOHN: "Outlines of Cosmic Philosophy," pt. II, chap. XXI, Boston, 1903.

FORD, HENRY J.: "The Natural History of the State," Princeton, 1915.

GALTON, FRANCIS: "Hereditary Genius," pp. 337–348, London, 1914.

GETTELL, RAYMOND G.: "Problems in Political Evolution," chap. II, pp. 41–43, Boston, 1914.

HIBBEN, J. G.: "A Defense of Prejudice and Other Essays," chap. VIII, New York, 1911.

KELLY, EDMOND: "Evolution and Effort," chaps. III, V, XIV, New York, 1898.

KIDD, BENJAMIN: "Individualism, and After," "Herbert Spencer Lectures, 1904–1914," Oxford, 1917.

McCABE, JOSEPH, "The Evolution of Civilization," New York, 1922.

McDOUGALL, WILLIAM: "Is America Safe for Democracy?" chap. I, New York, 1921.

McGEE: "The Trend of Human Progress," AA, vol. I, 1899.

MARVIN, FRANCIS S.: "The Century of Hope," Oxford, 1919.

————: "Recent Developments in European Thought," chap. XII, pp. 293–306, New York, 1920.

MÜLLER-LYER, F.: "History of Social Development," New York, 1921.

OGBURN, WILLIAM F.: "Social Change," pt. II, pp. 61–79, 103–108; pt. III, pp. 146–196, New York, 1922.

PARMELEE, MAURICE F.: "Poverty and Social Progress, chap. XXX, pp. 449–455, New York, 1916.

PARSONS, FRANK: "Legal Doctrine and Social Progress," chaps. VI–VII, X–XI, New York, 1911.

PETRIE, WILLIAM FLINDERS: "Revolutions of Civilization," chap. VII, New York, 1912.

RITTER, WILLIAM E.: "War, Science and Civilization," chaps. II–IV, Boston, 1915.

RIVERS, W. H. R.: "The Contact of Peoples," in "Essays and Studies Presented to William Ridgeway," Cambridge, 1913.

————: "History of Melanesian Society," Cambridge, 1914.

————: "Presidential Address," *Folk-Lore*, 1921.

ROSS, EDWARD A.: "Ossification," *Amer. Jour. Sociol.*, vol. 25, 1920.

————: "Principles of Sociology," p. 25 and chap. XLVI, New York, 1920.

SHELDON, W. H.: "The Defect of Current Democracy," *Jour. Phil., Psych. and Sci. Method*, vol. 16, 1919.

SIKES, E. E.: "The Anthropology of the Greeks," chap. II, London, 1914.

SMITH, WILLIAM C.: "Acculturation," *Jour. Appl. Sociol.*, **7**: 175–186.

SPENCER, HERBERT: "Principles of Sociology," vol. I, chaps. I–IV, 3rd ed., New York, 1914.

TUFTS, JAMES H.: "Our Democracy," New York, 1917.

———: "The Real Business of Living," New York, 1918.

WALLIS, WILSON D.: "Geographical Environment and Culture," *Social Forces*, 4: 702–708, 1926; reprinted in WALLIS, WILSON D., and WILLEY MALCOLM M., "Readings in Sociology," pt. III, New York, 1930.

———: "An Introduction to Anthropology," pp. 101–105, 481, New York, 1926.

———: "An Introduction to Sociology," chap. VIII, New York, 1928.

WEST, WILLIS M.: "The Story of Modern Progress," pp. 1–11, 352–369, chap. XLII, Boston, 1927.

ZIMMERN, ALFRED E.: "Nationality and Government," pp. 331–362, London, 1918.

CHAPTER XI

ADAMS, HENRY: "The Degradation of Democratic Dogma," pp. 140–311, New York, 1920.

ADAMS, JAMES T.: "Diminishing Returns in Modern Life," *Harpers Mag.*, 160: 529–537, 1930.

"Are We Better than Starfish?" Editorial, *The Nation*, 118: 470, 1924.

BAGEHOT, WALTER: "Physics and Politics," New York, 1902.

BATESON, WILLIAM: "Biological Fact and the Structure of Society," in the "Herbert Spencer Lectures, 1905–1914," Oxford, 1917.

BRADLEY, JOHN H.: "The Delusion of Progress," *Sci. Monthly*, 30: 450–457, 1930.

BRIFFAULT, ROBERT: "The Making of Humanity," London, 1919.

BURNS, C. DELISLE: "Common Ideals of Social Reform," in MARVIN, F. S. (editor), "The Unity of Western Civilization," chap. XI, New York, 1922.

CARPENTER, EDWARD: "Pagan and Christian Creeds," App. I, New York, 1920.

CASE, CLARENCE M.: "What is Social Progress?" *Journal of Applied Sociology*, 10: 109–119.

CHASE, STUART: "Are You Alive?" *The Nation*, 115: 68–70, 1922.

CHATTERTON-HILL, GEORGE: "Heredity and Selection in Sociology," pt. II, chap. I, pp. 226–232, London, 1907.

COOLEY, CHARLES H.: "Social Process," chaps. XV–XVII, XXXIV, New York, 1920.

CROZIER, JOHN B.: "Sociology Applied to Practical Politics," bk. II, chap. V, pp. 132–136, New York, 1911.

CROOKER, ORIN: "Civilizations and the Food Supply," *The Nation*, 110: 764, 1920.

CUNNINGHAM, W.: "Christianity and Economic Science," chap. II, London, 1914.

DAWSON, CHRISTOPHER: "Progress and Decay," *Sociol. Rev.*, 16: 1–11.

"Degeneracy and Degeneration," in "New International Encyclopædia."

FOX, R. N.: "The Triumphant Machine: A Study of Machine Civilization," London, 1928.

GILLETTE, JOHN M.: "Sociology," chaps. X–XII, pp. 110–146, Chicago, 1916.

GREG, WILLIAM R.: "Enigmas of Life," Boston, 1880.

HEADLAM, J. W.: "The Unity of Western Education," in MARVIN, F. S. (editor), "Unity of Western Civilization," New York, 1922.

"Hesiod," ERE.

HETHERINGTON, H. J. W., and MUIRHEAD, J. H.: "Social Purpose," chap. IX, pp. 178–205, New York, 1918.

"History as Fiction," *Living Age*, vol. 306, 1920.

HOBHOUSE, LEONARD T.: "Sociology," sec. 2a, ERE.

———: "Social Evolution and Political Theory," chaps. V, VII, New York, 1911.

HOUSTON, P. H.: "The Humanist and Progress," *North Amer. Rev.*, 214: 401–409, 1921.

HUME, DAVID: "Essay on the Populousness of Ancient Nations," in "Essays, Literary, Moral, and Political," chap. 33, London, 1870.

Independent, The, **108**: No. 3816, p. 431, 1922.

KIDD, BENJAMIN: "The Science of Power," chap. V, New York, 1918.

KELSEY, CARL: "Physical Basis of Society", chap. IX, pp. 331–351, New York, 1928.

KIRCHOFF, ALFRED: "Man and Earth," chap. VIII, pp. 221–223, New York, 1914.

LEARY, O. B.: In Internat. Jour. Ethics, **32**: 306–329.

LOWIE, ROBERT H.: "Primitive Society," chap. XIV, New York, 1920.

MACGREGOR, DAVID H.: "The Evolution of Industry," "Home University Library," New York, 1912.

MACIVER, R. M.: "Community," bk. III, chap. II, pp. 200–213, London, 1920.

MADAY, ANDRÉ DE: "Le progrès," Revue Internat. de Sociol., 1913.

MARVIN, FRANCIS S.: "Is the West Christian?" Hibbert Journal, vol. 20, 1922.

MARVIN, FRANCIS S. (editor), "Progress and History," chap. III, New York, 1916.

———: "Recent Developments in European Thought," chap. VII, pp. 181–215, New York, 1920.

MECKLIN, JOHN M.: "An Introduction to Social Ethics," chaps. IV, XIII–XIX, New York, 1920.

MENCKEN, HENRY L.: "Prejudices, Third Series," chap. I, New York, 1922.

MILLS, W. T.: "The Struggle for Existence," Berkeley, 1914.

MITCHELL, ARTHUR: "The Past in the Present," pt. II, Lectures III–IV, New York, 1881.

NASMYTH, GEORGE: "Social Progress and the Darwinian Theory: A Study of Force as a Factor in Human Relations," New York, 1916.

NORDAU, MAX S.: "Degeneration," New York, 1895.

PARODI, D.: "Progrès," in the "Grande Encyclopédie."

PETRIE, W. M. FLINDERS: "The Outlook for Civilization," Yale Review, **11**: 225–241, 1922.

"Production," ERE.

"Risk of Being Alive," Living Age, **304**: 737–739, 1920.

ROBINSON, JAMES HARVEY: "Is Mankind Advancing?" Survey, **26**: 247–252, 1911.

ROSS, EDWARD A.: "Social Decadence," Amer. Jour. Sociol., p. 23, 1918–1919.

———: "Principles of Sociology," chap. XLIII, New York, 1920.

"Savagery," Red Book Mag., January, 1921.

SCHOLZ, RICHARD F.: "Visions and Revisions," Mills Quart., **2**: 49–55, 1921.

SHAW, BERNARD: "The Revolutionist's Handbook," chap. VII–IX (Suppe'-ment to "Man and Superman") Cambridge, 1903.

SMALL, ALBION W.: "Progress," Amer. Jour. Sociol., **28**: 554–573, 1923–24.

SPENCER, HERBERT: "Progress, Its Law and Cause," London, 1874.

SPENGLER, OSWALD: "The Decline of the West," Engl. transl., New York, 1925, 1928.

TAGORE, RABINDRANATH: "Nationalism," London, 1917.

TEGGART, FREDERICK J.: "Prolegomena to History," pt. V, pp. 239–277, Berkeley, 1916.

THOMPSON, DAVID G.: "Social Progress," London, 1889.

THORNDIKE, A. H.: "Literature in a Changing Age," chaps. V, IX, New York, 1920.

TROTTER, W.: "Instincts of the Herd in Peace and War," pp. 13–19, London, 1920.

TYLER, JOHN M.: "The Coming of Man," chap. VII, Boston, 1923.

TYLOR, EDWARD B.: "Anthropology," chap. I, New York, 1881.

TUFTS, JAMES H.: "The Real Business of Living," chap. XXIX, New York, 1918.

VARLEY, HARRY: "The Modern Workman: He Has Lost the Joy of Creative Work," *The Outlook*, May 26, 1920.

WAGNER, CHARLES: "The Simple Life," New York, 1903.

WALLACE, ALFRED R.: "Social Environment and Moral Progress," New York, 1914.

WEST, WILLIS M.: "The Story of Modern Progress," pt. VI, Boston, 1927.

WHITE, ANDREW D.: "A History of the Warfare of Science with Theology in Christendom," vol. I, chaps. VIII–X, New York, 1910.

WHITE, WILLIAM A.: "A Theory of Spiritual Progress," Emporia, 1910.

WRIGHT, HENRY W.: "Faith Justified by Progress," New York, 1916.

———: In *Quart. Jour. Univ. No. Dakota*, **12**: 263–278.

ZIMMERN, ALFRED E.: "The Greek Commonwealth," pt. III, chap. II, pp. 218–225, 2nd ed., Oxford, 1915.

———: "Nationality and Government," New York, 1918.

Theories of Progress

AULT, NORMAN: "Life in Ancient Britain," chaps. XI, XVI, New York, 1920.

BALDWIN, J. MARK: "Social and Ethical Interpretations in Mental Development," chap. XIV, New York, 1902.

BANCROFT, H. H.: "The Necessity, the Reality, and the Promise of Progress of the Human Race," Proc., New York Historical Society, 1854–1855.

———: "Native Races of Pacific States of North America," vol. I, pp. 3–64, London, 1875.

BENTLEY, ARTHUR F.: "Relativity in Man and Society," chap. XXIV, New York, 1926.

BLACKMAR, FRANK W.: "Elements of Sociology," bk. IV, chap. VII, New York, 1905.

———: "The Story of Human Progress," Leavenworth, Kan., 1896.

——— and GILLIN, J. L.: "Outlines of Sociology," pt. IV, chap. VII, New York, 1923.

BOWEN, EZRA: "Progress—by Accident or Plan?" *Sci. Monthly*, **20**: 159–162, 1925.

BRUNHES, B.: "Degradation," Paris, 1908.

BURY, J. B.: "The Idea of Progress; an Inquiry into Its Origin and Growth," London, 1920.

CARLYLE, R. W. and A. J., "A History of Mediæval Political Theory in the West," New York, 1903.

CARRAN, L.: In *Revue des Deux Mondes*, October, 1875.

CLOW, F. R.: "Principles of Sociology," pt. III, New York, 1920.

CONKLIN, E. G.: "Heredity and Environment in the Development of Men," pp. 270–273, 3rd ed., Princeton, 1919.

———: "The Direction of Human Evolution," New York, 1922.

DAVIDSON, WILLIAM L.: "Political Thought in England: The Utilitarians from Bentham to J. S. Mill" ("Home University Library"), New York, n. d.

DAVIES, G. R.: "National Evolution," chap. IV, Chicago, 1919.

———: "Progress and the Constructive Instinct," *Amer. Jour. Sociol.*, **26**: 212–223, 1920.

DEALEY, JAMES: "Eudemics, the Science of National or General Welfare," *Publ. of American Sociological Society*, **15**: 1–15, 1921.

DELVAILLE, JULES: "Histoire de l'idée du progrès," Paris, 1910.

DEWEY, JOHN: "Reconstruction in Philosophy," chap. VII, New York, 1920.

DOLE, CHARLES F.: "The Ethics of Progress, or the Theory and the Practice by Which Civilization Proceeds," New York, 1909.

DOW, GROVE S.: "Introduction to Principles of Sociology," chap. XXV, Waco, Texas, 1920.

DRESSER, HORATIO: "Psychology in Theory and Application," chap. XXXV, New York, 1924.

DUNNING, W. A.: "A History of Political Theories from Rousseau to Spencer," pp. 106–110, New York, 1926.

DURANT, WILL: "Is Progress a Delusion?" *Harper's Mag.*, **153**: 742–751, 1926.

EMERSON, RALPH W.: "Progress of Culture," in "Letters and Social Aims," Boston, 1903.

EDMAN, IRWIN: "Human Traits," pp. 407–410, New York, 1920.

GAULT, ROBERT H.: "Social Psychology," chap. IX, New York, 1923.

GIDDINGS, FRANKLIN H.: "Elements of Sociology," chaps. XXIII, XXV, New York, 1898.

GODDARD, E. A., and GIBBONS, P. A.: "Civilization or Civilizations," New York, 1926.

GOOCH, G. P.: "Political Thought in England from Bacon to Halifax," London, 1915.

GUMPLOWICZ, LUDWIG: "Outlines of Sociology," pt. V, Philadelphia, 1899.

————: "Rassenkampf," Innsbruck, 1909.

GUTHRIE, WILLIAM B.: "Socialism before the French Revolution; A History," New York, 1907.

HARRISON, FREDERICK: "Order and Progress," London, 1875.

HENRY, C. S.: "Social Welfare and Human Progress," New York, 1861.

HERTZLER, JOYCE O.: "Social Progress," New York, 1928.

HIBBEN, JOHN G.: "A Defence of Prejudice," chap. II, New York, 1911.

HOBHOUSE, LEONARD T., WHEELER, and GINSBERG: "Material Culture and Social Institutions of the Simpler Peoples," chaps. I–II, London, 1915.

INGE, W. R.: "The Idea of Progress," Romanes lecture, Oxford, 1920.

JAVARY, L. AUGUSTE: "De l'idée du progrès," Paris, 1851.

KELSEY, CARL: "Physical Basis of Society," chap. XI, 2nd ed., New York, 1928.

LANGDON-DAVIES, JOHN: "The New Age of Faith," New York, 1925.

LANKESTER, E. RAY: "The Kingdom of Man," chap. I, New York, 1911.

LEROUX, PIERRE: "Doctrine de la perfectabilité et du progrès continu," Paris, 1850.

MACKENZIE, JOHN S.: "Outline of Social Philosophy," pp. 241–258, New York, 1918.

McDOUGALL, WILLIAM: "The Group Mind," chaps. XIX–XX, Cambridge, 1927.

MECKLIN, JOHN M.: "Introduction to Social Ethics," chap. XI, New York, 1920.

MERRIAM, JOHN C.: "Earth Sciences as the Background of History," *Sci. Monthly*, **12**: 7–17, 1921.

MILL, JOHN STUART: "Considerations on Representative Government," chap. II, New York, 1905.

MITCHELL, ARTHUR: "The Past in the Present," pt. II, New York, 1881.

MITCHELL, WESLEY C.: "Statistics and Government," *Quart. Publ., Amer. Statist. Assoc.*, **16**: 228–232, 1918.

MOUGEOLLE, PAUL: "Les problems de l'histoire," pp. 71–96, Paris, 1886.

MUZZEY, D. S.: "Mr. Wells' Utopian Pessimism," *Polit. Sci. Quart.*, **26**: 298–303, 1921.

"Population and Progress," *Edin. Rev.*, vol. 232, 1920.

ROBERTSON, JOHN M.: "Buckle and His Critics: A Study in Sociology," chap. IX, London, 1895.

RUSKIN, JOHN: "Political Economy of Art," New York, 1878.

RUSKIN, "Unto This Last," New York, 1901.

SABATIER, L. AUGUSTE: "Outlines of a Philosophy of Religion based on Psychology and History," New York, 1902.

SARGERET: "La guerre et le progrès," Paris, 1917.

SCHNEIDER, HERBERT W.: "Science and Social Progress: A Philosophical Introduction to Moral Science," Lancaster, 1920.

SIMONDS, J. P.: "Progress," *Sci. Monthly*, **24**: 537–547, 1927.

SMALLWOOD, W. M.: "Man the Animal," chap. XI, New York, 1922.

SOREL, GEORGES: "Les illusions du progrès," 2nd ed., Paris, 1911.

TOY, CRAWFORD H.: "Judaism and Christianity," "Introduction," pp. 1–46, Boston, 1892.

TYLER, JOHN M.: "The New Stone Age in Northern Europe," chap. XI, New York, 1921.

VICO, GIOVANNI B.: "La science nouvelle," Paris, 1844.

WARD, HARRY F.: "New Social Order," chaps. V, XII, New York, 1919.

WARNE, FRANK J.: "The Tide of Immigration," chap. XII, New York, 1916.

WEEKS, ARLAND D.: "Psychology of Citizenship," chap. VII, Chicago, 1917.

WELLS, HERBERT G.: "Outline of History," vol. II, pp. 572–575, New York, 1920.

"What Is Progress?" *Living Age*, **306**: 222–227, 1920.

WHITE, WILLIAM C., and HEATH, L. M.: "A New Basis for Social Progress," Boston, 1917.

ZIMMERN, ALFRED E.: "Nationality and Government," chaps. VII–VIII, London, 1918.

CHAPTER XII

"Ages of the World," ERE.

BARING-GOULD, S.: "Legends of the Patriarchs and Prophets and Other Old Testament Characters from Various Sources," chap. IV, New York, n. d.

BEER, MAX: "Social Struggles in Antiquity," chap. I, Boston, n. d.

BÖKLEN, E.: "Adam und Quain im Lichte der vergleichenden Mythenforschung," *Mythologische Bibliothek*, vol. I, Hefte 2–3, Leipzig, 1907.

DELVAILLE, JULES: "Essai sur l'histoire de l'idée du progrès jusqu'à la fin du xviiie siècle," chap. I, Paris, 1910.

FLIGHT, JOHN W.: "The Nomadic Idea and Ideal in the Old Testament," *Jour. Bibl. Liter.*, **42**: 158–226, 1923.

FLINT, ROBERT: "History of the Philosophy of History," pp. 87–90, Edinburgh, 1893.

FRAZER, SIR JAMES G.: "Folk-Lore in the Old Testament," vol. I, New York, 1923.

HERTZLER, JACOB O.: "The History of Utopian Thought," chaps. I, II, New York, 1923.

HSU, LEONARD S.: "The Confucian Concept of Progress," *Chinese Soc. and Polit. Sci. Rev.*, **10**: 582–599, 1926.

LAIDLER, HARRY W.: "A History of Socialist Thought," chap. I, New York, 1927.

LENORMANT, F.: "Les origines de l'histoire," Paris, 1880.

MASSINGHAM, H. J.: "The Golden Age," chap. II, New York, 1928.

McCOWN, CHESTER C.: "The Genesis of the Social Gospel," chaps. V–VII, New York, 1929.

McFAYDEN, JOHN E.: "Civilization Criticised at the Source: A Study of Genesis, I–XI," *Hibbert Jour.*, **19**: 702–711, 1921.

ROTH, R.: Über den Mythus von den fünf Menschengeschlechtern bei Hesiod und die indische Lehre von den vier Weltaltern (Thesis), Tübingen, 1860.

"Schlaraffia Politica. Geschichte der Dichtungen vom besten Staate," pp. 1–8, 29–32, Leipzig, 1892 (anonymous).

SCHWALLY, FRIEDRICH: "*Die biblischen Schöpfungsberichte,*" *Archiv f. Religionswiss.*, **9**: 171*ff*., 1906.

SUZUKI, DAISETZ: *A Brief History of Early Chinese Philosophy*, 2nd ed., London, 1914.

TAYLOR, HENRY O.: "Freedom of the Mind in History," chap. III, London, 1923.

WALLIS, WILSON D.: "Messiahs: Christian and Pagan," chap. I, Boston, 1918.

———: "An Introduction to Sociology," pp. 48–49, 203–204, New York, 1928.

WILLIAMS, EDWARD T.: "Chinese Political Thought," New York, 1927.

WU, Y. C. L.: "The Social Thought of Confucius," *Chinese Soc. and Polit. Sci. Rev.*, **12**: 294–309, 1928.

YETTS, W. PERCIVAL: "The Chinese Isles of the Blest," *Folklore*, **30**: 35–62, 1919.

CHAPTER XIII

ARISTOTLE: "Politics."

BARKER, ERNEST: "Greek Political Philosophy: Plato and His Predecessors," London, 1918.

BASSETT, E. O.: "Plato's Theory of Social Progress," *Internat. Jour. Ethics*, **38**: 467–477, 1928.

BEER, MAX: "Social Struggles in Antiquity," chaps. II–IV, Boston, n. d.

BURNS, C. DELISLE: "Political Ideals: Their Nature and Development," chap. II, Oxford, 1915.

COPELAND, EDITH A.: "The Institutional Setting of Plato's 'Republic,' " *Internat. Jour. Ethics*, **34**: 228–242, 1923–1924.

DELVAILLE, JULES: "Essai sur l'histoire de l'idée du progrès jusqu'à la fin du xviiie siècle," chaps. II, III, Paris, 1910.

FLINT, ROBERT: "History of the Philosophy of History," pp. 89–92, 136–150, Edinburgh, 1893.

HAYS, HEBER M.: "Notes on the Works and Days of Hesiod," Chicago, 1918.

"Hesiod," ERE.

HESIOD: "Works and Days."

LAIDLER, HARRY W.: "A History of Socialist Thought," chap. II, New York, 1927.

LICHTENBERGER, JAMES P.: "Development of Social Theory," chaps. I, II, New York, 1923.

MAIR, A. W.: "Hesiod: The Poems and Fragments Done into English Prose with Introduction and Appendices," Oxford, 1908.

MEYER, EDUARD: "Theopomps Hellenika mit einer Beilage über die Rede an die Larisæer und die Verfassung Thessaliens," Halle, 1909.

PERRY, W. J.: "The Isles of the Blest," *Folklore*, **32**: 150–180, 1921.

PLATO: "The Republic," New York, 1904.

———: "The Laws," New York, 1921.

PLUTARCH: "Lives" ("Lycurgus"), London, 1910.

SALIN, EDGAR: "Platon und die griechische Utopie," München und Leipzig, 1921.

———: "Civitas Dei," pp. 1–10, Tübingen, 1926.

"Schlaraffia Politica. Geschichte der Dichtungen vom besten Staate," pp. 7–19, Leipzig, 1892 (anonymous).

SWAIN, JOSEPH W.: "The Hellenic Origins of Christian Asceticism," New York, 1916.

TAYLOR, HENRY O.: "Freedom of the Mind in History," pp. 102–117, London, 1923.

VOIGT, ANDREAS: "Die sozialen Utopien," chap. II, Leipzig, 1906.

WALLIS, WILSON D.: "An Introduction to Sociology," chap. V, New York, 1928.

WATSON, JOHN: "The State in Peace and War," chaps. I, II, Glasgow, 1919.

ZELLER, E.: "A History of Greek Philosophy," Engl. transl., London, 1881.

———: "Outlines of the History of Greek Philosophy," Engl. transl., London, 1905.

CHAPTER XIV

ADAMS, JAMES: "The Vitality of Platonism and Other Essays," pp. 104–189, Cambridge, 1911.

"Ages of the World" (Greek and Roman), ERE.

ARNOLD, E. V.: "Roman Stoicism," Cambridge, 1911.

AURELIUS, MARCUS: "To Himself," London, 1915.

BEER, MAX: "Social Struggles in Antiquity," chap. VI, Boston, n. d.

BEVAN, EDWYN: "Stoics and Sceptics," Oxford, 1913.

BURNS, C. DELISLE: "Political Ideals; Their Nature and Development," chaps. III, IV, Oxford, 1915.

CASE, SHIRLEY J.: "The Evolution of Early Christianity," chaps. III, VIII, Chicago, 1914.

CROISET, MAURICE: "Hellenic Civilization," pp. 224–234, New York, 1925.

DAVIDSON, WILLIAM L.: "The Stoic Creed," Edinburgh, 1907.

DAVIS, CHARLES H. S.: "Greek and Roman Stoicism and Some of Its Disciples: Epictetus, Seneca and Marcus Aurelius," Boston, 1903.

DELVAILLE, JULES: "Essai sur l'histoire de l'idée du progrès jusqu'à la fin du xviiie siècle," chaps. IV, V, Paris, 1910.

DIODORUS SICULUS: Bk. II, chap. IV, Engl. transl. by G. Booth, London, 1814.

EPICTETUS: "Discourses," London, 1915.

FARRAR, F. W.: "Seekers after God," London, 1884.

FLINT, ROBERT: "History of the Philosophy of History," pp. 92–96, 109–123, Edinburgh, 1893.

GRENFELL, B. P., and HUNT, A. S.: "Hellenica Oxyrhynchia, cum Theompompi et Cratippi Fragmentis," Oxford, 1909.

HALLIDAY, W. R.: "The Pagan Background of Early Christianity," chaps. IV, V, Liverpool, 1925.

HOLBACH, PAUL H. T.: "Système social, ou principes naturels de la morale et de la politique," vol. I, chap. VIII, Londres, 1774.

LAIDLER, HARRY W.: "A History of Socialist Thought," chap. III, New York, 1927.

LICHTENBERGER, JAMES P.: "Development of Social Theory," chap. III, New York, 1923.

LUCRETIUS: "On the Nature of Things," bk. V, New York, 1916.

MEYER, EDUARD: "Theopomps Hellenika mit einer Beilage über die Rede an die Lariser und die Verfassung Thessaliens, Halle, 1909.

MURRAY, SIR GILBERT: "Tradition and Progress," chap. IV, New York, 1922.

OVID: "Metamorphoses," lines 89–124.

PATRICK, MARY M.: "The Greek Sceptics," New York, 1929.

ROHDE: "Der griechische Roman und seine Vorläufer," Leipzig, 1914.

SALIN, EDGAR: "Platon und die griechische Utopie," pp. 181–265, München und Leipzig, 1921.

"Schlaraffia Politica. Geschichte der Dichtungen vom besten Staate," pp. 20–29, Leipzig, 1892 (anonymous).

SCHWARTZ, E.: "Fünf Vorträge über den griechischen Roman," Berlin, 1896.

SWAIN, JOSEPH W.: "The Hellenistic Origins of Christian Asceticism," chaps. IV–VI, New York, 1916.

TAYLOR, HENRY O.: "Freedom of the Mind in History," pp. 63–73, London, 1923.

———: "Ancient Ideals," vol. I, pp. 371–385, New York, 1900.

WALLIS, WILSON D.: "An Introduction to Sociology," chap. V, New York, 1928.

WATSON, JOHN: "The State in Peace and War," pp. 53-63, Glasgow, 1919.

WENLEY, R. M.: "Stoicism and Its Influence," Boston, 1924.

CHAPTER XV

ALLEN, P. S. and H. M. (editors): "Sir Thomas More. Selections from His English Works and from the Lives by Erasmus and Roper," Oxford, 1924.

BAXTER, RICHARD: "A Holy Commonwealth," London, 1659.

BEER, MAX: "Social Struggles in Antiquity," pp. 45-50 and chap. VII, Boston, n. d.

BEGLEY, WALTER: "Nova Solyma the Ideal City, or Jerusalem Regained. An Anonymous Romance Written in the Time of Charles I. Now First Drawn from Obscurity, and Attributed to the Illustrious John Milton," London, 1902.

BELLERS, JOHN: "Proposals for Raising A Colledge of Industry of All Useful Trades and Husbandry with Profit for the Rich, A Plentiful Living for the Poor, and A Good Education for Youth," London, 1696.

———: "Essays about the Poor, Manufacturers, etc.," London, 1699.

———: "Essays for the Employing the Poor to Profit," London, 1723.

The Bible, the New Testament, especially Acts, II, IV-V.

BOGARDUS, EMORY S.: "A History of Social Thought," 2nd ed., Los Angeles, 1928.

BRANDT, L.: "Pierre Dubois, Who Dreamed of a League of Nations 600 Years Ago," *Survey*, **41**: 121, 1918.

BRIFFAULT, ROBERT: "The Mothers: A Study of the Origins of Sentiments and Institutions," vol. III, pp. 360-375, London, 1927.

CLARK, WILLIAM: "Savonarola: His Life and Times," Chicago, 1891.

DELVAILLE, JULES: L'histoire de l'idée du progrès jusqu'à la fin du xviiie siècle," chap. VI, Paris, 1910.

DE WULF, MAURICE: "Philosophy and Civilization in the Middle Ages," chap. XII, Princeton, 1922.

DUFF: "Spinoza's Political and Ethical Philosophy," Glasgow, 1903.

"Essenes," ERE.

FIGGIS, JOHN N.: "Political Aspects of St. Augustine's 'City of God,' " London, 1921.

FISHER, GEORGE P.: "The Beginnings of Christianity," New York, 1891.

FLINT, ROBERT: "History of the Philosophy of History," pp. 96-234, Edinburgh, 1893.

GIBBINS, H. DE B.: "English Social Reformers," 2nd ed., London, 1902.

GOOCH, G. P.: "The History of English Democratic Ideas in the Seventeenth Century," Cambridge, 1898.

GOTHEIN, EBERHARD: "Reformation und Gegenreformation," pp. 209-274, München und Leipzig, 1924. (Vol. II of "Schriften zur Kulturgeschichte der Renaissance, Reformation und Gegenreformation," herausgegeben von Edgar Salin.)

HANSLER, GEORGE C.: "The Theories of Pierre Dubois as Expressed in His Writings, Especially in 'De Recuperatione Terre Sancte' " (A. M. thesis, University of Minnesota, 1925).

HEARNSHAW, FOSSEY J. C. (editor): "The Social and Political Ideas of Some Great Thinkers of the Sixteenth and Seventeenth Centuries," London, 1926.

———: "The Social and Political Ideas of Some Great Mediæval Thinkers," London, 1926.

HERAUD, J. A.: "The Life and Times of Girolamo Savonarola: Illustrating the Progress of the Reformation in Italy during the Fifteenth Century," London, 1843.

HERTZLER, JOYCE O.: "The History of Utopian Thought," New York, 1923.

HOOKE, S. H.: "Christianity in the Making," London, 1926.

HORSBURGH, E. L. S.: "Girolamo Savonarola," London, 4th ed., 1911.

HUMPHREY, EDWARD F.: "Politics and Religion in the Days of Augustine," New York, 1912.

KAUTSKY, KARL: "The Position of 'Utopia' in Socialist History," Social. Rev., 26: 208–217, 1925–1926.

——: "Thomas More and His Utopia; with a Historical Introduction," Engl. transl., London, 1927.

——: "Vorläufer des neueren Sozialismus."

KENT, CHARLES F.: "The Work and Teachings of the Apostles," New York, 1916.

LAIDLER, HARRY W.: "A History of Socialist Thought," chaps. III–VII, New York, 1927.

LANGDON-DAVIES, JOHN: "A Short History of Women," chap. IV, New York, 1927.

LANGLAND, WILLIAM: "The Vision of William Concerning Piers the Plowman," edited by WALTER A. SKEAT, 10th ed., Oxford, 1924.

LANGLOIS: "De Recuperatione Terre Sancte. Traité de politique générale par Pierre Dubois," Paris, 1891.

LEGGE, F.: "Forerunners and Rivals of Christianity, Being Studies in Religious History from 330 B.C. to 330 A.D.," Cambridge, 1915.

LIGHTLEY, J. W.: "Jewish Sects and Parties in the Time of Jesus," London, 1925.

LIPPMANN, WALTER: "A Preface to Morals," pp. 205–210, New York, 1929.

LUCAS, HERBERT: "Fra Girolamo Savonarola: A Biographical Study Based on Contemporary Documents," London, 1899.

MATTHAEI, OTTO: "Konrad von Megenberg's Deutsche Sphaera," Berlin, 1912. (Vol. 23 of "Deutsche Texte des Mittelalters," herausgegeben von der K. Preussischen Akad. der Wissenschaften.) Contains an account of De Bosco (Pierre Dubois).

McCABE, JOSEPH: "St. Augustine and His Age," New York, 1903.

McCOWN, CHESTER C.: "Genesis of the Social Gospel," New York, 1929.

MORE, SIR THOMAS: "Utopia," New York, 1891.

MUMFORD, LEWIS: "The Story of Utopias," New York, 1922.

RENAN, E.: Études sur la politique réligieuse," Paris, 1899. (Contains an account of Pierre Dubois.)

SALIN, EDGAR: "Civitas Dei," Tübingen, 1926.

"Schlaraffia Politica. Geschichte der Dichtungen vom besten Staate," pp. 33–210, Leipzig, 1892 (anonymous).

SIHLER, ERNEST G.: "From Augustus to Augustine," Cambridge, 1923.

SPINOZA, BENEDICT: "Tractatus Theologico-Politicus," London, 1862.

——: "Tractatus Politicus," The Hague, 1882.

VEDDER, HENRY C.: "Socialism and the Ethics of Jesus," New York, 1912.

VOIGT, ANDREAS: "Die sozialen Utopien," chap. III, Leipzig, 1906.

VOLTAIRE: "Le siècle de Louis XIV, chap. XXXII, New York, 1852.

WALLIS, WILSON D.: "An Introduction to Sociology," chap. VI, New York, 1928.

WARD, C. OSBORNE: "The Ancient Lowly," chap. XXIII, Chicago, n. d.

WATSON, JOHN: "The State in Peace and War," pp. 76–79, 92–102, Glasgow, 1919.

WINGFIELD-STRATFORD, ESMÉ: "The History of British Civilization," vol. I, pp. 260–265, London, 1928.

WINSTANLEY, GERRARD: "Law of Freedom in a Platform, or True Magistracy Restored," London, 1652.

Utopias

ANDREÆ, JOHN VALENTINE: "Republicæ Christianopolitanæ Descriptio," 1619.

"Les Aventures de Jacques Sadeur," 1692, Engl. transl., London, 1693.

BACON, SIR FRANCIS: "New Atlantis," London, 1617 or 1623.

BARCLAY, J.: "Argenis," Paris, 1621.

BERGERAC, S. DE CYRANO: "Histoire de la lune," 1656.

BERNARD, RICHARD: "Isle of Man, or The Legal Proceeding in Man-shire Against Sin," 1627.

BIDERMANNUS, JAC. S. J.: "Utopia," 1640.

BISSEL, J.: "Icaria," 1637.

BUNYAN, JOHN: "Pilgrim's Progress," 1678.

CAMPANELLA, TOMASSO: "La Citta del Sole," Lugano, 1836.

"La Citta Felice," 1553.

ERYTHRÆUS, J. N.: "Eudemia," 1637.

FÉNELON, "Telemachus," 1698.

GRIMMELSHAUSEN: "Simplicissimus," 1671.

HALL, JOSEPH: "Mundus Alter et Idem," 1607.

HAPPEL, WERNER: "Der insularische Mandovelt," 1682.

———: "Der wohleingerichtete Staat Ophir," Leipzig, 1699.

HARRINGTON, JAMES: "Oceana," 1656.

HARTLIB: "Kingdom of Macaria," 1641.

HOLBERG, LUDWIG: "Niels Klims Wallfahrt in die Unterwelt," Boston, 1889.

INGELO: "Bentivolia and Urania," 1660.

"Man in the Moon, The," 1638.

MARANDE, LEONARD DE: "Ariades," Venice and Paris, 1629.

POMBAL, EMANUEL: "Relacão Abbreviado da Republica de los Jesuitas," 1757.

"Rélation du Pays de Jansenie," 1660, Engl. transl., 1668.

SADEUR, NICHOLAS: "La Terre Australe," 1676.

SADLER, JOHN: "Olbia, the New Island," 1660.

STIBLIN, CASPAR: "Commentariolus de Eudæmonensium Republica," 1555.

VAIRASSE: "Histoire des severambes," Paris, 1677.

CHAPTER XVI

ALBIER, RAOUL: "The Mind of the Savage," chap. I, New York, n. d.

ATKINSON, GEOFFROY: "Les rélations des voyages du xviiie siècle et l'évolution des idées," chaps. IX, X, Paris, n. d.

BAUDRILLART, HENRI J. L.: "Jean Bodin et son temps," Paris, 1853.

BEARD, CHARLES A. and MARY R.: "The Rise of American Civilization," vol. I, pp. 442–456, New York, 1927.

BODIN, JEAN: "Les six livres de la republique," Genève, 1608.

BRUNETIÈRE, FERDINAND: "Études critiques sur l'histoire de la littérature française," 5th ser., pp. 183–250, Paris, 1896.

BURNS, C. DELISLE: "Political Ideals: Their Nature and Development," pp. 156–173, 239–244, Oxford, 1915.

BURY, J. B.: "The Idea of Progress," London, 1920.

CAHEN, LEON: "Condorcet et la Révolution Française," Paris, 1904.

CHASTELLUX, FRANÇOIS J.: "De la félicité publique," Bouillon, 1776.

CHAUVIRE, ROGER: "Jean Bodin, Auteur de la Republique," pp. 304–378, Paris, 1914.

CONDORCET, M. J. A. N. C.: "Historical View of the Progress of the Human Mind," Baltimore, 1802.

———: "Historical View of the Progress of the Human Mind," pt. I, The Sociological Press, Hanover, N. H., 1928.

CROCE, BENEDETTO: "La Filosofia di Giambattista Vico," Bari, 1922.

DAIRE, EUGÈNE: "Œuvres de Turgot," Tome II, Paris, 1844; in "Collection des Principaux Economistes," vol. IV.

DELVAILLE, JULES: "Essai sur l'histoire de l'idée du progrès jusqu'à la fin du xviiie siècle," pp. 99–292, 605–718, Paris, 1910.

DIANNÈYRE: "Esquisse d'un tableau historique des progrès de l'esprit humain. Ouvrage posthume de Condorcet," nouvelle édition, Paris, 1797.

DOUGLAS, DOROTHY W.: "P. J. Proudhon: A Prophet of 1847," *Amer. Jour. Sociol.*, **34**: 781–803, 1929.

DROUET, JOSEPH: "L'Abbé de Saint-Pierre, l'homme et l'œuvre," Paris, 1912.

FÉNELON: "François de Salignac de la Mothe, aventures de Télémaque" (1699), Paris, 1859.

FLINT, ROBERT: "History of the Philosophy of History," pp. 190–350, Edinburgh, 1893.

——: "Vico," Edinburgh, 1884.

DE FONTENELLE: "Nouveaux dialogues des morts," Amsterdam, n. d.

GOTTSCHALK, LOUIS R.: "Communism during the French Revolution, 1789–1793," *Polit. Sci. Quart.*, **40**: 438–450, 1925.

DE GRAFFIGNY, FRANÇOISE D'ISSEN-BOURG: "Lettres d'une Peruvienne. Augmentée de plusieurs lettres et d'une introduction à l'histoire," Paris, 1755.

HODGSON, W. B.: "Turgot: His Life, Times and Opinions," London, 1870.

HOLBACH, PAUL H. T.: "Système social, ou principes naturels de la morale et de la politique, avec un examen de l'influence du gouvernment sur les mœurs," Londres, 1774.

MARTIN, KINGSLEY: "French Liberal Thought in the Eighteenth Century," Boston, 1929.

MICHELET, JULES: "Principes de la philosophie de l'histoire, traduits de 'La Scienza Nuova' de J. B. Vico," Bruxelles, 1855.

MICHIELS, ALFRED: "Histoire des idées littéraires en France au xixe siècle," Paris, 1842.

MORELLY: "Système d'un sage gouvernement," Paris, 1751.

MORIZE, ANDRÉ: "L'Apologie du luxe au xviiie siècle et 'Le Mondain' de Voltaire," Paris, 1909.

MORLEY, JOHN: "Condorcet," London, 1923.

——: "Turgot," London, 1923.

MORNET, D.: "Les sciences de la nature en France au xviiie siècle," pp. 237–246, Paris, 1911.

——: "Le sentiment de la nature en France de J. J. Rousseau à Bernardin de Saint-Pierre," Paris, 1907.

MUMFORD, LEWIS: "The Arts," in BEARD, CHARLES A. (editor), "Whither Mankind," chap. XII, p. 304, New York, 1928.

NEFF, EMERY: "Carlyle and Mill, Mystic and Utilitarian," chaps. III, IV, New York, 1924.

PERRAULT, CHARLES: "Paralelle des anciens et des modernes en ce qui regarde les arts et les sciences. Dialogues. Avec le poème du siècle de Louis le Grand, et une epistre en vers sur le génie," 2nd ed., Paris, 1692.

PLISCHKE, HANS: "Von den Barbaren zu den Primitiven. Die Naturvölker durch die Jahrhunderte," Leipzig, 1926.

RIGAULT, HIPPOLYTE: "Histoire de la querelle des anciens et des modernes," Paris, 1856.

SAINT-PIERRE, JACQUES H. B. DE: "Arcadie," Angers, 1781.

SAINT-PIERRE, L'ABBÉ DE: "Observations sur le progrès continuel de la raison universelle," Rotterdam, 1737.

——: "Projet pour rendre la paix perpetuelle en Europe," Utrecht, 1713.

SAY, LEON: "Turgot," Paris, 1887.

"Schlaraffia Politica. Geschichte der Dichtungen vom Besten Staate," pp. 135–210, Leipzig, 1892 (anonymous).

SIEGLER-PASCAL, S.: "Un contemporain égaré au xviiie siècle. Les projets de l'abbé de Saint-Pierre, 1658–1743," Paris, 1900.

STEPHENS, W. WALKER. "The Life and Writings of Turgot," London, 1895.

"Turgot's Second Sorbonne Discourse of 1750: On the Progress of the Human Mind," The Sociological Press, Hanover, N. H., 1928.

VERON, EUGÈNE: "Du progrès intellectuel dans l'humanité," Paris, 1862.

VILLEGARDELLE: "Code de la nature par Morelly. Reimpression complète augmentée des fragments importants de la Basiliade avec l'analyse raissonée du système social," Paris, 1841.

VOIGT, ANDREAS: "Die sozialen Utopien," chap. IV, Leipzig, 1906.

VOLTAIRE: "Essay on Toleration," New York, 1912.

———: Siècle de Louis XIV," New York, 1852.

WATSON, JOHN: "The State in Peace and War," pp. 104–118, 147–159, Glasgow, 1919.

Utopias

ATKINSON, GEOFFROY: "The Extraordinary Voyage in French Literature before 1700," New York, 1920.

———: "The Extraordinary Voyage in French Literature from 1700 to 1720," Paris, 1922.

———: "Les rélations des voyages du xviie siècle et l'évolution des idées, Contribution à l'étude de la formation de l'esprit du xviiie siècle," Paris, n. d.

BEAURIEU, G. G. DE: "L'élève de la nature," Amsterdam et Lille, 1777.

BEFFROY DE REIGNY: "La constitution de la lune," Paris, 1793.

BEHN, MRS.: "Oronoko, ou le Prince Nègre," Londres et Paris, 1769.

BELLIN, DE LA LIBORLIÈRE: "Voyage de M. Candide Fils au Pays d'Eldorado, vers la fin du dix-huitième siècle," Paris, 1803.

BERINGTON, SIMON: "La republique des philosophes ou histoire des Ajoiens. Ouvrage posthume de Fontenelle," 1768.

BIDERMAN: "Utopia didaci Bemardini seu Jacobi Bidermani,"Dilingæ,1691.

BOISSE, FRANÇOIS: "Le catéchisme du genre humain, que, sous les auspices de la nature et de son véritable auteur, qui me l'ont dicte, je mets sous les yeux et la protection de la Nation Françoise et de l'Europe éclairée, pour l'établissement essentiel et indispensable du véritable ordre moral, et de l'éducation sociale des hommes, dans la connaissance, la pratique, l'amour et l'habitude des principes et des moyens de se rendre et de se conserver heureux, les uns par les autres," Paris, 1789.

BORDELON, L'ABBÉ: "Mital, ou aventures incroyables, et toutefois, et cetera," Paris, 1708.

———: "Gomgam, ou l'homme prodigieux, transporte dans l'air, sur la terre et sous eaux," Paris, 1713.

BOUGEANT, L. P.: "Voyage merveilleux du Prince Fan-Feredin dans la Romancie; contenant plusieurs observations historiques, géographiques, physiques, critiques et morales," Paris, 1738.

BRETONNE, RESTIF DE LA: "The Year 2000."

BRUN, L'ABBÉ: "Le triomphe du nouveau monde; réponses académiques, formant un nouveau système de confédération, fondé sur les bésoins actuels des nations chrétiennes-commerçantes, et adapté à leurs diverses formes de gouvernement," Paris, 1785.

CABET: "Colonie icarienne aux États-Unis d'Amérique. Sa constitution, ses lois, sa situation matérielle et morale après le premier semestre," Paris, 1856.

———: "Voyage en Icarie," Paris, 1848.

CHATEL: Le code de l'humanité ou l'humanité ramenée à la connaissance du vrai Dieu et au véritable socialisme," Paris, 1838.

COYER, L'ABBÉ F. G.: "Chinki, histoire cochinchinoise qui peut servir à d'autres pays," Londres, 1768.

COYER, "Bagatelles morales et disserta-
tions, avec le testament littéraire
de M. l'Abbé Desfontainew,"
Londres et Francfort, 1757.

DELORMEL: La grande période, ou le
retour de l'âge d'ôr," Paris, 1790.

DEL PRATO, L'ABBÉ: "Dissertation sur
la possibilité d'une félicité universelle et durable sur la terre,"
Paris, 1814.

FIELDING: "Julien l'Apostolat, ou voyage
dans l'autre monde; traduit de
Fielding par M. Kauffmann," Amsterdam et Paris, 1788.

FOIGNY, GAB.: "Les avantures de Jacques
Sadeur dans la decouverte et le
voyage de la Terre Australe,"
Paris, 1676.

GARNIER, CHARLES G. T.: "Voyages
imaginaires, songes, visions et romans cabalistiques," 39 vols., Amsterdam et Paris, 1787–89.

"Gouvernement primitif, d'ou sont
deduit les principes de tout
gouvernement tant politique qu'-
hyerarchique," 1789.

GRIVEL: "L'Isle inconnue, ou mémoires
du chevalier des Gastines," Paris,
1783–87.

"Histoire de Camouflet, souverain
potentat de l'empire d'Equivopolis,"
1751.

HOLBERG, LOUIS DE: "Voyage de
Nicolas Klimins dans le monde
souterrain, contenant une nouvelle
théorie de la terre, et l'histoire
d'une cinquième monarchie, inconnue jusqu'à present," Copenhague
et Leipsic, 1753.

LA BEAUMELLE: "Mélanges de morale et
de litérature, publiés par M. Bar,"
Strasbourg, 1754.

LA DEXMERIE, BRICAIRE DE: " La Sibyle
Gauloise ou la France, telle qu'elle
fut, telle qu'elle est, et telle a peu
près qu'elle pourra être," Londres et
Paris, 1775.

———: "L'Isle taciturne et l'isle enjouée
ou voyage du génie Alaciel dans ces
deux isles," Amsterdam, 1759.

"La lune comme elle va, ou anecdotes
interéssantes pour les habitants
des contrées profondes," 1785.

LA PIERRE, J. DE: "Le grand empire de
l'un et l'autre monde, divisé en
trois royaumes, le royaume des
aveugles, des borgnes et des clair-
voyants," Paris, 1630.

LA PORTE, L'ABBÉ J. DE: "Voyage en
l'autre monde, ou nouvelles littéraires de celui-cy," Londres et
Paris, 1752.

LA VICOMTERIE: "Republique sans im-
pot," Paris, 1792.

"Le dernier cri du monstre, vieux conte
indien," 1789.

LEGER, F. P. A.: "John Bull, ou voyage
à l'Île des Chimères," Paris, 1818.

LE GRAVEREND: "Manuscrit tombé de
la lune, ou histoire rapide et légère
du peuple Ornithien," Paris, 1829.

LE MAINGRE DE BOUCICAULT, DON
LOUIS: "Les Amazones revoltées,
roman moderne, en forme de paro-
die sur l'histoire universelle et la
fable," Rotterdam, 1730.

LE MERCIER DE LA RIVIÈRE: "L'heureuse nation, ou rélation du gouvernement des féliciens, peuple
souverainement libre sous l'empire
absolu de ses loix; ouvrage contenant des détails interéssants sur
leurs principales institutions civiles,
réligieuses et politiques," Paris,
1792.

"Le retour de Babouc à Persepolis, ou
la suite du monde comme il va,"
Concordopolis, 1789.

LESCONVEL, P. DE: "Rélation du voyage
du Prince de Montberaud dans
l'Île de Naudely," 1706.

STEHLE, BRUNO· "Fenelon, 'Die Erlebnisse des Telemach,' Übersetzt, mit
einer Einleitung und erläuternden
Anmerkungen versehen," Münster,
1892.

LOUIS, DOM: "Le ciel ouvert à tout
l'univers, 1782.

MANN, W. E.: "Robinson Crusoe en
France," Paris, 1916.

MERCIER: "Year 2440."

MESLIER, J.: "Le bon sens du curé J. Meslier, suivi de son testament," Paris, 1802.

MONTPENSIER, MLLE. DE: "Rélation de l'isle imaginaire," Paris, 1805.

MOREAU, J. N.: "Nouveau memoire pour servir à l'histoire des Cacouacs," Amsterdam, 1757.

MORELLY: "Code de la nature, ou le véritable esprit de les loix, de tous temps negligé ou meconnu," 1755.

VOLNEY: "Ruins."

CHAPTER XVII

BAIN, ALEXANDER: "Mental and Moral Science," pp. 593–598, 2nd ed., London, 1868.

BURKE, EDMUND: "A Vindication of Natural Society: Or, a View of the Miseries and Evils Arising to Mankind from Every Species of Artificial Society. In a Letter to Lord * * * by a Late Noble Writer. 1756," in "The Works of the Right Honourable Edmund Burke," vol. I, London, 1803.

———: "Reflections on the Revolution in France, and on the Proceedings in Certain Societies in London Relative to That Event. In a Letter Intended to Have Been Sent to a Gentleman in Paris. 1790," in BURKE, "Select Works," vol. II, edited by E. J. Payne, Oxford, 1921.

DELBOS, VICTOR: "Les idées de Kant sur la paix perpétuelle," *Nouvelle Revue*, vol. 7, 1899.

DELVAILLE, JULES: "Essai sur l'histoire de l'idée du progrès jusqu'a la fin de xviiie siècle," pp. 99–292, 427–601, Paris, 1910.

"Die glückliche Nation, oder der Staat von Felizien. Ein Muster der vollkommensten Freiheit unter der unbedingten Herrschaft der Gesetze. Aus dem Französischen [?]," Leipzig, 1794.

ERSKINE, THOMAS E.: "Armata," London, 1818.

FERGUSON, ADAM: "An Essay on the History of Civil Society," Edinburgh, 1767.

———: "Institutes of Moral Philosophy," Edinburgh, 1773.

FIELDING, HENRY: "A Journey from This World to the Next," London, 1783. (Published in *Novelist's Mag.*, vol. 12, London, 1787.)

FLINT, ROBERT: "The Philosophy of History in France and Germany," London, 1874.

GIBBON: "Decline and Fall of the Roman Empire," chap. 38, App., New York, 1902.

GOOCH, G. P.: "Germany and the French Revolution," chaps. VI–XII, London, 1920.

HARTLEY, DAVID: "Observations on Man, His Frame, His Duty and His Expectations," 6th ed., London, 1834.

HERDER: "Outlines of a Philosophy of the History of Man," London, 1800.

HUME, DAVID: "Philosophical Works," Edinburgh, 1826.

ISELIN, ISAAK: "Philosophische Mutmassungen über die Geschichte der Menschheit," 1764.

KANT, IMMANUEL: "Anthropologie," Koenigsberg, 1798.

———: "The Idea of a Universal History on a Cosmo-political Plan," transl. by Thomas De Quincey, The Sociological Press, Hanover, N. H., 1927.

KAYE, F. B.: "The Fable of the Bees: Or, Private Vices, Publick Benefits. By Bernard Mandeville, with a Commentary Critical, Historical, and Explanatory," 2 vols., Oxford, 1924.

KIPPENBERG: "Robinsonaden in Deutschland bis zur Insel Felsenburg," Hanover, 1892.

LESSING, GOTTHOLD E.: "The Education of the Human Race," London, 1881.

LOCKITT, C. H.: "The Relations of French and English Society (1763-1793)," London, 1920.

LUNDEN, WALTER A.: "Adam Ferguson," thesis, University of Minnesota, 1930.

MANDEVILLE, BERNARD: "The Grumbling Hive," London, 1714.

———: "The Fable of the Bees," London, 1723.

MILLAR, JOHN: "Observations Concerning the Distinctions of Rank in Society," London, 1771.

PALEY, WILLIAM: "Moral and Political Philosophy," London, 1785.

PRICE, RICHARD: "A Review of the Principal Questions and Difficulties in Morals," London, 1758.

———: "Observations on the Importance of the American Revolution, and the Means of Making It a Benefit to the World," London, 1784.

PRIESTLEY, JOSEPH: "An Essay on the First Principles of Government; and on the Nature of Political, Civil, and Religious Liberty," London, 1768.

———: "Lectures on History and General Policy," Birmingham, 1788.

SCHILLER, J. C. F.: "Letters upon the Æsthetic Education of Man," Boston, 1845.

SMITH, ADAM: "Theory of the Moral Sentiments," London, 1759.

———: "Inquiry into the Nature and Causes of the Wealth of Nations," London, 1776.

———: "Essays on Philosophical Subjects," London, 1795.

SWIFT, JONATHAN: "A Project for the Advancement of Religion and the Reformation of Manners," London, 1801.

TINKER, CHAUNCEY B.: "Nature's Simple Plan. A Phase of Radical Thought in the Mid-Eighteenth Century," Princeton, 1922.

TURNBULL, GEORGE: "The Principles of Moral Philosophy, An Inquiry into the Wise and Good Government of the Moral World," London, 1742. ,

TURNBULL, "Observations upon Liberal Education," London, 1742.

VON HALLER, ALBRECHT: "Fabius und Cato," 1774.

———: "Usong," Carlsruhe, 1778.

———: "Alfred," Bern, 1773.

WILDE, NORMAN: "Mandeville's Place in English Thought," Mind, 23: 219–232, 1898.

CHAPTER XVIII

ALEXANDER, H. B.: "Religion and Progress," Hibbert Jour., 9: 169–187, 1910.

ATKINSON, CHARLES M.: "Life and Works of Jeremy Bentham," London, 1905.

BALFOUR, ARTHUR J.: "Essays and Addresses," pp. 241–332, 3rd ed. Edinburgh, 1905.

BEARD, CHARLES A.: "The Political Heritage of the Twentieth Century," Yale Rev., 18: 456–479, 1929.

BERGSON, HENRI L.: "Creative Evolution," New York, 1911.

BERNARD, L. L.: "The Concept of Progress: The Metaphysical Phase," Social Forces, 3: 617–622, 1924.

———: "The Concept of Progress: The Scientific Phase," ibid., 4: 36–43, 1925.

———: "The Concept of Progress: The Theological Phase," ibid., 3: 207–212, 1924.

———: "The Conditions of Social Progress," Amer. Jour. Sociol., 28: 21–48, 1922–1923.

———: "Invention and Social Progress," ibid., 29: 1–33, 1923–1924.

BLACKMAR, F. W.: "Mutations of Progress," Jour. Appl. Sociol., 9: 83–90.

BONNER, G. H.: "Progress," Nineteenth Century, 97: 10–19, 1925.

BOOTH, A. J.: "Robert Owen, the Founder of Socialism in England, London, 1869.

———: "Saint-Simon and Saint-Simonism: A Chapter in the History of Socialism in France," London, 1871.

BOWDEN, A. O.: "The Meaning of Social Progress," *School and Society*, **22**: 537–542, 1925.

BUTLER, SAMUEL: "Evolution Old and New," New York, 1914.

———: "Life and Habit," London, 1924.

CAILLARD, E. M.: "Progress and the Ideal," *Contemp. Rev.*, **121**: 491–495, 1922.

CARO, E.: "Le progrès social." *Revue des Deux Mondes*, October, 1873, pp. 743–774; November, 1873, pp. 116–149.

CARPENTER, EDWARD: "Art of Creation," London, 1905.

———: "Civilization: Its Cause and Cure," 9th ed., London, 1906.

———: "England's Ideal and Other Papers on Social Subjects," London, 1906.

CASE, CLARENCE M.: "Religion and the Concept of Progress," *Jour. Relig.*, **1**: 160–173, 1921.

———: "What Is Social Progress?" *Jour. Appl. Sociol.*, **10**: 109–119.

CAZAMIAN, LOUIS: "Le Roman social en angleterre (1830–1850)," 2nd ed., Paris, 1904.

CHATTERTON-HILL, GEORGE: "Heredity and Selection in Sociology," London, 1907.

CHESTERTON, GILBERT K.: "Utopia of Usurers and Other Essays," New York, 1917.

CLARK. FREDERICK C.: "A Neglected Socialist," (Wilhelm Weitling), *Ann. Amer. Acad. of Polit. and Soc. Sci.*, **5**: 718–739, 1895.

CLUTTON-BROCK, ARTHUR: "William Morris: His Work and Influence" ("Home University Library"), New York, 1914.

COCKERELL, T. D. A.: "Principles of Human Progress," *Sci. Monthly*, **5**: 61–63, 1917.

COOPER, J. FENIMORE: "The Monikins," especially chap. XXXI, New York, n. d.

COURNOS, JOHN: "Will Culture Survive?" *Yale Rev.*, **17**: 320–332, 1928.

CROSS, WILBUR: "The Mind of H. G Wells," *Yale Rev.*, **16**: 298–315, 1927.

CROZIER, JOHN B.: "Civilization and Progress," 3rd ed., New York, 1892.

DAVIES, G. R.: "Population and Progress," *Sci. Monthly*, **19**: 598–610, 1924.

DAWSON, CHRISTOPHER: "Progress and Religion. An Historical Enquiry," London, 1929.

DICEY, A. V.: "Influence of Opinion upon Law in England in the Nineteenth Century," London, 1914.

DOLE, CHARLES F.: "The Citizen and the Neighbor," Boston, 1884.

———: "The Coming People," New York, 1897.

———: "The Ethics of Progress, or the Theory of the Practice by which Civilization Proceeds," New York, 1909.

DOVE, PATRICK E.: "The Theory of Human Progression," New York, 1910.

DOW, GROVE S.: "Society and Its Problems, chap. 28, New York, 1929.

DRACHSLER, J.: "Racial Diversities and Social Progress," *Nat. Conf. of Soc. Work*, pp. 97–105, 1922.

DUPREEL, E.: "Deux essais sur le progrès," Brussels, 1928.

ELLWOOD, C. A.: "The Educational Theory of Social Progress," *Sci. Monthly*, **5**: 439–450, 1917.

FERRIÈRE, ADOLPHE: "La loi du progrès en biologie et en sociologie et la question de l'organisme social," Paris, 1915.

FITZPATRICK, F. W.: "The Law of Progress," *Open Court*, **36**: 472–480, 1922.

FLINT, ROBERT: "History of the Philosophy of History," pp. 340–706, Edinburgh, 1893.

FLOWER, B. O.: "How England Averted a Revolution of Force. A Survey of the Social Agitation of the First Ten Years of Queen Victoria's Reign," Trenton, 1904.

FOSDICK, H. E.: "Christianity and Progress," New York, 1922.

FOURIER, F. M. CHARLES: "Social Destiny of Man; or, Théorie des Quatres Mouvements," New York, 1859.

——: "Traité de l'association domestique agricole," Paris, 1812.

FREEMAN, R. AUSTIN: "Social Decay and Regeneration," Boston, 1921.

GARRAU, LUDOVICI: "La philosophie de l'histoire et la loi du progrès," Revue des Deux Mondes, pp. 568–586, October, 1875.

GARRETT, GARET: "Ouroboros," New York, 1926.

GIBBINS, H. DE B.: "English Social Reformers," chaps. IV–VI, 2nd ed., London, 1902.

GIDDINGS, F. H.: "The Ethics of Social Progress," Internat. Jour. Ethics, 3: 137–164, 1893.

HALL, CHARLES: "Effects of Civilization on the People in European States," London, 1805.

HARRIS, GEORGE: "Civilization Considered as a Science, London, 1861.

HARRIS, GEORGE: "Inequality and Progress," New York, 1897.

HARRISON, FREDERIC: "The Philosophy of Common Sense," New York, 1907.

HARRISON, MILTON: "Mental Instability as a Factor in Progress," Monist, 32: 189–199, 1922.

HART, HORNELL: "The Technique of Social Progress," New York, 1929.

VON HELMHOLTZ-PHELAN, ANNA A.: "The Social Philosophy of William Morris," Durham, N. Carolina, 1927.

HAYES, EDWARD C.: "La raison et le progrès moral," Revue de l'Inst. de Sociol., 1: 51–81, 1920.

HENKE, F. D.: "A Note on the Relation of Ethics to Progress," Internat. Jour. Ethics, 27: 485–494, 1917.

HENRY, CALEB S.: "Considerations on Some of the Elements and Conditions of Social Welfare and Human Progress," New York, 1861.

HIMES, NORMAN E.: "Robert Dale Owen, the Pioneer of American Neo-Malthusianism," Amer. Jour. Sociol., 35: 529–547, 1930.

HOBHOUSE, LEONARD T.: "Morals in Evolution," vol. I, pp. 33–40; vol. II, pp. 280–284, London, 1908.

HOWARD, C.: "Progress," Atl. Monthly, 105: 120–123.

HUGHES, CHARLES E.: "Conditions of Progress in Democratic Government," New Haven, 1910.

HULL, MARY: "Progress by Telic Guidance," World Unity, July, 1928.

HUXLEY, THOMAS H.: "Evolution and Ethics," New York, 1893.

JENNINGS, HERBERT S.: "Diverse Doctrines of Evolution," Science, 65: 19–25, 1927.

JOAD, C. E. M.: "The Future of Man," Harper's Monthly Mag., 157: 492–500, 1928; reprinted in WALLIS, WILSON D., and WILLEY, MALCOLM M., "Readings in Sociology," New York, 1930.

JORDAN, D. S.: "Democracy and World Relations," Yonkers-on-the-Hudson, 1920.

KELSEY, CARL: "The Physical Basis of Society," chap. XVII, 2nd. ed., New York, 1928.

KRACHT, G. V.: "Social Ideals and Social Progress," Internat. Jour. Ethics, 27: 472–484, 1917.

KROPOTKIN, PRINCE: "Ethics: Origin and Development," New York, 1924.

DE LABORDE, ALEXANDRE (COMTE): "De l'esprit d'association dans tous les interêts de la communauté, ou essai sur le complément du bien-être et de la richesse en France par le complément des institutions," Paris, 1818.

LIBBY, WALTER: "Introduction to Contemporary Civilization," chaps. I, XVIII, XIX, New York, 1929.

LITTLE, ARTHUR D.: "The Handwriting on the Wall," New York, 1928.

McCLELAND, HARDIN T.: "The Meliorability of Man's World," *Open Court*, **42**: 759–768.

McDOUGALL, WILLIAM: "Was Darwin Wrong?" *Forum*, **79**: 244–253, 1928.

MASON, E. S.: "Fourier and Anarchism," *Quart. Jour. Econ.*, **42**: 228–262.

MICHELS, ROBERTO: "Le caractère partiel et contradictoire du progrès," in, *Ann. de l'Inst. Internat. de Sociol.*, **14**: 460, 1913.

MILL, JOHN STUART: "Considerations on Representative Government," chap. II, Oxford, 1924.

———: "On Liberty," New York, 1921.

———: "A System of Logic," New York, 1900.

———: "Utilitarianism," New York, 1910.

MOORE, DAVID: "The Age of Progress; or a Panorama of Time, in Four Visions," New York, 1856.

MORRIS, WILLIAM: "A Dream of John Ball," New York, 1920.

———: "News From Nowhere," New York, 1901.

MURRAY, R. H.: "The Idea of Progress," *Quart. Rev.*, **234**: 100–118, 1920.

NICEFERO, ALFREDO: "Les indices numériques de la civilisation et du progrès, Paris, 1921.

ODUM, HOWARD W.: "Man's Quest for Social Guidance: the Study of Social Problems," chap. XXXII, New York, 1927.

OWEN, ROBERT: "A New View of Society," London, 1812.

———: "Lectures on the Rational System of Society, Derived Solely from Nature and Experience, as Propounded by Robert Owen, versus Socialism. Derived from Misrepresentation, as Explained by the Lord Bishop of Exeter and Others, and versus the Present System of Society, Derived from the Inexperienced and Crude Notions of our Ancestors, as it now Exists in all the Opposing, Artificial, and Most Injurious Divisions in all Civilized Nations, but most Especially in the British Empire and in the United States of North America," London, 1841.

———: "Life of Robert Owen, by Himself," London, 1857.

———: "Millenial Gazette; Explanatory of the Principles and Practices by which, in Peace, with Truth, Honesty, and Simplicity, the new Existence of Man upon the Earth may be Easily and Speedily Commenced," 2nd ed., London, 1857, (No. 11, Aug. 1, 1857).

———: "Observations on the Effect of the Manufacturing System: With Hints for the Improvement of those Parts of it Which are Most Injurious to Health and Morals," 2nd ed., London, 1817.

———: "The Revolution in the Mind and Practice of the Human Race; The Coming Change from Irrationality to Rationality," London, 1849.

PAGE, KIRBY (editor): "Recent Gains in American Civilization," esp. chaps. XII–XV, New York, 1928.

PATTEN, S. N.: "The Measure of Progress," *Ann. Amer. Acad. Polit. and Soc. Sci.*, vol. 44, supplement.

REYBAUD, M. R. LOUIS: "Études sur les reformateurs," Paris, 1864.

ROSENBERRY, M. B.: "Law and Social Progress," *Proc. Nat. Conf. of Soc. Work*, 76–91, 1926.

RUSKIN, JOHN: "The Political Economy of Art," New York, 1888.

———: "Unto This Last," New York, 1901.

SARGANT, WILLIAM L.: "Robert Owen, and his Social Philosophy," London, 1860.

SIMON, HELENE: "Robert Owen, sein Leben und seine Bedeutung für die Gegenwart," Jena, 1925.

SIMONDS, J. P.: "Progress," *Sci. Monthly*, **24**: 537–547, 1927.

SMALL, A. W.: "The Category 'Progress' as a Tool in Social Research," *Amer. Jour. Sociol.* **28**: 554–576, 1922–1923.

SOMERVILLE, BOLLING: "Social Progress and the Good Man," *Internat. Jour. Ethics*, **38**: 416–426, 1928.

SPENCER, HERBERT: "Data of Ethics," New York, 1890.

———: "Illustrations of Universal Progress," New York, 1880.

SPRAGUE, FRANKLIN M.: "The Laws of Social Evolution," Boston, 1895.

STEPHEN, LESLIE: "The English Utilitarians," New York, 1900.

TAYLOR, W. COOKE: "The Natural History of Society, in the Barbarous and Civilized State: An Essay towards Discovering the Origin and Course of Human Improvement," New York, 1841.

URWICK, EDWARD J.: "The Social Good," chaps. IV, V, London, 1927.

———: "The Philosophy of Progress," London, 1912.

WAENTIG, HEINRICH: "August Comte und seine Bedeutung," Leipzig, 1894.

WALLACE, A. R.: "Social Environment and Moral Progress," New York, 1913.

WEISS, ALBERT P.: "The Aims of Social Evolution," *Ohio Jour. Sci.*, **23**: 115–134, 1923.

WELLS, HERBERT G.: "New Worlds for Old," New York, 1908.

———: "Outline of History," New York, 1926.

———: "The Salvaging of Civilization," New York, 1921.

———: "The World of William Clissold," vol. II, bk. V, pp. 547–672, New York, 1926.

WHEELER, WILLIAM M.: "Emergent Evolution and the Development of Societies," New York, 1928.

WILLCOX, W. F.: "A Statistician's Idea of Progress," *Internat. Jour. Ethics*, **32**: 275–298, 1922.

WILLIAMSON, C. C. H.: "Progress," *Internat. Jour. Ethics*, **31**: 394–407, 1920–21.

WILSON, MABEL V.: "Auguste Comte's Conception of Humanity," *Internat. Jour. Ethics*, **38**: 88–102, 1927.

WOODS, E. G.: "Progress as a Sociological Concept," *Amer. Jour. Sociol.*, **12**: 779–821, 1906–07.

WRIGHT, HENRY W.: "Faith Justified by Progress," New York, 1916.

YARROS, VICTOR S.: "Human Progress: The Idea and the Reality," *Amer. Jour. Sociol.* **21**: 15–29, 1915–16.

———: "Is There a Law of Human Progress?" *Internat. Jour. Ethics*, **31**: 146–156, 1920–21.

CHAPTER XIX

ALLEN, HENRY F.: "The Key of Industrial Cooperative Government," St. Louis, 1886.

AMERSIN, F.: "Das Land der Freiheit," Graz, 1874.

ANONYMOUS: "The Beginning," Chicago, 1893.

———: "The Great Analysis," New York, 1913.

———: "Im Reiche der Frauen: Jedem das Seine," Berlin, 1891.

———: "The Legal Revolution of 1902," Chicago, 1898.

AUGUST, B.: "Wie kam es doch? Ein von Eugen Richter vergessenes Kapital," Leipzig, 1892.

BELLAMY, EDWARD: "Equality," Boston, 1897.

———: "Looking Backward," Boston, 1888.

BOUTON, J. BELL: "The Enchanted," New York, 1891.

BROWNE, WALTER: "2894, or the Fossil Man," New York, 1894.

CASWELL, EDWARD A.: "Toil and Self," Chicago, 1900.

CHAPMAN, R. M.: "Vision of the Future," New York, 1916.

CHAVANNES, ALBERT: "The Future Commonwealth," New York, 1892.

CHAVANNES, "In BrighterClimes," Knoxville, Tenn., 1897.

CLEGHORN, SARAH N.: "Utopia Interpreted," Atl. Montbly, 134: 55–67, 1924.

CRAIG, ALEXANDER: "Ionia: Land of Wise Men and Fair Women," Chicago, 1898.

CRAM, R. A.: "Walled Towns," Boston, 1919.

CRIDGE, ALFRED D.: "Utopia: The History of an Extinct Planet," Oakland, Calif., 1884.

CROCKER, SAMUEL: "That Island, by Theordore Oceanic Islet," Kansas City, Mo., 1892.

DILLINGHAM, G. W.: "The Sixteenth Amendment," New York, 1896.

DODD, ANNA B.: "The Republic of the Future, or, Socialism a Reality," New York, 1887.

DONNELLY, HENRY I.: "Cæsar's Column, Sensational Story of the 20th Century," London, 1892.

———: "Atlantis," New York, 1882.

DUDGEON, ROBERT ELLIS: "Colymbia," London, 1873.

EDSON, MILAN C.: "Solaris Farm," Washington, 1900.

ERDMANNSDÖRFFER, H. C.: "Ein Phantasiestaat," Leipzig, 1891.

EVERETT, HENRY LEXINGTON: "The People's Program," New York, 1892.

FERBER, EDNA, "A Few Things Altered or Abolished," The Nation, 126: 609–610, 1928.

FINGER, CHARLES J.: "Utopia—Made to Suit," The Nation, 126: 715–716, 1928.

FISKE, AMOS K.: "Beyond the Bourne," New York, 1891.

FLOWER, BENJAMIN O.: "Equality and Brotherhood," Boston, 1897.

FORBES, ALLYN B.: "The Literary Quest for Utopia, 1800–1900," Social Forces, 6: 179–189, 1927.

FORBUSH, ZEBINA: "The Co-opolitan," Chicago, 1898.

FRANCE, ANATOLE: "The Revolt of the Angels," New York, 1927.

———: "Sur la Pierre Blanche," Sec. V–VI, Paris, n. d.

FULLER, ALVARADO, "A. D. 2000," Chicago, 1891.

GAUIVET, ANGEL: "La Conquista del Reino de Maya por el Ultimo Conquistador Español, Pio Cid." Madrid, 1910.

GREGOROVIUS: "Der Himmel auf Erden," Leipzig, 1892.

GREGORY, O.: "Meccania, the Superstate," London, 1918.

GRIFFIN, CRAWFORD: "Nationalism," Boston, 1889.

GRIGSY, ALCANOAN O.: "Nequa: or the Problem of the Ages," Topeka, Kan. 1900.

HARBEN, WILLIAM N.: "The Land of the Changing Sun," New York, 1894.

HAUPTMANN, GERHARD J. R.: "Die Insel der grossen Mutter, oder, das Wunder von Îles des Dames: Eine Geschichte aus dem utopischen Archipelagus," Berlin, 1924.

HAWTHORNE, NATHANIEL: "The Blithdale Romance," Boston, 1880.

HELM, RUDOLF: "Utopia," Rostock, 1921.

HENRY, W. O. "EQUITANIA," Omaha, 1914.

HERTZKA, THEODOR: "Freeland; a Social Anticipation," London, 1891.

HERTZLER, JOYCE O.: "The History of Utopian Thought," New York, 1922.

HEYWOOD, D. HERBERT: "Twentieth Century," Chicago, 1890.

HOLFORD, CASTELLO N.: "Aristopia," Boston, 1895.

HOWARD, ALBERT W.: "The Miltillionaire," Boston, 1895.

HOWE, FREDERICK C.: "A Political Utopia," The Nation, 127: 178–179, 1928.

HOWELLS, WILLIAM D.: "Through the Eye of the Needle," New York, 1907.

———: "A Traveller from Altruria: Romance," New York, 1908.

JUSTINUS: "In der Zehnmillionenstadt: Berliner Roman A.D. Ende des 20. Jahrhunderts," Dresden, 1890.

KAUFMANN, M.: "Utopias; or, Schemes of Social Improvement from Sir Thomas More to Karl Marx," London, 1879.

KINGSLEY, CHARLES: "Alton Locke," New York, 1910.

LAICUS, PHILIPP: "Etwas Später," Mainz 1891.

LASSWITZSCHEN, KURT: "Bilder aus der Zukunft," Berlin, 1879.

LEWIS, SINCLAIR: "Mr. Lorimer and Me," *The Nation*, **127**: 81, 1928.

LINDELOF, O. J. S.: "Trip to the North Pole, or 'The Discovery of the Ten Tribes,'" Salt Lake City, 1903.

LIPPMANN, WALTER: "A Preface to Morals," chap. VIII, New York, 1929.

LÖWENTHAL, EDUARD: "Der Staat Bellamys und seine Nachfolger," Berlin, 1892.

MASSO, GILDO: "Education in Utopias," in Teachers' College, Columbia University, *Contrib. to Educ.*, No. 257, New York, 1927.

McDOUGALL, WALTER H.: "The Hidden City," New York, 1891.

MEHRING, F.: "Herrn Eugen Richters Bilder aus der Gegenwart," Nürnberg, 1892.

MERRILL, ALBERT ADAMS: "The Great Awakening," Boston, 1899.

MILLER, JOAQUIN: "The Building of the City Beautiful," Trenton, N. J., 1905.

MOORE, M. LOUISE; "Al-Modal," Cameron Point, La., 1892.

MÜLLER, E.: "Aus den Erinnerungen des Mr. Julian West," Berlin, 1891.

"New Britain, a Narrative of a Journey, by Mr. Ellis, to a Country So Called by Its Inhabitants, Discovered in the Vast Plain of the Missouri, in North America, and Inhabited by a People of British Origin, Who Live under an Equitable System of Society, Productive of Peculiar Independence and Happiness, Also, Some Account of Their Constitution, Laws, Institutions, Customs and Philosophical Opinions: Together with a Brief Sketch of Their History from the Time of their Departure from Great Britain," London, 1820 (anonymous).

NISWONGER, CHARLES E.: "The Isle of Feminine," New York, 1894.

OELRICH, HENRY: "A Cityless and Countryless World," Holstein, Ia., 1893.

OST, FRIEDRICH: "Erlebnisse in der Welt Bellamys," Wismar, 1891.

PATAUD, E., and POUGET, E.: "Syndicalism and the Cooperative Commonwealth," Oxford, 1913.

PECK, BRADFORD: "The World a Department Store," Lewiston, Me., 1900.

PERRYCOSTE, FRANKE H.: "Towards Utopia (Being Speculations in Social Evolution). By a Free Lance," New York, 1894.

REEVES and TURNER: "Looking Ahead, Not by the Author of Looking Backward," London, 1892.

REHM, WARREN S.: "The Practical City," Lancaster, Pa., 1898.

RICHTER, EUGEN: "Zukunftsbilder," Berlin, 1891.

ROBERTS, J. W.: "Looking Within," New York, 1893.

ROSEWATER, FRANK: "96, a Romance of Utopia," New York, 1894.

RUSSELL, A. P.: "Sub Cælum: The Skybuilt Human World," Boston, 1893.

SANDERS, GEORGE A.: "Reality," Cleveland, 1898.

SCHINDLER, SOLOMON: "Young West, a Sequel to Edward Bellamy's Celebrated Novel 'Looking Backward,'" Boston, 1894.

"Schlaraffia Politica. Geschichte der Dichtungen vom besten Staate," pp. 195–293, Leipzig, 1892 (anonymous).

SCHUETTE, H. G.: "Athonia, or the Original Four Hundred," Manitowoc, Wis., n. d.

SHAW, BERNARD: "Back to Methuselah," New York, 1921.

SHEPLEY, MRS. MARIE A. B.: "The True Author of Looking Backward," New York, 1890.

SIMPSON, WILLIAM: "The Man from Mars," San Francisco, 1891.

THOMAS, CHAUNCEY: "The Crystal Button," Boston, 1891.

TIBURTIUS: "Bellamy als Lehrer," Berlin, 1892.

TINCKER, MARY A.: "San Salvador," Boston, 1892.

TRUTH, HEINRICH: "Am Ende des Jahrhunderts," Basel, 1891.

VINTON, ARTHUR DUDLEY: "Looking Further Backward," Albany, N. Y., 1890.

WELCOME, S. BRYON: "From Earth's Centre," Chicago, 1894.

WELLS, HERBERT G.: "A Modern Utopia," New York, 1905.

WHEELER, DAVID H.: "Our Industrial Utopia and Its Unhappy Citizens," Chicago, 1895.

WILLIAMS, FRANCIS: "Atman," New York, 1891.

WOODBRIDGE, C. W.: "Perfecting the Earth," Cleveland, 1902.

WORLEY, FREDERICK U.: "Three Thousand Dollars a Year," Washington, 1890.

Inverted Utopias

BUTLER, SAMUEL: "Erewhon," New York, 1927.

———: "Erewhon Revisited Twenty Years Later," New York, 1920.

ELLIS, HAVELOCK: "The Nineteenth Century: An Utopian Retrospect," Boston, 1901.

HALL, JOSEPH: "Mundus Alter et Idem," Ultraiech, 1643; reprinted in part in MORLEY, "Ideal Commonwealths."

MORLEY, HENRY: "Ideal Commonwealths," London, 1885.

NORTH, FRANKLIN H.; "The Awakening of Noahville," New York, 1900

RICHTER, EUGEN: "Pictures of the Socialistic Future," London, 1912.

RUSSELL, FRANCIS T.: "Satire in the Victorian Novel," New York, 1920.

SATTERLEE, W. W.: "Looking Backward and What I Saw," Minneapolis, 1890.

SWIFT, M. I.: "The Horroboos," New York, 1911.

Communism and Socialism

BEER, MAX: "Social Struggles in Antiquity," Boston, n. d.

———: "Social Struggles in the Middle Ages," London, 1924.

BERNSTEIN, E.: "Die Voraussetzungen des Sozialismus und die Aufgaben der Sozialdemokratie," Stuttgart, 1899.

BERNSTEIN, PHILIP S.: "Where Communism Is Real," *The Nation*, **126**: 588–589, 1928.

The Bible, Acts, IV–V (New Testament).

BRISBANE, ALBERT: "The Social Destiny of Man," Philadelphia, 1840.

BRÜGGENMANN, FRITZ: "Utopie und Robinsonade. Untersuchungen zu Schabels Insel Felsenburg (1731–1743)," Weimar, 1914.

BURNS, C. DELISLE: "Political Ideals: Their Nature and Development," chap. XI, Oxford, 1915.

Committee on the War and the Religious Outlook, "The Church and Industrial Reconstruction," New York, 1921.

DICKINSON, G. LOWES: "Justice and Liberty," New York, 1908.

"Fabian Essays in Socialism," Boston, 1909.

FAY, C. R.: "Life and Labour in the Nineteenth Century," Cambridge, 1920.

HAWTHORNE, NATHANIEL: "The Blithdale Romance," Boston, 1880.

HYNDMAN, HENRY M.: "Historical Basis of Socialism in England," London, 1883.

JARRETT, BEDE: "Mediæval Socialism," chap. III, London, n. d.

JAURÈS, JEAN L.: "Studies in Socialism," New York, 1906.

KEYNES, JOHN M.: "Laissez-Faire and Communism," New York, 1926.

KIRKUP, THOMAS: "History of Socialism," London, 1900

KLEINWÄCHTER: "Die Staatsromane," Wien, 1891.

KLYCE, SCUDDER, "Universe," Sec. 123, Winchester, Mass., 1921.

KNORTZ: "Die christliche-kommunistische Kolonie der Trappisten in Pennsylvanien," Leipzig, 1892.

KÜRNBÜRGER, F.: "Der Amerika-müde," Frankfurt, 1855.

LAIDLER, HARRY W.: "A History of Socialist Thought," New York, 1927.

MACDONALD, RAMSAY: "The Socialist Movement," London, 1911.

MARX, KARL: "Capital," Engl. transl., London, 1887.

——— and ENGELS, FRIEDRICH: "The Communist Manifesto," London, 1848.

MORELLY: "Code de la nature," Paris, 1841.

NORDHOFF: "Communistic Societies of the United States," London, 1875.

PENTY, ARTHUR, J.: "Towards a Christian Sociology," New York, 1923.

SELDES, GILBERT: "The Stammering Century," chaps, VI, X, XIII, New York, 1928.

SEMLER, HEINRICH: "Geschichte des Socialismus und Communismus in Nordamerika," Leipzig, 1880.

SHAW, BERNARD: "The Intelligent Woman's Guide to Socialism and Capitalism," New York, 1928.

SOREL, GEORGES, "Les illusions du progrès," Pt. II, pp. 337-386, 3rd ed., Paris, 1921.

VEDDER, HENRY C.: "Socialism and the Ethics of Jesus," New York, 1912.

ZEHNDER-WEIL, LUISE: "Geläutert," München, 1889.

CHAPTER XX

ADAMS, JAMES TRUSLOW: "Our Business Civilization: Some Aspects of American Culture," New York, 1929.

ANDERSON, B. M.: "Social Value," New York, 1911.

BEARD, CHARLES A. (editor): "Toward Civilization," New York, 1930.

BERNACER, GERMAN: "Sociedad y Felicidad: Essays de Mecanica Social," Madrid, 1916.

BUCKLE, HENRY: "History of Civilization in England," vol. I, chap. IV, New York, 1913.

CARPENTER, EDWARD: "Civilization: Its Cause and Cure," New York, 1921.

CARVER, THOMAS N.: "Sociology and Social Progress," Boston, 1905.

CHASE, STUART: "Slaves of the Machine?" Harper's Monthly Mag., 158: 480-489, 1929.

———: "Men and Machines," New York, 1929.

"Civilization," EB, ERE.

COIT, STANTON: "Is Civilization a Disease?" Boston, 1907.

CONDORCET, MARIE J. A. N. C.: "Esquisse d'un tableau historique des progrès de l'esprit humain," Paris, 1829.

CROZIER, JOHN B.: "Civilization and Progress," 4th ed., London, 1898.

DICKINSON, G. LOWES: "Letters from a Chinese Official," New York, 1903.

DRAKE, DURANT: "Problems of Conduct," chap. III, pp. 25-36, Boston, 1921.

EPICTETUS: "Discourses," Bk. IV, New York, 1900.

EVERETT, WALTER G.: "Moral Values," New York, 1918.

FOSDICK, RAYMOND B.: "The Old Savage in the New Civilization," New York, 1928.

FROUDE, JAMES A.: "The English in the West Indies," New York, 1900.

GAUSS, CHRISTIAN: "The Threat of Science," Scribners Mag., 87: 467-478, 1930.

GEORGE, HENRY: "Progress and Poverty," San Francisco, 1899.

GOBINEAU, JOSEPH A.: "The Inequality of Human Races," chap. XIII, New York, 1915.

HALL, A. CLEVELAND: "Crime in Its Relation to Social Progress," "Columbia University Studies in History, Economics and Public Law," no. 15, 1912.

HARRIS, GEORGE: "Civilization Considered as a Science," 2nd ed., London, 1872.

HERTZ, FRIEDRICH: "Race and Civilization," chap. XI, New York, 1928.

HOBHOUSE, LEONARD T.: "Development and Purpose," London, 1913.

——: "Mind in Evolution," chaps. IV, VI, London, 1915.

——: "Social Evolution and Political Theory," New York, 1911.

HÖFFDING, HARALD: "Philosophy of Religion," New York, 1906.

HUXLEY, ALDOUS: "The Outlook for American Culture," *Harper's Mag.,* 155: 265–272, 1927.

INGE, WILLIAM R.: "Lay Thoughts of a Dean," pp. 216–222, New York, 1926.

JACKS, L. P.: "Moral Progress," in "Progress and History," edited by F. S. Marvin, New York, 1916.

KANT, IMMANUEL: "The Principle of Progress," in "Principles of Politics," Edinburgh, 1891.

LACOMBE, P.: "De l'histoire considerée comme science," Paris, 1898.

LOWIE, ROBERT H.: "Primitive Society," chap. XV, New York, 1920.

——: "Are We Civilized?" New York, 1929.

McDOUGALL, WILLIAM: "The Group Mind," chap. IV, Cambridge, 1927.

MARTIN, JOHN, MRS.: "Is Mankind Advancing?" London, 1908.

MARVIN, FRANCIS S.: "The Living Past: A Sketch of Western Progress," Oxford, 1917.

MASSINGHAM, H. J.: "The Golden Age," chap. III, New York, 1928.

MELLONE, SYDNEY H.: "The Price of Progress," London, 1924.

MENDELSSOHN, MOSES: "Jerusalem," vol. II, pp. 44–77, London, 1838.

MURRAY, SIR GILBERT: "Faith, War, and Policy," Boston, 1917.

O'BRIEN, FREDERICK: "Mystic Isles of the South Seas," chap. XXIV, New York, 1921.

PATTEN, SIMON N.: "Heredity and Social Progress," chaps. XIV–XVI, New York, 1903.

RADIN, PAUL: "The Story of the American Indian," New York, 1927.

REMARQUE, ERICH M.: "All Quiet on the Western Front," Boston, 1929.

RICHARD: "Les crises sociales et la criminalité," *L'année sociologique,* vol. 3, and *Revue Philosophique,* vol. 52.

RITCHIE, D. G.: "Natural Rights," chap. III, London, 1916.

SCHUMPETER: "On the Concept of Value," *Quart. Jour. Econ.,* 1909.

SAPIR, EDWARD: "Culture, Genuine and Spurious," *Amer. Jour. Sociol.,* 29: 401–429, 1924; reprinted in DAVIS, JEROME, and BARNES, HARRY E., "Readings in Sociology," New York, 1927.

"Slavery" EB, ERE.

SMART, GEORGE T.: "The Temper of the American People, Boston, 1912.

SPENCE, LEWIS: "The Civilization of Ancient Mexico," chap. VIII, Cambridge, 1912.

SPINDEN, HERBERT J.: "Ancient Civilizations of Mexico and Central America," pp. 207–210, New York, 1917.

——: "Can Civilized Man Keep Savage Virtues?" *Forum,* 78: 346–356, 1927.

TAYLOR, W. COOKE: "The Natural History of Society in the Barbarous and Civilized State: An Essay towards Discovering the Origin and Course of Human Improvement," New York, 1841.

TODD, ARTHUR J.: "Theories of Social Progress," New York, 1918.

URWICK, EDWARD J.: "A Philosophy of Social Progress," chap. X, London, 1912.

"Why Asia Scorns Our Culture," *Liter. Digest*, **81**: 36, 1924.

WINDELBAND, W.: "History of Philosophy," pp. 660–681, Engl. transl. by J. H. Tufts, New York, 1910.

WOOTON, J. W., MRS.: "Is Progress an Illusion?" *Hibbert Jour.*, vol. 18, 1919.

CHAPTER XXI

BOODIN, J. E.: "Value and Social Interpretation," *Amer. Jour. Sociol.*, **21**: 65–103, 1915–16.

BOUGLÉ, CELESTIN: "The Evolution of Values," Engl. transl., New York, 1926.

CALKINS, MARY W.: "Value—Primarily a Psychological Conception," *Jour. Phil. Studies*, 1928.

CHASE, STUART: "Men and Machines," New York, 1929.

DEWEY, JOHN: "The Quest for Certainty," Chaps. X, XI, New York, 1929.

DOLE, CHARLES F.: "The Ethics of Progress or the Theory and Practice by which Civilization Proceeds," pt. II, chap. I; pt. V, chap. I, New York, 1909.

EVERETT, WALTER: "Moral Values," New York, 1918.

FERGUSON, ADAM: "An Essay on the History of Civil Society," pt. I, Sec. 7–8, Edinburgh, 1767.

"Happiness," ERE.

HEADLAM, CECIL: "Friends That Fail Not," chap. XV, London, 1902.

HÖFFDING, HARALD, "Philosophy of Religion," London, 1906.

INGE, WILLIAM R.: "Lay Thoughts of a Dean," pp. 209–215, New York, 1926.

KEYSERLING, HERMANN (COUNT): "The Animal Ideal in America," *Harper's Mag.*, **159**: 265–276, 1929.

LINDSAY, KENNETH: "Social Progress and Educational Waste," London, 1926.

MILL, JOHN S.: "Utilitarianism," New York, 1910.

PERRY, RALPH B.: "The Philosophy of Value," New York, 1927.

RASHDALL, HASTINGS: "Theory of Good and Evil," London, 1924.

RUSSELL, DORA: "The Right to be Happy," London, 1927.

SCHOPENHAUER, ARTHUR: "Die Welt als Wille und Vorstellung," Halle, 1891.

SIDGWICK, HENRY: "The Methods of Ethics," chap. IX, New York, 1921.

THOMSON, J. ARTHUR: "The Control of Life," chap. IX, New York, 1921.

TURNER, J. E.: "The Philosophic Basis of Moral Obligation: A Study in Ethics," London, 1924.

CHAPTER XXII

ADAMS, JAMES T.: "Our Racial Amnesia," *Harper's Monthly Mag.*, **156**: 172–176, 1928.

BROWNELL, BAKER: "The New Universe: An Outline of the World in Which We Live," chap. VI, New York, 1926.

CARTER, E. H. (editor): "The New Past and Other Essays on the Development of Civilization," Oxford, 1925.

CRAM, RALPH A.: "Walled Towns," Boston, 1919.

D'ALBE, E. E. F.: "Hephæstus, or the Soul of the Machine," New York, 1925.

DAVIS, JEROME, BARNES, HARRY E., and others: "An Introduction to Sociology: A Behavioristic Study of American Society," chap. I, New York, 1927.

EAST, E. M.: "Population in Relation to Agriculture," in DAVENPORT, CHARLES B. (editor), "Eugenics in Race and State, Scientific Papers of the Second International Congress of Eugenics," vol. II, Baltimore, 1923.

FAIRCHILD, MILDRED, and HART, HORNELL: "A Million Years of Evolution in Tools," *Sci. Monthly*, **28**: 71–79, 1929.

FOLSOM, JOSEPH K.: "Culture and Social Progress," chap. I, New York, 1928.

GIBBS, SIR PHILIP: "Unshackling the Mind," *N. Y. Times Mag.*, Oct. 27, 1929.

HALDANE, J. B. S.: "Is History a Fraud?" *Harpers Mag.*, **161**: 470–478, 1930.

HEARD, GERALD: "The Ascent of Humanity," London, 1929.

ILES, GEORGE: "Why Progress Is by Leaps," *Pop. Sci. Monthly*, **49**: 216–230, 1896.

JENKS, ALBERT E.: "Prehistory Chart," Chicago, 1927.

KELLOGG, VERNON: "Evolution," chaps. XIII, XIV, New York, 1924.

MURRAY, SIR GILBERT: "Tradition and Progress," chap. IX, New York, 1922.

PEARL, RAYMOND: "Some Eugenic Aspects of the Problem of Population," in DAVENPORT, CHARLES B. (editor), "Eugenics in Race and State," *Sci. Papers*, Second International Congress of Eugenics, vol. II, pp. 212–214, Baltimore, 1923.

ROBINSON, JAMES H.: "The New History," New York, 1912.

———: "The Mind in the Making," chap. III, New York, 1921.

WALLIS, WILSON D.: "An Introduction to Anthropology," chaps. V, VI, New York, 1926.

———: "An Introduction to Sociology," chaps. XXXIII, XXXIV, New York, 1928.

——— and WILLEY, MALCOLM M.: "Readings in Sociology," New York, 1930.

WELLS, HERBERT G.: "An Outline of History," New York, 1920.

———: "The World of William Clissold: A Novel from a New Angle," New York, 1926.

———: "The Salvaging of Civilization," New York, 1921.

CHAPTER XXIII

DIXON, ROLAND B.: "The Building of Cultures," New York, 1928.

FOSDICK, RAYMOND B.: "The Old Savage in the New Civilization," chap. I, New York, 1928.

GOLDENWEISER, ALEXANDER A.: "Early Civilization," New York, 1922.

MARETT, ROBERT R.: "Anthropology," New York, 1912.

McCABE, JOSEPH: "The Evolution of Civilization," New York, 1922.

PARSONS, GEOFFREY: "The Stream of History," New York, 1928.

RADIN, PAUL: "The Story of the American Indian," New York, 1927.

READE, WINWOOD: "The Martyrdom of Man," 20th ed., London, 1912.

WALLIS, WILSON D.: "An Introduction to Sociology," pt. I, New York, 1928.

———: "An Introduction to Anthropology," New York, 1926.

CHAPTER XXIV

"Advances in Biophysics," *Sci. Monthly*, **26**: 189–190, 1928.

ANGELL, JAMES ROWLAND: "The Evolution of Intelligence," in LULL, R. S., "Evolution of Man," pp. 122–125, New Haven, 1922.

BALFOUR, ARTHUR J.: "A Fragment of Progress," in "Essays and Addresses," pp. 241–282, Edinburgh, 1905.

BERNARD, LUTHER L.: "Hereditary and Environmental Factors in Human Behavior," *The Monist*, 1927, pp. 1–22.

BURNS, C. DELISLE: "Progressive Morality," *Internat. Jour. Ethics*, **37**: 225–238, 1927.

CHENEY, EDWARD P.: "Law in History," *Amer. Histor. Rev.*, **29**: 231–248, 1924.

———: "Law in History and Other Essays," New York, 1927.

COOLEY, CHARLES H.: "Social Process," chap. XXXIV, New York, 1922.

CONKLIN, EDWIN G.: "The Trend of Evolution." in LULL, R. S., "Evolution of Man," chap. VI, New Haven, 1922.

CUTTEN, GEORGE B.: "The Threat of Leisure," New Haven, 1926.

DADOURIAN, H. M.: "Some Problems of Progress," *Sci. Monthly*, **15**: 348 ff., 1922.

DEWEY, JOHN: "Human Nature and Conduct," pt. IV, New York, 1922.

DIXON, ROLAND B.: "The Building of Cultures," chap. VIII, New York, 1928.

DOHRES, BONAMY, "Timotheus, or the Future of the Theatre," New York, 1925.

FOSDICK, RAYMOND B., "The Old Savage in the New Civilization," New York, 1928.

FRANCE, ANATOLE: "Penguin Island," bk. VIII, New York, 1922.

GRUENBERG, BENJAMIN C.: "The Chains of Prometheus," *Sci. Monthly*, **25**: 505–510, 1927.

HALDANE, J. B. S.: "Dædalus, or Science and the Future," New York, 1924.

HERTZ, FRIEDRICH: "Race and Civilization," chaps. XI, XIII, New York, 1928.

HOBHOUSE, LEONARD T.: "Morals in Evolution," pt. II, chap. VIII, 2nd ed., London, 1915.

LUCASSE, WALTER W.: "Progress and the Sciences," *Sci. Monthly*, **25**: 213–219, 1927; reprinted in WALLIS, WILSON D., and WILLEY, MALCOLM M., "Readings in Sociology," New York, 1930.

MARVIN, FRANCIS S.: "Science and Civilization," chap. XII, Oxford, 1923.

McCABE, JOSEPH: "The Evolution of Civilization," chap. VIII, New York, 1922.

MURRAY, SIR GILBERT: "Tradition and Progress," chap. X, New York, 1922.

SANTAYANA, GEORGE: "The Life of Reason," vol. I, New York, 1905.

SCHWEITZER, ALBERT: "The Decay and the Restoration of Civilization," London, 1923.

"Self-Sacrifice," ERE, **11**: 371, sec. 3.

"State of the Dead" (Christian), ERE, **11**: 836, sec. 7.

WALLIS, WILSON D.: "An Introduction to Anthropology," chap. XLII, New York, 1926.

———: "An Introduction to Sociology," chaps. XIX–XXXVII, New York, 1928.

——— and WILLEY, MALCOLM M.: "Readings in Sociology," New York, 1930.

WATSON, JOHN B.: "The Behaviorist Looks at Instincts," *Harper's Monthly Mag.*, **155**: 229–235, 1927.

WOODBRIDGE, F. J. E.: "The Purpose of History," chap. III, New York, 1916.

Index